THE UNIVERSITIES
OF EUROPE
IN THE MIDDLE AGES

THE DIVINITY SCHOOL, OXFORD

Photograph by J. R. H. Weaver

THE

UNIVERSITIES OF EUROPE

IN THE

MIDDLE AGES

BY THE LATE

HASTINGS RASHDALL

DEAN OF CARLISLE

A NEW EDITION IN THREE VOLUMES

EDITED BY

F. M. POWICKE

Regius Professor of Modern History
in the University of Oxford

AND

A. B. EMDEN

Principal of St. Edmund Hall, Oxford

VOLUME III

ENGLISH UNIVERSITIES—STUDENT LIFE

OXFORD UNIVERSITY PRESS

Oxford University Press, Amen House, London E.C.4
GLASGOW NEW YORK TORONTO MELBOURNE WELLINGTON
BOMBAY CALCUTTA MADRAS KARACHI LAHORE DACCA
CAPE TOWN SALISBURY NAIROBI IBADAN ACCRA
KUALA LUMPUR HONG KONG

FIRST EDITION 1895
NEW EDITION 1936
Reprinted lithographically in Great Britain
by LOWE AND BRYDONE (PRINTERS) LTD., LONDON
from sheets of the new edition
1942, 1951, 1958, 1964

CONTENTS OF VOLUME III

§ 7. THE PLACE OF OXFORD IN MEDIEVAL THOUGHT

§ 8. THE UNIVERSITY OF CAMBRIDGE

CHAPTER XIII

THE NUMBERS IN THE MEDIEVAL UNIVERSITIES

CHAPTER XIV

STUDENT-LIFE IN THE MIDDLE AGES

ILLUSTRATIONS

INTRODUCTION

IN the preface to the original edition of this book Rashdall expresses the hope 'that Oxford will soon cease to be almost the only important University in the world (exclusive, perhaps, of the Spanish Peninsula) whose earlier history cannot be studied in a tolerably complete series of published documents'. 'The work can only be done', he added, 'by the University itself. It is too extensive for private Societies.' Since Rashdall wrote these words much has been done to remove the reproach which they convey. But the initiative has come from a private society—the Oxford Historical Society; and the work so far achieved is in largest measure a monument to the scholarly industry of one man—Dr. H. E. Salter.[1] To-day there are available for students a score of printed volumes containing documentary evidence of great value for the history of medieval Oxford, whereas Rashdall had no readier means of access to this wealth of historical material than the crowded note-books of those untiring antiquaries, Robert Hare (d. 1611), and Brian Twyne (d. 1644). The medieval statutes and a selection of excerpts from the earliest surviving Chancellor's Register, alone of the primary sources for the history of the University of Oxford in the Middle Ages, were in print when Rashdall wrote. But the editing of *Munimenta Academica* had not been well done, as Rashdall himself noted. That disadvantage has now been removed. No better editions could be desired than that of the ancient statutes of the University by Mr. Strickland Gibson, and that of *Registrum Aaa* by Dr. Salter. Rashdall was no better served as regard the colleges. Before the publication of Robinson's series of popular histories of the Colleges, which began in 1898, the few monographs that had been written about individual colleges during the half-century preceding the issue of this book for the most part took the form of biographical registers.

[1] See below the bibliographical notes on pp. 4, 180, 191, 204.

It is no small testimony to Rashdall's industry and insight that his chapter on Oxford, prepared under these disadvantages, should have so long retained its freshness and importance. It possesses an originality which Rashdall did not feel attached in the same degree to those parts of his work in which he had been preceded by Denifle. But Denifle had only assigned twenty pages in his *Enstehung* to Oxford, and had made no claim to throw any new light on its history. As recently as 1886 the University of Oxford had been the subject of a separate historical study at the hands of an able archivist, Sir Herbert Maxwell-Lyte, then Deputy Keeper of the Public Record Office. Rashdall had no intention himself of writing a detailed narrative history of the university during the medieval period. He wanted to make a new approach to the subject. He felt strongly that the great defect in the writing of university histories had been the omission to apply the comparative method. In treating, therefore, of Oxford he set himself to trace the growth and development of the university in its European setting as one of the three archetypal universities, and in so doing to describe with tolerable fullness the conditions which governed the evolution of its constitution. The survey which Rashdall made from that angle has had no successor, and, in its essential features, needs none.

Even where it may be felt that his conclusions call for revision, it must be conceded that his argument is always stimulating. There are two chief points in which his account of the origin and growth of Oxford as an academic centre has been questioned. In his view the relationship of Paris and Oxford was demonstrably that of mother and daughter. He was convinced that the origin of the University of Oxford must be sought in a migration from Paris which he believed to have taken place in or about 1167 in consequence of the measures taken by Henry II to cut off Archbishop Becket from the support of his own countrymen so long as he remained in France. The novelty of this view had already led Rashdall into controversy with Professor, afterwards Sir, Thomas Erskine Holland in the pages of the *Academy*.[1] Rash-

[1] See below, p. 3.

dall's repetition and elaboration of it in the present work
drew immediate criticism. In the course of a review in *The
English Historical Review*[1] Mullinger remarked that if, as
Rashdall had himself stated, Paris and Bologna did not arise
until after 1170[2] and Oxford originated in a migration from
the former in 1167, 'then according to his showing the
daughter was born before the mother'. But Rashdall stood
firmly by his theory of a migration and defended it vigorously
against Leach's unduly pugnacious onslaught.[3] Even if it be
thought that Rashdall's case for a migration cannot be upheld
on the available evidence, there is no need on that score to
discount the importance that he attaches to the influence of
Paris upon Oxford during the formative years of the university movement. On the contrary, the extent and character of
that influence still need to be more fully explored. But in
directing attention to the importance of Paris for Oxford
history Rashdall was disposed to allow too little room for
the operation of intellectual activities in England capable of
developing contemporaneously along lines similar to those
which brought to birth the University of Paris. Mullinger
attributed this attitude in Rashdall to 'the determination
which he throughout evinces to dissociate as far as possible
the spirit which animated university culture from monastic
influences, and to exhibit the two as essentially hostile'. This
attitude certainly seems to have coloured Rashdall's treatment
of the question of academical origins at Oxford. He ruled
out the likelihood of any of the schools in connexion with
which the university grew up having been 'at any time dependent upon any capitular or monastic body in Oxford',[4] and
in so doing appears to exclude the possibility of any fruitful
contribution from such a quarter. But it is not necessary to
predicate actual dependence, if account is to be taken of the
influence that may have been exerted by the literary activities
of the secular canons of that short-lived foundation, Saint
George's-in-the-Castle.[5] The revival of learning in England

---

[1] *E.H.R.* ii (1896), p. 783.

[2] See above, i. 17.

[3] See below, p. 29, n. 2.

[4] See below, p. 10.

[5] See below, p. 9, n. 3.

during the first century after the Norman Conquest will have to be more fully studied before the earlier history of the schools of Oxford can be viewed in its proper perspective.

In his treatment of the development of a system of residence in *hospicia*—halls as they came to be known in Oxford or hostels in Cambridge, Rashdall also took his own line. He maintained that in their origin these little academical households were formed by parties of schoolboys who clubbed together for the purpose, appointing one of themselves to be responsible to their landlord for the rent. It has been doubted whether Rashdall's view of the originally democratic character and youthful control of the halls and hostels is supported by contemporary evidence.[1] But even if it be decided that Rashdall was mistaken in his view, there remain substantial grounds for gratitude to him for the stress which he laid, in this and other connexions, on the youthfulness of control that characterizes the medieval university. It has too often been overlooked that authority in academic affairs at Oxford lay chiefly in the hands of young graduates so long as the regency system lasted. Did not Archbishop Arundel in his indignation at being resisted in his visitation of the university complain to King Henry IV that he had been withstood by a pack of schoolboys?[2] The recurrent controversies that marked the relationship of the faculty of arts with the other faculties and with those religious orders who had *studia* in Oxford are the better understood when it is remembered that young graduates formed a majority in the Congregation which elected the chancellor and the proctors.

Rashdall was careful to point out that he was obliged, owing to considerations of space and time, to leave many aspects of university history untouched. It may be of service here if allusion is made to some of the directions in which subsequent investigations bearing upon Oxford history have been or are being pursued. Rashdall in his section on the University and the Church confined himself to constitutional issues. He did not find room to note the influence which the growth of a

[1] See below, p. 169.
[2] See *Snappe's Formulary*, ed. H. E. Salter (O.H.S.), pp. 103–4.

university in Oxford had upon appointments to the higher offices in the Church. Attention has been drawn recently to the importance of the advent of *magistri* to the ranks of the English episcopate during the reign of Henry III.[1] In her examination of the personnel of the episcopate during that reign Miss Marion Gibbs has attempted a classification of seventy-eight bishops. Summarily stated, her classification admits of the following statistics. Eight only of Henry's bishops were monks; forty-two are gathered into a group of 'administrators and magnates', of whom twenty-two were *curiales* of the normal type who had been employed in one or other department of the *Curia Regis*, and of whom fourteen seem to have been *magistri* who had spent some time in the schools of Paris or Oxford. A third group consists of forty *magistri* of whom thirty are noted as men 'whose academic experience seems to have been a factor in promotion or a real influence in their lives'. About half of these, it is pointed out, were scholars of some eminence, twenty-three had already had experience of diocesan work as members of cathedral bodies before their elevation to the episcopate. A fourth group is composed of diocesan and cathedral clergy, of whom it seems there were only half a dozen who had neither been *magistri* nor *curiales*. During previous reigns the bishops had been drawn in varying degrees from monasteries, cathedrals, and the king's court, but in the reign of Henry III the schools of Oxford began to make their influence felt in the composition of the episcopate. With the appointment of Master Edmund of Abingdon to the archbishopric of Canterbury in 1234 the young University of Oxford won a new prominence. For the first time a son of Oxford had been called upon to occupy the chief see in England. 'Henceforward', writes Miss Gibbs, 'there was a steady promotion of Oxford men: Grosseteste, who, with Edmund of Abingdon, had been the teacher most responsible for the early fame of the Oxford schools, and his younger colleagues or pupils: Ralph Maidstone (Bishop of Hereford), Richard Wych (Bishop of Chi-

[1] See M. Gibbs and J. Lang, *Bishops and Reform, 1215–1272*, Oxford, 1934, pp. 25–50.

chester), Sewal of Bovill (Archbishop of York)—successive Chancellors; Roger Weseham (Bishop of Coventry and Lichfield), Reader to the Franciscans; Nicolas Farnham (Bishop of Durham), the famous physician. And it is at least not improbable, considering the rising fame of the Oxford schools, that other *magistri* bishops had been there . . . Oxford, in short, was the common intellectual home of some of the most distinguished of the bishops of Henry III.'[1] Investigations of this kind need to be multiplied before any satisfactory attempt can be made to estimate the extent to which the English clergy during the Middle Ages were recruited from the Universities.

When he reaches the fifteenth century Rashdall is disposed to regard the spirit of Oxford as having been utterly crushed by the measures that Archbishop Arundel had taken to eradicate from it all traces of Wyclifism.[2] It has been assumed too readily perhaps by Rashdall and other writers that the University of Oxford entered upon a period of decline during the century preceding the Reformation and that this decline was the penalty which it had to undergo for having been the birth-place of the Wyclifite heresy. The latter assumption certainly rests on an exaggerated impression of the effects to be attributed to Archbishop Arundel's visitation.[3] The decrease in the numbers at Oxford during the course of the fifteenth century may well be due as much to external as to internal causes. The condition of the university during that period needs to be studied with full regard to the general condition of the Church and to the nature of the particular problems which confronted churchmen in England during that period. The complaints that were laid by the university before Archbishop Chichele in the Convocation of 1417 about the failure of graduates to obtain promotion to benefices reveal an

---

[1] Miss Gibbs names six bishops as probable *magistri* of Oxford: Walter Cantilupe (Bishop of Worcester), John Gervais (Bishop of Winchester), John Clipping and Stephen Berksted (successively Bishops of Chichester), Richard Gravesend (Bishop of Lincoln), and Henry Sandwich (Bishop of London). See *ibid.*, p. 35.

[2] See below, pp. 135, 270-1.

[3] See *Snappe's Formulary*, ed. H. E. Salter (O.H.S.), pp. 113-15.

unsatisfactory state of affairs for which Oxford cannot be held responsible, but which constituted a serious cause of discouragement to academical studies.[1] The criticisms with which the learned Thomas Gascoigne, chancellor of the university from 1442 to 1445, interspersed the pages of his *Liber Veritatum* are concerned with abuses that reflected on the reputation of the Church in England rather than on that of his own university.[2] No final verdict on fifteenth-century Oxford can be given until the difficulties with which the university and its colleges had to contend owing to the general unsettlement of the times have been more fully examined and the state of academical learning during this period has been made a subject of research. Meanwhile, there is comfort to be found in the conclusion reached by Kingsford. 'The University', he writes, 'cannot have been entirely dead which sent forth to the service of the State such men as Thomas Bekynton, William Waynflete, John Morton, and John Russell; they all owed their advancement in the first instance to their own merits and not to any chance of birth; they had all shared in the teaching and government of the university; they all retained their interest in learning in after life and showed their gratitude to Oxford in a practical fashion.'[3]

Rashdall felt obliged through lack of material for the earlier period to confine his account of the curriculum of Oxford almost entirely to the fifteenth century.[4] His description is based upon the evidence of the university statutes. Two other important sources of information have since become available. The *Registrum Annalium* of Merton College, the only record of its kind, which Dr. Salter has edited, usefully supplements the evidence to be derived from the statutes for

[1] See Professor E. F. Jacob's article 'Two Lives of Archbishop Chichele', in *The Bulletin of the John Rylands Library*, xvi (1932), p. 464. Important information on the difficult negotiations in which the archbishop and the university were concerned on this question is to be found in Chichele's Register, an edition of which Professor Jacob is preparing.

[2] A careful study of the life and works of Dr. Gascoigne has been made by Miss W. A. Pronger, St. Hugh's College, but is not yet published.

[3] C. L. Kingsford, *Prejudice and Promise in XVth Century England*, pp. 45–7.

[4] See below, p. 140.

the closing years of the Middle Ages.[1] A manuscript note-book, preserved in the Municipal Library of Assisi, which Dr. Little and Dr. Pelster have edited, furnishes material of great value for our knowledge of the theological schools at Oxford and Cambridge between 1280 and 1290.[2] In a learned introduction Dr. Pelster lays the foundation for a fuller inquiry into the activities of the theological faculties in both universities and to the methods of teaching employed.

'In writing the history of the medieval university our danger', as Dr. Salter has pointed out, 'is to over-estimate the importance of the colleges.'[3] The predominance which the colleges have come to exercise in the constitution and social life of the university since the end of the fifteenth century has been too readily assumed by older writers, like Twyne and Wood, to be equally true of the medieval period. Sir Herbert Maxwell-Lyte was perhaps the first of modern historians to draw attention to this fallacy. In the preface to his history of the university up to 1530 he warned his readers 'against the common error of supposing that the Colleges formed the component parts of the University to which they were affiliated';[4] and he was at pains to make clear that during the period covered by his book the history of the colleges had little bearing upon the general history of the university. Although Rashdall felt that 'the peculiar interest which our English colleges possess'[5] justified him in devoting separate sections to them, he was under no misapprehension as to the proper place to be accorded them in the working of the medieval university. But so completely have the Universities of Oxford and Cambridge become identified with the college

[1] *Registrum Annalium Collegii Mertonensis*, ed. H. E. Salter (O.H.S.), 1921. There is in the *Repertorium* of Dr. Stephen Patrington, O.C., preserved in St. John's College Library at Cambridge (MS. 103), a record of the academical acts performed when he proceeded to the doctorate in theology. Patrington, who subsequently became Bishop of Chi-chester, died in 1417.

[2] *Oxford Theology and Theologians, c. 1282–1302*, ed. A. G. Little and F. Pelster, 1934.

[3] See his article on 'The Medieval University of Oxford' in *History*, xiv (1929), pp. 58–9.

[4] *History of the University of Oxford*, p. ix.

[5] See below, p. 169.

system that to many it still comes as a surprise to be reminded that the colleges were not originally intended for undergraduates, but were designed to help men of promise who might otherwise have been prevented from graduating as Masters of Arts or from qualifying for the higher degrees owing to the length of the courses involved.[1] The numbers who were able to benefit from the facilities which colleges offered were comparatively small. Dr. Salter has estimated that in the middle of the fifteenth century University College numbered about six members, Queen's and Lincoln about eight each, Oriel about twelve, and Merton about twenty-four. The normal home of the medieval undergraduate must be sought in the halls, and his normal resort for instruction in the schools or lecture-rooms rented by regent masters. Until the foundation of New College, the colleges were not even designated as such in common speech: they were all termed halls. Dr. Salter goes so far as to say that down to 1450 the colleges of Oxford could have all been swept away and it would have made no great difference to the university. But if that be true as regards their place in the general organization of the university, it must be allowed that they made a distinctive and important contribution to the reputation of the university as a centre of learning. The history of Merton College during the medieval period affords striking evidence of the fame that a collegiate foundation might win through the scholarly achievements of its members.[2] But even so it is well to bear in mind that fellows of colleges did not remain in Oxford for the love of learning but were concerned to qualify themselves for promotion in the world outside.[3]

The section of Rashdall's chapter on Oxford in which he attempts to indicate the place which Oxford holds in the history of medieval thought is not endued with the same permanent qualities that distinguish his account of the growth of the constitution of the University. No part of the field

[1] See Dr. Salter's article cited above.

[2] See F. M. Powicke, *The Medieval Books of Merton College*, pp. 20–8.

[3] See Dr. Salter's remarks on this subject in his introduction to *Registrum Annalium Collegii Merton*. (O.H.S.), pp. viii–xi, and in the article already mentioned.

which Rashdall examined had been more neglected than that which relates to the history of Oxford studies in the Middle Ages. When Rashdall wrote, Dr. A. G. Little had pointed the way in a fine piece of pioneer work, *The Grey Friars in Oxford*, which was issued by the Oxford Historical Society in 1891.[1] But English students have been slow to follow. Dr. C. R. S. Harris's *Duns Scotus*, Dr. D. E. Sharp's *Franciscan Philosophy at Oxford in the XIIIth Century*, and Dr. R. Steele's editorship of the works of Roger Bacon are honourable exceptions. The great advance in our knowledge of the activities of medieval Oxford scholars is due chiefly to the labours of students from abroad—such as Baur, Chenu, Duhem, Grabmann, Longpré, Michalski, Pelster, Pelzer, Thomson, and Xiberta. As a result of the researches of these and other foreign scholars much light has been thrown on the output of the Oxford schools. But much work needs to be done before the importance of Oxford as a centre of learning during the Middle Ages can be adequately assessed. Rashdall felt that his constitutional study of Oxford would be unpalatable unless he touched upon its intellectual history. But if the review that he attempted was premature, it at least served to stimulate interest in a neglected subject. It is a pity that in attempting such an estimate Rashdall did not indicate the difficulties in the way—difficulties which, notwithstanding the important work that has since been done in this field, still exist. Scholars whose habit it was to move freely from one university to another and whose extant writings are often undated cannot readily be claimed as representative of one particular seat of learning. Oxford, for example, may claim the honour of having been the first university at which Duns Scotus studied and taught; but Cambridge, Paris, and Cologne also knew him as a teacher. The known facts

---

[1] For Dr. Little's other contributions to the history of the Franciscan School in Oxford see below, p. 66, n. 2. There is a great need for similar work to be done on the Dominicans. The Carmelite School in Oxford has fortunately found a historian in Fr. B. M. Xiberta, O.C. See his *De Scriptoribus scholasticis saeculi XIV in ordine Carmelitarum*, Louvain, 1931, and the articles mentioned below, pp. 265, n. 1, 267, n. 3.

about his career are meagre, the full list of his writings has not yet been identified, and the chronology of those that may safely be ascribed to him remains uncertain. It is, therefore, not to be wondered at that in the two recent studies of his teaching that have emanated from Oxford divergent conclusions should have been reached concerning his relationship to his Oxford predecessors and contemporaries.[1] Much patient investigation needs to be carried out along lines such as those that have in recent years brought to light new facts for the career of Duns himself, before these problems and others of the same kind can be resolved. In forming his estimate of Oxford's place in scholastic thought Rashdall confined his attention almost entirely to the achievement of five outstanding schoolmen, Robert Grosseteste, Roger Bacon, Duns Scotus, William Occam, and John Wyclif. Subsequent research has shown the importance of taking into account the work of lesser men, if the varied character and extent of Oxford's contribution to medieval learning are to be ascertained.

Rashdall has been criticized for the brevity of the section which he devoted to Cambridge.[2] He endeavoured to anticipate such criticism. 'I fear', he wrote, 'there may seem to be something almost disrespectful in the brevity with which I have disposed of so great a University as Cambridge. But the fact is that it is almost impossible to find anything to say about medieval Cambridge which has not already been said of Oxford.'[3] Unless his book was to have been extended to quite unwieldy proportions, it was clearly not possible for him to accord the same fullness of treatment to the seventy other universities that he accorded to 'the three great archetypal universities, Bologna, Paris, Oxford'. Moreover, it should be remembered that at the time when Rashdall wrote, Cambridge had received far more liberal attention in recent years at the hands of her own historians than had Oxford. Mullinger's learned history, which appeared in 1873, had set a new standard for the study of the history of English learning

[1] See C. R. S. Harris, *Duns Scotus*, i. 113–40; and D. E. Sharp, *Franciscan Philosophy at Oxford in the XIIIth Century*, pp. 280–2.

[2] See H. P. Stokes, *The Medieval Hostels of the University of Cambridge* (C.A.S.), p. 53.

[3] See below, p. 292.

and education. Willis and Clark's monumental history of the buildings of the University and Colleges of Cambridge—a work the historical value of which, as Rashdall pointed out, 'is by no means limited to the architectural side'—was published in 1886. The destruction of archives which the University of Cambridge suffered during the riots of 1381 has left her irremediably poorer than Oxford in historical material for the years preceding that melancholy event. It is only in the following century that the balance is redressed. Since the first edition of this book, Grace Book A (1454–88) and Grace Book B (1488–1511) have been admirably edited by Sir Stanley Leathes and Miss Mary Bateson, respectively. Recent years have shown that in Cambridge, as in Oxford, there still lies in college muniment rooms important material for the medieval period that is worthy of publication. Mr. H. Rackham's edition of the early statutes of Christ's College and Mr. A. H. Lloyd's account of the early history of the same college are welcome evidence of this. It is to be hoped that the work on the early statutes of Pembroke College upon which Mr. A. Attwater was engaged before his untimely death was sufficiently advanced to make publication possible. In the writing of college histories, whether at Cambridge or at Oxford, a notable defect has lain in the little attention that has been given to the history of the management of college estates and to all that pertains to the economic and financial aspects of college history. In the case of St. John's College, Cambridge, which does not come within the purview of this book, as it was not founded until 1511, this defect has been made good in exemplary fashion by Sir Henry Fraser Howard in his recently published volume: *An Account of the Finances of the College of St. John the Evangelist in the University of Cambridge, 1511–1926.* A proper understanding of the *milieu* and working of the colleges of medieval foundation in both universities will only be possible when their full activities as land-owning corporations have been investigated. There are college muniment rooms that are wonderfully rich in the requisite documentary evidence.

A. B. E.

CHAPTER XII

THE ENGLISH UNIVERSITIES

§ 1. THE ORIGIN OF THE SCHOOLS AND UNIVERSITY OF OXFORD

THE first investigations into the history of the university were prompted by the dispute for antiquity and precedence with Cambridge in the sixteenth century, beginning with the *Assertio Antiquitatis Oxoniensis Academiae* (by Thomas KAY or CAIUS), printed with Joh. Caius *De Antiq. Acad. Cantab.*, 1568 and 1574; also edited as *Vindiciae Antiquitatis Acad. Oxon.* by T. Hearne, 1730. But the first work that can be called a history is Bryan TWYNE, *Antiquitatis Academiae Oxoniensis Apologia*, 1608. Twyne's view of the antiquity of Oxford was as superstitious as that of Caius; but his Apology represents an immense amount of laborious research, while his twenty-four vols. of MS. collections formed the basis of all later work, a debt very inadequately acknowledged by his better-known successor, Wood. (G. LANGBAINE), *The Foundation of the Universitie of Oxford*, 1651, contains nothing but a short account of the colleges. The classical historian of Oxford is Anthony WOOD, whose immortal work appeared in a mutilated Latin translation as *Historia et Antiquitates Universitatis Oxoniensis*, 1674. *The History and Antiquities of the University of Oxford*, in its original dress of racy English (though not the actual work from which the Latin version was made), was only published by John GUTCH at Oxford in 1792–6. (References to Wood are always to this edition, where no work is specified.) Wood also wrote *The History and Antiquities of the Colleges and Halls in the University of Oxford*, ed. J. Gutch, 1786. His *Fasti Oxonienses* was published as an appendix to the last-mentioned work in 1790. (Another collection of *Fasti* is appended to the *Athenae*.) Wood's *Survey of the Antiquities of the City of Oxford* (written 1661–6) appeared in a much mutilated form as Sir John PESHALL's *Ancient and Present State of the City of Oxford*, 1773. The original manuscript has been edited in a most scholarly fashion by Andrew CLARK (Oxford Hist. Soc., 1889–99). The *Athenae Oxonienses*, consisting of biographies of Oxford 'Writers and Bishops' (ed. 1, 1691, and re-ed. P. Bliss, 1813–20), only begins with the year 1500. Wood's successor as chief antiquary of Oxford was Thomas HEARNE, whose rather trifling contributions to the medieval history of Oxford are scattered through his various works and editions, e.g. *Roberti de Avesbury Historia*, 1720, App. i (where the 'Bedel's Book' is printed); Leland's *Itinerary*, vol. ii (chiefly on the monasteries), 1710–12, &c. There is a complete list of Hearne's writings in *The Life of Mr. Thomas Hearne*, 1772. John AYLIFFE, *The Antient and Present State of the University of Oxford*, 1714, is a readable abridgement of Wood continued to the writer's own times, with some documents. [Mr. Strickland Gibson has drawn attention to this writer in an article entitled, 'A neglected Oxford historian', in *Oxford Essays in Medieval History, presented to H. E. Salter*, Oxford, 1934.] The only really valuable work done upon our history from the time of Wood down to the present decade was that of William SMITH, by far the acutest and most critical of our Oxford

CHAP. XII, antiquarians, who, in his *Annals of University College* (Newcastle-on-
§ 1.   Tyne, 1728), was the first to dissect and expose the whole tissue of lies
about Mempric, Alfred the Great, &c., which have, however, hardly
yet disappeared from serious histories. Of Sir John PESHALL's (Anon.)
History of the University of Oxford to the death of William the Conqueror,
1772, the title is a sufficient criticism; his *History of the University of
Oxford from the death of William the Conqueror*, 1773, is a dry compilation
from Wood, with a few documents *in extenso*. The *History of the University
of Oxford* (printed for R. Ackermann, London, 1814), though in folio
form, is little more than an illustrated guide-book. *Oxoniana* (printed for
Richard Phillips, London: no date, but about 1810) is a collection of
gossiping extracts relating to the university. Alex. CHALMERS, *History
of the Colleges, Halls, and Public Buildings attached to the University of
Oxford*, 1810, and J. K. INGRAM, *Memorials of Oxford*, 1837, deal almost
entirely with the colleges and buildings. J. SKELTON's illustrated *Oxonia
Antiqua Restaurata*, 1823; ed. 2, 1843, enables the reader to see what old
Oxford was like. His *Pietas Oxoniensis or Records of Oxford Founders*,
1828, is of less value. V. A. HUBER, *Die Englischen Universitäten*, Cassel,
1839 (abridged Eng. trans. ed. Francis W. Newman, London, 1843), is
one of the most worthless university histories which it has been my lot to
peruse: it may be described as a history written without materials. The
English translation contains, however, as an appendix, Thomas WRIGHT's
valuable *Historical Doubts on the Biography of Alfred attributed to Bishop
Asser*, &c. Cardinal NEWMAN contributed a popular sketch of 'Medieval
Oxford' to the *British Critic* for 1838 (also in *Historical Sketches*, London,
1872). The same writer also deals with the history of Oxford in an article
on 'The Rise and Progress of Universities', originally published in the
Catholic University Gazette, 1854; but these charming bits of writing have
no great value as history. J. C. JEAFFRESON, *Annals of Oxford*, 1871, is a
lively *réchauffé* of the old materials, not without flashes of historical insight,
but can hardly rank as serious history. James PARKER, in *The Early
History of Oxford* (Oxford Hist. Soc., 1885), has dealt very thoroughly
with the early history of the town and the growth of the Oxford myth.
Sir H. C. MAXWELL-LYTE, *History of the University of Oxford*, 1886, is the
first critical history of the university, and is generally accurate: I am especially indebted to Sir H. C. Maxwell-Lyte's references. G. C. BRODRICK,
History of the University of Oxford, 1886, is a condensed sketch of Oxford
history which becomes increasingly valuable after the medieval
period. S. F HULTON, *Rixae Oxonienses* (Oxford, 1892), is a lively
popular sketch.

G. V. COX (formerly Esquire Bedel), *Recollections of Oxford* (ed. 2,
1870), is full of interesting notices of old customs. A. G. LITTLE, *The
Grey Friars in Oxford* (O.H.S., 1892), is a most learned and pains-
taking piece of work. There is an earlier and very slight, but still useful,
study on *The Blackfriars in Oxford*, by W. G. D. FLETCHER (Oxford,
1882). W. D. MACRAY's learned *Annals of the Bodleian* (1868; ed. 2, 1890)
has only a few pages relating to our period. C. W. BOASE's delightful
volume on Oxford in *Historic Towns* (London, 1887) must not be passed
over, nor Andrew LANG's brilliant sketch entitled *Oxford: brief historical
and descriptive notes*, 1890. *The Colleges of Oxford: their history and traditions, xxi chapters by members of the Colleges* (ed. A. CLARK, 1891), contains
more original research on the history of Oxford than any book that has
appeared in the nineteenth century. There are some fragments of univer-

sity history in *A History of the Church of S. Mary the Virgin, Oxford* (E. S. CHAP. XII, § 1.
FFOULKES), 1892. The few pages devoted to a comparison between Oxford
and Paris in Mr. GLADSTONE's eloquent and characteristic *Academic Sketch*
(Romanes Lecture, Oxford, 1892) are full of interest.

Prof. T. E. HOLLAND has an article on 'The Origin of the University of
Oxford' in the *Eng. Hist. Review* of 1891, which summarizes the ascertained
facts, and there are some suggestive remarks in his article on 'The Ancient
Organization of the University of Oxford' in *Macmillan's Magazine* for
July, 1877. I have already explained my view of the origin of the university in the *Church Quarterly Review* for 1887 and in the *Academy*, No.
839, in a letter which was followed by a controversy between Prof. Holland
and myself in Nos. 847, 848, 849, 850, 890.

A *Registrum Privilegiorum almae Universitatis Oxoniensis*, containing the
Charters of Edward IV and Henry VIII, was printed at Oxford in 1770.
But the early statutes remained unpublished till 1868, when they were
edited (not well) by H. ANSTEY in *Munimenta Academica* (Rolls Series),
with an interesting introduction. *The Register of the University of Oxford*
(1449–63; 1505–1622) has been edited by C. W. BOASE (vol. i, 1885) and
A. CLARK (vol. ii, 1887–9: O.H.S.), a most laborious and important piece
of work. A few—too few—medieval documents are printed in *Collectanea*
(O.H.S., vol. i, ed. C. R. L. FLETCHER, 1885; vol. ii, ed. M. BURROWS,
1890). The *Laudian Code of Statutes* (first printed at Oxford in 1634
before its final revision), by which with little modification the university
was governed down to 1851, has been re-edited by J. GRIFFITHS (with
introduction by C. L. SHADWELL), Oxford, 1888. *The Statutes of the
Colleges of Oxford* were printed 'by the desire of the Commissioners' of
1851 (London, 1853). J. GRIFFITHS, *Enactments in Parliament relating to
the University of Oxford*, 1869, is very incomplete for the early period.
Some documents relating to the university appear in J. E. THOROLD
ROGERS, *Oxford City Documents* (O.H.S., 1891), and O. OGLE, *Royal
Letters addressed to Oxford, and now existing in the City Archives*, 1892.
There is a *Rough List of Manuscript Materials relating to the History of
Oxford contained in the printed catalogues of the Bodleian and College
Libraries*, 1887, by F. MADAN, who has also catalogued the *Oxford City
Documents* (1887: not published). I may also refer to the very valuable
Catalogue of MS. Authorities used by Wood, which Dr. Clark has added
to the last vol. of his edition of *Wood's Life and Times*.

My greatest obligations are after all to the invaluable collections of
Bryan TWYNE (cited as Twyne), with the two earlier MS. collections of
Robert HARE, known as the *Privilegia* and the *Memorabilia*. Of the first
there are two copies, one in the Bodleian (Bodley, No. 906), the other in
the archives of the university. I have used the Bodleian copy. The
Memorabilia is in the archives. I have also consulted the Smith MSS. in
the Library of the Society of Antiquaries. All references to documents in
Twyne and Hare have been verified and corrected by the originals (except
where these are lost), but I have thought it convenient to add the references to their collections, except of course when the documents have
been printed.

[Since the first publication of this work in 1895 much valuable material
for the history of medieval Oxford has been made available in print,
chiefly through the laudable enterprise of the Oxford Historical Society
and its successive editors. The earliest extant letter-book of the university
has been edited in two volumes by the Rev. H. ANSTEY under the title

Epistolae Academicae (O.H.S., 1898): the letters and documents contained in this collection range from 1421 to 1508. *The Mediaeval Archives of the University of Oxford* (O.H.S., 1917–19), carefully edited by Dr. H. E. SALTER, includes in vol. i privileges and similar deeds preserved in the university archives and in the Public Record Office, and the title-deeds of university property in the Middle Ages; and in vol. ii the Proctor's accounts ranging from 1464 to 1497, together with other documents relating to municipal rather than to academical history. In *Registrum Cancellarii Oxoniensis*, 1439–69 (O.H.S., 2 vols., 1932), Dr. SALTER has made available for study the earliest surviving register of the acts of the chancellors of the university: this most valuable work is prefaced by an important introduction. A scholarly edition of the pre-Laudian statutes of the university, *Statuta Antiqua Universitatis Oxoniensis*, 1931, has been compiled by Mr. Strickland GIBSON, with a very useful introduction. In *Snappe's Formulary* (O.H.S., 1923), Dr. SALTER has brought together in one volume extracts from the Formulary of Dr. John Snappe, who was commissary at Oxford in 1399, significations of excommunication, confirmations of the chancellors of the university by the bishops of Lincoln, a collection of documents of particular interest for the history of the repression of Wyclifism in Oxford, and for Archbishop Arundel's visitation of the university, and some miscellaneous deeds about Oxford, some of which concern academical affairs.

The cartularies of the religious houses that existed in Oxford and its immediate neighbourhood during the Middle Ages contain much information of importance for the history, especially the topographical history, of the university and its constituent halls and colleges. *The Cartulary of the Monastery of St. Frideswide at Oxford* (O.H.S., 2 vols., 1895–6) has been edited by the Rev. S. R. WIGRAM. A third volume may be expected, edited by Dr. SALTER. *The Cartulary of the Abbey of Eynsham* (O.H.S., 2 vols., 1906–8); *A Cartulary of the Hospital of St. John the Baptist* (O.H.S., 2 vols., 1914–15); *The Oseney Cartulary* (O.H.S., 4 vols., 1928–34; vol. v has yet to be published) have all been admirably edited by Dr. SALTER. Some further documents relating to the property of the Priory of S. Frideswide in Oxford will be found calendared in the *Cartulary of the Mediaeval Archives of Christ Church*, edited by N. DENHOLM-YOUNG (O.H.S., 1931). To the sources of topographical information there should be added the 'Description of Oxford, from the Hundred Rolls of Oxfordshire, 1279', edited by Miss Rose GRAHAM, in *Collectanea*, vol. iv (O.H.S., 1905). Mr. H. HURST has attempted a survey of medieval Oxford in *Oxford Topography* (O.H.S., 1900), as a companion volume to *Old Plans of Oxford* (O.H.S., 1899). Dr. SALTER has composed a *Map of Medieval Oxford*, Oxford, 1934, which places at the disposal of students the fruits of all his investigations into the medieval topography of Oxford. 'An Inventory of the Muniments of the University', made in 1631 by Brian TWYNE, has been printed by Dr. R. L. POOLE as an appendix to his interesting *Lecture on the History of the University Archives*, Oxford, 1912.

In *A History of the University of Oxford*, 3 vols., London, 1924–7, Sir Charles MALLET, with notable industry, has compiled a detailed and very readable history of the university, its colleges and halls. The first volume covers the medieval period. Dr. L. H. D. BUXTON and Mr. Strickland GIBSON, *Oxford University Ceremonies*, Oxford, 1935, although primarily concerned with modern practice, give valuable information for the medieval period. Mr. Aymer VALLANCE's handsome volume, *The Old*

Colleges of Oxford, London, 1912, contains an important architectural CHAP. XII,
survey. The Rev. B. H. STREETER, *The Chained Library*, London, 1931,   § I.
is valuable for the older library buildings and equipment.]

THE connexion of the University of Paris with the Pala- The Al-
tine Schools of Charles the Great rests only upon a series legend.
of arbitrary assumptions. The theory which traces the origin of
Oxford to Alfred the Great aspires to a foundation in contemporary evidence. The Oxford myth was long accepted on the
authority of a passage in the Annals of Asser, Bishop of
St. David's. This passage is found neither in any extant manuscript nor in the earliest printed editions, but made its first
appearance in Camden's *Britannia* in 1600; whence, three
years afterwards, it was transferred to his edition of Asser.[1]
The spuriousness of the passage, which is, indeed, sufficiently
betrayed by its affected classicality of style, was demonstrated as
long ago as 1843 in a dissertation appended to the English translation of Huber's *English Universities*.[2] The myth received its
coup de grâce at the hands of Mr. James Parker.[3] As the result
of that writer's laborious investigation into the matter, Sir
Henry Savile, of Bank,[4] is left under a grave suspicion of
having perpetrated the patriotic fraud and the illustrious
Camden of having not quite innocently inserted it in his edition.
When the supposed authority of Asser is put out of court, the
Alfredian legend, even in its simplest and least elaborate form,
cannot be traced farther back than the *Polychronicon* of Ralph
Higden, who died in 1364.[5] In fact, the whole story, with

[1] *Asser's Life of King Alfred*, ed.
W. H. Stevenson, p. 70; W. Camden, *Britannia*, London, 1600, p.
331. In Savile's ed. of Ingulf
(*Rerum Anglicarum Scriptores post
Bedam*, London, 1596, fol. 513 b)
there is a somewhat similar inter-
polation, making the writer study
at Oxford in the twelfth century,
as also at Westminster. Camden
was Head Master of Westminster
School.
[2] In the preceding year Mr.
Thomas Wright (*Archaeologia*, xxix.
192) had called attention to the
legendary character of the whole
life; but the first modern historian

who pointed out the probability of
an insertion appears to have been
Lappenberg in his *Gesch. von England*, Hamburg, 1834, i. 339 *sq.*
[3] *The Early History of Oxford*
(O.H.S.), pp. 40 *sqq.* [See also
Asser's Life of King Alfred, ed.
W. H. Stevenson, pp. xxiii–xxviii.]
[4] To be distinguished from the
better known Sir Henry Savile,
Warden of Merton College, and
Provost of Eton.
[5] Ed. C. Babington (R.S.), vi.
354. The *Historiola* incorporated
in the Chancellor's and Proctors'
books (Anstey, *Mun. Acad.* ii.
367) is probably of about the same

the vast cycle of legend of which it is the nucleus—the foundation by King Mempric, a contemporary of David, the Greek
professors who came over with Brute the Trojan after the fall
of Troy, and were established at Greeklade, or Cricklade, in
Wiltshire, and the subsequent removal of the university to
Oxford—may now be abandoned to students of comparative
mythology and of the pathology of the human mind.

The pains which have been expended in tracking to its
origin every single thread in the elaborate web of fiction
which is solemnly presented in the guise of history by Bryan
Twyne, and with more reserve by Anthony Wood, can hardly
be regretted on account of the light which Mr. Parker's researches have thrown upon the early history of the town. It
is practically certain that the growth of a town, or indeed of
any considerable settlement, on the site of the existing city is
certainly posterior, and in all probability much posterior, to
the Roman period. The story of S. Frideswide supplies the
earliest evidence which even can pretend to be called historical
of the existence of Oxford. That story is subjected by Mr.
Parker to a no less exhaustive examination than the Alfredian
cycle. Its details—King Didanus and his consecrated daughter,
her persecution by a wicked King of Leicester, the miraculous
blinding of the King and his messengers, the spring that burst
forth at Binsey in answer to her prayers—must of course be
treated as legendary embellishments, but we may probably
recognize in the legend a germ of historical fact, and accept it
as pointing to the establishment of a community of nuns
ascribing their origin to S. Frideswide, somewhere about the
traditional date 721. The foundation of this house—whether
or not on the exact site of the modern Christ Church—is the
earliest presumptive evidence for the existence of even the
later town.[1] The first actual notice of Oxeneford does not

date. [*Statuta Antiqua Universitatis
Oxoniensis*, ed. S. Gibson, pp. 17–
19, who dates it 'before 1350'.]
The Mempric story appears for the
first time in the *Historia Regum
Angliae* of John Rous or Rosse, the
Chantry-priest of Warwick, whose
history (if such it is to be called)

ends with 1486 (ed. T. Hearne, p.
20 *sq.*). [On the legendary history
of the university see Dr. Hans
Matter, *Englische Gründungssagen
von Geoffrey of Monmouth bis zur
Renaissance*, Heidelberg, 1922, pp.
394–402.]
   [1] [No evidence for the existence

occur till the year 912. In that year, according to the Anglo- Saxon Chronicle, Edward the Elder 'took possession of London and Oxford, and of all the lands which owed obedience thereto'.[1] Mr. Parker conjectures that it was on this occasion that the city was for the first time fortified, and finds in the Castle Hill the sole surviving relic of tenth-century Oxford, and a second centre round which houses must have congregated.[2]

Little more is heard of Oxford till the eleventh century, when it becomes a frequent place of meeting for the National Gemot as well as for ecclesiastical councils. We are not, however, writing the history of the town, but of its university. Yet the fact just mentioned may serve in some measure to answer what is in many respects a perplexing question. Why should Oxford of all places have become the earliest and greatest national university? Ecclesiastically it was a place of very minor importance, and no historical prestige. It was not the see of a bishopric. Its earliest ecclesiastical foundation— the house which, first as a nunnery, then as a college of secular canons, lastly as a priory of Augustinian Canons, occupied what is now known as Christ Church—was a poor and insignificant foundation, when compared with such abbeys as Abingdon or Glastonbury. The Collegiate Church of S. George-within-the-Castle, built by Robert d'Oilly, Constable of the Conqueror, and Roger d'Ivri in 1074,[3] was very small. Even the stately Oseney, also a house of Augustinian Canons, was a house of the second rank, and was not

of this community of nuns has been found in any charter or other reliable record. The church of S. Frideswide first appears as a parish church: later it was served by secular canons. See The Cartulary of the Monastery of S. Frideswide at Oxford, ed. S. R. Wigram (O.H.S.), i. 2, and the article by Dr. H. E. Salter in A History of Oxfordshire (V.C.H.), ii. 97.]

[1] J. Parker, The Early History of Oxford (O.H.S.), pp. 116, 324.

[2] [More recent archaeological opinion favours a Norman ascription. See R. H. Gretton, The Ancient Remains of Oxford Castle, Oxford, 1925, p. 5.]

[3] Annales Monastici (Oseney), ed. H. R. Luard (R.S.), iv. 9; J. Parker, The Early History of Oxford (O.H.S.), p. 206 sq. [See also the article by Dr. H. E. Salter in A History of Oxfordshire (V.C.H.), ii. 160; The Cartulary of Oseney Abbey, ed. H. E. Salter (O.H.S.), iv. 1-9.]

CHAP. XII, founded till 1129, the Cistercian Abbey of Rewley not till
§ 1. after the rise of the university. The foundation-bulls for
erecting new universities commonly recite in their preambles
that the place in question is adapted, by reason of the amenity
and salubrity of the air and the cheapness and abundance of
victuals, for the use of students. Medieval writers exhaust
the resources of their vocabulary in praise of the climate of
Paris. Oxford, then almost as completely water-girt as Cambridge, could never have offered many attractions of that kind.
The other recommendation, cheapness and abundance of
victuals, it may have well possessed. Another essential qualification for a university town often insisted upon in foundation-bulls is facility of access. Oxford was marked out as a
convenient meeting-place, alike for the magnates attending a
council or parliament and for the assemblage of teachers and
students from all parts of England, by its central position. It
was situated on the border between Wessex and Mercia—the
two great divisions of the southern and then most important
and civilized half of the kingdom.[1] It was not inaccessible
from London, not too distant from the Continent, and yet as
conveniently situated as any southern town could be for
students from the far north and the far west. Not least
important, it was on the great water-way of the Thames. The
strategic value which resulted from such a position led in the
Conqueror's time to the building of the existing castle tower,
which is still the first historic object that attracts the visitor's
attention upon arriving at Oxford by the railway, and later
to the construction of those venerable city-walls which still

[1] [The attachment of the prefixes
'north' and 'south' to Northampton and Southampton well exem-
plifies the central position which
Oxford came to acquire. See
J. E. D. Gover, A. Mawer, and
F. M. Stenton, *The Place-names
of Northamptonshire* (Engl. Place-
name Soc., vol. x), Cambridge,
1933, p. xix: '*South*ampton was
already so distinguished by the
year 980, while the full form *North*-
ampton first appears on the eve of
the Norman Conquest. These prefixes doubtless arose spontaneously
in common speech. Northampton
and Southampton were connected
by one of the best-recorded lines
of early medieval travel, the road
through Brackley, Oxford, Abingdon, Newbury, Whitchurch, and
Winchester. It is suggestive that
the full form Southampton first appears in the Old English Chronicle
in a version written at Abingdon.']

impart so unique a charm to the most delightful of college CHAP. XII,
gardens. To its position, too, must be ascribed the rapid § 1.
increase in the commercial importance of Oxford after the
final cessation of Danish devastations and especially after the
beginning of the twelfth century. Its early selection by Jews
as a business centre marks this development.[1] In short,
Oxford must be content to accept its academic position as an
accident of its convenient situation.

Of course, it would be absurd to attempt a demonstration The uni-
a priori that the first and most important English university a develop-
could have arisen nowhere but at Oxford. But when it is ment of
remembered that a central position was a great *desideratum*, schools.
that only one of the largest towns in the kingdom would be
equal to the housing and feeding of many hundreds or
thousands of strangers, and that a royal vill would be preferred
for security and protection alike against hostile townsfolk and
oppressive ecclesiastical authorities, it will be evident that
hardly one other town could be named which satisfied in
equal perfection the requirements of the case.

There was something like a consensus among English
writers before Sir H. Maxwell-Lyte[2] in connecting the origin
of the Oxford schools with some one or other of the conventual churches of Oxford—with the Priory of S. Frideswide's,
with Oseney Abbey, or with the Church of the canons secular
of S. George-in-the-Castle.[3] But, amid all the obscurity

[1] As to the whole history of the
Jews in Oxford, see Dr. Neubauer's
essay in *Collectanea* (O.H.S.), ii.
277 *sq.*

[2] J. B. Mullinger, *Cambridge*,
i. 80; *Mun. Acad.*, ed. H. Anstey
(R.S.), i. xxxv; G. C. Brodrick,
Hist. of Oxford, p. 3; S. S. Laurie,
*Rise and early Constitution of Uni-
versities*, p. 236. Sir H. Maxwell-
Lyte (*History of the University of
Oxford*, p. 12) sees that the nature
of the chancellorship is fatal to a
direct continuity between any monastic school and the university,
but (p. 9) still seems to attach too
much importance to these earlier

and purely hypothetical monastic
schools. Prof. Laurie positively
tells us that 'before the time of
Alfred there were Schools in connexion with the Priory of S. Frideswide's'. If S. Frideswide's existed
before Alfred, it was a nunnery. It
is contrary to all analogy to suppose
that a university grew out of a
monastery of monks, to say nothing
of a nunnery.

[3] [Dr. H. E. Salter has pointed
out (see his article on 'The
Medieval University of Oxford' in
History (1929), xiv. 57–8) that S.
George's-in-the-Castle cannot be
treated as of no account in this

CHAP. XII,
§ 1.

which hangs over the origin of the university, one thing may be taken as absolutely certain—that the schools in connexion with which the university grew up were never at any time dependent upon any capitular or monastic body in Oxford. Had they been so, the masters and scholars would have been under the jurisdiction of some officer of that body, as the masters of Paris were under the authority of the Chancellor of Notre Dame. The situation of the schools sufficiently testifies to the improbability of the hypothesis. The schools are first found established in the neighbourhood of S. Mary's —a parish church which came to be used by the University for its assemblies—and not in the neighbourhood of S. Frideswide's. As soon as the constitution of the university becomes known to us, the masters and scholars are under the authority of the Chancellor of Oxford, an official elected by the masters, but deriving his authority from the Bishop of Lincoln, and in no way connected with any monastic or collegiate church in Oxford. Had the schools at one time been connected with S. Frideswide's or Oseney, they could only have emancipated themselves from the jurisdiction of the prior or abbot by a tremendous struggle, which could not have passed into utter oblivion without leaving a trace or a vestige of itself behind.[1]

connexion. Walter, Archdeacon of Oxford (c. 1112–c. 1151), a learned man of considerable repute, was Provost of S. George's, and a patron of Geoffrey of Monmouth, who was himself resident in Oxford between 1129 and 1150. See also the articles by Dr. Salter in *A History of Oxfordshire* (V.C.H.), ii. 5–6, and *Engl. Hist. Rev.* (1919), xxxiv. 383, and the references to Walter, the archdeacon, in *Facsimiles of Early Charters in Oxford Muniment Rooms*, ed. H. E. Salter, pp. 60, 80, 81, 96, 101; and also the article on Walter Calenius by H. Bradley in *Dict. Nat. Biog.* Robert de Chesney, Bishop of Lincoln, 1148–66, had previously been a Canon of S. George's; see *The*

Cartulary of the Abbey of Eynsham, ed. H. E. Salter (O.H.S.), i. 418. But any encouragement to establish schools in Oxford that may have been given from this quarter must have been terminated by the transference of the short-lived foundation of S. George's to Oseney Abbey, or Priory as it was then, in 1149. See *The Cartulary of Oseney Abbey,* ed. H. E. Salter, (O.H.S.), iv. 37–8.]

[1] The sole connexion between the university and S. Frideswide's lay in the fact that the University chest was lodged for safe custody at S. Frideswide's. Had the masters recently emancipated themselves from the jurisdiction of the priory, this is the last place where they

These considerations are amply sufficient to establish a
probability, which in the minds of those who have followed §1.
the preceding account of the origin of other universities will Its origin must be
perhaps amount to a kind of intuitive certainty, that the origin sought *ab extra.*
of the Oxford school must be sought *ab extra.* In northern
Europe the universities which originated by spontaneous
development are always found in connexion with a cathedral
or great collegiate church, never in connexion with a monastery; and Oxford possessed neither cathedral nor collegiate
church to account for the growth of its schools. In northern
Europe the schools are invariably found to be under the
immediate supervision of some local ecclesiastical authority;
while at Oxford the masters seem at first to have enjoyed
practical independence; and when at length their schools
were subjected to ecclesiastical regulation, they were allowed

would have put it. The authority
quoted for the statement that S.
Frideswide's was at one time,
before the Conquest, in the hands
of the monks of Abingdon is Cap-
grave (*Nova Legenda Anglie*, ed.
C. Horstman, i. 460), who says
'Abendoniensi abbati ecclesia sancte
Frideswide cum possessionibus suis
a rege quodam donata fuit' (based
on MS. Cartulary of S. Frid.,
Ch. Ch. Library, No. 340, p. 8
[*The Cartulary of the Monastery of
S. Frideswide at Oxford*, ed. S. R.
Wigram (O.H.S.), i. 9]). But this
state of things did not continue 'for
two generations after the Norman
Conquest' (G. C. Brodrick, *Hist. of
Oxford*, p. 48). On the contrary,
Capgrave says that Abingdon was
in possession 'per annos aliquot'.
It is certain that the church was in
the hands of secular canons at the
date of Domesday and up to the
time of the intrusion of the regular
canons. Bryan Twyne (ap. Dugdale, vi. 1622) speaks of a 'Monastery of S. Aldate's' as founded
in 1122. The 'Monastery' of S.
Aldad is mentioned in the *Chron.
Mon. de Abendon*, ed. J. Stevenson

(R.S.), ii. 174, 213, on which his
statement is based; [but here, as
often in the first half of the twelfth
century, *monasterium* is merely used
to designate a church]. There is
indeed no good evidence that there
was any Benedictine house in Oxford till the foundation of the
Benedictine halls or colleges, still
less for connecting the origin of
the university with any Benedictine schools, a theory which Mr.
Mullinger (*Cambridge*, i. 80, 83)
seems inclined to accept—in spite
of his previous ascription to Oxford
of an 'origin similar to that assigned
to the university of Paris'. [Mr.
A. F. Leach (*National Review*,
Sept. 1896, pp. 99–102), in an
article vigorously criticizing Rashdall's theory of the origin of the
University of Oxford, contends
that 'Oxford is as much, there is
every reason to believe, a natural
growth from the schools and schoolmaster of S. Frideswide's as Paris
from those of Notre Dame'. Evidence of the activities of the schools
and schoolmaster of S. Frideswide's
has yet to be discovered.]

to elect their own superior, who was dependent only on the distant Bishop of Lincoln. The natural inference from these facts is that the school must have originated—probably at the time of some ecclesiastical confusion—in a migration from one of the great archetypal universities. No doubt a reader unacquainted with the history of other universities will be disposed to ascribe an *a priori* improbability to a theory which places the origin of a great university in some sudden and catastrophic movement of this kind. There will, however, be no such prejudice in the mind of the student familiar with the migratory habits of the medieval scholar and acquainted with the early history of academic constitutions. In ascribing the origin of Oxford to an academic migration I am at least ascribing it to a *vera causa*, which is known to have produced the universities of Reggio, Vicenza, Vercilli, Padua, Leipzig, and other permanent universities, to say nothing of the enormous number of merely temporary migrations.

Presumably in a migration from Paris. If Oxford originated in an academic migration, it will hardly be disputed that its original masters and scholars must have come from Paris, then the ordinary place of higher education for English ecclesiastics. Is there any trace of such a movement in actual history? Previous inquirers seem to have entirely overlooked the allusions to this movement, probably because they are of a kind which could not be discovered by turning out the word Oxford in the indexes of the various contemporary chroniclers.

Exodus of English scholars from Paris in 1167. These allusions are sufficient to establish a high probability that the University of Oxford owes its origin to the quarrel of Becket with Henry II.[1] In 1167 the exiled John of Salisbury, in a letter to one Peter the Writer, speaks of certain ominous events which had gone far to fulfil an astrological prediction about the issues of the current year. This prophecy contained the enigmatic statement that the votaries of Mercury (*Mercuriales*) should be depressed; and in that year, the writer continues, 'the *Mercuriales* were so depressed that France, the mildest and most civil of nations, has expelled her alien

[1] [See below, p. 29, n. 2.]

scholars'.[1] Is it not more than probable, having regard to the state of relations between England and France, that the alien scholars were, or at least included, the subjects of the English king, especially since the English then formed by far the largest body of foreign students at Paris? The event thus obscurely alluded to may have been a measure of hostility aimed by the French King against the oppressor of Holy Church and the English ecclesiastics, who as a body sided with their king against their not yet canonized primate; or this expulsion may be only rhetorically attributed to France, and the incident may really have been a voluntary exodus such as we have independent reasons for believing to have taken place at about this time. In any case, the movement must have been one of considerable magnitude, since it struck the imagination of contemporaries as worthy of being associated with the disastrous retreat of Frederick I from Rome and other events of European importance.[2]

Among a series of ordinances directed against the partisans of Becket by Henry II occurs a provision that henceforth no clerk shall cross from the Continent to England or from England to the Continent without leave of the King or his Justiciar in England. Moreover, at the same time all clerks who possessed 'revenues' in England were to be summoned by the Sheriffs to return within three months 'as they loved their revenues'.[3] There can be no doubt that in the middle of

Recall of English scholars by Henry II.

[1] 'Bella et seditiones ubique fervent; Mercuriales adeo depressi sunt ut Francia, omnium mitissima et civilissima nationum, alienigenas scholares abegerit', *Materials for the History of Thomas Becket*, ed. J. C. Robertson (R.S.), vi. 235, 236. Cf. Denifle, *Chartul. Univ. Paris*, Introd., No. 20, where 'Mercuriales' is explained by 'professores bonarum litterarum'.

[2] See the context of the passage cited above. [Rashdall's interpretation of this allusion to the expulsion of foreign scholars from France is open to the criticism that John of Salisbury is here not so much concerned to record recent events of 'considerable magnitude' as to note those which seem to bear out an astrological forecast for the year 1167. All the other events alluded to by John of Salisbury are selected for their significance in this latter connexion rather than for their fitness to rank with so important an event as the retreat of the Emperor.]

[3] 'Nullus clericus vel monachus vel conversus vel alicuius conversationis permittatur transfretare vel redire in Angliam, nisi de transitu suo habeat litteras iustitiae et de reditu suo litteras domini regis. Siquis aliter inventus fuerit agens,

CHAP. XII, the twelfth century scores, in fact hundreds, of masters and
§ I.   scholars beneficed in England must have been studying in the
schools of Paris.[1] Equally little doubt can there be that a
large proportion of them 'loved' their benefices. Hence we
are absolutely bound to infer the return to England in obedience to the royal command of a large body of Parisian
masters and scholars. At all events, all communication with
the Continent would have been cut off for the Parisian
students passing a vacation in England, and for the intending
freshmen of the year, at a time when probably some hundreds
of young Englishmen annually left the shores of England for
the schools of Paris. What became of this repulsed scholastic
host? Nobody who knows anything at all of the habits of the
medieval scholar will doubt that somewhere or other—in one
town or in several—at least a portion of these scholars would
be sure to congregate under their old masters, and to transfer
to English soil their old studies, their old discipline, and—so
far as altered circumstances permitted—their old organization.
As a matter of fact, we hear of no such congregation of scholars
except at Oxford. If the recalled scholars did not go to
Oxford, where did they go?

capiatur et incarceretur. . . . Ut
omnes clerici qui reditus habent in
Anglia sint submoniti per omnes
comitatus ut infra tres menses veni-
ant in Angliam ad reditus suos,
sicut diligunt reditus suos, et si non
venerint ad terminum statutum,
reditus in manu regis capiantur.'
Vita S. Thomae, auctore Willelmo
Cantuariensi, printed in Materials
for the History of Thomas Becket
(R.S.), i. 53, 54. Here the constitutions appear under 1165; in Hoveden's Chronica, ed. W. Stubbs
(R.S.), i. 231-2, under 1164; in the
Chronica of Gervase of Canterbury,
ed. W. Stubbs (R.S.), i. 215, and in
Materials, vii. 148, 149, under
1169. See the notes of Bishop
Stubbs on Hoveden, loc. cit., and
of Robertson in Materials. I may
add that the two provisions do not
seem quite consistent with each

other, and that they are not placed
consecutively in spite of their relation to the same subject-matter
which seems to suggest that they
may have been issued at different
times. [Bishop Stubbs in the note
here referred to expresses the
opinion that 'these instructions
were not issued in 1165, nor probably before 1169'.]

[1] [Dr. H. E. Salter considers
that 'this greatly exaggerates the
number. When Oxford and Cambridge were in full swing there
were not more than a hundred incumbents residing in the two universities, and it would be strange
if more than fifty were affected by
the command of Henry II.' See
History, 1929, xiv. 57. There is no
means of estimating the number of
unbeneficed English clerks studying in Paris at this period.]

The date of these ordinances is not quite certain. By some CHAP. XII,
of the chroniclers they are given under the year 1165, by §1.
others (with some variations) under 1169. The best authori- Date of the ordi-
ties agree in referring them to 1169, and there is no doubt nances.
that, if the whole collection is to be referred to the same year,
they cannot be placed earlier. In that case the 'expulsion'
alluded to by John of Salisbury cannot be connected with the
action of Henry II. But it seems quite probable that the
ordinances collected together by the chroniclers may really
have been issued at different dates; and that this particular
edict may have been issued towards the close of 1167, when
John of Salisbury's letter must have been written.[1] That hypothesis will account for the discrepancy between the various
chroniclers. In that case we may definitely assign the birth of
Oxford as a *studium generale* to 1167 or the beginning of 1168.
If any doubt be entertained as to whether an edict against the
'transfretation' of 'clerks' would really have affected the
scholars of Paris, we may appeal to a passage in a letter of one
of Becket's supporters, in which he complains that the King
'wants (or wills) all scholars to return to their country or be
deprived of their benefices',[2] while other correspondence of

[1] [This hypothesis would have gained in cogency if Rashdall had been able to point to any turn in the course of the quarrel between Henry II and Becket that would explain why this particular edict should have been issued towards the close of 1167.]

[2] 'Vult etiam ut omnes scholares repatriare cogantur aut beneficiis suis priventur.' *Materials* (R.S.), vii. 146. This letter is referred by Robertson to 1169, but apparently only in consequence of his view as to the date of the Edict. [In referring this letter to 1169 the editors of volume vii of the *Materials for the History of Thomas Becket* may well have been guided by the reference which it contains to the precautions being taken by Henry against the delivery of papal letters of interdict in England: such pre-

cautions would have been premature if they had been taken before the year 1169.]

The following passage from the letters of John of Salisbury, though it does not mention Oxford, seems to point to the existence of a university town somewhere in England : 'Unde et studiis tuis congratulor, quem agnosco ex signis perspicuis in urbe garrula et ventosa (ut pace scholarium dictum sit) non tam inutilium argumentorum locos inquirere, quam virtutum.' *Materials* (R.S.), vi. 6. The letter is dated 1166 by Canon Robertson, and it must have been written after Whitsunday in that year when the Archdeacon of Poitou was excommunicated, but it may well have been written a year later. That his correspondent Black was in England cannot be proved: I can only appeal

the Becket circle is full of allusions to the strictness with which the ports were watched in execution of the royal orders.

Schools of Oxford before 1167. In connecting the sudden rise of Oxford into a *studium generale* with the recall of the English scholars from Paris by Henry II in or about the year 1167, I am far from denying that there were already, or had been at an earlier date, schools of considerable importance at Oxford. A certain scholastic reputation may well have been one of the causes which attracted the recalled Parisians to Oxford rather than to any other of the few English towns whose size and situation fitted them equally well for the sudden reception of a large body of scholars.

Theobaldus Stampensis. There are two indisputable pieces of evidence, and one very questionable piece of evidence, which tend to prove the existence of not unimportant schools at Oxford before the year 1167. The first, and by far the most conclusive, of these has been overlooked by all the more recent historians of Oxford. Two letters are preserved from a certain Theobaldus Stampensis (Thibaut d'Estampes), one of them addressed to Faritius, Abbot of Abingdon from 1100 to 1117; the other to the illustrious Roscellinus after he had been compelled to flee (possibly to England) from the violence of his theological opponents. The writer is described as 'Master at Oxford'. In other and earlier letters he appears as 'Doctor at Caen'.[1] A comparison of dates then makes it clear that at

to the general tone of this and the preceding letter. He appears to have kept John of Salisbury informed as to the doings of the English bishops. [As Ralph Niger (or Black, as Rashdall calls him), to whom John of Salisbury wrote the letter here referred to and that which precedes it in *Materials* (R.S.), vi. 1–5, is known to have studied at Paris under Gerard Pucelle, subsequently Bishop of Coventry, who was lecturing there about this time, it seems more probable that Paris and not Oxford is the *urbs garrula et ventosa* to which allusion is made. See the article on Ralph Niger by Dr. C. L. Kingsford in *D.N.B.* Moreover, it may be remarked as

regards the date of this letter that the Archdeacon of Poitou, Richard of Ilchester, was released, by order of the Pope, before the end of 1166 from the sentence of excommunication under which Becket had placed him. See *Materials* (R.S.), vi. 1–5, 84–6; the article on Richard of Ilchester by Miss Kate Norgate in *D.N.B.*; and F. M. Powicke, *Stephen Langton*, pp. 33, 56.]

[1] Theobaldus Stampensis is mentioned by Wood (*Annals*, i. 140) as an Oxford doctor *sub anno* 1129; but later writers have probably been misled by the authority of Bale and Fabricius, who place him in the thirteenth century. Five letters of Theobald are printed in

some time before the year 1117 this French or Norman ecclesiastic, who had hitherto taught at Caen, transferred his
school to Oxford. A little tractate of his against the monks,
preserved in a Bodleian MS., proves that he was not a monk,
though he may very well have been teaching under the
authority of the canons of S. Frideswide's.[1] An anonymous
reply to this very violent onslaught contains the interesting
statement that he had under him at Oxford 'sixty or a hundred
clerks, more or less'.[2] The subject-matter of these literary

D'Achery's *Spicilegium* (1723), iii. 445, and *Patrologia Latina*, clxiii. 759–70. They are as follows:

(1) 'Ad episcopum Lincolniensem —De quibusdam in divina pagina titubantibus.' D'Achery gives the date 1108. The Bishop of Lincoln at this time (1093–1123) was Robert Bloet. The mistake as to the author's date seems to have arisen from confusion with the better-known Robert Grosseteste, Bishop of Lincoln 1235–53. The object of the letter is to uphold the efficacy of *poenitentia* in all cases, even without *confessio oris*, where that is impossible.

(2) *Inc.* 'Pharitio venerando Habendonensis Ecclesiae praelato, domino suo et indubitanter amico Theobaldus magister Oxenefordiae.' On the certain damnation of unbaptized infants, &c.

(3) *Inc.* 'Margaritae praecellenti reginae, praecellentis regis filiae, Theobaldus Stampensis, doctor Cadumensis.' This Margaret must be Queen Margaret of Scotland, who died in 1093.

(4) *Inc.* 'Theobaldus magister Cadumensis Philippo amico suo desiderabili.' A violent attack on monasticism; in fact, an apology for clerical marriage or concubinage.

(5) *Inc.* 'Roscelino Compendioso magistro Theobaldus Stampensis magister Oxenefordiae.' A violent reply to Roscellinus's attack on the preferment of priests' sons.

There is, of course, no authority

for the statement of the authors of the *Histoire littéraire de la France* (xi. 91) that Roscellinus 'excita de nouveaux troubles en Angleterre, dans l'académie d'Oxford, en soutenant que les enfans des prêtres ne pouvoient pas être élevés aux ordres sacrés'. These letters, unknown to any historian of Oxford, are mentioned by Cousin, *Ouvrages inédits d'Abélard*, p. xcvii.

[1] The MS. (Bodley 561), written in the first half of the twelfth century, is an 'Improperium cuiusdam in Monachos' which begins—'Turstano dei gratia laudabili eboracensium archiepiscopo T. stampensis, magister Oxinefordie' (f. 61), and is directed chiefly against the practice of impropriating parish churches and serving them by monastic priests. The tone of the document may be inferred from one of the opening sentences: 'Aliud est ecclesia, aliud est monasterium. Ecclesia namque est conuocatio fidelium, monasterium uero locus et carcer damnatorum, i.e. monachorum qui se ipsos damnauerunt ut damnationem euitarent perpetuam.' Since Thurstan was Archbishop of York from 1119 to 1139, we get a *terminus a quo*. This treatise cannot have been written before 1119.

[2] The passage is worth quoting in full:
'Et si uagorum noveras uicia clericorum (f. 68 b), debueras tamen honorem deferre timori magistrorum et religioni canonicorum. O

C

CHAP. XII, remains makes it plain that he was a theologian, while he
§ 1. appears to be also included by his opponent among the category of 'liberal masters'. Another theologian is mentioned Robert as teaching in Oxford in the year 1133. This was Robert Pullen. Pullus or Pullen,[1] the author of one of the most important

Coridon, Coridon, que te dementia cepit! Nunquid non sunt ubique terrarum liberales magistri qui dicuntur et clerici? Tu quoque nescio quis nonne magistri uice sexagenos aut centenos plusue minusue clericos regere diceris quibus uenditor verborum cupidus efficeris, forsitan ut eos incautos nequissime fallas, sic ut et ipse falleris? Unde ergo ista tua clericorum penuria?' Wood had apparently only seen the extracts from this manuscript in James's MS. Ecloga (in the Bodleian), but Twyne (Antiq. Acad. Oxon. Apol., p. 224) had read the original manuscript. This extract appeared in The Academy, no. 890: Prof. Holland has published further extracts in Collectanea (O.H.S.), ii. 156.

It is observable that the monastic Apologia throughout opposes canons to monks. The controversy forms part of the great struggle of the time between the monks and the secular (and usually married) canons. At the same time it should be observed that even regular canons seem to be included with the 'clerici' and grouped against the 'monachi'. The tractate is largely occupied with proving the necessity of celibacy for canons (whether regular or secular) as well as for monks. The following extract will illustrate these remarks: 'Veruntamen cum ait quia monasterium est locus et carcer damnatorum, i.e. monachorum, cur oblitus est, ut quidem uulgo loquar, et regularium canonicorum? An ignorat quod sanctus Augustinus ypponium ueniens concedente Ualerio tunc episcopo monasterium

fundauerit, in quo se et fratres quos ad seruitium Christi de mundana conuersatione predicando subtraxerat aggregauit? Sic enim de illo scriptum legimus. . . . Constat itaque monasterium esse tam canonicorum quam et monachorum. Quare ergo oblitus est et canonicorum? Forsitan ne damnarentur canonici sicut et monachi' (f. 63 a).

Whether the regular or Augustinian canons turned out the seculars at S. Frideswide's in 1111 or in 1122 appears to be doubtful (see Dugdale, Monasticon Anglicanum, ed. Caley, ii. 134; Matt. Paris, Chron. Mai., ed. H. R. Luard (R.S.), ii. 139; William of Malmesbury, Gesta Pontificum, ed. N. E. S. A. Hamilton (C.R.S.), p. 316; Wood, Annals (O.H.S.), i. 138, 139). According to the S. Frideswide's Cartulary [Cartul. Mon. St. Frideswide, ed. S. R. Wigram (O.H.S.), i. 9], the transference took place c. 1122, and this is probably the true date. If so, Theobald must have taught before the expulsion of the seculars; in any case, he was no doubt a secular himself, teaching probably more or less under the authority of the canons. [But a more likely patron is Walter, Archdeacon of Oxford (c. 1112–c. 1151), and Provost of S. George's-in-the-Castle, who is known to have been a secular canon and married, two points for which Theobald offered support. See above, p. 9, n. 3.]

[1] The passage in the Oseney Chronicle runs: 'MCXXXIII. Magister Rob' pulein scripturas divinas que in Anglia obsoluerant, apud Oxon. legere cepit. Qui postea cum ex

collections of 'Sentences' eventually superseded by the more CHAP. XII,
famous work of Peter the Lombard, which is, however, § I.
largely based upon the work of his English predecessor. He
was afterwards a cardinal and chancellor of the Holy Roman
Church.[1]

Far more doubtful is the received opinion that the eminent Case of Vacarius doubtful.
Lombard jurist Vacarius taught at Oxford in the year 1149.
It is certain that some years before this date he was brought
to England by Theobald, Archbishop of Canterbury, to assist
in the settlement of that prelate's dispute with Henry of Blois,

doctrina eius ecclesia tam Anglicana
quam Gallicana plurimum pro-
fecisset a papa Lucio secundo vo-
catus et in cancellarium Sancte
Romane ecclesie promotus est' (ed.
H. R. Luard (R.S.), *Annal. Monast.*,
iv. 19, 20). The *Continuatio Bedae*
(Bodl. MS. 712, f. 275) says:
'Eodem anno (1133) venit magister
Robertus cognomento pullus de
ciuitate Exonia Oxenfordiam ibique
scripturas divinas, que per idem
tempus in Angliam (*sic*) absolute
erant, et scolasticis quippe nec-
glecte fuerant, per quinquennium
legit, omnique die dominico uer-
bum dei populo predicavit, ex cuius
doctrina plurimi profecerunt. [Qui
postea ob eximiam doctrinam et
religiosam famam a papa Lucio
uocatus et in cancellarium sancte
romane ecclesie promotus est.]' The
manuscript was written for Robert
Wyvill, Bishop of Salisbury, 1330–
75. The statements in the last two
clauses are no doubt a rhetorical
flourish and have a suspicious resemblance to the passage about
Cambridge in the Ingulfine forgery
(see below, p. 276). The passage
is probably a rhetorical amplification of the Oseney Chronicler's
statement. [Dr. R. L. Poole (see
'The Early Lives of Robert Pullen
and Nicholas Breakspear' in *Essays
in Mediaeval History presented to
T. F. Tout*, pp. 61–4) considers
it more likely that Robert Pullen

taught at Exeter than at Oxford,
and in support of this view suggests
that the fourteenth-century copyist of the Oseney Annals mistook
Exonia for *Oxonia* in the original
version, which is Cotton MS. Vitell.
E. xv. This manuscript was among
those that suffered in the fire at
Ashburnham House in 1731, and
all but the first two letters of the
word in question have been burnt
away. But Dr. H. E. Salter (see
History, 1929, xiv. 57) has pointed
out that the writer of this manuscript 'did not use *Oxonia*, a word
which had not been invented at
that time, but *Oxeneford*', and
further that 'Brian Twyne, who
saw the manuscript before it was
burnt, gives the word in full'. It is
evident, therefore, that when the
fourteenth-century copyist wrote
'Oxoniam' he had *Oxenefordiam*
and not *Exoniam* before him in the
original edition.]

[1] Some doubt has been expressed
about the identity, but see John
of Hexham in *Symeonis Monachi
Opera*, ed. T. Arnold (R.S.), ii. 319.
His *Sententiae* are published in
Migne, tom. 186: for an account of
the book see J. E. Erdmann, *Hist.
of Phil.*, pp. 337–40. [See also the
article on Robert Pullen by Dr.
Rashdall in *D.N.B.*; and A. Land-
graf, 'Some Unknown Writings of
the Early Scholastic Period', in *New
Scholasticism* (1930), iv. 11–14.]

CHAP. XII,
§ 1.

Bishop of Winchester.[1] Several historians mention the fact that he was the first teacher of the civil law in England.[2] But only one of them, Gervase of Canterbury, mentions that this teaching was at Oxford.[3] From the way in which John of Salisbury speaks of these civil law lectures, it is more than probable that he means them to have taken place in the 'household' of Archbishop Theobald, in which it is independently certain that lectures and disputations were held on a scale which leads Bishop Stubbs to speak of this Palatine School as a kind of 'University'.[4] John of Salisbury was a

[1] [For a discussion of the reasons for Vacarius coming to England see F. Liebermann, *E.H.R.* (1896), xi. 305–14.]

[2] [See *Iohannis Saresberiensis Policraticus*, ed. C. C. J. Webb, ii. 399; Robert of Torigny, *Chronica*, in the *Chronicles of the Reigns of Stephen, Henry II, and Richard I*, ed. R. Howlett (R.S.), iv. 158–9; and Gervase of Canterbury, *Actus Pontificum Cantuar*, ed. W. Stubbs (R.S.), p. 384. The relevant passages in these writers have been conveniently collected by Prof. Holland in *Collectanea* (O.H.S.), ii. 165.]

[3] It is observable that Gervase evidently knew very little about the history of legal study, since he makes Gratian teach at Rome. The *Actus Pontificum* was written at the earliest in 1199 (i. xxviii–xxix); the manuscript is after the second half of the thirteenth century.

Cf. also Bacon, *Opera Inedita*, ed. J. S. Brewer (R.S.), p. 420. Of modern writers who have dealt with Vacarius, the most important is Wenck, *Magister Vacarius*, Leipzig, 1820; *Leipziger Literatur-Zeitung*, 1821, nos. 273, 274. [See also the article on 'Vacarius' by Prof. T. E. Holland in *D.N.B.* and the authorities there cited; Pollock and Maitland, *History of English Law*, ed. 2, i. 118–19; Dr. F. Liebermann, *E.H.R.*, 1896, ii. 305–14, 514–15; Vacarius, *Liber Pauper-*

um, ed. Prof. F. de Zulueta, Selden Society, 1927; and the note on 'The All Souls Fragments of Vacarius', by the same in the *Bodleian Quarterly Record*, iii. 164–5.]

[4] On these archiepiscopal schools see Bishop Stubbs's delightful *Lectures on Med. and Mod. Hist.*, pp. 130–1, 142 *sq.* By a singular coincidence Peter of Blois (Ep. vi, *Patrol. Lat.* ccvii, c. 17) actually speaks of the clerks in the archbishop's household as a 'Universitas': 'quod si Deus minori quae potiora sunt revelaverit, eius sententiae sine omni invidia et depravatione universitas acquiescit'. Of course, the word is used nontechnically. The study of the Roman law in England during the second half of the twelfth century was much more vigorous than is commonly supposed. It was not till the following century that it was finally decided that the old common law of England was not to be superseded or modified by the civil law of Rome (as was the case in so large a part of Europe), and that the common-law bar was not to be supplied by university-bred ecclesiastics and civilians. For the number of books on civil or canon law composed in England about 1180–1200 see Caillemer, 'Le Droit civil dans les provinces Anglo-normandes au xii siècle' in *Mém. de l'Ac. des Sciences etc. de Caen*, 1883, p. 156 *sq.*

member of the archbishop's household at the time and cannot
have been mistaken. If therefore his statement is inconsistent
with that of Gervase, there can be no doubt which of them is
to be accepted, since Gervase wrote at the beginning of the
following century. But it should be observed that Gervase
does not explicitly put the Oxford teaching in 1149. His
language is consistent with the supposition that this teaching
took place at some later date, and it is certain that Vacarius
was living in England as late as 1198. It is likely enough that
Gervase made a mistake about the date, if not about the place,
of Vacarius's law teaching.[1] The fact that Vacarius's *Liber
Pauperum*, a compendium of the civil law, occupied a prominent place in the studies of Oxford towards the end of the
century confirms Gervase's statement that he did teach at
Oxford, but it is quite as likely that the teaching was after
1167 as before it.[2]

[1] My doubts on the subject of Vacarius were suggested by Schaar-schmidt (*Johannes Saresberiensis*, Leipzig, 1862). At the same time I must point out that he unjustifiably passes over in silence the testimony of the Oseney Chronicler and makes the statement as to Pullus rest on that of the anonymous continuator of Bede only. His view that the *studium* had no existence (in post-Saxon times) till 1229 (p. 19) is simply absurd, and could hardly have been made even by Schaar-schmidt since publication of the *Munimenta Academica*. This excessive scepticism is the more remarkable in a writer who appears inclined to swallow the Alfredian story. [Dr. F. Liebermann in his excellent note on the career of Vacarius (*E.H.R.*, 1896, ii. 305–14, 514–15) is inclined to accept Gervase's testimony. He remarks that 'a Canterbury monk would be the last man intentionally to diminish the literary glory of his church by transferring the father of civil jurisprudence from his city to Oxford', and concludes that the known use

of the *Liber Pauperum* as the text-book of the Oxford civilians at the close of the twelfth century 'weighs so strongly in favour of Oxford's claim that Gervase's statement seems right after all'. Dr. R. L. Poole, in a footnote to 'the Early Lives of Robert Pullen and Nicholas Breakspear' in *Essays in Mediaeval History presented to T. F. Tout*, p. 62, summarily disposes of Gervase's statement as a mistake; but Prof. F. de Zulueta, in his judicious recapitulation of the evidence in the introduction to his edition of Vacarius's *Liber Pauperum* (Selden Society, 1927), pp. xiii–xix, endorses Liebermann's conclusions, and gives substantial grounds for the opinion that 'to doubt whether Vacarius ever taught at Oxford is to doubt against the evidence'. As regards the date when Vacarius taught in Oxford, Prof. de Zulueta (*op. cit.*, p. xvii) sees little to object to in Rashdall's supposition that the date should be reckoned to have been some twenty or more years after 1149.]

[2] See the account of Daniel of

CHAP. XII,
§ I.
Position as
studium
generale
due to
Parisian
migration.
But whatever may be thought as to the place or date of Vacarius's teaching, the question has little bearing upon the problem with which we are now concerned. The question is not how there came to be schools in Oxford, but how these schools grew into a *studium generale*. Up to 1167 we have no evidence of the existence in Oxford of more than one master at a time: a single master does not make a university.[1] There were other schools in England quite as important as we have any reason for believing Oxford to have been in the time of Theobald or Pullen or Vacarius, if the last really taught here before 1167. The question is 'Why did Oxford alone of all these Schools grow into a *studium generale*?' It is, of course, in itself conceivable that such a *studium* may have grown up by purely spontaneous evolution. I have already given reasons for believing that Oxford did not develop in this way. Unless we are to reject all the evidence that we

Merlac or Morley, who, arriving from Toledo some time between 1175 and 1200, describes England as wholly given up to the study of law ('Pro Titio et Seio penitus Aristoteles et Plato oblivioni darentur'), and continues 'Tum ne ego solus inter Romanos Graecus remanerem, ubi huiusmodi studium florere didiceram, iter arripui'. (There can be little doubt that the place was Oxford; observe that the *studium* seems to have sprung up since the writer left England.) The passage is printed by Holland, *Collectanea* (O.H.S.), ii. 171–2 (cf. below, p. 31, n. 2). In 1187–1200 Giraldus Cambrensis tells a story 'de clerico Oxoniensi, nomine Martino', from which it appears that the Oxford law-students were styled 'Pauperistae'. But see below, Appendix II. In 1195 Giraldus Cambrensis, *Opera*, ed. J. S. Brewer (R.S.), ii. 345, makes the archbishop hold a Court at Oxford 'praesentibus scholaribus multis et iurisperitis'.

[1] Prof. [later Sir T. E.] Holland (*Collectanea* (O.H.S.), ii. 151–92)

has made a very useful collection of the twelfth-century allusions to Oxford hitherto pointed out, but he adds nothing to the above notices for this period except a passage about Robert of Cricklade, afterwards Prior of S. Frideswide, of whom he says: 'There is no reason to suppose that the schools in question' (in which he was 'Magister Scholarum' when young) 'were situated elsewhere than at Oxford, in which city and its neighbourhood this great scholar seems to have passed his life' (p. 142). Of the gratuitousness of this last assumption readers may judge from the fact that Robert became a canon regular at Cirencester (see below, p. 28). Prof. Holland is evidently influenced by the tacit assumption that there were schools nowhere else but at Oxford. Theobaldus Stampensis tells us that there were schools at this time in every town and village: 'non solum in urbibus et castellis, uerum etiam et in uillulis, peritissimi scholarum magistri quot fiscorum regalium exactores et ministri' (Bodley MS. 561, f. 68 *b*).

possess as to the schools of the twelfth century in France and England, we must suppose that Theobald and Pullen taught in connexion with one of the great churches, probably S. Frideswide's. Or if a great master of established repute from Caen or Paris or Bologna may conceivably have been allowed to lecture in defiance of the usual rule without any special authorization, this supposition cannot be allowed in the case of the humbler masters of arts who formed at Oxford and Paris the true nucleus of the university. The hypothesis of a migration is the only one which will account for the independence of the Oxford masters and the absence of any organic connexion with an Oxford church. Evidence has been given to show that such a migration from Paris to England did take place about the year 1167. No doubt we cannot prove that the masters and scholars expelled or recalled from Paris in or about 1167 came to Oxford. All we can show is that the prohibition to study at Paris would naturally tend, sooner or later, to the formation of a *studium generale* in England; that we hear nothing of a *studium generale* half a century after 1167 except at Oxford; that at Oxford there is no evidence of a *studium generale* before 1167, while there is such evidence within a very few years after 1167. The method of exclusions is accounted a good one even in physical science. A hypothesis which alone explains all the facts, and which is alone in accordance with all known analogies, is entitled to at least a provisional acceptance.[1]

The last link in this chain of circumstantial evidence Allusions after 1167 testify to the generality of *studium*.

[1] I do not assert that the connexion of the migration with Oxford is direct and immediate. For (1) the expelled scholars may have halted at and temporarily studied in some other town or towns. (2) Or several *studia* may have been set up while only one prospered: as happened with the migration from Oxford in 1209 (see below, p. 33). (3) Less probably, the *studium* may have been originally formed by students prevented from going to Paris. In this case most of the masters must have been Paris masters, since most highly educated Englishmen (except lawyers) had studied at Paris; and these would naturally have been joined by new arrivals from the Continent. The first suppositions are in accordance with numerous analogies; at the same time there is no evidence for them. What we can be morally certain of is some causal connexion between the proved interruption of intercourse with Paris, *c.* 1167, and the proved emergence of Oxford into a *studium generale* soon afterwards.

CHAP. XII, remains to be set up.[1] It is not merely in their number but in
§ 1. their character that the allusions to Oxford schools after 1167
differ from the earlier notices. One master, even if he enjoys
a following of 'sixty or a hundred scholars, more or less', does
not make a *studium generale*. After 1167 the notices are
precisely of a kind which do point to the existence of a
studium generale in the looser and earlier sense of the word,
i.e. to the existence of schools in more than one faculty,
taught by many masters, attended by a numerous body of
scholars, and by scholars from different regions. Some of them
likewise show slight traces of a germinal organization similar
to that which had just begun to ripen in the schools of Paris.

[1] We should indeed have to add a most important piece of evidence to those already adduced if there were any ground for the theory that John of Salisbury studied and taught at Oxford in the middle of the twelfth century, and that his description of the scholastic logomachies of his day refers to the schools not of Chartres and Paris but of Oxford. It is sufficient here to say that the theory is devoid of all direct evidence, is very difficult to accommodate to what we know of the facts of John of Salisbury's life, and has arisen merely from an uncritical acceptance of Wood's conjecture (i. 143) that because John of Salisbury mentions Robert Pullus as one of his masters, and Pullus is recorded to have at one time taught at Oxford, it was at Oxford that John of Salisbury heard him. The theory, accepted by Huber, was elaborately defended by Christian Petersen in his edition of John of Salisbury's *Entheticus de Dogmate Philosophorum* (Hamburg, 1843, pp. 68–81), where the above-mentioned description occurs. Moreover, in the celebrated piece of autobiography in *Metalogicon*, ii, c. 10 [ed. C. C. J. Webb, p. 82, ll. 3–8] we read 'Extraxerunt me hinc (i.e. from Paris) rei familiaris angustia, sociorum petitio, et consilium amicorum, ut officium docentis aggrederer. Parui. Reuersus itaque in fine triennii repperi magistrum Gillebertum, ipsumque audiui. . . . Successit Rodbertus Pullus.' The 'return' was probably to Paris, though it may conceivably have been to Chartres. Petersen assumes that the return was from England. [Dr. C. C. J. Webb says that the return was to Paris, *op. cit.*, p. 82, note to l. 6.] Schaarschmidt (pp. 13–21) successfully shows the baselessness and extreme improbability of this view, though some of his reasoning is not conclusive. The 'officium docentis' was more probably exercised somewhere in the country (not necessarily at one place) than (as Schaarschmidt supposes) at Ste Geneviève. Mr. Mullinger tells us that 'John of Salisbury, writing about the year 1152, relates how, when he *returned* to Oxford after his residence at Paris, whither he had gone to study the canon law, he found the wordy warfare raging with undiminished vigour' (*The Univ. of Cambridge*, i. 56), thus bringing John to Oxford not once but twice; while an Oxford historian says 'We have the positive testimony of John of Salisbury', &c.

The earliest allusion to the schools of Oxford after 1167 which previous historians have had before them is contained in the amusing account given by the Welsh traveller and historian, Giraldus Cambrensis, of his visit to Oxford about the year 1184 or 1185 when, as he recounts in the most flattering of all autobiographies, he read his recently composed book, the *Topographia Hibernica*, before the assembled masters and scholars. But the story shall be given in his own words. He is modest enough to put his self-panegyric into the third person:

'In course of time, when the work was completed and corrected, desiring not to hide his candle under a bushel, but to place it on a candlestick so that it might give light, he resolved to read his work at Oxford, where the clergy in England flourished and excelled in clerkship, before that great audience. And as there were three divisions in his work, and each division occupied a day, the reading lasted three successive days. And on the first day he received at his lodgings all the poor scholars of the whole town; on the second all the Doctors of different Faculties, and such of their pupils as were of greater fame and note; on the third the rest of the scholars with many knights, townsfolk, and burghers. It was a costly and noble act, for the authentic and ancient times of the poets were thus renewed, nor does the present or any past age recall anything like it in England.'[1]

Here then we have suddenly revealed to us the existence of A large a *studium* on a very much larger scale than ordinary cathe-
A large body of masters.
dral or monastic school. One at least of the characteristics which differentiate the *studium generale* from such schools is presented to us in the number of masters, and of masters in several faculties, who attended these readings of Giraldus.

[1] Giraldus Cambrensis, *Opera*, ed. J. S. Brewer (R.S.), i. 72, 73. For other allusions to the same event, *loc. cit.* i. 221, 409; iii. 92. In the last passage the versifier and satirist Walter Mapes or Map, Archdeacon of Oxford, is spoken of as 'Magister Oxoniensis'. [See *Collectanea* (O.H.S.), ii. 173–5. About 1253 Michael of Cornwall, a wandering poet, recited a poem in praise of Cornwall and England before the Chancellor of Cambridge together with 'the university of masters'. See J. C. Russell, 'Master Henry of Avranches', in *Speculum*, iii (1928), 42. See also L. Thorndike, 'Public Readings of New Works in Mediaeval Universities', in *Speculum* (1926), i. 101–3.]

CHAP. XII,
§ I.

This is the first piece of evidence which supplies the smallest reason for attributing to Oxford any scholastic reputation beyond what was possessed by Lincoln or Hereford or St. Albans; and now, we are told, the reputation of the Oxford 'clergy' exceeded that of any other city in England. The suddenness of this rise of the Oxford school is a phenomenon which can hardly be accounted for by any other hypothesis than the one here propounded. But the evidence relates to the year 1184 or 1185. Is it probable, it may be asked, that so large a body of scholars as the migration theory postulates should have congregated in Oxford even for a period of some eighteen years without any other evidence of their existence? I believe it is possible to push back the direct evidence for the existence of a *studium generale* to within a few years of the date at which we have circumstantial evidence of migration of Parisian scholars into England.

A north-country scholar here, c. 1180.

There is contained among the *Acta Sanctorum* a very curious account, written by the then prior of the monastery, of the 'translation' of the body of S. Frideswide to the new shrine erected for its reception in 1180. Among the miracles which Prior Philip records as having taken place before and after the translation, we read of the cure of a scholar. The mere fact that there was one scholar in Oxford will not prove much for the importance of its *studium* any more than the existence of a single master in 1110 or 1133. But the significant fact is that the scholar was a native of Yorkshire and had come all the way to Oxford 'for the sake of his studies'.[1] The schools were already *de facto* what would afterwards have been called a *studium generale*.

Extensive book trade, 1170–80.

The second evidence of a university prior to 1185 is an undated conveyance. Bryan Twyne relies much, in proof of his preposterous theories as to the antiquity of the university, upon the bonds and similar documents in relation to property which are preserved amongst the archives of the university.

---

[1] 'Morabatur eo tempore apud Oxenefordiam studiorum causa clericus quidam Stephanus nomine, de Eboracensi regione oriundus', &c. *Acta Sanctorum*, October 19, viii. 579. I owe this reference to the kindness of the Rev. W. D. Macray of the Bodleian; but it had not escaped Twyne (MS. xxi, f. 13).

An examination of these documents, however, discloses only CHAP. XII, one which proves the existence of a *studium* at an earlier date $\S$ 1. than 1200.[1] This document is a transfer of property in 'Cattestreet',[2] close to S. Mary's Church. Among the parties or witnesses appear the names of one bookbinder, three illuminators, one writer, and two parchmenters—all evidently residing in the immediate neighbourhood of S. Mary's, close to the School Street of later times. However they got there, it is evident that by this time that Oxford is a city of schools. On palaeographical grounds it is certain that the document cannot be much later than 1180,[3] if it is not a little earlier, while an examination of the names and subsequent appearances of the witnesses makes it clear that the date cannot be pushed back much before that year.

Another fresh piece of evidence brings us still closer to University 1167. Among the persons cured at the tomb of S. Thomas sermons soon after 1170.

[1] It is true that Wood (*Annals*, i. 136) declares that 'in the ancientest evidences' which he had seen concerning tenements in Oxford, there occur allusions to the 'Vicus Scholarum' and 'Vicus Schediasticorum', but on such a matter none of the older university antiquaries can be trusted where they do not produce their evidence. And it is to be noted that Wood does not explicitly state, though he insinuates, that these 'ancientest evidences' belong to the reign of Stephen. Such inquiries and investigations as I have been able to make as to the College Muniments lead me to believe that no such documents of King Stephen's reign exist in Oxford. There are certainly none in the University Archives.

[2] By a blunder of the now extinct Local Board this ancient thoroughfare (leading from Broad Street to the High Street along the front of Hertford College) is now officially designed Catherine's Street, as though the ancient 'Cat-street' was an abbreviation of Catherine Street,

an assumption for which there is no evidence. [This misnomer has since been rectified. This street is once more officially designated 'Catte Street'.]

[3] Such is the opinion of Mr. Macray; and he inclines to place it rather earlier. On the other hand, the use of the form 'Oxonia', which elsewhere, I think, does not occur before 1190, is an argument against pushing it back many years before 1180. With reference to the form 'Oxonia', it is remarkable that it first occurs in notices of the schools: it is somewhat rare before 1200. Was it a piece of classical affectation on the part of the scholarly immigrants disgusted with the cumbrous 'Oxenefordia'? [Dr. H. E. Salter has pointed out that this deed cannot be dated before 1200 and probably not before 1205; see *The Medieval Archives of the University of Oxford* (O.H.S.), i. 291–2. Rashdall had a collotype illustration of this deed inserted in the original edition of this work as a frontispiece to vol. ii, part ii.]

CHAP. XII, was Robert, Prior of S. Frideswide's at Oxford. In giving
§ 1. an account of his previous sufferings, the prior reminds his hearers how he used to ask to be allowed a chair when preaching in the presence of 'clerks from various parts of England'.[1] The Icelandic Saga on the death of Thomas shows that the cure cannot have occurred later than 1172.[2] At this date, then, we have established the existence at Oxford of precisely what constituted a *studium generale* in the earliest sense of the word—i.e. of a body of scholars, large enough to demand university sermons, and coming from distant regions. Sermons would hardly have been provided for less than a few hundred scholars. Such are the numbers of the Oxford *studium* within a few years after 1167.[3] At about the same time, Oxford is mentioned in a contemporary letter, in significant juxtaposition to Bologna and Paris.[4] Alexander Neckam, who wrote before 1200, associates Oxford with Salerno, Montpellier, Paris, and Bologna, and remarks that thereby a prophecy of Merlin was fulfilled which declared that 'wisdom· flourished at Oxford'.[5]

[1] 'Testis est mihi populus civitatis nostrae, quem cum in festis diebus, quando loquebar ad eos ... cum interessent etiam clerici diversorum locorum Angliae, praetendebam excusationem standi', &c. *Materials for the History of Thomas Becket*, ed. J. C. Robertson (R.S.), ii. 99.

[2] See *Thómas Saga Erkibyskups*, ed. E. Magnússon (R.S.), ii. lxxiv *sq.*, 92 *sq.* From frequent allusions in the Saga it is clear that Robert was one of the biographers of S. Thomas.

[3] [In the account that he gives of his own sufferings Robert of Cricklade states that it was in Sicily that he contracted the malady of which he was cured by the water of S. Thomas. He is known to have been in Italy and Sicily in 1158. It is quite likely, therefore, that it was before 1167 that he first had to use a chair when he preached; and, as he had been Prior of S. Frideswide's since 1141, his sermons may

have been popular among clerks in Oxford for several years before he visited Sicily. See *The Cartulary of S. Frideswide*, ed. S. R. Wigram (O.H.S.), i. 20, 27, 33; the article on Robert of Cricklade by Dr. Hutton in *D.N.B.*; the note on his career in *Collectanea* (O.H.S.), ii. 161–5; and C. H. Haskins, *Studies in the History of Mediaeval Science*, pp. 168–71.]

[4] 'Verumtamen indomita cervice ferox post vocationis meae litteras nunc agere causas Parisiis, nunc reverti Bononiam, nunc Lincolniam proficisci, nunc morari Oxenefordiae ordinas et disponis' (*Patrol. Lat.* ccvii, c. 185). This passage occurs in a letter from Geoffrey (Plantagenet), Bishop-elect of Lincoln to a Magister Robertus Blondus, and must belong to the period between 1173 and 1182.

[5] 'Iuxta vaticinium etiam Merlini, viguit ad Vada Boum sapientia', Alex. Neckam, *De Naturis Rerum*, ed. T. Wright (R.S.), p.

After such evidence it may seem scarcely worth to mention CHAP. XII, § 1. an allusion to a certain 'Chaplain and scholar of honest conversation' in a fragment of the Llanthony Chronicle preserved by Twyne, but it is significant that the incident relates to the time 'when the blessed Thomas, Archbishop of Canterbury, was in exile';[1] and also that the chaplain is described both as a master and a scholar, i.e. a master of arts and a scholar in a superior faculty. Here then we have evidence of more than one faculty within some two years after our presumed migration.

The conclusion to which all this evidence points is that the real beginning of the *studium generale* at Oxford is due to the settlement therein of a body of masters and scholars in or about 1167, in consequence of an exodus fom Paris caused by the royal edict, and the cutting off of free access to the great centre of European education. The case is not proved, but the evidence for it is as strong as circumstantial evidence can well be.[2] It must be added that the evidence is of a kind

311. Mr. T. A. Archer was good enough to point out to me that this prophecy does not occur among the earlier editions of Merlin's predictions. Would not a sudden immigration be more likely to give rise to new prophecies or interpretations of prophecy than a slowly evolved university? [On Neckam see the article by J. C. Russell on 'Alexander Neckam in England' in *E.H.R.* xlvii (1932), 260–8. Mr. Russell draws attention to a passage in Neckam's 'Commentary on the Song of Songs', in which Neckam states that he had been a lecturer in theology at Oxford.]

[1] 'Ex relatu Magistri Ricardi de Buleia, quidam capellanus erat Oxoniae pauper et scholaris honestae conversationis tempore scilicet quo beatus Thomas Archiepiscopus Cantuariensis futurus Martyr exulabat in partibus transmarinis', Twyne MS. xxii, f. 162. [Rashdall has misunderstood this passage. Mag. Richard de Buleia is not the chaplain to whom reference is made. The chaplain is nowhere described as master in Twyne's excerpt; and it may well be doubted whether *scholaris* is used in this passage in the special sense claimed by Rashdall. Twyne's authority is *Corpus Christi Coll.: Oxon., MS. xxxiii*, f. 93 *sq.*]

[2] [Rashdall's arguments in support of his theory of the migration from Paris to Oxford have not satisfied all students of the subject. The fullest criticism of Rashdall's theory has come from Mr. A. F. Leach, who stated his reasons for rejecting Rashdall's contentions in an article on 'The Origin of Oxford' in the *National Review*, Sept. 1896, and reaffirmed his dissent in the course of his introduction to *Educational Charters and Documents: 598 to 1909* (p. xxiv). Rashdall took exception to this criticism in his review of Mr. Leach's book in *The Oxford Magazine* (1911–12), xxx. 278–9. This drew a long and

CHAP. XII, which at every point appeals to the reader's familiarity with
§ 1.   the state of education in the Middle Ages; everything turns
upon a due appreciation of two facts, first, the close dependence of the schools in northern Europe upon cathedral or
other important churches, and secondly, the habit of grega-
rious migration characteristic of medieval scholars. Even
the evidence produced in this book gives but a faint idea on
the one hand of the universality of this dependence upon the
cathedral chancellor or master of the schools, on the other
hand of the frequency with which wholesale migrations
appear from university records to be threatened or contemplated even when they are not actually carried out. The
reader may be reminded of a single illustration: a century later
Walter de Merton was afraid to localize his college in Oxford
lest perchance the *studium* should be transferred elsewhere.[1]

Possible   We need not suppose, indeed, that the academic population
fluctua-
tion of of Oxford continued to be as large as it probably was during
numbers. the continuance of the edict against clerical 'transfretation'.
We have seen what rapid vicissitudes of fortune attended
the infancy even of later and more formally instituted universities. The numbers attending the Oxford schools would
naturally fluctuate with every change in the political relations
between France and England; and in the years 1175–85 there
was a succession of ruptures between the two countries, each

interesting, though somewhat unduly combative, rejoinder from Mr.
Leach, in explanation of his rejection of Rashdall's theory. Rashdall
defended his position in a subsequent letter. As this controversy
gave Rashdall an opportunity of
reviewing his theory of a migration
from Paris in the light of Mr.
Leach's criticism, his letter to *The
Oxford Magazine* (1911–12), xxx.
384–5, and Mr. Leach's (*ibid*. xxx.
331–3) which evoked it, have been
reprinted as an appendix. With
the exception of a few passages that
do not warrant inclusion the letters
are given in full. See Appendix I.
Sir Charles Mallet (*A History of
the Univ. of Oxford*, i. 22–4) is

disposed to accept Rashdall's argument for the derivation of the University of Oxford from a migration
from Paris; but Dr. H. E. Salter
(*History* (1929), xiv. 57) rejects it.
In criticism of Rashdall's view Dr.
Salter writes: 'The late Dr. Rashdall started the theory that Oxford
as a University sprang into being
by a migration from Paris in 1167,
but we must return to the old theory
that Oxford, throughout the twelfth
century, was a place of study which
gradually developed into a university, no one can say when. For
the theory of a migration there is
really no evidence.']

[1] See below, p. 194.

of which might divert a fresh party of intending students from their projected journey to the French capital, while each short-lived peace would lead to a depletion of the Oxford *studium* in favour of its more famous prototype.[1] But, though there must no doubt have been fluctuations, there is every reason to believe that on the whole the numbers of the university must have rapidly increased, especially during the last decade of the twelfth and the first decade of the thirteenth century.

The difficulty of supposing that the schools of Oxford can have, gradually and unaided by any sudden accession from without, grown to the size and importance which they have attained by about 1170 without further evidence of their existence than is supplied by the mention of two or three solitary masters is enhanced by the frequency with which, when once this date is passed, the allusions pour in upon us. I have already spoken of the notices belonging to the years before Giraldus's visit in 1184 or 1185. Later on, about the year 1190 we read of a student from the low countries crossing the seas to go to 'the common *Studium* of letters which was at Oxford'.[2] 'Common' is, of course, a synonym of 'General', and this is perhaps the first instance of the occurrence of this technical expression in any of its forms. In 1192 Richard of Devizes speaks of the clerks of Oxford as so numerous that the city could hardly feed them.[3]

[1] The effect of an outbreak of hostilities between England and the French king is well illustrated by an incident in the life of Giraldus Cambrensis, who was thus prevented from going to study theology at Paris in 1192 and went to Lincoln instead. *Opera*, ed. J. S. Brewer (R.S.), i. 93.

[2] 'Qui cum mare versus Angliam anno etatis sue quasi 20, transisset communis causa studii litterarum quod fuit Oxonie, estuabat uberius liberalibus artibus se implicare.' *Emonis Chronicon*, ap. Pertz, *Mon. Germ. Hist. SS.* xxiii. 467. The *Chron. Menkonis* (*ibid.*, p. 524, cf. p. 531) makes him study the 'Decreta,

Decretales, Librum Pauperum' (&c. of Vacarius) at 'Paris, Orleans, and Oxford'. It is natural to conjecture that he studied arts and Vacarius at Oxford, and pursued the higher legal studies at Orleans or Paris. I am indebted for this reference to Dr. Poole.

[3] 'Oxonia vix suos clericos, non dico satiat, sed sustentat.' Richard of Devizes, 'De Rebus Gestis Ricardi Primi' in the *Chronicles of Stephen, Henry II, and Richard I*, ed. R. Howlett (R.S.), iii. 437. One manuscript, however, reads 'homines', which from the context can hardly be the true reading.

CHAP. XII,   In the seventh and eighth years of Richard I there occur
§ 1.
Richard I's   entries in the Pipe Rolls of payments to scholars maintained in
scholars.   the schools of Oxford by the royal bounty.[1] In 1197 an abbot
The Abbot   of St. Edmund's Bury—the Abbot Samson immortalized by
Samson.
               Thomas Carlyle—entertained a numerous party of Oxford
masters on a visit to the town.[2] At about the same date
Thomas de Marleberge, afterwards Abbot of Evesham, taught
canon and civil law at Oxford;[3] while a correspondent of the

[1] 'Nicholao clerico de Hungria viii^{li} et xvj^s et viii^d ad sustentandum se in scolis a festo sancti Michaelis anni preteriti usque ad pascha. per breue R.' Rot. Pip., 7 Ric. I (ap. Maxwell-Lyte, Hist. Univ. of Oxford, p. 14). [Pipe Roll, 1 Richard I (1195), Pipe Roll Society, N.S. vi. 142.] In this and a similar entry in the following year Oxford is not mentioned, but as they occur under the County of Oxford there can of course be no doubt as to the place meant. [Payment from the Oxford account for the maintenance of this clerk seems first to have been sanctioned in 1193; see Pipe Roll, 5 Richard I (1193), Pipe Roll Society, N.S., iii. 122, and Pipe Roll, 6 Richard I (1194), Pipe Roll Society, N.S. iv. 88. In her introduction to the Roll of 1193 (p. xxiii) Mrs. Stenton suggests that Nicholas of Hungary was a poor scholar who came to England in the train of German agents engaged in the business of the King's ransom.]

[2] 'Quatuordecim monachos de Conventria, qui ibi [Oxneford] convenerant, recepit in hospitio suo, et sedentibus monachis ad mensam ex una parte domus, et ex alia parte magistris scholarum, qui summoniti fuerant, laudabatur abbas magnanimus et magnificus in expensis.' Jocelini de Brakelonda Chronica, ed. T. Arnold, Memorials of S. Edmund's Abbey (R.S.), i. 295. Carlyle talks about 'the veritable Oxford Caput' (whatever that may mean)

'sitting there at dinner', without a shadow of justification from the Chronicle. (Past and Present, Bk. ii, ch. 16.) [The editor of the chronicle in a footnote to this passage suggests that they were schoolmasters from the neighbourhood of Oxford.]

[3] 'In ingressu suo attulit secum libros utriusque iuris, canonici scilicet et civilis, per quos rexit scholas ante monachatum (c. 1200) apud Oxoniam et Exoniam.' A number of other works are mentioned, books of Cicero, Isidore, Lucan, and Juvenal. Chron. de Evesham, ed. W. D. Macray (R.S.), p. 267. It is remarkable that among the books of 'Physics' which follow is a 'liber Democriti'. [See the article on Thomas de Marleberge by Miss Mary Bateson in D.N.B.] I may add that Denifle (i. 250) is disposed to underrate the importance of the Oxford School of Civil Law. The complaints of Roger Bacon (Op. Maius (R.S.), 446) against the civilians cannot refer exclusively to those who studied abroad. So in 1244 Henry III obtained the opinion of the 'Magistros Oxonie in Iure legentes' in favour of his appeal against William de Ralegh, Bishop of Norwich, elected to the see of Winchester. (Rot. Pat. 28 Henry III, m. 10 dorso [Cal. Pat. Rolls, Henry III, 1232–47, p. 413]; Twyne MS. ii, f. 38 a; cf. too Mon. Francisc. (R.S.), i. 113, where is also an allusion to an Oxford 'Medicus'.) William of Drogheda, who taught

Prior of Oseney alludes in the inflated style of the period to the neighbouring city 'in which abound men skilled in mystic eloquence, weighing the words of the law, bringing forth from their treasures things new and old'.[1] Finally, the year 1209 introduces us to an academic population of no less (according to a contemporary estimate) than 3,000 souls. It was in this year that the event occurred which ushers in the documentary period of Oxford history.

There is a remarkable parallelism between the events of the year 1209 at Oxford, and the events which in 1200 led to the grant of the charter of Philip Augustus at Paris. The killing —quite accidental as we are assured by our clerical historian —of a woman by a scholar provoked a raid by the mayor and burgesses upon the offender's hostel. Several clerks were apprehended. All England was now distracted by the great quarrel between Innocent III and John. The country at large lay under interdict: the property of the bishops was under sequestration: the King himself was excommunicated or threatened with excommunication. Under such circumstances it is not surprising to hear that John eagerly gave his con-

---

at Oxford in the thirteenth century, was a civilian of considerable importance, quoted even by the Bologna doctors. See M. A. von Bethmann-Hollweg, *Der Civilprozess des gemeinen Rechts*, vi. 123, 124; Albericus Gentilis, *Laudes Academiae Perusinae et Oxoniensis*, Hanover, 1605, p. 38. He wrote his *Summa Aurea* at Oxford. [See also F. W. Maitland, *Canon Law in the Church of England*, pp. 100–31, and F. de Zulueta's important article on William of Drogheda in *Mélanges de Droit Romain dédiés à Georges Cornil*, 1926, pp. 641–57]. It is true of course that in England civil law was studied chiefly for use in the Ecclesiastical Courts (and the Admiralty Court), but Bacon complains that the ecclesiastical lawyers cared more for the civil law than for the canon.

[1] Senatus, Prior of Worcester (1189 to 1196). He expresses surprise that he should be consulted on a point of canon law by one living near Oxford: 'Quod et uobis propono propter adiacentem urbem in qua abundant prudentes eloquii mistici, ponderantes uerba legis, proferentes omni poscenti de thesauro suo noua et uetera.' The first of the questions propounded was, 'utrum sacerdotes omnes sicut ordine ita indifferenter uti queant clauium potestate ligare sese et soluere, transeuntes quoque et scolares maxime, qui egressi proprium ouile, in pascuis alienis commorantur' (Bodley MS. 633, f. 209). The question forcibly illustrates the ecclesiastical anomalousness of the Oxford scholastic community and is corroborative evidence for the non-existence of a chancellor at this time.

CHAP. XII, sent to the execution of two or—as some accounts say—three
§ 1. of the imprisoned scholars.[1] The clerks pitched upon by the
townsmen were, as we are again assured, other than the actual
offenders, who had sought safety in flight. The masters and
scholars, after the manner of their class throughout Europe,
Disper- hastily dispersed. Some went to Reading, the nearest town
sion. of importance; others to the great mother-university of Paris;
Origin of others to Cambridge. What attracted them to that distant
Cam-
bridge. marsh town we know not. Schools of some kind there may
conceivably have been there already, but we hear nothing of
them before this. In any case, the *studium generale* of Cambridge owes its existence to the Oxford 'suspendium clericorum' of 1209. Altogether, according to Matthew Paris, 3,000
scholars left Oxford; and there is no reason to suspect that
estimate of more than the usual medieval exaggeration.
Though we hear afterwards of some 'profane masters' who
persisted in lecturing in defiance of ecclesiastical or academical authority, the majority of the schools must have been
closed, and the existence of the university practically suspended, till the reconciliation of the King of England with the
Pope compelled the citizens of Oxford to humble themselves
before his legate. A legatine ordinance of 1214—the year of
John's grovelling submission—addressed to the burgesses, is

[1] The story is told in *Chron. de Lanercost*, ed. J. Stevenson, p. 4; *Chron. Petroburg.*, ed. T. Stapleton (Camden Society), p. 6; Matt. Paris, *Chron. Mai.*, ed. H. R. Luard (R.S.), ii. 525–6, 569, and *Hist. Anglorum*, ed. F. Madden (R.S.), ii. 120; Roger de Wendover, ed. H. G. Hewlett (R.S.), ii. 51, 94; *Chron. de Mailros* (Bannatyne Club), p. 107; Walter of Coventry, ed. W. Stubbs (R.S.), ii. 201. Wood (*Annals*, i. 183) says that 'intelligence was immediately sent to the Diocesan (the Bishop of Lincoln) and at length to the Pope, who . . . did forthwith inter-dict the Town'. And Sir H. C. Maxwell-Lyte, *Hist. Univ. of Oxford*, p. 18, speaks of 'an interdict, more stringent apparently than that which Innocent III had laid on England in general'. The fact is that none of the authorities speak of any interdict other than the one laid on the country generally, and the 'interdict' of the scholars them-selves. Moreover, Hugh de Wells was consecrated Bishop of Lincoln on 20 Dec. 1209, and was conse-crated abroad. Hence Wood's 'in-telligence to the Diocesan' is the creature of his own imagination. The Chronicle of Mailros repre-sents the place as already deserted in 1208, on account of the King's tyranny: 'pauci autem remanentes non multi post propter divinorum suspendium ex toto villam inter-dicendo recesserunt'.

the first document in the nature of a charter of privilege which CHAP. XII,
the University of Oxford can boast.[1] It possesses for Oxford §1.
constitutional history something more than the importance The re-
which the charter of Philip Augustus possesses for that of turn and
Paris. It enjoined that those who had confessed to or had legatine
been convicted of the hanging of the clerks were, as soon as of 1214.
the interdict was relaxed, to do penance by marching in procession, barefoot and without coats or cloaks, to their victims'
graves, followed by the whole commonalty of the town,
whence they were to escort the bodies to the cemetery for
burial. For ten years one half the rent of existing *hospicia*
occupied by the clerks was to be altogether remitted; and for
ten years more rents were to remain as already taxed before
the secession by the joint authority of the town and the
masters.[2] Further, the town was for ever to pay an annual
sum of fifty-two shillings to be distributed among poor scholars twice yearly, and to feed on the festival of S. Nicholas,
the patron of scholars, a hundred poor scholars on bread and
beer, pottage, and flesh or fish. Victuals were to be sold at
a reasonable rate, and an oath to the observance of these
provisions was to be taken by fifty of the chief burgesses and
to be annually renewed by as many of them (not exceeding
fifty) as the Bishop should require. The masters and scholars were to be free to return and resume their lectures except
those who had irreverently persisted in lecturing after the
dispersion: these latter were to be suspended from lecturing
for three years.

The payment of the annual fine was forthwith transferred, Origin of
by an agreement with the town, to the Abbot and Convent of chests.
Eynsham.[3] By an ordinance of Bishop Grosseteste in 1240

---

[1] See the document in *Mun.
Acad.*, ed. H. Anstey (R.S.), i. 1 *sq.*
[This document and others con-
nected with this incident are given
in full by Dr. H. E. Salter, *The
Mediaeval Archives of the Univ. of
Oxford* (O.H.S.), i. 2–4.] Matthew
Paris, *Chron. Mai.*, ed. H. R. Luard
(R.S.), ii. 569.
[2] [See Sir C. E. Mallet, *A History*

of the *Univ. of Oxford*, i. 32 n.; and
A. B. Emden, *An Oxford Hall in
Medieval Times*, pp. 11, 12.]
[3] *Mun. Acad.* i. 4 *sq.* Since the
Dissolution, £3 1s. 6d. has been
paid by the Crown, and goes to
the Vice-Chancellor for a poor
scholar. [*The Cartulary of Eynsham Abbey*, ed. H. E. Salter
(O.H.S.), i. xx–xxi, ii. 163; *The*

CHAP. XII, this money was applied to the foundation of an institution
§ 1. which is peculiarly characteristic of the English universities, if not absolutely confined to them.[1] Endowments (such as we find elsewhere) left to be expended in loans without interest to the poor were no doubt a wise and useful form of charity at a time when the Jews were the only money-lenders, and when it was necessary to prevent the Jews of Oxford from charging over forty-three per cent. as annual interest on loans to scholars.[2] This institution was now introduced at Oxford for the especial benefit of scholars. The money accruing to the university was placed in a chest at S. Frideswide's in which the borrower was required to deposit some pledge—a book or a cup, or a piece of clothing—exceeding the value of the loan. Pledges not redeemed within a year were sold by public auction. In time private bequests were added to the Frideswide chest, and the foundation of similar chests became a favourite form of benefaction, the recipients being required to make some recompense for the founder's liberality by saying a stipulated number of prayers for the repose of his soul. Some twenty of these chests were established at Oxford in the course of the Middle Ages.[3]

Mediaeval Archives of the Univ. of Oxford, ed. H. E. Salter (O.H.S.), i. 6, 7; and Registrum Antiquissimum of Cathedral Church of Lincoln, ed. C. W. Foster, ii. 63–4.]

[1] Mun. Acad. i. 8 sq. [Statuta Antiqua Universitatis Oxoniensis, ed. S. Gibson, pp. 74, 75.]

[2] Mun. Acad. ii. 778. [Med. Arch. Univ. Oxford, ed. H. E. Salter (O.H.S.), i. 18, 19.]

[3] Mun. Acad. i. 10, 62 sq., 95 sq., 102 sq., ii. 745 sq. [Stat. Antiq. Univ. Oxon., ed. S. Gibson, pp. 71–8, 101–6, 113–16, 118–21, and index under 'Chests'. See also Sir C. E. Mallet, Hist. Univ. of Oxford, i. 322–4.] Some of the ordinances allow the university or a college to borrow. [The administration of these chests was generally governed by conditions laid down in their deeds of foundation. A sum of money having been given for the formation of a chest, the university appointed keepers to be responsible for its administration. The keepers of a chest usually held office for a year and a month. A fixed scale of loans was laid down, varying in amount according to the academic standing of the borrower, and it was the duty of the keepers to accept adequate pledges (cauciones) as security for the money lent. Books were a very usual form of caucio. Before a book was accepted by the keepers of a chest, it was required that it should be valued by one of the stationers of the university, so as to ensure as far as possible that the loan was sufficiently covered by the caucio that was to be deposited in the chest in consideration of the loan.]

But by far the most important provision in its bearing upon CHAP. XII, § I. the development of the university constitution is the clause Institution which requires that a clerk arrested by the townsmen shall be of chancellorship. at once surrendered on the demand of 'the Bishop of Lincoln, cellorship. or the Archdeacon of the place or his Official, or the Chancellor, or whomsoever the Bishop of Lincoln shall depute to this office'.[1] Another clause provides that the poor scholars to be feasted on S. Nicholas's Day shall be selected by the Abbot of Oseney and the Prior of S. Frideswide's by the advice of the Bishop, the Archdeacon of the place or his Official, or 'the Chancellor whom the Bishop of Lincoln shall set over the scholars therein'.[2] These are the first allusions in any authentic document to the existence of the chancellorship, and the words just quoted seem distinctly to imply that at present no chancellor of Oxford existed. The alternative allowing the archdeacon to act in matters purely affecting the scholars is hardly explicable except upon the supposition that the arrangements for the appointment of a chancellor had still to be made, and that some delay might take place in carrying them out. The words 'whom the Bishop of Lincoln *shall* appoint' seem added, not merely because no chancellor was actually in office, but because the office itself was not yet in existence, and its nature consequently required explanation. The only document bearing an earlier date which mentions a chancellor of Oxford is stamped alike by the character of its contents and by palaeographical evidence as the most transparent of forgeries.[3]

[1] 'Si uero contingat aliquem clericum a laicis capi, statim cum fuerint super eo requisiti ab episcopo Lincolniensi uel archidiacono loci eius officiali uel a cancellario seu ab eo quem episcopus Lincolniensis huic offitio deputauerit, captum ei reddent.' Archives (W. P.-P. xii. 1). [*Med. Arch. Univ. Oxford*, ed. H. E. Salter (O.H.S.), i. 3.]

[2] 'De consilio uenerabilis fratris Hugonis tunc Lincolniensis episcopi et successorum suorum uel archidiaconi loci seu eius officialis aut cancellarii quem episcopus Lincolniensis ibidem scolaribus preficiet.' *Ibid.* [In the draft charter of the mayor and burgesses (*c.* Aug. 1214) the chancellor is called 'Cancellarius scolarum Oxon.', not 'scolarium'. See *Med. Arch. Univ. Oxford*, ed. H. E. Salter (O.H.S.), i. 8–9. See also Sir C. E. Mallet, *Hist. Univ. Oxford*, i. 27, n. 3.]

[3] The document purports to bind the university never to cite into its courts any one residing within the precincts of S. Frideswide's; and was obviously forged

If the *studium* was in full working order by 1184 or earlier, while no chancellor was appointed till 1214, the question may be raised, 'How were the masters and scholars governed during the former period?' To this question our data do not admit of our giving a complete answer. The ordinary jurisdiction over masters and scholars would of course fall to the ecclesiastical authorities. It is possible that even the licence was granted by the archdeacon;[1] or we may suppose either that the masters of Oxford, like the Parisian masters who seceded to Angers and other places in 1219, conducted the inceptions of new masters on their own responsibility,[2] or that they ventured (like the masters of Paris

to aid the convent in a suit against the university. I was convinced of the spuriousness or later date of the document, from which the above words are cited by Wood (Appendix to *Hist. and Antiq.*, &c., p. 7), (1) by the improbability that the University of Oxford should have attained a so much higher degree of corporate development than the Mother University of Paris as would be implied by its possession of a common seal, common funds, and special university courts with considerable jurisdiction; (2) by the use of the expression 'domus congregationis' which implies a building more or less appropriated to university purposes. I afterwards saw the document (Archives, W. E. P.-Y. I) and found affixed to it a note by Mr. Macray of the Bodleian Library assigning the manuscript (which has the seal complete) to *c.* 1380. William Smith, the acute and learned historian of University College, notes it as a forgery (*Annals of University College*, p. 202), and its genuineness was questioned by the older scholars such as Sir Robert Cotton, and Spelman (see Twyne MS. iii, f. 140, where Twyne and Wood are clearly arguing against their convictions). Sir H. Maxwell-Lyte has the merit

of being the first of the professed historians of the university who has escaped the pitfall into which even Denifle has slipped (i. 244)! [This document is printed in *Med. Arch. Univ. Oxford*, ed. H. E. Salter (O.H.S.), i. 1, 2, with a note by Dr. H. E. Salter on its forgery.] Another document of the same kind, forged by the same versatile canons, occurs in a manuscript in Bodley (*Cat. of Oxford Charters*, ch. 127).

[1] The archdeacon is mentioned rather prominently in connexion with the schools by the ordinance of 1214, and it is possible that he had some control over them. He may even have conferred the licence; it is certain that he had some jurisdiction over the grammar schools (*Mun. Acad.* i. 85, [*Stat. Antiq. Univ. Oxon.*, ed. S. Gibson, p. 22], and below, p. 346). It may be worth noticing that the Chancellor of Lincoln's jurisdiction was confined to the archdeaconry of Lincoln. Linc. Reg. Dalderby, f. 214 *b*. [On the university and archidiaconal jurisdiction, see the important introduction to *Registrum Cancellarii Oxon. 1434–1469*, ed. H. E. Salter (O.H.S.), i. xv–xvii.]

[2] Notice an expression in the university's letter asking for the

on another occasion[1]) to elect an official of their own to give
the licence.

At all events it seems pretty clear that some kind of official head of the schools must have been in existence (whatever the mode of appointment and whatever his exact functions) before the secession; for in 1210 a Papal Bull (if we may trust Twyne's report as to the contents of a lost Abingdon cartulary) is addressed to the Prior of Oseney, the Dean of Oxford, and 'Magister Alardus, Rector of the Schools'.[2] It is probable that this rector of the schools must by this time have received some kind of episcopal recognition and authority; and quite possible that he may have been in popular parlance styled chancellor in imitation of the cathedral chancellor of Notre Dame and other famous schools connected with cathedral bodies. But nothing further can be stated as to the character of this mysterious office until it received a definite canonical status and the higher style of chancellorship from the legatine ordinance of 1214.

Not unimportant in accounting for the spontaneous evolu-

canonization of S. Edmund (*Collectanea* (O.H.S.), ii. 188): 'Ad studium theologie se transtulit, in quo tam mirabiliter in breui profecit, quod cito post paucos annos, suadentibus multis, *cathedram magistralem ascendit.*' It is likely enough that he was the first D.D. who incepted at Oxford. [For the full text of the university's letter see A. B. Emden, *An Oxford Hall in Medieval Times*, p. 268.]

[1] See above, i. 337, 399.

[2] It is a natural inference that this official stood in something like the position of the chancellor (like the 'Master of the Schools' mentioned below, p. 41), but (i) 'Rector Scholarum' may mean simply a regent master though it is not often so used as an official designation after a name; (ii) if it were an official dignity, we should expect the addition of 'Oxoniensis' or the like. The question must, therefore, be left doubtful. Another document is cited by Wood (*Fasti*, p. 5) to show that a chancellor existed in *c.* 1150, but (i) the date depends upon an uncertain identification, (ii) the document relates to one of the tithe-cases precisely similar to the one referred to the Chancellor of Oxford and others, *c.* 1221: we may therefore, with tolerable confidence, ignore this piece of evidence. The document is, so far as I can ascertain, lost. Cf. below, p. 41. [On the identity of Magister Alardus see *Snappe's Formulary*, ed. H. E. Salter (O.H.S.), pp. 318–19. Dr. Salter (*ibid.*, p. 318) draws attention to an earlier example of a precursor of the later chancellors in a deed of 1201 in which Mag. J. Grim is described as *magister scolarum Oxonie*. See also *The Cartulary of the Abbey of Eynsham*, ed. H. E. Salter (O.H.S.), ii. 45–6.]

CHAP. XII,
§ 1.
Vacancies
in see of
Lincoln.

tion of the Oxford *studium* and its presiding official is the fact that the see of Lincoln was vacant during by far the greater portion of the period under discussion—a period beginning (it will be remembered) with Henry II's quarrel with Becket and ending with John's embroilment with the Pope and the whole ecclesiastical order throughout the realm.¹ During this time of ecclesiastical confusion we can understand how easy it would have been for the masters to free themselves from the ecclesiastical yoke against which their brethren were beginning to rebel even at Paris. That masters were sometimes even after this period admitted to inception and so allowed to lecture without any regular ecclesiastical licence is rendered more than probable by a Bull of Innocent IV in 1246 addressed to Bishop Grosseteste, from which it appears that even then—more than twenty years after the institution of the chancellorship—certain persons presumed to ascend the magisterial chair without examination.² It is therefore ordered that in future none shall be allowed to teach in Oxford 'unless according to the custom of Paris he shall have been examined and approved' by the bishop or his representative. Such a state of things is hardly explicable except as a survival of an older régime such as must have prevailed up to 1214.

No recog-
nized
chancel-
lorship
before
1214.

Whether or not a 'Master of the Schools' or a so-called chancellor existed before 1214, it is practically certain that he was not recognized by the bishop as entitled to the latter appellation. Indeed, even after the issue of the legatine ordinance, it would seem to be doubtful whether the papal orders were fully obeyed. It would appear that the

¹ From Jan. 1166 to 1183 there was no bishop or no consecrated bishop, and there were vacancies amounting to seven years after 1184.
² 'Ut nullum ibi docere in aliqua facultate permittas, nisi qui secundum morem Parisiensem a te vel his quibus in hac parte tuas vices commiseris examinatus fuerit et etiam approbatus.' Lincoln Reg. Wells, Bull 15 (Wood, *Annals*, i.

236). [Sir Charles Mallet (*Hist. of Univ. of Oxford*, i. 28 n.) points out that Rashdall has followed Wood, who has in his turn followed Twyne, in mistakenly referring this passage to Bishop Wells's Register: Bishop Wells died eleven years before the issue of the Bull in question. The Bull is printed in *Snappe's Formulary*, ed. H. E. Salter (O.H.S.), pp. 299–300; see also *Cal. Papal Registers (Letters)*, i. 225.]

Bishop, jealous of his authority over the Oxford schools, delayed to appoint a chancellor, or to recognize as such the existing master of the schools. The famous Grosseteste, when he presided over the schools of Oxford, was, as was afterwards alleged, only allowed to assume the older and more modest title of 'Master of the Schools',[1] and a Bull addressed to the Chancellor of Oxford and two other ecclesiastics in 1221 remained unexecuted on the ground that no chancellor of Oxford was then in existence.[2]

If in the period of scholastic anarchy the masters had been in the habit of electing a *soi-disant* chancellor, this will explain the fact that the chancellor, though emphatically the bishop's officer, was from the first—so far as we know—elected periodically by the masters from their own number. However the title originated, the office is clearly an imitation of the Parisian chancellorship. It is the cathedral dignity reproduced in a university town which possessed no cathedral.[3] And this fact is the key to the peculiar character of the

[1] In 1295, in the course of one of his controversies with the envoy of the university, Bishop Sutton 'adiecit quod beatus Robertus quondam Lincolniensis episcopus qui huiusmodi officium gessit dum in Universitate predicta regabat, in principio creationis sue in episcopum dixit proximum predecessorem suum episcopum Lincolniensem non permisisse quod idem Robertus uocaretur Cancellarius sed magister scholarum'. Lincoln Register (Sutton), f. 117. (Twyne MS. xii. 7.) [On the occasion of Bishop Sutton's confirmation of the election of Roger de Wesenham to the chancellorship in 1295; see *Snappe's Formulary*, ed. H. E. Salter (O.H.S.), pp. 52, 319.]

[2] See the document in Appendix III. [But this can only mean that the office of chancellor was vacant at the time, as it is known from his mention in a Bull of Pope Honorius III that there was a chancellor at Oxford before March 1221. See

Med. Arch. Univ. Oxford, ed. H. E. Salter (O.H.S.), i. 15.] In 1225 there is a prohibition to the Archdeacon, Chancellor, and Dean of Oxford, who had cited the Dean of the King's Free Chapel of S. Martin's in a tithe-suit under a Papal Commission (Rot. Claus. 9 Hen. III. m. 8 *dorso*). The Dean 'gerens vices Cancellarii Oxon.' also decides a dispute as to the tithes of Yatton delegated to the Chancellor with others, in 1230. (*Registrum Malmesburiense*, ed. J. S. Brewer and C. T. Martin (R.S.), ii. 30, 59.) The Bull had been addressed to the Chancellor and the Dean of Oxford with the Abbot of Evesham. See also below, Appendix III. In a document in the burned Cottonian Cartulary of Oseney Grosseteste speaks of 'illius qui auctoritate diocesani iurisdictionem scholarium Oxon. habuerit'. (Twyne MS. xxii, f. 288.)

[3] [On the origin of the office of chancellor at Oxford and on the

CHAP. XII, Oxford chancellorship—its almost unique combination of the
§ 1.   functions of a continental chancellor with those of a continental rector. On the one hand we find the Chancellor of
Functions Oxford entrusted with all the functions exercised by the
of chan-
cellor same Parisian chancellor at the same period, before his rights had
as at Paris. begun to be curtailed by the usurpations of the magisterial
university and the papal bulls by which those usurpations
were supported. Scholars were in England, as in France,
treated as clerks and therefore entitled to trial in the ecclesiastical courts. This jurisdiction was in ordinary cases exercised
by the chancellor, though at first his jurisdiction did not
exclude the occasional interference of the bishop or even of
the archdeacon. The analogy between the Oxford and the
Paris chancellorships at the beginning of the thirteenth century—though not after that—is complete in everything but
the connexion of the former with the cathedral.[1] As an
ecclesiastical judge, the Chancellor of Oxford enforces his
process by excommunication or deprivation of the magisterial licence, suspension or deprivation of the scholastic
privileges.[2] Entrusted with a general supervision of the
schools, he issues proclamations against bearing arms, against
disturbance of the peace, against the formation of conspiracies, against going out after curfew without grave necessity,
against playing at noxious or other games, from which
dissensions may arise, in the meadows or elsewhere, against
keeping 'mulierculae' or 'concubines' in scholars' houses;
and the privilege of the university is denied to all whose

confirmation of the chancellor by
the Bishop of Lincoln, see the
introductory note by Dr. H. E.
Salter to the processes of nomination, 1290–1369, extracted from
the registers of the Bishops of
Lincoln and printed in *Snappe's
Formulary* (O.H.S.), pp. 40–89.]
   [1] Almost the only clear parallel
is the chancellorship of the Medical
University at Montpellier, which
originated at almost the same
period. See above, ii, p. 123 *sq.*
   [2] [On the subject of excom-

munication and the jurisdiction of
the Chancellor's Court at Oxford,
see Dr. H. E. Salter's introductory
note to 'Significations of Excommunication by Chancellors of the
University' in *Snappe's Formulary*
(O.H.S.), pp. 23–39; *Stat. Antiq.
Univ. Oxon.*, ed. S. Gibson, pp.
lxxviii–lxxx; *Med. Arch. Univ.
Oxford*, ed. H. E. Salter (O.H.S.),
i. 35, 36, 138, 147, 192, 205, 224;
*Registrum Cancellarii Oxon., 1434–
1469*, ed. H. E. Salter (O.H.S.),
i. xi.]

names are not borne upon the register of a master from whom they hear at least one 'ordinary' lecture every day. The chancellor enforces his injunctions both by excommunication and (in cases of offences against the peace) by imprisonment or banishment from Oxford, as well as by forfeiture of the privileges of the university.[1] In one point only does the parallel with the situation at Paris fail, and that is only one result of the fundamental difference in the conditions—the absence of a capitular body. At Oxford there was no episcopal prison; Lincoln was a long way off; nor was there any great church like Notre Dame at Paris in whose cloister or precinct a convenient chancellor's prison could be found. Consequently the chancellor had to send his prisoners either to the King's prison in the Castle or to the town prison over the Bocardo gate.[2] This necessity was calculated to prepare the way for that confusion between ecclesiastical and secular jurisdiction which was such a remarkable feature of the Oxford chancellor's position.

Originally then, it should be clearly understood, the chancellor's authority was derived from the bishop and from the bishop only. Primarily the chancellor was an officer not of the university but of the bishop.[3] The jurisdiction given him over scholars by the bishop was derived from the fact of their clerical status, not from the fact that they were members of a university: his jurisdiction extended to laymen only so far as

---

[1] 'Auctoritate domini Cancellarii excommunicati sunt omnes illi solemniter qui pacem Universitatis Oxoniae perturbaverint, *Item*, omnes qui ad hoc foedus inierint vel societatem. . . . *Item*, prohibet Cancellarius, sub poena excommunicationis, ne aliquis ferat arma', &c., *Mun. Acad.* i. 16; [*Stat. Antiq. Univ. Oxon.*, ed. S. Gibson, pp. 78–82.] They are clearly made by the chancellor on his own authority, not by that of the masters. It was just this kind of proclamation which provoked the hostility of the masters of Paris against the chancellor. See above,

i. 309 *sq.*
[2] See below, pp. 83, 84.
[3] [See Dr. H. E. Salter's important introductory note to the confirmations of chancellors by the Bishops of Lincoln printed in *Snappe's Formulary* (O.H.S.), pp. 40–8. When in 1302 the Bishop of Lincoln objected that Walter de Wetheringsete had exercised the office of chancellor before he had been confirmed by him, it was answered that the chancellor had not exercised any spiritual jurisdiction, but only 'de hiis que contingunt regiam potestatem'. See *op. cit.*, p. 61.]

laymen were subject to the authority of the ordinary ecclesiastical courts.[1] In so far as the chancellor was an officer
specially deputed by the bishop to superintend the *studium*,
the law which he administered was the ordinary canon law.

But at Ox-
ford the
chancellor
became an
officer of
the uni-
versity.
On the other hand, though originally and constitutionally
the functions of the Oxford chancellor exactly corresponded
with those of the Chancellor of Paris, yet practically even
from the first his position was very different. We have seen
how at Paris the schools and the rights of the cathedral over
them were more ancient by some centuries than the university proper. At Oxford the university, instead of being an
innovation, was probably in some rudimentary form coeval
with the chancellorship. Whatever degree of association
existed between the masters of Paris in the time of Johannes de
Cella[2] must no doubt have been reproduced at Oxford from
the days of the original Parisian settlement to which we have
seen reason to trace the origin of the *studium generale*. With
the Parisian masters, and the Parisian modes of lecture and
disputation, would naturally come the Parisian custom of
inception and the periodical congregations which that custom
implied. At Paris the chancellor was a member of a corporation incomparably richer, more eminent, and more splendid
than the new society of poor, obscure, and mostly plebeian
teachers who at the end of the thirteenth century began to
claim a share in the admission of new masters and the regulation of their professional conduct. At Oxford all the causes
which could tend to throw the chancellor into collision with
the university were absent. The chancellor was a member of
no hostile corporation; he owed his own existence to the
university. The bishop was too far off, and his diocese too
enormous, for him to meddle much with the details of
administration.

[1] [Rashdall does not emphasize
sufficiently the special character of
the chancellor's jurisdiction. The
chancellor had jurisdiction in any
suit in which a clerk of Oxford was
a party, e.g. in an action for debt.
It was a unique ecclesiastical court,
and tried cases which no other
ecclesiastical court tried. See H. E.
Salter, *History* (1929), xiv. 60-1;
Snappe's Formulary, ed. H. E.
Salter (O.H.S.), pp. 25-9; and
*Registrum Cancellarii Oxon., 1434-
1469*, ed. H. E. Salter (O.H.S.),
i. xv, xx-xxv.]

[2] Cf. above, i. 292, 293.

And on their side the scholars had no ground for viewing with jealousy the jurisdiction of the chancellor. If the chancellor was not from the first elected by the masters themselves, which there is no reason to doubt, he was at least chosen from their own ranks.[1] It is practically certain that the university proper, the society of masters, could, by the beginning of the thirteenth century, have had no permanent officers of its own: in all probability it continued longer than Paris in the acephalous condition from which that university emerged mainly for the purpose of resistance to the chancellor's autocracy. Under these circumstances the Chancellor of Oxford passed naturally and insensibly into the position of the head of the university. While the bishop's representative thus gained a position in the magisterial guild from which the Paris chancellor was always jealously excluded, the university practically appropriated to itself the judicial powers of the chancellor. The distinction between the jurisdiction which

---

[1] Adam de Marisco in a letter to Grosseteste speaks of the appointment of a Master Ralph of Simplingham [Sempringham] as chancellor 'de multitudinis assensu'. (*Monumenta Franciscana*, ed. J. S. Brewer (R.S.), i. 100–1.) The word *multitudo* is very suggestive of the rudimentary state of the Oxford 'congregation' or guild at this time. The letter clearly shows how completely the chancellor was at this time the representative of and responsible to the bishop; yet already he is identifying himself with usurpations on the part of the university of which the bishop complains. The chancellor is never found siding (as at Paris) with the bishop against the masters. [In his note on the episcopal confirmations of the chancellors, Dr. Salter writes: 'Much as the members of the University would have liked to assert that they elected to the chancellorship, and not merely nominated, they could not maintain it, and the form of the document which they obtained from the bishop, stating that *de gratia* he committed the office of chancellor to the man, until he revoked it, showed clearly what was the position of the office': *Snappe's Formulary* (O.H.S.), pp. 43, 44. See also *Stat. Antiq. Univ. Oxon.*, ed. S. Gibson, pp. xxxvii–xxxviii, lxxii–lxxiii. The election rested with the regents in the fourteenth century; but in a letter in a fifteenth-century treatise on *dictamen*, apparently from the University of Oxford to Archbishop Arundel, there is reference to the election of Archdeacon Hallam to the chancellorship having been made in a congregation of regents and non-regents: 'in quadam magna congregacione regencium et non regencium solemniter celebrata, aspirante Domino, sedatis nonnullis perniciosis dissencionum materiis, unanimi consensu et cordialissimo non regencium et omnium facultatum decreto.' See W. A. Pantin's article 'A Medieval Treatise on Letter-writing', in *The Bulletin of the John Rylands Library* (1929), xiii. 326–82.]

CHAP. XII,
§ I.

Conse-
quences of
this differ-
ence.

the chancellor exercised as the representative of the bishop and the jurisdiction which he wielded as head of the master's guild was rapidly lost sight of. The chancellor, by becoming dependent on the university, made himself practically more and more independent of the bishop from whom he derived his authority.[1] Hence the enormous superiority of Oxford to Paris in point of privilege and independence. To the masters and scholars of Paris privileges were, indeed, dealt out by pope and king with no niggard hand. But, though exempted from the jurisdiction of the ordinary tribunals, they were not placed under that of their own officers. Everything was done for the university, very little by it. When these privileges were first conferred, the university itself possessed no recognized head, and it would hardly have occurred to any one to confer a very extensive legal jurisdiction upon the ever-changing rector of the artists. At Oxford the original jurisdiction which the chancellor possessed as the bishop's representative served as a basis for further extensions by king or pope, and the power of the chancellor meant in the long run the power of the university. In process of time the amalgamation of authority, academic and ecclesiastical, civil and criminal, in the hands of the Chancellor of Oxford was such as has scarcely been wielded by the head of any other university except Cambridge. All the functions which at Paris were divided between the Apostolic Conservator, the Provost of Paris, the Chancellor, the Bishop's Court, and the Rector, were united in the hands of the Oxford Chancellor, as well as a share in the government of the town for which at Paris there is no parallel at all. And here we may take occasion to observe the importance to Oxford of its position as a city which was neither a capital nor a see-town. It would have been impossible for a university which had grown up beneath the shadow of an episcopal palace to have completely shaken off the authority of the bishop: it would have been impossible for the most clerically minded monarch to have placed a great

[1] [As Professor L. Halphen has pointed out, there was not in Oxford the same necessity as in Paris to seek papal support in order to secure freedom from diocesan authority; see his article, 'Les Universités au XIIIe siècle', in *Revue historique*, clxvi (1931), 235-6.]

capital in subjection to even the most dignified of academical CHAP. XII, dignitaries.

In dealing with the early history of the schools of Paris, I insisted strongly on the necessity of distinguishing between the growth of the schools and the growth of the university. We have seen reason for presuming that at Oxford the first rudiments of university organization were introduced by the immigrants of 1167-8. It remains for us to call attention to two slight positive traces which are found—in addition to what is implied by the custom of inception—of the existence of some such organization. Both of them occur in the already mentioned legatine ordinance of 1214. Among the legate's injunctions there is the proviso that masters who 'irreverently lectured after the recession of the scholars' shall be suspended from the office of lecturing for three years.[1] It is therefore probable that some kind of formal cessation or dispersion had been decreed by the masters immediately after the outrage: and the issue of such a decree implies a certain amount of organization or at least a habit of combination and co-opera-tion. Moreover, half the rent of existing *hospicia* 'as taxed by the common consent of the clerks and the burghers' was to be remitted for ten years: while in future *hospicia* were to be taxed by a joint board of four burghers and four clerks.[2] Whether or not there had been regular taxors before 1209 (which is the most natural inference), the masters must at least have possessed some organization which admitted of their negotiating with the burghers in a corporate capacity. In either case it is worthy of notice that the office of taxor apparently was the earliest university office at Oxford, as presumably it must have been in the Mother University of Paris. But how low a degree of organization is implied by these indications is illustrated by the fact that while copies of the legatine ordinance are addressed to the burghers, to the bishop, and to 'all the faithful of Christ', none was ap-parently sent to the masters themselves, who were not looked upon as a corporation sufficiently definite to be capable even

The uni-versity of masters in rudimen-tary form probably dates from 1167.

---

[1] See *Med. Arch. Univ. Oxford*, ed. H. E. Salter (O.H.S.), i. 4.　　[2] *Ibid.* i. 2-3, 8.

CHAP. XII, of receiving a letter. The process by which the university
§ I. emerged out of this rudimentary condition will be considered
in the next section.[1]

[1] I am glad to be able to claim the adhesion of Bishop Creighton to my hypothesis of a Parisian migration. *Archaeol. Journal*, 1892. xlix. 272 [reprinted in *Historical Essays and Reviews*, 1902, p. 279].

§ 2. THE CONSTITUTIONAL DEVELOPMENT

THE University of Oxford, in its primitive form, may be CHAP. XII, looked upon as an imitation, perhaps we ought rather to §2. say an unconscious reproduction, of the Parisian society of Imitation masters. It will be remembered that, up to the date at which of Paris. the existence of a *studium generale* at Oxford is first revealed to us, the University of Paris was what has been called a merely customary society without officers, written statutes or any other attributes of a recognized legal corporation. At Oxford as at Paris the bare existence of such a guild is all that we can trace till after the close of the twelfth century. The university is as yet an idea rather than an institution.

During the thirteenth century the intercourse between Custom Paris and Oxford was so close that every fresh development before statute. of corporate activity on the part of the masters of Paris was more or less faithfully imitated or reproduced at Oxford, though the process of development was modified at every step by the different position of the Oxford chancellorship. Written statutes, a common seal, elected officers were pretty sure sooner or later to make their appearance. But an attentive examination of the earliest documents connected with the Oxford schools shows that for the first half-century of their existence the university retained to a large extent its primitive character of a customary rather than a legal corporation. The right of the university to a common seal was disputed as late as the episcopate of Grosseteste.[1] Even after the date of the earliest written statutes we hear more of the 'customs' of the university than of its statutes; and we do not hear anything at all of statutes—at least of statutes avowedly owing their authority to the university and not to the chan- First cellor—till 1253.[2] In that year (March, 1253) we find the statute, 1253.

[1] Adam de Marisco thus writes to the bishop to apologize for the chancellor: 'Signo illo quod dicitur universitatis Oxoniae, quo in simplicitate sua *sicut et plures antecessorum suorum* usus est, de caetero si iusseritis nequaquam usurus, et ad nutum beneplaciti vestri suo cedet officio.' *Mon. Francisc.*, ed. J. S. Brewer (R.S.), pp. 100–1.

[2] [On the subject of the earliest statutes of the university see *Stat. Antiq. Univ. Oxon.*, ed. S. Gibson, pp. xlii–xlv.]

CHAP. XII, university enacting, or reducing to a written form,[1] what has
§ 2.   ever since remained a characteristic feature of the Oxford
constitution—the requirement that no one should be admitted to the licence in theology who had not previously
been a regent in arts.

Irish riot: To the preceding year belongs the settlement of a dispute
oath to the
peace.   between the Northern and the Irish scholars;[2] for there was

[1] *Mun. Acad.* i. 25 [*Stat. Antiq.
Univ. Oxon.*, ed. S. Gibson, p. 49];
Mon. Francis. (R.S.), pp. 346–8.
Notice the expression 'Statuit . . .
et si statutum fuerit, iterato consensu corroborat' (*loc. cit.*), as showing the uncertainty and informality
of any earlier resolutions of the university. [See also *Stat. Antiq.
Univ. Oxon.*, ed. S. Gibson, pp.
xlii, xliii.]

[2] *Mun. Acad.*, i. 20 *sq.* [*Stat.
Antiq. Univ. Oxon.*, ed. S. Gibson,
pp. 84–7.] A similar agreement
was made in 1267 by twenty-four
of each side after exchanging the
kiss of peace. For the settlement
of future disputes five persons were
to be elected from each of the
northern counties: the northern
were to elect 'tres capitaneos', each
Irish province likewise to elect
eight persons to name one captain:
all disputes were to be settled by
the four captains; if they could not
agree they were to appeal to arbitrators, and only in the last resort
to the chancellor or the *Hebdo-
madarii* (see below, p. 137). Most
of the 24 seals remain; it is noticeable that several of them are impressed from ancient gems; another
copy of this agreement (*ibid.* i.
136; *Med. Arch. Univ. Oxford*, ed.
H. E. Salter (O.H.S.), i. 28) is also
preserved bearing only the chancellor's seal, which consists of a
man holding, not (as Wood says)
either a crucifix or a rosary, but a
chained book. For the text of this
document see *Med. Arch. Univ.
Oxford*, ed. H. E. Salter (O.H.S.),
i. 26–8. Another agreement of the

same kind was made in Lent 1274,
'inter Australes, Marchiones, Hy-
bernienses et Walenses ex una parte
et Boriales et Scotos ex altera'. For
the text of this agreement see *Med.
Arch. Univ. Oxford*, ed. H. E.
Salter (O.H.S.), i. 30–3. 'Omnes
et singuli de Uniuersitate tam
maiores quam minores' swore to
observe it, and agreed that 'ad
mandatum Cancellarii insurgent'
against perturbers of the peace.
Persons suspected of violence were
to be required to give security 'per
pignora aut per clericos benefi-
ciatos', or be expelled, and all
swore to assist the chancellor in
forcibly carrying out this sentence.
The agreement was made 'de pleno
consensu omnium magistrorum regencium et non regencium, dominorum et bachelariorum, maiorum
et minorum Uniuersitatis'. One of
the masters mentioned in this agreement was John of London. Was
this the mathematician praised by
Roger Bacon (below, p. 249)? [See
L. J. Paetow, '*Morale Scolarium*' of
John of Garland, Berkeley, Cali-
fornia, 1927, p. 84, n. 17 and n. 20.
Professor Paetow in referring to
this footnote stated in error that
the name of Master John of London
is given by Rashdall as appearing
in a document of the year 1252.
Professor Paetow's suggestions as
to dates for the career of Master
John of London, the mathematician, will need to be reconsidered
if he is to be identified with Master
John of London who is mentioned
in the agreement made in 1274.
Professor Paetow was also unfortu-

an Irish question even then. The document reads like a
treaty of peace between hostile nations rather than an act of university legislation. Twelve arbitrators were chosen on each side, and thirty or forty 'rich men whether Regents or otherwise' were sworn to observe the conditions of peace and to denounce any violation of them to the chancellor. At the same time it was provided that a similar oath should in future be taken by 'inceptors in whatsoever Faculty together with the accustomed oath', as well as by nobles. The punishment denounced in the event of refusal is 'withdrawal of the fellowship of the masters'. It is noteworthy that in these early enactments no special appeal is made to the authority of the chancellor so long as the penalty is one which the university itself had the power to inflict.[1] Even formal statutes run in the name of the university only, nor are they even entrusted to the chancellor for execution. Whether the chancellor was or was not actually present, whether or not he in any sense 'presided' at the earliest Congregations, it is impossible to pronounce with certainty. Moreover, the above-mentioned agreements or treaties of peace appear to be made at general mass-meetings of the whole university, including students (or at least bachelors) as well as masters.[2] Indeed, for a time we almost seem to trace a democratic organization of masters and scholars (after the fashion of Orleans or Angers) existing side by side with the strictly magisterial university—an

nate in his suggestion that the time when John of London lectured in Oxford may be taken 'to have been about 1210–1213', as these years coincide with the *Suspendium clericorum* which lasted from 1209 to 1214. See *op. cit.*, p. 84.]

[1] 'Alioquin Magistrorum et Scholarium eis societas subtrahatur', *Mun. Acad.* i. 22 [*Stat. Antiq. Univ. Oxon.*, ed. S. Gibson, p. 86]. So in the statute about theological degrees: 'Ipso facto a societate Magistrorum et privilegiis Universitatis privatus existat' (above, p. 50). We learn from Adam de Marisco (*Mon. Francisc.*, ed. J. S. Brewer (R.S.), i. 346) that the

chancellor assented to this last statute, but the statute is actually enacted by the university 'Statuit: Universitas Oxoniensis', *Mun. Acad.* i. 25; *Stat. Antiq. Univ. Oxon.*, ed. S. Gibson, p. 49. [Rashdall has misconstrued what Adam Marsh has written. It appears from the letter in question that 'the chancellor and masters and certain bachelors' approved this statute in the form in which it had been drafted by a committee of seven.]

[2] [For two instances of the association of bachelors with masters in legislation see *Stat. Antiq. Univ. Oxon.*, ed. S. Gibson, p. xxii.]

CHAP. XII, organization which in 1267 (and possibly in 1252) even elected
§ 2. four captains for the preservation of the peace.[1] However,
this democratic university (if such it can be called) may have
been little more than a temporary expedient: in any case it
never seems to have taken upon itself any functions except the
preservation of the peace and the support, by armed force if
necessary, of the chancellor's authority, and was gradually
superseded by the more regular guild of masters.

Position of   A strictly magisterial statute of about the same period
the chan-
cellor. against dancing or other riotous celebrations in churches upon
the festivals of the patron saint of a 'nation' or diocese, shows
with great clearness the purpose for which the co-operation
of the chancellor was originally sought, and indeed the origin
of his position as president of the university as well as the
bishop's representative in the *studium*. The 'Decree and
Statute' is issued 'by the authority of the Chancellor and
Masters Regent with the unanimous consent of the Non-
Regents'.[2] The masters conclude by enjoining its observance
'by the authority of the Chancellor' under pain of imprisonment and the greater excommunication. If the chancellor did
not from the first preside in the university Congregations, the
convenience of obtaining the sanctions of excommunication
and imprisonment for the decrees of the university proper
made it expedient to obtain his approval for its acts. It soon
became usual (if it was not from the first) for the chancellor
to be present whenever a Congregation of all faculties was to
be celebrated.[3] Indeed, since he was himself a doctor of
theology, or of canon law, as well as chancellor, he would
necessarily attend all such meetings; and, at a time when the
university itself had no permanent officers of its own (unless

---

[1] See above, p. 50, n. 2. These
were, however, apparently taken
exclusively from the Northerners
and Irish.

[2] 'Auctoritate domini Cancellarii
et magistrorum regencium, cum
unanimi consensu non-regencium,
decretum est et statutum', &c.
(*Mun. Acad.* i. 18). [In his reference to this statute Rashdall relied

on the date 'A.D. 1250?' which is
assigned to it in *Mun. Acad.* i. 18.
The Rev. H. Anstey gives no
authority for this date. Mr. Strickland Gibson (*Stat. Antiq. Univ.
Oxon.*, pp. 82–3) gives this statute
no more precise date than 'before
1350'.]

[3] [See *Stat. Antiq. Univ. Oxon.*,
ed. S. Gibson, pp. 187–8.]

the taxors are regarded in that light), it was natural that he CHAP. XII, §2.
should more or less occupy the position of president at any
assembly in which he appeared.[1]

And yet there remained, and remain to this day, in our The proc-
academical constitution clear indications of the fact that the original
chancellor was originally an extra-university official, and was university
not the proper executive of the masters' guild. It was the executive.
proctors, not the chancellor, who in 1252 were empowered
to demand the oath for the conservation of the peace. It is to
the proctors a few years later that the execution of the sentence of suspension denounced for violation of the statutes is
entrusted.[2] In certain cases at all events it is the proctors who
summon Congregation. To this day it is the proctors who
administer all oaths and declarations, who in the regent congregation submit graces to the house and in all Congregations
count the votes and announce the decision. In these and in
other ways we from the first find the proctors jointly performing many of the functions naturally incident to the presidency of an assembly or the executive of a society and as such
discharged at Paris by the rector. The fact is the more
remarkable since the Oxford proctors, like the Parisian rector

[1] *Mun. Acad.* i. 22, 30: 'Faciant
Procuratores congregationem fieri.'
[On the position and functions of
the chancellor see *Stat. Antiq. Univ.
Oxon.*, ed. S. Gibson, pp. lxxi–lxxiv,
and *Reg. Cancell. Oxon., 1434–
1469*, ed. H. E. Salter (O.H.S.),
i. xiii–xxvi.]

[2] Note that in the early statutes
the chancellor's presence is not
expressly mentioned except where
non-regents were summoned as
well as regents. [See *Stat. Antiq.
Univ. Oxon.*, ed. S. Gibson, pp. 86,
108. For an ordinance of 1312,
made 'per Cancellarium et uni-
uersitatem regencium', see *Stat.
Antiq. Univ. Oxon.*, ed. S. Gibson,
p. 109, and for subsequent examples
see *ibid.*, pp. 24, 35, 202.] It is not
impossible that at first the proctors
presided over Congregations of
regents in all faculties as they un-

doubtedly did over Congregations
of regents in arts. Even in the fifteenth century Register (Archives,
Aa) we find that in a regent Congregation the graces are 'pronounced' (i.e. declared carried) by
a proctor, while in the Great Congregation (i.e. of regents and non-
regents) the chancellor performs
that function. [For an example of
pronouncement by the chancellor
in a Congregation of Regents and
Non-regents see *Stat. Antiq. Univ.
Oxon.*, ed. S. Gibson, p. 157.] In
our modern 'Convocation' and
'Congregation of the University of
Oxford' the question is put by the
vice-chancellor, but the decision is
announced by the senior proctor;
but in the 'Ancient House of Congregation' the graces are still put
to the house, as well as 'pronounced', by the senior proctor.

CHAP. XII,
§ 2.
of the thirteenth century, always remained primarily the officers of the regents in arts, not of the whole university. At Paris the university was obliged to employ the rector as its executive because it had no proper executive of its own. At Oxford, though the chancellor early became, if he was not from the first, the acknowledged head of the university, he is still so far felt to be above and outside the teaching corporation that many of the functions which would naturally attach to such a position, devolve upon the more democratic proctors. In the documents which mention the consent of the chancellor, he appears rather as an external authority whose approval might in certain cases be necessary to give effect to the decisions of the university than as an essential element in the university itself. The masters are bound by oath or solemn promise to obey both chancellor and university;[1] each authority is supreme in its own sphere. The statutes assume at times the form of treaties between two independent contracting parties.[2] This state of things could not or at all events did not last long: the two authorities were fused into one, and the developed Oxford constitution is the result of the fusion. The chancellor loses his independent position and becomes the presiding head of the university.[3] The university submits to the presidency of the bishop's officer, but at the same time, by as it were absorbing the chancellorship into itself, is able to arrogate to itself all the powers of that

The chan-
cellor
absorbed
into the
university.

[1] 'In fide qua teneris Domino et Universitati' (*Mun. Acad.* i. 30). 'Dominus' might conceivably mean the bishop. [Rashdall has been misled here. The reference is to 'God and the University'. In Register D this passage reads, 'Deo et uniuersitati'; in Register C, 'Domino et uniuersitati', see *Stat. Antiq. Univ. Oxon.*, ed. S. Gibson, p. 108.]

[2] So in 1257 (the statute prescribing the form for denouncing a master suspended), 'In hanc formam consentiunt Cancellarius et Universitas Magistrorum regentium Oxoniae' (*Mun. Acad.* i. 30),

[*Stat. Antiq. Univ. Oxon.*, ed. S. Gibson, pp. 107-8]. His consent is here necessary, since a suspension of a regent from lecturing involved a temporary withdrawal of the chancellor's licence. Notice that in this statute the usual purpose of Congregations is to celebrate (1) inceptions, (2) funerals. It was the same at Paris, above, vol. i.

[3] [For the succession of chancellors see the lists compiled by Dr. H. E. Salter, *Snappe's Formulary* (O.H.S.), pp. 318-35; *Reg. Cancell. Oxon., 1434-1469* (O.H.S.), i. xxxv-xxxix.]

office. Some of the anomalies which resulted from such a CHAP. XII, fusion will be traced hereafter.[1] §2.

A year after the date of the earliest extant statute, the University of Oxford, at about the same time as the Mother University of Paris, received the confirmation of all its 'immunities, liberties, and laudable, ancient and rational customs, and approved and honest constitutions' from Innocent IV. It is worthy of notice, as showing that the chancellor is still hardly regarded as an integral part of the university, that the Bull is addressed not to the chancellor and university but (after the manner of Bulls addressed to the masters of Paris) simply to the 'masters and scholars sojourning at Oxford in the diocese of Lincoln'.[2] At the same time the university obtained for its members a privilege against being summoned by papal delegates to answer outside Oxford in respect of contracts made within it.[3]

Papal confirmation of statutes, 1254.

Though by placing itself virtually under the presidency of the chancellor, the University of Oxford as a whole acquired a head earlier than Paris, separate meetings of the faculty of arts were essential, if it was only for the celebration of

The nations.

[1] It is impossible to say to what extent in the early days of the university the chancellor would have claimed the right of vetoing a statute in the name of the bishop, who certainly asserted a very paternal control over the university (see below, p. 115). In the later constitution of the university there is no trace of such a veto, which, however, the chancellor or vice-chancellor obtained by the Laudian statutes and still possesses.

[2] *Mun. Acad.* i. 26–30. The reader of Wood should be warned that the Bull of Alexander IV, maintaining the jurisdiction of the bishop over the 'universitas clericorum castri Oxon.' referred to by Wood, *Annals*, i. 250, has nothing to do with the University, but refers to the clergy of the churches within the Castle precinct. It is given *in extenso* in Twyne MS. ii, f. 19, and again in vii, f. 345, where

it is mistakenly referred to the year 1209. [This document is printed in *Snappe's Formulary*, ed. H. E. Salter (O.H.S.), p. 300. Twyne transcribed it from a Lincoln register which has since disappeared. Rashdall's warning does not hold good, as he was mistaken in supposing that *castrum* refers to the castle and not to the town of Oxford. Dr. H. E. Salter points out in a footnote that *castri Oxon.* cannot refer to the Castle of Oxford as there was no body of clerks in the castle at this time, and he has elsewhere noted the use of *castrum* as meaning 'town' in papal documents: see *Cartulary of Oseney Abbey* (O.H.S.), iii. 346, n. 2.]

[3] *Calendar of Papal Letters relating to Great Britain and Ireland*, i. 306. The grant was for five years only—a fact which no doubt accounts for its disappearance from our muniments and statute-books.

CHAP. XII, the all-important inceptions. The example of the Parisian
§ 2. masters of arts in dividing themselves into nations and placing
elective officers at their head was early imitated at Oxford.
It is somewhat tempting, indeed, to conjecture that at one
time the mystic number four, which had spread from Bologna
to Paris in the first or second decade of the century, was
reproduced at Oxford also. At all events in 1228 (a few years
after the first appearance of proctors at Paris) we read that
a dissension broke out between the scholars and the townsfolk, and that an agreement was made that in future all such
disputes should be composed by 'arbitration of the four
masters who should then be the chief'.[1] This seems to point
to four nations, even if the four masters were rather 'captains'
or 'arbitrators' of the type appointed to preserve the peace in
1267 than a reproduction of the Parisian proctorate. For
four nations, however, the composition of the magisterial
body at Oxford hardly supplied the materials. If a few
French masters came over from Paris in consequence of some
faction-fight or 'cessation' at Paris, the great majority were

[1] 'Arbitrio quatuor magistrorum qui tunc essent precipui', *Ann. de Dunstaplia* (ed. H. R. Luard), in *Ann. Monast.* (R.S.), iii. 110. So too *four* taxors are appointed in 1214 (*Mun. Acad.* i. 2; *Med. Arch. Univ. Oxford*, ed. H. E. Salter (O.H.S.), i. 3); and it is significant that when there were undoubtedly only two nations, the taxors were also two only. It is conceivable that these four masters may have been the taxors themselves; but whether called proctors, or taxors, or captains, there would probably be little difference between these officers and the primitive proctors appointed 'ad iniurias ulciscendas' at Paris (see above, i. 311), except that, if we suppose the captains to be meant, the students joined in their election. But cf. above, p. 30. [On the reduction of the number of university taxors from four to two, see A. B. Emden, *An Oxford Hall in Medieval Times*, pp. 13, 14. In 1231 the king directed that a board should be set up consisting of two masters and two responsible townsmen. When it is stated in the collection of statutes and customs of the university which Mr. Strickland Gibson dates 'before 1350' that four taxors were customarily elected by the proctors in the first Congregation after Michaelmas (*Stat. Antiq. Univ. Oxon.*, ed. S. Gibson, p. 71), the four may be taken to include the two laymen representing the town whose names, it may be supposed, were announced in Congregation together with those of the two masters of arts who were to represent the university. In an Oseney rental for 1324–5 in which the 'taxation' of a house is noted, the names of the four taxors are given, two masters of arts, and two laymen, see *Cartulary of Oseney Abbey*, ed. H. E. Salter (O.H.S.), iii. 183.]

no doubt of British or even English birth.¹ Though Irish
scholars were numerous and troublesome, Irish masters were
few, and the same was probably the case with the Welsh.²
Among Englishmen there was only one marked racial or
geographical distinction—the distinction between the English
north of the Trent and the English south of the Trent. Hence,
instead of the four nations of Paris, we find at Oxford only
two—the *Boreales* and the *Australes*. Scotchmen—probably
at this time only Lowlanders would'be likely to find their way
to Oxford—were included among the Northerners, Welshmen and Irishmen among the Southerners. The Northern
and Southern masters of arts were presided over by their
respective proctors.³ The two proctors are first heard of in
1248, when they appeared before Henry III at Woodstock
to prefer the complaints of the university against the misdoings of the Jews and the burghers. In the charter which
they succeeded in obtaining for the university they are
granted, in conjunction with the chancellor, the right of being
present at the assize of bread and beer.⁴

Two
proctors
first men-
tioned in
1248.

Whether the nations at Oxford were originally four or two,
it is pretty certain that they were originally more distinct
than they afterwards became, and it is probable that in the
earliest congregations the votes were taken by nations. For
in 1274 the articles of peace drawn up after one of the great
faction-fights between north and south⁵ solemnly provide

Abolition
of nations.

¹ Many foreign friars were sent
to study in Oxford (A. G. Little,
Grey Friars in Oxford (O.H.S.),
p. 66, *et passim*). In 1369, however,
Edward III ordered the expulsion
of all French scholars [*Munim. Civ.
Oxonie*, ed. H. E. Salter (O.H.S.),
p. 144].
² *Mun. Acad.* i. 23, [*Stat. Antiq.
Univ. Oxon.*, ed. S. Gibson, p. 87].
³ Chosen by a process of indirect
election, like the rectors of Bologna
and Paris. *Mun. Acad.* i. 81. [*Stat.
Antiq. Univ. Oxon.*, ed. S. Gibson,
pp. lxxiv, 64–6, 133–4, 143. No
evidence has been found to support
Rashdall's suggestion that the
Northern proctor presided over the

Northern masters of arts, and the
Southern proctor over the Southern. So far as is known the authority of both proctors extended over
the whole body of masters.]
⁴ 'Presentibus apud Woodstocke
tam procuratoribus scolarium universitatis quam burgensibus Oxon.'
Rot. Claus. 33 Hen. III, m. 15
dorso. [*Close Rolls, Henry III,
1247–51*, pp. 114, 216–17], *Med.
Arch. Univ. Oxford* (O.H.S.), i. 18,
19. [It is not stated in this grant of
privileges that the number of the
proctors of the university was two.]
⁵ See the 'Solennis Concordia
inter Australes, Marchiones, Hy-
bernienses et Walenses ex una parte

CHAP. XII, that in future the two bodies of Northerners and Southerners
§ 2.   should be amalgamated into a single nation; and from this
time, though one proctor was always an *Australis* and one a
Borealis, the term 'nation' ceases to be used, and the faculty
of arts votes as a single body.[1] The early extinction of nations
in the English universities is a symbol of that complete
national unity which England was the first of European
kingdoms to attain.

Rectors or   It will be remembered that in the chapter on Paris the
proctors.   origin of the nations and their proctors was traced back to the
four universities of Bologna and their rectors. It is interesting
to observe that, though at Paris the four rectors (if indeed that
title was ever applied to the four heads of nations) rapidly
disappeared and were superseded by one rector and four
proctors, at Oxford the proctors on one of their earliest
appearances in history are styled 'Rectors' instead of proctors.[2]
At Oxford the title rector is rarely used afterwards. At Cam-

et Boreales et Scotos ex altera'
(quoted above, pp. 50–1). *Med.
Arch. Univ. Oxford*, ed. H. E.
Salter (O.H.S.), i. 30–3, 332.

[1] 'Prouiso insuper quod de cetero
partes non fiant seu nominentur in
universitate, set unum sit collegium
et unum corpus; aliis nichilominus
obligationibus penalibus per universitatem prius ordinatis in suo
robore duraturis.' The last clause
seems to imply that the previous
statutes had been carried by the
consent of distinct nations. [It may
be doubted whether a reference to
voting by nations, as Rashdall
suggests, is implied in this clause.
It would seem more in keeping
with the sense and context of the
clause if it were taken as referring to
provisions made in the articles of
peace between North and South
of 1267, whereby the two bodies
of Northerners and Southerners
obliged themselves 'ad penam tri-
ginta librarum' to keep the peace.
See *Med. Arch. Univ. Oxford*, ed.
H. E. Salter (O.H.S.), i. 27–8.]
Cf. *Mun. Acad.* i. 92 (Statute of

1313) [*Stat. Antiq. Univ. Oxon.*, ed.
S. Gibson, p. 110]. 'Cum separatio
nationum Australium et Borealium,
cum nationes diversae non sint, tam
clericis quam laicis sit summo opere
detestanda', &c. An earlier statute
[dated by Mr. Strickland Gibson
'before 1275'] has a clause about
perturbations of the peace: 'na-
ciones tanquam diuersas, que non
diuerse sunt, defendendo, seu fatue
impugnando'. [See *Stat. Antiq.
Univ. Oxon.*, p. 108, ll. 14, 15,
App. B, ll. 2–4.]

[2] Adam de Marisco says that the
statute requiring theologians to be
M.A. (see above, p. 50, and below,
p. 68) was subscribed by the regents of the superior faculties (note
how the practice of the superior
doctors subscribing individually is
copied from Paris, see above, i. 328)
and by 'duo rectores pro artistis'.
Mon. Francisc. (R.S.), i. 347. There
is a reference to 'procuratores, sive
rectores' as late as 1377 in the contemporary *Chronicon Angliae*, ed.
E. Maunde Thompson (R.S.), p.
173.

bridge both titles continued in use throughout the medieval period. This alternative use of titles which at Paris denoted separate offices may be accounted for in one of two ways. It is certain that the heads of the nations appeared at Paris earlier than the common rector of the artists; it is possible that they were once called indifferently rectors or proctors, and there are slight independent reasons for believing that such was the case.[1] In that case the national rectorships or proctorships may have been reproduced at Oxford before the institution of the single rectorship ar Paris.[2] On the other hand it is a significant fact that these Oxford rectors or proctors are first heard of at a time when we know that there was a schism in the faculty of arts at Paris, three of the nations having elected one rector in opposition to the rector of the French nation alone. It is quite conceivable that our Oxford proctorships may represent the perpetuation of this anomalous, but then by no means unusual state of schism in the Mother University.[3]

The constitution of Oxford may be said to represent an arrested development of the Parisian constitution modified by the totally different relation of the chancellor to the masters. It is the Parisian constitution transplanted to Oxford after the establishment of the nations and national officers, but before the final establishment of the single common rectorship and before the organization of the superior faculties into distinct colleges or corporations with officers, statutes, and seals of their own. At Oxford the need of a distinct head of the university was never felt, because the chancellor, here on friendly terms with the university, served the turn. The need of a common head of the faculty of arts was unfelt, because there were only two nations, and those less sharply divided either by nationality or organization[4] than the nations of Paris.

No single rector.

---

[1] See above, i. 312.

[2] i.e. before 1237 or 1244.

[3] See Bulaeus, iii. 222; *Chartul. Univ. Paris.* i, No. 187. As late as 1266, certain arbitrators appointed to adjust a schism of this character at Paris provide that one or more nations shall be authorized for just cause to separate from the rest and elect a separate rector. *Chartul. Univ. Paris.* i, No. 409.

[4] The reader will remember that it was the necessity of joint resistance to the chancellor that led to the formation of the four national seals which necessitated the separate congregations. See above, i. 304 *sq.*

CHAP. XII,
§ 2.
There were (at least after the peace of 1274) no separate meetings of the *Australes* and *Boreales*: in the separate congregations of the artists the senior proctor presided.[1]

Prerogative of faculty of arts.
We have seen how at Paris the university proper was for a time almost supplanted by the nations. The faculty of arts habitually took the initiative in university business, the doctors of the superior faculties being merely called in to confirm the resolutions already arrived at by the great national assemblies. At Oxford the predominance of the faculty of arts was still more conspicuous than at Paris.[2] At Paris the general predominance of that faculty and in particular its exclusive initiative in university business was, as we have seen, eventually broken down by the growth of the faculties into organized bodies governed by officials, statutes, and congregations of their own. At Oxford the superior faculties never acquired a separate existence of this kind; no deans of faculties appear upon the scene. The initiative of the faculty of arts remained a permanent principle of the university constitution, and even passed into a claim to an actual veto upon the proceedings of the university.[3] Every statute had to be promulgated in the

[1] *Mun. Acad.* ii. 481. [The date of the 'Forma Congregacionis magne' to which reference is here made is about 1480-8; see *Stat. Antiq. Univ. Oxon.*, ed. S. Gibson, pp. 291-2. According to this 'forma' the senior proctor may convene all the regents to a 'Black Congregation' to discuss the agenda to be laid before the Great Congregation of regents and non-regents. For earlier references to the relations of the senior and of the junior proctor to the Congregations of the university, see *Stat. Antiq. Univ. Oxon.*, ed. S. Gibson, pp. 128 (1325), 144-7 (1344), 156-7 (1357).]

[2] Father Denifle (i. 78) remarks that the assertion 'universitatem (i.e. Parisiensem) fundatum esse in artibus' was never made in the medieval period. But see a document of 1387 in *Chartul. Univ. Paris.* iii, No. 1537: while at Oxford we find the faculty of arts in 1339 boasting that it is 'fons et origo ceteris' (*Mun. Acad.* i. 142). [*Stat. Antiq. Univ. Oxon.*, ed. S. Gibson, pp. xxiii, 142.] It is quite possible that this statement is historically true, i.e. that the migration of 1167-8 consisted entirely of masters of arts. At the end of the twelfth century there was, indeed, clearly a great deal of law-teaching at Oxford (for the evidence see above, p. 21, n. 2, and below, p. 65, n. 2). But, as has been suggested (above, p. 39, n. 1), S. Edmund may probably have been the first theologian to incept at Oxford.

[3] [In this connexion Prof. L. Halphen remarks: 'Cette particularité même a plutôt pour effet de renforcer la cohésion du corps universitaire en empêchant les Facultés de s'isoler et de vivre chacune de sa vie propre'; see his article, 'Les Universités au XIIIe siècle' in *Revue historique*, clxvi (1931), pp. 236-7.]

Congregations of regent masters of arts summoned and pre- CHAP. XII,
sided over by the proctors at S. Mildred's[1] before it could be §2.
submitted to the whole university at S. Mary's. The claim of
the faculty—at least when unanimous[2]—to prevent the further
progress of a statute negatived in this 'Previous Congregation'
is frequently asserted in the proctors' books, but never in
the register kept by the chancellor.[3] The superior faculties
admitted the right of the faculty of arts to a separate and previous deliberation, but not the right to bar the further progress
of a statute.[4] An attempt, however, to give the force of statute
to the contrary opinion in 1357 failed,[5] and this important
question of constitutional principle remained undecided till
the fifteenth century, when the faculty of arts seems to have
claimed an absolute negative only in the granting of graces,[6]
i.e. dispensations from some of the conditions necessary for
taking a degree.

---

[1] A church which formerly stood
to the north of the site of Lincoln
College (Wood, *City* (O.H.S.), ed.
A. Clark, ii. 94). It was also used
for the vespers of artists. *Mun.
Acad.* ii. 408. [*Stat. Antiq. Univ.
Oxon.*, ed. S. Gibson, pp. 177, 197.
On the subject of the Congregation
of Artists see below, pp. 63–4.]

[2] 'Nihil expeditum penitus habeatur facultate artium *integre* reclamante.' *Mun. Acad.* ii. 429
(where Registers B and C read
'penitus'), [*Stat. Antiq. Univ.Oxon.*,
ed. S. Gibson, p. 179, l. 29]. Cf.
the '*penitus* non reclamante' of p.
483. [*Stat. Antiq. Univ. Oxon.*, ed.
S. Gibson, p. 293, l. 20.]

[3] *Mun. Acad.* i. 117, 331, ii. 429,
481–3. [*Stat. Antiq. Univ. Oxon.*,
ed. S. Gibson, pp. 127–8, 179,
264–5, 291–3.] Of this last statute
there is a late copy in the chancellor's book. [Rashdall's statement that there is no record in the
Chancellor's Book (*Registrum A*)
of the claim of the faculty of arts to
exercise control over the course of
university legislation is not correct.
See *Mun. Acad.* ii. 429, 484; *Stat.*

Antiq. Univ. Oxon., ed. S. Gibson,
p. 179, ll. 24–9. See also *ibid.*,
p. 124, ll. 28–33.]

[4] [See *Stat. Antiq. Univ. Oxon.*,
ed. S. Gibson, pp. xxiii–xxiv. Mr.
Strickland Gibson points to an
ordinance of 1325 as furnishing
'the earliest dated reference to this
right of previous deliberation', but
see *ibid.*, p. 124, for a reference to
it in a statute of 1322.]

[5] *Mun. Acad.* i. 188–9. [*Stat.
Antiq. Univ. Oxon.*, ed. S. Gibson,
pp. xxvi–xxvii, 156–7.] This decla-
ration was passed by a majority
consisting of the non-regents and
two faculties, the theologians and
the civilians; but as the faculty of
arts opposed, they would of course
not recognize the authority of the
statute, though the chancellor pronounced it carried. See below,
p. 65.

[6] In 1441, *Mun. Acad.* i. 331.
[*Stat. Antiq. Univ. Oxon.*, ed. S.
Gibson, pp. 264–5.] This purports
to be a statute of the regents and
non-regents, but is found only in
the proctors' books.

CHAP, XII,
§ 2.
Origin of
proctorial
veto.

It may be added that the mere necessity of a promulgation in the 'Previous Congregation' of artists gave a practical veto to the proctors (by whom alone that faculty could be summoned), at least when agreed. In 1344 a statute was passed enabling one proctor, with the consent of the chancellor, to promulgate a statute;[1] but the two proctors united could still oppose a barrier to any proposed legislation. The proctorial veto, which was embodied in the Laudian Statutes and still survives, may no doubt be traced back to this ancient supremacy of the faculty of arts.[2]

The proctors are the executive of the whole university.

A further consequence of this predominance was that the proctors, being only the representative officers of the magisterial body, acted as the executive of the whole university, just as it was left to the Parisian rector, originally the head of the artists only, to execute the decrees of the whole university at a time before his actual 'Headship' was admitted by the superior faculties. At Oxford the rise of the proctors to the headship of the university was barred by the established position of the chancellor; but from the first the proctors are officers of the university as well as of the faculty of arts.[3] To this day the proctors are the assessors of the vice-chancellor in most of his public acts. Down to 1868 they kept the university accounts and administered its whole finance subject to audit by a Committee of Auditors or 'Judices'.[4]

[1] *Mun. Acad.* i. 146. [*Stat. Antiq. Univ. Oxon.*, ed. S. Gibson, p. 146.]

[2] The only other trace of a direct proctorial veto which I have come across in the Middle Ages is in 1461, when a great disturbance took place because the commissary adjourned a Congregation of Regents 'utroque procuratore reclamante' (Aa, f. 121 a). It thus appears that the consent at least of one proctor was necessary to the adjournment of a Lesser Congregation. [See L. H. D. Buxton and S. Gibson, *Oxford University Ceremonies*, p. 54.]

[3] [On the functions of the proctors see *Stat. Antiq. Univ.*

Oxon., ed. S. Gibson, pp. lxxiv–lxxvii. On the succession of proctors see the lists compiled by Dr. H. E. Salter, *Snappe's Formulary* (O.H.S.), pp. 318–25; *Reg. Cancell. Oxon., 1434–1469* (O.H.S.), i. xliv–xlv.]

[4] [Fifteen proctors' accounts, ranging from 1464 to 1496, are extant and are printed in *Med. Arch. Univ. Oxford*, ed. H. E. Salter (O.H.S.), ii. 272 sq. Dr. H. E. Salter notes that the average income of the university at this time was about £58 and the average expenditure less than £45, the balance being probably devoted to buildings under construction.]

A peculiarity of the Oxford constitution was the important position occupied by the non-regents. At a very early date we find the presence of the non-regents essential to all permanent statutes and other important acts of the university. When they attended, they gave a collective vote like a distinct faculty. Elections and all merely administrative business remained, as at Paris, in the hands of the regents.

There were thus at Oxford three distinct congregations:[1]

(1) The Congregation of the regents in arts commonly called the 'Black Congregation'. Besides the celebration of inceptions in arts and the election of proctors, this Congregation met at S. Mildred's Church for the preliminary

CHAP. XII, § 2. The non-regents.

Three Congregations.

(1) Black or previous.

[1] [Dr. H. E. Salter (*Bodl. Quarterly Record*, 1926, v. 19–22) suggests that there were only two Congregations before 1500, and 'that the phrase *congregatio artistarum* is a loose way of speaking of the Congregation of Regents, in which the artists always had a large majority'. Mr. Strickland Gibson (*Stat. Antiq. Univ. Oxon.*, pp. xxiii–xxxii: it was this section of his introduction as it previously appeared in *Bodl. Quarterly Record*, 1925, iv. 296–307, that evoked Dr. Salter's statement of the case for two instead of three Congregations) corroborates Rashdall's account. Sir Charles Mallet, who gives a careful summary of both these views (*Hist. Univ. Oxford*, iii, App. B, and see also *ibid.* i. 176–7), is disposed to favour that held by Rashdall and Mr. Gibson, but indicates a possible line of compromise. He notes that 'Mr. Gibson, dwelling on the early statutes, is impressed with the passages in which the separate activities of the Artists are referred to again and again', and that the points which Dr. Salter makes are 'mostly founded on passages dating from the middle or end of the fifteenth century, a time when the Congregation of Artists had probably sunk into decay, when its meeting-place had vanished, and when the activities of the Congregation of Regents were beginning almost to efface the recollection of the other' (*loc. cit.*, p. 508). See also L. H. D. Buxton and S. Gibson, *Oxford University Ceremonies*, p. 51, n. 5. If the Congregation of Regents in arts had a separate existence, it is evident from the passages in which this designation is found that it was essentially a deliberative body whose main function was to discuss beforehand the agenda of the next Congregation of Regents and Non-regents. The celebration of inception in arts and the election of proctors are not, as Rashdall states, found included among its functions. See *Stat. Antiq. Univ. Oxon.*, ed. S. Gibson, pp. xcvi–xcvii for inception in arts. The election of proctors took place in the Congregation of Regents, see *ibid.*, pp. xxiii, lxxvi. While there is reference to be found to 'Congregacio arcistarum preuia ad congregacionem regencium et non regencium apud sanctam Mildredam facienda' (*Stat. Antiq. Univ. Oxon.*, ed. S. Gibson, pp. 146, 156), no example appears to be known of the abbreviated form 'Previous Congregation', as given by Rashdall.]

CHAP. XII, discussion of proposed statutes. When assembled for this
§ 2.   purpose, it was often called the 'Previous Congregation'.[1]

(2) Lesser   (2) The Congregation of Regents (of all faculties) or 'Lesser
or regent.   Congregation' (*Congregatio minor*) met at S. Mary's. To this
Congregation belonged, in all ordinary cases, the grant of
leases, the ordinary finance of the university, and the control
of all matters relating to lectures, studies, and degrees, especially the grant of dispensatory graces where not specially
reserved by statute to the 'Great Congregation'.[2] This power
grew in course of time (as we shall see) into the power of
conferring the degree itself. From the completion of the Congregation-house in about 1327, the regent Congregation met
in that building. It is a detached building standing on the
north side of the choir of S. Mary's Church.[3]

[1] At the Previous Congregation
non-regents in arts at times appear
(*Mun. Acad.* i. 188), but not always
(*ibid.*, p. 481). It was probably at
the discretion of the proctors to
summon them or not. [In stating
that non-regents in arts sometimes
appeared at this Congregation, Rashdall was misled by the erroneous
inclusion of 'et Non-Regentibus' in
Mun. Acad. i. 188; see *Stat. Antiq.
Univ. Oxon.*, ed. S. Gibson, p. 156;
Mallet, *Hist. Univ. Oxford*, i. 177,
n. 4.]

[2] [See *Stat. Antiq. Univ. Oxon.*,
ed. S. Gibson, pp. xxii–xxiii, xxv–
xxvi; Mallet, *Hist. Univ. Oxford*,
i. 178, 200–1. There may be added
to the functions of the Congregation
of regents enumerated here the
election of the chancellor, proctors,
and bedels. The title *congregatio
minor* does not appear to have been
commonly used. Dr. H. E. Salter
has noted two even less common
forms: *congregacio prima* and *congregacio basteres*; see *Bodl. Quarterly
Record*, 1926, v. 21, 22; *Reg. Cancell. Oxon., 1434–1469*, ed. H. E.
Salter (O.H.S.), i. 73, 88, 89.]

[3] This building was begun in
1320 by Adam de Brome, Rector
of S. Mary's and Founder of Oriel

College, at the expense of Thomas
de Cobham, Bishop of Worcester,
a room above it being appropriated
to the library left to the university
by that prelate. It was left not
quite completed on the death of the
bishop in 1327. See the document
in *Collectanea* (O.H.S.), ii. 62 *sq.*,
which recounts the violent dispute
between Oriel College (as Rectors
of the Church) and the university
for the possession of the library,
which lasted till 1410, when the
Oriel Archbishop Arundel compensated the college for its claim.
(Rot. Pat. 11 Hen. IV, p. 2, m. 22.);
[*Cal. Pat. Rolls, Henry IV, 1408–
13*, p. 190. See also E. H. Pearce,
*Thomas de Cobham, Bishop of Wor-
cester*, pp. 244–8; *Oriel College
Records*, ed. C. L. Shadwell and
H. E. Salter (O.H.S.), pp. 24–7;
and Mr. F. Madan's note on
'Bishop Cobham's Library' in
Bodl. Quarterly Record, vi. 50–1.]
The chaplain of the university
served as librarian (*Mun. Acad.*
i. 227. [*Stat. Antiq. Univ. Oxon.*,
ed. S. Gibson, p. 166.] It may
be noted that this congregation-
house is the only part of S. Mary's
Church (it is really, however, a
separate building) over which the

(3) The Congregation of Regents and Non-regents, com- CHAP. XII,
monly called the 'Full' or 'Great Congregation' (*Congregatio* §2.
plena or *magna*), was the supreme governing body of the (3) Full or great.
university and was alone competent to make a permanent
statute.[1] It met at S. Mary's. In the 'Great Congregation'
the voting was by faculties; and there is no reason to doubt Voting by faculties.
that here as at Paris the principle which obtained throughout
the thirteenth century was that a statute required the consent
of all four faculties[2] with the addition, in the case of Oxford,
of the non-regents.[3]

university has the smallest right of property or control. The church is merely *lent* for university sermons. [In 1899 the university took over from Oriel College responsibility for the repair and maintenance of Adam de Brome's Chapel, see *Statt. Univ. Oxon.*, 1934, p. 663. See also L. H. D. Buxton and S. Gibson, *Oxford University Ceremonies*, p. 111.]

[1] The term 'Convocatio' is rarely used in the Middle Ages: where it occurs, it is a synonym of 'Congregatio'. In the sixteenth century 'Convocatio' was gradually appropriated to the Great Congregation, 'Congregatio' to the Lesser Congregation. The Black Congregation was by this time practically obsolete. [See *Stat. Antiq. Univ. Oxon.*, ed. S. Gibson, pp. xxi–xxii, xxv–xxvi, xxix–xxxi; Mallet, *Hist. Univ. Oxford*, i. 178–9, 200–1.] The Congregation of Regents and Non-regents both 'statuerunt' and 'ordinauerunt'; the 'Acta' of the Congregation of Regents took the form of ordinances only. The enactments of the regents only are never called *Statuta*, but *Ordinationes*. In a form of statute imposed upon the university by a Royal Commission in 1376, we find 'quibuscunque ordinacionibus magistrorum regencium, vel statutis magistrorum regencium et non-regencium'. Rot. Pat. 50 Ed. III, pt. i, m. 10 (Hare,

Mem., f. 72. [*Cal. Pat. Rolls, Edward III, 1374–7*, pp. 290–3.] The regents must not be confounded (as is done by a learned writer) with 'the Masters of less than two years' standing', who are the 'necessario regentes'. Though a new M.A. was obliged to lecture for one year (the period of necessary regency has since been extended to two years), he could continue to teach, and therefore to enjoy the rights of regency as long as he pleased. It is only since the regents ceased to lecture that M.A.s of two years' standing (with the deans of colleges, the doctors, and a few officials) became the only regents. [See *Stat. Antiq. Univ. Oxon.*, ed. S. Gibson, p. xxii.]

[2] Civil and canon law are sometimes spoken of as two faculties, and generally appoint two representatives upon university delegacies (divinity and medicine appointing one each and arts four), but on a division they appear at times to vote as one (see below, p. 72, but cf. p. 77). [See also *Stat. Antiq. Univ. Oxon.*, ed. S. Gibson, pp. xxxvi–xxxvii, 254–5, 292.]

[3] Their position seems established by 1280: 'Magistri non-regentes in partem se trahentes per se' (*Mun. Acad.* i. 41; cf. p. 43). [*Stat. Antiq. Univ. Oxon.*, ed. S. Gibson, pp. 96–7; see also *ibid.*, pp. cii, 118, 146–7, 292–3.]

CHAP. XII,   The beginning of the fourteenth century introduces us to
§ 2.   a great constitutional crisis in the history of the university.
Constitu-
tional   Here as at Paris the constitutional development of the univer-
changes in
fourteenth sity is intimately bound up with a struggle against the intru-
century.   sion of the Mendicant Friars. About the year 1303 a statute was
passed which distinctly affirmed the principle that a majority
of the faculties (the non-regents being reckoned as one) could
bind the whole university. To understand the circumstances
which provoked this constitutional revolution, a glance at the
history of the Oxford Mendicants is indispensable.

Establish-   Impelled by a vague desire to establish a hold upon the
ment of the
Mendicant thought of the age as well as by the more definite purpose of
Orders in
Oxford.   gaining converts for their Orders,[1] the friars everywhere
seized upon the university towns as the basis of their opera-
tions. We have seen the storm which followed upon their
advent at Paris. At Oxford the Dominicans made their
appearance in 1221, soon after their first landing in England.[2]
They established themselves in the heart of Oxford on the
east side of the street called the Jewry.[3] Though the conversion of the Jews was a prominent part of their work,[4] they
early connected themselves with the university by opening a
school in which theology was taught by a 'converted' doctor
of divinity, Robert Bacon. The Franciscans followed in

---

[1] Jordan of Saxony, the third
Dominican General, as he wanders
from one university to another,
recounts the number of his 'cap-
tures'. Thus at Oxford in 1229 he
writes, 'Apud studium Oxoniense,
ubi ad praesens eram, spem bonae
capturae Dominus nobis dedit'.
Lettres, ed. P. C. Bayonne, p. 126; [*B.
Jordanis de Saxonia Opera*, ed. J.-J.
Berthier, Fribourg, 1891, p. 72.]

[2] Trivet, *Annales*, ed. T. Hog,
p. 209. For details as to the establishment of this and other Orders
in Oxford see Wood, *City* (O.H.S.),
ii. 312 *sq.*, and A. G. Little, *Grey
Friars in Oxford* (O.H.S.). [See
also Dr. A. G. Little's articles on
the Oxford Friaries in *Victoria
County History of Oxford*, ii. 107-

52; the same author's *Studies in
English Franciscan History*, pp.
192–221; and his article 'The Franciscan School at Oxford in the 13th
Century', in *Archivum Franciscanum Historicum* (1926), xix. 803–74.
Unfortunately no adequate history
has yet been written of the Dominican school in Oxford. Reference
may be made to Bede Jarrett, O.P.,
The English Dominicans, London,
1921; *The English Dominican Province*, London, 1921, containing
articles by various authors.]

[3] [Now the north-west corner of
the site of Christ Church.]

[4] [See L. M. Friedman, *Robert
Grosseteste and the Jews*, Cambridge, U.S.A., 1934.]

1224,[1] and were given a site on the west side of S. Ebbe's CHAP. XII,
Church, where the Order was joined by many students of § 2.
noble birth; before long they expanded and included the land
outside the town wall as far as the Trillmill stream on the
south.[2] In 1245 the Dominicans moved to a suburb, and
established themselves on a spot still known as Black Friars
Road, upon what was then an island formed by the Trillmill
stream and the Thames, between Folly Bridge and Oseney.[3]
In 1256 the Carmelites acquired a house on the west of
Stockwell (now Worcester) Street in the northern suburb,
where they remained till 1318, when Edward II, in fulfilment
of a vow made at Bannockburn, granted them his Palace in
Beaumont Fields, the site of which is still commemorated by
the name of the neighbouring 'Friar's Entry'.[4] In 1268 the
fourth great Mendicant Order, the Augustinians, are found
obtaining from the King a piece of ground for a convent in
Holywell—on the site now occupied by Wadham.[5] The
Friars of the Sack established themselves near the Castle
about the year 1262;[6] the Trinitarians obtained a house outside
the East Gate in 1293;[7] and the Crutched Friars are heard of
in the following century.[8] But the houses of these last Orders
played no considerable part in the history of the university.

Both at Paris and at Oxford, in the first flush of their repu- Harmony
tation for sanctity and asceticism, the friars were well received between
friars and
by the university, though often annoyed by the opposition of university.
the higher ecclesiastics. At Paris the new-comers very quickly
outlived their welcome. At Oxford the harmony between

---

[1] *Mon. Francisc.* (R.S.), i. 9.
Cf. *ibid.*, p. 633.
[2] *Ibid.* (R.S.), i. 15; Little,
Grey Friars (O.H.S.), pp. 1 *sq.*,
295 *sq.*
[3] *Ann. Monast.* (Oseney) (R.S.),
iv. 94–8.
[4] Dugdale, *Monasticon*, vi. 1575;
documents in Wood, *City* (O.H.S.),
ii. 415 *sq.*; Linc. Reg., Dalderby,
f. 388 (Twyne MS. i, f. 4 *b*);
Chronicles of Edward I and II, ed.
W. Stubbs, ii. 300; cf. Ogle, Nos.
xiv, xv, xxi.
[5] Documents in Dugdale, vi.

1596, and Wood, *City* (O.H.S.), ii.
447 *sq.* [See *Cartulary of the
Hospital of St. John the Baptist*,
ed. H. E. Salter (O.H.S.), i. 25–9,
for their first site.]
[6] Dugdale, vi. 1608; Wood, *City*
(O.H.S.), ii. 473. The Order was
suppressed in England in 1307.
[7] Wood, *City* (O.H.S.), ii. 478.
In the Lincoln Register, Dalderby,
f. 308 (Twyne MS. ii, f. 30), is the
approval of a chantry for them in
1315, with the royal licence of 1304.
[8] Dugdale, vi. 1586; Wood, *City*
(O.H.S.), ii. 478.

CHAP. XII, regular and secular was of much longer duration. Even the
§ 2. Dominicans forgot to quarrel: while the more humble-
minded Franciscans employed secular doctors of divinity to
lecture for them in their conventual school.[1] The illustrious
Grosseteste was the first of the Franciscan lectors and showed
himself throughout his life a warm friend and patron of the
Order. Oxford was indeed just touched by the storm which
rent the University of Paris in sunder for so many years. In
$125\frac{1}{2}$, a few weeks after the passing of the first statute against
the friars at Paris,[2] we find a statute passed at Oxford[3] with
the same general intention of setting a limit to the multiplication of friar doctors and of securing the control of the university over regular graduates. Like the Parisian statute it
requires an inceptor in theology to have previously ruled in
arts. The further objects of the Parisian statute are secured
in another way. Instead of setting a fixed limit to the number
of friar doctors, it merely forbids the graduation in theology
of men who have not previously been masters of arts.[4] This
would at the same time secure that the candidates should
already have taken the promise or oath of obedience to the

Statute
of $125\frac{1}{2}$
requiring
gradua-
tion in
arts.

[1] *Mon. Francisc.*, ed. J. S.
Brewer (R.S.), i. 37–9, 550.

[2] Bulaeus, iii. 245; *Chartul.
Univ. Paris.* i, pt. i, No. 200. See
above, i. 376. The Paris statute
was passed in Feb. $125\frac{1}{2}$, the Oxford statute was carried on the 9th
of the following March (*Mon.
Francisc.* (R.S.), i. 346), and was
probably suggested by the news
from Paris. [The correct date of
the passing of the Oxford statute
is 9 Mar. $125\frac{2}{3}$. Rashdall was
misled by Wood into giving $125\frac{1}{2}$
as the year. This Oxford statute
was unconnected with affairs in
Paris. The dispute in Oxford arose
over a petition from the friars that
Friar Thomas of York should be
allowed to proceed to the degree of
D.D., although he had not incepted
in arts. This was the first occasion
so far as is known that this question
had been raised in Oxford. Cer-

tainly, as regards the Franciscans,
the first four *lectores* were seculars,
and the next three had incepted as
M.A. before joining the Order.
See A. G. Little, *The Grey Friars
in Oxford* (O.H.S.), pp. 37–9, 134–
40; and his article, 'The Franciscan School at Oxford in the 13th
century', in *Archivum Franciscanum Historicum* (1926), xix. 823–
31.]

[3] *Mun. Acad.* i. 25. [*Stat. Antiq.
Univ. Oxon.*, ed. S. Gibson, pp.
cxiii, 49.]

[4] 'Nisi prius rexerit in artibus
in aliqua Universitate.' The statute is similarly quoted in the
friars' pleadings in 1313 (*Collectanea* (O.H.S.), ii. 225), but in their
Act of Appeal it runs 'nisi prius in
arte dialectica gradum seu statum
Magistri *uel saltem bacullarii* ha-
buisset'. *Ibid.*, p. 239.

statutes,[1] which, it will be remembered, was the great bone CHAP. XII, §2.
of contention at Paris. In one respect, indeed, the objects of
the two statutes were different. The Paris statute was enacted
by the theological faculty and was designed to protect the
secular theologians from the competition of their Mendicant
rivals. At Oxford there is less trace of dislike for the Mendicants as such.[2] The Oxford statute was passed by the university itself, and was inspired by the jealousy of the faculty of
arts for its own authority and for the studies of which it was the
guardian. The statute would not touch men who had entered
a religious order after completing their regency in arts. But
the friars, though they professed to give their novices a philosophical training in their own schools,[3] considered it inconsistent
with their principles to allow graduation in secular branches
of learning. To the mind of the secular academic the study
of philosophy was an essential preliminary to that of theology: even when he applied himself to the study of theology,
he was disposed to attach more importance to the Sentences
than to the Bible, and to apply to the doctrine of the Holy
Trinity or to the psychology of angelical beings the philosophical distinctions in which he had revelled as an artist.[4] The
secular masters of arts were not disposed either to allow
theology to be approached without adequate instruction in
philosophy or to permit that instruction to be given by any
but authorized masters of their own faculty. At the same

[1] Even if the oath was not yet required upon inception in theo-logy, as it undoubtedly was later, *Mun. Acad.* ii. 374 [*Stat. Antiq. Univ. Oxon.*, ed. S. Gibson, p. 19], we have no doubt a relic of this conflict with the friars in the pro-vision that an inceptor in any other faculty is merely required *dare fidem*, while a master of theology is required *iurare* 'ponendo manum ad pectus' (*loc. cit.*, cf. ii. 421). [*Stat. Antiq. Univ. Oxon.*, ed. S. Gibson, p. 57.]
[2] But see *Mon. Francisc.* (R.S.), i. 338, 346 *sq.*, and cf. *Collectanea* (O.H.S.), ii. 200, 245.
[3] See *Collectanea* (O.H.S.), ii.

217. At an earlier date secular edu-cation had been forbidden alto-gether. Cf. *Chartul. Univ. Paris.* i, Nos. 57, 335, 342.
[4] Even among the Mendicants, Roger Bacon complains that the biblical lecturer 'mendicat horam legendi secundum quod placet lec-tori Sententiarum'. *Opp. Inedita*, ed. J. S. Brewer (R.S.), p. 329. [Denifle urged that it has been too readily assumed that more attention was paid to the study of the Sentences than to that of the Bible. See his article, 'Quel livre servait de base à l'enseignement des Maîtres à l'Université', in *Revue Thomiste*, 1894, i. 149–61.]

CHAP. XII, time a dispensing power was reserved to the chancellor and
§ 2. regents. According to the admissions of the friars themselves,
such dispensations were at first liberally granted;[1] and the
friendly relations between the university and the Orders seem
to have been little disturbed by the new statute.[2]

Movement The inevitable conflict broke out at the beginning of the
against
friars, following century. About the year 1303 begins a series of
1303. statutes obviously directed against the obnoxious Mendicants,

Vespers especially the ever-combatant Order of S. Dominic. In that
and ser-
mons year the university transferred the 'Examinatory Sermons'
transferred
to S. required of bachelors of theology as a condition of inception
Mary's. from the Dominican and Minorite convents down by the
quiet river-side, where they had commonly been preached, to
the more central but (as the friars contended) more noisy and
incommodious S. Mary's. In 1310 the theological vespers—
the disputation on the eve of inception—which had hitherto
been given in any master's school, were likewise required to
be held in the University Church. The measure was really
aimed at the friars, since the usual practice had been to borrow
or hire one of the large and well-built schools of the Friars

The Minor or Friars Preachers. A little later (1310 or 1311) friars
Sentences
before the were required to take the degree of bachelor of theology in
Bible. the university, and not merely (as heretofore) to obtain the
authorization of their own superiors, before they could
lecture upon the Bible. As the degree of bachelor of theology
was taken by lecturing on the Sentences,[3] which required a

---

[1] *Collectanea* (O.H.S.), ii. 256.
[2] For the whole of this conflict
the chief and almost only authority
is a Roll containing a record of the
proceedings in the Roman Court
upon the appeal of the friars,
which I have edited in *Collectanea*
(O.H.S.), ii. 195 *sq.* For further
details I may refer to the Introduction prefixed thereto. Rot. Claus.
6 Ed. II, m. 8 *dorso* may be added
to the documents there published:
in it the King intervenes on the side
of the friars. [See *Cal. Close Rolls,
Edward II, 1307–13*, pp. 445, 456,
567–8; *1313–18*, p. 535; *1318–23*,

pp. 31, 32. See also *Hist. MSS.
Comm. 4th Report*, App., p. 379 *sq.*]
[3] Usually, but in *Collectanea*
(O.H.S.), ii. 233, the university
contradicts the friars' statement
that the B.D. could only be taken
in this way. Perhaps the allusion
is to the old and obsolete permission to read the *Magister Historiarum*. See *Mun. Acad.* i. 25.
[*Stat. Antiq. Univ. Oxon.*, ed. S.
Gibson, pp. cxiii–cxiv, 49. See
A. G. Little, 'The Franciscan
School at Oxford in the 13th Century', in *Archivum Franciscanum
Historicum* (1926), xix. 826–7.]

philosophical education, this pressed heavily on the friars, CHAP. XII,
then the only students of theology who cared much about the § 2.
exegetical study[1] of the Bible as a practical preparation for the
duties of the preacher and the pastor. The university statute,
as they not unreasonably contended, was 'irrational' and
changed the proper 'order of doctrine', since there were many
simple friars quite fitted for lecturing on the Bible who were
not equal to grappling with the intricacies of scholastic
theology: though to the university it appeared that such
teaching only led to the diffusion of 'errors'. Besides these
formal, corporate attacks upon the position which the friars
had hitherto occupied in the university, they now began to
be annoyed by the stricter enforcement or abuse of their
prerogative on the part of individual masters. Graces dispens- Graces
ing from the obligation to graduate in arts, which had hitherto the uni-
been granted almost as a matter of course, began to be re- versity.
fused; and a single master of arts, according to the interpretation which the university put upon the statute, could obstruct
the grace. Again, the statutes required that candidates for
theological degrees should have disputed in the school of
every master of the faculty; and now secular masters began
to refuse admission to the friar candidates. Finally, not only
did the university decline to admit friars to its degrees without
an oath to obey the statutes of the university[2] (here the old
Parisian grievance comes to the front), but existing masters
were required to swear obedience to the new statutes; and
upon his refusal the Dominican doctor, Hugh of Sutton, was Expulsion
expelled from the university.[3] To complete their list of minican
grievances, the university got the contumacious friars excom- friar.
municated by the Archbishop of Canterbury, which exposed
them to a host of petty vexations. They were preached
against in the pulpits of the seculars: their own sermons, their
schools, and their confessionals began to be avoided by scholars

[1] 'Legere Bibliam biblice', sometimes explained as 'sive textualiter',
as opposed to the scholastic discussion of 'questiones' arising out
of the text.
[2] *Collectanea* (O.H.S.), ii. 218;
Mun. Acad. ii. 374. [*Stat. Antiq.*

Univ. Oxon., ed. S. Gibson,
p. 19.]
[3] [Hugh of Sutton (de Suctona)
is also known as Hugh of Dutton
or Dytton (de Ductona). See H.
Rashdall, *Collectanea* (O.H.S.), ii.
219.]

and townsfolk alike. People were afraid to speak to them or give them money or food, lawyers to act as their counsel: even their own students (as the friars alleged) had been driven by this storm of obloquy and persecution to run away from their convents: those who remained had their 'necessary living, good fame, and affection of their friends' taken away from them.[1]

Majority of faculties defined by statute, 1302–3.   It was to carry through this programme of anti-mendicant legislation—these 'exquisite and secret machinations', as the friars pathetically phrased it—that an innovation was attempted in the university constitution exactly parallel to that which we have traced at Paris. At Paris, however, we were unable to fix the exact period at which the principle of statute-making by a mere majority of faculties was introduced, if indeed the revolution was not too silent and gradual to be assigned to any precise moment. At Oxford we are able to give a definite date. About the year 1302 or 1303 the university enacted that the regents in two faculties with a majority of the non-regents should have the power to make a permanent statute binding on the whole university; and the statutes about the place of vespers and the priority of the Sentences to the Bible were in fact carried only by the required majority, the two faculties being the faculty of arts and the always closely allied faculty of medicine, which was for the nonce embodied in the person of a single doctor.[2]

Appeal to Roman Court.   The result of the embroglio with the Mendicants was an appeal to the Roman Court,[3] and in this appeal the constitu-

---

[1] *Collectanea* (O.H.S.), ii. 217–37, 256–61.

[2] Ibid. ii. 218, 226. [*Stat. Antiq. Univ. Oxon.*, ed. S. Gibson, p. 109.] The faculty of theology would of course include many regulars; still the two dissentient faculties do not appear to have opposed the constitutional innovation or sided with the Mendicants in the ensuing struggle. The secular theologians as individuals certainly joined in the campaign against the friars.

[3] In Feb. 1312 (*Collectanea* (O.H.S.), ii. 237 *sq.*), the pleadings of the friars give an amusing account of their proctor's efforts to serve the notice of appeal upon the chancellor and proctors. The chancellor's servant prevented Brother Lawrence of Warwick from entering his master's school. He then repaired to S. Mary's, where a Congregation was being held, but was forcibly ejected ('exiit conturbatus protestans se dictas prouocationes et appellationem velle prosequi cum effectu et earum copiam offerens postquam hostium Ecclesie recluserunt'). Thereupon the un-

tional statute, upon the validity of which the legality of the whole proceedings turned, formed one of the subjects of complaint. The case was partly heard by a cardinal at Rome in 1313,[1] but only with the result that, upon the petition of the university, the case was referred to arbitrators—two seculars and two friars—in England.[2] Their award in the main decided the case for the university. As a slight concession to the friars on the merits of the question, it was provided, however, that every bachelor of divinity, after completing his course upon the Sentences, should preach one sermon in the Dominican Church before proceeding to the degree of doctor. On the more important constitutional questions at issue it was ordered:

(1) That when a grace was asked for a friar, every master should be required to swear that he would not refuse the grace 'out of malice or hatred or rancour', but only 'for the common utility and honour of the university'. If after this precaution a regent should refuse the grace, he was to be required forthwith to state his reasons to the chancellor, proctors, and regent masters of theology, by whom an investigation was to be held into their sufficiency. If in the opinion of a majority of the theological regents the objection was not sustained, the grace was to be deemed *ipso facto* granted.

(2) The principle of majority-voting was upheld; but it was ordered that the majority should consist of three faculties instead of two, of which the faculty of arts must be one, besides the non-regents. Moreover, the friars had complained that statutes were passed without sufficient notice to the superior faculties. It was therefore enjoined that no statute should be passed without previous promulgation in a

Margin notes: CHAP. XII, § 2.

Award of arbitrators, 1313.

---

daunted friar mounted a tombstone on the south side of the chancel and shouted through an open window that he would leave a copy of the appeal on the church-door; after which he retired amid the maledictions of the scholars' servants, who shouted 'peccatum esset uobis fratribus subuenire et pium hostia uestra obstruere et uos tamquam superbissimos ibi comburere qui

cum sitis miseri et mendici audetis contra tantam congregationem tam reuerendarum et excellentium personarum appellationem aliquam commouere' (*ibid.*, p. 245).

[1] *Collectanea* (O.H.S.), ii. 224. [*Cal. Papal Registers* (*Letters*), i. 111–12.]

[2] *Regesta Clem. V* (Rome, 1888), No. 9253; *Collectanea* (O.H.S.), ii. 263.

CHAP. XII, General Congregation of regents,[1] at which copies should be
§ 2. handed to a master of each faculty fifteen days before the time
of voting.

The award was confirmed by royal letters patent on 7 April
1314.[2] But the litigious preachers found means of prolonging
the suit for six years longer and getting a succession of Bulls
Submis- in their favour from John XXII.[3] At last in 1320, however,
sion of
friars in they were compelled to renounce these papal favours, and to
1320. make an unconditional submission to the university.[4] The
royal writ of 1314 must henceforth be considered as settling
the general principles of the university constitution. In the
fifteenth-century registers there is, indeed, no trace of the
observance of the provisions about the sermon in the Dominican Church, or of the provisions about friars' graces, but
there is abundant evidence of the practice of 'voting by faculties' throughout the period with which we are concerned.

Later con- The controversy between the university and the Mendicants
flicts. continued to smoulder until it was lost, so to speak, in the
wider issues raised by the outbreak of the Wyclifite heresy.[5]
The quarrel in Oxford was in truth but a symptom of the
great feud between the friars and the seculars which divided
the whole Church of England—indeed the whole Church
of Europe—throughout the fourteenth century. In England
as in France the universities were but the organs of the secular clergy at large. The expenses of the university litigation

---

[1] Such are the words of the
royal brief (*Collectanea* (O.H.S.),
ii. 271), but in that case the non-
regents would get no notice. A
certificate of the publication of a
citation in connexion with this suit
is preserved among the manuscript of the Dean and Chapter of
Lincoln.

[2] *Collectanea* (O.H.S.), ii. 264–
72. [*Cal. Pat. Rolls, Edward II,
1313–17*, p. 115; *Stat. Antiq.
Univ. Oxon.*, ed. S. Gibson, pp.
116–18.]

[3] Mr. Bliss has kindly communicated to me transcripts of these
Bulls, which are now in the Public

Record Office. (Cf. A. G. Little,
Grey Friars (O.H.S.), p. 40.) [See
also *Cal. Papal Registers (Letters)*,
i. 167, 199.] On some points the
friar-ridden Edward II was induced
to write in their favour to the Pope,
in the teeth of his own injunctions.
Rymer's *Foedera* (1706), ii. 588.

[4] *Collectanea* (O.H.S.), ii. 272;
cf. *Med. Arch. Univ. Oxford*, ed.
H. E. Salter (O.H.S.), i. 99–100.

[5] It is interesting to see that
William of Saint-Amour was still
read at Oxford. This appears from
a manuscript poem in the Bodleian
(James MS. vii, f. 86). He is often
referred to by Wyclif.

against the friars were defrayed by a tax upon the ecclesias- CHAP. XII,
tical property of the realm imposed by the two convocations.[1] §2.
After the settlement of the academic questions just noticed,
the controversy turned chiefly upon the question of the age
at which the friars might admit novices. In 1357 Richard
Fitz-Ralph, Archbishop of Armagh—the great champion of
the seculars at Oxford, commonly known to the Middle
Age as Armachanus—proceeded to the court of Avignon
to expose the system of kidnapping or inveigling young Arma-
scholars, for which the popularity of the friars as confessors Avignon.
chanus at
afforded great facilities. The allurements held out by the
friars to boys so young as not to be uninfluenced by a present
of apples[2] had inspired the parental mind with such alarm that
the numbers of the universities were, it was alleged, falling off
with astounding rapidity.[3] Fitz-Ralph died at Avignon and
the university did not send another legation. They, however,
took the matter into their own hands by passing statutes
against the admission into the Mendicant colleges of boys
under eighteen years of age.[4] On this point, however, the
friars triumphed over the university at the Parliament of 1366;

[1] Wilkins, *Concilia*, ii. 551; 8th
Report of Hist. MSS. Commission,
p. 354; Linc. Reg., Burghersh, f.
351 (Twyne MS. ii, f. 5 b); *Letters
from Northern Registers*, ed. J.
Raine (R.S.), pp. 346–9.

[2] 'Uncinis pomorum, ut populus
fabulatur, puerulos ad religionem
attrahitis, quos professos doctrinis
non instruitis vi et metu, sicut
exigit aetas illa, sed mendicativis
discursibus sustinetis intendere
atque tempus quo possent addis-
cere, in captandis favoribus amicorum consumere sinitis, in offen-
sam parentum, puerorum pericu-
lum et ordinis detrimentum':
Richard de Bury, *Philobiblon* (ed.
E. C. Thomas), p. 51. So *Mun.
Acad.* i. 207: 'Pomis et potu, ut
populus fabulatur, puerulos ad religionem attrahunt.' [See also G. R.
Owst, 'Some Franciscan Memorials
at Gray's Inn', in *Dublin Review*
(1925), clxxvi. 282–4.]

[3] The discourse which he then
delivered, *Defensorium Curatorum*,
is printed in E. Brown's *Appendix
ad Fasciculum rerum expetendarum*,
pp. 466–86. Wyclif declares that
Armachanus was assisted by the
English bishops. *Fasciculi Zizaniorum* (R.S.), ed. W. W. Shirley, p.
284. Cf. R. L. Poole in *Dict. Nat.
Biog.*, and below, p. 326. [By a
statute of 1402 the reception of
children under 14 years of age into
any one of the four Mendicant
Orders, without the consent of their
parents, was forbidden. See 4 Hen.
IV, c. 17; *Rot. Parl.* iii. 502;
Johannis de Trokelowe Annales
(R.S.), p. 349.]

[4] In 1358, *Mun. Acad.* i. 204–5.
[*Stat. Antiq. Univ. Oxon.*, ed. S.
Gibson, pp. 164–5. Mr. Strickland
Gibson dates this entry in Register
C (the junior proctor's book)
'? 1365'.]

CHAP. XII, though they were forbidden to use any papal bulls which
§ 2.
they might have obtained to the prejudice of the universities.[1]

A friar's   Occasional bickerings between the secular masters and the
apology.
friars continued, however, to be among the normal incidents
of university life.[2] An amusing illustration of the sort of feud
that was ever going on in Oxford occurs in 1358 (just after the
mission of Armachanus), when a friar preacher, having in a
sermon attacked the 'Sophists' as persons who want to seem
wise but who never attain to true wisdom, was supposed to be
aiming at the faculty of arts (whose students were technically
known by that designation), and was compelled to make a
public retractation and apology.[3]

Consti-   It is, however, no part of my plan to enter into a detailed
tution
fixed, history of the later relations between the university and the
c. 1314. friars.[4] The university constitution as it emerges from the
great dispute of 1312–20 continued in its main lines unaltered.
We have no evidence to show how far the amendment imposed by the royal letter of 1314 was observed. But, whether
the majority had to be composed of three faculties or two (in
addition to the non-regents), there is no doubt that a statute
could be carried by a majority of faculties.[5] It should be
added that, as at Paris, only one Mendicant doctor of each
Order might sit in Convocation at the same time.[6]

[1] *Rot. Parl.* ii. 290. [*Cal. Papal
Registers* (*Letters*), iv. 52–3.]
[2] [See *Cal. Close Rolls, Richard
II, 1385–9*, pp. 378–9, 511, dated
17 Mar. and 1 Aug. 1388, respectively.]
[3] *Mun. Acad.* i. 211–12. A dispute between the Austin friars and
the university terminated in the
submission of the former in Jan.
1358. *Med. Arch. Univ. Oxford*,
ed. H. E. Salter (O.H.S.), i. 171–5.
An original document relating to
this affair is pasted into the Twyne
MS. ii, f. 380. (Cf. *Mun. Acad.* i.
208.) In the fifteenth century we
often find a regular who had graduated elsewhere admitted to the
privileges of regency 'excepto quod
non intret domum Congregationis'.

[4] [For the later history of the
relations between the university
and the religious orders in Oxford,
see *Stat. Antiq. Univ. Oxon.*, pp.
cxiv–cxviii.]
[5] There were other constitutional
disturbances at about this time. In
1327 a 'pugna' took place which led
to the deposition of the chancellor
and proctors of the university. See
Chronicles of Edw. II and III, ed.
W. Stubbs, i. 332. [See also Wood,
Annals, i. 409–19.] Cf. *Mun. Acad.*
i. 119 *sq.* [*Stat. Antiq. Univ. Oxon.*,
ed. S. Gibson, pp. 128–31.]
[6] *Mun. Acad.* i. 353, [*Stat.
Antiq. Univ. Oxon.*, ed. S. Gibson,
p. 290]: the Dominicans appear to
have here enjoyed no special privilege.

In a document belonging to the latter half of the fourteenth CHAP. XII, century or later we find the whole process of voting on a § 2. Procedure statute described in elaborate detail.[1] The proceedings are to at Great be spread over five days. On the first day the proposal is to be Congregation. promulgated by the proctors in the Black Congregation.[2] On the second day it is to be discussed. On the third day the chancellor summons a Great Congregation, when the non-regents elect their 'scrutators' and through them receive a copy of the proposed statute.[3] At another Congregration the statute is discussed and voted on by the separate sections of the university, who retire for the purpose to different parts of S. Mary's Church. The non-regents presided over by the scrutators 'are to remain in the choir; the Theologians in the Congregation House; the Decretists in the Chapel of S. Ann; the Physicians in the Chapel of S. Thomas; the Proctors with their Regents in the Chapel of the Glorious Virgin'. After a second discussion on the next day the votes of each of the six bodies concerned are handed in.[4] This elaborate

[1] *Mun. Acad.* ii. 481–3. [*Stat. Antiq. Univ. Oxon.*, ed. S. Gibson, pp. 291–3.] The document is apparently not a statute but merely a memorandum for the use of the proctors. Since in the chancellor's book it is inserted only in a later hand, the earlier part of the book being written *c.* 1350, it is probable that it belongs to the second half of the century. S. Mildred's is not mentioned as the place of session for the Black Congregation, which might suggest a still later date. [Rashdall gives this document too early a date. Mr. Strickland Gibson (*Stat. Antiq. Univ. Oxon.*, p. xxx) dates it about 1480–8.]

[2] [Mr. Gibson's account of the successive meetings specified in this 'Forma Congregacionis Magne' accords more closely with the text than that given by Rashdall; see *Stat. Antiq. Univ. Oxon.*, pp. xxix–xxxi, 291–3. According to the Forma, the second day is occupied by the summoning of the

Great Congregation and the election of 'scrutators', and not as Rashdall states by another session of the Black Congregation. The business, therefore, which Rashdall assigns to the third and fourth days should be assigned to the second and third. and the second discussion and the voting which Rashdall assigns to the fifth day should be assigned to the fourth and fifth days respectively.]

[3] In the sixteenth-century registers we find that statutes were usually drawn up by *eight* delegates appointed for the purpose—precisely the number which we have seen to be usual from an earlier period at Bologna and Paris.

[4] The last relic of the system of voting by faculties is the formula still in use, 'Placetne vobis, Domini Doctores? Placetne vobis, Magistri?' though, upon a scrutiny, no notice is taken of the division into faculties.

CHAP. XII, procedure, extending over five days, was of course only
§ 2. observed when a statute in the proper sense of the word, as
opposed to temporary decrees or dispensatory graces of the
university, had to be passed.

Statutes of It should be added that we do very rarely find occasional
separate
faculties instances of the separate faculties, as at Paris, making statutes
rare. for the regulation of their own internal discipline,[1] but as a
general rule statutes relating to all faculties—even those
dealing with educational details or with internal discipline—
were enacted by the Congregation of the whole university.
The want of independent corporate life on the part of the
superior faculties and their complete subordination to the
inferior faculty of arts, is one of the most remarkable pecu-
liarities of the Oxford University constitution. The University
of Paris was distinctly a federal constitution consisting of four
distinct corporations, one of which was itself a federation.
The Oxford Congregation was rather a parliament of several
estates and one in which the predominance of the most
democratic element—the regents in arts—was as marked as
that of the House of Commons in the modern English Parliament.[2]

[1] In *Mun. Acad.* ii. 402 there is
a list of regulations 'expedita Facultate Decretorum'. [This example will not serve. The rubric
'expedita Facultate Decretorum'
which only occurs in Registrum C
(see *Stat. Antiq. Univ. Oxon.*, p. 43)
is simply a heading marking the
end of the canon law section and
the beginning of the civil law
section.] See too *Mun. Acad.* ii.
411. [*Stat. Antiq. Univ. Oxon.*, ed.
S. Gibson, p. 24.] 'Auctoritate
domini Cancellarii et Procuratorum Universitatis, necnon et omnium Magistrorum in facultate
artium regentium, *ordinatum est et
provisum.*' In 1385 the faculty of law
obtained a royal letter allowing
them to hold meetings 'pro omnibus negotiis vos ac gradus et facul-
tates vestras concernentibus', but
this was only to enable them to

carry on a pending suit against
the university, notwithstanding the
king's prohibition against unlawful
assemblies. Rot. Pat. 8 Ric. II, pt.
2, m. 35; Ayliffe, ii, App., p. xxxv.
[*Cal. Pat. Rolls, Richard II, 1381–
5*, p. 526.]

[2] It is doubtful, however, how
long the Black Congregations continued to be held. In 1570, when
a movement took place for the
reform of the university's utterly
uncodified and mostly obsolete
statutes, it was summoned by the
proctors at the command of the
vice-chancellor; but we are expressly told that it had become
obsolete, and that doubts were
entertained as to whether it had
not been repealed by statute.
(Register KK 9, f. 94 b.) [See *Stat.
Antiq. Univ. Oxon.*, ed. S. Gibson,
pp. xxxi–xxxv.] The church in

§ 3. THE UNIVERSITY AND THE TOWN

I HAVE thought it well to reserve a separate section for the curious history of the process by which a society of teachers succeeded first in sharing, then in almost monopolizing, the government of an important English town. The inquiry is an interesting one because it explains the origin of those singular liberties which still survive among us—almost the last relic perhaps in all Europe of the old clerical immunities. But our subject possesses a higher and more solid interest on account of the light which it incidentally throws upon the conduct of local government, the administration of justice, and the realities of clerical and academic life in medieval Europe generally.

In inquiries of this kind we are, as it were, sinking a shaft into the accumulated rubbish of ages; and it may be doubted whether from any other boring we could extract more precious historical ore than from the documentary remains of the universities, especially of Oxford and Cambridge. We are struck in reading these records with the minuteness of the control exercised by the King and his council over local affairs. The government of a medieval town was carried on in accordance with what still remains, under altered forms, the

which it was held had been pulled down by 1437. (Wood, *City* (O.H.S.), ii. 95.) This circumstance may by itself have assisted the disappearance of the Black Congregation, which was also promoted by the extinction of all regents in arts except the most junior masters, i.e. the necessary regents. See below, p. 163. I have not thought it necessary to mention the various university officials. Bedels do not appear to be mentioned at a very early date, but doubtless existed as in all universities. [On the appointment and duties of the bedels see *Stat. Antiq. Univ. Oxon.*, ed. S. Gibson, pp. xxxvii–xxxviii, lxxvii–lxxviii; see also *Registrum Cancellarii Oxon., 1434–69*, ed. H. E. Salter

(O.H.S.), pp. xlv–xlviii.] The *scriba* or *tabellio Universitatis* or registrar is not expressly mentioned till the fifteenth century. Cf. *Med. Arch. Univ. Oxford*, ed. H. E. Salter (O.H.S.), ii. 284. [See also *Stat. Antiq. Univ. Oxon.*, ed. S. Gibson, pp. xx, 285–6.] The chaplain of the university, whose duty it was to say Mass for the university's benefactors on certain days was made librarian and assigned a salary in 1412. *Mun. Acad.* i. 261–3. [*Stat. Antiq. Univ. Oxon.*, ed. S. Gibson, pp. 217–18.]; *Med. Arch. Univ. Oxford*, ed. H. E. Salter (O.H.S.), ii. 286–7; but the office probably existed before this [see *Stat. Antiq. Univ. Oxon.*, ed. S. Gibson, pp. 98, 102, 113, 119, 134, 138, 165–6].

CHAP. XII, distinctly English system of administration—a system neither
§ 3. of centralization nor of decentralization, but of local self-government subject to central control and inspection.[1] Then as now the ordinary administration was in the hands of elected local officers; but no matter was considered unworthy of the interference of the King and his council, when once attention was called to any neglect on the part of the local authorities. The rights of Parliament were never so understood as to exclude administrative action of a kind which would now be looked upon as actual legislation. Thus at Oxford we find constant royal orders upon such matters as the repair and cleansing of the streets, or the slaughtering of cattle within the city.[2] The clerks being imperfectly acclimatized were more fastidious than the townsmen in such matters. Thus in 1300 a royal letter to the sheriff complains that 'the air is so corrupted and infected' by the filth in the streets 'that an abominable loathing' (or perhaps 'ague') is 'diffused among the aforesaid masters and scholars', a state of things aggravated by the practice of regrators melting tallow before their houses.[3] There are frequent orders requiring each inhabitant to repair as well as clean the pavement in front of his own

Sanitary door. In the minuteness of its sanitary inspection medieval
inspection. administration far surpassed anything that obtains in these days of social science and hygenic civilization.[4] In 1293, for

[1] [Rashdall seems disposed to treat the frequency of royal intervention in the municipal affairs of Oxford as typical of an English medieval town, whereas it was exceptional. The reasons for this exceptional treatment are clearly explained by Dr. H. E. Salter in the section dealing with the Royal Writs to Oxford in his Introduction to *Munimenta Civitatis Oxonie* (O.H.S.), pp. xiii–xvi. 'Nine out of ten', he writes, 'would not have been called for, but for the existence of the University'.]

[2] e.g. Rot. Pat. 13 Ed. III, p. 2, m. 28 (Ayliffe, ii, App., p. xlii). [*Cal. Pat. Rolls, Edward III, 1338–40*, pp. 186, 306; *Munim. Civ.*

Oxon., ed. H. E. Salter (O.H.S.), pp. 10–11, 13–14, 18.]

[3] 'Per fimos et fimaria, et plures alias feditates que in stratis et venellis ville predicte ponuntur et colliguntur aer ibidem in tantum corrumpitur et inficitur quod magistris et scolaribus predictis et aliis ibidem conversantibus et transeuntibus horror abhominabilis incutitur.' Rot. Claus. 29 Ed. I, m. 14 *dorso* (Hare, *Priv.*, f. 19 *b*; Wood, i. 362. [*Cal. Close Rolls, Edward I, 1296–1302*, p. 484; *Munim. Civ. Oxon.*, ed. H. E. Salter (O.H.S.), pp. 11, 13.]

[4] [This statement should not be taken too strictly.]

instance, a royal letter was directed to the sheriff forbidding CHAP. XII, § 3.
the use of the corrupt water of Trillmill stream (on the south
of Oxford beyond Pembroke College) for brewing and baking
purposes. Anthony Wood laments that in his own day 'very
unwholesome liquor' was still brewed from the dilute sewage
of the offending rivulet, 'which without doubt', he adds, 'is
the author of several diseases among us'.[1] The Crown ever
exercised a fatherly supervision over the well-being of the
scholars. Tournaments and jousts were forbidden in Oxford
and its neighbourhood lest they should be distracted from
their studies,[2] and to this day the vice-chancellor retains the
right of prohibiting or exercising a censorship over theatrical
entertainments in the town. Disputes between town and
university were constantly referred to the King and Council,
and also (though more rarely) those between conflicting
university authorities. There were practically no limits to
the interference of the Crown when once interference was
provoked, though the general policy of the English kings was
to uphold and protect local liberties. Instances occur of both
chancellor and proctors being removed by royal writ.[3] There
was of course no notion of the university having legal rights
which it could enforce against the Crown. So far as secular
authority was concerned, the Crown was practically absolute.
Few of the privileges either of town or university rested upon
any parliamentary basis, nor were they part of the common law.
They were the creation of the Sovereign's favour and were
liable to suspension or revocation at his pleasure. A churchman might of course have claimed the scholar's exemption
from lay tribunals as an indefeasible right. But, though in all
but very grave cases the cognizance of clerical offences was left
to the ecclesiastical tribunals, the King in Council would never
hesitate to imprison a clerk in Oxford or anywhere else.

It has already been pointed out that the chancellor's power Chancel-
was in its origin purely ecclesiastical.[4] The jurisdiction which lor's juris-
diction
originally a
spiritual

[1] Placita coram Rege de Term.
S. Mich. 21 & 22 Ed. I, Rot. Scacc.
5; Wood, i. 345. There is still a
Brewers Street here.
[2] Rot. Claus. 33 Ed. I, m. 2 *dorso.*

[Cal. Close Rolls, Edward I, 1302–7, jurisdic-
pp. 355, 361; Rymer, Foedera, ed. tion over
1816, i, pt. ii. 977, dated 12 Nov. scholars.
1305.]   [3] See above, p. 76, n. 5.
[4] [See above, pp. 41–7.]

the official of the bishop or archdeacon exercised over other
ecclesiastics was specially delegated to the chancellor in the
case of masters and scholars of Oxford, and (as time went on)
of a gradually increasing class of dependants to whom the
favour of the university extended some of the least of the then
very real benefits of clergy.[1] This jurisdiction was originally
claimed in all criminal cases, though in earlier times the more
serious cases were reserved for the bishop's ordinary tribunal.
The chancellor's jurisdiction was enforced by excommunication and penance: imprisonment was regarded rather as
a preliminary to trial than as a normal form of punishment.
Over laymen the chancellor had at first no jurisdiction, except
in so far as the exercise of such jurisdiction might be incidentally necessary to the enforcement of his authority over his
clerical subjects, or to their protection from lay violence; and
then his jurisdiction was spiritual only. It is, however, easy to
understand that in cases arising out of quarrels between a
scholar and a townsman it might often be difficult to say with
precision which of the parties was plaintiff and which defendant. Moreover, at a time when the spiritual courts exercised
an extensive control over the private lives of laymen, it is
not very surprising that the chancellor's jurisdiction should
occasionally have been extended beyond the limits which the
theory of his office would seem to prescribe; and this extension would be facilitated by the fact that there was no bishop's
court at Oxford, but only that of the archdeacon. At all
events, in one way or another, the chancellor as a spiritual
judge seems to have gained a good deal of jurisdiction over
townsmen before he received any express recognition of his
authority from the Crown.

Early
quarrels
with
town. Of the first recorded collision with the townsfolk and its
sequel enough has been said. The ordinance of 1214 produced no change in the constitutional position beyond dividing
between the bishop and archdeacon on the one hand and the
chancellor on the other the rights hitherto enjoyed only by the
former—namely, the right of demanding the surrender of an

---

[1] [On the chancellor's archi-
diaconal powers see *Reg. Cancell.*
Oxon., 1434-1469, ed. H. E. Salter
(O.H.S.), i. xv–xvii.]

imprisoned scholar, and (where the bishop allowed it) con- CHAP. XII,
§ 3. ducting the trial. The affair was settled by the papal legate and the Bishop of Lincoln without any interference of the King.[1] A fatal affray which took place between town and gown in 1228 was likewise settled by purely ecclesiastical authority, the offender being positively allowed (such a thing would have been impossible a century later) to be sent to Rome for trial.[2] The promptness of the ecclesiastical authorities to protect the scholars of Oxford contrasts strangely with the apathy shown on the somewhat similar collision of the following year at Paris, and England profited by the reputation which it enjoyed as a safe place for clerks by receiving a colony of the dispersed Parisians. They were specially invited to England by a letter of Henry III.[3] Many of them certainly settled at Cambridge, but others no doubt came to Oxford. The increased importance given to the university by this augmentation of numbers may be traced in a succession of royal writs. In 1231 the King ordered that the mayor and bailiffs should allow the chancellor to use the town prison for the confinement of refractory clerks;[4] and a few years later

Leave to use town prison, 1231.

[1] The privilege of 56 Henry III (Ap. 28, 1272) speaks of 'libertates per chartas *predecessorum nostrorum* Regum Angliae et nostras concessas'. [See *Cal. Pat. Rolls, Henry III, 1266–72*, p. 697. The 'privilege' here referred to was, in fact, a commission to Godfrey Giffard, Bishop of Worcester, and Roger de Mortimer, to hear and settle certain contentions that had arisen between the university and the town.]

[2] *Ann. Monast.* (Dunstable), ed. H. R. Luard (R.S.), iii. 109–10. [The Dunstable chronicler does not state that the offenders were sent to Rome for trial. They were required to make a pilgrimage to Rome to obtain pardon: this was the regular procedure when laymen were found guilty of assaulting clerks.]

[3] Rot. Pat. 13 Hen. III, m. 6. [*Pat. Rolls, Henry III, 1225–*

32, p. 257; *Med. Arch. Univ. Oxford*, ed. H. E. Salter (O.H.S.), i. 17, 18.] In 1231 a royal writ about the taxation of lodgings declares that 'apud villam nostram Oxon. studendi causa e diversis partibus tam cismarinis quam transmarinis scolarium confluit multitudo'. Rot. Claus. 15 Hen. III, m. 13 *dorso* (Hare, *Priv.*, f. 1). [*Close Rolls, Henry III, 1227–31*, p. 587.]

[4] *Letters of Hen. III*, ed. W. W. Shirley (R.S.), i. 397. [*Close Rolls, Henry III, 1227–31*, p. 586. This writ is directed to the Sheriff of Oxford and not to the mayor and bailiffs, and relates to the King's prison and not to that of the town.] At a later date the town was directed to provide a separate prison for scholars and other slight offenders 'of good condition', and not to imprison them 'inter latrones' (Twyne MS. iv, f. 64). [The date of this order is 8 Nov. 1313,

CHAP. XII,
§ 3.

the constable is directed to allow the use of the King's prison in the Castle for the same purpose.[1] The fact that there was at Oxford no regular bishop's prison such as was to be found in every episcopal city or (if there was one) the fact that the chancellor was not allowed to use it, no doubt contributed to that confusion between spiritual and temporal jurisdiction which is at a very early period traceable in the relations between the Chancellor of Oxford and the townsmen.[2] It is natural to find that the chancellor always experienced a certain difficulty in obtaining the assistance of the secular arm in executing his decrees, though the sheriff, mayor, and bailiffs are constantly enjoined to render such assistance. [But for carrying out the verdicts of his court the chancellor needed no staff of constables or sergeants. All who appeared in his court, both laymen and clerks, were bound by oath to obey the decision of the court, and any one who was condemned to prison walked there accompanied by the bedel. If he refused, he was guilty of perjury and incurred excommunication. If it were a clerk who refused, there was the further penalty of banishment from the university.[3]] In the year 1231 another important step was taken towards the establishment of discipline among the motley crew with which the fame of its schools had flooded the streets of the town by a royal writ directing the sheriff to expel all so-called scholars who were not under a regular master.[4]

Expulsion of masterless scholars, 1231.

see *Munim. Civ. Oxon.*, ed. H. E. Salter (O.H.S.), p. 25. An earlier direction to this effect (22 Aug. 1311) is given in Twyne MS. iv, f. 66; and see also *Med. Arch. Univ. Oxford*, ed. H. E. Salter (O.H.S.), i. 333.] The prison actually used was the chamber over Bocardo Gate, which then stood close to the tower of S. Michael's, Northgate.

[1] Rot. Claus. 21 Hen. III, m. 19 *dorso* (Hare, *Priv.*, f. 2). [*Close Rolls, Henry III, 1234–7*, pp. 514, 519.]

[2] [Rashdall over-estimates the importance of the question of a prison as affecting the relations between the chancellor and the townsmen.]

[3] *Mun. Acad.* i. 94. [*Stat. Antiq. Univ. Oxon.*, ed. S. Gibson, p. 112. The passage inserted here takes the place of the following two sentences in Rashdall's text: 'It seems, indeed, to have been the custom, when a scholar was sentenced, for the bedel simply to invite him to go to prison on his own account. If the invitation was declined, he was merely banished from the university.']

[4] *Letters of Hen. III* (R.S.), i. 397–8. [*Close Rolls, Henry III, 1227–31*, p. 586.]

The first important extension of the chancellor's juris- CHAP. XII,
diction took place in the year 1244. In that year a raid was Charter
made upon the Jewry by a body of scholars. Forty-five of 1244.
them were imprisoned and Grosseteste had some difficulty in
producing their surrender.[1] But about a fortnight later a
charter was granted by which the Jews of Oxford were forbidden to take more than 2*d*. in the pound per week as interest
from scholars, and all disputes of the kind which had no doubt
led to the anti-semitic outbreak were referred to the chancellor's decision. By this charter the chancellor acquired
jurisdiction in actions of debt, disputes about rents or prices,
and all other 'contracts of movables' in which one party was a
clerk.[2] A charter of 1248 authorized the chancellor and Jurisdic-
proctors to assist at the assaying of bread and beer by the contracts,
mayor and bailiffs, and imposed upon the latter an oath to Mayor's
respect the liberties and customs of the university, to be taken oath, 1248.
on admission to office.[3] The town was also made liable in its
corporate capacity for injuries to scholars. Otherwise no
change was made in the limits of the chancellor's jurisdiction.
To the jurisdiction over the clerks of the university which he

---

[1] *Chron. of Abingdon*, ed. J. O.
Halliwell, p. 5. *Fourth Report of
the Deputy Keeper of the Public
Records*, p. 142. [*Close Rolls,
Henry III, 1242-7*, p. 181.]
    [2] 'In causis clericorum ex mutuis
datis aut receptis aut taxationibus
seu locationibus domorum, aut
equis conductis, uenditis seu com-
modatis seu pannis et uictualibus
ortum habentibus seu aliis quibuslibet rerum mobilium contractibus
in municipio aut suburbio Oxon.
factis nostra prohibicio non currat'
(Rot. Pat. 28 Hen. III, m. 6 *dorso*;
Ayliffe, ii, App. p. vi). [*Cal. Pat.
Rolls, Henry III, 1232-47*, p. 424.]
This and all the more important
later privileges are printed from the
Inspeximus of Edward IV, in the
Registrum privilegiorum of 1770. It
should be noticed that this was
simply a local grant of what the
clergy were everywhere at this

time contending for as a matter of
right, elsewhere with little success.
Cf. Stubbs, *Constitutional Hist. of
England*, ed. 1880, iii. 370. [The
procedure of 'cession of debts',
which grew up, enabling a townsman who had difficulty in collecting a debt from another townsman
to give his right to some clerk and
so transfer his case to the chancellor's court, led to long controversy between the university
and the town; see *Reg. Cancell.
Oxon., 1434-69*, ed. H. E. Salter
(O.H.S.), i. xxxiii-xxxv.]
    [3] *Med. Arch. Univ. Oxford*, ed.
H. E. Salter (O.H.S.), i. 18, 19, 24;
Mun. Acad. ii. 777. [*Close Rolls,
Henry III, 1247-51*, pp. 114, 132.
On the control of the assize of bread
and ale by the university see *Reg.
Cancell. Oxon., 1434-1469*, ed.
H. E. Salter (O.H.S.), i, xv.]

CHAP. XII, had from the beginning and the jurisdiction over laymen in
§ 3. civil actions which was conferred in 1244, the charter of 1255
Jurisdiction in for the first time added a criminal jurisdiction even over lay-
breaches men, for breach of the peace. By this charter[1] it was provided
of peace, that if a layman did any grievous injury to a clerk, he should
1255. be imprisoned in the Castle, and detained there 'until he
satisfy the clerk and that at the discretion of the Chancellor
and University, if the clerk be unreasonable in his claims; if
the injury be a minor one, he should be committed to the
town prison'.[2]

The disputes between the town and the university led in
England, as everywhere, to frequent secessions.[3] Half the
universities in Europe owed their origin to such migrations
Secession —Oxford itself probably among the number. A similar
to North-
ampton, migration from Oxford in 1209 led to the establishment of a
1263. permanent university at Cambridge. In or about the year
1261 one of the usual conflicts with townsmen led in turn
to an exodus from Cambridge to Northampton. At first
the new university seems to have been encouraged by the

[1] 'Si laicus inferat clerico grauem
uel enormem lesionem statim capiatur, et si magna sit lesio incarceretur in castro Oxonie et ibi
detineatur quousque clerico satisfiat, et hoc arbitrio Cancellarii et
Uniuersitatis Oxonie, si clericus
proteruus fuerit; si minor uel leuis
sit iniuria, incarceretur in uilla.'
Med. Arch. Univ. Oxford, ed. H. E.
Salter (O.H.S.), i. 20; Mun. Acad.
ii. 776. [Cal. Pat. Rolls, Henry III,
1247–58, p. 413; Rymer, Foedera,
ed. 1816, i, pt. i. 323.]

[2] In 1261 a jury found that the
chancellor's jurisdiction extended
to Jews who, as the King's chattels,
would have been exempt from the
ordinary ecclesiastical courts; Rot.
Pat. 45 Hen. III, m. 19 dorso; Rot.
Claus. 45 Hen. III, m. 14 (Hare,
f. 6); Inquis. post mortem no. 50
(Hare, f. 6). [Cal. Pat. Rolls,
Henry III, 1258–66, p. 105;
Close Rolls, Henry III, 1259–61,

pp. 360–1; Snappe's Formulary
(O.H.S.), pp. 282–4; and Cal.
Inquisitions, Miscell. i. 93.] Cf.
Peshall, p. 26. This jurisdiction was
expressly confirmed in 1286; see
Med. Arch. Univ. Oxford, ed. H. E.
Salter (O.H.S.), i. 40.

[3] [Dr. R. L. Poole has pointed
out that the oath never to consent
to the reconciliation of Henry
Symeonis which all bachelors were
required to take before inception
down to 1827 had its origin in a
fatal affray in which Henry, son of
Symeon, and another townsman
were concerned about the year
1242. The subsequent pardon
granted to Henry by the King and
his return to Oxford appears to
have been one of the causes of the
secession to Northampton in 1263.
See E.H.R. (1912), xxvii. 515–17;
Stat. Antiq. Univ. Oxon., ed. S.
Gibson, p. 36.]

King,[1] then he ordered its dissolution; but in 1263 a distur- CHAP. XII, bance at Oxford, followed by a writ ordering the dispersion of §3. the Oxford schools partly perhaps in view of the session of the Parliament,[2] which was to be held there in the spring, had the effect of still further reinforcing the Northampton settlement. The motive for this order seems to have been the sympathy shown by the scholars of Oxford for the King's enemies in the Barons' War. At the siege of Northampton in 1264 the scholars did much execution among the King's forces with bows and arrows—weapons with which they may have been familiarized by occasional practice in the streets of Oxford. On the capture of the town the clerks narrowly escaped hanging at the hands of the indignant monarch.[3] After the King's defeat at Lewes, the scholars were commanded by a writ issued in the King's name to return to Oxford,[4] and soon afterwards a similar order decreed the 'entire cessation of the University of Northampton'.[5]

It is highly probable that the emigrants of 1262-4 must have found a body of scholars already established in Northampton. At all events an earlier migration from Oxford had Earlier migration taken place in the year 1238 when a quarrel arose at Oseney to North- between the scholars and the Legate Otho, who was lodging in ampton,

---

[1] Rot. Pat. 45 Hen. III, m. 17 (Ayliffe, ii, App., p. ix). [Cal. Pat. Rolls, Henry III, 1258-66, p. 140, 1 Feb. 1261.]

[2] Ann. Monast. (Winton), ii, pp. 100-1; (Oseney) iv, pp. 139-41; Chron. of Abingdon, ed. J. O. Halliwell, p. 16; Rishanger, Chron., ed. H. T. Riley (R.S.), p. 20 sq.; Chronicles of Edw. I and Edw. II, ed. W. Stubbs (R.S.), i. 61; Dyer, Privileges of Cambridge, i. 6; Rot. Pat. 48 Hen. III, m. 17. [Cal. Pat. Rolls, Henry III, 1258-66, p. 307, 13 Mar. 1264.] Flores Historiarum, ed. H. R. Luard (R.S.), ii. 487. Walter of Hemingburgh declares that the university was moved 'iussu baronum', Chronicon, ed. H. C. Hamilton (E.H.S.), i. 311, while Higden (ed. J. R. Lumby (R.S.), viii. 248), says, 'Rex Henricus eiecit universitatem de Oxonia'. [See Victoria County History of Northants, ii. 16-17, and Mallet, Hist. Univ. Oxford, i. 52, n. 2.]

[3] Upon hearing the King's threats, 'raserunt capita sua multi' (Knighton, ap. Twysden's Scriptores Decem, c. 1652, Walter of Hemingburgh, loc. cit.). [Knighton, Chronicon, ed. J. R. Lumby (R.S.), i. 242-3.] Cf. Chron. Abendon. ap. Twyne MSS. xxiv, f. 626.

[4] Rot. Pat. 48 Hen. III, m. 12 (Hare, Priv., f. 8 a). [Cal. Pat. Rolls, Henry III, 1258-66, p. 320, 30 May 1264]; Med. Arch. Univ. Oxford, ed. H. E. Salter (O.H.S.), i. 24-6.

[5] Rot. Claus. 49 Hen. III, m. 10 dorso (Ayliffe, ii, App., p. x).

CHAP. XII, the monastery. A party of scholars had come to the monastery
§ 3.   to salute the legate, but were rudely repelled by his servants.
At the same time a poor Irish chaplain was begging at the
kitchen door, when a cauldron of hot water was thrown in his
face by the legate's brother, who filled the office of 'Master of
the Cooks' to his Eminence. The enraged scholars fell upon
the master-cook, and killed him. The legate had to take refuge
in the tower of the abbey church and at night fled for his life.
Oxford was laid under interdict, the university suspended,
and the offenders proceeded against with much vigour by the
King.[1] The result was a dispersion. Some of the fugitives
established themselves at Northampton, and it is not unlikely
that as a *studium* of some kind maintained themselves in that
and to city continuously from 1238 to 1264: others went to Salis-
Salisbury,
1238. bury,[2] where we have interesting evidence of the continuance
of the *studium* then established as late as 1278. In that year
we find a compact drawn up between the chancellor and the
Sub-dean of Salisbury with respect to the limits of their
respective jurisdictions over the scholars of the place. There
is nothing in this by itself to denote the presence of a *studium
generale*. The chancellor of the Cathedral church everywhere claimed spiritual jurisdiction over the scholars of the
cathedral city, and granted licences to their masters. Still the
number of their masters, the circumstance that they belong
to more faculties than one,[3] and the fact that the causes and
contracts spoken of are evidently not the disputes of mere
schoolboys, make it probable that the schools here were of
a character which we have no reason for believing to have
permanently existed at such places after the growth of the
universities. A century earlier, or at some cathedral town
much more remote from a university than Salisbury is from

---

[1] Matt. Paris, *Chron. Mai.*, ed.
H. R. Luard (R.S.), iii. 481–5;
Hist. Min. ii. 407–8. [*Close Rolls,
Henry III, 1237–42*, pp. 53, 92,
127, 133–6; *Cal. Pat. Rolls, Henry
III, 1232–47*, pp. 218, 226, 236.]

[2] Walsingham, *Ypodigma Neustriae*, ed. H. T. Riley (R.S.), p.
141. [*Eulogium Historiarum*, ed.

F. S. Haydon (R.S.), iii. 118.]
[3] 'Inter omnes scolares, cuiuscunque facultatis existant, studiorum causa in civitate ipsa commorantes.' See the document in
Appendix VIII, and also reference
there to Bishop Bridport's foundation of a college of *Scholares de
Valle Scholarium*.

Oxford, such a *studium* would excite no surprise. But at Salisbury in 1278 we can have little doubt that such an agree-ment reveals the continued existence of the Oxford colony of 1238. Salisbury was still in fact a university town. It would be vain to speculate how far the colony may have been rein-forced by the troubles of 1264, or by one of the many distur-bances between North and South or town and gown which marked the years 1264–78. It is vain to speculate which of these causes may have led to the attempt to found or develop a *studium* at Salisbury. It is of more importance to notice how immediately it is assumed that the local scholastic authority has the same jurisdiction over the new-comers that they had exercised over the mere grammar-boys before their advent. This is exactly what would have happened at Oxford had it possessed a cathedral or important collegiate church.

It is in all probability to the capture of Northampton by Henry III that we owe the fact—on the whole a regrettable one—that England possesses no more than two ancient universities. Another very determined effort to found a new university at Stamford was made by the Northern scholars of Oxford, worsted in their battles with the Southerners, in the year 1334, or, as another account has it, by masters beaten in an encounter with scholars.[1] It required the most strenuous

Secession to Stam-ford, 1334.

---

[1] It seems to me essentially mis-leading to say with Dr. Henson, now Bishop of Durham, (*Collec-tanea* (O.H.S.), i. 3) that the Car-melite schools, established *c.* 1265, 'formed the nucleus, around which there soon gathered an University in all but name'. There is no evidence that there were any but purely claustral schools at Stamford till 1334. See *Collectanea* (O.H.S.), i. 3–16. [Dr. H. E. Salter (*E.H.R.* xxxvii (1922), 249–53) has drawn attention to the misdating of cer-tain of the documents printed by Dr. Henson in *Collectanea*, vol. i. Dr. Salter shows reason to believe that the migration to Stamford began with the Michaelmas Term of 1333, and that Oxford had been in a disturbed state since 1331 and more particularly so in the early part of 1333.] On the secession to Stamford see also Knighton, *Chronicon*, ed. J. R. Lumby (R.S.), i. 472 (ed. 1821), ii, pt. ii. 891, 898, 903–4; Rot. Claus. 8 Ed. III, m. 17 *dorso* (Hare, *Mem.*, f. 37). [*Cal. Close Rolls, Edward III, 1333–7*, p. 330, dated 2 Aug. 1334.] Peck, *Academia tertia Anglicana*, Lon-don, 1727. [See also *Collectanea* (O.H.S.), iii. 133–4; *Med. Arch. Univ. Oxford*, ed. H. E. Salter (O.H.S.), i. 126–7.] According to a fragment from an apparently lost chronicle preserved by Twyne and printed in Appendix IV, the

CHAP. XII, exertion of the royal authority to disperse the seventeen
§ 3.
masters who persisted in lecturing in spite of the royal
prohibition;[1] and until 1827 an oath not to lecture at Stamford
was exacted from all candidates for the mastership at Oxford.[2]
Once more in the seventeenth century the jealousy of the older
universities was unfortunately allowed to prevent the execution of Cromwell's project of founding a northern university
at Durham. It is impossible to doubt that the cause of learning in England has been injured by the paucity of its universities, or that the stagnation of Oxford and Cambridge at certain
periods of their history has been aggravated by the total
absence of competition. Perhaps even at the present day
[1895] English education suffers from the too exclusive
prestige of her two ancient universities.

Charter of   There were very serious disturbances at Oxford in the first
Edward I,
1275.   years of the reign of Edward I. In 1274, after a great fight
between North and South, no less than fifty persons accused

secession was due to the defeat of
the masters in a bloody encounter
with their rebellious scholars. Was
it some earlier fracas of this description which induced Master William
Wheteley to retire to Stamford and
there solace his leisure by writing
a commentary on Boethius's *De
disciplina Scholarium*, now in the
Exeter Coll. Library (MS. No. 28)?
If so, certainly his choice of subject
is intelligible enough. The words
'qui rexit scolas Stamfordie anno
ab incarnatione Domini millesimo
tricentesimo nono' might be used
of a mere grammar-school master,
but this is scarcely probable. The
manuscript has very much the
appearance of being a course of
academic lectures. [For the list of
seventeen masters who persisted in
teaching at Stamford in spite of
royal prohibition see *Cal. of Inquisitions, Miscell., 1307–49*, pp.
352–3. As Mr. A. F. Leach has
remarked, these seventeen masters
were all northerners. For the fullest
account of Stamford University see
Mr. Leach's article in *Victoria*

County History of Lincoln, ii.
468–72. See also *Brasenose College
Monographs* (O.H.S.), ii. 15–20,
and Mallet, *Hist. Univ. of Oxford*,
i. 157–8. The evidence is against
Rashdall's surmise that Master
William Wheteley was not 'a mere
Grammar-school Master'. Wheteley was subsequently master of
Lincoln Grammar School. There
is preserved among the New College
manuscripts a volume (No. 264)
which chiefly consists of a commentary by Wheteley on Boethius's
Consolatio Philosophiae, to which
he appended two hymns written by
himself in 1316. Moreover, the *De
disciplina Scolarium* of pseudo-Boethius was, as Mr. A. F. Leach has
pointed out, a school-book and not
a university one. See A. F. Leach,
V.C.H., Lincoln, ii. 423, 470–1.]
    [1] Rot. Escaet. 10 Ed. III, No.
172 (Hare, *Mem.*, f. 45). [*Cal. of
Inquisitions, Miscell., 1307–49*, pp.
352–3.]
    [2] *Mun. Acad.* ii. 375; *Laudian
Code*, ed. Shadwell, p. 111.

of homicide were sent up to London for trial.[1] A new era,
therefore, in the development of the Oxford privileges is
opened by the letters patent of 1275.[2] This document confers upon the chancellor the cognizance of all personal
actions whatever wherein either party was a scholar,[3] whereas
it is not clear that the former privileges gave a civil jurisdiction except when the scholar was defendant. In the same
reign we find a legal recognition by the verdict of a jury of the
immunity of halls or houses occupied by scholars from a
variety of fiscal and civic liabilities.[4] This immunity would
appear to rest, not (as Wood assumes) upon previous charters,
but upon simple custom, approved perhaps by the King or
his sheriffs, but not hitherto enjoying any legal sanction. In
tracing the growth of the university privileges in this period,
it must be remembered that we are at present in an age which
was governed by custom rather than by written law, and an
age in which a precedent of a very few years was held quite
sufficient to establish a custom whereof the memory of man
went not to the contrary.[5]

[1] [See *Cal. Close Rolls, Edward I, 1272–9*, pp. 66–7, and *Med. Arch. Univ. Oxford* (O.H.S.), i. 30, for an important prefatory note by Dr. H. E. Salter to the terms of peace agreed between North and South on this occasion.]

[2] In Rot. Pat. 8 Ed. I, m. 21 (Hare, *Mem.*, f. 18) [*Cal. Pat. Rolls, Edward I, 1272–81*, p. 366, dated 14 Mar. 1281], the King orders the 'custodes cambii sui' to send £3,000 to the chancellor and proctors 'ad utilitatem scholarium'. This was no doubt connected with the calling-in of false and clipped coin. Wood, i. 303.

[3] Rot. Pat. 3 Ed. I, m. 6 (Hare, *Priv.*, f. 13). [*Cal. Pat. Rolls, Edward I, 1272–81*, p. 108, dated 30 Oct. 1275.] The privilege contains a clause 'non obstante pro-
hibitione nostra'. This is inter-
preted by Wood to mean that the King had at a former period prohibited the exercise of this juris-
diction; but of course its real effect was to bar an application for a pro-
hibition to the King's Court. [Its real effect were better stated to be that of making inoperative any sort of prohibition which might be obtained by the defendant.]

[4] 'A sectis, visibus Franci plegii, auxiliis, tallagiis, vigiliis, finibus, redemptionibus, amerciamentis, contributionibus, aut aliis quibuscunque oneribus emergentibus,' &c. Wood, *Annals*, i. 302, who, how-
ever, gives no reference to the original.

[5] I cannot precisely determine the origin of the chancellor's power of imprisoning prostitutes. It was probably asserted as part of his general power of dealing with disturbers of the peace of the univer-
sity, and is assumed in the petition of the university and the answer given to it in the Parliament of 1305 (*Memoranda de Parliamento*, ed. F. W. Maitland (R.S.), p. 44),

CHAP. XII, §3.
Taxation of halls.

Another important right of the university, which was in the first instance probably due to mere assertion, was the principle that houses once occupied by scholars for halls or schools should never be let to lay tenants so long as there were masters who wanted to take them.[1] The taxation of halls by a joint board of burgesses and masters is a custom which was established from the earliest times in all medieval *studia*. At Oxford it obtained canonical sanction from the ordinance of 1214, and royal approval by the general confirmation of the university customs in 1244 and 1248. But the scholars of Oxford, as of some other universities, claimed that when once a hall was let to a scholar, it should never be let to a layman, unless the owner might himself wish to occupy it. This claim of the university was sanctioned by a writ of Edward I in 1303.[2] A further custom grew up in the university whereby buildings which had once been used as lecture-rooms could not be occupied as dwelling-houses, but must continue to be used as lecture-rooms, so long as they were required for that purpose.[3]

Dispute with bailiff of northern suburb, 1288.

Towards the close of the thirteenth century we find abundant evidence of the growing powers of the university.

where the chancellor finds a difficulty in dealing with such characters when they lived beyond his then jurisdiction, 'ultra peti-pount in parochia S. Clementis'. The answer is that he must catch them when they enter the town. By a writ, dated 16 Mar. 1305, the King required the town to keep two separate prisons, one for men, and one 'pro mulieribus publicis'; see *Munim. Civ. Oxon.*, ed. H. E. Salter (O.H.S.), p. 5. [The jurisdiction of the chancellor over prostitutes was derived from his exercise of the functions of an archdeacon in the university. See *Reg. Cancell. Oxon., 1434-1469*, ed. H. E. Salter (O.H.S.), i. xvii-xix.]

[1] *Mun. Acad.* i. 14. [*Stat. Antiq. Univ. Oxon.*, ed. S. Gibson, p. 79.] Cf. below, p. 172.

[2] *Med. Arch. Univ. Oxford*, ed.

H. E. Salter (O.H.S.), i. 81-2. [This writ, dated 19 Sept. 1303, and addressed to the mayor and bailiffs reiterated a request which the King had recently made to them at the instance of the university that the townspeople should let to the scholars all such premises as they were wont to let to them and any other premises that could be spared for their residence. There is no mention of any claim by the university to any privilege with regard to the letting of houses.]

[3] [On the taxation of halls and schools see A. B. Emden, *An Oxford Hall in Medieval Times*, pp. 35-6; *Oriel Records*, ed. C. L. Shadwell and H. E. Salter (O.H.S.), p. 224; and *Reg. Cancell. Oxon., 1434-69*, ed. H. E. Salter (O.H.S.), i. xxix-xxx.]

In 1288 disputes arose out of the attempts of a certain Robert de Welles, the King's Bailiff of Northgate Hundred, to resist the jurisdiction of the chancellor, in the suburb outside the North gate. The open space then called Beaumont fields, which embraced not only the present university park but also the wide street or open space known as S. Giles's, appears to have been at that time the usual students' playground—the 'Pré-aux-clercs' of Oxford: hence it is easy to understand how collisions between the university and the bailiff would arise. The bailiff had been excommunicated for imprisoning a bedel and refusing to obey the citation of the chancellor. In retaliation he procured by a royal writ the attachment of the chancellor's commissary, one of the proctors, and other members of the university to make answer in the court of the Northgate Hundred. But, on the matter coming before the King's Council, the rights of the university were upheld and the officious bailiff removed from his office.[1] On this occasion we find the university employing the favourite weapon of their Parisian brethren, a threat of 'Cessation', in the event of the obnoxious official being restored. Two years later the whole question of the relations between the town and university became the subject of discussion before the King in Parliament. By this time it is no longer a question of protecting defenceless scholars from the tyranny of brutal burghers, but of protecting respectable citizens from oppression by the Chancellor's Court and the hundreds of quarrelsome boys who were always ready to annoy their lay neighbours by the abuse of its process. The jurisdiction, sometimes salutary enough, but too often petty and inquisitorial, exercised by the ecclesiastical courts everywhere and not during the Middle Ages only—is too much lost sight of by historians in estimating the real relations between Church and people. At Oxford the system would be exceptionally galling in proportion to the number and ubiquitousness of the clerical population interested in asserting the rights of their

[1] *Mun. Acad.* i. 43 *sq.*, 68. The King had ordered the excommunication to be raised till the session of Parliament; Rot. Pat. 14 Ed. I, m. 7 *dorso* (Hare, *Mem.* f. 19 *b*) [*Cal. Pat. Rolls, Edward I, 1281–92*, p. 258]; documents from City Red Book in Twyne MS. iv, f. 28.

CHAP. XII, order against offending laics. Already it is complained that
§ 3. the chancellor sets free prisoners committed by the mayor
and bailiffs, appropriates to himself the forfeited victuals of
regrators and flesh or fish confiscated as unfit for human
food, imposes ruinous fines on imprisoned laymen and the
like. By the judgement of the King and Parliament (1290),[1]
the chancellor's jurisdiction is for the first time exactly
defined. But though provisions are inserted against the abuses
complained of, the net result—as in all subsequent cases of
similar dispute—was a substantial addition to the authority
which the academic monarch had hitherto legally enjoyed.
He now obtained jurisdiction in cases of all crimes committed
in Oxford, where one of the parties was a scholar, except pleas
of homicide and mayhem.[2] His jurisdiction over the King's
bailiffs is affirmed, but with leave to them to apply to the
King's Court if aggrieved by the chancellor's proceedings. In
civil cases it was to extend to all contracts where one party was
a scholar and the cause of action arose in Oxford.[3] The victuals
—including the stinking fish about which the civil and ecclesiastical authorities were so strangely at issue—or rather perhaps

[1] *Mun. Acad.* i. 46 *sq.*; *Rot. Parl.*
i. 33; Ogle, *Royal Letters to Oxford*,
No. 13. [Cf. *Med. Arch. Univ.
Oxford*, ed. H. E. Salter (O.H.S.),
i. 88–94; and L. Toulmin Smith,
'Parliamentary Petitions relating to
Oxford', in *Collectanea* (O.H.S.),
iii. 102–3, 118–20.]

[2] 'Exceptis placitis de morte hominis et mayhemio.' The successive confirmations of the privileges
continue this limitation till a
charter of Richard II (Rot. Cart. 14
Ric. II, No. 14; Hare, *Mem.*, f. 107)
[for the text of this charter see
Med. Arch. Univ. Oxford, ed. H. E.
Salter (O.H.S.), i. 221–3, and *Cal.
Charter Rolls, 1341–1417*, p. 320],
which substitutes 'felonia et ma-
hemio dumtaxat exceptis', which
long continued to be the legal limit
of the chancellor's jurisdiction
(see Appendix IX). [See also *Cal.
Charter Rolls, 1341–1417*, pp.
430–1.] It would be assumed that

pleas affecting freehold held in lay
fee would be excluded from the
jurisdiction of the chancellor as
of all other ecclesiastical courts.
(Cases affecting college property
were constantly tried in the town
court of Hustings.) Cf. the Bull of
Boniface IX, 'tribus casibus, videlicet homicidio, mutilatione, et
libero tenemento duntaxat exceptis' (*Mun. Acad.* i. 79). In the first
two cases, scholars would be surrendered to the bishop after trial
at assizes. One other class of cases
was exempted from the chancellor's jurisdiction, i.e. pleas which
'touch the Crown'. This exception is made in the verdict of
the jury about the Jews, above,
p. 86, n. 2.

[3] [On the chancellor's jurisdiction in civil disputes see the important note by Dr. H. E. Salter,
Reg. Cancell. Oxon., 1434–1469
(O.H.S.), i. xx–xxiii.]

the pecuniary fines imposed upon their vendors, were to go as chap. xii, § 3. royal alms to the hospital of S. John, which then stood outside the eastern gate near Magdalen bridge.[1] The liberties of the university were affirmed to extend to the 'families' (i.e. servants) of clerks, as well as to the bedels, parchment makers, illuminators, writers, barbers, and 'others who wore the livery or robes of the clerks'.[2] If, however, the latter engaged in 'merchandise', they were to be tallageable like the burgesses.

It was customary for the university, like other corporate bodies, to apply from time to time for a confirmation of its privileges and charters, particularly on the accession of a new sovereign. A curious notice has been preserved as to the terms on which these renewals were granted. Scholars were a poor class, but all clerks could read and pray, and in those days prayers were a marketable commodity. Accordingly, when a confirmation of charters was applied for in 1315, it was granted in return for 1,500 whole psalters,[3] in consideration of which the fee for sealing was remitted. Would it be rash to infer that in the number of whole psalters prescribed we have an approximate estimate of the number of scholars then studying at Oxford?

Confirmation granted for prayers.

Passing over some grants of minor privileges of no great interest we come in 1355 to a great crisis in the history of the university. To give the reader some idea of what the medieval Town and Gown war really was, I propose to relate the story of this particular engagement (for such it may be fairly called)

---

[1] 'Forisfacturae, emendae, et amerciamenta de carnibus et piscibus putridis et non competentibus.' *Mun. Acad.* i. 51. Cf. *Med. Arch. Univ. Oxford*, ed. H. E. Salter (O.H.S.), i. 154, 356.

[2] 'Nisi clerici et eorum familiae et servientes pergamenarii luminatores scriptores et alii homines de officio qui sunt de robis ipsorum clericorum.' *Mun. Acad.* i. 52. The last clause can hardly mean persons engaged in making the clerks' robes (i.e. tailors), as Mr. Anstey supposes. To be 'de robis' of a noble meant to be a member of his household or suite, a companion or servant. [On the servants of clerks see *Reg. Cancell. Oxon., 1434–1469*, ed. H. E. Salter (O.H.S.), i. xxxi–xxxiii. See also L. H. D. Buxton and S. Gibson, *Oxford University Ceremonies*, p. 121.]

[3] 'Per ipsum Regem et consilium et pro mille et quingentis psalteriis, et sint quieti de feodo sigilli.' *Rot. Pat.* 8 Ed. II, pt. ii, m. 11 (Hare, *Priv.*, f. 32). [For the text of these letters patent see *Med. Arch. Univ. Oxford*, ed. H. E. Salter (O.H.S.), i. 95–6.]

in some detail. But the relation of the events of this one war
will give a false impression unless it is remembered that the
kind of fighting which we shall have to describe was perpetu-
ally going on in the streets of Oxford on a smaller scale and
with less fatal results. There is probably not a single yard of
ground in any part of the classic High Street that lies between
S. Martin's and S. Mary's which has not, at one time or
other, been stained with blood. There are historic battle-
fields on which less has been spilt.[1]

'The
Slaughter'
of 1355.　Like nearly every disturbance of the kind, the affair of
1355 broke out in a tavern. Its origin cannot be better
described than in the racy language of old Anthony Wood.
'On Tuesday, 10 Feb. (being the feast of S. Scholastica the
Virgin), came Walter de Springheuse, Roger de Chesterfield,
and other Clerks, to the Tavern called Swyndlestock (being
now the Meermaid Tavern at Quatervois, stiled at this day
in leases Swynstock), and there calling for wine, John de
Croydon, the Vintner, brought them some, but they disliking
it, as it should seem, and he avouching it to be good, several
snappish words passed between them. At length the Vintner
giving them stubborn and saucy language, they threw the wine
and vessel at his head.[2] The Vintner therefore receding with
great passion, and aggravating the abuse to those of his family
and neighbourhood, several came in, encouraged him not to
put up with the abuse, and withal told him they would faithfully stand by him.'[3] That was all: the same narrative would
be a sufficiently exact description of scores of similar conflicts

[1] There was a very serious disturbance in 1298 in which the town
claimed that they had received
damage to the extent of £3,000.
The whole of the pleadings on each
side are printed in *Med. Arch.
Univ. Oxford*, ed. H. E. Salter
(O.H.S.), i. 43–81, with a valuable
prefatory note by Dr. H. E. Salter.
The 'concord' is printed in *Med.
Arch. Univ. Oxford* (O.H.S.), i.
333–4, and *Mun. Acad.* i. 67. No
damages were paid on either
side.

[2] 'Et cum quarta caput eius fre-

git.' Robert of Avesbury, *De gestis
Edw. III*, ed. E. M. Thompson
(R.S.), p. 421. [Rashdall's whole
account of this outbreak is based
upon that given by Wood in
Annals, i. 456–61. Wood's description of the origin of the affray is an
embroidered version of the statement of grievances prepared by the
burgesses after the conclusion of
the rioting. For the text of these
grievances see *Munim. Civ. Oxon.*,
ed. H. E. Salter (O.H.S.), pp.
126–8.]

[3] Wood, *Annals*, i. 456.

at Oxford, Paris, or any other university town. After this the affairs took the stereotyped course. The vintner's friends rang the bell of the town church of S. Martin. The commonalty 'in an instant were in arms, some with bows and arrows, others with divers sorts of weapons'. The scholars, at present defenceless, were shot at. The chancellor appeared upon the scene to 'appease the tumult': he was shot at, and had to flee for his life back into Gown-land. By his order S. Mary's bell is rung. Ere long he is at the head of an army of English archers. With such weapons it is difficult to understand how the fight could have been maintained till even the close of a February day without a single man on either side being killed or mortally wounded. But neither townsmen nor gownsmen were as skilled with their weapons as the yeomen of Cressy. The fight had begun on a holiday: the next day was a 'legible' one. The chancellor made proclamation against breaches of the peace. The obedient scholars, we are assured, betook themselves meekly to the schools. But not so the townsmen. The bailiffs had ordered the citizens to prepare for a renewal of hostilities, and had even hired reinforcements of peasants from the surrounding country. A 'determination' which was going on at the convent of the Austin Friars (the present Wadham College) was broken in upon by a band of armed townsmen. Fourscore citizens, armed with bows and arrows, laid wait in S. Giles's Church till after dinner, when the scholars began to appear in their accustomed recreation-ground in Beaumont fields. This time some of the scholars were mortally wounded. Again the rival bells of S. Mary's and S. Martin's were heard, and preparations made for a pitched battle. The gownsmen shut the town gates, for the rustics were seen swarming in from Cowley, Headington, and Hinksey; but it was too late to prevent a party of some 2,000 entering, with an ominous black flag displayed, by the West gate. Hatred of the secular clergy was a pretty strong passion in the rustic mind of the fourteenth century.[1] Now was a fine

[1] [Wood's story of the course of the conflict is derived from the account sent by the university to the Bishop of Lincoln (Twyne MS. v, ff. 137–40) and from two Latin poems describing these events (*Collectanea* (O.H.S.), iii. 169–79, 183–7).]

CHAP. XII, opportunity for paying off old scores against the parish priest.[1]
§ 3.
Some twenty inns or halls were pillaged.[2] Scholars were killed or wounded; their books torn to pieces; the halls themselves were fired. The next day the chancellor is dispatched, at the head of a deputation, to the King at Woodstock. Meanwhile proclamation is made that the scholars (who had been outnumbered and completely overpowered on the preceding day) shall remain in their houses. But again the halls are broken into. More scholars are killed outright in cold blood and their bodies mutilated. Others, horribly wounded, are carried off to the town prison. 'The crown of some chaplains, viz. all the skin so far as the tonsure went, these diabolical imps flayed off in scorn of their clergy.' Churches supply no sanctuary. The fugitives are beaten and wounded, clinging to the very altars, nay, to the tabernacle itself. The friars, forgetting for the moment their own bitter differences with the university, come out in solemn procession bearing the host and chanting a litany for peace. The crucifix is planted in the midst of the rioters with a 'procul hinc ite profani'; but the sacred symbol is dashed to the ground. One scholar is killed even while clinging to the friar who bears the host. At last the scholars begin to flee the town, and no further mischief remains to be done.[3] But for the scholars of Merton, safe

---

[1] [There is no evidence that this motive actuated the rioters.]

[2] [Robert of Avesbury (*De Gestis Edwardi Tertii*, ed. E. M. Thompson (R.S.), p. 422) gives the number of halls broken into as 'about 20'. In the account of the conflict sent by the university to the Bishop of Lincoln (Twyne MS. v, f. 139) the number given is five.]

[3] The account sent to the bishop by the chancellor and masters, and the bishop's interdict, &c., are given in Linc. Reg. Gynwell, ff. 67–70 (partly copied in Twyne MS. v, f. 137; where also are extracts from the lost City Red Book; see also Twyne MS. xxii, ff. 316–40); the petition of the burgesses and the answer of the university in Twyne

MS. iv, ff. 76–8 [*Munim. Civ. Oxon.*, ed. H. E. Salter (O.H.S.), pp. 126–8], and several writs relating to the affair in Twyne MS. iv, ff. 570, 571. See also Robert of Avesbury, ed. E. M. Thompson (R.S.), pp. 421–3; Leland's *Itinerary*, vi. 141–6; Thomas Walsingham, *Hist. Anglicana*, ed. H. T. Riley (R.S.), i. 278; *Chron. Angliae auctore monacho S. Albani*, ed. E. M. Thompson (R.S.), p. 31; [*Chronica Iohannis de Reading, &c.*, ed. J. Tait, pp. 126, 266–7]; Bodley MS. 859, ff. 292 *b*–294 *b* [Latin poems relating to the riot: they have been edited by the Rev. H. Furneaux and printed in *Collectanea* (O.H.S.), iii. 165–87]; Rot. Pat. 29 Ed. III, p. 1, mm. 13, 16 *dorso*, 36; p. 2,

behind their solid walls, and a few others, the town is deserted.[1]

But now comes the day of vengeance. For more than a year the town lies under an interdict, which is proclaimed in all the churches with the accustomed paraphernalia of bells, curses, and extinguished tapers.[2] The King issues a special commission for the investigation of the affair and the punishment of the offenders. The mayor and bailiffs are sent to the Marshalsea prison; the sheriff—who was held, we may presume, responsible for not preventing the inroad of the rustics —is removed from his office. The further hearing of the affair is adjourned to London. Both university and town surrender all their privileges and charters—the university including even those received from the Holy See—into the King's hands. The university had, of course, decreed a 'cessation', and indeed most of the scholars had of their own accord fled into the country. Not till a general pardon was proclaimed for the offences of the clerks—an indication, by the way, that the scholars' conduct in the affair had not been altogether as lamb-like as their advocates represented—and published throughout the country did they begin to flock back to their old haunts. As late as 11 June 1355[3] it was necessary for the King to send a writ to Oxford to entreat the masters to resume their lectures.

As the outcome of the whole affair there resulted fresh New privileges for the university.

m. 26 [*Cal. Pat. Rolls, Edward III, 1354–8*, pp. 234, 235, 239, 240, 304, 343–4]. A few of the documents are printed by Thorold Rogers in *Oxford City Documents* (O.H.S.), p. 245 *sq.*, and others by O. Ogle, *Royal Letters*, Nos. xxxiv–xlv; App. No. iii [*Cal. Close Rolls, Edward III, 1354–60*, pp. 146–8, 200–1, 213–14]; *Med. Arch. Univ. Oxford*, ed. H. E. Salter (O.H.S.), i. 148–60, 342–3. See also W. H. Turner's *Catalogue of Charters in the Bodleian Library*, p. 282.

[1] 'Nonnulli in eadem Villa prae timore Laicorum latent in abscondito.' O. Ogle, *Royal Letters to Oxford*, No. xxxiv. [It is to be

inferred from the account given by Robert of Avesbury that members of other collegiate halls besides those of Merton remained in residence: 'scholaribus aulae de Mertone et aliarum aularum consimilium paucisque aliis scholaribus dumtaxat exceptis' (*De Gestis Edw. Tertii*, ed. E. M. Thompson (R.S.), p. 422.]

[2] [The interdict was removed on 15 Mar. 1356. See *Munim. Civ. Oxon.*, ed. H. E. Salter (O.H.S.), pp. 132–4.]

[3] Rot. Claus. 29 Ed. III, m. 23 *dorso* [*Cal. Close Rolls, Edward III, 1354–60*, p. 201].

CHAP. XII, privileges for the university, fresh humiliation for the town.
  § 3.   The assize of bread, wine, and ale; the assize of weights and
measures; the cognizance of cases of forestalling and regrat-
ing; the 'correction of victuals';[1] the punishment of both
clerks and laymen for carrying arms; the cleansing and paving
of the streets (which was to be enforced by ecclesiastical
censure); the 'assessment and taxation' of privileged persons
—all these matters were now placed under the sole and exclusive jurisdiction of the chancellor.[2] The forfeitures for
unwholesome or 'incompetent' victuals were still to go to the
Hospital of S. John. This provision might be held to throw an
unpleasant light upon the obscure question of medieval hospital
management, but here (as in former cases) it is not quite clear
whether it was the victuals themselves or merely pecuniary
fines for selling them that were devoted to charitable uses and
the benefit of the Sovereign's soul. On every one of the long-
standing subjects of contention between town and university
the latter scored a permanent triumph. From this time forward
the town of Oxford was practically governed by the university.[3] The university thrived on her own misfortunes.

[1] [There is plenty of documentary evidence about the way in
which these jurisdictions were exercised. Records of the courts held
in connexion with the assize of
bread, the assize of ale, and the
assize of weight and measures,
ranging from 1309 to 1351, are
edited by Dr. H. E. Salter in *Med.
Arch. Univ. Oxford* (O.H.S.), ii.
129–267. This volume also contains a record of cases under the
Statutes of Labourers, ranging
from 1390 to 1394 with a fragment
of a roll for 1355, edited by Miss
B. H. Putnam (*ibid*. ii. 1–128). The
chancellor, with the mayor and
others, was a justice for the local
enforcement of these statutes. See
also *Reg. Cancell. Oxon., 1434–1469*,
ed. H. E. Salter (O.H.S.), i. xv.]

[2] [*Med. Arch. Univ. Oxford*, ed.
H. E. Salter (O.H.S.), i. 152–7,
ii. 139–40: 27 June 1355; O. Ogle,

Royal Letters, pp. 57–8, 60–4;
Munim. Civ. Oxon., ed. H. E.
Salter (O.H.S.), pp. 135–7; *Cal.
Charter Rolls, 1341–1417*, pp.
143–6, 152.]

[3] Rot. Chart. 29 Ed. III, n. 5
(Hare, *Priv.*, f. 74; *Registrum*, p. 23).
[For the text of this ordinance see
Med. Arch. Univ. Oxford, ed. H. E.
Salter (O.H.S.), i. 158–60. For the
royal writ relating to the payment
of this fine see O. Ogle, *Royal
Letters*, pp. 58–60. For a list of
property stolen from scholars during the rioting and subsequently
restored, see *Munim. Civ. Oxon.*, ed.
H. E. Salter (O.H.S.), pp. 129–32.]
At the same time the power of the
chancellor to punish breaches of
the peace by laymen, even when no
scholar was aggrieved, was explicitly
recognized and the sheriff of Oxford
required to take oath to respect the
privileges of the university.

No less than £250 was to be raised by the citizens and paid chap. xii,
to the chancellor and scholars as compensation for all injuries § 3.
except death and mayhem; the goods of the scholars which Penalties
for the
had been seized by the townsmen were to be forthwith town.
restored.[1] Besides the material compensation which they
received from the Crown, the scholars were accorded an
ample measure of what may be called ecclesiastical satisfaction
at the hands of the bishop. He enjoined on the city as a condition of the relaxation of the interdict what was nothing less
than an annual penance to be performed by the mayor and
chief citizens for ever. On every anniversary of S. Scholastica's day the mayor, bailiffs, and sixty burghers were to
appear in S. Mary's Church at the celebration of Mass with
deacon and subdeacon (at their own expense) for the souls
of the slaughtered scholars, and at the offertory each one of
them was to offer one penny at the high altar.[2] Of this sum
forty pence was to be distributed by the proctors among poor
students and the rest to go to the curate of the church.[3] The
length of time during which this penance has been performed
is one of those curious links between past and present which
would hardly have been possible in any country but our own.
After the Reformation the town availed itself of the opportunity of neglecting the popish ceremony. But upon the university bringing an action against the city upon their old bond
for its observance, the council ordered that the Mass should
be commuted to a sermon and communion, the offering to be
made as heretofore. After a few years the service was changed
to a litany. In the year 1800 the municipality once more
attempted to shake themselves free from the humiliating
observance. Once more the fine of 100 marks provided for
in the bond was demanded by the university and paid by the
town. It was only in 1825 that on the humble petition of the
city the university was graciously pleased to forgo its rights,

[1] Rot. Claus. 29 Ed. III, m. 17.
[*Cal. Close Rolls, Edward III,
1354-60*, pp. 146-8; Rymer, *Foedera*, ed. 1816, iii, pt. i. 309.]

[2] [Any scholar molesting any
townsman taking part in the procession to or from S. Mary's on

this occasion was to be severely
punished. See *Stat. Antiq. Univ.
Oxon.*, ed. S. Gibson, pp. 230-1.]

[3] *Mun. Acad.* i. 190-202; Rot.
Pat. 31 Ed. III, pt. ii, m. 26
(Ayliffe, ii, App., p. lv). [*Cal. Pat.
Rolls, Edward III, 1354-8*, p. 564.]

CHAP. XII, and that the citizens of Oxford ceased to do annual penance
§ 3.   for the sins of their forefathers on S. Scholastica's day, 1354.[1]

No execu-   The most curious part of the whole business is that we hear
tions.   nothing of the sentence passed on the actual criminals. Several
of the chief offenders are expressly excepted from the writ
granted after the settlement of the affair, by which the accused were allowed to go out on bail. These were apparently
reserved for trial at the assizes.[2] There can, however, be
little doubt that they escaped hanging. Even the mayor who
had been the principal offender seems to have spent some
years in prison, but he died rich and a liberal benefactor to
Mother Church.[3] The contrast between the mildness of the
penalties inflicted on the actual ringleaders, and the severity
of those imposed on the community, is very characteristic of
medieval notions. Corporate privileges carried with them
corporate responsibility.

Clerks of   It was to secure the better exercise of the supervision over
the market.   the market conferred upon it at this time that the university
appointed the officers known as 'supervisors', or 'clerks' of
the market.[4] The office still remains, though many of its

[1] Archives, A. 13; Cox, Recollections, pp. 112, 113.

[2] Rot. Claus. 29 Ed. III, m. 17.
[Cal. Close Rolls, Edward III,
1354-60, pp. 213-14.] O. Ogle,
Royal Letters to Oxford, Nos.
xxxvii, xliv. The last document is
dated 17 Nov. 1357. Yet by the
Order in Council of 17 July 1355
(O. Ogle, App. No. iii) it would
seem that even the mayor was to be
bailed. It is not improbable that
some of the offenders may have
continued in outlawry (some possibly even in prison) till the general
pardon at the King's jubilee in
1362, O. Ogle, No. xlv. [Rymer,
Foedera, ed. 1816, iii, pt. i. 309.]

[3] [John de Bereford, the mayor,
was certainly at large on 1 Aug.
1356, when he witnessed a concord
in the Hustings court: see Twyne
MS. xxiii, ff. 398-9.]

[4] We hear of 'supervisores panis',
'vini', and 'cerevisiae' from 1454.

'Supervisores mercati' are not mentioned till 1507. On the whole
subject see the article in Collectanea (O.H.S.), ii. 1-135, by Octa-
vius Ogle, who filled this office for
many years. For clerks of the
market when the city still had control, see O. Ogle, No. xxii. [In the
charter granted to the university,
dated 27 June 1355, a clause was
inadvertently omitted which should
have transferred to the university
the privilege which the burgesses
of Oxford had enjoyed at least
since 1327, that the King's clericus
mercati should not interfere in their
market when the King was in Oxford or its neighbourhood. This
omission had been rectified by
1359. The words by which this
privilege was eventually conveyed
to the university have been misconstrued as conveying the clerkship
of the market. See the remarks on
this subject by Dr. H. E. Salter in

functions have disappeared with the abolition of the old state- CHAP. XII,
regulation of prices and other restrictions on trade; but the § 3.
clerk still exercises the power of summarily confiscating false
weights and measures, and butter which is under weight.

Only one important accession of privilege remains to be Jurisdic-
recorded. Henry IV gave the university the right to claim the univer-
surrender of 'privileged persons' indicted for felony, who steward,
were thereupon to be tried by a newly constituted officer of 1406.
the university, the seneschal or steward, to be appointed by
the chancellor, provided the lord high chancellor were satisfied of his competence. The trial was then to take place
according to secular law by a jury composed half of privileged
persons out of a panel returned by the bedel, and half of
townsmen summoned in the ordinary way by the sheriff of the
county.[1] The commons petitioned against this unconstitu-
tional if not illegal charter, but in vain, and the university
still retains this anomalous privilege as well as the older
jurisdiction conferred on the Chancellor's Court,[2] both being
now sanctioned by a special Act of Parliament.

It should be clearly understood that in its origin the privi- Not ex-
lege affected only the case of privileged laymen, servants of clerks.
scholars, and members of privileged trades, such as writers
and stationers.[3] Where the offender was a clerk, even in those

Med. Arch. Univ. Oxford (O.H.S.),
i. 176, 186; and in Munim. Civ.
Oxon. (O.H.S.), 194, 197, 263 n.]
    [1] Rot. Cart. 6 and 7 Hen. IV,
No. 3; Registrum, p. 47. [The
charter making this grant bears
date 2 June 1406; for the text see
Med. Arch. Univ. Oxford, ed. H. E.
Salter (O.H.S.), i. 231–4; and Cal.
Charter Rolls, 1341–1417, pp.
430–1.]
    [2] The steward also held a court
leet in the name of the university.
See Twyne MS. xiii. [For the
steward's oath see Reg. Cancell.
Oxon., 1434–1469, ed. H. E. Salter
(O.H.S.), ii. 14. On the Court of
the High Steward see L. H. D.
Buxton and S. Gibson, Oxford
University Ceremonies, pp. 125–6.]

[3] In 1454 they are thus defined
(Mun. Acad. i. 346): 'the styward
of the Universitie and fredmen of
the same Universite wyth their
menyall men, also alle Bedells with
dailly servants and their house-
holdes, alle staciones, alle boke-
bynders, lympners, wryters, per-
gemeners, barbours, the belle-
rynger of the Universite, with alle
their housholdes, alle catours,
manciples, spencers, cokes, laven-
ders, povere children of Scolers or
clerkes (i.e. boy-servitors) within
the precinct of the said Universite,
also alle other servants taking clothing or hyre by the yere, half-yere,
or quarter of the yere, takyng atte
leste for the yere vi shillings and
viii pence, for the half iii shillings

CHAP. XII,
§ 3.

more serious cases which were not triable by the chancellor, he was after conviction at assizes[1] surrendered to the bishop to be dealt with according to ecclesiastical law.[2] In the majority of cases he was probably 'admitted to purgation', i.e. allowed to get a number of other tonsured ruffians to swear that they believed him to be innocent, and was thereupon discharged. If he was refused purgation, or failed in his purgation, he was liable to whatever period of imprisonment in the bishop's prison the ecclesiastical judge might order.

and iv pence, and the quarter xx pence, of any doctour, Maister, graduat, Scoler, or clerc, withoute fraude, or malengyne; Also, all common caryers, bryngers of Scolers to the Universite, or their money, letters, or eny especiall message to any Scoler or clerk, or fetcher of any Scoler or clerk fro the Universite', &c.

[1] Sir James Stephen speaks of this principle—that a clerk should not be surrendered till after conviction—as settled by the practice of the courts by the time of Henry VI (*Hist. of the Criminal Law*, ed. 1883, i. 460). But it was the usual practice much earlier. The jury was impanelled 'ut sciatur quales liberari debent Episcopo' (i.e. whether as guilty or not guilty). See the proceedings at the Oxford 'Eyre' of 1285 in *Oxford City Documents*, ed. Thorold Rogers (O.H.S.); and the same usage seems to have generally prevailed. Moreover, a constitution of Archbishop Pecham enacts that 'clerici pro suis criminibus detenti a publica potestate, et tandem *pro convictis Ecclesiae restituti*, non facile liberentur, nec perfunctorie pro eis Purgatio admittatur'. See the text with Lynwood's comments in *Provinciale*, l. v, tit. 14, *Clerici*. At times it would appear that bishops actually issued commissions to the King's justices to try clerks (so Bishop Burghersh in 1322: Linc.

Reg., f. 51 *b*). There were exceptional cases—at Oxford as elsewhere—in which a clerk was hanged, e.g. in 1327, when scholars assisted the citizens of Abingdon in plundering the monastery. See documents in Twyne MS. xxiii, f. 220 *sq.*; Wood, i. 412. So in 1285, when Rogers (*loc. cit.*, pp. 191, 223) thinks that the offender had previously pleaded his clergy. At about the end of the fifteenth century the judges would only surrender clerks in grave cases *sine purgatione*, with directions that the bishop was to imprison them for life (Stephen, *loc. cit.*; Hale, *Precedents and Proceedings*, London, 1847, p. lvii *sq.*). In 1489 we find a somewhat anomalous commission for the trial of a scholar issued to the Duke of Suffolk, the mayor, and five others (*Materials Illustrative of the Reign of Henry VII*, ed. W. Campbell (R.S.), ii. 482); [*Cal. Pat. Rolls, Henry VII, 1485–94*, p. 283. On the subject of Benefit of Clergy see Sir W. S. Holdsworth, *History of English Law*, iii. 294–9].

[2] This was the usual course, but in 45 Henry III a commission to the Judge of Assize at Cambridge provides 'ita tamen quod ad suspensionem vel mutilationem clericorum non procedatis sed eos *alio modo per concilium Universitatis Cantabr. castigetis*' (Fuller, *Hist. of Camb.*, ed. Prickett and Wright, p. 29).

But in a majority of cases the convicted clerk probably got off CHAP. XII,
with a very moderate penalty. Lay dependants of the univer- § 3.
sity of course enjoyed no such privileges; hence the necessity
for the Steward's Court. After the Reformation, however,
clerks could no longer claim any further benefit of clergy
than laymen, nor were members of the university treated as
clergymen. Consequently the provisions of the charter became applicable to all members of the university convicted of
treason or felony, and were not unfrequently put into force.

In the same reign the hitherto vague limitation of the The pre-
chancellor's jurisdiction to the 'precinct of the university' univer-
received a more exact definition.[1] It was declared to extend sity.
to the Hospital of S. Bartholomew on the east, to Botley on
the west, to Godstow Bridge on the north, and to Bagley
Wood on the south.[2]

[1] [By letters patent dated 8 Apr.
1336, the jurisdiction of the
chancellor 'de contractibus et
transgressionibus factis scolaribus'
had been extended to the suburbs
outside the walls. See *Med. Arch.
Univ. Oxford*, ed. H. E. Salter
(O.H.S.), i. 128.]

[2] Rot. Cart. 2 Hen. IV, pt. i,
No. 2 (Hare, *Mem.*, f. 116) [for the
text of this charter, which bears
date 13 May 1401, see *Med. Arch.
Univ. Oxford*, ed. H. E. Salter
(O.H.S.), i. 226–30; and *Cal.
Charter Rolls, 1341–1417*, pp.
409–10]. The power of banishment
beyond the limits of the town itself
was probably assumed in the first
instance as a part of the chancellor's ordinary criminal jurisdiction, being a usual punishment in
town-courts. It was exercised early
in the fourteenth century (Linc.
Reg. Dalderby, f. 27 *b*); and it is expressly recognized in 1355 (O. Ogle,
[*Royal Letters to Oxford*, p. 63; see
also *Med. Arch. Univ. Oxford*, ed.
H. E. Salter (O.H.S.), i. 189]). In
1444 it is defined as extending, in
the case of 'contumacious and rebellious persons', to twelve miles

round Oxford (*Mun. Acad.* ii. 504).
[See *Stat. Antiq. Univ. Oxon.*, ed. S.
Gibson, p. xix, n. 1, and *Reg. Cancell. Oxon., 1434–1469*, ed. H. E.
Salter (O.H.S.), i. xvii–xix, 100,
107.] A later charter of 1459 (Rot.
Pat. 37 Hen. VI, pt. i, m. 7 [*Cal.
Pat. Rolls, Henry VI, 1452–61*, p.
479]; O. Ogle, No. lxxv) limits it
(while professing merely to extend
the existing power of banishment)
to ten miles with reference to
'omnes pronubas et mulieres incon-
tinentes'. In this last case the power
has been exercised very recently
[i.e. *c.* 1895]. In 1482 we find in
the proctors' accounts, 'Pro dela-
cione collistrigii ad quadrivium
pro punitione unius mulieris ban-
nite, iiiid'. (Archives, W. P.—Y.
28.) [*Med. Arch. Univ. Oxford*, ed.
H. E. Salter (O.H.S.), ii. 334.] As
to the power of 'discommuning'
still occasionally exercised by the
university, Twyne (MS. xxiii, f.
491) declares that he knows of no
express grant of it. It must be taken
to be simply a part of the university's disciplinary power to
interdict its own members from
'commercium cum oppidano'.

CHAP. XII,
§ 3.
Subjection
of town.

By the middle of the fifteenth century the town had been crushed, and was almost entirely subjugated to the authority of the university. The burghers lived henceforth in their own town almost as the helots or subjects of a conquering people. Whatever ups and downs there may have been from time to time in the battles of the streets, the constitutional relations between the two populations continued to be regulated in the main by the settlement of 1355.[1] It is difficult at the present day to realize the extent of interference with the private lives of individuals which the system of godly ecclesiastical discipline really involved; though it must of course be remembered that lay town-government was hardly less minutely paternal. At Oxford a very peculiar mode of enforcing this discipline was established at an early period—a mode which appears to have been practised as regards the 'excesses' of scholars as early as 1280,[2] and to have gradually extended itself to the misdoings of the laity. At irregular intervals what was termed

General inquisition.

a 'general inquisition' was instituted into the morals of the inhabitants. The town was mapped out into districts, to each of which a theological doctor and two masters of arts were appointed. These 'delegate judges' sat in the different churches of the town and there held a general investigation into the characters of the inhabitants, a jury of citizens being summoned before them to give evidence on oath.[3] A report

[1] Among the relics of this state of things which have survived till to-day or yesterday is the fact that the night-police of the city were wholly controlled and paid by the university till the Oxford Police Act of 1868. In the medieval proctors' accounts we get charges of some £2 or £3 'pro expensis factis in nocturnis vigiliis pro custodia pacis toto anno', but excessive expenditure on this head is often surcharged by the auditors to the over-zealous proctors personally (Archives, W. P.—Y. 28). [On the sums paid to the proctors for the night watch, see Dr. H. E. Salter's introduction to the proctors' accounts in *Med. Arch. Univ. Oxford*

(O.H.S.), ii. 282–3. It is not known on what evidence Rashdall formed the conclusion that 'over-zealous proctors' were made personally liable for 'excessive expenditure' on this head.]

[2] *Mun. Acad.* i. 42. [*Stat. Antiq. Univ. Oxon.*, ed. S. Gibson, p. 97]. Mr. Anstey's summary misrepresents the meaning. The 'tam per scholares . . . quam laicos' means by the evidence of a jury of scholars or laymen.

[3] This 'Inquisition' was probably a local survival of the episcopal inquisitions by means of synodal witnesses, or synodsmen (whence the more modern 'sidesman'), which elsewhere became extinct—

was made to the chancellor, before whom the offenders were chap. xii,
summoned with a view to excommunication and penance.   § 3.
One of these reports which has been preserved gives us
full statistics as to the exact number of common scolds
(*obiurgatrices consuetudinariae* or *intolerabiles*), as well as of
notorious evil-livers of a more serious order who were found
in the parishes of S. Peter's-in-the-East and S. Clement's in
the year 1448.[1] Some of the offenders were reported merely
for keeping late hours, a habit which in the fifteenth century
exposed people to the gravest suspicions.[2]

In spite of the inquisitorial character of medieval police, the Mildness
annals of Oxford produce an impression of the extreme mild-   of law in medieval
ness of English criminal law in the Middle Ages—at least in   towns.
corporate towns. It might have been very often quite otherwise with the villeins of rural lords. One meets with no such
sentences as perpetual imprisonment or demolition of the
offender's house, which were occasionally the fate of an oppressor of the clerks in Paris, though even there murder could
generally be compounded for. When bows and arrows or
daggers were employed in every street-brawl, a very slight
disturbance might often terminate fatally. At Oxford homicide was so frequent that the proctors were directed to keep
lists of such offenders[3] and of those who had been banished
from the town. An execution was of the rarest possible occurrence. As a general rule homicides of a kind which in modern
times would be more often treated as murder than as

on the Continent largely because
superseded by the papal inquisition.
Grosseteste had revived this inquisition throughout his diocese.
See H. C. Lea, *Hist. of the Inquisition*, i. 312 *sq.*

[1] *Mun. Acad.* ii. 580–1. [*Reg.
Cancell. Oxon.*, *1434–1469*, ed.
H. E. Salter (O.H.S.), i. 161–2.
Mr. Anstey has the date 1441 in the
margin; this is wrong: it should
be 1448.]

[2] Instance the following: '*Item,
dicunt iidem iurati, quod Isabella
Hay custodit vigilias suspiciose et
frequenter usque ad mediam noc-

tem.' So Mauricius Kariore 'con-
suetudinarie custodit vigilias sus-
piciosas ultra tempus' (*loc. cit.*).

[3] *Mun. Acad.* i. 24, ii. 494.
[*Stat. Antiq. Univ. Oxon.*, ed. S.
Gibson, p. 88, ll. 9–13. The evi-
dence of as many of the Oxford
Coroners' Rolls as have survived
goes to prove that homicide was
not frequent, though wounding
may have been common. See
Oxford City Documents (O.H.S.),
J. E. Thorold Rogers, pp. 150–
74; *Records of Mediaeval Oxford*
(*Coroners' Inquests*, &c.), ed. H. E.
Salter, pp. 1–56.]

CHAP. XII, manslaughter were punished by a few months' imprisonment,
§ 3. or excommunication, or both, terminated by some kind of
penance, of which a payment for the spiritual benefit of the
deceased, and (if the victim was a scholar) for the temporal profit of his surviving brethren, in general formed
a prominent part.[1] Banishment from the place was in fact
the only severe secondary punishment which seems to
have been practically known to the jurisprudence of a
medieval town.[2] To the medieval mind the main object of
punishment was to produce submission and promises of
future amendment. Almost the only deterrent punishment
(besides banishment) consisted in fines and ecclesiastical
penances, humiliating perhaps but not severe. There was a
quite intelligible feeling against the infliction of a punishment, such as prolonged imprisonment, which did not re-
dound to the advantage of the persons inflicting it, and
which would certainly have imposed a severe tax upon the
innocent community. A man was only imprisoned as a
means of compelling him to submit to the court, pay his
fine and swear 'not to do it again'. If he could not be caught,
he was excommunicated with a like object.[3] A curious instance of this domestic system of jurisprudence occurred in
the case of an 'organ pleyer' of All Souls, who was imprisoned
for adultery, but upon his 'weeping bitterly' the warden was
inspired with 'good hope of him for the future', and became

[1] [It is to be presumed that in making this generalization Rashdall had in mind the loss of life inci-dental to many of the major out-breaks between North and South, and between Town and Gown during the medieval period; but it should be remembered that on these occasions the authorities were dis-posed to regard any loss of life as the responsibility of the factions or communities concerned and not of particular individuals. Im-prisonment and excommunication were inflicted preliminary to and not consequently upon an official investigation. If executions were rare, they were so because flight was easy.]

[2] Townsmen were frequently pilloried—not so, of course, the clerks. [See *Reg. Cancell. Oxon.*, *1434-1469*, ed. H. E. Salter (O.H.S.), i. 332-3, ii. 101.]

[3] In the earliest period, as we have seen, the chancellor generally proceeds by excommunication. When he had acquired the power of imprisonment both of clerks and laymen, he was disposed to rely chiefly on the secular arm, though excommunication as well as im-prisonment is frequently threat-ened in his edicts.

surety for him.[1] Whereupon he was discharged without further penalty after three hours' incarceration.

The great mass of the criminal business of the Chancellor's Court consisted in the settlement of assault cases of one kind or another.[2] It must be remembered that in the Middle Ages it was not merely freshmen or young noblemen who were involved in street-brawls and assaults, but masters of arts, friars, beneficed clergymen, principals of halls, even heads of colleges. Thus, within a period of ten years, we find two successive vicars of S. Giles's in trouble. One of them was merely bound over to keep the peace; the other 'forfeited his club and paid two shillings'.[3] A schoolmaster is imprisoned for inciting his scholars to drag from the pulpit a priest who was reading his excommunication.[4] Some of his devoted pupils afterwards joined him in jail for attempting a nocturnal rescue. The Warden of Canterbury College was convicted of consenting to his scholars violently seizing the beer of others to the value of 12d.[5] He was merely required to pay the value of the beer to the complainants. There was a regular tariff of charges for various kinds of breaches of the peace varying from 12d.—about a week's battels for a scholar—for threats to 40s. for 'resisting justice' or 'nocturnal wandering'. This last enormity, it is curious to note, is punished twice as severely as 'shooting an arrow with intent to injure', nor was the usual punishment increased even when the victims chanced to be the 'Northern Proctor and his attendants',[6] the offender being

[1] Mun. Acad. ii. 674–5. [Reg. Cancell. Oxon., 1434–1469, ed. H. E. Salter (O.H.S.), i. 413.]

[2] [On the chancellor as a justice of the peace see Reg. Cancell. Oxon., 1434–1469, ed. H. E. Salter (O.H.S.), i, pp. xxiii–xxv.]

[3] Mun. Acad. ii. 588, 668. [Reg. Cancell.Oxon.,1434–1469,ed.H.E. Salter (O.H.S.), i. 174, 348, 382, 383. Owing to an error in transcription on the part of Mr. Anstey, Rashdall was misled into assuming that two successive vicars of S. Giles's were guilty of breaches of the peace. The second sentence

mentioned by Rashdall was imposed on Owen, a servant of the same vicar, Richard Andrew.]

[4] Mun. Acad. ii. 601. [Reg. Cancell. Oxon., 1434–1469, ed. H. E. Salter (O.H.S.), i. 212, 324.]

[5] Mun. Acad. ii. 506. [Reg. Cancell. Oxon., 1434–1469, ed. H. E. Salter (O.H.S.), i. 8.]

[6] Mun. Acad. ii. 666. [Reg. Cancell. Oxon., 1434–1469, ed. H. E. Salter (O.H.S.), i. 364.] The scale is fixed by a Statute of 1432 (ibid. i. 314) [Stat. Antiq. Univ. Oxon., ed. S. Gibson, pp. 204–6; Reg. Cancell. Oxon., 1434–1469, ed. H. E. Salter

CHAP. XII, merely imprisoned till his fine was paid. It should be added
§ 3.   that in the Chancellor's Court—as in England generally—
        immense use was made of the system of sureties. There are
        half a dozen cases where sureties to keep the peace or be of
        good behaviour are required for one in which any actual
        penalty is inflicted.[1]

Inquisi-   There really seems to have been hardly any limit to the
torial
juris- extent to which the private life of citizens as well as scholars
diction.
        was liable to regulation in the Chancellor's Court. Its proce-
        dure was no doubt much the same as that of town courts
        elsewhere; but in ordinary municipalities the system was
        administered by elected magistrates.[2] Brewsters and taverners
        are pilloried or (if incorrigible) banished for brewing bad beer,[3]
        bakers for giving light weight. A manciple is punished for
        playing at dice all night.[4] Certain tradesmen are required
        solemnly to abjure the game of 'tennys' within Oxford and its
        precincts:[5] two others are imprisoned for speaking words
        against the office of proctor, until they swear to be faithful to
        the university in word and deed.[6] Every species of quarrel in
        which a scholar or privileged person was concerned was

(O.H.S.), i. xix–xx], which remarks
in the preamble that 'there is no
better means of punishment in
these days' than fines, which are
more feared than anything else.
[Mr. Strickland Gibson dates this
statute c. 1410 (op. cit., p. 204). It
was re-enacted with emendations
in 1432. See op. cit., pp. 242–3.]

[1] The amount annually returned
into the University Chest by the
proctors 'pro de transgressoribus
et perturbantibus pacem' was often
only some twenty or thirty shillings. (Archives, W. P.—Y. 28)
[Med. Arch. Univ. Oxford, ed.
H. E. Salter (O.H.S.), ii. 294–355,
for the years 1464–5, 1469–75,
1477–83, 1488–9, 1492–3, 1494–5,
and 1496–7. See also Reg. Cancell.
Oxon., 1434–1469, ed. H. E. Salter
(O.H.S.), i. xxiv.]

[2] [This comparison with town
courts is not apposite. The pro-

cedure of the Chancellor's Court
was that of all ecclesiastical courts.
There were no essoins; the case, if
it was a civil action, opened with
the production of a libellus; all
statements were on oath; and all
the parties took an oath to accept
the verdict.]

[3] Acta Curiae Cancellarii (Aaa)
[Reg. Cancell. Oxon., 1434–1469,
ed. H. E. Salter (O.H.S.)], passim.

[4] Mun. Acad. i. 530. [Reg.
Cancell. Oxon., 1434–1469, ed.
H. E. Salter (O.H.S.), i. 69.]

[5] Mun. Acad. ii. 602. [Reg.
Cancell. Oxon., 1434–1469, ed.
H. E. Salter (O.H.S.), i. 213–14.]

[6] Mun. Acad. ii. 556. [Reg.
Cancell. Oxon., 1434–1469, ed.
H. E. Salter (O.H.S.), i. 141. A
barber and a bookbinder, both
privileged persons who were bound,
therefore, to support proctorial
authority.]

brought into the Chancellor's Court, and, in nine cases out of CHAP. XII, ten, referred to arbitration or settled by an agreement drawn § 3. up under the auspices of the chancellor.[1]

In this way servants often settled their wages with their Amicable masters, writers with the stationers who employed them, and settle-
ments. so on.[2] In one case an agreement between a schoolmaster and the Prior of the Canons Regular, who had quarrelled, contains a clause providing that the parties should partake of an amicable meal together in the hall of the Prior's college.[3] In another, bad blood having arisen between two halls, it was agreed that the principals should kiss, and be reconciled.[4] This parental system of adjusting disputes was no doubt well adapted to the wants of an age in which full-grown and well-educated men fought and quarrelled and informed against one another on the slightest provocation, like children in a nursery. Few things are more calculated to make one realize the enormous extent to which civilization has succeeded in curbing and controlling the natural passions even of the lowest strata of modern society than the annals of a medieval university.

It is instructive, by the way, to notice that by the beginning Expulsion of the fifteenth century Saxon oppression had already, it of Irish,
1423. seems, developed the well-known characteristics of the Irish race.[5] Their turbulence, exceptional even in the university towns, led in 1413 to the passing of an Act of Parliament banishing them from the universities. Religious and graduates were excepted from the provision, but even these were required to find security for their good behaviour.[6] After a

---

[1] [On the chancellor's offices as an arbitrator see *Reg. Cancell. Oxon., 1434–1469*, ed. H. E. Salter (O.H.S.), i. xxv–xxvi.]

[2] The cream has been skimmed from the *Acta Curiae Cancellarii* in *Mun. Acad.* ii. 505–727. [The full text of the Register containing these *Acta* is contained in the two volumes of *Reg. Cancell. Oxon., 1434–1469*, ed. H. E. Salter (O.H.S.).]

[3] *Mun. Acad.* ii. 713. [*Reg.*

Cancell. Oxon., 1434–1469, ed. H. E. Salter (O.H.S.), ii. 175.]

[4] *Mun. Acad.* ii. 553. [*Reg. Cancell. Oxon., 1434–1469*, ed. H. E. Salter (O.H.S.), i. 131–2.]

[5] [See the case of *Hogonona v. Friar Austin* in *Select Cases before the King's Council, 1243–1482* (Selden Soc.), ed. I. S. Leadam and J. F. Baldwin, pp. 85–6.]

[6] *Rot. Parl.* iv. 13 (1 Hen. V, c. 8); Wood, *Annals*, i. 557; Rot. Claus. 1 Hen. V, m. 8. [*Cal. Close*

CHAP. XII, temporary relaxation, the expulsion was actually carried out
§ 3. in 1423, except in the case of clerks producing certificates
from the English authorities in Ireland that they were subjects of the King of England.[1]

Purgation. We have noticed the incessant oaths of amendment on the
part of accused persons. Still more at variance with modern
notions was the practice of allowing a plaintiff who confessedly
could not prove his case to require the defendant to clear
himself on oath. Sometimes persons merely suspected or
accused by common report of discreditable conduct appeared
in court to set their character right with their neighbours.
Thus on one occasion the Principal of White Hall insisted on
being allowed to swear that he was not a Scotsman.[2] In
some cases—in charges of immorality, of theft or fraud, and
even in actions of debt—the extraordinary system of compurgation, everywhere employed by the ecclesiastical courts in
dealing with the offences of the clergy, was adopted in the
Chancellor's Court. In these cases, besides the defendant's
own oath to his innocence, twelve or some smaller number of
other clerks were called upon to swear that he had spoken
truly. This was the usual termination of all criminal prosecu-
tions against the clergy in other courts for all offences from
murder downwards. The only way in which the procedure
of the Chancellor's Court differed from that of the ordinary
Bishop's Courts is that at Oxford clerks really did suffer
minor punishments—fine and banishment—whereas elsewhere they would too often have gone scot free. Another

Rolls, Henry V, 1413–19, i. 110–11;
L. Toulmin Smith, 'Parliamentary
Petitions relating to Oxford' in
Collectanea (O.H.S.), iii. 154–5.]
    [1] Rot. Parl. iv. 190 (1 Hen. VI,
c. 3).
    [2] It is entirely misleading with
Mr. Anstey (Mun. Acad. ii. 631) to
call the admission to compurgation
a 'trial by a jury of twelve men
before the Chancellor'. In ordinary
ecclesiastical courts, when a clerk
offered to purge himself, no evidence could be offered for the
prosecution. [Evidence could be

offered against him, and it was invited, but no one took the trouble
to come forward.] At Oxford
people could, indeed, object to the
clerk being admitted to purgation,
but only, as Chancellor Gascoigne
remarks, at the risk of death or
mutilation: hence that excellent
chancellor warns his successors
against too great facility in admitting to purgation, which was at
Oxford 'causa intollerabilis ne-
quicie'. Ibid. ii. 536. [Reg. Cancell.
Oxon., 1434–1469, ed. H. E. Salter
(O.H.S.), i. 94.]

peculiarity of the Chancellor's Court was its jurisdiction over
the very large number of scholars' servants, and persons
belonging to various trades specially connected with the
university, who had been admitted to the same privileges as
actual scholars.[1] The wide extension thus given to university privilege is specially characteristic of the English universities.[2]

[1] [See above, p. 95, n. 2.]

[2] [See Dr. H. E. Salter's remarks on the special character of
the Chancellor's Court: *History*
(1929), xiv. 60–1. The real peculiarity of the Chancellor's Court,
Dr. Salter points out, lay in the
fact that it dealt 'not only with
ecclesiastical offences and the
ordinary matters of an archdeacon's court, such as wills and
matrimony, but also with civil
matters, debt, breach of contract,
injuries by assault, and all that
could be tried in the Hustings
Court of the city, with the one
exception of cases of freehold'. See
also *Snappe's Formulary*, ed. H. E.
Salter (O.H.S.), pp. 25–9. Concerning appeals from the Chancellor's Court see *Med. Arch.
Univ. Oxford*, ed. H. E. Salter
(O.H.S.), i. 189–91.]

§ 4. THE UNIVERSITY AND THE CHURCH

CHAP. XII,
§ 4.
Original
position of
bishop.

THE relation of the university as a body and of its individual members to the ecclesiastical authorities is, as we have seen, an entire blank up to the year 1214. The university was in a sense the child of ecclesiastical anarchy, and its subsequent history was not unworthy of such an origin. But the restoration of ecclesiastical order for a time placed the university entirely under the control of the Bishop of Lincoln. In the closeness of the relations between the university and the bishop, Oxford in its earliest days resembles rather some of the smaller universities of France, such as Orleans or Montpellier, than Paris, where a powerful chapter and a capitular chancellor stood between the bishop and the university. What differentiates the position of Oxford from that of Angers or Orleans is the distance of the episcopal city. The closest, indeed the only close, parallel to the Oxford constitution is found in the medical university of Montpellier, where alone we find an elective chancellor, who is at once the bishop's officer and the head of the university—where also the university was not actually in the bishop's see, though Maguelone is only a few miles from Montpellier, while Oxford is some 120 miles from Lincoln; and this latter circumstance is the determining factor in the process by which Oxford became emancipated from the jurisdiction, first of the bishop of the diocese, and eventually even of the Metropolitan and Primate of all England.

The chancellor the bishop's delegate.

In the period immediately after 1214 the bishop, besides exercising his ordinary jurisdiction over masters and scholars, claimed at times to regulate matters of purely academical concern. The chancellor was merely his officer, and enjoyed just so much authority as the bishop chose from time to time to delegate to him. His jurisdiction was merely concurrent with that of the bishop and archdeacon and their respective officials. Thus in the case of a serious crime we find Henry III refusing to allow the surrender of a batch of imprisoned clerks to the chancellor, and requiring it to be made to the bishop or his official.[1] So long as the see of Lincoln was filled by Robert Grosseteste—the most distinguished son that the infant university had yet produced—almost unbroken harmony prevailed between the university and the diocesan. The university was encouraged and protected by the bishop, who addressed to the masters truly paternal admonitions as to the method of their studies, which seem to have been received in the spirit in which they were given.[2] It was not till the accession of his successor, Henry of Lexington, in 1254, that the first disagreements broke out. It was possibly in consequence of this bishop's interferences with the liberties of the university that the masters in that year procured from Innocent IV the confirmation of their statutes. At the same time the bishops of London and Salisbury were appointed conservators of the 'rights, liberties, and immunities of the university'.[3] This provision did not, however (like the corresponding arrangement at Paris), materially affect the development of the university. The jurisdiction which at Paris was entrusted to the apostolic conservator was at Oxford exercised by the chancellor himself. It was only against the bishop of the diocese,

[1] Adam de Marisco, *Mon. Francisc.* (R.S.), i. 115. [Rashdall appears to have misunderstood the facts of this incident recorded by Adam Marsh. Wood has set them out correctly in *Annals*, i. 243–4. The number of clerks in prison was two. The King did not refuse to surrender them to the chancellor. 'Liberavit dominus rex', writes Adam Marsh, 'prefatos clericos duos incarceratos ad petitionem scholarium absolute.' But the King expressed his unwillingness to concede it as a precedent that clerks concerned 'in atrocibus criminibus' should be handed over to the chancellor rather than to the Bishop of Lincoln or his official.] The reason given is that the offences might be such as to require 'deposition' or 'degradation'. This power the chancellor appears never to have possessed, even in the height of his

importance. Yet after 1369 it would seem that no one else (except the Pope) could have legally passed such a sentence. The punishment was, however, one which (except in case of heresy) was almost as unknown to the ecclesiastical courts in the Middle Ages as it is unhappily at the present day.

[2] *Epistolae*, ed. H. R. Luard (R.S.), pp. 346–7. [With the assent of the university he instituted the S. Frideswide Chest, see *Stat. Antiq. Univ. Oxon.*, ed. S. Gibson, pp. xl, 74–6.]

[3] *Mun. Acad.* i. 27, 29. [*Cal. Papal Registers* (*Letters*), i. 306.] It is observable that the liberties of the university are recognized as in part resulting from the concession of the bishop. Cf. 'libertates et immunitates ab *Episcopis*, Regibus, Magnatibus et aliis Christi fidelibus rite concessas'.

CHAP. XII, who could not well be excommunicated by his own chancellor,
§ 4. that the university required external conservators, and it
would be difficult to produce an instance of the exercise of
these powers by the papal conservators. No regular Court of
Conservation ever sat at Oxford.[1]

Settlement   The dispute with Bishop Lexington went on till 1257,
of 1257. when a peace was arranged before the King in Parliament at
St. Albans.[2] What were the terms of the arrangement is not
known, but from an incident which occurred in the following
year it would appear that the bishop objected to all manifestations of autonomy on the part of the university. The real
question was whether the University of Oxford should be
governed by itself or by the bishop. It will be remembered
that it was but very recently that the university had begun
to reduce its unwritten customs to written statutes, and the
opposition which it encountered from Lexington was nearly
as decided as that which the masters of Paris experienced at
the hands of the chapter and chancellor at a precisely similar
stage in their constitutional development some forty years
before. The masters had passed a statute denouncing the
penalty of suspension from regency (which was to be inflicted
not by the chancellor but by the proctors) for non-attendance
at congregation. As the masters lectured by virtue of the
licence which the chancellor bestowed as the bishop's repre-

[1] There is, indeed, a letter in the University Letter-Book (F, f. 38; Twyne MS. vii, f. 91) [*Epist. Acad.*, ed. H. Anstey (O.H.S.), i. 126] calling upon the Bishop of London to act as 'nostre Universitatis conservator specialis' (? *c.* 1411). [A similar letter was addressed at the same time to the Bishop of Salisbury, 'nostro conservatori'. The date of these letters is 1435.]

[2] Matt. Paris, *Chron. Mai.* (R.S.), v. 618. It was on this occasion that the historian, pleading for the university with the King, used the celebrated expression about Oxford being 'the second school of the Church'—'Universitas enim Parisiensis, tot altrix et magistra sanc-

torum praelatorum, non mediocriter perturbatur; si similiter uno tempore perturbetur Oxoniensis universitas, cum sit scola secunda ecclesiae, immo ecclesiae fundamentum, timendum est vehementer, ne ecclesia tota ruinam patiatur'. [A deputation of about nine masters of arts waited on the King at St. Albans on 9 Mar. and were given an audience in the Abbey Church in the chapel of S. Oswin. The King gave them a day for stating their complaint before Parliament. The Parliament at which they appeared was held in London. Rashdall has confused the two occasions. See Matt. Paris, *Chron. Mai.* (R.S.), v. 618, 622.]

sentative, the bishop regarded the new statute as an infringe- ment of his prerogatives. The chancellor, though theoretically the bishop's officer, was already completely identified with the interests of the university, and had expressly assented to the statute. But the Archdeacon of Derby (perhaps as the Bishop's Official) entered a protest on behalf of the diocesan. It does not appear, however, that anything came of it beyond a formal acknowledgement on the part of the university that they did not intend by their statutes 'to prejudice the said bishop or his successors or the Church of Lincoln'.[1]

Originally, as has been said, the chancellor's right to demand the surrender of imprisoned scholars was shared with the archdeacon and the ordinary official of the bishop. The bishop was at any moment entitled to supersede the authority of the chancellor, and there was of course an appeal from him to the bishop. The later royal grants of privilege were, how-ever, made in favour of the Chancellor's Court only; and the chancellor thus obtained an exclusive right to demand the surrender of scholars in all cases to which his jurisdiction extended, i.e. all except homicide and mayhem or (later) felony. In those cases the surrender was presumably made to the bishop, but only after indictment at Assizes,[2] and the clerk was punished, or more often escaped punishment, in the same way as other clerks. The independent jurisdiction con-ferred upon the chancellor by successive extensions of royal privilege, combined with the unique character of the office, the vague and mysterious authority supposed to reside in the university, the facility with which in the Middle Ages the cus-tom of a decade or two was held to establish inalienable rights, combined to make the chancellor practically independent of the distant prelate from whom he derived his commission,[3]

The royal jurisdic-tion granted to chancellor only.

---

[1] *Mun. Acad.* i. 30. [*Stat. Antiq. Univ. Oxon.*, ed. S. Gibson, pp. 107–8.] *Ann. Monastici* (Burton), ed. H. R. Luard (R.S.), i. 436.

[2] See above, p. 104, n. 1.

[3] The favourite residence of the Bishops of Lincoln was at Bugden or Buckden in Huntingdonshire, some sixty miles from Oxford.

[The Bishops of Lincoln used also to reside at their manor of Fingest (or Tinghurst), Bucks., which is only about twenty miles from Oxford; see the itinerary of Bishop Grosseteste, *Rotuli Roberti Grosse-teste* (C.Y.S.), pp. x–xii, and that of Bishop Gravesend, *Rotuli Ricar-di Gravesend* (C.Y.S.), pp. 353–8.]

CHAP. XII,
§ 4.
even before he obtained canonical immunity from the great sanctioner of all successful ecclesiastical usurpation in the medieval world.

Growth of chancellor's powers under Bishop Gravesend and Archbishop Pecham.
In the episcopate of Lexington's successor, Richard of Gravesend (1258-79), we hear little of any conflict between the bishop and the university, and during the reign of this peaceable prelate it would seem that the university managed to effect considerable inroads on the episcopal prerogatives. In the last year of this episcopate (1279), Archbishop Pecham and his comprovincials assembled in council at Reading solemnly confirmed the privileges of the university and provided for the effective exercise of the chancellor's power of excommunication by enjoining that his sentences should be duly executed in any diocese to which the offender might have escaped and denouncing a penalty of three years' sequestration against beneficed disturbers of the university's peace.[1]

Privileges asserted against Bishop Sutton, 1280.
The next bishop, Oliver Sutton, from the moment of his accession became involved in a dispute with the university.[2] In the year 1280 we find Congregation solemnly swearing to maintain against the bishop the four following rights as based on custom 'from time out of mind': (1) that a scholar might cite a lay defendant before the chancellor;[3] (2) that the

[1] *Mun. Acad.* i. 39. [*Med. Arch. Univ. Oxford*, ed. H. E. Salter (O.H.S.), i. 35-6; Wilkins, *Concilia*, ii. 39.] The original with the seals of the archbishop and his comprovincials is in Archives, Pyx I (W.P.) 2 (but some of those mentioned in *Mun. Acad.* i. 41 are wanting and were never there). [The only seals still fairly complete are those of the Archbishop of Canterbury and the Bishop of Exeter. See the note on this document by Dr. H. E. Salter in *Med. Arch. Univ. Oxford* (O.H.S.), i. 36 n.] It should be added that the decree distinctly recognizes the university itself as sharing the chancellor's right of excommunication: 'sentenciis per Cancellarium Uniuersitatis uel iudices inferiores deputatos ab eo, uel per ipsum

Cancellarium una cum tota Uniuersitate, quandoque solorum regencium, quandoque regencium et non-regencium', &c.

[2] The excommunication (renewed by Dalderby in 1314) against those who make or introduce statutes or customs 'que magis proprie abusiones et abhominationes dicuntur' against the rights of his see, probably belongs to this period. Reg. Dalderby, f. 265 (Twyne MS. vii, f. 376 *b*).

[3] At this time the chancellor certainly possessed such jurisdiction by royal privilege in civil matters (see above, pp. 85, 90); it might be disputed how far it extended to spiritual cases. [To this right there is attached the qualification that the defendant should be found 'infra libertates antedicte uniuersitatis'.]

probate of scholars' wills belonged to the chancellor;[1] (3) that the right of 'inquisition' into the moral delinquencies of scholars belonged to the university; (4) that no master could be compelled to plead in any court but the chancellor's in respect of contracts entered into within the university or outside.[2] In the following year we find the chancellor, proctors, and other masters summoned to Buckden to answer before the bishop for their 'contempt' in resisting his visitatorial power, and a batch of other masters and scholars summoned to answer charges of incontinence which had been brought against them at the recent visitation. The chancellor and proctors pleaded that a general commission had been given to the chancellor by the bishop's predecessor,[3] and that by long custom the jurisdiction in such cases belonged to the bishop only 'in defect of the chancellor and university' or by way of appeal in the last resort, after appeal had been made in vain to the congregation of the university.[4] Of this appellate jurisdiction in spiritual cases claimed by the university I shall have something to say hereafter: at present it may be noted that, though apparently recognized by the bishops at Reading, it rested originally upon no legal or canonical basis whatever, and is one of the most astonishing instances in history of the success of barefaced assertion and bold usurpation. On the

[1] 'Et procuratores' is found in the proctors' book but is erased and then written over in the chancellor's book. If it is genuine, the usurpation is the more remarkable as the proctors had certainly never been entrusted with spiritual jurisdiction. [Mr. Strickland Gibson is of the opinion that 'et procuratores' was not in the original deed. It is an addition in Register D, the oldest of the proctors' books. See *Stat. Antiq. Univ. Oxon.*, p. 96. The probate of scholars' wills is limited to the wills of those scholars who died within the bounds of the university. See also L. H. D. Buxton and S. Gibson, *Oxford University Ceremonies*, p. 120, n. 5.]

[2] [*Stat. Antiq. Univ. Oxon.*, ed. S. Gibson, pp. lxxi, lxxx, 96–7.]

[3] [They plead that this jurisdiction had been granted to the chancellor 'ex generali commissione domini Lincolniensis episcopi cuilibet Cancellario Uniuersitatis tempore prefeccionis sue facta'. Rashdall's references to the bishop's predecessor is misleading. See *Med. Arch. Univ. Oxford*, ed. H. E. Salter (O.H.S.), i. 37.]

[4] The university alleged that 'correcciones huiusmodi nonnisi in defectum Cancellarii et Universitatis iuxta gradus et ordinem per uiam appellacionis in causarum cognicionibus obseruatum ad cognicionem episcopi pertinerent'. Original in Archives, I (W.P.) 5 (Twyne MS. i, ff. 65–6, xvii, f. 418). *Med. Arch. Univ. Oxford*, ed. H. E. Salter (O.H.S.), i. 37.

CHAP. XII, other hand, we may see in it a case of mistaken analogy;
§ 4. because the university had, as was natural, the right to hear
appeals from the chancellor in matters of its own internal
discipline, it was assumed that it could also claim such a right
in cases wherein the chancellor was exercising a jurisdiction
which came to him only by the special privilege of king or
bishop. The question was at length brought before a provincial synod or convocation, when the archbishop and his
colleagues warmly took the part of the university, and the
bishop was compelled to concede nearly all that the university wanted, with a barren protest that he did it as an act
of pure and voluntary grace.[1] From this time forward the
chancellor's jurisdiction was practically exclusive of the
bishop's in all ordinary cases. Of course, there remained
extraordinary exertions of the episcopal jurisdiction which
the chancellor did not claim, such as the power of interdict,
deprivation, or degradation. There remained also a doubt as
to the relations between the chancellor and the archdeacon
of Oxford, which culminated in a suit between the university
and Cardinal de Mota, Archdeacon of Oxford, in consequence
of the extortions and encroachments of the officials to whom
the absentee archdeacon had farmed out the archdeaconry.
It appears that the dispute related chiefly to (1) jurisdiction
over clergy beneficed or serving churches in Oxford, (2)
privileged persons other than scholars and the probate of
their wills. The controversy, which began before 1325, was
settled by consent in 1345, when it was decided that the
chancellor alone had archidiaconal jurisdiction over scholars
(except those serving Oxford cures) as well as over a limited
number of privileged tradesmen, except in respect of the
probate of wills of writers. Over scholars serving parochial

---

[1] A synodal constitution of the
bishop giving a general confirmation of privileges was made in Aug.
1280 (original lost); Twyne MS.
vii. f. 366. A 'Compositio' leaving
the visitation of masters and
scholars to the chancellor by
special favour is dated 18 May
1281, but it contains no mention
of appeal to the university (Original
in Archives, I (W.P.) 5). For the
text of this agreement see *Med.
Arch. Univ. Oxford*, ed. H. E.
Salter (O.H.S.), i. 37–9. The
Council of Bishops there referred
to will probably be the convocation
at Lambeth in 1280 (Wilkins, *Concilia*, ii. 42).

churches the archdeacon retained his jurisdiction in respect CHAP. XII,
§ 4. of the fabric, goods and services of the church, but without prejudice (apparently) to the chancellor's general power of correction.[1] But Sutton was the last bishop who seriously attempted to interfere with the ordinary course of appeal from the Chancellor's Court to the Regent Congregation and thence to the full Congregation of Regents and Non-regents.[2] There remained the right of appeal to the bishop, though even that would appear to have fallen into practical desuetude before it was formally abrogated. Formal assertions of the bishop's ancient rights continued to be made from time to time, but by the beginning of the fourteenth century the university had practically become the stronger power of the two.[3]

[1] *Mun. Acad.* i. 148–52. See also the documents (ed. Henson) in *Collectanea* (O.H.S.), i. 8–9, 16–27; Wilkins, *Concilia*, ii. 526–8; Rymer, *Foedera* (1707), iv. 189–91, 375, 385, 411–13; *Med. Arch. Univ. Oxford*, ed. H. E. Salter (O.H.S.), i. 114–16; [see also *Stat. Antiq. Univ. Oxon.*, ed. S. Gibson, p. lxxi].

[2] The bishop appended to his confirmation a protest against a number of usurpations on the part of the masters, especially their claim 'se non posse aliquo modo trahi coram episcopo extra municipium Oxonie si de ipsis querela deponeretur uel eciam ab ipsis appellaretur episcopus, quodque non posset admitti appellatio interposita ad episcopum a Cancellario nisi servaretur gradus appellando primo a Cancellario ad Universitatem regentium et secundo regentium et non-regentium'. Linc. Reg. (Sutton, f. 3); [*Snappe's Formulary*, ed. H. E. Salter (O.H.S.), p. 46]. The commission was granted 'donec aliud vobis super hoc dederimus in mandatis'. Again in 1291 the bishop raises technical objections before he would consent to confirm the chancellor 'de gracia speciali', and declares that the university 'reuerti

ad antiquam stulticiam suam' (Reg. ff. 50, 51); [*Snappe's Formulary*, pp. 47–8.] In 1297 he grumbles at the university speaking of their electing instead of nominating a chancellor (Reg. f. 178 b); [*Snappe's Formulary*, pp. 53–5.] In 1314 Bishop Dalderby drew up a letter against those who infringed the episcopal rights in the University of Oxford by their 'illicit confederacies and mutual conspiracies', 'sed non fuit ista littera executa' (Reg. f. 260). He renewed, however, Sutton's excommunication against those who made statutes to the prejudice of his see (Reg. f. 264 b), and fulminated 'contra usurpantes iurisdictionem in universitate Oxon. Cancellaria vacante' (Reg. f. 265 b). Bishop Beck in 1343 also objects to the term 'election', and confirms 'de gracia speciali' (Reg. f. 88 b). [On the subject of these disputes between the Bishops of Lincoln and the university see below, p. 123, n. 2. See also *Stat. Antiq. Univ. Oxon.*, ed. S. Gibson, p. xl, n. 2; and L. Toulmin Smith, 'Parliamentary Petitions relating to Oxford', in *Collectanea* (O.H.S.), iii. 129.]

[3] In 1284 it is still necessary for the archbishop to write to the

CHAP. XII,
§ 4.
Metro-
political
visitations.

In England the archiepiscopal jurisdiction was a very formidable reality. The archbishop claimed and exercised a general power of hearing in the first instance or calling up into his court cases from all parts of his province without waiting for the decision of the diocesan judge. Metropolitical visitations, during which the whole authority of the bishop was suspended, were not of an infrequent occurrence.[1] Two very important visitations of the university were held in the course of the thirteenth century, by Kilwardby in 1277, and by Pecham in 1284. Although the first-mentioned prelate was himself a Dominican who had graduated both at Paris and at Oxford, the main object of his visitation was to condemn a number of doctrines—grammatical, logical, philosophical, and theological—which had recently begun to be taught by the Oxford Dominicans and some of which claimed the authority of the great S. Thomas himself.[2] The condemnation was renewed at a similar metropolitical visitation by the Primate's Franciscan successor Pecham in 1284.[3] There are

Bishop of Lincoln on behalf of the university. (Wilkins, *Concilia*, ii. 111, 113.) Lastly, in 1322 Bishop Burghersh revokes his commission to the chancellor, John Lutterell. *Med. Arch. Univ. Oxford*, ed. H. E. Salter (O.H.S.), i. 105; cf. Rot. Claus. 16 Ed. II, m. 29). [*Cal. Close Rolls, Edward II, 1318–23*, p. 675. See also the article on John Lutterell by Dr. C. L. Kingsford in *D.N.B.*; *Hist. MSS. Comm. 4th Report*, pp. 379–91; *Snappe's Formulary*, ed. H. E. Salter (O.H.S.), p. 44; and *Cal. Chancery Warrants, 1244–1326*, p. 533.]

[1] [On the general subject of metropolitical visitations see I. J. Churchill, *Canterbury Administration*, i. 288–94].

[2] [Rashdall in the original edition of this work gives 1276 as the year in which Archbishop Kilwardby carried out his visitation, and Dr. T. F. Tout does the same in his article on Kilwardby in *D.N.B.* Both Rashdall and Dr. Tout appear

to have been misled either by Wood (*Annals*, i. 305–6) or by the marginal date given by the editor of the Oseney Chronicle in the Rolls Series (*Annales Monastici*, iv. 270). Kilwardby visited Oseney Abbey on Sunday, 7 Mar., and the university on 18 Mar. 127$\frac{6}{7}$. Rashdall gives the correct date in a later passage (see below, p. 251) where he records the contemporaneous proscription of Dominican errors by Stephen Tempier, Bishop of Paris, and by Archbishop Kilwardby in Mar. 1277.]

[3] The errors now condemned are printed in a black-letter pamphlet (without date or place-mark) entitled *Mag. Stephani formalitates in doctrinam Scoti*, and by d'Argentré, *Collectio Judiciorum*, i. 234; Wood, *Annals*, i. 306; Wilkins, *Concilia*, ii. 107 *sq.*; *Annales Monastici* (Oseney), ed. H. R. Luard (R.S.), iv. 297–9. Among the grammatical errors was the assertion that 'Ego currit' is good Latin.

also many instances of appeals to the Archbishop's Court, and CHAP. XII, §4. the archbishop systematically supported the authority and independence of the chancellorship against the Bishops of Lincoln. It was largely, no doubt, through the archbishop's interference that Sutton was compelled to yield to the claims of the university.[1]

After the episcopate of Sutton, the disputes between the bishop and the university related mainly to the formalities to be observed on the presentation of a new chancellor to the bishop.[2] Already in Sutton's time the question had been raised whether the chancellor-elect was bound to appear in person to seek for confirmation. In 1288 the dispute led to a long cessation.[3] In 1290 the King compelled the newly elected chancellor to appear in person, but the bishop agreed that in future confirmation might be sued for by proxy if the bishop were not within a reasonable distance of Oxford.[4] Under Sutton's successor the question was raised in 1300 at the

Disputes as to chancellor's confirmation.

This doctrine was of course a logical theory about the copula, not a piece of mere grammatical ignorance, as is supposed by Wood and others. [See *Reg. Joh. de Pontissara, Ep. Wynton.* (C.Y.S.), i. lxxiii–lxxv, 301–8. See also J. L. Peckham, *Archbishop Peckham as a Religious Educator* (Yale Studies in Religion, No. 7), p. 44.]

[1] *Mun. Acad.* i. 39. [*Med. Arch. Univ. Oxford,* ed. H. E. Salter (O.H.S.), i. 38.]

[2] [On this subject reference should be made to the records of the confirmation of chancellors by the Bishops of Lincoln in *Snappe's Formulary* (O.H.S.), pp. 46–89, and to the prefatory article by Dr. H. E. Salter (*ibid.,* pp. 40–5), and also to the note by Mr. Strickland Gibson in *E.H.R.,* 1911, vol. xxvi. 501–12. See also *Cal. Papal Registers* (*Letters*), iv. 66, 83.]

[3] *Annales Monastici* (Oseney), ed. H. R. Luard (R.S.), iv. 316–18; Capgrave, *Chron. of England,* ed. F. C. Hingeston (R.S.), p. 168.

[It seems that it is Rashdall who is guilty of confusion here. The dispute with Bishop Sutton was consequent upon the election of William de Kingscote to the chancellorship 'apparently in the beginning of 1289'. See *Snappe's Formulary,* ed. H. E. Salter (O.H.S.), pp. 323–4. It appears that studies were resumed in the university when the bishop consented to admit Kingscote to hold office for one year pending a decision of the question by the King.]

[4] *Annales Monastici* (Oseney), iv. 324; *Rot. Parl.* i. 16, where the bishop pleads 'quod Commissio illa est de pura et libera voluntate sua'. Sir H. C. Maxwell-Lyte (*Hist. of Univ. of Oxford,* p. 127) appears to confound the settlement by the King of the dispute which arose in 1288 with the parliamentary settlement of 1290. Cf. also Reg. Sutton, f. 117 (Twyne MS. xii, f. 7). [*Snappe's Formulary,* ed. H. E. Salter (O.H.S.), pp. 46–7.]

CHAP. XII, confirmation of James de Cobham. Bishop Dalderby asked
§ 4. the university's proctor why the chancellor-elect did not
appear in person, and objected to the terms of the university's
letter, which described the choice of a chancellor as an 'election', whereas the bishop held it to be 'nomination'. The
bishop, however, eventually granted the commission 'of
special favour', without insisting on Cobham's personal
appearance, on the ground that the chancellor was a relation
of the Archbishop of Canterbury.[1]

Confirmation by the archbishop.
The controversy smouldered till the year 1350, when
Bishop Gynwell vexatiously delayed the chancellor's confirmation. The university appealed to Archbishop Islip, who,
upon the bishop's refusing to obey his monition to proceed
with it, himself issued a commission for the confirmation.
An appeal to the Pope followed, which ended in a decision
recognizing the bishop's right to confirm in the first instance,
but establishing the archbishop's right to do so in default of
the Bishop of Lincoln.[2] By this decision the confirmation
was obviously reduced to a mere formality, and eventually
seems to have disappeared in practice even before it was
dispensed with by papal authority in 1367.[3] The university

[1] Reg. Dalderby, f. 5 b, 6 (Twyne
MS. ii. 4; xii. 13). [*Snappe's Formulary*, ed. H. E. Salter (O.H.S.),
pp. 55-7.]

[2] In the course of this dispute
the archbishop laid Banbury, where
the bishop was then residing (including his own chapel), under an
interdict: whereupon the latter
claimed a papal exemption from
all obedience to the see of Canterbury. This privilege, alleged to
have been granted by Clement VI
(Wilkins, *Concilia*, ii. 751) through
inadvertence, was revoked by Innocent VI in 1353 (Wilkins, iii. 29).
The other documents are printed
in *Mun. Acad.* i. 168, and more
fully by Wilkins, *Concilia*, iii. 3-9:
also Lambeth Reg. Islip, ff. 20 a,
27 a-28 b, 35 a; Linc. Reg. Gynwell, f. 21. [See also *Snappe's
Formulary*, ed. H. E. Salter

(O.H.S.), pp. 44-5.] The archbishop claimed that the confirmation had 'devolved' 'ad audientiam
suam propter negligentiam dicti
domini Episcopi', the bishop replying that it was 'extra casum et
causas appellacionis et negligentie
cuiuscumque', and the further
citation of the bishop was 'tam
directe quam tutorie'.

[3] Wilkins, *Concilia*, iii. 75. Yet
in 1369 Bishop Buckingham directs
the Archdeacon of Oxford's Official
to cite Adam Tonesworth for acting
without confirmation (Reg. f. 70),
but this is the last trace of the
confirmation being insisted on
which I have found in the Lincoln
Registers. [See *Snappe's Formulary*, ed. H. E. Salter (O.H.S.),
pp. 45, 86-9.] The Bull of Urban V
in 1367 dispensing with confirmation does not appear to have been

had thrown off the episcopal yoke. A good illustration of the chap. xii, independence which it now asserted occurs as early as 1322, §4. when it arrogated to itself the right of deposing a chancellor by its own authority.[1]

It was during this period of academical liberty that Wyclif- Liberty ism grew up, and it can hardly be doubted that the Wyclifite Wyclifism movement was powerfully aided by the practical exemption at Oxford. of the university from direct episcopal control.[2] We are not concerned here with the history of Wyclifism as a religious movement; but it falls strictly within the limits of our subject to notice the extent to which the alienation of the university from the dominant ecclesiastical system was at this time carried, and the boldness with which the university as a corporation ventured on resistance to ecclesiastical authority. In 1377 Wyclif's doctrines had been condemned by the Pope, in 1382 by the so-called Earthquake Council, and by the archbishop and his assessors—bishops, doctors of law, and friar-theologians—at the Blackfriars' Chapter-house in London.[3] Among the doctrines condemned on the last occasion it is sufficient to notice the explicit denial of transubstantiation

inserted in the Lincoln Register till the time of Bishop Repingdon (f. 15).

[1] *Mun. Acad.* i. 108. [*Stat. Antiq. Univ. Oxon.*, ed. S. Gibson, p. 123.] We have seen that the bishop had begun to complain of the exercise of spiritual power during a vacancy in the chancellorship, which suggests that the custom was already establishing itself by which the senior D.D. acted as *cancellarius natus* during a vacancy. [*Cal. Pat. Rolls, Richard II, 1381–5*, p. 153; Wilkins, *Concilia*, iii. 166; Rymer, *Foedera*, ed. 1816, iv. 150; *Med. Arch. Univ. Oxford*, ed. H. E. Salter (O.H.S.), i. 216–18, dated 13 July 1382.]

[2] The proceedings against Wyclif in his lifetime were taken under special apostolic authority. By Rot. Pat. 6 Ric. II, pt. i, m. 32

(Twyne MS. vii. f. 43) [*Cal. Pat. Rolls, Richard II, 1381–5*, p. 153], the chancellor and proctors are appointed 'ad inquisitionem generalem' (sc. 'heretice pravitatis') 'assistentibus vobis omnibus Theologis universitatis predicte regentibus'; but, as will be seen, they did not take kindly to the office. [On the procedure for the deposition of a chancellor who proved 'intolerabilis' see *Stat. Univ. Oxon.*, ed. S. Gibson, p. lxxiii. For the *cancellarius natus* in the fifteenth century see *Reg. Cancell. Oxon.*, ed. H. E. Salter (O.H.S.), i. xlii–xliv.]

[3] See the documents in J. Lewis, *Life of Wiclif*, ed. 1830, p. 356 *sq.*; Walsingham, *Hist. Angl.*, ed. H. T. Riley (R.S.), ii. 57–9; *Fasciculi Zizaniorum*, ed. W. W. Shirley (R.S.), pp. 105 *sq.*, 275 *sq.* [See also H. B. Workman, *John Wyclif*, ii. 253–73.]

and of the medieval doctrine of the Sacrifice of the Mass, the very foundations of the wealth and power of the medieval priesthood, and perhaps the still more alarming assertion that the State might lawfully take away their property from 'habitually delinquent' clergy. There was no period in the history of the University of Paris at which such a manifesto would have attracted the smallest sympathy. At Oxford the utmost efforts of Pope and archbishop could not prevent an open resistance on the part of a considerable and respectable body of attached adherents.[1] It was apparently in the summer of 1381 that Wyclif's anti-sacramental theses were publicly maintained; yet on Ascension Day, 1382, his former disciple, Nicholas Hereford, made a violent attack on the Mendicants in a sermon preached in the churchyard of S. Frideswide's before the university, boldly asserted his sympathy with Wyclif, and in his Bidding Prayer omitted the name of the Pope. It was known that Hereford's sermon and his open defence of Wyclif on other occasions had given offence in high places; yet its author was allowed without opposition to proceed as a doctor of divinity, and on Corpus Christi of the same year was again appointed to preach before the university by the chancellor, Robert Rugge.[2] Before the festival arrived, a mandate from the Archbishop of Canterbury was served upon that official, directing him to publish the condemnation of Wyclif's theses in the usual way by sending the bedel of theology round the university schools. The chancellor, alleging (it is difficult to say on what grounds) the exemption of the

---

[1] It was with good reason that Walsingham exclaimed when the university hesitated to enforce the Pope's Bull against Wyclif in 1377 (Wilkins, *Concilia*, iii. 116), 'Oxoniense studium generale ! quam gravi lapsu a sapientiae et scientiae culmine decidisti! quod quondam inextricabilia atque dubia toti mundo declarare consuesti, iam ignorantiae nubilo obfuscatum dubitare non vereris, quae quemlibet e laicis Christianis dubitare non decet'. Walsingham, *Hist. Angl.* (R.S.), i. 345. [See H. B.

Workman, *John Wyclif*, ii. 252–3, 276–7.]

[2] [Rashdall has here confused Nicholas Hereford with Philip Repingdon. It was Repingdon who preached before the university on Corpus Christi Day. He proceeded subsequently to the degree of D.D. As regards his doctorate see H. B. Workman, *John Wyclif*, ii. 274 n. Hereford had proceeded to the doctorate before he preached his Ascension Day sermon; see *ibid.* ii. 133.]

university from metropolitan jurisdiction, flatly refused to CHAP. XII, comply with the injunction.   At Corpus Christi the long- § 4. expected sermon was delivered, and the preacher boldly defended the orthodoxy of Wyclif's doctrine of the Eucharist (about the nature of which there could in Oxford be not the smallest doubt) as the true doctrine of the Universal Church. As the chancellor retired in state from S. Frides-wide's, followed by the whole concourse of doctors and masters, he made a point of waiting for the preacher at the church door, and walked home with him 'laughing and great joy came upon the Lollards at such a sermon'.[1]

The chancellor was subsequently forced to beg pardon of The chan- the archbishop on his knees.[2] It is pleasant to notice that he cellor's apology. received it on the intercession of the wisest and most moder-ate leader of the prelatic party, the aged statesman William of Wykeham. At the same time the chancellor professed that he dared not, for terror of his life, publish the condemnation of Wyclif in Oxford. 'Then is Oxford' exclaimed Courtenay, himself once Chancellor of Oxford, 'the University of heresies, if she will not allow orthodox truths to be published.' And the archbishop spoke no more than the truth.[3]

It was not till a full generation after Wyclif's death that the subjugation of the university to the ecclesiastical yoke was really effected, or that Wyclifism, notwithstanding the recan-tation of its most promising leaders, ceased to command

---

[1] Walsingham, *Hist. Angl.* (R.S.), ii. 189–91; *Fasc. Zizan.* (R.S.), pp. 295–301. [See also H. B. Work-man, *John Wyclif*, ii. 273–5.] The first sermon is preserved in Bodley MS. No. 240. Cf. T. Arnold in *Academy*, No. 526, p. 397. In 1398 the archbishop attempted to visit Gloucester College, not (as Sir H. Maxwell-Lyte assumes, p. 291) the university. [This visitation took place in 1389 and not in 1398. Archbishop Courtenay visited Ose-ney Abbey on 13 Nov., S. Frides-wide's Priory on 14 Nov., and Merton College on 15 Nov. 'Visi-tauit Collegium aule Merton in

uniuersitate Oxoniensi ac nonnulla inibi coram eo comperta debite reformauit', see Reg. Courtenay, f. 143 v. See also *Visitations of Religious Houses in the Diocese of Lincoln*, ed. A. Hamilton Thomp-son (C.Y.S.), i. xxix–xxx. For the resistance to visitation offered by the Benedictines in Oxford see Walsingham, *Hist. Angl.*, ed. H. T. Riley (R.S.), ii. 190–2; *Historia Regni et Vitae Ricardi II*, ed. T. Hearne, 1729, pp. 115–17.]

[2] *Fasc. Zizan.* (R.S.), p. 308. [See H. B. Workman, *John Wyclif*, ii. 278–82.]

[3] *Fasc. Zizan.*, p. 311.

CHAP. XII, a large amount of scarcely veiled sympathy in Oxford. Arch-
§ 4.   bishop Courtenay, indeed, who imagined that he had succeeded in completely purging the university of heresy, even
aided it in procuring its culminating privilege. In 1395
Bull of Boniface IX[1] granted a Bull exempting the university from
Exemp- the jurisdiction of all archbishops, even *legati nati*, bishops,
tion, 1395. and ordinaries. Even exempt persons, such as the Mendicants and monks of exempt monasteries, and exempt cases,
such as assaults on clerks, which continually sent the clerks
of Paris to seek absolution from special papal delegates, were
now expressly placed under the jurisdiction of that most
anomalous of dignitaries, the Chancellor of Oxford. It is not
surprising to learn that the conservative instincts of the
faculty of law, as well as the ultramontane sympathies of the
regulars, had led them to oppose the university's petition for
the Bull.[2] A possibility of appealing to the Holy See no doubt
theoretically remained; but attempts at such appeal were
stopped by royal authority.[3]

Wyclifism.   As a matter of fact, however, the university had no sooner
entered upon its greatest theoretical independence than the
period of its greatest practical enslavement began. In another
chapter we shall have to observe how the practical freedom

---

[1] Wood clearly shows (*Annals*, i. 365) that the Bull must have been granted by Boniface IX (though at times he appears unconvinced by his own reasoning): in spite of which Mr. Anstey (*Mun. Acad.* i. 78) ascribes it to Boniface VIII and the year 1300. [See *Cal. Papal Registers* (*Letters*), vi. 304.] The provision as to assaults on clerks may be an illustration of the Roman policy of granting privileges to authorize acts which they could not prevent. Assaults on clerks were by canon law *casus papales*; yet it appears that Bishop Dalderby had authorized the chancellor to absolve in such cases for assaults committed in Oxford: assailants of clerks in the suburbs were to go for absolution to the sacrist of Oseney.

Linc. Reg. Dalderby, f. 391 *b* (Twyne MS. ii, f. 15). There is no trace of any papal authorization.

[2] Cotton MS. Faustina C. vii, f. 164. [Dr. H. E. Salter has edited this manuscript in *Snappe's Formulary* (O.H.S.), pp. 90–193. For the text of the Bull see *ibid.*, pp. 144–6. See also H. B. Workman, *John Wyclif*, ii. 342, n. 7. As regards Archbishop Courtenay's attitude towards the procuring of this Bull, see *Snappe's Formulary* (O.H.S.), p. 152. It appears that Courtenay had first been adverse, but had later acquiesced.]

[3] [See *Med. Arch. Univ. Oxford*, ed. H. E. Salter (O.H.S.), i. 349–50, 189–92; and *Cal. Fine Rolls, 1369–77*, pp. 173–4.]

of which Oxford had enjoyed so large a measure—freedom CHAP. XII,
§ 4.
from papal legates and heresy-hunting bishops and Dominican inquisitors—culminated in a great outburst of free religious thought, of thought free and also fruitful, of religious
activity founded upon and springing out of free speculation.
The university had, as it were, burst the ecclesiastical shell
within which the germinal principle of the institution had long
been confined. The ecclesiastical world felt that this spoiled
and now rebellious daughter of the Church must be put back
into the leading-strings to which her elder sister, the University of Paris, had long grown accustomed. I shall have
hereafter to dwell more at length upon the higher aspects of
this crisis in the history of Oxford. At present we must
confine ourselves to its relation to the privileges of the
university. Throughout the struggle the dominant party
among the seculars was for Wyclif; but the hand of the
university was forced by the bishops and the King. The zeal
of the English Court and prelates against the heresy was
greater than their respect for the letter of the papal privilege.
The Bull of Exemption had been procured (as we have seen)
by the aid of Courtenay, the ex-Chancellor of Oxford. A
year later he was succeeded by Arundel, a much more
vigorous opponent of Lollardism than his predecessor. At
the Convocation of 1397,[1] there appeared two bodies of
petitioners from the University of Oxford—one from the Privileges
faculty of law to urge certain grievances against the other renounced
in Convo-
faculties, and another from the orthodox minority of the cation of
1397.
university to complain of the continued teaching of Wyclifism in its schools. The proctor for the university also appeared and put in a copy of the papal Bull[2] in bar of the

[1] Wilkins, *Concilia*, iii. 227 *sq.*
[The Bull is also printed in
Snappe's Formulary, ed. H. E.
Salter (O.H.S.), pp. 146–51]. Even
before the death of Courtenay, in
Nov. 1395, the university had been
compelled to submit absolutely to
the King. Rot. Claus. 19 Ric. II,
m. 20 *dorso* (Twyne MS. vii,
f. 67). [*Cal. Close Rolls, Richard II,
1392–6*, p. 482.]

[2] 'Quandam scedulam privatam
in manibus suis tenens, nullatenus
bulla apostolica, sigillove autentico,
aut cuiuscunque notarii publici
signo, subscriptioneve munitam.'
It is afterwards alleged that certain
masters and bachelors of arts 'quod-
dam absurdum exemptionis privilegium, nomine totius dicte Universitatis . . . a Romana curia iam
tarde subdole impetrarunt'. The

CHAP. XII, archbishop's jurisdiction. In spite of the Bull, however, the
§ 4.   archbishop, pretending to doubt its authenticity, announced
that he would, after the convocation, take measures for the
redress of the alleged grievances, and compelled the proctor
to renounce the privilege there and then in his presence. It
is remarkable how light orthodox ecclesiastics will make of
ecclesiastical authority when the supposed interests of orthodoxy are at stake.

Measures   Very shortly afterwards the archbishop procured a royal
against
Lollard- writ peremptorily requiring the university to renounce its
ism.   'unwonted and unheard of exemption', and another declaring
the right of visitation to belong solely to the Archbishop of
Canterbury.[1] A political impeachment for the present put a
check upon the archbishop's proceedings, and the Oxford
masters were left undisturbed for some years. At length in
1408 a synod was held in Oxford, and in the ensuing Convocation of Canterbury a number of constitutions were issued
against the teaching of Wyclifism in the schools or elsewhere,[2]
and directing a monthly inquisition into the orthodoxy of
the scholars in each college or hall by the head or principal.
These constitutions for the first time introduced a censorship

archbishop is styled (in the official
record of the Convocation) 'dicte
Universitatis ordinarius superior
immediatus'. [Rashdall's account
of these proceedings is confused.
The chancellor's commissary, Dr.
Nicholas Faux, put in a copy of the
papal Bull. The archbishop did
not compel him to renounce the
privilege there and then. The
privilege was renounced voluntarily
by Dr. Michael Cergeaux, proctor
for the faculty of laws. In protest
the chancellor, Dr. Thomas Hende-
man, left the assembly 'cum verbis
contumeliosis'. See *Snappe's Formulary*, ed. H. E. Salter (O.H.S.),
pp. 148, 151, and H. B. Workman,
John Wyclif, ii. 343.]
   [1] [Rashdall began this paragraph
with the statement: 'The University was not likely to consider
itself bound by a renunciation made

behind its back by a proctor not
specially commissioned for the
purpose.' In view of Rashdall's
misunderstanding with regard to
the action of the proctor concerned,
this sentence has been deleted.]
Rot. Pat. 20 Ric. II, pt. 3, mm.
32, 9 (Hare, *Mem.*, f. 93 b). [*Cal.
Pat. Rolls, Richard II, 1396–9*,
pp. 109, 143; *Snappe's Formulary*,
ed. H. E. Salter (O.H.S.), pp. 99,
153–5; H. B. Workman, *John
Wyclif*, ii. 345.]
   [2] Wilkins, *Concilia*, iii. 314–19.
[The correct date of the meeting
of the Southern Convocation in
Oxford is 27 Nov. 1407, and not
1408, as Rashdall gives it. 'The
Synod' and 'the ensuing Convocation' referred to by Rashdall are
identical. See Dr. Workman's note
on the Constitutions of Oxford, *John
Wyclif*, ii. 417–19 (Appendix V).]

of the press, or rather of the pen, into the university. No CHAP. XII,
book written in the time of John Wyclif was to be lectured   § 4.
upon till it had been licensed both by the university or its
delegates and by the archbishop, and the stationers were
forbidden to copy and sell books not so licensed. On this
occasion no open resistance was offered by the university,
though it is likely enough that the constitution remained very
much of a dead letter.¹ In 1409, however, the Convocation of
Canterbury called upon the university itself to condemn
the heresies of Wyclif. But when the proposal to appoint
delegates for the purpose came before the Great Congregation, it was rejected by a majority of the faculties.

Even after the twelve delegates were appointed (not before Opposition of university.
1410), John Birch submitted a resolution to a Great Congre-
gation rescinding the appointment and suspending all further
proceedings against the heretics. As proctor the same John
Birch declared the motion carried. The chancellor hastily
dissolved the congregation; and was afterwards forced into
resignation. But the proctors called a Congregation of Regents
at which they appointed a number of 'sufficiently suspected'
persons as the judges of heresy. Eventually even this 'suspected' board were compelled to condemn the incriminated
articles or some of them; and the 267 propositions were
duly burnt at Carfax.²

It is evident, however, that a majority of the university

¹ It appears that the constitutions in Wilkins, *Concilia*, iii. 314,
were published both at Oxford and
in the Convocation at S. Paul's: the
exact date seems to be uncertain.
[On these events see H. B. Workman, *John Wyclif*, ii. 355–9.]

² The chief authority for these
transactions is Cotton MS. Faustina, C. vii. f. 135 (described by
Wood as a fragment of a Register:
if so, it must be largely interspersed
with Lollard comments) and the record of the archbishop's visitation
in the Oriel Coll. Treasury. [The
contents of this manuscript, and the
records of the inquisition held at
Oriel in 1411 have been edited by

Dr. H. E. Salter with full introductory notes; see *Snappe's Formulary*
(O.H.S.), pp. 90–215.] See also
Wilkins, *Concilia*, iii. 322–30; Reg.
Arundel, pt. ii, ff. 126, 127 (Twyne
MS. xxiv, f. 122). [No evidence has
been found to support Rashdall's
statement as to the burning of the
267 propositions. There is reason
to believe that a list of 61 errors of
Wyclif was condemned by a vote
in Congregation on 26 June 1410,
and that this was followed by the
burning of 14 of Wyclif's works at
Carfax. See *Snappe's Formulary*,
ed. H. E. Salter (O.H.S.), p. 100;
H. B. Workman, *John Wyclif*, ii.
366.] It is impossible to pretend

CHAP. XII,
§ 4.
Arch-
bishop
Arundel's
attempted
visitation,
1411.

really sympathized with Lollardism, or at least cared more for their academical privileges than for the suppression of heresy; and in 1411 the archbishop, in spite of the papal exemption, cited the university to appear before him as visitor in S. Mary's.[1] This brought matters to a head. The chancellor, Richard Courtenay, and the proctors, Benedict Brent and

to chronological exactness in reproducing the events of this troubled year. Wilkins (*Concilia*, iii. 339) places the actual condemnation of the articles in 1412. At the Convocation which began 2 Dec. 1411, there are still complaints of the rampant heresy of Oxford and the imprisonment of those who appealed to the Holy See, which makes it probable that the condemnation had not already taken place. [For the chronology of these events see *Snappe's Formulary*, ed. H. E. Salter (O.H.S.), pp. 98, 115, and H. B. Workman, *John Wyclif*, ii. 366–73. The correct date of the condemnation of the articles is 1410 and not 1412.] A passage in the report of the Convocation of Dec. 1411 bearing on the celebrated testimonial alleged to have been given by the university in this year in favour of Wyclif, and produced in defence of Hus at Prague, seems to have escaped observation: 'Quasdam etiam literas falsitatis, testimonium perhibentes in defensionem brigarum, haeresium, et errorum, sigillo communi universitatis, inconsultis magistris et doctoribus, clam sigillant, ad regna et loca extranea transmittunt' (Wilkins, *Concilia*, iii. 336). [This testimonial was dated 6 Oct. 1406. The passage cited by Rashdall from the report of Convocation had previously been noticed by Sir H. C. Maxwell-Lyte (*Hist. Univ. Oxford*, p. 279).] The persons referred to are the 'gerentes officia' of the university: this seems to make it certain that the testimonial was actually sealed with the real university seal by the university officials whether regularly or irregularly. As it was customary for the regents to grant themselves a general leave to have what testimonials they required passed under the university seal (Register Aa, *passim*), the testimonial was even less than most testimonials an indication of the deliberate opinion of the testimonialists. [On the university's testimonial to Wyclif see H. B. Workman, *John Wyclif*, ii. 347–55; and A. B. Emden, *An Oxford Hall in Medieval Times*, pp. 138–43.]

[1] [There are some points in Rashdall's account of Archbishop Arundel's visitation that need correction. As Dr. H. E. Salter has pointed out (*Snappe's Formulary*, O.H.S., p. 114), the resistance offered to the archbishop does not necessarily signify that the sympathy of the majority of the university was with Lollards, but that the whole thing turned on the Bull of Pope Boniface. The statement that the scholars appeared in the streets with bows and arrows is derived, as Dr. Salter explains, from 'some flowery words in one of the King's letters' (*ibid.*, p. 109), and need not be taken too literally. S. Mary's Church, and not the whole town, was laid under an interdict (*ibid.*, p. 200). The archbishop had left Oxford before John Birch, the proctor, celebrated High Mass in S. Mary's notwithstanding the interdict. Rashdall is misled by Wood into stating that the university decreed a cessation; see *Annals*, i. 548. The university did

CHAP. XII,
§ 4.
Gallant
resistance
of proc-
tors.

John Birch (their names deserve to be recorded) positively refused to allow the archbishop to enter Oxford as visitor; S. Mary's was fortified against him. The scholars appeared in the streets armed with bows and arrows, and showed themselves quite prepared to use them against the primate and his retinue should the attempt be persisted in. When the town was laid under an interdict, John Birch broke open the doors of S. Mary's and said Mass as usual.[1] Eventually the archbishop judged it prudent to beat a retreat, after arriving at an understanding that the matter should be referred to the King. To the King accordingly the archbishop wrote to explain 'with what insolency he had been received by a company of boys'. The King's wrath fell heavily on the masters. The chancellor and proctors were sent for to London and required to resign their offices into the King's hands. The university decreed a cessation, and an animated correspondence flowed between the King and the university. When required to elect a new chancellor and proctors, the masters had the spirit to re-elect the old ones; and, by the mediation of Henry, Prince of Wales, these champions of privilege were at last allowed to retain their offices.[2] Meanwhile measures were taken to deprive the university of what had hitherto been their

no more than state that it would be obliged to do so, if its privilege of exemption was violated; see *Snappe's Formulary*, ed. H. E. Salter (O.H.S.), pp. 158–60.]

[1] Lambeth Reg. Arundel, f. 91*b*; Capgrave, *Chron. of England*, ed. F. C. Hingeston (R.S.), p. 299. It is charged against two Fellows of Oriel that they 'fuerunt consentientes . . . castellationi ecclesie beate Virginis contra suum pastorem Archiepiscopum visitantem et stante interdicto', &c., Oriel Register. [*Snappe's Formulary*, ed. H. E. Salter (O.H.S.), p. 200.]

[2] Cotton MS. Faustina, C. vii, f. 137 *sq.* (Twyne MS. ii, f. 205 *sq.*) [*Mun. Acad.* i. 251; *Stat. Antiq. Univ. Oxon.*, ed. S. Gibson, p. 210.] Cf. also Wood, *Fasti*, p. 39.

The statement in Wood that the young men who had resisted the archbishop 'were as truants corrected by the rod and ferula' (followed by Maxwell-Lyte, *Hist. Univ. Oxford*, pp. 294–5) appears to be founded upon a misunderstanding of the King's letter. The university had pleaded that the disturbers of the peace 'subduntur virgis et ferulis', i.e. were mere boys; whereupon the King recommends that 'trutannos tales quoscumque virgis acrioribus et ferulis subdendos esse'; but it does not appear that the suggestion was or was meant to be literally complied with. [See *Snappe's Formulary*, ed. H. E. Salter (O.H.S.), pp. 103–4.] Cf. *Correspondence of Bekynton*, ed. G. Williams (R.S.), i. 278.

unquestionable plea of legality. The Bull of Boniface IX was revoked by John XXIII, in November, 1411;[1] in the same month the university submitted itself unreservedly to the archbishop,[2] and in the Parliament held at the close of the year the archbishop's right of visitation was solemnly asserted.[3] The constitutional struggle had been, it should be added, merely the formal side of a contest the real object of which was the suppression of Lollardy—in other words, the suppression of free speech and thought—in the schools and pulpits of Oxford. The issue of the struggle practically closes the history of Lollardism as a recognized force in English politics, and with it the intellectual history of medieval Oxford.

Mixed motives of opposition.   We must not, indeed, suppose that all the scholars or all the masters who took part in the resistance to the archbishop were moved by pure zeal either for freedom of speculation or for evangelical truth. On the side of Wyclif were enlisted not only the religious zeal of the Lollard, but the local patriotism of the North-countryman, the chronic antipathy of the secular scholar to the friars, the antipathy of the realist to the nominalist, the antipathy of the artist to the higher faculties, and also the academic pride of loyal Oxonians. Attachment to corporate privilege and tradition amounted in the Middle Ages to a passion which can hardly be understood in modern times, except, indeed, from the experience of life in an English public school. And, if any reliance whatever is to be placed upon the statements contained in the record of the archbishop's visitation at Oriel, a good deal of pure ruffianism must have been called in to the support of what might possibly be called the Protestant party. Three Fellows of Oriel who were accused of being aiders and abettors of John Birch (himself an Oriel man) are further charged with habitual

Lawless Fellows of Oriel.

---

[1] [For the text of the Bull of John XXIII see *Snappe's Formulary*, ed. H. E. Salter (O.H.S.), pp. 176–9. See also *Cal. Papal Registers (Letters)*, vi. 302–4. In *Snappe's Formulary* (pp. 94, 176, 179) Pope John XXII has been printed in error for Pope John XXIII.]

[2] Reg. Arundel, pt. 2, f. 90 *sq.* (Twyne MS. vii, f. 59; xxiv, f. 121).

[3] *Rot. Parl.* iii. 651; J. Griffiths, *Enactments in Parliament*, p. 1 *sq.*

night-walking (*noctivagio*), spending their days and nights in CHAP. XII,
taverns, breaking into college at unreasonable hours, intro- §4.
ducing armed men within its walls, knocking up the provost
at 10 p.m., calling him a liar and challenging him to fight,[1]
and finally with taking part in a great onslaught upon the
chancellor's house on the vigil of S. Peter, in which a scholar
of law was killed. On another occasion also one of the accused
Fellows had collected an 'army of night-walkers' and headed a
riot in which many were slain.

The reader must judge for himself as to the exact amount State of
of credence to be attached to such accusations. It is certain versity in
that charges of personal immorality are generally forthcoming 1411.
when orthodoxy demands that the character of a heretic shall
be blackened. On the other hand it is equally clear that
during some months of the year 1411 Oxford was a scene of
the wildest disorder; and clerks of the character indicated by
these accusations were no doubt to be found among the
archbishop's assailants. From the record in the Oriel Treasury
we gather that the visitation was eventually carried out by
the archbishop's commissary. Some at least of the colleges
were visited individually. Obstinate Lollards were deprived
of their fellowships;[2] the rest were compelled individually to
abjure the condemned propositions.

So utterly crushed was the spirit of the once proud univer- The uni-
sity that in 1414 it seems tamely to have submitted to a crushed.
visitation *quoad haereticam pravitatem* by its diocesan, Bishop by Bishop
Repingdon, though the papal Bull established the au- Reping-
thority of the archbishop only.[3] The ardent spirits among the

---

[1] 'Vocando ipsum falsum dicen-
do quod mentiebatur in caput eius,
indicans eum ut surgeret et exiret
ad pugnandum secum.' (Document
at Oriel.) I have combined in the
above paragraph charges some of
which were only made against one
or two of the Fellows. [For the
text of this document see *Snappe's
Formulary*, ed. H. E. Salter
(O.H.S.), pp. 196–215.]

[2] [No evidence has been found
for this statement.]

[3] Linc. Reg. Repingdon, f. 136
(Twyne MS. ii, f. 13 *sq.*). It is not
certain that the visitation was
actually held, but the university
submitted so far as to dispatch to
the bishop a list of resident graduates. Besides the chancellor and
proctors, there were nine doctors of
theology (only three seculars), one
of decrees, four D.C.L.s, one
M.D., ten B.D.s, twelve regent
M.A.s, eighteen non-regents, four
bachelors of law. The numbers

CHAP. XII, masters were either intimidated or bribed into submission,
§ 4. though an undercurrent of Lollardism may have flowed on
to the very eve of the Reformation. So submissive had the
The Ex- university become to ecclesiastical tutelage that in 1479 she
emption
restored, was allowed to obtain a Bull from Sixtus IV, legally restoring
1479. her proud exemption from all English ecclesiastical authority.[1]

In 1490 the office of chancellor received its last accession
of dignity, the privilege of licensing (with the theological
faculty) preachers to preach in every diocese in England—
a privilege which, though obsolete, the university still retains
—and that of conferring minor orders.[2]

Anomalous   Anomalous as was the spiritual jurisdiction wielded by the
appeal to
Congre- chancellor, still more extraordinary was the appellate tribunal
gation. of the university. The system of appeal from the Rector's
Court first to the faculty of arts and then to the whole university, which was in force in Paris, was copied at Oxford in
complete disregard of the entirely different origin and char-

testify to the depletion of the university, but it is likely that the list
is incomplete, since but six M.A.s
are mentioned as fellows of colleges:
there must certainly have been
more. Possibly the visitation took
place in vacation. [Rashdall is
among the writers who have mis-
interpreted this entry in Bishop
Repingdon's register. The number
of graduates named in the list to
which Rashdall refers only com-
prises those whom the chancellor
had personally cited, i.e. those
who attended the Congregation at
which the bishop's letter was read.
There is no evidence for any depletion of the university in consequence of the recent controversy.
It is open to question whether
Rashdall has not exaggerated the
effect of Archbishop Arundel's
victory in crushing the spirit of the
university. On this subject see
Snappe's Formulary, ed. H. E.
Salter (O.H.S.), pp. 114-15, 181-6.]
In 1458 the university refused to
accept the Bishop of Lincoln, who

had been appointed arbitrator by
the King, on the ground that to do
so would involve an infringement
of its liberties. Registrum Aa, f.
115 a (Twyne MS. vii, f. 130 b).
[Mun. Acad. ii. 754.]

[1] Printed by Wood, Annals, i.
632–5. It also gives the chancellor
the power of absolving for perjury,
which, however, he had probably
exercised without papal authorization. The university had before
this resumed its old independent
attitude. In 1461 it imprisoned
two bachelors of law for serving
an inhibition from the Arches
Court. Registrum Aaa, f. 183.
[Mun. Acad. ii. 683; Reg. Cancell.
Oxon., 1434–1469, ed. H. E. Salter
(O.H.S.), i. 38–9.]

[2] MS. Letter-book F, f. 164 b,
165 a; Wood, i. 648. [The documents here referred to are printed
in Epist. Acad. Oxon., ed. H.
Anstey (O.H.S.), ii. 564, 567. They
do not state that these privileges
were granted.]

acter of the two tribunals. The appeal was first from the
Hebdomadarius, i.e. the bachelor of law appointed every
week to hear minor cases[1] (if the hearing had been before
him), to the chancellor in person or his commissary, then to the
Congregation of Regents, finally to the Great Congregation.[2]
The appeals were heard then as in modern times by delegates
of the two assemblies; the necessity for the representation of
all faculties on the board of 'delegates of appeals in Convocation' marks the antiquity of an institution which has only just
disappeared from our midst.[3] A system of fines, increasing
with the wealth of the appellant and the number of courts
through which the appeal was carried, had to be devised to
check the tendency to a frivolous prolongation of litigation.
The appellate procedure was exactly the same in spiritual as
in criminal and civil causes. And thus it happened that the
decision of the most purely spiritual causes—subject indeed,
where the King thought fit to permit, to papal revision—in
the case of priests or even bishops who might be studying in
Oxford, belonged to a co-opting popular assembly, many of
whose members, though not in the medieval sense laymen,
were not in orders at all.[4] And this jurisdiction, though ultimately sanctioned by papal authority, was in the first instance
acquired simply by usurpation, based as we have seen on
nothing but a false analogy.

The mere accident that the chancellor's deputy has usually Surviving
anomalies.

[1] *Mun. Acad.* i. 73–6. [*Stat.
Antiq. Univ. Oxon.*, ed. S. Gibson,
pp. 91–4.] These appeals have just
been abolished [i.e. in 1894]. See
below, Appendix IX. [See also *Stat.
Antiq. Univ. Oxon.*, ed. S. Gibson.
p. lxxx.]
[2] *Mun. Acad.* i. 69 *sq.* [*Stat.
Antiq. Univ. Oxon.*, ed. S. Gibson,
pp. 89 *sqq.*] The system seems to
be sanctioned by John Romanus,
Archbishop of York in 1295, since
he directs the enforcement of sentences 'per Cancellarium Universitatis eiusdem, vel iudices inferiores
deputatos ab eo, vel per ipsum
cancellarium una cum tota uni-

versitate quandoque solorum regentium, quandoque regentium et
non regentium', Winchelsey Reg.,
f. 171 *b*. [Wilkins, *Concilia*, ii. 214.
See also *Reg. Joh. de Pontissara,
Ep. Wynton.* (C.Y.S.) i. lxxv–lxxvi.
205–6.] The mode of expression
seems to indicate that it was felt to
be necessary that even the sentences reversing his own judge-
ments should somehow emanate
from the chancellor's authority.
[3] [In 1894.] See Appendix IX.
[4] [It should be remembered in
this connexion that archdeacons
sometimes, and their officials often,
were only in minor orders.]

CHAP. XII, been in priest's orders disguises the singular fact that since
§ 4. the Reformation a spiritual jurisdiction as complete as that
exercised by their medieval predecessors has been vested in
the lay Chancellors of Oxford and Cambridge and in assemblies
of their lay graduates.¹ Up till a recent period the representative of the lay Chancellor of Cambridge was in the habit of
solemnly absolving from the guilt of perjury and restoring to
the sacraments of the church persons who had committed
unavoidable breaches of the statutes to which they had sworn
obedience.² There is a touch of historic irony in the fact that
the leader of a party whose members have gone to prison
rather than disuse a vestment in obedience to a lay tribunal
should have acknowledged the spiritual validity of the cen-
sures of a court which derived its authority from a lay
chancellor by citing his opponent before it on a charge of
heresy—an authority whose ultimate source must be supposed
to be either the Roman bishop or the English Sovereign.³

The chan-   An important change in the character of the chancellor's
cellorship
becomes office, which began in the fifteenth century, now demands
perma-
nent. a moment's attention. The election to the chancellorship was
originally biennial,⁴ and the chancellor was of course—as has
been implied throughout—the resident head of the university.
In the fourteenth century, however, re-election was not infrequent, and, in the one instance of a chancellor called directly
from the university to hold the Great Seal of England, he was
invited to retain his university office as a non-resident.⁵ In

¹ [On the office of the chancellor's commissary or vice-chancellor see *Stat. Antiq. Univ. Oxon.*,
ed. S. Gibson, p. lxxiv; and *Reg.
Cancell. Oxon., 1434–1469*, ed.
H. E. Salter (O.H.S.), i. xxxix–xlii.
The title vice-chancellor is used
from 1450 onwards.]

² The formula ran as follows:
'Authoritate nobis commissa' (? by
Pope Martin V, or by the Sovereign), 'nos absolvimus vos ab
omni levi negligentia, forisfac-
tione seu transgressione statutorum
privilegiorum et consuetudinum et
Deo et sacramentis ecclesiae vos

restituimus. In nomine Patris et
Filii et Spiritus Sancti. Amen.'
G. Peacock, *Observations on the
Statutes of the University of Cam-
bridge*, p. 17.

³ In the case of *Pusey and Others*
v. *Jowett*, 1863.

⁴ *Mun. Acad.* i. 107. [*Stat.
Antiq. Univ. Oxon.*, ed. S. Gibson,
pp. 122–3; and *Snappe's Formulary*, ed. H. E. Salter (O.H.S.), pp.
318–25. The office was made
biennial in 1322.]

⁵ Robert de Stratford, who became Bishop of Chichester and
Lord Chancellor in 1337. [See

the course of the fifteenth century the chancellors at both universities gradually became practically permanent and habitually non-resident.[1] In this way John Russell, Bishop of Lincoln (1484), succeeded as chancellor in getting into his hands that control over Oxford which his predecessors had struggled in vain to retain in right of their see. The change in the position of the chancellor was however no mere accident. In spite of formal papal exemptions, the universities were more and more passing under the control of a court at once more despotic and more ecclesiastically minded, and of a hierarchy more courtly than of old. It became a matter of importance to the university to have a protector at court and for the court to have a trusted agent for the coercion of the university. From this time the chancellorship—once the symbol and the organ of academic autonomy—became practically the instrument of its subjection to an autocratic court and an Erastian prelacy.[2] It may be added that at the present day the chancellorship has passed into a merely honorary office; but at Oxford the chancellor still appoints the vice-chancellor, though pledged by usage to appoint the heads of colleges in order of seniority.[3] The Duke of Wellington was the first chancellor who dispensed with the formality of asking confirmation of his nominee by Convocation. It is to be regretted that the university should so tamely have submitted to so gross an infraction of her ancient liberties.

Tame submission of the university.

Stat. Antiq. Univ. Oxon., ed. S. Gibson, p. lxxiii, note; Collectanea (O.H.S.), i. 33, 35; and Snappe's Formulary, ed. H. E. Salter (O.H.S.), pp. 326–32.]

[1] [For the fifteenth-century chancellors see Snappe's Formulary, ed. H. E. Salter (O.H.S.), pp. 332–5; and Reg. Cancell. Oxon., 1434–1469, ed. H. E. Salter (O.H.S.), i. xxxv–xxxix.]

[2] Yet as late as 1495 the university had the independence to elect Morton in preference to either of the two bishops suggested by the Crown. MS. Letter-book F, f. 176 sq. [Epist. Acad. Oxon., ed. H. Anstey (O.H.S.), ii. 618–20, 621–35.]

(The King's letter may have arrived too late, but the university had been ordered to await the royal pleasure.)

[3] A division was taken on the appointment of Dr. Symons, Warden of Wadham, in 1844. In 1845 a division was challenged, but the vice-chancellor took no notice of the opposition. The consent of Convocation is still asked for, but no 'placetne vobis' follows. The nineteenth century has thus revived the arbitrary practice introduced by the Earl of Leicester, chancellor in 1569. G. Cox, Recollections, pp. 339, 340, 351. [See also L. H. D. Buxton and S. Gibson, Oxford University Ceremonies, p. 137, n. 3.]

§ 5. THE STUDIES OF OXFORD

THE system of study and graduation pursued at Oxford is so largely formed on the Parisian model that it will be unnecessary to do more than notice the few points upon which they differ. We are unable at Oxford to trace the gradual growth or modification of the educational curriculum even with that approach to completeness which has been possible in the case of Paris. Most of what follows must be taken to represent the system in vogue in the fifteenth century. If the records of both universities had come down to us in greater fullness, some of the points of apparent difference, small as they are, would possibly disappear: as it is, our knowledge only becomes ample at a period when the intercourse between them was much less frequent and intimate than was the case in the thirteenth century. Still, where no difference is noticed, it may be taken that so far as our knowledge goes the system was alike in the two universities as regards their main outlines: details—the exact number of disputations required for a degree, the period at which they were performed, and so on —were of course frequently changed even in the same university. It would have been an almost hopeless task to give a perfectly accurate account of them as they existed at any given moment in the course of our period.

It is a striking illustration of the rapidity with which every development of the Parisian system reproduced itself in Oxford that a few years after the statute making the Lenten Determination compulsory at Paris we find a statute regulating Determination at Oxford, and treating the exercise as an habitual part of the arts student's course.[1] The same statute—belonging to the very year in which 'Responsions' are first mentioned at Paris[2]—assumes the existence
of a preliminary *Responsio de quaestione* in the preceding

---

[1] *Mun. Acad.* i. 34-6. [*Stat. Antiq. Univ. Oxon.*, ed. S. Gibson, pp. 25-7. The date of this statute is 1268.] This 'Ordinance' is made by the 'Masters and Bachelors'.

[2] [This can hardly be so: the Oxford statute is dated 1268, and the Paris regulations, as Rashdall himself states, came into force 'in 1275, if not earlier'. Cf. above. vol. i, p. 452.]

summer.[1] The nature of these exercises appears to have been CHAP. XII, § 5. precisely the same in the two universities.

In connexion, however, with the bachelor's degree, we Points of contrast. encounter the first of the points of contrast which we have to notice:

(1) We have seen that the Parisian chancellor had nothing Chancellor confers bachelor's degree. to do with determination or with the bachelor's degree. At Oxford the chancellor was the head of the university proper, as well as the bishop's delegate—in fact (for many purposes) the Parisian rector and the Parisian chancellor in one.[2] Accordingly, at Oxford, it was the chancellor who conferred the licence to 'lecture on any book of the Faculty of Arts', after which a student was in practice called bachelor, though he was not considered to have fully taken the degree till his determination in the following Lent.[3]

(2) The word 'Examination' had even at Paris a wider sense No literary examination for mastership. than it bears in modern times. It included any process of inquiry into the candidate's fitness, as well as a direct testing of his scholastic attainments. We have seen, however, that at Paris there was always an examination in the modern sense by the chancellor and the faculty or examiners selected therefrom. If in the superior faculties this examination was reduced to a mere formality, that was not the case in the faculty of arts, and in all cases there were real examinations at earlier stages of the candidate's career. At Oxford it is a curious fact that we have no express evidence of the existence of examination in the literary sense of the word. For the

---

[1] Afterwards, apparently, the time was extended to Christmas (or a fortnight after), as at Paris. *Mun. Acad.* i. 242 [*Stat. Antiq. Univ. Oxon.*, ed. S. Gibson, p. 200].

[2] A minor point of difference is that the proctors, here the executive of the whole university, took part in the graduation ceremonies of all faculties, their chief business being to administer the oaths.

[3] Sometimes, but not always, in the fifteenth-century register (Aa) he is admitted on condition of determining next Lent. At Cam-

bridge the vice-chancellor after the Determinations or 'Second Tripos' pronounced: 'Authoritate qua fungimur, decernimus, creamus, et pronunciamus omnes huius anni determinatores finaliter determinasse, et *actualiter esse in Artibus Baccalaureos.*' Gunning, *Ceremonies of the University of Cambridge*, Cambridge, 1828. [For a careful analysis of the Oxford regulations concerning Determination see *Stat. Antiq. Univ. Oxon.*, ed. S. Gibson, pp. lxxxviii–xcii.]

CHAP. XII, §5.

inception or licence the statutes are silent about the existence of any examination whatever. When a candidate presented himself before the chancellor for the licence in arts, he had to swear that he had read certain books, and nine regent masters (besides 'his own' master who presented him) were required to testify or 'depose' to their 'knowledge' of his sufficiency (*de scientia*), and five others to their 'belief' therein (*de credulitate*).[1] In the faculty of theology all the masters were required to depose *de scientia*, a single adverse vote being fatal to the degree.[2] Whether the masters had any other means of judging of the candidate's knowledge and capacity than had been afforded by his performances in the various disputations required for the degree,[3] cannot be pronounced with certainty.[4] In the superior faculties they undoubtedly had not. In the faculty of arts there seems an *a priori* improbability in supposing Oxford and Cambridge to have been in this particular totally unlike all other known universities. Yet it is practically certain that there can have been no regular board of examiners or temptators such as existed everywhere else, who formally examined the candidate in the subject-matter of his books. Had such examiners existed, we must have met

---

[1] *Mun. Acad.* ii. 424. [*Stat. Antiq. Univ. Oxon.*, ed. S. Gibson, pp. xciii–xcvi, 29, ll. 24–30, l. 5.]

[2] *Ibid.* ii. 379. [*Stat. Antiq. Univ. Oxon.*, ed. S. Gibson, pp. cx, 224–5.]

[3] At Cambridge we are told that 'All the Determiners do sit in the new Chapell within the Schools from one o'clock till five upon Munday, Tuesday, Wednesday, and Thursday in the week before Shrove Sunday, abiding the examination of so many Mrs. as will repair for that cause hither. And from three to four all they have a potation of Figgs, Resons, and Almonds, Bunns and Bear, at the charge of the said Determiners, . . . and upon Thursday they be only examined in song and writing' (Harl. MS. 7037, p. 103, quoted by Abdy Williams, *Hist. Account of*

Degrees in Music, p. 62)—a survival which may suggest the kind of informal examination which may have taken place in the Middle Ages.

[4] Every bachelor had to dispute a certain number of times with a master of arts at the Augustinian Convent, a disputation which, reduced to a formality, was kept up till within living memory [1895] under the name of 'doing Austins', *Mun. Acad.* i. 313. [*Stat. Antiq. Univ. Oxon.*, ed. S. Gibson, p. 247. For examples of the form taken by these disputations in the fifteenth century see *ibid.*, Appendix C.] For the superior faculties the candidate had to dispute with every master (*ibid.* ii. 396, 399, 407). [*Stat. Antiq. Univ. Oxon.*, ed. S. Gibson, pp. 42, 47, 49–50.] Cf. above, p. 71.

with some trace of their appointment in the statutes or registers: moreover, their existence would have made the interposition of the nine deposing masters (selected by the candidate) superfluous and unintelligible. We can only suppose that each master who was asked by the candidate to depose to his attainments was at liberty to subject him, whether in private or in conjunction with other deposing masters, to such examination in his books as he thought fit.[1] This supposition is borne out by the way in which the examination is spoken of in the solitary allusion to any such institution which has come down to us, though the latitude with which the term was used must not be forgotten. William Wheteley, the Stamford master, in his commentary on the pseudo-Boethian *De disciplina Scholarium* says that a candidate is to go from school to school 'before exposing himself to the examination of the masters by whose grace and favour he is to be crowned, that is, to incept and be licensed',[2] and to 'oppose' in each of them.

As to the admission of bachelors, four masters (as at Paris) were undoubtedly appointed to conduct the admission of bachelors to determination; but it is uncertain whether they supplemented their inquiries into a candidate's attendance at lectures and so on by questions on the subject-matter of the books taken up. There is no positive evidence that they did; on the other hand, it appears that, just as before the licence the 'deposition' of nine masters was necessary, so at determination nine (afterwards reduced to six) masters or bachelors who had already determined, had to depose to the sufficiency

Examination for B.A. doubtful.

[1] For a somewhat similar mode of examining for Oxford scholarships see C. Hole's *Life of the Ven. W. W. Phelps* (Reading, 1871), p. 51 *sq.*

[2] 'De scola unius magistri ad scolas alterius magistri, antequam incipiat vel se examinationi magistrorum exponat *quorum gratia et fauore ipse est coronandus*, i.e. quorum magistrorum gratia ipse incepturus et licentiandus', Exeter Coll. MS. No. 28. It further appears

that 'magistri examinantes scolares qui debent licentiari in artibus debent eos examinare in moribus sicut in scientiis', which shows that the examination was not *purely* literary, and suggests that the term *may* imply merely the conference among the masters in congregation as to whether his grace should pass (see above, i. 465 *sq.*), but the view I have taken seems to me most probable.

CHAP. XII,
§ 5.

of the candidate's attainments.[1] The existence of this 'deposition' may by itself perhaps be held to supply a presumption that there was no literary examination by the admitting masters. On the other hand, due weight must be allowed to the intrinsic improbability of the total absence in 'the second School of the Church' of examinations such as certainly existed everywhere outside England.

Determining for others.

(3) We get at Oxford a distinction between determining 'for oneself' and determining 'for others', which demands a brief explanation. Previous writers have seen in the latter phrase a permission to perform the exercise by deputy. But, though it is not easy precisely to explain the nature of the arrangement, it is abundantly clear that it was the pecuniary expense attendant upon graduation, and not the duty of disputation itself, that was vicariously discharged. This is placed beyond the reach of doubt by the University Register, from which it appears that the only candidates who determined for others were rich and well-born students. Had it been the intellectual part of the performance that was transferable, the poor would have been more likely to determine for the rich than vice versa. When a Neville, or an Audley, or a Courtenay determined, he was allowed to 'take under him' a certain number of poor bachelors, whose expenses he paid,[2]

[1] In 1268 it is simply 'Magistri vel Bachilarii' (*Mun. Acad.* i. 35); in 1409 six masters or three masters and three inceptors. [According to the Statute of 1268 the depositions at Determination had to be made before four regent masters nominated by the proctors in the congregation of regents to regulate the admission of properly qualified candidates. On this subject see *Stat. Antiq. Univ. Oxon.*, ed. S. Gibson, pp. xc, 25, 28, 203. The requirement as to six masters, or three masters and three inceptors in arts, only applied to those who wished to determine for others. See *ibid.*, pp. xci, 201.]

[2] 'Quod possit . . . pro aliis determinare ita quod possit accep-

tare sub se tot inceptores quot sibi placuerit, dummodo formam et cetera pertinentia ad gradum compleuerint.' Register Aa, f. 80 *b*. Cf. ff. 94 *a*. Again, 'accipere sub se certum numerum ipsorum qui tenentur ex statuto dare liberatam et conuiuare regentes'; *ibid.*, f. 103; [*Mun. Acad.* ii. 744–5]. Cf. *Reg. Univ. Oxford*, ed. C. W. Boase (O.H.S.), i. ix. The above explanation is confirmed by the position of the 'Sub-determiner' at Paris. [See also *Stat. Antiq. Univ. Oxon.*, ed. S. Gibson, p. xci. Sir Stanley Leathes has put forward another explanation for determination by proxy in his introduction to *Grace Book A* (Cambridge Antiquarian Society), p. xxiii. He notes

while the banquet which he gave on the occasion was no CHAP. XII,
doubt on a scale which was considered to do duty for the §5.
whole party.

(4) It is exceedingly important to notice that only the regent Inception
masters of the faculty had any share in advising the chancellor reserved to the
as to the fitness of a candidate for the licence.[1] Similarly, in faculties.
the actual admission to the mastership—the inception—none
but the regents of the faculty took part except the chancellor
and the proctors, who attended in the name of the university
to take the oath imposed by the university on inceptors in
all faculties.[2] But the actual ceremony of inception—the

that the statute required that those
determining for others should be
of higher standing than those who
determine for themselves, and
makes the suggestion 'that determining for others is the full bachelor's share of the disputation *in
quadragesima: determinatio pro se* is
the ordinary exercise of determination as observed by commencing
bachelors only. In the latter case
the questions to be solved are those
that the determiner has propounded
for himself; in the other case they
are propounded independently,
and the student is not forewarned
of the questions he will have to
determine'. In his review of *Grace
Book A* in *E.H.R.* xv (1900),
p. 578, Rashdall considered this
suggestion and stated that he felt
strongly inclined to adopt it, although 'the question is still not
free from difficulty'. The explana-
tions put forward by Rashdall and
Sir Stanley Leathes do not take
account of all the evidence available. The position of the sub-
determiner at Paris does not furnish the confirmation which Rashdall claims for it. See vol. i, p. 455.
At Paris the sub-determiner was a
poor student of good ability who
was allowed to relieve a wealthier
student of the necessity of determining throughout Lent, and to
have his fees for determination paid

for in return. Nothing is said in
the Oxford statutes about the
poverty of those who determined
for others, but it is required that
they should be able to find masters
who would state that they were
sufficiently well advanced in their
studies to have been ready to determine the previous year. It might
be inferred that they had not
determined earlier because they
had not means sufficient of their
own to meet the necessary fees, and
that, as at inception so too at determination, the wealthier men were
allowed to pay for the poorer so
that the arts course should not
be closed to the deserving for lack
of means. There is no reason to
suppose that the practice of Oxford
and Cambridge differed from that
of Paris in this matter.]
[1] Under certain circumstances
civilians might 'depose' for canonists and vice versa [and masters of
arts for the licence of a bachelor
of medicine]. *Mun. Acad.* ii. 425.
[*Stat. Antiq. Univ. Oxon.*, ed. S.
Gibson, pp. 30–1.]
[2] 'Item, cum in tractatibus fa-
ciendis super inceptoribus in theologia et baculariis pro legendis
sententiis licentiandis omnes et
singuli Magistri regentes in illa
facultate de usu more et consuetudine cum Cancellario et procuratoribus debeant si uoluerint inter-

CHAP. XII,   tradition of the book and the ring, and the imposition of the
§ 5.   *biretta* with the kiss of fellowship—was performed, as at Paris,
not by the chancellor, but by a regent of the faculty.[1]   Even as
late as the seventeenth century this ceremony was kept up at
the annual act.   The regius professors of theology, civil law,
and medicine conducted the inception in their respective
faculties: while in the faculty of arts it was performed by the
senior proctor, the ancient head and representative of that
faculty.[2]   At Cambridge some at least of the ancient ceremonial of creation was kept up till fifty or sixty years ago [as
reckoned in 1895].[3]

Modern   On no point is the modern constitution of Oxford so
consti-   misleading as in this matter of the 'conferment of degrees'.
tution
mislead- The formula still in use testifies to the fact that the ceremony
ing.   now commonly called taking a master's degree is in reality
the ancient ceremony of receiving the chancellor's licence to
incept; and the inceptor does not legally become a master or
take his seat in convocation till the beginning of the following
term.   But the 'Act'—that is, the ceremony of inception, at
Cambridge called 'the Commencement'—has disappeared
from the life, though not from the calendar, of our universities.   It is true that in this part of the university system, and
in this part only, has the now fictitious distinction between
regents and non-regents been preserved.   Only regents sit in
the 'Ancient House of Congregation', which for the purposes
of the conferment of degrees has survived the havoc which
the seventeenth century and the nineteenth between them

esse,' &c. *Collectanea* (O.H.S.),
ii. 240. Cf. *Mun. Acad.* i. 120, ii.
489. [*Stat. Antiq. Univ. Oxon.*, ed.
S. Gibson, pp. 63, 177.]
    [1] [See *Stat. Antiq. Univ. Oxon.*,
ed. S. Gibson, p. xcviii, note 4.]
    [2] *Laudian Statutes*, ed. J.Griffiths
with introduction by C. L. Shadwell, pp. 72–4; *Diary of John
Evelyn*, ed. Bray, i. 290.
    [3] [Rashdall printed in the original
edition of this work an Appendix
containing a description of the
Cambridge Commencement from

Henry Gunning's *Ceremonies of the
University of Cambridge*, London,
1828, pp. 120–5, as 'an illustration
of one of the last survivals in
Europe of the ancient *Inceptio* or
Principium'. As it is now nearly a
hundred years since Commencement ceased to be observed at
Cambridge, it has not been thought
necessary to reprint Gunning's
account. On the subject of Commencement see H. P. Stokes, *Ceremonies of the University of Cambridge*, 1927, pp. 36–7.]

have made in the ancient institutions of Oxford. In the requirement that nine regents shall be present in the House of Congregation for a degree to be conferred we have no doubt a survival of the ancient 'deposition' of nine masters in the faculty of arts. But the distinction of faculties has been lost; we have the anomaly of masters of arts voting on the conferment of superior degrees.. And this has tended to obscure the fact that the licence was originally conferred by the chancellor with the advice of the masters of the respective faculties, not by the university itself. A modern English Dictionary would probably define a university as a 'body empowered to grant degrees'. This was just what in medieval times the university, properly speaking, did not do. The licence came from the chancellor:[1] the inception or actual mastership from the faculty. Even when all inceptions at Oxford took place in a full Congregation of the university, the actual inception was still, as has been said, performed not by the chancellor, but by a master of the faculty.

So far there was no difference between medieval Paris and medieval Oxford, except that the proctors—the officers of the faculty of arts—figured in the inceptions even of the superior faculties in a way unknown at Paris. But there was one great point of difference which arose indeed out of the fundamental contrast between the two constitutions, but which proved in its ultimate results a matter of much more than technical importance. The greatest constitutional peculiarity of Oxford—more remarkable even than the position of the chancellor—is the almost entire absence of separate faculty organization. At Oxford we find, as we never find at Paris, the university itself settling every detail of the curriculum and internal discipline of all faculties. And the regulations which the university made the university alone could

The University legislates for the faculties,

---

[1] It is true that at Oxford, where the chancellor was so soon identified with the university and separated from the bishop, the distinction was early forgotten. The chancellor conferred degrees 'auctoritate mea et totius Universitatis' (*Mun. Acad.* ii. 383); [*Stat. Antiq. Univ. Oxon.*, ed. S. Gibson, p. 36.] Notice that at Oxford degrees were never conferred in the name of the Pope.

CHAP. XII, dispense.[1] Thus a candidate who had complied with every
§ 5. minute regulation prescribed for a degree by custom or
statute, had in the Middle Ages no need of the 'grace' of
congregation; but the moment a dispensation was needed,
and retains an application to the congregation of regents became neces-
power of
dispensa- sary. A grace originally meant in fact a dispensation. But
tion. even by the fifteenth century the neglect of the elaborate and
complicated regulations had become so habitual that a 'grace'
was necessary in the great majority of cases. It seems that
in this way a grace eventually came to be asked as a matter
of course, so that at last it was supposed that it was the
assembly of regents who really conferred the degree.[2]

Condi- There is an immense and arbitrary variety in the 'con-
tions of
'graces'. ditions' imposed upon the granting of these 'graces'. Sometimes the condition is the performance of some additional
exercise—a responsion, a disputation, a 'variation',[3] a sermon,

[1] The constitutional principle
would seem to have been that the
power of dispensation lay with the
regents, except where it was
specially reserved by statute to the
Great Convocation. In practice
most graces were granted by the
regents, but sometimes we find
precisely similar graces granted by
the Great Congregation. [It is
more in keeping with the available
evidence to assume that the constitutional principle was that the
power of dispensation lay with
the Great Congregation, i.e. with the
whole body of the university; but
that in practice the non-regents
were usually relieved from the
necessity of taking part in the
granting of graces 'propter fatiga-
ciones et uexaciones frequentes in
uocacione non regencium eui-
tandas'. See *Stat. Antiq. Univ.
Oxon.*, ed. S. Gibson, p. 18, ll. 19–
21; Sir C. E. Mallet, *Hist. Univ. of
Oxford*, i. 200, n. 5. On the whole
subject of graces and dispensations
see *Stat. Antiq. Univ. Oxon.*, ed.
S. Gibson, pp. cxviii–cxix.]

[2] This is beautifully illustrated

by the following inscription in a
book once belonging to the chancellor Thomas Gascoigne, and now
Magd. Coll., Oxford, MS. No.
103: 'Compleui formam meam complete in sacra theologia anno gratie
1434, ita quod nullam graciam
habui in uniuersitate de aliquo
actu, sed tantum de tempore, nam
respondi ix uicibus et nunquam
concursorie (i.e. always *ordinarie*),
et omnia alia feci debita ex statutis.'
See also as to the statutes of New
College, below, p. 221.

[3] 'Quod bis variet in Parviso.'
Dr. A. Clark (*Reg. Univ. Oxford*,
O.H.S., ii, pt. i. 21) explains 'in
Parviso' as equivalent to 'in par-
visiis', i.e. the *little things*, logic and
grammar. But we do not find the
plural in the fifteenth century, and
do find 'in Paraviso': cf. *Mun.
Acad.* i. 242. [*Stat. Antiq. Univ.
Oxon.*, ed. S. Gibson, p. 200.]
('Parvisum . . . frequentantes'.)
The word 'Parvis' appears to be a
corruption of 'Paradisus', and is
used of the Cloister of Notre Dame
at Paris, the Palace Yard at Westminster, &c. See Ducange, *sub*

a course of lectures, or two or more lectures in place of the
regent doctor.[1] In other cases (where the dispensation was
more extensive or the candidate worth bleeding), a contribution was imposed for the benefit of the 'New Schools', or the
repair of a window in the Convocation-house, or the pavement
of S. Mary's. At other times the condition is for the personal
benefit of the regents. The candidate is to feast all the regents
or the regents actually present[2] on the occasion, or to present
them with new gowns, or with knives, 'according to ancient
custom', or to pay the regent doctor for the lectures which
he has been dispensed from attending. Already in the middle
of the fifteenth century the number of these graces is so great
that it may almost be said that each case was considered on
its own merits. It was assumed that the full requirements of
the university could not be practically complied with.
When a candidate thought he had studied sufficiently to have
earned his degree, he presented his *supplicat*, stating the
number of terms which he had kept, the exercises he had
performed, and asking for the degree.[3] There was no doubt

voce 'Paradisus', and Somner, *Glossarium* ad Twysden *Decem Scriptores*, *s.v.* 'Triforium'. In Chaucer (*Prologue*, l. 312) we hear of a serjeant of the law 'that often hadde yben at the parvis', which Pulling (*Order of the Coif*, p. 3) understands of the Parvis of S. Paul's. [See *Oxford English Dictionary* under 'Parvis'.]

[1] 'Quod semel (*or* bis *or* ter) excuset doctorem.' This was only in the case of the higher faculties. The following facts are from the fifteenth-century register (Aa) in the Archives. [See *Mun. Acad.* ii. 730–4, 737–9, &c.]

[2] The same conditions are some-times imposed on persons seeking 'reconciliation' with the university, e.g. a payment 'pro vino et ostriis' (oysters) pro Magistris Regentibus'.

[3] A student's 'time' is often made up in a very curious way by count-ing a specified number of long vaca-tions 'and many short ones'. Terms

kept in one faculty are allowed to count towards graduation in another: an odd term or long vaca-tion is kept at Cambridge; terms passed in the country (with or without attendance at lecture) 'causa pestilencie' are counted; while the lectures given and exer-cises performed are enumerated as though no special number was prescribed by statute. On the other hand, the 'forma' of books to be heard is pretty strictly adhered to, except where a special dispen-sation is given from part of them, or where other books are allowed to be substituted for those pre-scribed by statute. Many 'graces' are granted as to the number of lectures which will constitute a 'term', sometimes for a whole batch of candidates, sometimes for individuals. As a rule sixteen 'ordinary' lectures counted as a term kept. At times we find very curious graces enabling candidates

CHAP. XII, a certain roughly defined understanding as to the conditions
§ 5.   which were dispensable and those which were not. The
candidates for B.A., for instance, were usually made to go
through the whole course of books, though the number of
terms was sometimes reduced. In the attainment of the M.A.
degree, on the other hand, there was more elasticity. In this
The grace way it would seem to have gradually come about that a 'grace'
becomes
necessary. became necessary in the case of all graduates, and was asked
for as a matter of course. The process was completed by the
Revival of Learning, which created a divorce between the
statutable requirements and the actual practice of the university. The old unrepealed statutes of the university still required so many ordinary lectures to be heard on Aristotle in
Schools Street; while the real educational work of the place
was done in hall or college lectures—still largely but no longer
exclusively upon Aristotle—which did not satisfy the statutable definition of 'ordinary lectures'. Another circumstance
which helped forward the tendency to substitute college for
university was the enormous number of 'non-legible' days
which the growing piety or gratitude of the university had
introduced into its calendar. A mere glance at the extant
calendar, wherein eleven days in the month of November are
holidays so far as the university is concerned, besides Sundays
and three days on which only cursory lectures might be given,
will make it clear that serious education would have been
impossible had not the college prelectors and tutors taken
upon themselves the burden which the university regent was
becoming more and more eager to shirk, and less and less
competent to perform.[1]

And here we may pause to notice how merely constitu-

---

to go to an extra lecture or course
of lectures 'pro ordinariis minus
attente auditis sed non completis
istius termini', or the like. Such
scrupulosity was due to the desire
to avoid perjury.

[1] *Mun. Acad.* i, p. cxlix. Besides
the legal holidays the regents were
constantly voting themselves 'a
day', i.e. of exemption from all

academical duties, or short vaca-
tions besides those prescribed by
the calendar, which were roughly
identical with the statutable vaca-
tions of modern times, except that
there was a short vacation at Whit-
suntide. [See also C. Wordsworth,
*The Ancient Kalendar of the Uni-
versity of Oxford* (O.H.S.), pp. 28,
35–8, 180–2.]

tional differences have modified the educational organization of different universities and the culture of different nations during whole generations of men. The practical extinction of all the higher faculties in the English universities is partly due no doubt to the absence of endowments for university teachers and to the presence of these endowments in the colleges, enabling them to monopolize that instruction which the universities themselves were unable to supply. Partly, too, it is accounted for, as regards the legal faculty, by the non-Roman and unscientific character of English law, and as regards medicine by the comparatively small size of the university towns. But the suppression of all effective instruction in the higher faculties was also promoted by the control which, here alone among the universities of the world, the regents in arts—that is to say, after the decay of university lectures, the youngest masters—had acquired over the degrees in the higher faculties. In other universities each faculty regulated the conferment of its own degrees. At Oxford and Cambridge an unlimited power of dispensation was vested in the regents of all faculties, the majority of whom of course were regents in arts. The extent to which this power was abused, even in the middle of the fifteenth century,[1] was already such as to prepare the way for the total suspension of the residence and study required by the statutes for these

[1] Thus we find the regents frequently dispensing themselves wholesale from a year's study in any faculty in which they should hereafter proceed, or even at times from the necessity of taking the bachelorship in civil or canon law (Reg. Aa, f. 79 *b*), or in any faculty but theology (*ibid.* 122 *b*) before the doctorate, or allowing one of their brother M.A.s to 'create' them (i.e. conduct their inception) as doctors of civil or canon law if no doctor were present (e.g. Aa, f. 81 *a*; Letter-book F, f. 64 *a*. [*Epist. Acad.*, ed. H. Anstey (O.H.S.), i. 218–19.]) Cf. the testimony of Gascoigne: 'Iam enim in Anglia periit cura animarum per ecclesias appropriatas, et per non residenciam curatorum . . . et per pessimam collacionem gradus scolastici et concessionem graciarum indignis et viciosis et insciis personis in Oxonia, et in aliis studiis, quae collacio mala graduum scolasticorum non erit destructa quousque potestas dispensandi cum bonis statutis retrahatur a regentibus et a procuratoribus Universitatis, qui pessima concedunt pro lucro proveniente eisdem per graduatos et graduandos per eosdem.' *Loci e libro Veritatum*, ed. J. E. Thorold Rogers, p. 3. Cf. p. 20.

CHAP. XII, degrees, while the professors lacked the power or the inclina-
§ 5. tion to convert the remaining 'exercises' into effective tests
of competence. The higher degrees continued to be taken
almost as much as formerly, especially degrees in theology.
In many cases college statutes bound the fellows by the most
solemn obligations to study and graduate in some superior
faculty, and the title of doctor has always been more or less
in request. But mere 'standing' was at last unblushingly
treated as equivalent to residence and study.[1]

Difference (5) When we come to compare the details of the require-
in curri-
culum. ments of the two universities for the various degrees, we shall
find that as a rule the books 'taken up', the exercises, and the
'time' required at Oxford correspond roughly with those of
Paris. The most noticeable differences are:

(*a*) At Oxford the enormous length of the course required
(from the fourteenth century onwards) at Paris for D.D. is
considerably reduced.

(*b*) We observe no such tendency at Oxford towards
shortening the arts course, at all events towards shortening
the time required for B.A. At Oxford the tendency was to
put the baccalaureate and determination late, and to reduce
the requirements for M.A. till at last—within the present
century—the last relics of residence and of 'exercises' after
B.A. have finally disappeared.[2]

(*c*) In the actual curriculum we shall find that there
was rather more elasticity than at Paris. The dominion
of Aristotle was somewhat less exclusive. Importance was
attached to keeping up the theory that a university arts course
included the *Trivium* and *Quadrivium* of the earlier Middle
Ages, as well as the 'three Philosophies' introduced by the
rediscovery of Aristotle in the thirteenth century. More
importance was attached to mathematics and astrology, and

---

[1] [Rashdall concluded this paragraph with the remark: 'and thus
at the present day the highest
degree which it is in the power of
the University of Oxford to bestow
has come to be the reward of eleven
years passed in forgetting the minimum of knowledge required in the
pass schools of the faculty of arts';
but this criticism of the doctorate
of divinity has lost its point since
the revision of the regulations for
the degree in 1924.]

[2] See G. Cox, *Recollections*, p. 60.

more alternatives were offered to the choice of the individual student. CHAP. XII, § 5.

The *chief* requirements for the various degrees may be thus briefly summarized:[1]

Requirements for degrees.

ARTS

For B.A. (*Admissio ad lecturam alicuius libri Facultatis Artium*):
Four years' study.

For Determination,[2]
(A) In 1268:
To have heard : (1) The Old Logic, i.e. Porphyry's *Isagoge*, the *Categoriae* and *De Interpretatione* of Aristotle, the *Sex Principia* of Gilbert de la Porrée, twice; and the Logical works of Boethius (except *Topics*, bk. iv), once. (2) In the New Logic, *Priora Analytica, Topica, Sophistici Elenchi,* twice; *Posteriora Analytica*, once:
With (1) Grammar, i.e. Priscian, *De constructionibus,* twice; Donatus, *Barbarismus,* once.
and (2) Natural Philosophy, i.e. Aristotle, *Physica, De Anima, De Generatione et Corruptione Animalium.*
To have responded *de Sophismatibus* for a year or have heard the *Posteriora Analytica* twice, instead of once.[3]
To have responded *de quaestione.*[4]
(B) (In 1409)[5]:
To have disputed for at least a year as a general sophister *in Parviso.*

[1] [In compiling these summaries of the chief requirements for the various degrees Rashdall has relied chiefly on the provisions embodied in university statutes. It should be borne in mind that the evidence on this subject to be derived from extant statutes is incomplete, particularly for the thirteenth century. Rather fuller summaries based on the evidence of the statutes will be found in *Stat. Antiq. Univ. Oxon.,* ed. S. Gibson, pp. xciii–cxviii. The extent to which valuable additional information concerning the curriculum may be derived from MS. copies of *quaestiones* disputed at Oxford is well illustrated, as regards the faculty of theology, by A. G. Little and F. Pelster, *Oxford Theology and Theologians, c. 1282–1302,* (O.H.S.), pp. 25–56.]

[2] *Mun. Acad.* i. 35, 36; [*Stat. Antiq. Univ. Oxon.,* ed. S. Gibson, pp. 25–7. See also *ibid.,* pp. lxxxviii–xciii].

[3] Determiners *pro aliis* who had not previously determined *pro se* were required further to have heard the *Magnum* of Priscian and three books of the *Meteorics* of Aristotle. [On the creation of general sophisters see *Stat. Antiq. Univ. Oxon.,* ed. S. Gibson, p. lxxxix, n. 4.]

[4] [See *Stat. Antiq. Univ. Oxon.,* ed. S. Gibson, p. xci, n. 8. The questionist represented a definite grade in the arts course; see *ibid.,* p. lxxxix, n. 7.]

[5] *Mun. Acad.* i. 241 *sq.*; [*Stat. Antiq. Univ. Oxon.,* ed. S. Gibson, pp. 199–201. See also L. J. Paetow, *The Arts Course at Medieval Universities,* Champain, Illinois, 1910, p. 9, n. 8].

To have heard: Donatus, *Barbarismus*; Porphyry, *Isagoge*; Gilbert de la Porrée, *Sex Principia*; Aristotle, *Sophistici Elenchi*; Arithmetic (*Algorismus integrorum*); the method of finding Easter (*Computus ecclesiasticus*); [Joannes de Sacro Bosco], *Tractatus de Sphaera—lectionatim* in College or Hall.[1]

The Old and New Logic, except the Boethius, *Topics*, bk. iv *cursorie* from bachelors in the public schools.

To have responded *de quaestione*.

For Licence and Inception:[2]

Three years' additional study.[3]

To have been admitted to determine (?).[4]

To have been admitted *ad lecturam alicuius libri Aristotelis*, and to have lectured thereon.[5]

To have responded *apud Augustinenses*, and taken part in a certain number of other disputations.[6]

To have heard, in addition to the books already read for B.A.:[7]

---

[1] 'Secundum sufficientem expositionem a magistro vel bachillario in collegio aut in aula se lectionatim integre audiuisse cum recitacione debite subsecuta, ita tamen quod in primo biennio, quo scholares fuerint facultatis arcium, huiusmodi audicionem lectionariam, ut praefertur, aggredi non praesumant,' *Mun. Acad.* i. 242; [*Stat. Antiq. Univ. Oxon.*, ed. S. Gibson, p. 200]. Determiners *pro aliis* were further required to have heard the Posterior Analytics in college or hall.

[2] [*Stat. Antiq. Univ. Oxon.*, ed. S. Gibson, pp. xciii–cii.]

[3] *Mun. Acad.* ii. 416; [*Stat. Antiq. Univ. Oxon.*, ed. S. Gibson, p. 34, ll. 20–7]. Those who have not determined were required to complete *eight* years.

[4] This I infer from the fact that *supplicats* for inception always mention determination; but the extant statutes do not actually require it, and it is clear that it was not necessary actually to determine. [On this point see *Stat. Antiq. Univ. Oxon.*, ed. S. Gibson, pp. xciii, 33, ll. 21–7, 34, ll. 26, 27; and Sir C. E. Mallet, *Hist. Univ. of Oxford*, i. 188, n. 4.]

[5] *Mun. Acad.* ii. 414; [*Stat.*

Antiq. Univ. Oxon., ed. S. Gibson, p. 34, ll. 14–19].

[6] For details see *Mun. Acad.* ii. 416; [*Stat. Antiq. Univ. Oxon.*, ed. S. Gibson, p. 32, l. 15. For examples of early disputations, contained in MS. Magd. Coll. 38, see *Stat. Antiq. Univ. Oxon.*, ed. S. Gibson, pp. 643–4; and the article 'The Order of Disputations', by Mr. Gibson in *Bodleian Quarterly Record*, vi (1930), 107–12. This manuscript also contains examples of the forms to be observed by an inceptor at vespers and at commencement. Mr. Gibson notes other manuscripts in which similar disputations are preserved.]

[7] *Mun. Acad.* i. 285 *sq.*; [*Stat. Antiq. Univ. Oxon.*, ed. S. Gibson, pp. 234–5. This list of books is contained in the 'Forma' prescribed by the Statute of Dec. 10, 1431. For early fourteenth-century notes as to the requirements for inception in arts, preserved in MS. Merton Coll. 261, see F. M. Powicke, *The Medieval Books of Merton College*, p. 34]. The statute-books contain two other 'Formae' (nearly identical) for inceptors (*Mun. Acad.* ii. 413–15) [*Stat. Antiq. Univ. Oxon.*, ed. S. Gibson, pp. 33, l. 28; 34, l.

IN THE SEVEN ARTS:

Grammar   Priscian 'in majore vel minore'. (One term.)[1]

Rhetoric   The *Rhetoric* of Aristotle. (Three terms.)
Or the *Topics* of Boethius, bk. iv.
Or Cicero, *Nova Rhetorica.*
Or Ovid's *Metamorphoses.*
Or 'Poetria Virgilii'.[2]

Logic   Aristotle, *De Interpretatione.* (Three terms.)
Or Boethius, *Topics* (first three Books).
Or Aristotle, *Prior Analytics,* or *Topics.*

Arithmetic Boethius. (One term.)

Music   Boethius. (One term.)

Geometry One book of Euclid, but ? six books.[3]
Or Alhaçen. (Two terms.)
Or Vitellio, *Perspectiva.*[4]

Astronomy *Theorica Planetarum.* (Two terms.)
Or Ptolemy, *Almagesta.*

IN THE THREE PHILOSOPHIES:

Natural Philosophy   Aristotle, *Physica* or *De caelo et mundo.*
(Three terms.)
Or *De proprietatibus elementorum,* or
Meteorica, or *De vegetabilibus et plantis,*
or *De Anima,* or *De Animalibus,* or
'any of the smaller books'.[5]

19; 32, l. 33; 33, l. 27], which contain fewer books than the above and assign shorter time for them (e.g. eight days for arithmetic), which seems to show that the 'term' assigned to a subject was practically a very short course of lectures. Another 'Forma' is printed in Appendix V.

[1] 'Per terminum anni', which Mr. Anstey is probably wrong in translating 'for one year', since in all other cases the time is given in *terms.*

[2] The last three alternatives are perhaps recent additions. If so, they supply an interesting illustration of the dawn in Oxford of the Latin (as distinct from the Greek) Renaissance. [See also L. J. Paetow, *The Arts Course at Medieval Universities,* pp. 61, 69–70.] In 1448 we find a bachelor characteristically supplicating that a lecture upon the 'Georgics' of Virgil

imposed upon him by the 'Magistri Determinatorum' should be commuted for a lecture on the 'De Anima' (Aa, f. 21 b). It is also interesting to note that in 1453 the regents debated 'an videatur expediens universitati ut conducantur v regentes an pauciores ad perficiendum lecturam scientiarum per necessarios regentes non lectarum' (Aa, f. 76 b), but this proposal to widen the university course by the foundation of professorships seems to have come to nothing.

[3] Six books are required according to 'Forma' contained in *Mun. Acad.* ii. 415; [*Stat. Antiq. Univ. Oxon.,* ed. S. Gibson, p. 33, l. 17; dated '? before 1350'].

[4] This reading is a correction in Register B (Sen. Proctor's book). [*Stat. Antiq. Univ. Oxon.,* ed. S. Gibson, p. 234, l. 30.]

[5] 'Aliquem de minutis libris', i.e. the Parisian 'Parva naturalia'.

Moral Philosophy   Aristotle, *Ethica*, or *Economica*, or *Politica*. (Three terms.)

Metaphysic Philosophy Aristotle, *Metaphysica*. (Two terms.)[1]

MEDICINE[2]

For M.B.[3]

For Licence and Inception:

For M.A. candidates, six years' study (in all).

To have lectured cursorily, for theory, on the *Liber Tegni* of Galen, or *Aphorismi* of Hippocrates, 'pro majori parte'.

To have lectured cursorily, for practice, on the *Regimenta Acutorum* of Hippocrates, or the *Liber Febrium* of Isaac, or the *Antidotarium* of Nicholas.

To have responded in the schools of the regents for two years.

For others, to have been admitted to practice, as above: eight years' study (in all): to have given the above lectures.

For admission 'ad practicandum' in Oxford:[4]

For M.A. candidates, four years' study.

To pass an examination conducted by the regent doctors.

For others, eight years' study and examination.

CIVIL LAW[5]

For B.C.L. (Licencia legendi aliquid cursorie in iure ciuili):[6]

For M.A. candidates, four years' study.

For others, six years' study.

For Licence ad Volumina (e.g. *the Digestum Novum* or *Infortiatum*).

To possess *libri apparitati* of the Civil Law [on which lectures must be given for one year from the feast of St. Denys (Oct. 9) to the feast of St. Peter ad Vincula (Aug. 1)].

---

[1] Three for candidates who had not determined. It is clear that the majority of M.A.s had determined, but the lists of determiners in Register Aa are somewhat shorter than those of 'Admissi *ad lecturam*, &c.', or B.A.s.

[2] *Mun. Acad.* ii. 406–9; [*Stat. Antiq. Univ. Oxon.*, ed. S. Gibson, pp. 16–20, 40–2, 177, and *ibid.*, ciii–cv. See below, additional note, p. 168.]

[3] Rarely one of the books mentioned below is substituted. No examination or practice was apparently required for an M.A. to become an M.D. Such was the belief in healing by Aristotle. By a statute of 9 Hen. V, cap. 11 (*Rot. Parl.* iv. 130), the council is empowered to make regulations for preventing non-graduates practising anywhere in England, but in the dearth of M.D.s in England any such regulations must have been quite futile.

[4] In Register Aa usually conferred with the M.B. [See *Stat. Antiq. Univ. Oxon.*, ed. S. Gibson, pp. civ–cv.]

[5] *Mun. Acad.* ii. 402–5; [*Stat. Antiq. Univ. Oxon.*, ed. S. Gibson, pp. 43–5, 177. See also *ibid.*, pp. cv–cvii].

[6] Occasionally the licence is to read some other book of the civil law.

For Inception as D.C.L.:

(No additional *time* specified.)

To have lectured on the *Libellus Institutionum*, the *Digestum Novum*, and the *Infortiatum*, [one year being devoted to each of the latter two subjects].

To have given an ordinary lecture for each regent doctor.

To have opposed and responded in the school of each Decretist.[1]

[To have lectured cursorily on one legal volume, the *Libellus Institutionum*, or the *Corpus authenticorum*, or the three extraordinary books of the *Codex*.]

CANON LAW[2]

For Bachelor of Decrees: (Admissio ad lecturam extraordinariam alicuius libri Decretalium):

Five years' study of civil law.

To have heard the Decretals twice, and the Decretum for two years.[3]

For Inception as Doctor of Decrees:

To have lectured *extraordinarie* on two or three 'causes' or the tractate *De symonia*, or *De consecracione*, or *De penitencia* (parts of the *Decretum*).

To have opposed and responded to the questions of every regent of the faculty.

To have given one lecture for each regent.

(After inception, two years, afterwards one year of necessary regency.)

[1] A statute found in the Proctors' Books (B and C), and in the chancellor's (A), and probably later than the above, requires the reading of 'unam collationem, vel unum librum de [tribus] libris extraordinariis codicis' (*Mun. Acad.* ii. 405 [*Stat. Antiq. Univ. Oxon.*, ed. S. Gibson, p. 45]), but whether in addition to or substitution for the above *volumina*, does not appear. [The statute here referred to is dated by Mr. Strickland Gibson 'before 1380', that summarized above 'before 1350'.]

[2] [See *Stat. Antiq. Univ. Oxon.*, ed. S. Gibson, pp. cvii–cix and index.]

[3] It is impossible to adjust this provision (*Mun. Acad.* ii. 398;

[*Stat. Antiq. Univ. Oxon.*, ed. S. Gibson, p. 46, ll. 2–3]) with the (? later) statute relating to inception which requires that inceptors in canon law who have not been regents in civil law, 'iura civilia ad minus per triennium, bibliam, quatenus legitur in studio, per biennium, decreta per triennium, ac decretales integraliter se jurent audisse', *Mun. Acad.* ii. 399; [*Stat. Antiq. Univ. Oxon.*, ed. S. Gibson, p. 47, ll. 17–20. Mr. Strickland Gibson dates both these provisions 'before 1350'. See also Wilkins, *Concilia*, iii. 228, 400]. There is no information as to the standing for the doctorate except what is contained in the passage cited above.

THEOLOGY[1]

For Opponency:[2]

For M.A. candidates, four or five years' study (i.e. apparently to be in the fifth year),[3] presumably divided between the Bible and Sentences,[4] since three years' auditio of the Bible are required for inception.

For others, eight years in the study of arts;[5] six or seven years in theology.[6]

[1] Mun. Acad. ii. 388–97. [Stat. Antiq. Univ. Oxon., ed. S. Gibson, pp. 178, 57, 48, 226, ll. 3–6, 49, 178–9, 50–1, 52, 267, 195, 268, 49–50, 52–3. See also ibid., pp. cix–cxiii. An admirable account of the exercises required of a theological student in Oxford is given by Dr. A. G. Little in his article 'The Franciscan School at Oxford in the 13th Century' in Archivum Francisc. Hist. xix (1926), pp. 825–30. Dr. Little and Dr. Pelster have provided valuable material for the study of the curriculum for graduation in theology at Oxford during the latter part of the thirteenth and the early part of the fourteenth century in Oxford Theology and Theologians, c. 1282–1302 (O.H.S.). See especially Dr. Pelster's section on the theological lecture and on the various disputations, ibid., pp. 25–56.]

[2] In the fifteenth-century register (Aa) there are two regular steps or degrees in theology for which 'supplicats' are presented —'Admissio ad opponendum et respondendum', and 'Admissio ad lecturam libri Sententiarum'. Only the latter seems to confer the style 'Baccalarius in Theologia', though this is not quite clear. A probably fourteenth-century statute (Mun. Acad. ii. 389; [Stat. Antiq. Univ. Oxon., ed. S. Gibson, p. 48, l. 13 sq. Mr. Strickland Gibson dates this statute 'before 1350']) requires the fifth year for 'opponency' and the seventh for 'respondency'. That being so, I cannot understand the provision 'quod quilibet ad lectu-

ram libri sententiarum de cetero licentiandus, in admissione sua iuret quod postea non opponet in theologia, publice et in scholis, in statu minore quam status Bacularii in eadem', Mun. Acad. ii. 390; cf. p. 394. [Stat. Antiq. Univ. Oxon., ed. S. Gibson, p. 178; cf. p. 52. The provision last referred to only applied to candidates coming to Oxford from other universities. See Stat. Antiq. Univ. Oxon., ed. S. Gibson, p. cix, n. 1.]

[3] [Stat. Antiq. Univ. Oxon., ed. S. Gibson, p. 48: 'ante quintum annum audicionis theologie opponere non presumant.']

[4] [During the first half of the thirteenth century the Historia Scholastica of Peter Comestor was studied as an alternative text-book. See Stat. Antiq. Univ. Oxon., ed. S. Gibson, p. 49, ll. 19–20, and A. G. Little and F. Pelster, Oxford Theology and Theologians, c. 1282–1302 (O.H.S.), pp. 25–6.]

[5] At least if the candidate wanted to proceed to B.D. From a university letter (Ep. 62. F, f. 23 a [Epist. Acad., ed. H. Anstey (O.H.S.), i. 77–8]) it appears that 'monachi artium scholares in nostra universitate' had to pay the collecta to the regents, but from the 'graces' it is clear that the regulars might keep their time in arts by study in the conventual schools, in Oxford if not elsewhere. [For concessions made to Benedictine students by the university see Stat. Antiq. Univ. Oxon., ed. S. Gibson, pp.

(For note 6 see opposite page.)

For B.D. (Admissio ad lecturam libri Sententiarum):
For M.A. candidates, two years more, i.e. seven years in all.
For others, two years more, i.e. eight years in all.
Certain opponencies, number not specified.[1]
For Licence [i.e. for the Doctorate].
Two years' further study.
To have lectured on one book of the Bible and on the Sentences.[2]
An examinatory sermon at S. Mary's.[3]
Eight responsions to non-graduate opponents.[4]
To dispute (as opponent) with every regent D.D.
Vespers.[5]

cxv–cxvi. A regular was only re- quired to spend one year studying theology at the schools in Oxford before his opponency. The rest of the period of study to be devoted to acts and theology could be spent elsewhere so long as his studies were under the direction of a master. See *Stat. Antiq. Univ. Oxon.*, ed. S. Gibson, p. 78, l. 29 *sq.*, and Dr. A. G. Little's article, 'The Franciscan School at Oxford in the 13th Century' in *Archivum Francis- canum Historicum* (1926), xix. 825.]

[6] [*Stat. Antiq. Univ. Oxon.*, ed. S. Gibson, p. 48: 'ante septimum annum opponere . . . aliqualiter non attemptent.']

[1] [At the close of the fifteenth century a candidate for the degree of B.D. does not appear to have been required to make more than one opponency or one responsion. See *Reg. Annalium Coll. Merton.*, ed. H. E. Salter (O.H.S.), pp. xxvi–xxvii.]

[2] In *Mun. Acad.* ii. 391; [*Stat. Antiq. Univ. Oxon.*, ed. S. Gibson, p. 50. See also *ibid.*, pp. cxii– cxiii]; lectures on both Bible and Sentences are required (cf. *Col- lectanea* (O.H.S.), ii. 218). Yet on p. 396 [*Stat. Antiq. Univ. Oxon.*, ed. S. Gibson, pp. 49–50] we find 'aliquem librum de canone bibliae *vel* sententiarum Oxoniae in scholis theologiae publice legant'. In Register Aa we find that a candi- date usually enumerates among his exercises 'introitus Biblie', as well

as 'lectura libri Sententiarum'. We may presume that the lecture on the Bible had now sunk for the majority of secular candidates to a formal introductory discourse upon a book which was never finished. The real lectures on the Bible which had still to be *heard* by every candidate were no doubt delivered (as at Paris) by regulars. [See also A. G. Little and F. Pelster, *Oxford Theology and Theologians, 1282– 1302* (O.H.S.), pp. 26, 34–42.]

[3] [See *Stat. Antiq. Univ. Oxon.*, ed. S. Gibson, p. cxi, n. 1; *Reg. Annalium Coll. Merton.*, ed. H. E. Salter (O.H.S.), p. xxviii; G. R. Owst, *Preaching in Medieval Eng- land*, pp. 259–62; A. G. Little and F. Pelster, *Oxford Theology and Theologians, 1282–1302* (O.H.S.), pp. 172–7.]

[4] [See *Stat. Antiq. Univ. Oxon.*, ed. S. Gibson, p. cx, n. 6. On the exercises of respondents see A. G. Little and F. Pelster, *Oxford Theology and Theologians, 1282– 1302* (O.H.S.), pp. 31–6. Re- sponding at vespers and at inception was included in the eight respon- sions, see *Stat. Antiq. Univ. Oxon.*, ed. S. Gibson, p. 179, ll. 15, 16.]

[5] [See Dr. A. G. Little's article, 'The Franciscan School at Oxford in the 13th Century' in *Archivum Franciscanum Historicum* (1926), xix. 828–9, and A. G. Little and F. Pelster, *Oxford Theology and Theologians, c. 1282–1302* (O.H.S.), pp. 42–52, 273–5.]

CHAP. XII,   In the fifteenth century an additional sermon was added by
§ 5.   statute.[1]

Degrees in   We have already noticed the comparative prominence of
music,
mathematics and the two sciences then most closely associated
with mathematics, i.e. music and astronomy or astrology.
In the fifteenth century we find actual degrees given in music.[2]
The candidate for the doctor's degree was required to compose a mass or a mass and a hymn (*cantilena*) to be performed
at S. Mary's at the annual act or general summer inception.
The bachelor's degree was taken by admission to 'read any
book of Music' or 'any book of the Music of Boethius'. This
graduation in music is a peculiarity of the English university
system which we have hitherto seen only in certain Spanish
universities. It is probably of late growth and little importance, except as an interesting indication of the growth of
Church music during the one period of its history at which
England took the lead in musical progress.[3] The title of
doctor carried with it no rights such as were enjoyed in the
case of other masters or doctors: the doctor of music was, it
would appear, academically on a level with the humble master
and in   of grammar—a title which, at this time, was also conferred
grammar.
Study of   after the manner of a 'degree'.[4] It does not appear that actual
astrology. degrees were given in astronomy, but we have frequent

[1] *Mun. Acad.* ii. 396; [*Stat.
Antiq. Univ. Oxon.*, ed. S. Gibson,
pp. cxi, n. 7, 268, ll. 1–9]; constantly
alluded to in Register Aa as the
'novum statutum'. A candidate
sometimes supplicates to be allowed
to preach in English at S. Peter's-
in-the-East, instead of in Latin at
S. Mary's. The afternoon sermons
in Lent were preached at S. Peter's
till 1828. See G. Cox, *Recollections*, p. 241 *sq*.
[2] Registers, *passim*. [See *Stat.
Antiq. Univ. Oxon.*, ed. S. Gibson,
pp. xciii, xciv, n. 2. The earliest
record of a degree in music at
Oxford that Mr. Strickland Gibson
has discovered is that of Richard
Ede in 1507.] At Cambridge
musical degrees occur as early as

1464. [See *Grace Book A*, ed.
S. M. Leathes, pp. xxvi, 41.] For
a full account of their history see
C. F. Abdy Williams, *A Short
Historical Account of the Degrees
in Music at Oxford and Cambridge*,
an interesting work which would
be the better for the omission of
the very uncritical chapter on 'The
Origin of Academical Degrees in
general'.
[3] Cf. C. F. A. Williams, *loc. cit.*,
p. 12.
[4] As to the degree in grammar see Clark, *Reg. Univ. Oxon.*
(O.H.S.), ii, pt. i, 8, 218, and
below, p. 599 *sq*. [See also *Stat.
Antiq. Univ. Oxon.*, ed. S. Gibson,
pp. lxxxv–lxxxviii.]

allusions to courses of astronomy apparently more extended CHAP. XII,
than what was included in the ordinary arts course,[1] and in § 5.
the sixteenth century there is an instance of a scholar admitted
'to practice in astronomy'.[2]

Another peculiar institution which we find introduced into
the university at the end of the fifteenth century is the practice of creating poets laureate by their actual investiture with Poets
a laurel crown.[3] In some cases the laureation seems to be Laureate.
combined with a degree in rhetoric.[4]

The Greek and Hebrew professorships ordered by the
Council of Vienne in 1311 were actually founded, or at

---

[1] e.g. 'quatuor anni in medicinis
et astronomia' (Aa, f. 121 b).
William Rede of Merton, bishop
of Chichester 1369–85, drew up
some astronomical tables. For
these and other fragments of Oxford astronomy cf. Twyne MS.
ii, f. 92 sq. [See F. M. Powicke,
The Medieval Books of Merton
College, pp. 162, 167. Bishop
Rede was only part author of the
volume of astronomical calculations to which Rashdall refers. See
also P. Duhem, Le Système du
monde, 1916, iv. 70–4; and R. T.
Gunther, Early Science in Oxford,
ii. 42–67, 337–70, the chapter on
'The Merton School of Astronomy',
descriptions of the Oriel College
Astrolabe, c. 1340, and those of
Merton College, c. 1350 and c.
1390, ibid. ii. 206–13, and the text
of the treatises of Richard of
Wallingford on the Rectangulus,
1326, and the Albion, 1326–7. As
a result mainly of the work of
fellows of Merton the Alfonsine
tables were recast for the latitude
of Oxford and furnished the means
for making calendars constructed
for the meridian of Oxford. To
William Merle, fellow of Merton,
belongs the credit of having led the
way in the keeping of scientific
records of the weather. See ibid.
ii. 315–17. See below, p. 267.]

[2] Early in the sixteenth century

we find a general grace for regents
in arts, 'Quod si contingat aliquem
eorum studere in astronomia possit
practicare in eadem'. Register H.
7, f. 4 a. Licences were also granted
(without degrees) 'ad practicandum
in arte Cyrurgie in Universitate et
infra precinctum eiusdem'.

[3] Bernard Andrew, poet laureate,
received a royal annuity in 1486 on
account of his teaching at Oxford
and elsewhere. Materials illustrative of Henry VII, ed. W. Campbell, ii. 62. Cf. Wood, Athenae
Oxon. (1691), i. 22; Cooper, Annals
of Camb. i. 241, whence it appears
that Skelton was a laureate of
Cambridge. It appears that at
Cambridge bachelors of other
faculties wore floral wreaths at the
festivities of the act (Caius, Hist.
Cantebr., p. 122). The custom of
laureating poets perhaps originated
in Italy. We hear of it at Padua in
the fourteenth century (Tomasinus,
De Gymn. Patav., p. 169). There is
a letter of Petrarch (Chartul. Univ.
Paris. ii, No. 1038) where the
poet declares that he received in-
vitations on one and the same day
'ad percipiendam lauream poeti-
cam' from Rome and from the
chancellor of Paris. Only the first
invitation was accepted.

[4] Reg. Univ. Oxford, ed. C. W.
Boase (O.H.S.), i. 299.

2994·3   M

CHAP. XII, least money was collected for the payment of the pro-
§ 5.
Greek and fessors.[1]
Hebrew.
French. Another study which occupied a somewhat anomalous
position was the French language. It was decidedly regarded
in the light of an 'extra'. There were, it appears, certain
persons who taught and others who learned 'the art of writing
and composing and speaking the Gallic idiom', as also the
art of 'composing charters and other scripts', and of holding
lay courts or the English mode of pleading—an indication of
the purpose for which French was in demand. But it struck
the academic mind as irregular that there should be students
of these subjects when the university provided no 'ordinary'
lectures on them. Accordingly it was provided that such
scholars should attend lectures on the subjects which approached most nearly to their own, i.e. grammar and rhetoric:
while the teachers were required to swear obedience to the
statutes of the university, and at the same time to divide
between them a tax of 13s. 4d. to the masters of arts by way
of compensation for the damage which was inflicted upon
them by the withdrawal of pupils from their more regular
instructions.[2] Even this very qualified encouragement to the
study of a foreign modern language is unparalleled in any
other medieval university.[3]

[1] Linc. Reg. Burghersh, f. 11 b
'pro stipendiis cuiusdam conversi
catholici nunc docentis Oxon. lin-
guam Ebraicam atque Grecam',
with the significant addition 'et pro
negociis communibus ecclesie', &c.
[Mr. A. F. Leach has noted that
an item of 12d. appears in the
chamberlain's account of Worcester
priory for 1320–1 as paid to the
master of the Greeks at Oxford
('Magistro Grecorum Oxonie').
'This 12d.', he points out, 'was at
the rate of a farthing in the pound
of the Chamberlain's total income,
ordered by the Convocation of
Canterbury in 1320 to be paid for
carrying out the decree of the
Council of Vienne.' See A. F.
Leach, Early Education in Wor-

cester (Worc. Hist. Soc.), pp. xxxix,
42. See also G. R. Stephens, The
Knowledge of Greek in England in
the Middle Ages, 1933, p. 90.]
[2] 'In recompensam praejudicii
per eorum doctrinam Artistis illati,'
Mun. Acad. i. 303; [Stat. Antiq.
Univ. Oxon., ed. S. Gibson, pp.
240–1. See also ibid., p. lxxxvii].
The same statute provides that in
future the collecte received by the
regents in arts shall be divided
equally between them. [See also
L. H. D. Buxton and S. Gibson,
Oxford University Ceremonies, p. 5,
n. 2.]
[3] [A fifteenth-century MS. bequeathed to All Souls College in
1483 (All Souls Coll. MS. No. 182)
contains treatises on the art of

For information as to a great number of details which might naturally find a place in this section, the reader must once again be referred back to the chapter on Paris. The system of university teaching was exactly the same in the two places. In both universities the teachers were dependent upon their *collectae*;[1] in both universities want of adequate support for university teaching, and the youth and inexperience of the 'necessary regents', led eventually to the breakdown of university teaching, at least in the faculty of arts.[2]

In the fifteenth century some attempt was made at Oxford to supply the deficiency by Humphrey, Duke of Gloucester, who, in 1437, temporarily founded certain lectureships in the Seven Arts and the Three Philosophies.[3] But these lectureships were not permanently endowed, and came to an end upon the Duke's death. The need was actually met by the gradual growth of college teaching, which practically made the wealth of the colleges intended for other purposes

---

speaking and writing French, on French grammar, on the conjugation of French verbs, on French spelling, and other aids to learning the language. See *Registrum Epistolarum Fr. J. Peckham, Archiepiscopi Cantuar.*, ed. C. T. Martin (R.S.), i, pp. xliv–liii.]

[1] [See the important article on 'Masters' Salaries and Student-fees in the Medieval Universities', by Dr. Gaines Post in *Speculum*, vii (1932), 181–98.]

[2] [See *Stat. Antiq. Univ. Oxon.*, ed. S. Gibson, p. c, n. 5.]

[3] Presumably one in each; Letter-book F, f. 42 *a*; [*Epist. Acad.*, ed. H. Anstey (O.H.S.), i. 139–40]. These are frequently alluded to in subsequent letters of the university. See especially F, f. 61 *b* [*Epist. Acad.*, ed. H. Anstey (O.H.S.), i. 210], in which the university boasts itself to be the only one in the world where 'non pro vili precio et particulatim seu in priuato, ut olim consueuerunt, sed gratis, integre et in publico

omnes artes, omnes philosophie leguntur' (1442). [See K. H. Vickers, *Humphrey Duke of Gloucester*, p. 402.] A royal lectureship of the same kind for theology is mentioned in 1482 (F, f. 143) [*Epist. Acad.*, ed. H. Anstey (O.H.S.), ii. 478–9], which was perhaps absorbed in the Margaret Professorship. The only earlier evidence of anything like an endowment for teachers is in 1275, when Franciscus Accursii, having returned to England with Edward I, was provided with free quarters in the 'King's Manor' at Oxford, i.e. Beaumont Palace. Rot. Pat. 4 Ed. I, m. 35 (Twyne MS. ii, f. 43 *b*); [*Cal. Pat. Rolls, Edward I, 1272–81*, p. 127. There appears to be no evidence to support the suggestion that Francis Accursii taught in the university. It is not known that he acted in England in any other capacity than that of confidential adviser or *secretarius* to the King. See J. Selden, *Ad Fletam Dissertatio*, ed. D. Ogg, p. 145.]

CHAP. XII,
§ 5.
Margaret
professor-
ship.

available for the endowment of university teachers. In the higher faculties such teaching as continued to be given at all was supplied by the endowed professorships, of which only one was instituted within our period—the Professorship of Divinity, founded by the Lady Margaret, mother of Henry VII, in 1497.[1]

Buildings.

The architectural history of the university lies beyond the scope of this work, except in so far as it bears upon its constitutional and educational organization. In the Church of S. Mary—the centre of University life and the scene of its earliest Congregations—the university possessed of course no rights whatever. The church[2] was simply borrowed by the university for its congregations and Latin sermons just as S. Peter's-in-the-East was borrowed for English sermons, and

The Con-
gregation-
house.

S. Mildred's for meetings of the faculty of arts. The adjoining Congregation-house, which was rebuilt at the end of the fifteenth century, was begun by Thomas Cobham, Bishop of Worcester, in 1320, with an upper chamber to hold his library.[3] The executors of the bishop pawned the library to defray the expenses of his funeral and pay his debts. Oriel College, at their suggestion, redeemed the books, and being also the impropriating rectors of the church, claimed to treat both building and library as its own property; but in 1337 the masters asserted their supposed rights of ownership by coming 'with a great multitude' and forcibly carrying away the books from Oriel, 'in autumn' when the fellows were

---

[1] Wood, *Annals*, i. 654, iii. 826; Letter-book F, f. 180 *b*; [*Epist. Acad.*, ed. H. Anstey (O.H.S.), ii. 646–7. See also *Stat. Antiq. Univ. Oxon.*, ed. S. Gibson, p. c, n. 5. A royal licence for the foundation of a lecturership in theology was granted to Margaret, Countess of Richmond, in 1497, and a lecturer was appointed; but it was not until 1502 that the lecturership was endowed. The *Ordinatio dominae Margaretae* founding the lecturership is printed in *op. cit.*, pp. 300–8. See also *ibid.*, pp. 309–10].

[2] The church was almost entirely reconstructed (except the tower) at the end of the fifteenth century, the chancel in 1462, the nave in 1490–5. Wood, *City* (O.H.S.), ii. 17–19; Maxwell-Lyte, *Hist. Univ. Oxford*, p. 378; Archives F, f. 156 *sq.*, 176; [*Epist. Acad.*, ed. H. Anstey (O.H.S.), ii. 525–7]. An account of these letters is given by E. S. Ffoulkes, *Hist. of the Church of S. Mary*, p. 201 *sq.* [See also Sir T. G. Jackson, *S. Mary the Virgin, Oxford*, Oxford, 1897.]

[3] [See above, p. 64, n. 3.]

CHAP. XII,
§ 5.

mostly away, lodging them in the upper chamber.[1] The quarrel smouldered till the year 1410, when Oriel was induced to acknowledge the university's proprietary rights, subject to a quit-rent of one penny, in consideration of a present of fifty marks from Archbishop Arundel, who also provided for the endowment of the university chaplaincy.[2] In respect of schools, the masters continued throughout our period dependent upon hired rooms; though inceptions and determinations had to be performed in the schools of School Street or its immediate neighbourhood. Many of these schools were afterwards situated in residential halls.[3] In 1439, however, Thomas Hokenorton, Abbot of Oseney, pulled down a number of the isolated schools belonging to his abbey, and erected

The Schools.

[1] See the article on Cobham by Dr. R. L. Poole in *D.N.B.*, and the interesting narrative printed from the Oriel Register by Mr. Shadwell in *Collectanea* (O.H.S.), i. 62–5. [See also E. H. Pearce, *Thomas de Cobham, Bishop of Worcester*, pp. 244–8; and *Oriel College Records*, ed. C. L. Shadwell and H. E. Salter (O.H.S.), pp. 24–9.] Mr. Ffoulkes (*loc. cit.*, pp. 24, 59, 61) speaks of an 'old Congregation-house', the building of which he attributes to S. Hugh of Lincoln. What evidence there may be for the existence of such a building, I know not, but certainly Mr. Ffoulkes produces none, nor can I suppose that 'S. Hugh evidently meant his new erection to serve for a Chapter-house, which was then wanting in Oxford' (p. 25), when there was no chapter at S. Mary's to use it. S. Frideswide's, of course, possessed both a chapter (i.e. of regulars) and a chapter-house. There was, indeed, a university chapel at S. Mary's from 1274, with an endowed chaplain who said Mass for the benefactors of the university. Rymer, *Foedera* (ed. 1816), i. 519.

[2] See Document in Ayliffe, ii. lxxx. Sir H. C. Maxwell-Lyte (*Hist. Univ. Oxford*, p. 100)

assumes that Oriel recovered the books, but of this there is no evidence.

[3] At the beginning of the fifteenth century thirty-two in number. *Mun. Acad.* i. 239, 240 (cf. ii, p. 453); [*Stat. Antiq. Univ. Oxon.*, ed. S. Gibson, pp. 287–8, dated 'before 1477']. Denifle (i. 682) had been misled by Mr. Anstey into supposing that in 1278 there were thirty-one schools in various parts of the town, citing a document from *Mun. Acad.* i. 38 [*Stat. Antiq. Univ. Oxon.*, ed. S. Gibson, p. 106], which describes the number of 'Regentes' in each part of the town, including regions where no schools are ever heard of. Mr. Anstey admits that in A the contraction 'Reg.' stands for 'Regratorum', and a petition of the university to the Parliament of 33 Edward I, complaining that the townsmen have increased the accustomed number of thirty-two regrators, places this reading beyond a doubt (*Memoranda de Parliamento* (R.S.), p. 45). [See *Stat. Antiq. Univ. Oxon.*, ed. S. Gibson, p. 106, n. to l. 8.] That there should afterwards have been this very number of thirty-two schools in School Street is certainly an odd coincidence.

CHAP, XII, 'a long pile of stone building consisting of two stories', which
§ 5. practically served as the principal arts schools of the university till the present 'Old Schools' were built in the time of James I.[1] The masters who taught in the 'Schools of Oseney' paid rent (13s. 4d. for each school) to the abbey, reimbursing themselves (as at Paris) by subletting to determiners.[2] About the year 1426,[3] the university began to collect money for the

Divinity present Divinity School, which when its ample window space
School. was filled with stained glass, must have been a gorgeous specimen of late Gothic art. The building absorbed the energy of the university and the liberality of its benefactors for half a century; it was not completed till 1488.[4] An upper chamber over the Divinity School was established for the valuable library given to the university by Humphrey, Duke of

Law Gloucester, in 1439 and 1443.[5] The schools of law lay in the
Schools. neighbourhood of S. Edward's Church. In 1465-88 we find the university collecting money for the repair of the Canon Law School and the Civil Law School, but it is clear that these buildings were the actual property of the principal

[1] Wood, *Annals.* iii. 759 *sq.*, 787 *sq.* [The Schools erected by Abbot Hokenorton were re-built in the reign of Queen Mary. They were contained in a long two-storey building comprising ten lecture-rooms. In the *Topographica Delineatio* prepared by Thomas Neale for Queen Elizabeth's visit to Oxford in 1566 they are depicted by John Berebloc with a verse by Neale below commemorating Queen Mary's bounty. See *Elizabethan Oxford*, ed. by the Rev. C. Plummer (O.H.S.), pp. 31, 166; *Collegiorum Scholarumque Publicarum Academiae Oxoniensis Topographica Delineatio*, with preface by F. Madan, Oxford, 1882, p. 33.]

[2] Wood, *Annals*, iii. 759, 760.

[3] Letter-book F, f. 6 *a*; [*Epist. Acad. Oxon.*, ed. H. Anstey (O.H.S.), i. 20-2]. The site was bought in 1427. Pyx, W. P.-B. 5.

(Other documents, nn. 2, 3, 4, have disappeared.)

[4] Wood (*Annals*, iii. 778) gives 1480, but see F, ff. 134 *b*, 160 *b*. [*Epist. Acad.*, ed. H. Anstey (O.H.S.), ii. 445-7, 547-8. See also *Med. Arch. Univ. Oxford*, ed. H. E. Salter (O.H.S.), ii. 288; *Adderbury 'Rectoria'*, ed. T. F. Hobson (Oxfordshire Record Soc.), pp. 32-8].

[5] *Mun. Acad.* ii. 758-72. Others were not received till after 1450, i.e. till at least three years after the Duke's death. W. D. Macray, *Annals of the Bodleian*, pp. 6-8. [See also K. H. Vickers, *Humphrey Duke of Gloucester*, pp. 406-7; and H. H. E. Craster, 'Index to Duke Humphrey's Gifts to the Old Library of the University in 1439, 1441, and 1444' in *Bodleian Quarterly Record*, i. 131-5, and 'Duke Humphrey's Library', *ibid.* iii. 45.]

doctors of canon and civil law, not of the university itself.[1] It is curious to observe how universally the fifteenth century is the era of 'university buildings'. About the year 1440 the universities all over Europe were endeavouring to provide themselves with buildings of their own. It is more than an accidental coincidence that this was about the period at which the universities began to lose their independence, and to fall more and more under the control of their respective governments. In their poverty had been their strength. In another way, however, the story of the buildings in which the masters of the fifteenth century took more delight than in teaching or in study, is one connected with the best movement of the age. The fifteenth century was everywhere an age of library-making; in the library the solitary student, weary of the disputations of an effete scholasticism, could find richer intellectual pastures for himself. Duke Humphrey's library contained, besides the usual contents of medieval libraries, a considerable number of Greek and Latin classics, together with some works of the Italian scholars.[2] It is the first irruption of the full-blown Italian Renaissance into Oxford, and no doubt helped on that spontaneous groping after an improved Latinity and a more literary education which, at Oxford as at Paris, prepared the way for the men of the Renaissance proper—the wandering Greeks and the Northern scholars who had studied in Italy.[3] The last years of the

Duke Humphrey's library.

---

[1] F, ff. 117 b, 143 b, 144 a; Wood, *Annals*, iii. 769; [*Epist. Acad.*, ed. H. Anstey (O.H.S.), ii. 377, 479–82]. The Canon Law School was rebuilt in 1489; F, f. 159 b [*Epist. Acad.*, (O.H.S.), ii. 540, 542–4, 546–8, 556, 571]. It is not clear whether the 'Civil School' was rebuilt. [The Canon Law School was the property of the university before 1279. It was let to the canonists who lectured there. See *Med. Arch. Univ. Oxford*, ed. H. E. Salter (O.H.S.), i. 275, ii. 289. The university did not collect money in 1465–88 for the repair of the Civil

Law School, which was not its property: but it enlisted subscriptions for the addition of a story to the Canon Law School for the accommodation of the Civil Law School. It appears that sufficient money was not forthcoming to make this addition possible. See *Epist. Acad.*, ed. H. Anstey (O.H.S.), ii. 480.]

[2] See Catalogue in *Mun. Acad.* ii. 758 *sq.*, and Macray, *loc. cit.*, p. 6 *sq.* [See also K. H. Vickers, *Humphrey Duke of Gloucester*, pp. 426–38.]

[3] [See J. E. Sandys, *Harvard Lectures on the Revival of Learning*, p. 197; G. R. Stephens, *The Know-*

CHAP. XII,
§ 5.
Growth of
human-
ism.

fifteenth century, as presented to us in the official records of the university, tell of nothing but the dreary routine of expiring scholasticism. As presented to us in the letters of Erasmus and his friends, they are full of bright promise—a promise which in Oxford was never wholly fulfilled. But the growth of humanism during the last ten years of the fifteenth century—the age of Colet and Grocyn, of Linacre and Erasmus—in many ways the most fascinating decade in all our Oxford annals, belongs not to the history of medieval university systems, but to the history of the movement by which that system was destroyed.[1]

ledge of Greek in England in the Middle Ages, Philadelphia, 1933, pp. 96–117.]

[1] The history of these years has been delightfully written by Mr. Seebohm in his *Oxford Reformers*, and by Prof. Montagu Burrows in *Memoir of William Grocyn* (*Collectanea* (O.H.S.), ii. 332 *sq.*). See especially his remarks (p. 339) on Thomas Chandler, Warden of New College from 1454 to 1475, who wrote good Latin, though there is no reason to believe that he had studied in Italy. [See also *Mediaeval Archives of the Univ. of Oxford*, ed. H. E. Salter (O.H.S.), i, pp. v, vi.]

Additional Note:
The number of medical doctors at Oxford was always small: the only one of much fame was John Gaddesden of Merton, author of the *Rosa Anglica* or *Practica medicinae a capite ad pedes*, who wrote 1305–17. See H. Haeser, *Lehrbuch*, i. 712. [See also H. P. Cholmeley, *John of Gaddesden and the Rosa Medicinae*, Oxford, 1912. Mention may also be made of Nicholas of Tingewick, physician to Edward I; see R. T. Gunther, *Early Science in Oxford*, iii. 9, and F. M. Powicke, *The Medieval Books of Merton College*, p. 157.]

§ 6. THE COLLEGES OF OXFORD

GREATLY as the originality of the English college-system has been exaggerated, there can be no doubt of the peculiar interest which our English colleges possess for those who are familiar with the towns to which they still impart that ecclesiastical and medieval tone which has so completely vanished from the university cities of the Continent. We may therefore be allowed to devote to the origins of Merton and New College, of Peterhouse and King's, somewhat more attention than has been bestowed upon the Sorbonne and the College of Navarre.

Something has already been said in connexion with Paris about the system of residence in halls or hostels and the gradual changes by which the hall passed from an independent and self-governing community into the position of a boarding-house kept and in the main governed—though not without vestiges of its ancient autonomy—by a master under the authority of the university. Indeed, we have been obliged to some extent to interpret the scanty notices of the Parisian system by the ampler evidence which Oxford supplies. Whatever doubt there may be as to the originally democratic character of the Parisian hostels, there can be none as to that of the Oxford halls,[1] while the Aularian Statutes of 1489 exhibit this ancient autonomy in the very act (as it were) of being superseded by that of the university of masters and of the individual principals.[2]

---

[1] [Rashdall's view as to the original democratic character of the Oxford halls has been subjected to criticism. See Dr. H. E. Salter's article, 'An Oxford Hall in 1424', contributed to *Essays in History presented to R. L. Poole* and *History*, 1929, N.S. xiv. 59–60; A. B. Emden, *An Oxford Hall in Medieval Times*, pp. 7–33, where the evidence is fully discussed. Such evidence as can be gleaned from the earlier statutes of the university and other sources rather supports the conclusion that the halls owed their origin to the initiative of graduates teaching in the university. It appears from the oldest surviving rentals of Oseney Abbey and S. John's Hospital that the principals who rented the halls belonging to these two corporations were in nearly all cases 'magistri'.]

[2] Similarly the 'Inns of Court' in London were originally hostels hired from a landlord by some

CHAP. XII,   It is instructive to trace the process by which the university
§ 6.
Growth of gradually asserted its supremacy over the hall-communities.
university The starting-point of the chancellor's jurisdiction over the
authority
over halls. relations between the principal and his 'fellows' (*socii*) was
simply the custom of giving security before the chancellor
for the rent of the house.[1] This proceeding was enforced
merely to secure the payment of the rent and prevent disputes
between competing applicants for halls: any scholar who
tendered the required amount had the right to be admitted
to the principalship. But it would at the same time enable
a chancellor to reject a principal to whom he had reason to
demur, and in certain cases the university threatens principals
offending against the university regulations about the manner
of hiring halls—as for instance by buying the succession to
a principalship from the last holder—with the loss of their
position. Gradually the chancellor seems to have arrogated to
himself a general power of removing an offending principal.[2]
In the time of Edward I it is said that the chancellor received
express authority from the university to veto the statutes
made by the *Aulares* and even to impose statutes upon them
at his own discretion,[3] though there is not much evidence of

group or society of 'Apprentices of
the Law'. (Pulling, *The Order of
the Coif*, p. 130.) They were
formerly ruled by a *Principal* and
Ancients, 'as it has continued to
this day in the lesser Inns' (*ibid.*,
p. 165). Since these societies were
not incorporated, their *status* was
very similar to that of the hall-
communities. It is probable that
their government was at one time
more democratic than now. [See
J. B. Williamson, *The History of
the Temple*, London, pp. 83–105.]

    [1] [On the annual *exposicio cau-
cionis* by principals of halls see
A. B. Emden, *An Oxford Hall*, pp.
25, 26; *Reg. Cancell. Oxon., 1434–
1469*, ed. H. E. Salter (O.H.S.), i.
xxvii–xxviii.]

    [2] *Mun. Acad.* i. 14, ii. 470;
[*Stat. Antiq. Univ. Oxon.*, ed. S.
Gibson, pp. 80, 224]. Principals

are also required, even in the more
ancient statutes, to report to the
chancellor scholars not attending
lectures and otherwise offending.
Ibid. i. 93, ii. 427; [*Stat. Antiq.
Univ. Oxon.*, ed. S. Gibson, pp.
110–11, 194].

    [3] 'Nullum statutum aulare in
Oxonia ligat nec obligat aliquem
de aula si Cancellarius contradicat;
et tunc eciam concessum fuit Cancellario Oxonie imperpetuum vt
ipse licite possit declarare, modifi-
care, et reuocare statuta aularia
studencium in Oxonia, et noua
statuta ex officio suo in aulis sta-
tuere, quociens expediens Cancellario visum fuerit; et istud priui-
legium concessum fuit Cancellario
quia olim principales aularum et
scolares fecerunt statuta derogancia
officio et potestati Cancellarii',
ibid. ii. 470; [*Stat. Antiq. Univ.*

the power having been actually exercised till the second half of the fifteenth century.[1] In 1411 principals were forbidden to receive scholars expelled from other halls for breaches of their statutes.[2] In 1421 Henry V enjoined that principals should receive only scholars of good character, and all scholars were required to reside in the halls of principals 'lawfully approved and admitted by the Chancellor and Regents'.[3] Probably at some earlier date a statute had been passed to forbid a maniciple or servant, though himself a scholar, from being principal of a hall,[4] and in 1432 the university took the important step of restricting the principalship to graduates (though even after this a principal might be merely a bachelor of arts); and it is noticeable that the statute now passed recognizes the principal as bound in some measure to assist his scholars in their studies.[5] At about the same time, during the chancellorship of Gilbert Kymer, M.D., a code of statutes was drawn up for the government of the halls by the chancellor with the 'advice and consent of the Congregation of Masters and of the Principals of Halls'.[6] Another

Oxon., ed. S. Gibson, p. 224. There is only fifteenth-century authority for the grant of this privilege to the chancellor. See A. B. Emden, *An Oxford Hall*, pp. 31–2]. Evidence of the existence of student-made statutes is also supplied by the Balliol Statutes. [See *Oxford Balliol Deeds*, ed. H. E. Salter (O.H.S.), p. 277.] See below, p. 181.

[1] Some of the proclamations by the chancellor or declarations of custom contained in the statute-books may perhaps be looked upon in this light, but the private statutes of the individual halls were not superseded.

[2] *Mun. Acad.* i. 252; [*Stat. Antiq. Univ. Oxon.*, ed. S. Gibson, pp. 210–11, 296. See A. B. Emden, *An Oxford Hall*, pp. 38–9, 218.]

[3] *Mun. Acad.* i. 279; [*Stat. Antiq. Univ. Oxon.*, ed. S. Gibson, pp. 226–7. The injunctions of Henry V confirmed previous university legis-

lation. The problem of the unattached student, or *chamberdekenys*, as they were known, was a recurrent one. See A. B. Emden, *An Oxford Hall*, pp. 30–1, 231].

[4] *Mun. Acad.* ii. 468; [*Stat. Antiq. Univ. Oxon.*, ed. S. Gibson, p. 183. Mr. Strickland Gibson dates this statute 'before 1380'. See also A. B. Emden, *An Oxford Hall*, p. 37].

[5] It complains of the appointment as principals of 'non-graduati et caeteris minus docti coaularesque suos inepti docere', *Mun. Acad.* i. 307; [*Stat. Antiq. Univ. Oxon.*, ed. S. Gibson, pp. 243–4].

[6] [There is no record of a special code of statutes having been drawn up during Dr. Kymer's chancellorship for the government of the halls. A statute made in 1489–90, when John Russell, Bishop of Lincoln, was chancellor, required that in future principals should convene the members of their halls

_{CHAP. XII,} code—probably the code still extant—appeared between 1483
_{§ 6.} and 1490.[1] By these statutes the authority of the principals
was still further reinforced and migration without the consent
of the principal or of the chancellor peremptorily forbidden.
We shall have more to say about the contents of these statutes.
Meanwhile we may note their significance as marking the
completion of the process by which the ancient hall or hostel
was transformed from a private house rented by a society of
students into a recognized university institution.

Taxation　　As at Bologna and Paris, and in fact in all towns where there
of halls: was any community of scholars, the principle of compulsory
principals. 'taxation' by a joint-board of masters and burghers was
established from a very early period: it is one of the very few
parts of the university-system which can be traced back to a
period anterior to the legatine ordinance of 1214.[2] At Oxford
the control of the university over halls was peculiarly ample.
Not only was the owner precluded from letting his house to a
layman so long as a clerk was willing to take it,[3] but, if he
refused to repair after three monitions, the tenant might
execute the repairs and deduct their cost from the rent.[4]

three times a year and read certain
ordinances and statutes to them,
especially those made in Dr.
Kymer's time and in that of the then
chancellor. Rashdall's reference to
the statutes made in Dr. Kymer's
time suggests the existence of a
code of Aularian statutes no longer
extant, whereas there can be no
doubt that the statutes referred to
are identical with the collection of
statutes published on 24 May 1432,
several of which related to matters
of discipline and were therefore of
concern to principals and their
scholars. See *Stat. Antiq. Univ.
Oxon.*, ed. S. Gibson, pp. 204–6,
238–48, and A. B. Emden, *An
Oxford Hall*, pp. 198–200.]
　　[1] *Mun. Acad.* i. 358 *sq.*; [*Stat.
Antiq. Univ. Oxon.*, ed. S. Gibson,
pp. 295–7. In the former edition
of this book this code of *Statuta
Aularia* was printed by Rashdall in

an Appendix, but it is not included
in the present edition, as these
statutes are contained in Mr.
Strickland Gibson's edition of the
ancient statutes of the university
(*op. cit.*, pp. 574–88). For an
analysis of the contents of these
statutes see A. B. Emden, *An
Oxford Hall*, pp. 202–21]. Chamberdekyns still survived in 1612.
(Reg. K. 22, f. 109.)
　　[2] [On the subject of the 'taxation' of halls see A. B. Emden,
An Oxford Hall, pp. 10–17; *Reg.
Cancell. Oxon., 1434–1469*, ed. H. E.
Salter (O.H.S.), i. xxix, xxx.]
　　[3] [See *Stat. Antiq. Univ. Oxon.*,
ed. S. Gibson, p. 79, ll. 11–18; and
A. B. Emden, *An Oxford Hall*,
pp. 17, 35–6.]
　　[4] [See *Stat. Antiq. Univ. Oxon.*,
ed. S. Gibson, p. 79, ll. 19–30; and
A. B. Emden, *An Oxford Hall*,
pp. 27–8.]

Although this custom is not everywhere on record, it is probable that it was widely diffused, since we find almost exactly the same regulations in universities of distant regions and widely divergent types. At Oxford the chancellor's ample powers of spiritual censure gave the university exceptional facilities for enforcing these somewhat high-handed 'customs'.[1]

Before the close of the medieval period, most of the halls passed into the possession either of monastic bodies or of colleges.[2] This circumstance helped to give the aspect of

[1] *Mun. Acad.* i. 15; [*Stat. Antiq. Univ. Oxon.*, ed. S. Gibson, p. 79]; *Stat. Artistarum Patav.*, f. xxxii *b*.

[2] [The connexion of monastic bodies with the halls, and the connexion of colleges with the halls, should not be identified. By the end of the thirteenth century religious houses in Oxford and its neighbourhood had become very considerable owners of property in the town, and consequently a large number of halls are to be found on their rent-rolls: this is notably so in the case of the Augustinian Houses of Oseney and S. Frideswide and of the Hospital of S. John the Baptist outside the East Gate. But the relationship between these corporations and the halls was only one of landlord and tenant. The colleges were brought into connexion with the halls under other circumstances. Many of the halls were acquired by the founders of colleges and subsequently by colleges themselves for the provision or extension of college sites. But there is also traceable from the fifteenth century onwards a connexion growing up between the older colleges and certain of the halls in their vicinity as the result of fellows of these colleges undertaking the principalships of halls as an additional source of income. Connexions which originated in this way were in some cases developed by colleges as a means whereby commoners, that is, the fee-paying undergraduates normally resident in halls, could be admitted to the benefits of a collegiate foundation. See A. B. Emden, *An Oxford Hall*, pp. 52–5, 225–6, 237–8, 260–2. For a list of halls existing during the middle years of the fifteenth century see Dr. H. E. Salter's valuable appendix to *Reg. Cancell. Oxon.*, *1434–1469* (O.H.S.), ii. 357–67. For their position and distribution see his valuable *Map of Medieval Oxford*. On the history of individual halls, see, for Broadgates Hall, D. Macleane, *A History of Pembroke College* (O.H.S.), pp. 1–145, and *Pembroke College*, pp. 1–48; for Hart Hall and Magdalen Hall, S. G. Hamilton, *Hertford College*, pp. 1–39, 100–40; for S. Edmund Hall, A. B. Emden, *An Oxford Hall in Medieval Times*. See also Wood, *City of Oxford* (O.H.S.), vol. i, *passim*. Dr. H. E. Salter has drawn attention to differences which distinguished the halls of artists from those of legists, the former being mainly undergraduate, the latter wholly graduate societies. See his article 'An Oxford Hall in 1424' in *Essays in History presented to R. Lane Poole*, pp. 432–4.]

CHAP. XII, public and permanent institutions to the few halls which
§ 6.   survived the Reformation and which are now in process of
extinction by one of the most vandalistic and unintelligent
of our university reforms.[1] The colleges, regarding the
principalship of their halls as a piece of patronage to be
bestowed upon one of their fellows, ceased to demand anything more than an accustomed quit-rent.[2] As no fresh halls
were allowed to be created, the principalships passed into
important preferments in the hands either of the chancellor
or of the college to which the hall belonged; and in the course
of time the lawyers being puzzled by the anomalous character
of these hall-communities, which *de facto* held and transferred
property without any legal incorporation or perpetual succession, devised the legal fiction that their property was held
in trust for them by the university. The Earl of Leicester
obtained from Queen Elizabeth the recognition of his right to
nominate to the principalship of the halls (though Queen's
afterwards succeeded in making good its claim to the nomination at S. Edmund Hall);[3] but even then traces of the demo-

[1] All are doomed with the solitary exception of S. Edmund Hall,
which is now placed in still closer
connexion than formerly with
Queen's College. The others have
been sacrificed to the cupidity of
neighbouring colleges. [Rashdall
here refers to the union of S. Alban
Hall with Merton College in 1882,
and of New Inn Hall with Balliol
College in 1887. Since the former
edition of this book S. Mary Hall
has gone, being united with Oriel
College in 1902 on the voidance of
its principalship by the death of
Dr. Chase. In 1903 S. Edmund
Hall was threatened with a similar
fate owing to the pending resignation of the principal, Dr. Moore,
but the requisite statute authorizing its union with Queen's College
was rejected by Congregation. In
1913 a statute preserving the independence of the last survivor of
the medieval halls was enacted by

the university and confirmed by
the King in Council.]
[2] An opinion of the attorney-
general was obtained at the time of
the foundation of the first Hertford
College (1740) to the effect that
Exeter College had lost the right
to raise the rent of Hart Hall.
[3] [Queen's College derived this
exceptional privilege from a composition made between the university and the college in 1559,
whereby the college was granted
the right of appointment to the
principalship of S. Edmund Hall
in return for its services, or rather
those of its provost, William
Dennyson, in saving the hall from
conversion to secular uses during
the critical period which followed
the dissolution of Oseney Abbey,
its former landlord. See A. B.
Emden, *An Oxford Hall*, pp.
235–63.]

cratic character of the institution remained, and it was still CHAP. XII,
considered necessary to summon the whole society (including §6.
the undergraduates) to elect the chancellor's nominee. This
ceremony was last gone through on the admission of Dr. Chase
as Principal of S. Mary Hall[1] in 1857.[2]

The earliest benefaction intended to support scholars at the Benefaction of
university was of a very simple character. To maintain or Alan
'exhibit' a scholar or two at a school or university was a Basset.
recognized 'good work' long before the age of colleges: to
found a chantry for the maintenance of a priest to say mass for
the founder's soul was an equally common expression of
medieval piety. Alan Basset, who died in or shortly before
the year 1243, conceived the idea of combining a chantry with
a scholarship. In accordance with instructions contained in
his will, the executors arranged with the prior and convent of
Burcester or Bicester (a house founded by a kinsman of the
testator) for the payment of eight marks a year to two chaplains who should say mass daily for the founder and his wife,
and at the same time study in the schools of Oxford or
elsewhere.[3] The chantries in Oxford churches no doubt
helped many a poor priest to get a university education; but
Basset's exact plan was not followed by later benefactors.
Though Alan Basset may claim the credit of providing the first
permanent endowment for an Oxford scholar, he can hardly
be called the founder of the first Oxford college.

UNIVERSITY COLLEGE (c. 1280)

William SMITH's *Annals of University College*, Newcastle-on-Tyne,
1728—by far the best of our earlier college-histories. Cf. WOOD's *City*, i.
554. The muniments are catalogued in the *Fifth Report of the Historical
MSS. Commission*, p. 477. William Smith also left a large collection of

[1] [On the absence of medieval
precedents for this custom see
A. B. Emden, *An Oxford Hall*,
pp. 20-1. It would seem more in
accord with the available evidence
to conclude that the custom of
electing to the headship grew up in
the halls in imitation of the mode
of appointment usual in the
colleges.]

[2] See Appendix VII.

[3] Twyne MS. i, f. 159. I have
been unable to trace the original.
Wood and Sir H. C. Maxwell-Lyte
refer to *Lincoln Reg. Wells*, f. 71,
but the register does not appear to
be extant. [Dr. H. E. Salter has
shown that the credit for the foundation of these two scholarships is
due rather to Bishop Grosseteste
than to Alan Basset. See *Snappe's
Formulary* (O.H.S.), pp. 297-9.]

manuscript transcripts of documents, &c., connected with the college, which is preserved in the college treasury. [A history of *University College*, by Mr. William CARR, was published in 1902. Two deeds relating to the early properties of the college are printed in *Med. Arch. Univ. Oxford*, ed. H. E. SALTER (O.H.S.), i. 324–6.]

William of Durham's bequest (1249). The original plan of what was in design, though not in actual erection, the earliest of existing college-foundations was hardly on a larger scale than the modest chantry of Alan Basset. William of Durham, a distinguished master of Paris, at one time rector of Wearmouth, at another Archbishop-elect of Rouen,[1] died in 1249, leaving to the university 310 marks to be invested in rents for the support of ten or more masters of arts studying theology.[2] The university placed the money in a chest and used it, partly 'on their own business' and partly in 'loans to others' which were never repaid.[3] In this way 160 marks had been spent; but a considerable part of the money was laid out soon after the founder's death in the purchase of houses in Oxford which produced an annual income of about 18 marks.[4] The purchase of these houses

[1] Matthew Paris calls him at one time 'eminentissime literatus', at another 'vir literatissimus'. He died in crossing the Alps upon his return from the Roman Court. *Chron. Mai.*, ed. H. R. Luard (R.S.), v. 91; *Hist. Minor*, ed. F. Madden (R.S.), iii. 67. [Rashdall has been misled by Matthew Paris, who in one passage recording the death of William of Durham says 'transalpinans', and in another 're-diens a curia Romana'. Actually Innocent IV was at Lyons.] He was one of the four masters who in 1229 left Paris for Angers (*Chron. Mai.* iii. 168), but I know of no evidence that he headed 'a migration to Oxford', as is confidently stated by Sir H. C. Maxwell-Lyte (*Hist. Univ. Oxford*, p. 31), though this may well have been the case. It is probable that he was not identical with William de Lanum, Archdeacon of Durham in 1234, though they are identified in an inscription in a window of the college. Le Neve, *Fasti*, ed. T. D. Hardy, iii. 302. [In his manuscript corrections for a new edition of this book Rashdall has struck out the statement that William of Durham was at one time Archbishop-elect of Rouen, but gives no authority for his change of view. Dr. A. F. Pollard in his article on William of Durham in *D.N.B.* credits William with the archdeaconry of Durham and admits the possibility of his election to the archbishopric of Rouen.]

[2] The facts which follow are found in the document mentioned on p. 177, n. 3.

[3] W. Smith, *Annals of University College*, pp. 9–13. Some of it was lent to the barons in the Barons' War. See Adam de Marisco's letter to the chancellor, *Mon. Francisc.* (R.S.), i. 257. [See also W. Carr, *University College*, p. 15.]

[4] One of these was a house at the corner of Schools Street, bought in 1253; another, bought in 1255, was the hall which the

may have been intended merely as a mode of investing the CHAP. XII,
money, and it is not clear whether the rents received were   § 6.
actually expended upon those whom the founder had designed
to benefit, and whether, if so, the recipients of the endowment
lived together in one of these houses or elsewhere.[1] If they
did, University College may fairly claim to be in actual fact
the oldest of Oxford colleges. But it was not till after a
precedent had been created by other benefactors that the
university drew up a scheme for a little community of four
masters who were to live together (with any other scholars
who might be willing to board with them) in a hall which had
been purchased as their residence. This hall is the germ of Great Uni-
the present University College, still legally styled Great Uni- versity
versity Hall.[2] The college, if it did not exist *de facto* already, *c. 1280.*
must have come into actual being in 1280 or soon after.
The earliest extant statutes were drawn up by the university
in that year,[3] but were superseded by a fuller code in

eminent canonist, William of Drogheda, in 1250 gave to the prior
and convent of Sherborne, who in
1255 sold it to the university
(Documents in Treasury). It is
still known as Drawda Hall (No.
33 High Street). [See W. Carr,
Univ. Coll., p. 14.]

[1] [See W. Carr, *Univ. Coll.*,
pp. 31, 32; Sir Charles Mallet,
Hist. Univ. Oxford, i. 87, n. 4.]

[2] It has usually been supposed
that the *Aula Universitatis in vico
Scolarum*, bought in 1253 (W.
Smith, *Annals of Univ. College*,
p. 61), was inhabited by William of
Durham's masters, but this is not
a safe assumption: the title only
denotes that the hall was the
property of the university. The
first tenement on the present site
in High Street was acquired for the
college in 1332 (Wood, *Colleges*,
p. 43). [See W. Carr, *Univ. Coll.*,
pp. 33, 34; Sir Charles Mallet,
Hist. Univ. Oxford, i. 89, n. 2.] The
title of the college varied during the
course of the fourteenth century.
In deeds between 1340 and 1360

the designation is 'Magistri et
Scholares Aulae Universitatis':
after 1360 'Magistri et scholares
Magistri Willelmi de Dunelm.' is
more frequent, and after 1380
'Magistri Magnae Aulae' appears.
In the earliest surviving bursar's
roll (1381) the designation is 'Collegium Willelmi de Dunelm., vulgariter appellatum Mickle Universitie Hall'. [See W. Carr, *Univ.
Coll.*, p. 36.] The style 'College of
William of Durham' was still sometimes used in the time of Elizabeth
(Conybeare, in *The Colleges of
Oxford*, p. 10). For an account of
the forgeries, lies, and impostures
which former masters and fellows
of University have perpetrated in
defence of its Alfredian origin, ending with the millenary banquet of
1872, see W. Smith, *Annals of
Univ. College, passim*, Conybeare,
pp. 101-4, [and W. Carr, *Univ.
Coll.*, pp. 1-19].

[3] In this year a scheme, containing a short code of statutes, was
drawn up for the foundation of
the society, as appears from a

1292.[1] [The purpose of the college was to enable masters of arts to complete the long course necessary for the degree of D.D.] Following the example set by the founder of Merton, the university made the masters to some extent a self-governing society under the senior fellow, who was to receive a double allowance in consideration of his administrative labours, and who gradually came to be known as master, and was eventually elected by the society.[2] At first he was to act in conjunction with an external master of arts, while, in the election to vacant places, the chancellor and theological masters of the university were to act with the members of the community.[3] In 1292, however, the external superintending master disappeared, but the college still remained under the government of the chancellor, the proctors, and the faculty of theology, and by them the vacant places upon the foundation were filled up.[4] How very gradually the little college fought its way to autonomy is illustrated by the fact that so late as 1311, the date of its third code of statutes, the community had no common seal and was therefore obliged to borrow the seal of the rural dean of Oxford in concluding the agreement between itself and the university.[5]

Additional endow- ments. In spite, however, of the want of any royal charter or formal incorporation, the college, according to medieval practice, experienced no difficulty in holding land and other property in its own name. Where the society resided during the first

document in the treasury, partially translated by Wood, *Colleges*, pp. 40, 41. I am much indebted to the master (Dr. J. F. Bright) for his kindness in giving me access to the original and to other college documents.

[1] *Mun. Acad.* i. 56.

[2] This change was made by a body of statutes drawn up for the college by Thomas Chandler, vice-chancellor in 1478; [see W. Carr, *Univ. Coll.*, p. 69].

[3] An attempt was made to elect a master in 1382, but was seemingly foiled. W. Smith, *Annals of Univ. College*, pp. 264–6.

[4] Compare the very similar con-

stitution of the Sorbonne at Paris, which very probably suggested this provision, above, i. 508. The university, however, retained and frequently exercised the right of hearing appeals from these delegates.

[5] W. Smith, *Annals of Univ. College*, p. 46. The original of these statutes is in the University Archives, I. (W.P.) 10 (printed from the statute-books in *Mun. Acad.* i. 87). [The text of these statutes is printed in *Med. Arch. Univ. Oxford* (O.H.S.), i. 84–6.] The earliest seal appears in 1320, W. Smith, *Annals of Univ. College*, p. 103. [See also W. Carr, *Univ. College*, pp. 223–4.]

years of its existence is uncertain. It was not until 1332 that it acquired a house known as Spicer's Hall which occupied part of the present site in High Street, and from about 1343 this became the home of the small community.[1] The college buildings grew by the successive annexation of neighbouring halls. None of these older buildings remain, the present college being chiefly of seventeenth-century design. The possessions of the college and number of its scholars were gradually increased by successive benefactions. The most important of these additions were three fellowships founded by Walter Skirlaw, Bishop of Durham, a former *alumnus*, in 1403, and three more out of the impropriation of the valuable rectory of Arncliffe in Craven by Henry Percy, Earl of Northumberland, in 1443.[2] In 1377 the college became involved in an extremely complicated lawsuit about some of the newly acquired property.[3] It was to extricate themselves from their legal embarrassments, by procuring a *supersedeas* to transfer the case to the King's Council, that the master and scholars of University first devised the impudent fiction of a royal foundation by Alfred the Great, which has now become part of the law of England by a judgement of the court of King's Bench after the verdict of a jury on the question of fact.[4] The stratagem was completely successful; and the King's Council assigned the disputed property to the college, apparently in the teeth of legal right as much as of history.

Alfredian myth.

BALLIOL (1261–6)

Balliol can boast of the earliest of college histories—a good one of its kind—*Balliofergus*, by Henry SAVAGE, then master (Oxford, 1668). *The Early History of Balliol College*, by MRS. DE PARAVICINI (London, 1891),

[1] [W. Carr, *Univ. College*, pp. 33–6.]

[2] W. Smith, *Annals of Univ. College*, p. 219; Wood, *Colleges*, p. 47; [W. Carr, *Univ. College*, pp. 57–8, 62].

[3] W. Smith, *Annals of Univ. College*, pp. 107–41; [W. Carr, *Univ. College*, pp. 37–48.] The litigation lasted till 1389. It involved an actual change in the law of the realm (9 Ric. II, c. 3).

[4] In 1726, when the visitation of the college was adjudged to the Crown (J. K. Ingram, *Memorials of Oxford*, i. 6), though there was not a single precedent for its exercise and numerous evidences of the visitatorial rights of the university—a characteristic illustration of the way in which English lawyers have manipulated history. [See also W. Carr, *Univ. College*, pp. 173–4.]

CHAP. XII, reprints most of the documents contained in Savage, and collects some
§ 6. documents and information about the college from other sources. The
college archives are calendared by Riley in the *Fourth Report of the
Historical Manuscript Commissioners*, 1874, p. 442 *sq*. [A history of *Balliol
College*, by Prof. H. W. C. DAVIS, was published in 1899. The important
collection of early deeds relating to the Oxford properties of the college
has been edited by H. E. SALTER (*Balliol Oxford Deeds*, O.H.S., 1913). For
the life of Dervorguilla see W. HUYSHE, *Dervorgilla, Lady of Galloway*
(1913).]

John de In or about the year 1260 Sir John de Balliol, father of the
Balliol's
penance. illustrious rival of the Bruce, incurred the wrath of one of
those militant prince-bishops whom the English kings employed to guard the northern border against the Scot. The
details of the outrage are not known, but we are told by
Matthew Paris that the Lord of Barnard Castle had 'unjustly
vexed and enormously damnified' the Church of Tynemouth
and the Church of Durham.[1] Certain it is, however, that in
the year above mentioned, the founder of Balliol College
knelt at the door of Durham Abbey, was there publicly
scourged by the bishop, and undertook to provide a perpetual
maintenance for certain poor scholars in the university.[2] The
outcome of this involuntary munificence was a college which
forms an exception to the general type of English colleges, and
well illustrates the difference between the English college-
system originated by Walter de Merton and the earlier foundations of Paris, of which Balliol's original scheme is an
obvious imitation.

College It is certain that the scholars were established in Oxford
ablished
before before June 1266.[3] They were at first supported by annual
1266.
payments from the founder, who allowed a commons of eight-
pence a week to his pensioners.[4] On this ground Balliol

[1] *Chron. Mai.*, ed. H. R. Luard,
(R.S.) v. 528. Cf. W. H. Bliss,
Transcripts, i. 573.
[2] *Chron. de Lanercost*, ed. J.
Stevenson (Maitland Club, 1839),
p. 69. The name of Balliol is not
mentioned, but the identification is
practically certain.
[3] The King directs the Mayor
and Bailiffs of Oxford to lend John
de Balliol £20 out of the fee-farm
of the town 'for the use of the

Scholars whom he maintains in the
said town'. *Cal. of Documents relating to Scotland*, i. 476.
[4] *Chron. de Mailros*, ed. J.
Stevenson (Bannatyne Club, 1835),
p. 217 (an. 1269). Sir H. C. Maxwell-
Lyte (*Hist. Univ. Oxford*, p. 71 *sq*.)
was apparently the first writer who
discovered this and the above allusions. [This was an adequate
and even a liberal allowance for an
undergraduate, but below the level

College may be said to possess a certain shadowy claim to CHAP. XII, be the oldest of Oxford colleges. But if the antiquity of a § 6. college is held to date from its existence as a legal corporation, it must yield to the claims of Merton.[1] For it was not till Formal 1282, thirteen years after Balliol's death, that his widow charter, 1282. Dervorguilla placed the 'House of Balliol' on a permanent footing. Though the statutes now drawn up[2] were later than Statutes. the earliest statutes of Merton, they seem to be entirely uninfluenced by that famous code, and probably embody a constitution already in working order. Balliol College was originally not a land-holding corporation like other Oxford colleges, but simply a hall of students presided over by a principal of their own election. The finances of the house were entrusted neither to the principal nor to the scholars, but to two extraneous 'Procurators'—a Franciscan friar[3] and External a secular master of arts,[4] who paid them their respective proctors. allowances weekly, elected to vacant places and generally governed the house after the manner of a Parisian board of 'gubernatores'. Like many Paris foundations, but unlike most Oxford colleges, the 'Hall of Balliol' was originally a A college college for artists only, who after they had obtained the of artists.

allowed by Walter de Merton for B.A.s. There can be little doubt that under the statutes of 1340, not many members of Balliol continued to reside in the college after they obtained the degree of M.A.]

[1] [On this subject see Sir Charles Mallet's note in *Hist. Univ. Oxford*, i. 83.]

[2] [For the text of these statutes see *Oxford Balliol Deeds*, ed. H. E. Salter (O.H.S.), pp. 277–9.] The establishment of the college was confirmed by Oliver Sutton, Bishop of Lincoln, in 1284 (*Linc. Reg. Sutton*, f. 74 *b*; Savage, *Balliofergus*, p. 18); [*Oxford Balliol Deeds* (O.H.S.), pp. 280–1]. The actual foundation belongs to the same year (*ibid.*, p. 25; *4th Report Hist. MSS. Comm.*, p. 442), but the language of the deeds makes it plain that the college existed *de*

facto before John de Balliol's death in 1269. A licence for an oratory was granted by the bishop in 1293 (*Linc. Reg. Sutton*, f. 75 *a*; Savage, *Balliofergus*, p. 30), and confirmed by Bull of Urban V in 1364 (*ibid.*, p. 36). [See *Oxford Balliol Deeds* (O.H.S.), pp. 314–18; H. W. C. Davis, *Balliol College*, pp. 26, 27.]

[3] We may perhaps trace the Franciscan influence in the fact recorded in Bishop Sutton's confirmation (*Linc. Reg. Sutton*, f. 7 4*b*), that many members of the house 'in religione et alibi magnum fructus cumulum produxerunt'.

[4] Later [in 1433] they are called 'rectores'—a term sometimes used for the 'gubernatores' at Paris. *4th Report Hist. MSS. Comm.*, p. 443 *a*; [*Oxford Balliol Deeds*, ed. H. E. Salter (O.H.S.), p. 302].

CHAP. XII, degree of M.A. were not allowed to proceed to some other
§ 6. faculty. Yet, though the members of the foundation must
have been mere boys, the principal was required to govern
them in accordance with statutes and customs made by themselves.[1] [But the duties of the principal were concerned with
the holding of disputations and other small matters, the real
power in regard to the exercise of discipline being in the
hands of the external procurators.] And herein we obtain a
most interesting clue to the mode of government (if such it
can be called) which prevailed in the ordinary halls whether
the principal was a master or not. The college assumed
something more like the form of the other Oxford colleges
after the foundation of six theological fellowships (in addition
Somer- to the existing sixteen) by Sir Philip Somerville in 1340;[2]
ville's twenty-four years after which the privilege of studying
founda-
tion, 1340. theology after regency in arts was extended to the original
fellowships by papal Bull.[3] Somerville's statutes were super-

[1] This was confirmed by a decision of the external procurators of the college in 1325. *4th Report Hist. MSS.Comm.*, p. 442; [*Oxford Balliol Deeds*, ed. H. E. Salter, (O.H.S.), pp. 285–6. Rashdall seems here to exaggerate the boyishness of the members of the college. It is certainly to be inferred from Dervorguilla's statutes of 1282 that her scholars on admission 'might be undergraduates, but it may be fairly supposed that, at any rate after the first two or three years of the foundation, a proportion of those in residence were at least bachelors of arts. The decision of 1325 shows that there might be masters of arts in the college; they were not obliged to resign their fellowships on inception.]

[2] The statutes for Somerville's foundation are issued by 'Edwardus (Balliol) Dei gratia Scotorum Rex, ex primaeva fundatione Magistri et Scholarium aulae sive domus de Balliolo in Oxonia Fundator'. [See *Oxford Balliol Deeds*, ed. H. E. Salter (O.H.S.), pp. 286–99.] A

somewhat varying copy is found in *Reg. Palatinum Dunelmense*, ed. T. D. Hardy (R.S.), iii. 381. Somerville created a master, but left the principalship untouched. It was clearly intended that (as in Paris colleges) there should be a master of the theologians with a separate head for the artists. [H. W. C. Davis, *Balliol College*, pp. 30–2.]

[3] College Register. [*Oxford Balliol Deeds*, ed. H. E. Salter (O.H.S.), pp. 299–300; H. W. C. Davis, *Balliol College*, pp. 32–7, 62.] The extended tenure of the fellowships and an increase of the commons from 8*d.* to 12*d.* per week were secured by the impropriation of Abboldesley in the diocese of Lincoln, given by Sir William Felton, in 1340 (Paravicini, *Early Hist. Balliol College*, p. 168), though the endowment did not become available by the death of the rector till 1361, when Wyclif as master took possession of the benefice. (*Linc. Reg. Guywell, Institutions*, pp. 367, 368; J. Lewis, *Life of John Wyclif*, Oxford, 1820, p. 4; [*Oxford Balliol*

seded by a code drawn up, under papal authority, by Simon CHAP. XII, Sudbury, Bishop of London, in 1364.[1] The statutes by which §6. the college was governed up to the date of the first parlia- Bishop Sudbury's mentary commission were framed in 1507 by the Bishops of statutes, 1364. Winchester and Carlisle, under a Bull of Julius II, at the Statutes of request of the master and fellows.[2] The original founder had 1507. omitted to place his college under a visitor (the effect of which was to make the Bishop of Lincoln visitor *iure ordinario*), and by Somerville's statutes the visitatorial powers were awkwardly divided between the chancellor of the university, the Bishop of Durham, the Prior of Durham College, and the two extrinsic masters.[3] The statutes of 1364 had made the Bishop of London visitor.[4] The new papal statutes bestowed upon the college the unique privilege of electing its own visitor.[5]

Deeds, ed. H. E. Salter (O.H.S.), p. 299]. Wyclif is mentioned as master in other documents from 1360. (*4th Report Hist.MSS.Comm.*, p. 447 *sq.*) [H. B. Workman, *John Wyclif*, i. 79. For particulars of the connexion of Wyclif with Balliol see H. B. Workman, *John Wyclif*, i. 70–81.] The scholars were at first established in hired halls occupying part of the present site. S. Margaret Hall, bought in 1284, was the first habitation of their own (*4th Report Hist. MSS. Comm.*, p. 447), and forms the nucleus of the present college. [S. Margaret Hall was not acquired until 1342. It seems more probable that the scholars lived in Old Balliol Hall, later known as Sparrow Hall, a property belonging to the university and situated immediately to the west of S. Margaret Hall. It was acquired by the college in 1427. See *Oxford Balliol Deeds*, ed. H. E. Salter (O.H.S.), pp. 19, 29.]

[1] Not extant. *Statutes of the Colleges of Oxford*, i (Balliol College), p. 2 and Pref.; *4th Report Hist. MSS. Comm.*, p. 443. [*Oxford Balliol Deeds*, ed. H. E. Salter (O.H.S.), pp. 301–2; H. W. C. Davis, *Balliol College*, pp. 32, 33.]

[2] *Statutes of the Colleges of Oxford*, i (Balliol College), p. 1. The former prelate was Richard Fox, the founder of Corpus. [H. W. C. Davis, *Balliol College*, pp. 63–75; *Oxford Balliol Deeds*, ed. H. E. Salter (O.H.S.), pp. 309–14. Prior to the Bull of Julius II, a Bull bearing date 13 Aug. 1504, had been addressed by Alexander VI to the Bishops of Winchester and Norwich for the revision of the statutes.]

[3] *Statutes of the Colleges of Oxford*, i (Balliol College), p. x. The master-elect had also to be presented to the lord of the founder's manor of Wichenore, *loc. cit.*

[4] *Statutes of the Colleges of Oxford*, i (Balliol College), pp. xx, 2. [H. W. C. Davis, *Balliol College*, p. 33; *Oxford Balliol Deeds*, ed. H. E. Salter (O.H.S.), pp. 302–9.]

[5] The other colleges mentioned are Oriel, Brasenose, and Lincoln. (Rymer, *Foedera*, ed. 1712, xiv. 757.) The intention may, however, be only to establish the rights of the bishop as ordinary, not as visitor. [The college does not appear to have exercised this privilege, with the exception of the appointment of Archbishop Laud, before 1691; see H. W. C. Davis, *Balliol College*, pp. 73–4.]

CHAP. XII, After the Reformation the intrinsic visitatorial right of the
§ 6. diocesan appears to have been restored by the foundation-charter of Christ Church. It is not very clear by what means the college has recovered the right of electing a visitor, and there seems some reason to fear that this ancient society, in acting upon the papal Bull in defiance of a royal charter, may at one time have been liable to the tremendous penalties of *Praemunire*; though any such defect in the visitor's title is no doubt cured by the new statutes.

Far more elaborate and original was the design of Walter de Merton, the true founder of the English college-system. But before approaching this part of our subject it will be well to notice the growth of those houses by which at Oxford as at Paris the conception of an academical college must have been to a large extent suggested—the colleges of the regulars. The establishment of the Mendicant Orders in Oxford has already been sufficiently dealt with. It will be enough, therefore, to notice the colleges of the older orders, which, being entirely designed as places of study, were more closely analogous to the secular colleges than the convents of the Mendicants.

THE MONASTIC COLLEGES

The example of the Mendicants was tardily followed by the older religious orders. The days were over in which the Benedictine monasteries had been the repositories of the learning of the age. As places of education they had been completely superseded by the growth of the universities: as houses of learning their reputation had decayed with the decay of the positive or contemplative theology which had once flourished within their walls. Only very tardily were they shamed by the intellectual activity and consequent fame and influence of the Mendicants into somewhat feeble efforts to rescue their orders from the reproach of entire ignorance.[1]

In 1279 a chapter-general of the Benedictines in the

[1] [It should also be remembered that co-operation between Benedictine houses was dependent upon the effective development of a system of general chapters.]

Province of Canterbury held at Abingdon[1] imposed a tax of
2*d.* per mark upon the revenues of all the Benedictine monasteries in the southern province, for the purpose of maintaining
a hall at Oxford as a *studium* for their monks.[2] Four years
later, Sir John Giffard, of Brimpsfield, established a priory
as Gloucester College for thirteen monks from the great
monastery of S. Peter at Gloucester; but in 1291 this house
was apparently thrown open to all Benedictine convents in
the southern province, though John Giffard's benefaction
must (it may be presumed) have still been enjoyed by Gloucester alone. Gloucester College thus became an independent
college, and its prior ceased to owe any special allegiance to
the Abbot of Gloucester. The house was under the general
government of the Benedictine chapter-general and its presidents, who elected the prior. The expenses of each monk
(except the thirteen from Gloucester) were defrayed by
his own house, each convent being obliged to send one or
more scholars to Oxford.[3] The old buildings of Worcester

[1] [Rashdall in error gave the date
as 1289. This new proposal was
made and accepted in 1277 at the
previous chapter of the Canterbury
Province, held at Reading: it pre-
sumably received confirmation at
Abingdon. See *Chapters of the
English Black Monks*, ed. W. A.
Pantin, Camden Society, 3rd
Ser. xiv. 75, 101, 102, and Mr.
Pantin's article on the same sub-
ject in *Transactions of the Engl.
Hist. Society*, 1927, x. 209–10; and
*New Documents about Gloucester
College*, ed. V. H. Galbraith in
Snappe's Formulary, ed. H. E.
Salter (O.H.S.), pp. 342–4, 354–6.]
[2] The documents are printed in
Reyner, *Apostolatus Benedictinorum
in Anglia*, Douai, 1626, App. pt. i.
53 *sq.*—some of them reproduced
in Dugdale, *Monasticon*, ed. J.
Caley, 1823, iv. 407 *sq.*; *Hist. Mon.
S. Petri Glouc.*, ed. W. H. Hart
(R.S.), i. 32; *Annales Monastici
(Worcester)*, ed. H. R. Luard (R.S.),
iv. 488; *Chron. Petroburgense*, ed.

T. Stapleton (Camden Soc. 1849),
p. 31. Wood deals with Gloucester
College in *City* (O.H.S.), ii. 248 *sq.*
I have been unable to find any con-
firmation for Wood's statement
that a *studium generale* of the
Benedictines at Oxford is men-
tioned in 1175. Cf. also Dr.
Daniel's article on Worcester Col-
lege in *The Colleges of Oxford*,
p. 425 *sq.* [See also Dr. Daniel's
and Mr. W. R. Barker's history of
Worcester College; A. F. Leach,
Early Education in Worcester (Worc.
Hist. Soc.), pp. xxxvi–xliii; and the
*New Documents about Gloucester
College*, ed. V. H. Galbraith, with
an excellent introduction, in
Snappe's Formulary, ed. H. E.
Salter (O.H.S.), pp. 338–86 *b*.]
[3] Wilkins' *Concilia*, ii. 595, 714,
&c. [The particulars given by
Rashdall need considerable revision in the light of Mr. V. H.
Galbraith's researches. An abor-
tive attempt was made about 1291
to transfer the college from S.

College still exhibit the arms of some of the chief English monasteries, which are no doubt to indicate the separate staircases built by and appropriated to their respective houses.[1]

Soon after the foundation of Gloucester Hall we find Benedictine monks from Durham—the greatest monastery of the northern province—sent by their then prior, Hugh of Derlington, to study at Oxford.[2] Richard of Hoton, who succeeded him in 1289, began the erection of a college-building.[3] Richard de Bury, Bishop of Durham, greatest of medieval

Peter's, Gloucester, to the Benedictine Order, so as to make it the common college of the whole Province of Canterbury. Eventually in 1298–9 a dual arrangement was made whereby Sir John Giffard transferred his college to the Abbey of Malmesbury, under whose care he was spending his closing years, reserving certain powers to the presidents of the general chapters of the province. The connexion with S. Peter's, Gloucester, was severed. The abbots of Malmesbury seem to have failed to compete successfully with the presidents of the chapters in exercising the chief control over the affairs of the college and the appointment of its prior. After Benedict XII by the constitutions of 1336 united the Provinces of Canterbury and York into one chapter, monks from the north were as free as those from the south to enter the college. This *locus communis* of Benedictine scholars in Oxford was unlike any other academical foundation in the university. Its peculiarity has been well described by Mr. Galbraith. 'Strictly speaking it was neither a college', he writes, 'nor a monastic "cell", nor an independent priory. It was not indeed a corporate body at all, but a collection of *camerae*, belonging each to a different monastery. The abbey of Malmesbury, which controlled the site and the General Chapters which framed its

rules, exercised a divided control, the effect of which was to give an unusual degree of independence to the individual communities which sent students to the college. Each house was allotted a small plot of ground on which it built at its own expense and according to its particular requirements. Certain buildings used in common, such as the hall and chapel, were maintained at the common expense. Over the whole presided a *prior studentium*.']

[1] The monks had their own regent in theology. Reyner, *Apostolatus Benedictinorum in Anglia*, Douai, 1626, App. pt. iii. 105, 107, 134–6, 162, 177, &c. [See also *Chapters of the English Black Monks* (Camden Soc.), ed. W. A. Pantin, 3rd Series, xlv. 174–5. For the regulations governing the college and the reports of the *prior studentium* see *ibid.*, vol. ii (3rd Series, xlvii), 55–8, 74–82, 90, 149 ff., 211–16.]

[2] 'Monachos misit Oxoniam ad studendum.' Robertus de Graystanes, ap. *Hist. Dunelm. SS. Tres*, ed. J. Raine (Surtees Soc.), pp. 72, 73.

[3] *Ibid.*, p. 73. The following statements rest on *op. cit.*, p. 138, with the documents printed by Raine in his Appendixes, and in Wilkins, *Concilia*, ii. 613 *sq.* Cf. Dugdale, iv. 676 *sq.*; Wood, *City* (O.H.S.), ii. 263 *sq.*; H. E. D.

bibliophils, contemplated its refoundation and permanent CHAP. XII,
endowment;[1] and actually bequeathed to it the invaluable   § 6.
library which he had collected at Auckland. His successor,
Thomas de Hatfield—the magnificent builder of the Castle
Hall and the episcopal throne at Durham—actually entered
into an agreement with the prior and convent for the joint-
endowment of a college for eight monks and eight secular
scholars; but the project was not completed till after his
death in 1381, when it was undertaken by the convent under
an agreement with Hatfield's executors.[2] By Bishop Hatfield's ordinance the monastic students of theology and
arts were placed in the position of what would afterwards
have been called fellows or full members of the society:
the secular students of arts and grammar, who held their
places for seven years only, waited upon the fellows, sat
at a second table in the hall with the servants, and were in
fact mere servitors of the lordly monks of Durham.[3] The
library built to hold the treasures accumulated by de Bury[4]
still forms a connecting link between the ancient monastic

Blakiston in *Colleges of Oxford*,
p. 323 *sq*. A number of documents
relating to the college (once in the
possession of the Dean and Chapter
of Durham) are copied in Twyne
MS. ii, f. 32 *sq*. [See also 'Some
Durham College Rolls', edited,
with an important introduction,
by the Rev. Dr. H. E. D. Blakiston,
in *Collectanea* (O.H.S.), iii. 3–76;
Trinity College, pp. 1–28, by the
same author; and *Durham Account
Rolls*, ed. J. T. Fowler (Surtees
Society), vols. i, ii, and iii.]

[1] He bound himself in 1338 to
fulfil a vow made to that effect by
Edward III on the field of Hali-
don, on condition that the King
would abandon his claim to the
advowson of Simondburn. *Reg.
Palatinense Dunelm.*, ed. T. D.
Hardy (R.S.), iii. 210, 211. [See
Wilkins, *Concilia*, ii. 613–14.]

[2] [See H. E. D. Blakiston, 'Some
Durham College Rolls' in *Collec-*

tanea (O.H.S.), iii. 12–16; *Cal.
Papal Registers* (*Letters*) *1396–
1404*, pp. 21, 600–1.]

[3] [Bishop Hatfield's 'Ordinacio
collegii' is printed in Wilkins,
Concilia, ii. 614–17.]

[4] That the bishop intended his
library for Durham College is
proved by *Philobiblon*, c. 18 *sq*.,
where he lays down elaborate regulations for its use. That he actually
gave it is doubted by his latest
editor, Mr. E. C. Thomas (*Philobiblon*, p. xxix), but without sufficient reason. [It cannot be claimed
that the library was built to hold
Bishop de Bury's books, as the
bishop's valuable collection had to
be sold by executors to pay his debts,
and the main part of the library of
Durham College was erected in
1417–18. See H. E. D. Blakiston,
'Some Durham College Rolls' in
Collectanea (O.H.S.), iii. 9–10, 20,
73–4.]

CHAP. XII, house and the modern Trinity College erected on its ruins
§ 6.   by Sir Thomas Pope in 1554.

Canter-   The monks of Christ Church, Canterbury, had a hall of
bury.   their own in or near the site of the present S. Edmund Hall
as early as 1331[1] (besides a house in Gloucester College),
which, however, they sold to the monks of Westminster after
acquiring a regularly endowed college of their own in Canterbury Hall, to which we shall return hereafter.[2]

Rewley.   The Cistercian Abbey of Rewley, founded by Edmund,
Earl of Cornwall, in or about 1280,[3] has usually been looked
upon as an independent monastic house rather than a college;
but it was founded to serve the purpose of a college for
Cistercian students from other houses, and is often spoken of as the
studium.   'Studium' of the Order.[4] Other Cistercians, however, resided
in halls temporarily hired for the purpose, till in 1437,[5]

[1] *Literae Cantuarienses*, ed. J. B.
Sheppard (R.S.), i. 358, 392. It is
described as 'situatam iuxta ecclesiam Sancti Petri in Oriente, ubi
sõlebat Dominus Archiepiscopus
manere'. S. Edmund Hall possibly marks the site, though others
often refer the name to a former
owner called Edmund. [This hall
was opposite S. Peter's Church
and is now incorporated in the site
of Queen's College. See Dr. H. E.
Salter's note in J. R. Magrath, *The
Queen's College*, i. 326–7.]
[2] *Ibid.* iii. 14.
[3] 'Anno 1280.—Petitionem nobi-
lisimi viri comitis Cornubiae, qui
petit propriis sumtibus aedificare
studium nostri ordinis Oxoniae in
Anglia, capitulum generale plenis
gratiis prosequens, approbat et
confirmat, committens executio-
nem negotii abbati de Thama in
plenaria ordinis potestate; ita quod
eisdem libertatibus, iuribus, et dis-
pensationibus per omnia gaudeat
ille locus, quibus gaudet studium
B. Bernardi Parisii (*sic*), et studentes monachi in dicto studio de
diversis abbatiis congregati; et dictus abbas de Thama curam habeat

dictae domus, sicut et studii sancti
Bernardi venerabilis frater domus
Clarae-vallis.' Document in Fortu-
nato de S. Bonventura, *Historia da
real Abbadia Alcobaça*, Lisbon,
1827, Provas, p. 7. [E. Martène et
U. Durand, *Thesaurus Anecdotorum*,
iv. 1472.] Some other notices
about Rewley are collected by Dr.
Little in *Engl. Hist. Rev.* (1893).
[See also Dr. H. E. Salter's article
in *A History of Oxfordshire* (Victoria County Histories), ii. 81–3.]
[4] *Annales de Dunstaplia*, in *Ann.
Mon.*, ed. H. R. Luard (R.S.), iii.
287; Dugdale, v. 697. [See also
E. Martène et U. Durand, *Thesaurus Anecdotorum*, iv. 1476, 1478,
1479–80; A. G. Little, 'Cistercian
Students at Oxford in the 13th
Century', in *E.H.R.* (1893), viii.
83–5; R. C. Fowler, 'Cistercian
Students at Oxford' in *E.H.R.*
(1908), xxiii. 84–5.]
[5] Dugdale, v. 745. The foundation deeds are preserved in a Cistercian Register of Privileges, Univ.
Coll. MS., f. 93 *b*. [Cf. Sir Charles
Mallet, *Hist. Univ. Oxford*, i.
406, n. 1. See also Dr. H. E.
Salter's article in *A History of*

Archbishop Chicheley, the founder of All Souls, founded, on CHAP. XII, the site now occupied by S. John's, a college of S. Bernard, § 6. though the provisor and scholars continued to be supported S. Bernard's by their respective houses.[1] College.

In the same way the canons regular of the Order of S. Augustine acquired in 1435 a college known as S. Mary's College, to which canons were sent from all the houses of the Order.[2] It was situated on the site of a house now known as Frewin Hall; and a touch of historical interest is still imparted to the little ruin in New Inn Hall Street by the remembrance that Erasmus took up his quarters there during his residence in Oxford.[3] In the same year the canons regular of Oseney

S. Mary's College.

Oxfordshire (V.C.H.), ii. 86; Sir Charles Mallet, Hist. Univ. Oxford, i. 406; and Cal. Patent Rolls, Henry VI, 1436–41, pp. 45–6, for royal licence dated 20 Mar. 1437.]

[1] Since the building was unfinished half a century later (Proceedings of Somersetshire Archaeol. Soc. vi. 60 sq.), and the monks were supported by their monasteries (Wood, City, ii. 308), it is clear that Chicheley could not have done very much for them. ['The founder', says Dr. Salter, 'gave little more than the site, part of which was acquired from Durham College.' A History of Oxfordshire (V.C.H.), ii. 86.] Cf. 4th Report Hist. MSS. Comm., p. 469. The statutes of 1446 were given not by Chicheley but by an abbot named by the chapter-general. (Smith MSS. xiii. 303.) [E. Martène et U. Durand, Thesaurus Anecdotorum, iv. 1638. The history of S. Bernard's College will be dealt with by Dr. H. E. Salter in a forthcoming publication of the Oxford Historical Society to be entitled The Early History of St. John's College.]

[2] Rot. Pat. 14 Hen. VI, p. 2, m. 19. [Cal. Patent Rolls, Henry VI 1429–36, p. 590, dated 24 Dec. 1435.] The statutes of this college, which had long disappeared,

I found in 1890 in an unnumbered volume of the 'Rawlinson Statutes' in the Bodleian Library. Cf. Wood, City, ii. 228 sq. [See Dr. H. E. Salter's article in A History of Oxfordshire (V.C.H.), ii. 102–3; and Miss E. Evans's article, 'St. Mary's College in Oxford for Austin Canons', in Report of Oxfordshire Archaeol. Soc., 1931, pp. 367–91. The founder of the College was Thomas Holden, of Clay Hall, Barking, Essex. The statutes of the college were drawn up by Thomas Hooknorton, Abbot of Oseney, in 1448. The appointment of the prior rested with the Chapter of the Austin Canons. The prior was responsible for the administration of the college. There were no fellows, but the prior was expected in certain cases to act with the advice of the senior students. 'The students at the College were of three main types: the Canons studying theology or canon law, for whom the college was primarily intended; the younger Canons still reading logic and grammar; and the secular students, who might be doing either, who paid for their rooms and brought their own servants.' See Miss Evans's article, pp. 378–9.]

[3] Richard Charnock, the prior of this house, is praised by Erasmus

CHAP. XII, turned their dependent house of S. George's-within-the-
§ 6.   Castle into a college for their own young canons as well as
S. George's
College. for other seculars under a warden chosen from their own
number.[1]

Unimpor-   These monastic colleges possess very little importance in
tance. the history either of learning or of education. Monks never
applied themselves cordially to the scholastic philosophy or
theology. The older monastic Orders never produced a
single great theologian from the days of S. Bernard till the
reign of the scholastic theology was over and was superseded
by an age of learned theology. The aim of these monastic
colleges was probably very simple and practical. It was only
a select few of the younger monks who were sent to them.
What the monastic houses wanted was not to produce great
theologians or to contribute to the advancement of learning,
but simply to have a few instructed theologians capable of
preaching an occasional sermon to their brethren and of
imparting an elementary theological education to the novices.
Another purpose which probably interested the average abbot
more than the educational needs of his house was the supply
of canonists competent to transact its legal business and to
represent it in the ecclesiastical courts.

Services of   The real services of the monks to literature in the later
monks to Middle Age lie in a field quite alien to the studies of the
literature.
universities. To the monasteries belongs the credit of producing the great medieval historians. The Benedictine monks of
this period were above all things men of the world: their

in *Ep.* xliv. (*Opera*, Leyden, 1703,
tom. iii, c. 42.) [*Erasmi Epistolae*, ed. P. S. Allen, i. 243, dated
Oct. 1499.] A letter dated from S.
Mary's College is printed, *ibid.*,tom.
iv, c. 1791. [*Ibid.* i. 249, dated
Oct. 1499. See also *ibid.* i. 265,
267, 268.]

[1] Cf. Wood, *City*, ii. 180. Sir
H. Maxwell-Lyte does not notice
the existence of this college. The
statutes are preserved in the same
volume as the S. Mary's statutes
mentioned above. [Rashdall places
the date of the foundation of this
college too early. Dr. H. E. Salter
gives the probable date of its
foundation as about 1480. It is
not evident on what authority
Rashdall states that the young
canons regular of Oseney were
educated there. Under the statutes
of the college the five secular priests
and the scholars who formed the
society were under no obligation
'that they should be in any way
connected with the Augustinian
rule'. See the article on the college
by Dr. H. E. Salter in *A History
of Oxfordshire* (V.C.H.), ii. 161.]

point of honour was a devotion to the interests of the house: their intellectual interests lay in its history and traditions. As a body they had as little interest in the controversies of the age as they had in the practical work of the Church. Both theology and preaching were abandoned to the friars. The consequence was that no great schoolman was a monk; while not more than two or three important historians were friars. It is worth noticing that as the monastic orders sank into a yet deeper quagmire of moral degradation towards the close of the fourteenth century, the number and quality of monastic historians began to fall off.[1] The connexion between intellectual and spiritual vitality, in societies if not in individuals, is much closer than is sometimes supposed.

MERTON (1263 or 1264)

G. C. BRODRICK, *Memorials of Merton College* (Oxford Hist. Soc. 1885), especially valuable for the biography of individual fellows and for the post-medieval period, has not altogether superseded the *Sketch of the Life of Walter de Merton* by Edmund (HOBHOUSE, then) Bishop of Nelson, 1859. The *Foundation Statutes of Merton College, Oxford*, with a few other documents, have been published in English by PERCIVAL, London, 1887. A number of documents are contained in that curious farrago, KILNER's *Pythagoras' School in Cambridge* (no place or date). The college muniments are calendared in the *Sixth Report of the Hist. MSS. Comm.* (1877), pp. 545–9. [A history of *Merton College*, by Dr. B. W. HENDERSON, was published in 1899. Dr. H. E. SALTER has edited the earliest register of the college (*Registrum Annalium Collegii Mertonensis 1483–1521*, O.H.S., 1921), which is a particularly valuable source of information for the administration of a college at the close of the Middle Ages. An important selection of documents from the college archives, with collotype facsimiles, has been edited by Dr. P. S. ALLEN and Mr. H. W. GARROD (*Merton Muniments*, O.H.S., 1926). The history of the property in Cambridge acquired by the founder has been written by Mr. J. M. GRAY, *The School of Pythagoras, Cambridge*, C.A.S., Quarto Series, 1932. Two interesting papers on the college library have been contributed to the *Transactions of the Bibliographical Society*: 'Early Documents connected with the Library of Merton College' (*The Library*, N.S. iv. 249 *sqq.*) by Dr. P. S. ALLEN, and 'The Library Regulations of a Medieval College' (*The Library*, N.S. viii. 312 *sqq.*) by Mr. H. W. GARROD. These documents have been edited by Prof. F. M. POWICKE and made the subject of a detailed study of the development of the collection of medieval books in the Library of Merton College (*The Medieval Books of Merton College*, Oxford, 1931). An important chapter on the Merton School of Astronomy

---

[1] Even in 1345 Richard de Bury complains that 'calicibus epotandis non codicibus emendandis indul- get hodie studium monachorum.' *Philobiblon*, ed. E. C. Thomas, pp. 42, 43.

CHAP. XII, is included by Mr. R. T. GUNTHER in *Early Science in Oxford* (O.H.S.),
§ 6.   ii. 42–69. The *Injunctions of Archbishop Kilwardby, 1276*, have been
printed by Mr. H. W. GARROD with an introductory note (Oxford, 1929).
Mr. H. W. GARROD has written a valuable paper on the *Ancient Painted
Glass in Merton College, Oxford*, Oxford, 1931.]

The   Walter de Merton was one of those ecclesiastical civil
founder. servants or statesmen who rose to high position in the Church
almost before university distinction had become the ordinary
passport to a public career. He may have been a student at
Oxford; but it is pretty certain that he never graduated there
or elsewhere. He resolved to devote the savings of a successful
life to secure to future scholars, and especially to his own
family, the advantages which he had not himself enjoyed.
The chief object of the college was to enable eleven bachelors
of arts to obtain the degree of M.A., after which they might
remain in the college as regents of arts, or might proceed
to the study of theology.[1] A limited number of the fellows
might be allowed to proceed in civil and canon law.

First   It was probably in the year 1263[2] that Walter de Merton
founda- made over his manor house and estate of Malden in Surrey
tion.   to a community of scholars. The formal and permanent
establishment of the college was effected, and the first
statutes granted, in the following year.[3] On the whole, there-

[1] [On the motives of the founder see B. W. Henderson, *Merton
College*, pp. 26–34. See also *Registrum Annalium Collegii Merton.*,
ed. H. E. Salter (O.H.S.), pp. ix–
xi.]

[2] For the following particulars it
seems sufficient to give a general
reference to the printed *Statutes*.
[Between 18 Oct. 1262 and 9 Sept.
1264; see *Merton Muniments*, ed.
P. S. Allen and H. W. Garrod
(O.H.S.), pp. 9, 10.]

[3] See the deed in E. Hobhouse,
Walter de Merton, p. 15 (as to the
date, cf. *loc. cit.*, p. 11). [For the text
and collotype facsimile of these
statutes see *Merton Muniments*
(O.H.S.), pp. 15–17. This code
of statutes or 'ordinatio' was preceded by an 'ordinatio' that has
been lost, but to which reference

is made in the deed by which the
manors of Malden and Farleigh
were assigned to the use of the
scholars. This earlier 'ordinatio',
in the opinion of Dr. P. S. Allen and
Mr. H. W. Garrod (*Merton Muniments* (O.H.S.), pp. 9, 10), 'has,
perhaps, as good a claim as that of
1264 to be regarded as the first
body of Statutes made for Merton
College'.] From a charter granted
by the Earl of Gloucester in 1262
it appears that the founder had
contemplated vesting the property
in trust with the Priory of Merton,
or some other religious house, on
the plan of Basset's foundation: *loc.
cit.*, pp. 9, 10. [See *Merton Muniments* (O.H.S.), p. 8. Dr. P. S.
Allen and Mr. H. W. Garrod (*op.
cit.*, p. 8), 'in view of the terms of
the licence granted by Richard of

fore, Merton has the best claim to be the earliest Oxford
college. Balliol existed before it, we may say, *de facto* but not
de iure, and University *de iure* but not *de facto*. Merton alone
existed both *de iure* and *de facto* in 1264.[1] The nature of this
'House of the Scholars of Merton' has often been strangely
misrepresented. It has been spoken of as if the founder had
conceived the design of planting a college of students in arts
and theology in the midst of the corn-fields of Surrey. So far is
this from being the case that the scholars, in whom the property of the house was vested, were nevertheless not allowed
by the statutes to reside within its walls for more than one week
in the year at the annual audit.[2] The house was to be occupied
by a warden (*Custos*), who was not (so far as appears) required
to be either a priest or a scholar, together with certain
'Brethren' (a name probably suggested by the lay brothers
who farmed the estate of a Benedictine abbey), at other times
spoken of as bailiffs or stewards, whose business it was to
manage the property and pay their allowances to the scholars.[3]
There was also a provision for certain 'ministers of the altar'
who were no doubt to serve the parish church, and who lived
with the brethren. The eight original scholars were all
nephews of the founder;[4] and their number was to be increased
to twenty from the descendants of his parents, or (failing a
sufficient number of these) other 'honest and capable young
men' with a preference for the diocese of Winchester. They

Clare', are inclined to suppose that
the property was originally vested
in the Priory of Merton, but that
this arrangement was revoked some
time before 9 Sept. 1264, when
Walter de Merton obtained licence
from Gilbert, Earl of Clare,
Richard's son, to dispose of the
property 'prout expedire voluerit'
for the sustentation of scholars 'in
scholis degentium'.]

[1] [See p. 181, n. 2.]

[2] [The passage here referred to
states 'ibidem per octo dies, si
velint . . . moram facturi'. There
is nothing said about the eight or
ten scholars who are to undertake
this annual audit at Malden not

being allowed to stay for more than
one week, if necessary. It is laid
down in the statutes that two or
three scholars might come to
Malden at other times to make
investigation in the event of the
negligence or the illness of the
warden.]

[3] It is curious to find the archbishop in 1295 writing '*fratribus
et scolaribus domus scholarium
de Merton*': he goes on to speak
of '*vestre congregacionis ceno-
bium*'. (*Lambeth Reg. Wynchelsey*,
f. 175 b.)

[4] [They were to have an annual
allowance ranging from £2 to
£2 13s. 4d.]

CHAP. XII,
§ 6.
were to live together at the university, in a hall and to wear a uniform dress.[1] The warden did not accompany them; he was not their master or instructor, but rather the representative of a rich uncle who intended for all time to serve at once the Church and his own family by providing for the education of his less wealthy relations; and as such he was no doubt to exercise a paternal control—but a control from a distance—over their conduct at the university.

Provision for possible transfer.
The uncertainty which the Statutes of 1264 express as to the place of study arose from the dangers with which dissensions within, and the civil war without, threatened the continuance of the Oxford *studium*.[2] The statutes are dated in the very year of the Northampton Secession, and the foundation clause contemplates not merely the possibility of a temporary removal of the *studium* from Oxford, but of a state of things in which it might be expedient for his scholars to settle elsewhere. It is worth mentioning that the founder in 1269–70 acquired a house at Cambridge for his college,[3] no doubt in view of the possibility of a migration to that university.

Statutes of 1270.
As a matter of fact, however, Walter de Merton's scholars were from the first established in a hall at Oxford. By the body of statutes, which was given to the community in 1270, their corporate life at Oxford is more fully regulated.[4] There is now to be one sub-warden at Malden and another to preside over the students at Oxford, who is called the 'interior warden'; but it does not very clearly appear whether the warden is still intended to reside at Malden. The founder had for some time been engaged in acquiring property in Oxford. In the course of the years 1265 and 1266 S. John the Baptist's

[1] [See *Merton Muniments*, ed. P. S. Allen and H. W. Garrod (O.H.S.), p. 9, n. 4.]

[2] [The wording of the passage in the Statutes of 1264 here referred to runs: 'ad perpetuam sustentationem viginti scolarium in scolis degentium Oxon., vel alibi ubi studium vigere contigerit', see *Merton Muniments*, ed. P. S. Allen and H. W. Garrod (O.H.S.), document ii, l. 5.]

[3] Afterwards known as Pythagoras Hall—the subject of Kilner's monograph. [Mr. J. M. Gray has made a detailed study of the history of the estate acquired by Walter de Merton in Cambridge. See *The School of Pythagoras, Cambridge* (Cambridge Antiquarian Society, Quarto Series), 1932.]

[4] [See B. W. Henderson, *Merton College*, pp. 14–19; Sir Charles Mallet, *Hist. Univ. Oxford*, i. 114.]

Church was bought from the Abbey of Reading and impropriated for the benefit of the college; and several houses in
its immediate neighbourhood were made over to the scholars.
The site thus acquired became the permanent home of the
college henceforward known as Merton Hall in Oxford.[1] In
1274 the founder, now Bishop-elect of Rochester, issued a new
code of statutes, by which the warden is definitely placed at
the head of the Oxford community.[2] The country-house at
Malden was still occupied by some of the stewards or
'brethren' as before, and stood in precisely the same relation
to the Oxford community, except that the college had by this
time acquired other estates, likewise farmed by bailiffs, upon
any one of which the audit might now be held; and upon
some of which presumably some of the 'brethren' might
reside. At Oxford the community had become responsible
for the services of the impropriated church: there were to be
four or at least three chaplains in priests' orders: the rest
were to attend the canonical hours 'when they could find
time for them', i.e. on Sundays and festivals. Three bursars
were to be appointed from among the scholars to receive and
administer the revenues of the society. Besides the sub-
warden, there were to be a 'vicenarius' placed over every twenty
or a 'decanus' over every ten, as might be thought desirable.[3]
The duty of these deans consisted mainly in keeping the
peace among the cousins. To assist them in the maintenance
of discipline, and especially to enforce the rule of Latin-
speaking, one of the seniors in each chamber was responsible.
This last provision when introduced into Wykeham's foundation at Winchester may be said to have originated what is
known as the 'monitorial system'. In the universities it is not
without parallel in other college statutes, but was naturally
superseded when the usual number in each chamber became

[1] E. Hobhouse, *Walter de Merton*, p. 17; G. C. Brodrick, *Memorials of Merton College* (O.H.S.), p. 5. [B. W. Henderson, *Merton College*, pp. 10–14.]

[2] [For the text and collotype facsimile of the Statutes of 1274 see *Merton Muniments*, ed. P. S. Allen and H. W. Garrod (O.H.S.), pp. 21–6; see also G. C. Brodrick, *Memorials of Merton College* (O.H.S.), pp. 317–40; B. W. Henderson, *Merton College*, pp. 19–24.]

[3] ['Vicenarii' were provided for in the Statutes of 1270.]

CHAP. XII,
§ 6.

limited in the later medieval period to two and still later to one; but the dean still remains, amid all changes in the character of the discipline enforced, the disciplinary officer in most English colleges.

The visitor.

The original visitor or 'patron' of the college was the Bishop of Winchester, in whose diocese Malden was situated; but in 1276 the right of visitation was transferred to the Archbishop of Canterbury.[1]

The rule of Merton.

This careful provision for the maintenance of reasonable order and discipline in the house will not seem superfluous to any one acquainted with the laxity and licence of life in the university towns of the period. Merton's regulations were destined eventually to produce a revolution in the character of university life in England.[2] His scholars were to be ready upon admission to their year's probation to begin the study of arts.[3] After completing their period of necessary regency in the arts schools, the majority were to study theology, a few were to be allowed to study canon, and, as subsidiary to it, civil law. As some of the scholars might often be only seven or eight years old,[4] it was natural that for many purposes only a certain number of the seniors, varying in different cases, should be associated with the warden in the government of the house. The society, however, possessed a higher degree of autonomy than most Parisian colleges. By the Statutes of 1264 the twelve senior fellows elected the warden. By this last code three candidates were to be presented to the visitor, who was to admit one of them. Vacancies were filled up by the warden and the thirteen seniors according to the Statutes of 1264, and by the warden and seven seniors

---

[1] B. W. Henderson, *Merton College*, pp. 24, 195. The statutes are singularly silent as to the rights of the visitor.

[2] [On the college exercise, called *variations*, in the second half of the fifteenth century, see *Reg. Annalium Collegii Merton.*, *1483-1521*, ed. H. E. Salter (O.H.S.), pp. xxiii–xxiv.]

[3] [In his introduction to *Reg. Annalium Collegii Merton.*, *1483-*

1521 (p. ix), Dr. H. E. Salter controverts the view taken by Rashdall and other writers that it was the intention of Walter de Merton that undergraduates should be admitted as scholars of the college.]

[4] [Dr. H. E. Salter points out that 'as they were Bachelors, they were probably not less than nineteen years old when elected'. See *Reg. Annalium Collegii Merton.*, *1483-1521* (O.H.S.), p. ix, n. 1.]

according to those of 1274. In case of disagreement in the election of warden they were to be starved into unanimity, like an old English jury, by a 'subtraction of victuals'.

Although the allowance which each might receive from the common fund was strictly limited, the scholars were in a different position to the 'bursars' of continental colleges. They were corporate landowners, not (like the scholars of Balliol and many Parisian colleges) pensioners receiving an endowment administered by others. The Archbishop of Canterbury as visitor had little power beyond that of enforcing the statutes. So far as appears, the scholars might reside in college throughout the year, whereas at Paris a scholar's connexion with his college usually ceased during the long vacation. In later English college statutes residence during a great part of the long vacation is actually enforced. Moreover, the provision did not terminate with the attainment of the mastership in the faculty wherein the scholar had been studying. A fellowship was always voidable upon promotion to a benefice of a certain amount; otherwise it was (as a rule) tenable for life, though the statutes of later colleges generally required holy orders to be taken sooner or later as a condition of its retention. We must not, however, fall (with some modern enthusiasts for the collegiate ideal) into the anachronism of attributing to our college founders the enlightened design of providing homes for lifelong study or 'research'. Long as was the education of the theologian or even of the canonist, it was gone through as a preparation for active service in Church or State elsewhere than in the university. It was assumed that fellows would be quite eager enough to take a good living as soon as they could get one: till then the English college founders[1] desired to provide for their scholars' maintenance. In so doing they were following the example of Walter de Merton who (it must always be remembered) was providing, as the successful medieval ecclesiastic was expected to provide, for the members of his own family. The

---

[1] In some of the Paris colleges theologians are allowed to remain till they can get a 'living'—it is not there contemplated that they should be allowed to stay after the offer of a living. But in most cases resignation after the degree is enforced.

CHAP. XII,
§ 6.
life-fellow, whether 'idle' or studious, was a being quite undreamed of by any early college founders.[1]

The 'parvuli.'
Walter de Merton undertook to provide for his nephews from their earliest childhood. Besides the full members of the society provision was made by the original statutes for the reception and education in the country-house of a few small boys of the founder's family, who might want the means of providing them with such preliminary instruction in 'Grammar' as would enable them to begin the study of arts at Oxford. When the society were lodged in their own house at Oxford, these 'parvuli' were moved into the college or its neighbourhood.[2] They were to be instructed by a grammar-master, whom the more advanced scholars might also consult 'without blushing' upon matters pertaining to his faculty.

Provision for increased numbers.
It should be added that Walter de Merton did not, like some college founders, definitely limit the number of his fellows. During the earliest years of its corporate life the college property was continually increasing through the supplementary liberality both of the founder and of other benefactors. It was provided that as many fellows should be elected as the revenues would maintain. A provision for a similar increase in the number of fellows proportionate to their increasing wealth is found in many college statutes even where the original and normal number is prescribed. It is probable that these provisions have very seldom been

[1] This is clearly evident in the statutes of Queen's (*Statutes of the Colleges of Oxford*, i (Queen's College), 15), which provide that the refusal of a benefice (by whomsoever offered) 'occasione morae in ipsa aula ulterius faciendae' shall vacate a fellowship.

[2] The Statutes of 1270 made provision for the *parvuli* of the founder's kin up to the number of 13 or 15, and a memorandum supplementary to this code made provision for 12 *scolares pauperes secundarii*, who were to receive 6*d.* a week. It would appear that the *parvuli* and the 'secondary scholars' are quite distinct. The statutes of 1274 limited the number of the *parvuli* to 13. [On the subject of the *scolares pauperes secundarii* see *Injunctions of Archbishop Kilwardby*, ed. H. W. Garrod, pp. 7–8. For particulars of Merton Grammar School see A. F. Leach, *The Schools of Medieval England*, pp. 165, 171–4, 195–7.] At one time the 'parvuli' appear to have been lodged in Holywell—later close to the college in Nun Hall (afterwards S. Alban Hall). G. C. Brodrick, *Memorials of Merton College* (O.H.S.), p. 12.

observed. Already in 1284 Archbishop Pecham complains of CHAP. XII,
the excessive and unstatutable salary which the Merton fellows   § 6.
had assigned to the brewer and the cook and of the increase
which they had voted to their own allowance of 50s. a
year to defray the cost of 'delicate living'.[1] By 1425 the
college had even ventured on diminishing the number of
fellows.[2] The history of the English colleges is one of increasing wealth and increasing luxury secured by unearned
increments and some perjury. Such a result is due largely to
that freedom from external financial control of which Walter
de Merton set the example. On the other hand, the interest
of English fellows in their property has perhaps prevented
the waste, dissipation, and loss of college revenues of which
the history of Paris supplies so many examples.

The founder's care of his academic family did not cease Advow-
with the conclusion of their studies. Advowsons were often sons.
acquired by college founders simply in order to impropriate
the rectories, which was, of course, very much the cheapest
way of securing a revenue. But in some of the advowsons
acquired by Walter de Merton the rectories were not impropriated. It appears, therefore, that it was distinctly a part of
his purpose at least to give his scholars their first step upon
the ladder of ecclesiastical promotion. Walter de Merton is
thus distinctly the founder of that system of college livings
which was almost unknown out of England[3] and which has
exercised so powerful an influence for good and for evil over
the English universities and the English Church.

A new class of foundationers was introduced when the Portion-
body of portionists (now corrupted into postmasters) was ists.
engrafted on to the Merton foundation by John Wylliott, at
one time chancellor of the university, about the year 1380.[4]
The portionists, though possibly not junior to the younger

---

[1] *Statutes of the Colleges of Ox-*
ford, i (Merton College), 41, 42.

[2] *Ibid.*, p. 46.

[3] Canonries and rectories were
often held and served by members
of colleges, but I do not remember
any case of a continental founder

making it part of his design to provide preferment for his collegians
after leaving the college.

[4] [*Reg. Annalium Collegii Mer-*
ton., *1483–1521*, ed. H. E. Salter
(O.H.S.), pp. 514–17.]

CHAP. XII, fellows,[1] were a distinctly inferior and poorer class, who had § 6. no share, and no prospect of rising to a share, in the government of the house, and were in fact the servitors of the individual masters, by whom at least from the end of the fifteenth century they were appointed.[2]

Buildings. It forms no part of my plan to trace in detail the architectural history of the universities; but a word must be said as to the growth of the buildings in this typical English college. It is important to notice the prominence given to the chapel in Merton's scheme; for, though the parish church already existed, the founder at once proceeded to build a new one on the scale not of a mere oratory, like other college chapels already existing at Paris or elsewhere, but of a considerable collegiate church. The high altar was dedicated in 1277, the year of the founder's death, though the building could only have just begun.[3] Walter de Merton thus at once emphasized the ecclesiastical aspect of the English college and founded a certain tradition of architectural magnificence in which there is some reason to believe that the English colleges long surpassed those of other countries. Another feature in which Merton served as the type of later colleges cannot be attributed to the deliberate design of the founder. It was only gradually that the buildings assumed the familiar form of an Oxford quadrangle. 'The system of this first College seems to have been to keep the buildings separate: the collegiate

---

[1] G. C. Brodrick, in *Colleges of Oxford*, p. 19.

[2] *Ibid.*, p. 69. [On the subject of the portionists see *Reg. Annalium Collegii Merton., 1483–1521*, ed. H. E. Salter (O.H.S.), pp. xii–xv. The register also reveals the existence of certain *communarii*, never more than four in number, who in return for their keep performed various duties as servitors in the college. There are also references to *pauperculi* who may possibly be identical with the *communarii*: see *op. cit.*, pp. xv–xvii.]

[3] [Dr. B. W. Henderson, *Merton College*, pp. 196–201, on the evidence of the account-rolls that he had examined, is disposed to conclude that the date of the building of the choir was 1294–7. He does not think that the dedication of a high altar in 1277 relates to the present structure. Mr. H. W. Garrod, *Ancient Painted Glass in Merton College*, p. 12, considers that 'the account-rolls of the College make it fairly certain that it was not begun before 1289', and gives the date of completion as above 1294. On either finding the possibility of the choir having been begun in Walter de Merton's lifetime is excluded.]

quire with its vestry on the right hand of the courtyard; the refectory (of which the doorway appears to belong to Merton's original plan) opposite to the entrance, with its kitchen and offices beyond; the master's *hospicium* on the left; and the scholars' *hospicium* as a separate dwelling also. On the south side of the church there is now a real quadrangle, called Mob Quadrangle, of great apparent antiquity, which nevertheless is the result of a gradual accumulation of buildings. The northern side is formed by a range of chambers of the sixteenth century standing within ten feet of the quire buttresses, but, previous to the building of this range, the northern side was formed by the church itself. The eastern side contains the vestry and the treasury, both of Merton's time; and it is completed by a range of chambers of uncertain date. The west side was at first formed by the wall of the south transept (now covered by the north range), and by part of the library, begun about 1376, long after Merton's time. This library returns and closes the quadrangle on the south.'[1] By the time that the venerable quadrangle was complete, other quadrangles already existed at Oxford and Cambridge. The earlier of them arose from the loose arrangement of buildings round a court, but at last the quadrangle was adopted as the natural form in which college buildings might be deliberately planned. The quadrangle of Corpus Christi College, Cambridge, is said to have been the first originally planned close quadrangle. At Oxford the form almost accidentally assumed by the buildings of Merton was deliberately adopted by the founder of New College, whose 'buildings served as a model for all the large foundations which were subsequently undertaken'.[2]

EXETER (1314–16)

Life of the founder in G. OLIVER, *Lives of the Bishops of Exeter*, 1861, p. 54 *sq.* [There is a biographical preface to *The Register of Walter de Stapeldon*, 1892, by Prebendary F. C. HINGESTON-RANDOLPH.]   C. W. BOASE, *Register of Exeter College* (privately printed), Oxford, 1879, with some documents and a preface which amounts to an interesting college history.

[1] Willis and Clark, *Architectural History of Cambridge*, iii. 250. [The library was begun in 1375, and completed in 1378, see H. W. Garrod, 'The Library Regulations of a Medieval College' in *The Library*, N.S. viii. 312.]

[2] Willis and Clark, iii. 256.

There is a second and enlarged edition of this very learned work, without the preface (Oxford, 1893–4), and another revised edition with the original preface expanded into an ample 'History' but without some of the Latin documents (Oxf. Hist. Soc., 1894). My references are to the first edition. The muniments are calendared in the *Second Report of Hist. MSS. Comm.*, p. 126 *sq.* The statutes of this college were not printed for the University Commissioners. [The statutes which were drawn up by Bishop Stapeldon for his foundation of Stapeldon Hall in 1316 are printed by Prebendary Hingeston-Randolph in his edition of the Bishop's Register, pp. 304–10. A history of *Exeter College*, by W. K. STRIDE, appeared in the Oxford series of the *College Histories* in 1900.]

In the college founded by Walter de Stapeldon, Bishop of Exeter, in or soon after the year 1314,[1] we return once more in some respects to the simpler type of college prevalent at Paris and represented at Oxford by Balliol. The main endowment of the college—consisting merely in two impropriate rectories and an acre of land in Cornwall—was vested in the hands of the Dean and Chapter of Exeter, who paid over the revenue to the college.[2] A single scholar served the college as chaplain and studied theology or canon law: the remaining twelve were all artists, to be chosen from the diocese of Exeter, and lost their places upon completion of two or three years' regency in arts. But, though a college of artists, the scholars enjoyed an even fuller autonomy—in everything except the management of their property—than other Oxford colleges.[3] The rector was elected by themselves, but held office only for a year. Stapeldon was a canonist, and it is impossible to doubt that he must have got the idea of this democratic arrangement while studying law at Bologna or some other southern university.[4] The scholarships were filled up by the college itself and were restricted to natives of the founder's diocese, with the exception of the

[1] *Reg. Exeter Coll.*, pp. i, 1. The first extant 'ordinance' of the founder is dated 1322, *ibid.*, p. xl. The statutes of Sir Wm. Petre give 1316 as the date of the foundation. [The Bishop obtained a licence in mortmain in 1312 for the great tithes of S. Gwinear in Cornwall and an acre of land there, which property formed the first endowment of the college. See W. K.

Stride, *Exeter College*, p. 9.]
[2] *Reg. Exeter Coll.*, pp. xii, xliv, xlvi, &c.; C. W. Boase, in *Colleges of Oxford*, p. 77.
[3] [For an analysis of the founder's statutes see W. K. Stride, *Exeter College*, pp. 10–17.]
[4] [It is not known on what authority Rashdall rested his surmise that Bishop Stapeldon studied in Italy.]

chaplain-fellow, who was nominated by the Dean and Chapter CHAP. XII,
§ 6. of Exeter;[1] an arrangement which lasted till the University Commission of 1877. The scholars were at first quartered in Hart Hall and Arthur Hall,[2] on the site of the present Hertford College: shortly afterwards three houses were acquired on the site of the present Exeter College—a name which eventually superseded the earlier designation of Stapeldon Hall. Although not entrusted with the management of their Cornish property, the college held its Oxford house in its own name, and most of the later benefactions were made to the college directly. In 1566 the rectorship became a permanent, instead of an annual office,[3] and the college was thus practically remodelled in accordance with the now accepted Oxford or Mertonian type of college constitution; but it did not acquire fellowships for theologians (in addition to the chaplain) till the new foundations by Sir William Petre in 1566.

ORIEL (1324)

The Charter of Foundation and Foundation Statutes were withheld from the Commissioners of 1853, but were privately printed for the Commission of 1855. I am indebted to Dr. Shadwell, Fellow and late Treasurer, subsequently Provost, for access to these statutes and to his transcripts from the college documents. Valuable instalments of the results of Dr. SHADWELL'S work upon the college documents has been given us in his contribution to *The Colleges of Oxford*, and in the first volume of his *Registrum Orielense, 1500–1700* (London, 1893). The statutes printed for the Commission of 1853 are those drawn up by the college in the year following the foundation. *Second Report of Hist. MSS. Comm.*, p. 136. [A history of *Oriel College*, by Mr. D. W. RANNIE was published in 1900. The Rev. Dr. G. C. RICHARDS has completed a register of the provosts and fellows begun by Dr. C. L. SHADWELL (*The Provost and Fellows of Oriel College, Oxford*, 1922). Besides the particulars which it gives of the medieval provosts and fellows, this book contains several useful appendixes, some of which deal with the medieval period of the history of the college: App. i. 'The Vicars of S. Mary's'; App. ii. 'Oriel and the Wycliffite Movement'; App. iii. 'Oriel and the Reformation'; App. viii. 'College Livings'; App. ix. 'Order of Succession of the Fellows

---

[1] Subject to a veto by two-thirds of the college.

[2] [Arthur Hall did not stand on the site of Hertford College, but lay to the north or north-east of the church of S. Peter-in-the-East. This is evidenced by deeds in the possession of the college.]

[3] *Reg. Exeter Coll.*, pp. lii, 40. The power of re-election had been granted in 1384. In case of disagreement the chancellor of the university appointed. In other matters the visitation belonged of course to the Bishop of Exeter.

CHAP. XII, of Oriel'. Dr. SHADWELL compiled a catalogue of the muniments of the
§ 6.   college (*Oriel College, Oxford, Catalogue of Muniments*, printed for private
circulation, in 10 parts, 1893–1905). Dr. H. E. SALTER has made this
work more accessible so far as it relates to the Oxford property of the
college in *Oriel Records* (O.H.S.), 1926, and included all deeds concerning the foundation and internal management of the college. He has also
edited, in conjunction with Dr. G. C. RICHARDS, *The Dean's Register of
Oriel, 1446–1661* (O.H.S.), 1926. 'An Inquisition at Oriel, Sept. 4–7,
1411' is included by Dr. SALTER in *Snappe's Formulary, &c.* (O.H.S.),
pp. 194–215; it consists of the interrogatories about the misdeeds of five
fellows of the college, in connexion with the visitation of the university
by Archbishop Arundel.]

Founda-   The fifth Oxford college was more important than any of
tion and
statutes. its predecessors except Merton; and its original statutes are
copied almost *verbatim* from the 'rule' of that house. In the
year 1324 Adam de Brome, Clerk in the Chancery, Almoner
of Edward II, and Rector of S. Mary's, Oxford, acquired a
hall known as Tackley's Inn on the south side of the High
Street[1] near S. Mary's Church; and therein established a
'College of Scholars in Theology and the Dialectical Art'.
A little more than a year later (1 Jan. 1326), however, the
possessions of the college were surrendered into the King's
hands and the college re-established with the King as its
nominal founder—an arrangement which brought the Royal
Chancellor into the position of visitor.[2] The endowment was

[1] As Adam de Brome obtained
a royal licence to buy a messuage
for the college, and Tackley's Inn
was bought, it is probable that this
was the actual residence of the college, if it ever came into substan-
tive existence prior to the royal refoundation. As to the locality of
the college after this, Dr. Shadwell
says, 'It probably was at first established either in S. Mary's Hall, the
Manse or Rectory House of S.
Mary's Church, or in Tackley's
Inn, a large messuage in the High
Street, on the site now occupied
by the house No. 106.' (Shadwell
in *The Colleges of Oxford*, pp. 89,
90.) [See Dr. H. E. Salter's note on
Tackley's Inn and the documents
relating to the purchase of it in
Oriel Records (O.H.S.), pp. 163–5.]

[2] The college was governed by

the second code (though there are
isolated cases of appeals to the
chancellor) till 1726, when the
Court of Common Pleas decided
that the first statutes were still in
force, and the Crown and not the
bishop visitor. See Shadwell in
The Colleges of Oxford, pp. 113,
118 *sqq.* This is a characteristic
piece of lawyer's history. [For the
text of the foundation statutes of
the college dated 21 Jan. 1326, and
other documents relating to the refoundation by Edward II see *Oriel
College Records*, ed. C. L. Shadwell and H. E. Salter (O.H.S.),
pp. 3–14. For the texts of the
statutes made by the college 23
May 1326, and 8 Dec. 1329, see
Statutes of the Colleges of Oxford, i
(Oriel College), 6–16. See also *Oriel
College Records* (O.H.S.), pp. 17, 19.]

partly supplied by the impropriation of S. Mary's Church, whose services were maintained by the college, and its choir used by its members.[1] A body of statutes was given to the college by the King in the year of the refoundation, which was, however, immediately superseded by a code drawn up by the college and confirmed by the bishop and later by Edward III.[2] This was due to the necessity of dissociating the college from the declining fortunes of Edward II, and the most important change made by the new statutes was to substitute the bishop as visitor for the King or his chancellor. The college consisted of a provost and ten scholars, at least bachelors of arts, who, after completion of regency, were to study theology, except three, who might be allowed to study civil or canon law. The smaller numbers of the college not calling (as at Merton) for many deans, the Oriel statutes provide for only one, who here alone is the second person in the college. The fellows enjoyed, moreover, still more completely than at Merton, the autonomy characteristic of the English college. All take part in the election of warden and the government of the house. Certain functions were, indeed, restricted to a limited number of the senior fellows, and in many later colleges the greater part of the ordinary business of the college was performed by some such 'seniority' (to use the Cambridge term); but the choice of a head and the right of assenting to the use of the common seal were here, as almost always in Oxford, vested in the whole body of fellows. Even the power of making new statutes is vested in the provost and 'ten or eight senior and discreter Fellows with the approval of the Visitor'.[3]

---

[1] A chapel in the college was built by Richard, Earl of Arundel, c. 1373 (Shadwell in The Colleges of Oxford, p. 112); [Oriel College Records, ed. C. L. Shadwell and H. E. Salter (O.H.S.), pp. 29–30; D. W. Rannie, Oriel College, pp. 35–6.]

[2] The then Bishop of Lincoln, Burghersh, was an adherent of the now triumphant Queen's party, who used his influence to secure the visitatorial rights for his see.

The consent of the bishop, which even the Royal Charter could not dispense with, was not given till after the change. [See Oriel College Records, ed. C. L. Shadwell and H. E. Salter (O.H.S.), pp. 14–17; and D. W. Rannie, Oriel College, pp. 11–13, where the differences between the two codes are indicated.]

[3] This provision is taken from Merton, where, however, the visitor's consent was not required.

Two other characteristics of the Oriel statutes deserve
notice as illustrating how a founder's will may modify the
whole history of an institution in totally unforeseen ways for
centuries after his death. All the original fellowships at Oriel
were unrestricted to any part of England, and there were no
'boys' or other inferior foundationers who enjoyed any right
or expectation of succeeding to them. Some close fellowships
were founded at later dates, but never more than six or seven.
The rest of the fellowships always remained open to public
competition. This peculiarity contributed largely to make an
Oriel fellowship the blue ribbon of university distinction, and
constituted it the home first of the liberal movement to which
the university owed its intellectual revival, and then of the
ecclesiastical movement which has borne so large a share in
the reawakening of the Church of England from its eighteenth-
century lethargy. It must not, however, be hastily concluded
that local restrictions were always bad. The older English
colleges exhibit (in their original constitution) less local restriction than those of Paris: most county fellowships are of
comparatively late origin and in some cases seem to have been
introduced simply to prevent the elections being influenced
by a county clique in the college. They certainly needed to
check the system of corrupt elections for which open colleges
like All Souls obtained so scandalous a notoriety.

Local
habitation.   Soon after 1327 the college moved into a new house, presented to it that year by Edward III and known as La Oriole,
a name which has now superseded its official title, the House
of the Scholars of S. Mary in Oxford.[1] The old rectory of
S. Mary's Church was let to a master and became an independent hall, though closely connected with Oriel, till once
again merged in the college originally (it would seem) partly
or entirely housed within its walls.[2] Besides its buildings,
S. Mary's College received from Edward III another addition
to its property in the ancient Leper-hospital of S. Bartholo-

---

[1] It was also known as the King's
Hall. 'La Oriole' was probably
occupied by the college in 1329
(Shadwell, in *The Colleges of Ox-
ford*, p. 91). [See *Oriel College*   *Records*, ed. C. L. Shadwell and
H. E. Salter (O.H.S.), pp. 114–15.]
[2] [S. Mary Hall was reunited with
Oriel College in 1902 on the death
of Dr. Chase, principal since 1857.]

mew, the remaining buildings of which may still be seen a few hundred yards off the Cowley Road, a mile beyond Magdalen Bridge.[1]

QUEEN'S (1341)

The muniments are described in *Second Report of Hist. MSS. Comm.*, p. 137, and *Fourth Report*, p. 451. For the life of Eglesfield see R. L. POOLE in *Dict. Nat. Biog.* [The unique Obituary Book of the college (*Liber Obituarius Aulae Reginae in Oxonia*) was worthily edited by the Provost, the Rev. Dr. J. R. MAGRATH in 1900 for the Oxford Historical Society. A compendious history of *The Queen's College*, in two volumes, by the Provost, was published in 1921. The archives of the college have been calendared by Mr. N. DENHOLM-YOUNG; a copy of the calendar in typescript is in the Bodleian Library.]

The Queen's Hall, now known as Queen's College, derived its name from Queen Philippa, Consort of Edward III, by whose chaplain, Robert de Eglesfield, it was founded in 1341. It was placed under the perpetual patronage of the Queens of England, a compliment which does not appear to have won for the college much material assistance from its original recipient, though many subsequent Queens consort have been among its benefactors. The statutes of this college are not based upon the 'rule of Merton', but are of a far more elaborate character, and aim at regulating the whole domestic life of the society down to such minutiae as the composition of the college pottage[2] and the washing of the fellows' heads.[3] In many respects the new departure now taken was followed

Founda-tion.

---

[1] For its history see Wood, *City* (O.H.S.), iii. 504. The college was afterwards accused by the hospital of stealing from it the skin of S. Bartholomew and other relics for the enrichment of S. Mary's. Inquisition of 14 Rich. II, n. 138 (Twyne MS. ii, f. 45). [Dr. H. E. Salter's article in *Victoria County History of Oxford*, i. 157–8; *Oriel College Records*, ed. C. L. Shadwell and H. E. Salter (O.H.S.), pp. 282–369.]

[2] 'Item quolibet die fiat potagium congruum et competens, in aliquo vase ad hoc specialiter ordinato, de fabis vel pisis vel utrisque mixtis, de mensura dimidii busselli Londonie, farina avenarum vel hordei competenter immixta, de communi emptis, et singulis diebus anni ad portam cum residuo fragmentorum pauperibus erogetur,' *Statutes of the Colleges of Oxford*, i (Queen's College), 33; [J. R. Magrath, *The Queen's College*, i. 58.]

[3] 'Lotrices eciam cameras scolarium vel habitancium quorumcunque in dicta aula non intrent, sed per eorundem barbitonsorem capita eorundem laventur.' *Ibid.*, p. 33; [J. R. Magrath, *The Queen's College*, i. 49].

by later college founders: other provisions represent the
somewhat eccentric whims of the founder of Queen's.

The original society was intended to consist (when the
state of its revenues should permit) of a provost and twelve
scholars,[1] in imitation of our Lord and his Apostles, who were
to sit on three sides of the high table only in imitation of the
conventional representations of the Last Supper (a custom
still observed at Queen's) and to wear blood-red or purple
robes in remembrance of Christ's Passion. The fellows—
these are the first statutes in which the term *socii* is the
ordinary technical name of the full members of the society[2]
—are still summoned together to dinner by the sound of a
trumpet; in this and other details the Court chaplain is very
anxious to have everything done in Court fashion (*curialiter*).
His scholars may talk French instead of Latin at table. Eglesfield is clearly desirous that his scholars shall live in rather
better style than the members of previous foundations.
Whereas at Oriel, founded but fifteen years before, the scholar's
commons were limited to a shilling a week, rising when the
price of corn was high to fifteen-pence, the fellow of Queen's
was to receive a table-allowance of not less than eighteenpence a week, which might rise to two shillings at the discretion of the college. The provision for servants is also peculiarly
ample. The establishment was to include a treasurer's clerk

---

[1] [It was required of a candidate
for a fellowship that he should have
already proceeded to the degree
of M.A. and have completed his
necessary regency, and that he
should be well fitted to study
theology. See J. R. Magrath, *The
Queen's College*, i. 33.]

[2] Originally the term was employed to denote the relations between those who boarded together
in the same hall. Eglesfield's example is followed by Wykeham,
the 'verus et perpetuus socius'
being distinguished from the pro-
bationer. The distinctive use of
scholaris for the *inferior* members
of the foundation is still later. They
are denoted by a great variety of
terms—*pueri, scholastici, sizatores*
(at Cambridge)—and appear to
have been required to act more or
less as servants or 'fags' or humble
companions to the actual fellows.
Gradually—in post-medieval times
—we find the class differentiating
itself into 'Scholars' or foundationers who had no share in government but who had no menial
duties, and 'servitors' or 'sizars',
who still performed such duties.
'The Master (or President) and
scholars' still forms the official
designation of the head and fellows
in many colleges.

(probably one of the chaplains[1]), a butler or steward, a cook, CHAP. XII,
and a scullion,[2] a baker, a brewer, and a miller to grind the § 6.
college corn, and a boy to help them, a porter-barber, a
gardener, a washerwoman, and a night-watchman,[3] besides
ordinary servants.

Another matter in which the statutes of Queen's mark Chaplains.
a stage in the development of the college-system is the increasingly ecclesiastical character of the foundation. A staff
of thirteen chaplains was to be maintained for service of the
college chapel or impropriated church, if such a church should
ever be acquired in the immediate neighbourhood of the
college.[4] Moreover, these are the first statutes which expressly require the fellows to take holy orders.[5] Here even
the canonists are required to take holy orders within a year[6]
and priest's orders within three years.

Besides the twelve 'true and perpetual' fellows, all of whom Poor boys.
were to be theologians or canonists, provision is made for the
maintenance of twelve 'poor boys'.[7] Their position was very
much like that of the 'parvuli' at Merton, but they enjoyed no

[1] 'Unum presbiterum, clericum thesaurarii nominandum cum provisoribus et dispensatoribus.' [See J. R. Magrath, The Queen's College, i. 52.]

[2] 'Unum garcionem coquinae.'

[3] The duties of this official are peculiar. He is appointed (Statutes, p. 32) [J. R. Magrath, The Queen's College, i. 49] because 'necessarie sunt nocturne vigilie, pro vitando ignis periculo' (it is a remarkable fact that there have been more fires at Queen's than at any other college), 'pro excludendo latronum incursu, pro variis eciam insolenciis explorandis . . . necnon pro horis et partibus noctium ‹ certius cognoscendis'. The latter function was to be performed by 'noctis temporibus fistulans consuetis, ut per hoc magis excitentur et sciant tam scolares quam eciam servientes quando melius quiescere debeant et quando melius laborare'. A night in medi-

eval Queen's must have had its horrors!

[4] The founder probably had his eye upon S. Peter's-in-the-East. [See J. R. Magrath, The Queen's College, i. 43–4.]

[5] Hitherto the only obligation to take orders arose from the obligation to take theological degrees. [See J. R. Magrath, The Queen's College, i. 39.]

[6] If illegitimate they are given three years, perhaps to allow time to procure a dispensation. The provision is remarkable, as many college-statutes expressly require legitimate birth. In some or all universities—certainly at Paris—it was necessary even for graduation.

[7] [Their status was that of a grammar-school boy and not that of an undergraduate. See J. R. Magrath, The Queen's College, i. 45–9.]

CHAP. XII, positive claim for vacant fellowships, although, in the event
§ 6.   of their candidature, they were to receive favourable consideration by reason of their previous education in the college.
For their instruction an artist and a grammarian are to be
provided: while two chapel clerks are to instruct them in
plain-song.[1] They are to be daily opposed or 'posed in
grammar and dialectic by the fellows at dinner before sitting
down to their own table. They are to earn the 'alms' that are
doled out to them by singing in chapel, and by waiting at
table on Sundays and festivals.[2] Besides the chaplains and
the 'poor boys', thirteen poor men and women are to be daily
fed at the side tables in hall; and broth is to be distributed
daily at the college gate.[3] Altogether in Eglesfield's statutes
the charitable and religious aspect of the college decidedly
predominates over the scientific. Next to the desire to provide for the future of his own soul and those of his benefactors
and relations, it was the founder's aim to strengthen the
Church in the wild regions of Cumberland and Westmorland:
natives of those counties and of parishes whose tithes were
impropriated to the college enjoyed a preference, though by
no means an exclusive right, in the election to vacant fellow-
Visitor. ships. The Archbishop of York, in whose diocese the chief
impropriated benefice was situated, became Visitor,[4] and the
college has always retained the character of a North-country
foundation.

CANTERBURY (1361)

The documents relating to this foundation are calendared in *Fifth Report
of Hist. MSS. Comm.*, p. 450 *sq*. Islip's statutes are printed in WILKINS,
Concilia, iii. 52 *sq*. Other notices occur in *Literae Cantuarienses*, ed. J. B.

[1] As nothing is said of their attending lectures in School Street,
and the 'artist' himself is not required to be a master or even a
bachelor, it is not clear whether the
boys were even to keep terms in the
university.

[2] They are to wait only 'cum
curialitatis honestas requirit' (p.
29). The name 'Taberdar' (originally given to these boys, but after-

wards apparently confined to those
of them who were B.A.) was derived from the fact that the tabard
was the ordinary dress of non-
masters. [J. R. Magrath, *The
Queen's College*, i. 47–8. See also
A. F. Leach, *The Schools of Medieval England*, p. 195.]

[3] [J. R. Magrath, *The Queen's
College*, i. 58.]

[4] [*Ibid.* i. 42.]

SHEPPARD (R.S.), in whose preface (ii. xxv *sq.*) the history of this college is fully dealt with. Cf. WOOD, *City*, ii. 275. [See also H. S. CRONIN, 'John Wycliffe, the Reformer, and Canterbury Hall, Oxford', in *Trans. Royal Hist. Soc.*, 3rd Series (1914), viii. 55–76; H. B. WORKMAN, *John Wyclif*, i. 171–84; and important documents in J. FOXE, *The Acts and Monuments*, ed. J. Pratt, ii. 922–38, especially 927–9, 935. Cf. Sir C. E. MALLET, *Hist. of Univ. of Oxford*, i. 304–7. An edition of the records of the college preserved in the Library of Canterbury Cathedral is being prepared for the Oxford Historical Society by Mr. W. A. PANTIN.]

Canterbury Hall, founded by Simon Islip, Archbishop of Canterbury, in 1361, is an earlier instance of the attempt successfully made by Bishop Hatfield of Durham to unite regulars and seculars on the same foundation.[1] Its failure was no doubt due to the fact that the seculars and regulars were here placed on a footing of entire equality, except, indeed, the chaplain who—as was usual with such 'inferior clergy'—was required to wait on the fellows and then dine at the second table. There is nothing in the founder's statutes to appropriate the college or any of its places to monks: on the contrary, there is the usual provision that a fellowship shall be lost by entering 'any religion'.[2] The warden was, however, to be chosen by the archbishop out of three persons presented to him by the prior and convent, and it appears that the first warden was actually a monk of Canterbury.[3] But in 1365 the archbishop changed his mind, turned out the monk Henry Wodhall from the wardenship and put in a secular master, one John Wyclif, by some identified with the Reformer.[4] An appeal to Rome followed, which was not

[1] [See *Cal. Patent Rolls, Edw. III, 1361–4*, pp. 139–40. The royal licence is dated 20 Oct. 1361.]

[2] [Rashdall is probably mistaken here in assuming Islip's undated statutes, so 'secular' in tone (Wilkins, *Concilia*, iii. 52–8), to be the original foundation statutes; see below, p. 212, n. 1. It is clear from the King's licence that a mixed body of monks and seculars was from the first (1361) intended; see *Literae Cantuarienses*, ed. J. B. Sheppard (R.S.), ii. 409. The monks' co-operation would be necessary for the appropriation of the church of Pagham, which was the principal endowment of the college. According to the *tenor fundacionis*, dated 13 Apr. 1363, the college was intended by the archbishop *pro duodenario studencium*. See *Lit. Cant.*, ed. J. B. Sheppard (R.S.), ii. 442 *sq.*]

[3] [*Lit. Cant.*, ed. J. B. Sheppard (R.S.), ii. 416.]

[4] Lambeth Reg. Islip, ff. 192 *b*, 306 *b*. This John Wyclif is identified with the Reformer by the Monk of S. Alban's in *Chron. Angl.* (ed. E. M. Thompson (R.S.), p. 115), and by Wodeford in Wyclif's lifetime (ap. W. W. Shirley, *Fasc*

CHAP. XII, decided till 1371, after the accession of a new archbishop, the
§ 6.   Benedictine Simon Langham, by whose favour the monks of
Canterbury got a decision assigning not merely the wardenship but the whole college to members of their own body.[1]
In this position the college remained till the Dissolution,
with the addition of certain secular servitorships after the
model of those in Durham College founded by Archbishop

Zizan. (R.S.), p. 517), but the balance of evidence seems to me to
point the other way. There are
arguments for the identification of
the Reformer with the Warden in
Church Quarterly Rev. v. 129 *sq.*,
and B. W. Henderson, *Merton College.* Against it see Shirley, *loc. cit.*;
G. Lechler, *Life of Wycliffe*, translated by Lorimer, new ed., p. 103
sq.; R. L. Poole, *Wycliffe and the
Movements for Reform* (1889), p. 68;
[and Rashdall's article on John
Wyclif in *D.N.B.*]. Wyclif alludes to the dispute about the
college in *De Ecclesia*, ed. J.
Loserth, p. 871. [Rashdall's rejection of the identification cannot be
commended. Dr. H. B. Workman
(*John Wyclif*, i. 171–94) has made
a full and careful survey of all the
available evidence, and shows good
reason for the conclusion that 'the
older opinion that Wyclif of Canterbury was the Reformer is correct' (*ibid.* i. 185).]

  [1] *Lit. Cant.*, ed. J. B. Sheppard
(R.S.), ii. 504; Higden, *Polychronicon* (continuation), ed. J. R. Lumby
(R.S.), viii. 365. If the decision was
based on Islip's statutes there must
have been a violent perversion of
justice. But Courtenay (*Lit. Cant.*
ii. xxx) cites these statutes as
providing that the warden shall be
'monachus ecclesiae nostrae'. Mr.
Sheppard thinks that Simon Langham issued fresh statutes which
Courtenay mistook for those of
Islip, 'since it would be unreasonable to charge Archbishop Courtenay with wilful misquotation'. It

is equally possible that a garbled
copy was produced by the monks
of Canterbury. [But as Dr. Workman rightly argues (*op. cit.* i. 174),
it is not likely that Archbishop
Courtenay either deceived himself
or was imposed upon by the monks.
Mr. W. A. Pantin suggests that the
sequence was as follows: (i) probably Archbishop Islip drew up
(*c.* 1361–5) a first set of statutes,
now lost, for the mixed college of
monks and seculars; it would be
these that Archbishop Courtenay
cites; cf. also the extract, *verba
ordinacionis*, in *Lit. Cant.* ii. 417;
(2) Archbishop Islip's second
statutes, for the secularized college,. printed in Wilkins, *Concilia*, iii. 52–8, under the year
1362, but in fact undated, and
probably a mere draft made not
before the middle of Mar. 1366; cf.
H. S. Cronin, *Trans. Royal Hist.
Soc.*, 3rd Series, viii (1914), 60–2; (3)
Archbishop Courtenay's statutes,
for the completely monastic college,
Jan. 1384, preserved in Canterbury
Cathedral, Reg. B, ff. 388ᵛ–92,
extracts given in *Lit. Cant.* ii,
xxx *sq.*; apparently this recasting
of the statutes had already been
begun by Archbishop Sudbury,
1375–81; see Reg. Courtenay, f.
42ᵛ. Under Archbishop Courtenay's statutes the college was to
contain a warden and monk-fellows
elected by the Prior and Chapter of
Christ Church, Canterbury. The
college accounts show the number of fellows varying from two to
six.]

Courtenay.[1] Its memory still lives in the Canterbury Gate CHAP. XII, and Quadrangle of Christ Church. § 6.

NEW COLLEGE (1379)

The old life of the founder (by MARTIN), *Historica Descriptio complectens vitam ac res gestas Guillelmi Wicami*, London, 1597, contains little information about the colleges. There are a few documents in the two scholarly Lives of Wykeham by Bishop LOWTH (2nd ed., London, 1759) and G. H. MOBERLY (Winchester, 1887 and 1893). WALCOTT, *William of Wykeham and his Colleges* (Winchester, 1882), still leaves something to be desired as a final work upon Wykeham and his foundations. *Cartae de fundatione Coll. B. Mariae Wynton. in Oxon.* (privately printed in 1879). There is a manuscript life ascribed to, but really only corrected by, Warden CHANDLER in the New College Library. For some other documents cf. OGLE, *Letters addressed to Oxford*, Nos. lv, lx, App. No. iv. Cf. also HARPSFIELD, *Hist. Anglicana Ecclesiastica*, Douai, 1622, p. 522 *sq.*, and *Second Report of Hist. MSS. Comm.*, p. 132. [A history of *New College* by Dr. RASHDALL and Dr. R. S. RAIT was added to the Oxford series of *College Histories* in 1901. *The Chaundler MSS.* have been finely edited by Dr. M. R. JAMES for the Roxburghe Club (1916). This volume contains admirable reproductions of the very interesting illustrations contained in the New College manuscript. An article on 'Wykeham's Books at New College' was contributed by Mr. A. F. LEACH to *Collectanea* (O.H.S.), iii. 213–44; and an article by Mr. A. H. M. JONES and Mr. K. MCGREGOR entitled 'Medieval Life in an Oxford College', will be found in *Discovery*, v (1924), pp. 231–4: it deals interestingly with the original arrangement of rooms in the college.]

It has often been observed that the great foundation of New era in William of Wykeham, Bishop of Winchester, marks a new college-building. era in the history of college foundations. Yet it is not so much in any one distinctly original feature as in the greater scale of the whole institution that New College can justly be said to represent a new idea.[2] In many of its features Wykeham's

---

[1] Document in *Lit. Cant.* (R.S.), xxxi; cf. iii. 184. [There were to be five of these 'pueri collegii'. A certain number of rooms required for the use of the fellows and the secular scholars of the college were let to '*commorantes*' or 'sojourners' who might be religious or secular. The secular 'sojourners' were generally scholars or beneficed ecclesiastics of senior standing, e.g. Thomas Chaundler, chancellor of the university.]

[2] [New College is an abbreviated form of the fuller designation 'novum collegium sancte Marie Wyntoniensis', which served to distinguish it from the older college of S. Mary in Oxford, commonly called Oriel College, which prior to Wykeham's foundation is to be found designated 'domus seu collegium sancte Marie Oxonie aliter dictum le Orialle'. See *Cartulary of the Hospital of St. John*, ed. H. E. Salter (O.H.S.), ii. 85, n. 2, and *Oriel College Records*, ed. C. L. Shadwell and H. E. Salter (O.H.S.), 27.]

CHAP. XII, design was but a more splendid realization of the ideal which
§ 6.   had floated before the mind of Robert Eglesfield, the founder
of Queen's, who had probably hoped that a large extension
would one day be given to his foundation by Philippa or one
of the future Queens consort of England under whose special
protection he had placed the college;[1] and he contemplated
the possibility of the increase of both the fellows and poor
boys till the latter equalled in number 'the seventy-two
disciples'. In these hopes, however, he was disappointed,
and it is doubtful whether the funds of the college at first
sufficed even for the maintenance of the elaborate establishment provided for in the statutes. What Eglesfield proposed,
Wykeham accomplished.

Founda-   Wykeham's New College at Oxford appears to have entered
tion.   upon a *de facto* existence not later than 1375, the scholars
being lodged in Hart Hall and other adjoining buildings;[2] but
the foundation charters were not granted till 1379. In 1387
the society entered in solemn procession into the splendid
habitation which their founder had been preparing for it in
an unoccupied corner within the walls of the town. To this
year also belongs the earliest extant draft of the founder's
statutes: in their final form they date from 1400.[3]

School   The originality of Wykeham as a college founder is almost
at Win-   eclipsed by his originality as the founder of the first English
chester. public school.[4] There had been indeed colleges for gram-

---

[1] Eglesfield passed his old age in
the college of his foundation, and
appears to have so completely im-
poverished himself by his munificence that his personal expenses
—down to the cost of shoeing his
horse—had to be defrayed by the
college. J. K. Ingram, *Memorials
of Oxford*, i. 3; [J. R. Magrath, *The
Queen's College*, i. 11–12. Mr. A. F.
Leach, *A History of Winchester
College*, pp. 79–84, emphasizes the
historic importance of Eglesfield's
statutes, and takes Rashdall to task
for giving Wykeham too much
credit for originality in introducing
features in which he had been

anticipated by Eglesfield.]
[2] Lowth, *William of Wykeham*
(ed. 1759), pp. 184, 185; Moberly,
William of Wykeham, p. 103; [H.
Rashdall and R. S. Rait, *New College*, pp. 37–8.]
[3] Lowth, pp. 189, 190. The
papal Bull confirming his statutes
and exempting his college from all
ecclesiastical jurisdiction, except
that of the Bishop of Winchester,
is dated 1398 (*ibid.* p. 194). [*Cal.
Papal Registers* (*Letters*), v. 171–3.]
[4] [Mr. A. F. Leach (*Educational
Charters*, pp. xxxiv–xxxv) has
pointed out that 'both colleges
were undoubtedly modelled on

marians only at Paris, and grammar colleges were not unknown in connexion with great cathedral schools elsewhere. Winchester College was the first elaborate foundation for the purely grammatical education of boys which had yet been established out of connexion with either a cathedral or a university.[1] In the place of the seventy-two young scholars whom Eglesfield had thought of establishing in his Oxford college, Wykeham more wisely provided for his seventy young scholars a separate college and school at Winchester. From the scholars of Winchester and from them only—with a preference for certain dioceses—were to be chosen the seventy scholars of 'S. Marie Colledge of Winchester in Oxford'. On arriving at Oxford the boy, already not less than fifteen years of age, was ready to enter at once upon the course in arts as a probationary scholar. After two years' probation he became a full fellow. As might be expected in so young a society, the officers—the sub-warden, five deans, and three bursars, together with a certain number of the seniors, varying in different cases, but usually eleven—were associated with the warden in the government of the house; but the youngest full fellow—even below the degree of B.A.—was accorded the essential right of full membership in an English college, a vote in the election of warden. In the conduct of its legal business a prominent share was assigned to the senior canonists and civilians. Ten fellows were to study canon, and ten civil law: the rest were to be students, first of arts, and then of theology. Artists, canonists, and civilians were required to proceed to Holy Orders after they had taken their respective degrees and had served their periods of necessary regency. Two fellows might be specially allowed to study medicine,

Merton College, and on the royal college of Navarre at Paris, founded by Joan, Queen of France and Navarre, in 1304, for 70 scholars in grammar, arts, and theology. Both models were improved on.']

[1] [See A. F. Leach, *A History of Winchester College* (1899), p. 81, where it is pointed out that a grammar school was a recognized appendix to a collegiate church. The originality of Winchester College lay in the fact that there 'for the first time a school was established as a sovereign and independent corporation existing by and for itself, self-centred and self-governed'. Cf. A. F. Leach, *The Schools of Medieval England*, pp. 205–6.]

CHAP. XII, and two others astronomy: even these were required eventu-
§. 6   ally to proceed to priest's orders.[1]

Tutors.   Among the other original features of the New College
which give Wykeham an important place in the history of
education is his provision for the tuition of his scholars. It
has already been observed that the resident head of a Parisian
arts college was a regent whose primary function was to supplement the education of the schools by private instruction.
At Oxford the primary function of the head was to manage
the property and rule the house: in the earlier college statutes
no provision is made for the education of the scholars. Wykeham's statutes supply this deficiency, not by entrusting
the educational supervision of the younger members of the
society to the head as at Paris, or to a single artist as in the
case of the 'parvuli' at Queen's, but by dividing it among
the older fellows, who draw in return an additional allowance
from the college funds besides what they may have received
from individual pupils.[2] At present, of course, this private
teaching was merely supplemental to the 'ordinary' lectures
of the public schools. But nevertheless by these provisions
Wykeham became the founder of the tutorial system destined
eventually to extinguish the lectures of the regents in the
public schools and in time to reduce to insignificance those
of the few salaried professors in the faculty of arts whom
Oxford gradually acquired.[3]

Liber-   We have already noticed the contrast which is presented
ality of
founder. by the meagreness of the college allowance at Paris and the

---

[1] In the case of 'Medici', 'postquam inceperint et rexerint per
triennium', since a priest was forbidden to be a regent in medicine.

[2] *Statutes of the Colleges of Oxford*, i (New College), 54. This
tuition lasted for three years.

[3] [See further on this subject
H. Rashdall and R. S. Rait, *New
College*, pp. 49–50. The inclusion
of this feature by Wykeham in his
statutes was incidental to the admission of undergraduates to his
foundation. It is probable that

Wykeham was not so great an in-
novator in this respect as Rashdall has claimed. The provision
of tutors appears to have been
the ordinary practice in academical
halls where undergraduates normally resided during the medieval
period before colleges began to
admit them. See Dr. H. E. Salter's
article 'An Oxford Hall in 1424', in
*Essays in History presented to R. L.
Poole*, pp. 421–35; A. B. Emden,
An Oxford Hall in Medieval Times,
pp. 36, 193, 195–6.]

comparative liberality of the Oxford founders. To some CHAP. XII, extent the tradition was begun by Walter de Merton, and this § 6. tendency is still further developed at Oriel and at Queen's, and still more at New College. The table allowance is here, indeed, smaller than at Queen's.[1] But the deficiency is amply compensated for by the increased scale of the extra allowance to the senior fellows for their services as priests, tutors, and officers. Still more striking is the contrast between the magnificent and still extant buildings of New College and the scanty remains which now survive of earlier collegiate dwellings. Of all the college buildings erected in Oxford before the foundation of New College not one stone remains beyond the earliest portion of Merton; and these were not finished till after the founder's death. At New College, the founder, who had been introduced to his sovereign's favour by his services as surveyor of the royal works,[2] was at least as much interested in the architectural designs for his foundation as in the compilation of its statutes, and the buildings remain to this day, in their main outlines, exactly as the founder designed them to be. Whatever may be thought of his originality as an educational reformer, Wykeham was unquestionably the creator of English collegiate architecture. The buildings of New College as a whole embody a complete and original architectural design, worthy of a prelate who, if in no strict sense a professional architect, had reached his exalted position through his services in supervising works of architecture. New College Chapel, still beautiful with the

[1] At Queen's the fellows were to be much better fed than the stipendiary chaplains and poor boys. At New College fellows, chaplains, and scholars alike are to receive 12*d.* weekly in plentiful seasons, which might be increased 'necessitate poscente' to 16*d.* in times of scarcity, and to 18*d.* when corn was at more than 2*s.* per bushel. At the same time it is provided that the members of the foundation are to be served 'habendo respectum debitum ad status et gradus . . . . aequalitate communarum . . . non

obstante'. Thus practically the theologian of New College might dine better than the theologian of Queen's.

[2] He is probably attacked on this score by Wyclif in his tract *Why poor Priests have no Benefices*: 'And ȝit þey wolen not presente a clerk able of kunnynge . . . , but a kechen clerk, or a penne clerk, or wis of bildynge of castelis or worldly doynge, þouȝ he kunne not rede wel his sauter.' *Eng. Works of Wyclif*, ed. F. D. Matthew (Early English Text Society, 1880), p. 246.

CHAP. XII, cold beauty of perfect proportion, once splendid with the
§ 6.   richest products of medieval sculpture and painting and glass-
staining, has well been called Merton Chapel idealized.[1]
Though some bays of its unfinished nave were then standing,
Merton Chapel perhaps suggested to Wykeham's mind the
plan of a choir with a nave stopping short at the transepts,
as the most appropriate form for a college chapel, which
wanted only a spacious choir for the choral masses and canonical hours, and room for a few side altars at which fellows
and chaplains might say their private masses.[2] Adjoining was
a burial-ground surrounded by a cloister which a cathedral
church might envy, for daily processions of chaplains and
choir 'according to the use of Sarum'. In an angle of the
town wall the college buildings cut off an ample garden for
the recreation of the scholars, or for the supply of vegetables
to the kitchen. For the first time perhaps in the history of
Europe a home was provided in which secular priests might
be as well housed and enjoy almost as complete seclusion
from the outer world as the novice in an old Benedictine
abbey.

Corporate   The bishop had once, it would appear,[3] thought of founding
dignity. a monastery; and he is the first English college founder[4] who
seems to have conceived the idea of making a college not a
mere endowed lodging-house for students, but a house of
community which could vie in the splendour of its buildings
and the dignity of its corporate life with the great capitular
and monastic establishments. In some of the earlier colleges
the head was only allowed one room in the college, and was
to dine with the fellows in the common hall. The Warden
of New College was to live like an abbot in a house of his own

[1] It has since regained some of
its ancient ornament.
[2] [On the form of Merton College Chapel and of New College
Chapel see B. W. Henderson, Merton College, pp. 205–6.]
[3] This seems to be a fair inference from Statutes of the Colleges
of Oxford, i (New College), § 68,
pp. 112–13. [It is open to question
whether the clause to which Rash-

dall refers can bear the interpretation which he extracts from it. Cf.
A. F. Leach, A History of Winchester College, p. 60.]
[4] In some respects an example
had been set by the College of
Navarre at Paris, whose chapel was
only dedicated in 1373. It is quite
likely that Wykeham may have
been to some extent influenced by
this example.

within the college walls, with separate hall, kitchen, and establishment.[1] His salary of £40 was princely compared with the 40s. assigned to the Master of Balliol, or even the 40 marks of the Warden of Merton.[2] Instead of the jealous provisions against burdening the college with the entertainment of guests which we meet with in the statutes of Parisian colleges, ample provision is made for the entertainment of important strangers by the warden in his own house, or in his absence by the sub-warden and fellows in the great hall, as they would have been entertained at the abbot's or prior's table in a wealthy Benedictine abbey. It had been recognized, indeed, by the founder of Peterhouse at Cambridge, that it would be 'indecent' for the master to go a-foot, and productive of 'scandal to the College' for him to hire a hack;[3] he was therefore allowed one horse of his own. But the Warden of New College was to have six horses at his disposal for himself and his attendants when he went on a progress round the college estates or otherwise. The most important of the earlier colleges had made use of an impropriated church for their chaplains to say masses for the founder's soul, and there the scholars assisted in surplices at the Sunday and festival services; though little oratories had been established at Balliol and elsewhere. Thus the Warden and Fellows of Merton occupied the choir of the unfinished church of S. John the Baptist; Oriel College made a similar use of S. Mary's. In the same way, at Cambridge,

[1] The warden's cook is a man of sufficient social position to dine with the fellows; his under-cook dines with the servants. 2nd Report Hist. MSS. Comm., p. 134. [Mr. A. F. Leach, A History of Winchester College, p. 80, takes exception to Rashdall's comparison of the warden's establishment to that of an abbot, pointing out that 'the separate house was, in fact, the characteristic of secular canons, their deans and provosts, not of the monks or regular canons, with whom it was an innovation.' Eglesfield had provided that in the event of an increase in numbers the pro-

vost might live in a residence of his own. See J. R. Magrath, The Queen's College, i. 31.]

[2] [Eglesfield had arranged that the salary of the provost should 'be increased gradually to £40 as the income of the College allowed the number of Fellows to be increased, the maximum to be reached when the number of the Fellows reached forty'. See J. R. Magrath, The Queen's College, i. 29.]

[3] 'Quum Magistrum non deceat ... ire pedes nec etiam cum domus et Scholarium scandalo conducere Hakenys.' Documents, Univ. and Colleges of Cambridge, 1852, ii. 14.

CHAP. XII, Michaelhouse used S. Michael's Church; Corpus, S. Benet's.
§ 6.   At New College the chapel forms an integral part, indeed the
most prominent feature, of the whole design—larger, richer,
and more important than the adjoining hall, as the common
hall towers above the humble chambers of the individual
fellows.[1]

Promi-   The prominence and splendour of the chapel in the new
nence of
ecclesias- foundation is indicative of something more than the com-
tical
aspect. pleteness of the founder's architectural design: it represents
an increased prominence of the religious—or perhaps we
should say ecclesiastical—aspect of the college as an institution. Wykeham had shared the feeling predominant among
the laity of his day against the monks, so far as to found a
secular house rather than a monastery. But this feeling arose
rather from experience of the almost universal unfaithfulness
of religious houses to their rule than from any want of sympathy with the monastic ideal itself. Wykeham, the leader
of the political party opposed to Wyclif and his patron, and
one of the greatest living pluralists, saw that he could better
contribute to a revivification of the old church-system by
sending out into the world a continual succession of highly
trained ecclesiastics than by filling some secluded valley with
the dwellings of contemplative recluses. All medieval charity
was largely inspired by the desire of providing a perpetual
succession of spiritual persons pledged to pray for the souls
of their benefactor and those in whom he was interested.
To pray for one's benefactors was the first duty of medieval
piety.[2] But a body of secular priests could sing masses and
canonical hours just as effectively as monks[3] and could in
general be provided at a much cheaper rate, while the actual
members of the society were set free for the active labours
of the school, and hereafter of the world. 'S. Marie Colledge

---

[1] The quadrangle was then a
story lower than at present.
[2] So Chaucer's 'Clerk of Oxenforde':
    'bisily gan for the soules praie
    Of hem that yaf him wher-withto
        scoleye.' *Prologue*, ll. 303–4.

[3] A disposition on the part of
church-benefactors to found collegiate chapters of secular priests
instead of monasteries is a noticeable feature of late medieval
times.

of Winchester' was in fact a seminary for ecclesiastical students combined with a college of secular priests bound to the incessant routine of masses and canonical hours.

But even the scholars were bound to attend mass daily and to make some return for their founder's liberality by repeating the Angelical Salutation fifty times with a 'pater' after every five: while in the great hall daily after dinner and supper 'De Profundis'[1] was said with prayers for 'the repose of the soul of William of Wykeham'. These requirements are the more remarkable when contrasted with the conspicuous absence of provision for college worship in the earlier college foundations except on Sundays and Saints' days.[2] In the statutes of the College of Harcourt, which were drawn up by the founder's brother, the Bishop of Coutances, in 1311, we even find artists expressly exempted on 'legible' days from attending the daily mass,[3] and daily attendance at chapel is clearly not contemplated by the earlier Oxford statutes.[4] Now, in the reaction against Wyclifism, the religious wants of the students receive more attention: though the religious duties enjoined upon them seem to be imposed more for the good of the founder's soul than their own; and there is as little provision for 'religious instruction' as in other pre-Reformation statutes. Still Wykeham may be allowed the credit of having been the first college founder who required his scholars to say their prayers morning and evening and to go to chapel daily.

A word must be said as to the origin of one most singular privilege which Wykeham is supposed to have acquired for

Prayers and chapel.

The New College privilege.

[1] The hymn *Te de Profundis* is or was a few years ago still sung in the college hall of Winchester after dinner on certain days.

[2] [Mr. A. F. Leach, *A History of Winchester College*, p. 81, refuses to consider these requirements as remarkable, 'when at Queen's half a page is devoted to dictating exactly the hymns to the Virgin that were to be sung daily in chapel by the scholars, and express direction is given for singing of *De Profundis* with certain specified prayers after dinner and supper in Hall', and further notes that 'Eglesfield made all his Fellows swear to take priest's orders, and his Doctors not actually teaching were obliged to attend canonical hours; neither of which requirements are to be found in Wykeham's statutes'.]

[3] Bulaeus, iv. 155.

[4] [See H. Rashdall and R. S. Rait, *New College*, pp. 53, 54.]

CHAP. XII, §6. his society—that of being admitted to their degrees without any 'grace' of convocation after examination by their own masters alone.[1] This privilege is said to have been obtained by an agreement between the founder and the university. But there is no evidence of the existence of any such agreement beyond the statement of Archbishop Bancroft in 1607 that the privilege had been enjoyed for more than 200 years.[2] The origin of this New College privilege being veiled in impenetrable obscurity, I venture to suggest the following hypothesis. Since no such document is to be found in the well-kept muniment-room of Wykeham's college, it is almost inconceivable that it can have originated in any express grant of Pope, King, or university. The only peculiar regulation on the subject of degrees which we meet with in the founder's statutes is the prohibition (except in certain specified cases) of suing for graces or dispensations from the time or exercises required by the university statutes.[3] Now it has been shown in another section[4] that originally no 'grace' was needed except where some of the statutable conditions were not performed, and it has been suggested that the grace gradually became necessary in all cases in consequence of the growing laxity in granting dispensations from these conditions. To New College men alone was it forbidden to avail themselves of such dispensatory luxuries. In course of time it is probable that this abstention on the part of Wykehamists from the 'supplications', which had come to be regarded as essential to all other candidates, was interpreted as a special privilege dating from a time whereof the memory of man ran not to the contrary. Moreover, Wykeham's statutes did not merely forbid exemption from the university's tests of competence:

[1] [An identical privilege was enjoyed by King's College, Cambridge; see below, p. 319.]

[2] So J. Ayliffe, *The Antient and Present State of the University of Oxford*, i. 315, 316. Fellows of New College are still exempt from the 'supplication' for their degrees. But, as no one can now be a fellow before taking or at least passing his examinations for B.A., the distinction has become purely formal. [See H. Rashdall and R. S. Rait, *New College*, pp. 219–20.]

[3] *Statutes of the Colleges of Oxford*, i (New College), 49 *sq*. I have already put forward this view in my chapter on New College in the *Colleges of Oxford*, p. 162, from which I have also borrowed some other paragraphs.

[4] Above, pp. 148–50.

they imposed an additional test from which other candidates CHAP. XII, §6. were free. They required an actual examination and that too at a time when the university can hardly be said to have imposed an examination at all in the modern sense.[1] Hence, when the Laudian Statutes introduced a university examination,[2] it was supposed that Wykehamists, who demanded their degrees as of right instead of supplication for them like other candidates, had the same mysterious claim to exemption from the new, that they had long enjoyed from the old, requirements of the university. Hence they continued to be examined by their own examiners only. It is a singular illustration of the irony of history that Wykeham's anxious care for the discouragement of idleness in his scholars should have grown into the means of increasing it in their successors. It is true that the Laudian Examination, even before it degenerated into a mere farce, would have been no formidable ordeal to a college recruited from Winchester. It was only from the institution of Honour Examinations at the beginning of last century to the voluntary resignation of the so-called privilege in 1834 that this curious historical accident became the means of excluding the noblest of medieval foundations from all participation in that revival of industry which the new Examination Statute brought with it.[3]

LINCOLN (1429)

The account of Lincoln by the Rev. A. CLARK in *Colleges of Oxford* (pp. 170–207) is a more than usually original and valuable piece of college history, to which the following paragraphs owe everything but what can be gathered from the printed statutes. *Second Report of Historical MSS. Comm.*, p. 130. [A history of *Lincoln College* by Dr. Andrew CLARK was published in 1898. Mr. S. A. WARNER's well-illustrated volume (*Lincoln College, Oxford*, 1908) does not claim to add to the information to be obtained from Dr. CLARK's history as regards the medieval history of the college.]

Richard Fleming, the founder of Lincoln College, was one of those Wyclifite leaders to whom the excesses of its extreme Foundation by Bishop Fleming.

[1] 'Si iudicio Custodis, Vice-Custodis, duorum Decanorum . . . ac sex aliorum seniorum . . . examinatus, habilis, sufficiens et idoneus repertus fuerit', *loc. cit.* See above, pp. 141–3.

[2] *Laudian Code*, ed. J. Griffiths, with introduction by C. L. Shadwell, p. 88.

[3] [See also H. Rashdall and R. S. Rait, *New College*, pp. 153–5, 219–20.]

followers or the prospect of preferment or the natural conservatism of maturer years had revealed the error of their youthful ways.[1] His timely tergiversation was rewarded by the bishopric of Lincoln; and the college which he founded in 1429 was specially for the benefit of the diocese whose name it bears and for the defence of the Catholic Faith against the heresies from which the founder had so successfully emancipated himself. An oath against heresy was exacted of all its fellows, and in other ways the ecclesiastical character of the foundation is prominent. The three parish churches—All Saints', S. Michael's, and S. Mildred's—were impropriated to a college to be styled the College of All Saints of Lincoln, and were to be served by the fellows themselves with the assistance of two chaplains.[2] The three churches were in fact united into a sort of collegiate church under the government of the rector and fellows.[3] The whole of the original endowment of the college was supplied by these impropriations; and the Church of S. Mildred was destroyed to make way for some of the buildings of Lincoln College.

The founder, dying little more than a year after the formal foundation, left his college in a very incomplete condition. It had a rector, possibly some fellows, but no statutes;[4] and the buildings had only been begun. [Its survival was largely due to the energy of its second rector, Dr. John Beke.] The

[1] [It is no longer believed that Fleming was a Wyclifite. Dr. H. E. Salter has shown that what was taken as evidence of Fleming's sympathy with Wyclifite doctrine ought not to be so interpreted. See Snappe's Formulary, ed. H. E. Salter (O.H.S.), pp. 95–100.]

[2] See Rot. Pat. 6 Henry VI, p. 1, m. 8 [Cal. Patent Rolls, Henry VI, 1422–9, p. 455] the Praefatio of the founder, and the Prooemium of the second founder, Rotheram; Statutes of the Colleges of Oxford, i (Lincoln College), 4–12.

[3] Two of the fellows were to be appointed for both All Saints' and S. Michael's annually to have 'totale regimen chori', the one at All Saints', the other at S. Michael's, see Statutes of the Colleges of Oxford, i (Lincoln College), 22. The college attended All Saints' on Sundays.

[4] [Dr. A. Clark (Lincoln College, p. 7) notes that in 1432 Dr. Thomas Gascoigne gave six manuscripts to the college, which he received back on loan from the 'Rector et Socii unanimi consensu'. See also op. cit., p. 15. As regards statutes it would appear from the Prooemium to Archbishop Rotheram's statutes that a draft of the statutes intended by Bishop Fleming for his college formed the basis of Rotheram's code.]

erection of the hall, kitchen, and library (now the sub-rector's CHAP. XII room) and the chapel (now a fellow's room) by John Forest, §6.
Dean of Wells, about the year 1437, has procured for him the Completed by Forest, position of co-founder; and the college gradually grew under the hands of successive benefactors, as was often the case with colleges scantily provided for by their original founder.[1] The title of 'second founder' is claimed for Thomas Rotheram, and Rotheram. Bishop of Lincoln, who in the course of a visitation at Oxford had been impressed with the unfinished condition of the college. He completed the front quadrangle by building its southern side, and· increased its endowments both by impropriations and by actual gift, making up the number of its fellows to twelve.[2] It was, moreover, by Rotheram's influence that the college was extricated from a legal embarrassment which at one time threatened its very existence. In 1461–2 the college, like many other owners of property, had thought it prudent, upon the change of dynasty which followed the deposition of Henry VI, to sue out a pardon and obtain a new charter in ratification of the old one, from the victorious Edward IV.[3] Even then the college had some difficulty in securing its endowments against rapacious adherents of the new dynasty, and about the year 1474 it was discovered that the draughtsman of Edward's charter, whether by accident or more probably through the machinations of interested persons, had omitted after 'Rector and Fellows' the words 'and their successors'. It was now suggested that on the death of the then existing rector and fellows the property had lapsed to the Crown—an interesting indication of the growth of stricter views as to the creation of corporations with perpetual succession than had existed at a time when societies like the university itself assumed to themselves the right of holding property without any royal incorporation at all. This legal defect was in 1478 cured by the issue of a new charter.[4]

The college owes its first Code of Statutes (1480) to Rotheram's statutes. Rotheram, who became Archbishop of York soon after this issue. They exhibit no feature of special interest. All the

---

[1] A. Clark, *Lincoln College*, p. 8.   [3] *Ibid.*, pp. 21–3.
[2] *Ibid.*, pp. 24, 27–9.   [4] *Ibid.*, p. 28.

members of the college were to be masters (or at least bachelors) of arts on election, to take priest's orders, and (with the
exception of one canonist) to study theology.[1] Both Fleming
and Rotheram were natives of York and Bishops of Lincoln,
and the medieval fellowships were divided between their
county and their diocese.

ALL SOULS (1438)

Montagu BURROWS, *Worthies of All Souls*, Oxford, 1874; *Catalogue of
the Archives of All Souls College*, ed. MARTIN, London, 1877; DUCK,
Vita Henrici Chichele, Oxford, 1617. [A history of *All Souls College* by
Sir C. Grant ROBERTSON was published in the Oxford series of *College
Histories* in 1899. Prof. E. F. JACOB has added important information in
the following articles, 'Two Lives of Archbishop Chichele with an appendix containing an early book-list of All Souls College, Oxford', in
The Bulletin of the John Rylands Library, xvi (1932), 'The Building of All
Souls College, 1438–1443', in *Historical Essays in honour of James Tait*,
1933, 'The Warden's Text of the Foundation Statutes of All Souls', in
The Antiquaries Journal, xv (1935), and a letter on 'The Chained Books
of All Souls', in *The Times Literary Supplement*, Jan. 31, 1932. He has
in preparation an edition of the Register of Archbishop Chichele.]

Founda-
tion.
    The next two Oxford colleges—All Souls and Magdalen—
are emphatically daughters of New College. The founder of
All Souls began life as a fellow of New College. The founder
of Magdalen had been head master of Winchester, and Wykeham's influence is obviously discernible in the whole plan
of the two foundations, in the composition of their statutes,
and in the architecture of their buildings. In 'the College of
the Souls of all the faithful departed', founded in 1438,[2] the
ecclesiastical aspect is even more prominent than at New
College. The college was designed to pray for the souls of
Henry V, the Duke of Clarence, and the Englishmen who fell
in the French War, which is believed to have been largely
inspired by its able founder,[3] the lawyer-diplomatist-states-

[1] [The original foundation of
Bishop Fleming consisted of a
rector and seven fellows. To this
Rotheram added five more fellows.
See *Statutes of the Colleges of Ox-
ford*, i (Lincoln College), 11.]
[2] The property was surrendered
to the King, and the charter of 1438
(Rot. Pat. 16 Hen. VI, m. 24; [*Cal.
Patent Rolls, Henry VI, 1436–41*,

pp. 172–3, dated 20 May]) is issued
in the name of the King. The foun-
dation-stone had been laid in the
preceding February, and the fellows previously lodged in 'a hired
hall at the founder's expense'. [See
Sir C. Grant Robertson, *All Souls
College*, pp. 5–8.]
[3] [The view that the war with
France was largely inspired by

man, Henry Chicheley, Archbishop of Canterbury. Chaplains are, indeed, provided to conduct the college services,
and the fellows are not bound to attend the daily mass; but
the daily prayers exacted from each fellow for the founder and
the souls for whose good he had built the college are longer
and more elaborate than at New College.[1] The endowments
were largely supplied by the confiscated property of the alien
priories bought by the Archbishop from Henry VI, who
by his charter became the nominal founder of the college.[2]
All Souls was the first college founded at Oxford by a great
ecclesiastical lawyer; and the proportion of law-students to
theologians is naturally large. But though the college was
intended to benefit the souls of the dead, its objects were by
no means primarily or exclusively devotional. The college
was to consist of twenty-four artists or theologians and
sixteen jurists; and the statutes are carefully designed to
maintain the balance between the two elements in the college.
On a vacancy in the wardenship, for instance, a jurist and an
artist or theologian are to be presented to the Archbishop of
Canterbury as visitor, and he is to choose freely between the
two. All the members of the foundation (except the chaplains) were to be of three years' standing in the university on
election and were to become full fellows after a year's probation. The buildings, though originally covering a rather
limited area, since the college was situated in the very centre
of academic Oxford at the corner of High Street and Catte
Street, were on a magnificent scale.[3] Alone among the colleges
of Oxford, All Souls still consists (but for four Bible-clerks)
exclusively of fellows without either scholars or non-founda-

Archbishop Chicheley is chiefly
based on the fictions of certain
sixteenth-century historians. See
C. L. Kingsford, *Henry V*, pp. 109–
10, *Prejudice and Promise in XVth
Century England*, pp. 11–12.]
    [1] [For an account of the foun-
der's statutes and a comparison of
them with those of New College,
to which they are indebted, see
Sir C. Grant Robertson, *All Souls

College*, pp. 17–26.]
    [2] [See *ibid.*, p. 16; *Cal. Patent
Rolls, Henry VI, 1436–41*, pp. 231,
261, 386, 394, 437, 563; *1441–6*,
pp. 19–20. See also E. F. Jacob,
'Two Lives of Archbishop Chichele', reprinted from *The Bulletin
of the John Rylands Library*, xvi
(1932), 40–1.]
    [3] [See Sir C. Grant Robertson,
All Souls College, pp. 5–16.]

CHAP. XII, tion members;[1] and at all events serves the function of
§ 6. reminding us that in their origin colleges were designed to be primarily bodies of students and not bodies of teachers.

MAGDALEN (1448)

J. BUDDEN, *Vita Gulielmi Patteni*, Oxford, 1602; R. CHANDLER, *Life of William Waynflete*, London, 1811; J. R. BLOXAM, *Register of Magdalen College*, Oxford, 1853, &c.; W. D. MACRAY, *Notes from the Muniments of Magdalen College*, Oxford, 1882; *Fourth Report of Hist. MSS. Comm.*, p. 468 *sq.* The *Register* unfinished by BLOXAM is now being continued by Mr. MACRAY in a New Series, of which vol. i has appeared (London, 1894). [The new edition of this *Register* in eight volumes was completed in 1915.] H. A. WILSON, *Magdalen College*, 1899 (*Oxford College Histories*). [*The Cartulary of the Hospital of St. John the Baptist*, ed. H. E. SALTER (O.H.S.), 3 vols., is concerned with property which, after the dissolution of the hospital, went to endow Waynflete's foundation.]

The foundation. The founder of the last Oxford college which falls within our period was William Patten, known, after his ordination, from his native place as William of Waynflete. When the first steps were taken towards the foundation of a college he had just been consecrated Bishop of Winchester.[2] The Royal Licence for the foundation of S. Magdalen Hall for a president and fifty fellows was granted in 1448;[3] and the new society was promptly established in some halls bought by the founder on the south side of High Street, between University

[1] Other than the probationers who are styled 'Scholares' in the statutes. The existing four Bible-clerks of All Souls are not provided for by the original foundation. The Bible-clerk was originally a poor scholar who read the Bible during dinner, and in many cases also waited on the head or fellows. At All Souls the statutes (p. 27) provide for 'unum clericum seu alium servientem honestum qui sibi in mensam (*sic*) in aula et camera sua aliisque locis debite ac diligenter deserviat', who very possibly acted as 'Lector Bibliae'. [As Sir Charles Mallet has pointed out the statutes provided that the Bible should be read at meals in hall by a clerk of the chapel, see *Hist. Univ. of Oxford*, i. 364, n. 3. The four Bible-

clerkships were abolished in pursuance of the Universities of Oxford and Cambridge Act, 1923.]

[2] It seems to me misleading to say (with Mr. Wilson in *The Colleges of Oxford*, pp. 234–5) that the foundation of 1448 was a hall, and that in 1456 Waynflete 'conceived the idea of improving his foundation at Oxford, by converting it from a Hall into a College'. Every medieval college was frequently called an *Aula* and the foundation was as much a college in 1448 as in 1456. [Mr. Wilson in his history of the college (*Magdalen College*, p. 9) avoids the wording to which Rashdall objects.]

[3] R. Chandler, *William Waynflete*, p. 323.

College and the present Schools. In 1456, however, Waynflete obtained from the King a grant of the ancient Hospital[1]
of S. John the Baptist, situated upon the Cherwell bank, just
outside the East Gate of the city; and the Royal Charter for
a new college to be built upon the site thus acquired was
granted in 1457. The actual deed of foundation is dated in
1458, when the bishop was Lord High Chancellor of England.
It is worthy of note that all the greater medieval colleges at
Oxford were founded by bishops who were also chancellors.
No considerable portion of the large fortunes accumulated by
English chancellors has ever been spent upon any public
object since chancellors ceased to be churchmen and became
married men.[2]

William of Waynflete may almost be said to have passed
his life under the shadow of the great monuments of Wykeham's genius. There is, indeed, no evidence that he was on
the foundation of New College before his appointment, but
he had been master of the school of Winchester College.[3]
Selected by Henry VI as head master and afterwards provost
of Eton (itself an imitation of Winchester), he lived under
the Royal Castle at Windsor, which owed so much to Wykeham's love of building: he ended his days as bishop of the
church whose nave the builder-bishop had recreated. His
foundation at Oxford shows how much he had imbibed alike
of the architectural taste and of the educational zeal of his
great predecessor. Both the institution and its lovely home
reproduce, on a smaller and compacter scale, almost every
feature of Wykeham's grander work. It is significant of
coming changes that the college was partly founded out of the
property of monastic houses which the bishop obtained leave
to suppress—the priories of Sele in Sussex and Selborne
in Hampshire.[4] Here Wolsey, whose career began with a

[1] As to its date see Clark's note
on Wood, *City* (O.H.S.), ii. 533;
[H. A. Wilson, *Magdalen College*,
p. 13].

[2] [The endowment was increased
in 1474 by the addition of a property at Caister in Norfolk left by
Sir John Fastolf, who died in 1459,
and originally intended for a college of priests at Caister, see H. A.
Wilson, *Magdalen College*, pp. 17–
18.]

[3] [H. A. Wilson, *Magdalen College*, p. 4.]

[4] *4th Report Hist. MSS. Comm.*,
p. 459.

CHAP. XII,
§ 6.

Attention
to gram-
mar:
demies.

fellowship at Magdalen, may have meditated on the advantages of a larger extension of the same policy.

Waynflete—perhaps the first of the great schoolmaster-bishops who have played such a conspicuous part in the history of the English Church—was as wisely solicitous as the founder of the oldest public school for the proper grammatical preparation of his scholars. But his scheme was to provide for grammar and arts within the same institution.[1] The forty fellows were to be at least B.A. on their admission to their probationary year, and were to proceed to degrees in theology or (with special leave) in law or medicine. But a younger body of thirty foundationers—called demies (*medii communarii*) from their receiving half a fellow's commons—were admissible at the early age of twelve, and were kept at school under the grammar-master (*informator*) of the college until considered by the president and master fit to enter upon the university course in arts.[2] The approaching Renaissance was heralded in England by a humble movement of purely indigenous growth in favour of an increased attention to Latin grammar. The movement had already begun at New College,[3] under the scholarly Warden Chandler, and the Magdalen College schoolmasters, Stanbridge and Whitting-

[1] [For an analysis of the founder's statutes see H. A. Wilson, *Magdalen College*, pp. 35–44.]

[2] There is a whiff of the Renaissance about the very words of the statute (*Statutes of the Colleges of Oxford*, ii (Magdalen College), 16), 'circa grammaticalia et poemata, et alias artes *humanitatis*, diligenter insistent et operam dabunt, quod non solum sibi ipsis proficere sed et alios instruere ac informare valeant'. [See also A. F. Leach, *The Schools of Medieval England*, p. 270.]

[3] The new method seems to have been originated by the first head master, John Anwykyll, who taught it to his usher and successor, John Stanbryge or Stanbridge, and to Robert Whittington, each of whom wrote numerous simplified gram-

mars; probably also to John Holte, author of *Lac Puerorum* (1497), dedicated to Cardinal Morton. (R. Chandler, *William Waynflete*, pp. 253, 254; J. R. Bloxam, *Magdalen Coll. Register*, iii. 7–25.) [See Foster Watson, *The English Grammar Schools to 1660*, pp. 235–42.] It was at Magdalen too that Colet learned the method which he embodied in his 'eight parts of speech' which he dedicated to the first high master of his school at S. Paul's, the famous Lily, a pupil of Whittington, to whose *Syntaxis* Wolsey wrote a prefatory epistle (J. R. Bloxam, *Magdalen Coll. Register*, i. 2). It may be remarked that the choristers lived in the fellows' chambers and waited on them. They waited in hall down to 1802. *Ibid.* i. xiii.

ton (the first a New College man), authors of the first Latin CHAP. XII, § 6.
grammars which drove Donatus and Alexander de Villedieu
out of English school-rooms, did something to promote its
progress: while the head-mastership of the same school
formed the first preferment of a patron of humanism no less
illustrious than Cardinal Wolsey.[1] Nor were the labours of
these eminent teachers without results for their own immediate pupils. Magdalen—the college of Grocyn (who received
his earliest education at New College) and possibly of Colet,[2]
the temporary abode of Erasmus—was essentially the home
of the Classical Renaissance in Oxford; a strange contrast to
the Magdalen of Gibbon's Autobiography, or of the still later
period in which its fellowships had become the wealthiest in
England.

Waynflete showed the wisdom of the practical school- No foun-der's kin.
master by giving his demies only a preference, and not an
actual claim, to vacant fellowships; and it is perhaps due to
his sympathy with masters and tutors that he abstains from
inflicting upon them the founder's-kin fellow, who was admitted by most previous college founders and who enjoyed
peculiarly preposterous privileges at New College and All
Souls.

Magdalen closes the list of Oxford colleges which fall College lecturers.
within our period. Two innovations in its statutes (1479) may
be noticed as indications of the progress of changes destined
ultimately to revolutionize the whole aspect and constitution
of the university. We have already noticed the introduction
of the tutorial system by Wykeham at New College. Wykeham's statute is reproduced almost *verbatim* by Waynflete;
and it seems probable that before the middle of the fifteenth
century the teaching of undergraduates (as distinct from
bachelors) was mainly in the hands of tutors[3] in the colleges

---

[1] [See A. F. Pollard, *Wolsey*, pp. 12, 13.]

[2] Such is the tradition, but there appears to be no good evidence for it. He may have been a commoner. See H. A. Wilson, *Magdalen College*, p. 59.

[3] The word used both at New College and Magdalen is *informator*. At Brasenose College the word *tutor* occurs for the first time, but only in reference to the fellow who is to be responsible for a commoner. The education of both undergraduates and B.A.s is there to be conducted entirely in

or principals and their assistant regents or non-graduate lectors in the halls;[1] though a formal attendance at a certain number of lectures in School Street was still required.[2] Now a further step was taken in the same direction. Waynflete founded three lectureships in theology, moral and metaphysical philosophy, and natural philosophy respectively.[3] It is probable that similar lectures were by this time not unknown in other colleges; and it thus became possible for a student in arts—and at Magdalen even a student in theology—to obtain the whole of his education within the college walls. But here a further innovation was introduced: the lectures were to be open to all members of the university, so that Waynflete may be considered in a sense the founder of the first endowed professorships of the university. In the statutes of the next Oxford college, Brasenose (founded in 1509), it is clearly assumed that the student need not go outside his college for lectures. Lectures continued to be given in the public schools, but were more and more superseded by the lectures of halls and colleges on the one hand and by Henry VIII's endowed professorships on the other. The statutes continued to impose upon regents the obligation of lecturing, but it became usual to grant more and more sweeping dispensations from necessary regency, and from the obligation of hearing such lectures,[4] till the latter

the college hall under a *lector*. It was only by a later change that the main teaching passed from the college praelectors or lectors to the single tutor strictly so called.

[1] In a *Supplicat* of 1456 a scholar in arts asked to count a term in which he was 'lector in aula' (Register Aa, f. 99 *b*).

[2] See the Statute of 1409 (*Mun. Acad.* i. 241 *sq.* [*Stat. Antiq. Univ. Oxon.*, ed. S. Gibson, p. 199 *sq.*]; above, p. 154), where it appears that a few books must still be heard *cursorie* from bachelors in the schools. Most of the books before determination are to be heard 'in collegio aut in aula lectionatim . . . cum recitacione (? i.e. repetitione)

debite subsecuta'. Notice that the 'repetitiones' are as at Paris characteristic of the college teaching; but even the more informal college lectures (*auditio lectionaria*) are too formal for beginners, and the scholar is forbidden to attend them for *his first two years*, during which he may be presumed to have been occupied with *Summulae* and catechetical instruction from his private tutor. The Oxford *Statuta Aularia* (*c.* 1489) require attendance at the 'matutina lectio' and the 'meridiana recitatio'.

[3] [See H. A. Wilson, *Magdalen College*, pp. 38–40.]

[4] In the middle of the fifteenth century the system of necessary

requirement was abolished by the Laudian Statutes, and CHAP. XII,
the former was satisfied by dispensing all the regents except   § 6.
a single 'ordinarius' in each of the 'seven Arts and the
three Philosophies'. These lecturers were paid by the fees
of the dispensed masters and continued till the end of the
eighteenth century to deliver their 'wall lectures' to empty
benches.[1]

The second notewothy innovation in Waynflete's statutes Gentlemen
is the provision permitting the admission of *filii nobilium* as commoners.
commensales.[2] The admission of persons not on the foundation to board with the fellows is contemplated in the statutes
of several of the smaller and poorer colleges of earlier date—
in the statutes of William of Durham's four masters, of Oriel,
and of Lincoln. But these were primarily colleges of theologians, and their *commensales* would be more likely to be
brother-students of theology than mere boys studying arts.
On the other hand Wykeham distinctly forbade the admission
of strangers (*extranei*) to live in college, though a few gentle-

regency is still in full vigour, though most of the books before B.A. could now be heard in college, and those still required to be heard 'in scholis' were heard *cursorie* from a bachelor. After the hiatus in our extant regis-ters (1463–1505) we find the system on its last legs. In 1449 we do in-deed find all the regents of the year allowed to lecture out of School Street (Register Aa, f. 31 *b*). Had this precedent been followed, the 'ordinary lectures' might simply have been transferred to colleges and halls and the university have retained its hold (as at Paris) over college lectures. But a different course was followed. After 1505 the necessary regency is either dis-pensed with altogether or reduced to a period of a few days, e.g. there is usually an annual dispensation allowing every regent to deliver 'unum ordinarium dispensativum omnibus bacallariis audientibus pro eorum lecturis privatis', or the like. The audience being thus

dispensed from attendance, we are not surprised to find that in 1518 the regents supplicating 'quatenus non teneantur legere ordinaria sua per maiorem partem hore. Causa est quod nulli audiunt eos legentes' (Register H 7, f. 6 *b*). But more than once before this we find all the masters present dispensing them-selves from necessary regency al-together, e.g. in 1511 (*ibid.*, f. 141), or after All Saints' Day (*ibid.*, f. 299). [On the subject of the length of the regency see *Reg. Annalium Collegii Merton.*, *1483–1521*, ed. H. E. Salter (O.H.S.), pp. xxi–xxii.]

[1] But when a professor was en-dowed for any art or philosophy, he became the *ordinarius*. There were still four unendowed *ordinarii* in the time of Gutch. *Collectanea Curiosa*, Oxford, 1781, ii. 39 *sq.* They had acquired the name of Wall Lectures even in Anthony Wood's time.

[2] [H. A. Wilson, *Magdalen College*, p. 41.]

CHAP. XII, men-commoners, educated at Winchester, were eventually
§ 6.   received.[1] Waynflete abandoned this restriction, but only
in favour of twenty high-born youths, who were not
merely to board but to be educated in the college. The
language of the statute clearly implies that the commoner-
system had by this time at least gained ground in the university. It is evident its progress would be likely to keep
pace with the growth of college-teaching. At Paris we have
seen .that both changes had been in progress since the
middle of the fourteenth century. As to the time at which
the two changes were introduced into Oxford we know
little but that the statutes of Queen's are the first which
contemplate arts-teaching within the college walls, that
the system was extended by Wykeham, and that Waynflete
is the first who expressly authorizes the admission as
commensales of boys or young men *in statu pupillari*. The
accounts at Queen's, however, make it probable that a
few boys were received as commoners at that college as early
as 1363.[2] On the whole it is probable that these changes
gained ground more slowly and gradually than at Paris; but
by the beginning of the sixteenth century the only real
teaching in arts was given within the colleges and halls, while
by the time of Edward VI the halls were reduced to a very
small number, so that a large proportion of students in arts
must by that time have been housed within college walls as

[1] At first, it would appear, without living within the walls.

[2] Among others, one John Wyclif,
who has been mistakenly identified
with the Reformer (*2nd Report
Hist. MSS. Comm.*, p. 141), e.g.
by W. W. Shirley, *Fasc. Zizan.*
(R.S.), p. xiii. [Rashdall here appears to confuse John Wyclif, the
Reformer, with Wyclif, a 'poor
boy' of Queen's College, whose
Christian name is not known.
There is no reason to doubt that
Wyclif who was assigned rooms in
Queen's in 1363–4 was identical
with the Reformer. He is also mentioned in the Long roll of the college for 1365–6; in that for 1374–5,
where he is expressly described as
'Magister Iohannes Wiclife', and
lastly in that for 1380–1. Among
the 'expense puerorum' in the Long
roll for 1371–2 there is mention of
a Wyclif; but it is known what was
the relationship of this young Wyclif to the Reformer. See J. R.
Magrath, *The Queen's College*, i.
111–15; H. B. Workman, *John
Wyclif*, i. 63–6. The 'pauperes
pueri' of Queen's who were maintained to act as choristers are in no
way equivalent to the subsequent
commoners.]

non-foundation members. It is well known that the Reformation in its earliest phase produced a great diminution in
the numbers of the university; and when, under Elizabeth,
the numbers began to expand again, no new halls were created
and the whole increase had to be accommodated in the colleges
and the few remaining halls.

§ 7. THE PLACE OF OXFORD IN MEDIEVAL THOUGHT[1]

CHAP. XII,
§ 7.
Oxford influential as a school, not as a corporation.

IN the political and ecclesiastical history of England the University of Oxford, as a corporation, played but a small part. Though its scholastic fame throughout Europe stood second only to that of Paris, and at one time hardly second, it had comparatively little international character: it was recruited mainly, though by no means exclusively, from the British Isles.[2] In purely insular politics there were times of disturbance when the students of Oxford could take a side; but the university as a corporation was rarely consulted and rarely ventured unasked to express an opinion, though it was at times invited to send representatives to Convocation and even to Parliament.[3] The political power of the University

[1] [The views expressed by Rashdall in this section are in many particulars so characteristic of his theological and philosophical outlook that it has been thought best to refrain from revision of his text, even where the views that he has expressed do not accord with those more generally held. Some of Rashdall's own notes for a new edition have been incorporated in the portion that deals with Roger Bacon. But for the rest, such amplification and correction as has been thought necessary has been for the most part confined to notes written within square brackets, where references have been given to the chief contributions made in this field of study since 1895. For fuller bibliographical information the reader is directed to F. Ueberweg, *Grundriss der Geschichte der Philosophie*, ed. B. Geyer (1920), vol. ii; M. de Wulf, *History of Medieval Philosophy*, trans. E. C. Messenger, 2 vols., 1926 (a sixth and revised French edition of this work is in process of publication); and L. J. Paetow, *A Guide to the Study of Medieval History*, ed. 1931.]

[2] We do of course hear of foreigners here, especially in the early part of our period. (See § 1 of this chapter, *passim*.) Later on, such intercourse was liable to be interrupted by war. By the Treaty of Brétigny in 1360 it was provided that the subjects of each king should be free to study and enjoy the privileges of each other's universities, 'comme ils povoient faire avant ces presentes guerres et comme ils font au présent' (Rymer, *Foedera*, vii (1708), p. 226). After the renewal of the French war (43 Edward III) we hear of a French scholar being attacked for disobeying the King's proclamation (Twyne MS. xxiii, f. 188). At Pembroke College, Cambridge, there was a preference for Frenchmen.

[3] It has usually been assumed that the university returned no members to Parliament before the time of James I, but Ayliffe, *Antient and Present State of Univ. of Oxford*, ii, App. p. lxxxviii, prints a

of Paris was due partly to its situation in the capital, partly
to the weakness of the French kings in face of factious princes
and powerful feudatories. Fortunately for England, the
English kings were rarely weak. More than once the university was rudely dealt with when it attempted to play an independent part in ecclesiastical politics; even on points of
theology or canon law its corporate decisions exercised
little influence.[1] It was not as a great semi-ecclesiastical
corporation, but as a centre of speculative thought and
of religious life, that Oxford contributed to the making
of English history. It was through her influence upon
the religious life of England that the University of Oxford
did, as we shall see, at one supreme moment open a new page
in the history of England and of the civilized world.

The internal development of the scholastic philosophy lies
beyond the limits of the present work. It is, however, impossible to understand even the bare external history, whether
of the universities or of the Middle Ages generally, without
knowing at least the nature of the questions debated in the
schools and the relations of the parties which arose out of

writ of 28 Ed. I requiring the chancellor to send 'quatuor vel quinque
de discretioribus et in iure scripto
magis expertes Universitatis predic-
tae' to Parliament, though the practice appears not to have been kept
up. [See *Cal. Close Rolls, Edward I,
1296–1302*, p. 410, dated 26 Sept.
1300. A similar writ was sent to
the Chancellor of Cambridge, except that the number of legal ex-
perts to be sent was limited to two
or three. The letter from the Chancellor of the University to the
King's Treasurer, Thomas Bek, *c.*
1279, which is given in *Snappe's
Formulary*, ed. H. E. Salter
(O.H.S.), p. 7, asking what sort of
persons should be sent to Parliament, refers not to university
members but to delegates who were
to represent the university in
certain matters touching the university that were to be decided in
Parliament.] It is just possible that

Wyclif's appearance in Parliament was in this capacity. See G.
Lechler, *John Wycliffe and his English Precursors*, Eng. trans. by P.
Lorimer, ed. 1884, p. 129 *sq.* [Dr.
Workman after a careful examination of the facts rejects Wyclif's
supposed membership of Parliament, but allows that 'as one of the
king's clerks he may well have been
present in the council'. See H. B.
Workman, *John Wyclif*, i. 237–9,
340–1.] As to Convocation, in 1408
'in concilio cleri celebrato Lon-
doniis, assistentibus Doctoribus
Universitatum Oxoniae et Can-
tabrigiae, tractatum est de censu
et obedientia Papae subtrahendis
vel non subtrahendis' (Walsingham, *Ypodigma Neustriae*, ed.
H. T. Riley (R.S.), pp. 424–5).

[1] [See Additional Note at the end
of this chapter on the connexion
of the university with the Great
Schism.]

CHAP. XII, these debates to the ecclesiastical and political movements of
§ 7. the time. I must therefore attempt briefly to point out the
distinctive part which Oxford played in the history of medieval thought, confining myself almost wholly to what may be
called the external history of its philosophical life, without
attempting to enter into the inner growth and movement of
that great scholastic system which found its first home in
Paris and its second in Oxford.

The
earliest Enough has been said of the relation between Oxford and
Oxford the mother University of Paris to make it unnecessary to enter
teachers. at length into the general character of Oxford studies. The
university was originally in all probability a colony of Parisian
schools transferred to English soil;[1] and, throughout the first
century at least of its existence, the relations between the two
studia were of the closest and most intimate character. Whatever was read and taught in Paris was sure sooner or later to
be read and taught in Oxford.[2] It by no means, however,
follows that the converse proposition would be equally true.
And, scanty as is our knowledge of the earliest generation of
Oxford teachers, enough remains to make it clear that the
intellectual life of the thirteenth-century Oxford was something more than a pale reflex of the intellectual life of Paris.[3]
Of the three most famous Oxford teachers of the thirteenth
century two at least were much more than mere scholastics.
One of the three, Edmund Rich,[4] afterwards Archbishop of

---

[1] [See above, pp. 12–16, 22–23.]

[2] Of course, the close intellectual connexion between England
and France began before the rise
of Oxford. See Professor C. H.
Haskins's article on the 'Introduction of Arabic Science into England' in *E.H.R.* (1915), xxx. 56 *sq.*,
[which forms ch. vi of *Studies in
the History of Medieval Science*,
1924, pp. 113–29].

[3] [John Blund, whose election to
the Archbishopric of Canterbury
was set aside by Pope Gregory IX
in 1233, may be noted as an example of a scholar who taught at
Paris and at Oxford during the first

half of the thirteenth century. See
L. J. Paetow, *Morale Scolarium of
John of Garland*, p. 177 n.; J. C.
Russell's article on 'Master Henry
of Avranches' in *Speculum*, iii
(1928), 45; and his article on 'The
Preferments and "Adiutores" of
Robert Grosseteste' in *The Har-
vard Theological Review*, xxvi
(1933), 165.]

[4] [He bore the name of Edmund
of Abingdon in his lifetime. His
father was Reginald le Rich, but
there is no evidence that S. Edmund was ever known by the name
of Rich before the seventeenth
century. It seems that Anthony

Canterbury, need only be mentioned here as the first master CHAP. XII, who is actually recorded to have taught the new logic in the § 7. Oxford schools and the first who is known to have taken the Edmund Rich. degree of doctor of divinity at Oxford.[1] But he was remembered in Oxford rather on account of the ascetic saintliness of his personal character than of any permanent contribution to the progress of thought. The other two, Robert Grosse-Robert Grosse- teste,[2] and Roger Bacon, are commonly numbered—it must be teste. admitted with only partial truth—rather among the critics of scholasticism than among its creators. Both of them were schoolmen, but both of them were something more. Grosseteste pioneers thirteenth-century Aristotelianism by his exertions in promoting better translations of the Aristotelian

---

Wood must be held responsible for having started the misnomer. See A. B. Emden, *An Oxford Hall in Medieval Times*, pp. 103–4.]

[1] He is often said to have been the first to teach the *Ethics* in Oxford, but the true reading of the passage in Roger Bacon is not 'Ethicorum' but 'Elencorum'. 'Etiam logicalia fuerunt tarde recepta et lecta. Nam Beatus Edmundus Cantuariensis Archiepiscopus primus legit Oxoniae librum elencorum temporibus meis': *Fr. Rogeri Bacon Compendium Studii Theologie*, ed. H. Rashdall, p. 34. Charles (*Roger Bacon*, p. 315) assumes that the *Soph. Elenchi* were not taught even at Paris till this date, but that is surely impossible. See above, i. 441. As to his doctorate see the letter of the university in *Collectanea* (O.H.S.), ii. 188, 189. [A full text of this letter is printed, together with a facsimile in photogravure, in A. B. Emden, *An Oxford Hall in Medieval Times*, pp. 267–70.] Some new documents are printed in W. Wallace, *St. Edmund of Canterbury*, London, 1893. [See also *D.N.B.*; A. Herbert, 'Edmund of Abingdon and the Universities', in *Dublin Review* (1898), cxxiii. 107–20; Baroness F. de Paravicini, *St.*

Edmund of Abingdon, Archb. of Canterbury; B. Ward, *St. Edmund, Archbishop of Canterbury*; article by Prof. H. W. C. Davis, *E.H.R.*, xxii. 84–92; A. B. Emden, *An Oxford Hall, &c.*, pp. 81–104; *La Merure de Seinte Eglise*, ed. H. W. Robbins, Lewisburg, Penn., n.d.; and G. Lacombe, *La Summa Abendonensis* in *Mélanges Mandonnet; Études d'histoire littéraire et doctrinale du moyen âge*, ii. 163–91.]

[2] There is no contemporary evidence that he studied at Paris, though this is asserted by Bulaeus and others. [Mr. F. S. Stevenson (*Robert Grosseteste, Bishop of Lincoln*, pp. 15–18) accepts the tradition that Grosseteste studied theology in Paris: 'Grosseteste's intimate acquaintance with such men as William de Cerda and William Arvernus [de Alvernia], Bishop of Paris, his familiarity with the details of the theological course of studies pursued there, as shown in his letter to the regents in theology at Oxford, and the references of Cardinal Egidius to his fame throughout the whole body of the French and of the English clergy, all tend to confirm the view expressed by Bulaeus.']

CHAP. XII, treatises than those hitherto in use. The first translation of
§ 7. the *Nicomachean Ethics* direct from the Greek was made under
his directions, though he can hardly be considered the actual
translator;[1] and it is tempting to trace back the peculiar and
undying affection of Oxford for that great work to the influence of her first recorded chancellor. But Grosseteste's
interests lay rather in the direction of mathematics and
Roger physical science on the one hand, and of theology on the
Bacon. other, than in the direction of logic and metaphysics.[2] His

[1] Roger Bacon says expressly: 'Graecum et Hebraeum non scivit sufficienter ut per se transferret, sed habuit multos adiutores' (*Op. Ined.*, ed. J. S. Brewer (R.S.), p. 472). Matthew Paris gives the name of his assistant, 'coadiuvante magistro Nicholao Graeco, clerico abbatis Sancti Albani' (*Chron. Mai.*, ed. H. R. Luard (R.S.), iv. 233). [Subsequent research has shown clearly that the importance of Grosseteste as a translator from the Greek was far greater than Rashdall imagined. See Prof. F. M. Powicke, 'Robert Grosseteste and the Nicomachean Ethics', *Proceedings of the British Academy*, xvi (1930); S. Harrison Thomson, 'The "Notule" of Grosseteste on the Nicomachean Ethics', in *Proceedings of the British Academy*, xix (1933), 'Grosseteste's Topical Concordance of the Bible and the Fathers', in *Speculum*, 1934, ix. 139–40, and his 'A Note on Grosseteste's Work of Translation', in *Journal of Theological Studies*, 1933, xxxiv. 48–52. In this latter article Dr. Thomson writes: 'The researches of Baur, Grabmann, Minges, Pelzer, and Powicke have shown him as beyond doubt the translator of the whole of the Nicomachean Ethics, the *De Bona Fortuna*, and probably the compendious comments of Eustratius, Aspasius, and Michael of Ephesus on the Ethics.' Grosseteste's revision of the translation by Burgundio of

Pisa of the *De Orthodoxa Fide* of Damascene, his translations of the *Testamenta XII Patriarcharum*, the section of Suidas's Lexicon on *'Ιησοῦς*, as well as the four principal works of Dionysius the Areopagite have, as Dr. Thomson points out, been well known since the thirteenth century. Other translations attributed to him by his earlier biographers remain to be identified. Dr. Thomson in the article cited above shows reason for adding to the list the *De Lineis Indivisibilibus*, 'one of the most difficult of the pseudo-Aristotelica'. See also E. Franceschini, *Roberto Grossatesta, vescovo di Lincoln, e le sue traduzioni latine*, Venice, 1933. See also A. G. Little, *Studies in English Franciscan History*, pp. 208–9. Monsignor Grabmann and Prof. F. M. Powicke have drawn attention to the work and career of another Oxford Aristotelian and chancellor of the university, Simon of Faversham (†1306). See M. Grabmann, 'Die Aristoteles-Kommentare des Simon von Faversham', in the *Sitzungs-berichte der bayerischen Akademie der Wissenschaften*, Philosoph.-hist. Abt. 1933, pp. 11–13; and Prof. Powicke's article 'Master Simon of Faversham' in *Mélanges d'histoire du moyen âge offerts à F. Lot*, Paris, 1925, pp. 649–58.]

[2] 'Unde dominus Robertus, quondam episcopus Lincolniensis sanctae memoriae, neglexit omnino libros Aristotelis et vias

writings show a range and versatility rare indeed among chap. xii,
medieval doctors:[1] he was a French poet, an agriculturist, a §7.
lawyer, a physician, and a preacher; if he can scarcely be
called a Greek or Hebrew scholar,[2] he was at least interested
in the study of these languages. Although himself a scholastic
philosopher largely instrumental in introducing the new
Aristotle to the Oxford schools, he was a decided opponent
of the rising Aristotelianism in theology. As Bishop of
Lincoln, he endeavoured to encourage biblical study,[3] and
to keep the line of demarcation between theology and philosophy where it had been placed by the old Latin Fathers and

eorum, et per experientiam pro-
priam, et auctores alios, et per
alias scientias negotiatus est in
sapientialibus Aristotelis et melius
centies millies scivit et scripsit illa
de quibus libri Aristotelis loquun-
tur, quam in ipsius perversis trans-
lationibus capi possunt' (Roger
Bacon, *loc. cit.*, p. 469). [See also
P. Duhem, *Le Système du monde*,
1915–17, iii. 277–87, v. 341–58.]

[1] Giraldus Cambrensis, ed. J. S.
Brewer (R.S.), i. 249. Pegge ap-
pends a catalogue of the Bishop's
works to his *Life of Robert Grosseteste*, London, 1793. On Grosseteste see Ludwig Baur, 'Die philo-
sophischen Werke des Grosseteste,
Bischofs von Lincoln' in *Beiträge
zur Geschichte der Philosophie des
Mittelalters*, Münster-i.-W., 1912;
the same, *Die Philosophie des Robert
Grossesteste, Bischofs von Lincoln*,
Münster-in-W., 1917. For Grosseteste's influence on Roger Bacon
see L. Baur, 'Der Einfluss des
Robert Grosseteste auf die wis-
senschaftliche Richtung des Roger
Bacon' in *Roger Bacon, Commemoration Essays*, ed. A. G.
Little, pp. 33–54. Dr. Baur has
shown the close dependence of
Bacon upon Grosseteste both for
his sense of the importance of
philology and for his scientific
ideas. [See also L. Baur, *Das
philosophische Lebenswerk des Robert
Grosseteste, Bischofs von Lincoln*,
Cologne, 1910. F. S. Stevenson,
*Robert Grosseteste, Bishop of Lin-
coln*, London, 1899, is still the fullest biography of Grosseteste. For
an analysis of his philosophy see
D. E. Sharp, *Franciscan Philosophy
at Oxford in the XIIIth century*,
pp. 9–46; for his connexion with
the Franciscan School at Oxford
see A. G. Little, *Studies in English
Franciscan History*, pp. 195–209,
and his article, 'The Franciscan
School at Oxford in the 13th century' in *Archivum Franciscum Historicum*, xix (1926), 807–10. For
fuller bibliography see Ueberweg-
Geyer, 371–7, 731–2. Of more
recent literature mention may be
made of the following articles by
Dr. S. Harrison Thomson: 'The
Text of Gosseteste's *De Cometis*',
Isis, 1933, xix. 19–25, 'The *De
Anima* of Robert Grosseteste', *The
New Scholasticism*, 1933, vii. 201–
21. It is to be hoped that Dr.
Thomson's important researches
will soon bear fruit in a catalogue
of Grosseteste's works.]

[2] [See above, p. 240, n. 1.]

[3] *Epistolae*, ed. H. R. Luard
(R.S.), p. 346. [See also A.
Kleinhaus, O.F.M., 'De Studio
Sacrae Scripturae in O.F.M. sae-
culo xiii', in *Antonianum*, vii (1932),
pp. 413–40.]

CHAP. XII, the earlier medieval doctors. The name of *Lincolniensis* stands
§ 7. high in the theological literature of the Middle Ages, but he
is appealed to on the one hand as a physicist, and on the
other as an independent theologian, as a great ecclesiastical
statesman, as a champion of the rights of the English Church
against both Pope and King[1] rather than as a logician or a
metaphysical thinker.

Much further apart from the main current of scholastic
thought stands the great Oxford Franciscan, Roger Bacon.
It is not altogether without justification that the medieval
schools, singularly happy in their choice of epithets for great
teachers, labelled him *Doctor Mirabilis*.[2] His contributions

---

[1] It should be observed, however, that the defiant letter to the Pope, preserved by Matthew Paris, to which he owes much of his fame as an Anglican ecclesiastic, is of very doubtful authenticity. See Jourdain's essay in *Excursions historiques*, p. 150 *sq.* [See also O. H. Richardson, *The National Movement in the Reign of Henry III*, pp. 24–35; A. L. Smith, *Church and State in the Middle Ages*, pp. 101–18.]

[2] He was born *c.* 1214, and died in 1292. The most important book by a single writer on Roger Bacon is E. Charles, *Roger Bacon, sa vie, ses ouvrages, ses doctrines*, Paris, 1861; a work of great value. I may also refer to Professor Adamson's address on Roger Bacon, *The Philosophy of Science in the Middle Ages*, Manchester, 1876; and to the important volume, *Roger Bacon, Commemoration Essays*, Oxford, 1914, edited with a valuable introduction and bibliography by A. G. Little. Some pages of Professor Adamson's address are there reprinted, see *op. cit.*, pp. 13–19. Bacon is also very frequently alluded to by F. Picavet in *Esquisse d'une histoire générale et comparée des philosophes médiévales*. For a minimizing view of Bacon's importance see the very learned article by Professor Thorndike in the *American Historical Review*, xxi (1916), 237–57, 468–80, and his chapter on Bacon in *History of Magic and Experimental Science*, ii. 616–91. Professor Thorndike has no doubt exploded many of the exaggerations about Bacon which have been largely due to ignorance of other medieval writers on the same subject, but though I have modified some passages in my first edition, I venture to think that Bacon is a more remarkable figure in the history of medieval thought than Professor Thorndike would admit. For recent editions of various works of Bacon by Mr. Robert Steele and others see Dr. A. G. Little's bibliography in *Roger Bacon, Commemoration Essays*. [For a list of authorities dealing with the writings of Roger Bacon see L. J. Paetow, *A Guide to the Study of Medieval History* (revised edition, 1931), pp. 444, 446, 460–1, 464–5, 472–3; Ueberweg-Geyer, ii. 466–73, 760–1; G. Sarton, *Introduction to the History of Science*, ii. 952–67; A. G. Little, 'The Franciscan School at Oxford in the 13th Century' in *Archivum Franciscanum Historicum*, xix (1926), 864, n. 3. An English translation of *The Opus Majus of Roger Bacon* by R. B. B. Burke, 2 vols., Philadelphia, 1928,

to the discussion of the metaphysical questions which absorbed his contemporaries, though they eventually exercised considerable influence, made little noise. Entirely free from the ignorant contempt for speculative philosophy too common among experimental inquirers, he realized none the less the fatal preoccupation of his age with logic and metaphysics—especially in the ordinary educational curriculum. Doubtless he was much more the child of his age than he himself imagined: his own diatribes against excessive reliance on authority are supported by long strings of quotations. Many other medieval writers sing the praises of experience, and there was more or less intelligent observation and experiment than is commonly recognized.[1] Bacon owed more to his predecessors than he acknowledges; and his criticisms on his contemporaries are often unfair and exaggerated. He was undoubtedly boastful and jealous. Still, it is true that the characteristic defects of the medieval schools are pointed out almost as fully by Roger Bacon as by the great namesake who has on somewhat slender grounds been styled Father of the Inductive Philosophy. The neglect of observation and experiment, the abuse of syllogistic reasoning, the blind deference to authority in science and philosophy as well as

has been made. Professor W. R. Newbold, *The Cipher of Roger Bacon*, ed. R. G. Kent, Philadelphia, 1928, believed that he had succeeded in deciphering the mysterious Voynich MS., but J. M. Manly, in his article 'Roger Bacon and the Voynich MS.', in *Speculum*, vi (1931), 345–91, doubts this solution of the cipher. See also D. W. Singer, 'Alchemical Works attributed to Roger Bacon' in *Speculum*, vii (1932), 80–6. Dr. A. G. Little's lecture on 'Roger Bacon', in *Proceedings of the British Academy*, xiv (1928), and Mr. Robert Steele's article, 'Roger Bacon and the state of science in the thirteenth century', in *Studies in the History and Method of Science*, ed. C. Singer, ii (1921), 121–50, furnish useful surveys of Bacon's importance and achievement. The position of the study of the natural sciences at Oxford during the time of Grosseteste and Bacon is summarized in an article by Stephen d'Irsay in *Archeion*, xv (1933), 225–31.]

[1] At bottom the defect of the better medieval writers on natural science was not so much contempt of experience as want of historical criticism. They believed that things had been experienced because ancient writers recorded them and sometimes declared that they had themselves experienced them, and did not appreciate the unreliability of tradition, popular belief, and travellers' tales.

CHAP. XII, in religion—on all these points Roger Bacon, writing in the
§ 7. thirteenth century, is as vigorous a censor of the ordinary
scholastic methods as Francis Bacon in the seventeenth, even
though he sometimes illustrates the very defects which he
condemns. It is difficult to believe that the later writer was
not, directly or indirectly, influenced by his thirteenth-century
namesake.[1] He is no doubt far from having escaped from
the meshes of scholasticism himself. His most penetrating
suggestions are often enveloped in a half-mystic haze, and
mixed up with astrological and other delusions, from which
the writings of the brilliant seventeenth-century man of
letters are free; but Francis Bacon's comparative immunity
from scientific superstition is due rather to the actual advances
in scientific discovery made by the contemporaries to whose
achievements he accorded so grudging a recognition than to
his own superior originality. Roger Bacon's actual discoveries
or anticipations of discovery have often been absurdly exaggerated; but the same may be said of those of the philosophic chancellor.[2] It may even be contended that he had
a truer conception of the value of mathematics, both in
education and in scientific inquiry, than was possible to the
unmathematical Francis; but the illustrations which he gives
show that he had a very clear conception as to where that
value lay. He was free from that petulant contempt for
ancient learning which has endeared the name of Francis

[1] For minor coincidences, cf. with
Francis Bacon's 'idola' Roger's
enumeration of the four 'compre-
hendendae veritatis offendicula',
viz. 'fragilis et indignae auctoritatis
exemplum, consuetudinis diutur-
nitas, vulgi sensus imperiti et pro-
priae ignorantiae occultatio cum
ostentatione sapientiae apparentis'
(*Opus Majus*, ed. Jebb, Lond. 1733,
p. 2), and the 'tres magnas praero-
gativas respectu aliarum scientiarum' (*ibid.*, p. 448) of experimental science. But the agreement
in general aim is much more remarkable.

[2] Francis Bacon's discovery of
the 'form of heat' may be paralleled
by Roger Bacon's attainments in
optics; but there are perhaps other
medieval writers for whom the
same claim might be made with as
much justice. Colonel Hime (*Roger
Bacon, Commemoration Essays*, p.
333) claims for him the invention of
gunpowder as an explosive though
not as a means of propelling pro-
jectiles; but Professor Thorndike
(*History of Magic and Experimental
Science*, ii. 688–91) has shown upon
what slender foundations this claim
rests. After all, the supposed discovery rests on an alleged crypto-
gram.

Bacon to the Philistines of every succeeding age. While he CHAP. XII, condemned the excessive authority attributed to the *ipse dixit* § 7. of Aristotle, he fully appreciated the value of Aristotle and other ancient thinkers; like all the *esprits forts* of the Middle Ages he was himself somewhat in bondage to the Arabians.[1] But unlike other medieval thinkers, orthodox or unorthodox, he saw that the study of Greek was the true key to the meaning of Aristotle,[2] and a knowledge of the Bible in the original the true foundation for a fruitful study of theology.[3] All the characteristic ideas of the sixteenth century are held in solution, as it were, in the writings of Roger Bacon, mixed up no doubt with much that is redolent of the age in which he lived; but, of all the anticipations of modern ways of thinking with which his works abound, the most remarkable is his plan of educational reform. He was convinced that the proper basis of a learned education was the study on the one hand of the ancient languages, on the other of mathematics: these were the proper foundation for the superstructure of philosophy and theology, of medicine and science.[4] Theology and philosophy must be studied philologically and

Bacon's educational theory.

---

[1] He was a disciple of Avicenna rather than of Averroës, whose 'Unity of Intellect' he rejected. Yet the influence of Averroës in Oxford may be due in part to a tradition dating from Roger Bacon.

[2] I agree with Dr. Little (*Roger Bacon, Commemoration Essays*, p. 14) that 'Bacon certainly exaggerated the badness of the later translations', i.e. those direct from the Greek. I suspect that wherever he found Aristotle unintelligible or unsatisfactory, he was apt to put it down to the badness of the translations. 'He nowhere gives credit to Albertus Magnus and Thomas Aquinas for their great commentaries on Aristotle, which are superior to any that he wrote': L. Thorndike, *History of Magic and Experimental Science*, ii. 634.

[3] *The Greek Grammar of Roger Bacon and a fragment of his Hebrew*

Grammar has been edited by the Rev. E. Nolan and Dr. S. A. Hirsch, Cambridge, 1902. M. F. Picavet thinks it established that Bacon 'connaissait bien l'hébreu' (*Essais sur l'histoire de théologie et philosophie médiévale*, p. 17). Dr. Hirsch (*Roger Bacon, Commemoration Essays*, p. 143) seems to put his knowledge of Hebrew a little lower. All that Bacon says about the importance of language study is a little discounted by his boast that he could teach all that was wanted in either Hebrew or Greek in three days (*Op. Tertium*, p. 65). [See also B. van de Walle, O.F.M., 'Roger Bacon dans l'histoire de la philologie', in *France Franciscaine*, xi (1928), 315–410; xii (1929), 44–90, 161–228.]

[4] 'Harum scientiarum porta et clavis est mathematica' (*Op. majus*, ed. Jebb, p. 57).

CHAP. XII, historically:[1] science must be studied mathematically and
§ 7.   experimentally. It is probable that he was nearer not merely
to the physical conception of measurable force but to the wider
conception of general laws harmoniously combining to form
an ordered system, than any thinker who lived before the
seventeenth century,[2] and this is a greater intellectual achievement than any real or supposed 'anticipations'.[3] No doubt
parallels to Bacon's ideas may often be discovered in other of
the more enlightened medieval writers, but it may be doubted
whether on the whole any other such writer could be mentioned who gives so striking a literary expression to the ideas
which have developed into modern science.

Bacon as   So isolated a thinker as Roger Bacon may be supposed to
school-
man.   throw little light upon the general tone of the university with
which he was—as it were accidentally—connected. But it is
a mistake to imagine that Bacon has no place in the history
of the scholastic philosophy understood in its narrower and

---

[1] 'Impossibile est quod textus Dei sciatur propter abusum libri Sententiarum' (Op. Minus in Op. Ined., ed. J. S. Brewer (R.S.), p. 329). He adds that 'Liber Historiarum (i.e. the Historia Scholastica of Petrus Comestor) solebat legi et adhuc legitur rarissime'. The 'Liber Historiarum' is recognized as a possible alternative to the Sentences in a Statute of 1252 (Mun. Acad. i. 25: [Stat. Antiq. Univ. Oxon., p. 49, l. 20. Mr. S. Gibson gives the date of this statute as 12 Mar. 1253.])—a remarkable peculiarity of Oxford, which, however, soon disappears. [See A. G. Little and F. Pelster, Oxford Theology and Theologians, c. 1282-1302 (O.H.S.), pp. 25, 26. The 'Liber Historiarum' was read and commented on in Paris by Hugh of S. Cher, see Ueberweg-Geyer, ii. 399.]

[2] Cf. Professor Adamson's remarks on this subject. Roger Bacon, Commemoration Essays, p. 16.

[3] Among his anticipations (in another sphere) may be mentioned the doctrine that the aged poor should be maintained by the state, see Op. Majus, ed. J. Bridges, ii. 351, quoted by Dr. Little, Roger Bacon, Commemoration Essays, p. 20. A passage in his writings suggesting the possibility of reaching the Indies by a voyage westward (Op. Majus, ed. J. Bridges, i. xxxiii, 292) is noted by Dr. Little (op. cit., p. 30) as having been quoted by Cardinal Pierre d'Ailly (Petrus Alliacus) without acknowledgement. Bacon's plea for a reform of the Calendar is another suggestion which bore practical fruit after several centuries (Op. Majus, ed. J. Bridges, i. xxxiv); but he was indebted to Grosseteste (L. Thorndike, History of Magic and Experimental Science, ii. 444), as he was for his interest in burning-glasses and optics generally. Grosseteste perfectly understood the principle of both the microscope and the telescope (ibid. ii. 441).

non-technical sense. In fact the result of the most recent CHAP. XII,
study of Bacon is rather to lower the popular estimate of his §7.
achievements in science, which is partly based on accidental
expressions of exuberant rhetoric, and to attribute to him a
scholastic importance hitherto insufficiently acknowledged.
All the germinal ideas of that antagonism to the Dominican
teaching in which Oxford philosophy had its origin may be
traced in the writings of the 'wonderful Doctor', though of
course, we cannot be sure how much of his thought was
original or how much was the common property of the
Franciscan Convent in Oxford.[1] The accidents which prevented any considerable part of his writings being printed till
the eighteenth century is responsible for the non-recognition
of his importance even from the purely scholastic point of
view, although he is often quoted with respect in the Middle
Ages and later.[2] In his criticism of the Thomist 'Unity of
Form' he is the predecessor of Scotus: in his doctrine of
Universals, of immediate perception without 'real intelligible
species', and of the 'principle of individuation' he anticipates

[1] [See A. G. Little, 'Thomas Docking and his relations to Roger Bacon', *Essays in History presented to R. L. Poole*, pp. 301–31.]

[2] This was more probably due to their desultory and unsystematic character than to any sort of persecution or theological reprobation. The schoolmen were chiefly printed by the Orders which had produced them. Bacon produced nothing but programmes or introductions to a great system of philosophy which was never written. 'He constructed a sort of intellectual portico more pretentious than he could have justified by his main building' (L. Thorndike, *History of Magic and Experimental Science*, ii. 635). The notion that Bacon was persecuted by his Order for his addiction to natural science or a too friendly attitude towards magic has been shown to be baseless. See L. Thorndike, *op. cit.* ii. 626 *sq.* If it is true that he was condemned in 1277 and sentenced to imprisonment for certain theological errors (which is not certain), we do not know that these had anything to do with his scientific investigations. For a critical examination of the subject see P. Féret, 'Les Emprisonnements de Roger Bacon', *Revue de questions historiques*, l (1891), 119–42. Bacon's condemnation was certainly connected with the controversies which prevailed at this time between the Franciscan and Dominican Orders, and was probably provoked by the disrespectful way in which he had spoken of both sides. He held a doctrine which might very well be supposed to approximate to the 'Unity of Intellect' theory, though really quite different. See P. Mandonnet, O.P., *Siger de Brabant et l'Averroïsme latin au XIIIme siècle*, Louvain, 1911, pp. 246–8. [See also A. G. Little, *Roger Bacon, Commemoration Essays*, pp. 26, 27.]

CHAP. XII, nearly all the fundamental ideas of Ockham.[1] The realistic
§ 7. side of his doctrine was, indeed, common to most Oxford
teachers of his time; but he must have contributed something
at least to the development of this Oxford criticism, if it
cannot all be traced back to him. His nominalistic side was
not developed till later, but it can hardly be doubted that
Ockham or Ockham's predecessors got their first inspiration
from the writings of this sometimes erratic schoolman.[2]

Bacon not Even on his mathematical and experimental side Roger
alone at
Oxford. Bacon was not without predecessors or like-minded contemporaries. He is full of praise for the first generation of Oxford
teachers, especially for Grosseteste[3] and Adam de Marisco,[4] of
whose school he must be considered the brilliant product.[5]

[1] 'Universale non est nisi con-
venientia plurium individuorum'
(ap. Charles, *Roger Bacon*, p. 383).
At the same time he avoided Ockham's mistake of inferring that
therefore only the particular is real.
Indeed the *dictum* was susceptible
of a Scotist as well as of an Ock-
hamist development.

[2] By way of authority for the
above, I must be content to refer
to M. Charles's admirable account of
Roger Bacon's position as a Schoolman (*ibid.*, pp. 164–294). It should
not be assumed that Père Mandonnet is necessarily right in pronounc-
ing Bacon 'en retard sur le mouve-
ment intellectuel de son siècle'
(*Siger de Brabant et l'Averroïsme
latin au XIIIᵐᵉ siècle*, Louvain,
1911, i. 244), because he withstood
the Dominican Aristotelianism.
After all Père Mandonnet with all
his learning and modernity is a
Dominican.

[3] In *Op. Tert.* (*Op. ined.* p. 75)
he styles them 'maiores clerici de
mundo'. Again, 'Nullus scivit lin-
guas nisi Boëtius de translatori-
bus famosis, nullus scientias nisi
dominus Robertus episcopus Lincolniensis', *ibid.*, p. 91). [On Grosseteste's influence on Bacon see L.
Baur's article, 'Der Einfluss des

Robert Grosseteste auf die wissen-
schaftliche Richtung des Roger
Bacon', in *Roger Bacon, Commemor-
ation Essays*, pp. 33–54, and A. G.
Little, *Studies in English Franciscan
History*, pp. 195–8.]

[4] [On Adam Marsh see A. G.
Little, 'The Franciscan School at
Oxford in the 13th century', in
*Archivum Franciscanum Histori-
cum*, xix (1926), 831–8; Ueberweg-
Geyer, ii. 396, 738.]

[5] [Mention may be made here of
one of Bacon's contemporaries at
Oxford whose teaching he severely
criticized—Richard Rufus of Cornwall, who was *lector* of the Franciscan school about 1256. Bacon
describes him as 'famosissimus
apud stultam multitudinem; sed
apud sapientes fuit insanus et
reprobatus Parisius propter errores
quos invenerat et promulgaverat
cum solemniter legebat sententias
ibidem'. See *Fr. Rogeri Bacon
Compendium Studii Theologiae*, ed.
H. Rashdall, pp. 52–3. Notwithstanding Bacon's denunciation, the
importance of Fr. Richard Rufus
of Cornwall has now come to be
recognized. See A. G. Little, 'The
Franciscan School at Oxford' in
Archivum Franciscanum Hist. xix
(1926), 842; F. Pelster, S.J., 'Zu

But, amidst all his laments at the aberrations of his own generation, we find that it was at Oxford that the best mathematics of the day were taught.[1] The two chief mathematicians of the thirteenth century (judged by the vogue of their writings) were Oxford men.[2] All through the Middle Ages the greatest mathematicians were either Englishmen or Italians,[3] though in the later Middle Age English mathematics did not come up to the promise of the thirteenth century.

It is not difficult to understand some of the causes of this contrast between thirteenth-century Oxford and thirteenth-

Richardus Rufus de Cornubia', in *Zeitschrift für Katholische Theologie*, xlviii (1924), 625–9, 'Roger Bacon und Richardus Rufus', in *Scholastik*, iv (1929), 410–16, and 'Neue Schriften des englischen Franziskaners Richardus Rufus von Cornwall (um 1250)', *ibid.* viii (1933), 561–8; W. Lampen, 'De Fr. Richardo Rufo Cornubiensi, O.F.M.', in *Arch. Francisc. Hist.* xxi (1928), 403–6; Little and Pelster, *Oxford Theology and Theologians, c. 1282–1302* (O.H.S.), p. 62, n. 1; and Ueberweg-Geyer, ii. 396–7, 733.]

[1] 'Haec autem scientia (i.e. Perspectiva) non est adhuc lecta Parisius nec apud Latinos, nisi bis Oxoniae in Anglia' (*op. cit.*, p. 37). So in *Op. Min.* (*ibid.*, p. 361) he praises the 'Anglici Naturales' as opposed to the Parisians. Again, 'Non sunt enim nisi duo perfecti (mathematici), scilicet magister Jo. London. et magister Petrus de Maharn-curia Picardus. Alii duo boni sunt, scilicet magister Campanus de Novaria, et magister Nicholaus, doctor domini Almarici de Monte Forti' (*Op. Tert.*, pp. 34–5). Of these the first was certainly, the second presumably an Oxonian. Cf. *ibid.*, pp. 43, 46. Bacon was no doubt indebted to all these men. [For John of London see above, p. 50, n. 2). For Petrus de Maharn-curia (Petrus Peregrinus

de Maricourt) see Ueberweg-Geyer, ii. 465–6, 760; and P. Duhem, *Le Système du monde*, 1915, iii. 237–8. For Campanus de Novara see P. Duhem, *op. cit.* iii. 317–26.]

[2] Cf. i. 442. Johannes de Sacro Bosco (Holywood), author of the 'Tractatus de Sphaera', to whom Europe was indebted for the theory of a 'crystalline heaven' and Johannes Pisanus (i.e. Pecham, the Franciscan Archbishop of Canterbury), whose work on optics perhaps owes something to Roger Bacon. See *Reg. Fr. Johannis Peckham*, ed. C. T. Martin (R.S.), iii. lviii *sq.* [For Johannes de Sacro Bosco see P. Duhem, *Le Système du monde*, 1915, iii. 238–40; R. T. Gunther, *Early Science in Oxford* (O.H.S.), ii. 27, 28, 159–60. For Archbishop Pecham see below, p. 255, n. 1. See also P. Duhem, *Le Système du monde*, 1915, iii. 515–17.]

[3] It is worth mentioning that a fifteenth-century eulogy of the university (Lambeth MS. 221, f. 308 *b* [M. R. James and C. Jenkins, *Descriptive Catalogue of MSS. in the Library of Lambeth Palace*, p. 360]) claims Campanus de Novara (i. 250) as an Oxonian. [On the contribution made by Oxford mathematicians see P. Duhem, *Études sur Léonardo de Vinci*, 1913, iii. 405–510, *Le Système du monde*, 1915–16, iv. 72–4, 280.]

CHAP. XII,
§ 7.
century Paris. Oxford had known no such wild outburst of heresy as the Almarician movement at Paris: consequently there was less reaction, less ecclesiastical repression, less exclusive absorption in theological controversy. Another circumstance which made in the same direction was the fact that the leading teachers of the thirteenth-century Oxford were either seculars or members of what ultimately proved the less conservative of the two great Mendicant Orders. It is true that the Franciscans had at first chosen what was on the whole the less enlightened side in the great scholastic debate. While the Dominican masters were for the most part inflexible adherents of the moderate and philosophically enlightened Aquinas, the Franciscans were divided in their allegiance between the thoroughgoing realist Alexander of Hales and the mystic Bonaventura.[1] But neither of these masters ever acquired the authority which was wielded over the Dominican mind by the Angelical doctor. In the Franciscan Order there was possibly for a time less intellectual emancipation and good sense, but there was more freedom, more originality.[2] And at Oxford, as in England generally,

[1] [The Oxford Franciscan School was not troubled by this division. Dr. Little in an article, 'Was St. Bonaventura a student in Oxford?' in *Archivum Franciscanum Historicum*, xix (1926), 289–91, reviews the evidence for S. Bonaventura having studied at Oxford and for his having visited Oxford in 1259 at the time of the death of Fr. Adam Marsh, O.F.M.]

[2] [In her important study, *Franciscan Philosophy at Oxford in the 13th Century*, Oxford, 1930, Dr. D. E. Sharp has treated of Grosseteste, Thomas of York, Roger Bacon, John Pecham, Richard of Middleton, and Duns Scotus. Dr. Sharp utters the warning that 'the writings of that School are still too little known to justify any closed conceptions of its activities such as are fostered by the vicious obsession of modern writers to label the

Oxford Franciscans as disciples of Augustine and of Bonaventura or as precursors of Scotus' (*op. cit.*, p. 51). As Rashdall makes no reference to Thomas of York, some mention of him seems called for here. Thomas of York stands fourth in the series of *lectores* at the Franciscan convent in Oxford (*c.* 1253). His *Sapientiale* justly won him a high reputation as a metaphysician. His work, like that of Grosseteste, is characterized by his familiarity with the recent translations of Greek, Arabic, and Jewish authors. On Thomas of York, besides Dr. Sharp's study of his work and the authorities cited by her, see A. G. Little, 'The Franciscan School at Oxford in the 13th century', in *Arch. Francisc. Hist.*, xix (1926), 839–41; F. Tresserat, 'Entorn del "Sapientiale" de Tomàs de York' in *Criterion* (Barcelona),

all through the Middle Ages, the speculative, enthusiastic, CHAP. XII,
§ 7. often democratic Franciscans were more influential than the sternly orthodox, authority-loving, persecuting Dominicans.

Unlike in many respects as these two earliest Franciscan doctors may appear, they agree in this—that they resisted the Aristotelianism which Albert and S. Thomas had introduced into the Dominican theology, and adhered to the old Augustinian traditions which in philosophy (though not in theology) had been abandoned by the Dominican doctor.[1] The Aristotelian innovations of S. Thomas at first met with much opposition even at Paris from Franciscans and seculars; and the Thomist doctrine which placed the principle of individuation in matter was condemned in 1277 by Stephen Tempier, Bishop of Paris, amid a host of Averroïstic theses.[2] But in Oxford the conservative Augustinian tendency was at first championed even by Dominicans.[3] Sixteen days after the Parisian condemnation, the Dominican Archbishop Robert Kilwardby, at a Council held at Oxford, condemned in a much more explicit manner the cardinal Thomist doctrine of the 'Unity of Form' in man,[4] and a number of other tenets

Conservative resistance to Aristotle.

v (1929), 5–45, 158–80, and 'De doctrinis metaphysicis Fratris Thomae de Eboraco' in *Analecta Sacra Tarraconensia*, v (1929), 33–102.]

[1] The view here taken of the origin of Franciscan tendencies in philosophy, which throws a flood of light upon the position of Oxford in scholastic history, I owe to Father [later Cardinal] Ehrle, 'Beiträge zur Gesch. der mittelalterlichen Scholastik', in *Archiv f. Kirchengesch. des Mittelalt.*, v. 603 sq.

[2] *Chartul. Univ. Paris.* i. 554, 556, note. The doctrine is attacked by Roger Bacon (ap. Charles, pp. 580, 581). [See also P. Mandonnet, O.P., *Siger de Brabant et l'Averroïsme latin au XIIIme siècle*, i. 214–32.]

[3] [For the early history of the Dominican School in Oxford see Ueberweg-Geyer, ii. 400, 739; F. Pelster, S.J., 'Die Bedeutung

der Sentenzenvorlesung für die theologische Spekulation des Mittelalters. Ein Zeugnis aus der ältesten Oxforder Dominikanerschule', *Scholastik*, ii (1927), 250–5, 'Das Leben und die Schriften des Oxforder Dominikanerlehrers Richard Fishacre', *Zeitschrift für Katholische Theologie*, liv (1930), 518–53, and 'Eine Handschrift mit Predigten des Richard Fishacre, O.P., und anderer Oxforder Lehrer', *ibid.* lvii (1933), 614–17; M.-D. Chenu, O.P., 'La Théologie comme science au XIIIe siècle', *Archives d'histoire doctrinale et littéraire du moyen âge*, ii (1927), 31–47.]

[4] 'Quod vegetiva, sensitiva, et intellectiva sint una forma simplex' (*Chart. Univ. Paris.* i, pt. i, No. 474). The Thomist doctrine was that the 'anima rationalis' was the only 'forma' of man, which in him performed the functions which the

CHAP. XII, which had evidently been maintained by younger men in the
§ 7.   Dominican School.[1] While the condemnation at Paris was
apparently the work of the bishop only, and was certainly in
opposition to the dominant tendency of the university, the
English archbishop expressly tells us that he had the consent
of the masters. The condemnation was renewed at the visitation of the Franciscan Archbishop Pecham in 1284.[2]
Four years later the same primate, sitting at S. Mary Arches

vegetable or sensitive souls or forms performed in the lower animals. The entire absence of Averroïstic theses in the list of errors is remark-able. Cf. Pecham's letter to the university (*Registrum*, ed. C. T. Martin (R.S.), iii. 840, 852, 864), which shows clearly that the opin-ions condemned were Dominican.

[1] [See P. Mandonnet, O.P., *Siger de Brabant et l'Averroïsme latin au XIIIme siècle*, 1911, i. 233 *sq.*]

[2] *Ann. Monast.*, Oseney (R.S.), iv. 298 *sq.* [On the anti-Thomist controversy see P. Glorieux, O.P., 'Comment les thèses thomistes furent proscrites à Oxford (1284–6)', in *Revue Thomiste*, xxxiii (1927), 259–91, and 'La Littérature des Correctoires', *ibid.* xxxiii (1928), 69–96; A. Callebaut, O.F.M., 'Jean Pecham, O.F.M., et l'Augustin-isme', in *Arch. Francisc. Hist.* xviii (1925), 441–72. See also Ueberweg-Geyer, ii. 492–7, 764. For Fr. Richard Clapwell or Knapwell, O.P., who was condemned for his Thomist teaching by Archbishop Pecham in 1286, see Ueberweg-Geyer, ii. 542, 773; M.-D. Chenu, O.P., 'La Première Diffusion du Thomisme à Oxford', in *Archives d'histoire doctrinale et littéraire du moyen âge*, iii (1928), 185–201; and F. Pelster, 'Richard von Knap-well, O.P., seine Quaestiones dis-putatae und sein Quodlibet' in *Zeitschrift für Katholische Theo-logie*, lii (1928), 473, 491. See, too, the biographical notice of him in A. G. Little and F. Pelster, *Ox-*

ford Theology and Theologians, c. 1282–1302 (O.H.S.), pp. 90–1. Other prominent supporters of Thomism in the Dominican School at Oxford were Fr. William de Hothum, who was Provincial in England at the time of Fr. Richard Knapwell's condemnation, Fr. Thomas Jorz, who succeeded Ho-thum as Provincial, Fr. Robert of Oxford, Fr. William Macclesfield, who is credited with having colla-borated with Knapwell in writing the 'Correctorium corruptorii' in answer to William de la Mare's 'Correctorium fratris Thomae', Fr. Thomas de Sutton, opponent of the teachings first of Henry of Ghent and later of Duns Scotus, and Fr. Nicholas Trivet, author of the 'Annales sex regum Angliae (1135–1307)'. For their writings see the bibliography in Ueberweg-Geyer, ii. 541–3, 773. To the authorities therein mentioned may be added Dr. F. Pelster's edition of Thomas de Sutton's *Quaestiones de reali distinctione inter essentiam et esse*, Münster-i.-W., 1929, and Dr. D. E. Sharp's article on 'Thomas of Sutton, O.P.', in *Revue néoscolastique de philosophie*, xli (1934), 332–54. For biographical notices see A. G. Little and F. Pelster, *Oxford Theology and Theo-logians, c. 1282–1302* (O.H.S.). See also J. Kraus, 'Die Stellung des Ox-forder Dominikanerlehrer Cra-thorn zu Thomas im Aquin', in *Zeitschrift für Katholische Theo-logie*, lvii (1933), 66–88.]

Church in London, condemned another batch of Dominican CHAP. XII, § 7.
opinions, among which significantly appears the position 'that
in such matters one is not bound to adhere to the authority
of the Pope, or of Gregory, or of Augustine, or of any other
Master whatever; but solely to the authority of the Bible and
of necessary reason'.

In this conservative Augustinianism, with the consequent The
antagonism to the Thomist views as to the principle of indi- Franciscan
philo-
viduation and the unity of form, lay the germ of all the later sophy.
developments of Franciscan philosophy.[1] Of this philosophical conservatism the centre was Oxford: yet in the long
run the Franciscan spirit proved more fruitful in new ideas,
both philosophical and theological, than the Thomism, with
its new-fangled but immovable Aristotelianism in philosophy and its conservative orthodoxy in theology, which
reigned at Paris. It is not till the beginning of the fourteenth
century that Oxford attained to European fame as a centre of
scholasticism. By this time the tendency towards an independent study of nature and towards fresh and unscholastic
modes of thought, of which there are slight traces in thirteenth-century Oxford, had nearly worn itself out; and Oxford
plunged more fiercely even than Paris into the great scholastic
strife. From this time forward the intellectual activity of
Oxford far surpasses that of Paris.[2] At Paris itself it is the
English Nation that takes the lead. Both the two great scholastic
innovations of the fourteenth century—the revival of realism in
a totally new form by Duns Scotus[3] and the nominalistic reaction
headed by Ockham—had their origin probably in Oxford,
certainly in English minds. The most important fourteenth-

[1] Peckham, *Regist.*, ed. C. T. Martin (R.S.), iii. 923. [Besides Pecham the chief representatives of the Franciscan School in Oxford in the latter part of the thirteenth century were Fr. Nicholas of Ocham and Fr. Roger Marston. See Ueberweg-Geyer, ii. 486–9, 762; A. G. Little, 'The Franciscan School at Oxford in the 13th century', in *Arch. Francisc. Hist.* xix (1926), 52–8; and A. G. Little and F. Pelster, *Oxford Theology and Theologians, c. 1282–1302* (O.H.S.), for biographical notices of Nicholas of Ocham, p. 89, and of Roger Marston, pp. 93–5, 119–20.]

[2] See above, i. 561 *sq.*

[3] Scotism may be conveniently treated as characteristic of the fourteenth century, though Scotus began to teach towards the end of the thirteenth.

CHAP. XII, § 7.

century schoolmen were Oxonians: nearly all the later schoolmen of any importance were Englishmen, or Germans educated in the traditions of the English nation at Paris.

Characteristics of fourteenth-century scholastics.

From one point of view the scholasticism of the fourteenth century exhibits a decline: the old battle between nominalism and realism was renewed, and with even more unphilosophic vehemence than before. It was at this time that philosophy literally descended from the schools into the street and that the *odium metaphysicum* gave fresh zest to the unending faction fight between north and south at Oxford, between Czech and German at Prague. And yet from another point of view this very descent into the streets exhibits an advance. The range of subjects debated in the schools of the fourteenth century is wider than that which bounded the horizon of the thirteenth. Scholasticism begins to come into contact with practical life. Out of the somewhat muddy metaphysics of the fourteenth-century schools there emerge present-day questions as to the foundations of property, the respective rights of King and Pope, of King and subject, of priest and people; at Oxford was struck the spark that kindled the torch which was soon to set Europe in a blaze and which was not extinguished at Constance.

Predecessors of Duns Scotus.

The way for Scotus had been prepared at Paris (perhaps at Oxford also) by the very important thinker, Henry of Ghent,[1] a schoolman at once cautious and original, who gave a more Platonic turn to the Thomist doctrine of Universals and maintained against Aquinas that matter might actually exist, without form; while at Oxford the Thomist doctrine of the unity of form was attacked by Roger Bacon, Robert Kilwardby,[2]

[1] Born 1223, died 1293. The received accounts of his life are unhistorical. See Ehrle in *Archiv*, i. 367 *sq.* [See also Ueberweg-Geyer, ii. 498–502, 764–5.] The manuscript mentioned on p. 249, n. 1, claims him as an Oxonian. [On the relation of Duns Scotus to Henry of Ghent see C. R. S. Harris, *Duns Scotus*, i. 238–53; and on his relation to Richard of Middleton see *ibid.* i. 165–8, 254–9, and on his

relation generally to contemporary schoolmen see D. E. Sharp, *Franciscan Philosophy at Oxford in the 13th Century*, pp. 279–82.]

[2] The importance of Kilwardby in the development of the Oxford School was for the first time revealed by his letter defending the Oxford condemnation published by Father [subsequently Cardinal] Ehrle (*Archiv*, v. 603), who shows its points of contact with the

Pecham,[1] and others. The polemic was continued by William CHAP. XII, de la Mare (probably an Englishman, possibly an Oxonian, §7. certainly a Franciscan),[2] who maintained in all its fullness the essential doctrine of Scotism, that of the plurality of forms in the same individual. According to Thomas there is but one form in man which constitutes his humanity, viz. the rational soul. With William de la Mare and Duns Scotus, corporeity, animality, rationality, and the like became

Augustinian tradition. Kilwardby (i) defends the substantial *reality* of the Augustinian 'rationes seminales sive originales rerum', and (ii) contends for a doctrine evolved by him out of Augustine as to the distinctions of the vegetative, sensible, and intellectual 'souls' in man—a doctrine which passed to Olivi, the Apostle of the Spiritual Franciscans, and blossomed into a much more extensive 'plurality of forms' in Gulielmus de Mara and Scotus. The letter is full of germinal Scotism; so too are the positions implied by the Oxford condemnations of Kilwardby and Pecham. [For Kilwardby see also the article by Prof. T. F. Tout in *D.N.B.*; Ueberweg-Geyer, ii. 493–5, 764; the articles by M.-D. Chenu, O.P., 'La Théologie comme science au xiiie siècle', in *Archives d'histoire doctrinale et littéraire du moyen âge*, ii (1927), 35–47, and 'Les Réponses de S. Thomas et de Kilwardby à la consultation de Jean de Verceil' in *Bulletin Thomiste*, vii (1930), 129–39; and F. Stegmüller, 'Les Questions des Commentaires des Sentences de Robert Kilwardby', in *Recherches de théologie ancienne et médiévale*, vi (1934), 55–79, 215 –28. Rashdall's reference to Olivi should not be understood as indicating a connexion between his teaching and that of Kilwardby.]

[1] Peckham, *Regist.*, ed. C. T. Martin (R.S.), iii. 871. [On John Pecham see the article by Dr. C. L. Kingsford in *D.N.B.*; Ueberweg-

Geyer, ii. 479, 484–5, 495, 762; D. E. Sharp, *Franciscan Philosophy at Oxford in the 13th Century*, pp. 175–207; A. G. Little, 'The Franciscan School at Oxford in the 13th century', in *Arch. Francisc. Hist.* xix (1926), 852–4; *Tractatus Tres de Paupertate*, ed. C. L. Kingsford, A. G. Little, and F. Tocco for the British Society of Franciscan Studies (1910) and the bibliography of Pecham's works there given; H. Spettmann, O.F.M., 'Der Sentenzencommentar des Franziskanerbischof Johannes Pecham', in *Divus Thomas* (Freiburg), v (1927), 327–45, and 'Pechams Kommentar zum vierten Buche der Sentenzen' in *Zeitschrift für Katholische Theologie*, lii (1928), 64–74; and V. Doucet, O.F.M., 'Notulae bibliographicae de quibusdam operibus Fr. Ioannis Pecham', in *Antonianum*, viii (1933), 307–28, 425–49.]

[2] A. G. Little, *The Grey Friars in Oxford* (O.H.S.), p. 215. [Dr. Little in his article, 'The Franciscan School at Oxford in the 13th century' in *Arch. Francisc. Hist.* xix (1926), 864–5, states that William de la Mare 'was certainly an Englishman, but until more is known of him, it is not safe to claim him as an Oxonian'. See also Ueberweg-Geyer, ii. 486, 495–6, 762; and F. Pelster, S.J., 'Les Declarationes et les Questions de Guillaume de la Mare' in *Recherches de théologie ancienne et médiévale*, iii (1931), 397–411.]

CHAP. XII, distinct and essential 'forms' coexisting in the individual
§ 7. Socrates. Thus with William de la Mare originated what has seemed to its opponents the fundamental Scotist heresy of 'multiplying entities without necessity'.[1] All these writers probably owed something to Roger Bacon.[2] At all events all with one consent fell upon the Dominican doctrine which places the *principium individuationis* in matter—a doctrine involving for the orthodox thinker angelogical difficulties which were more acutely felt than its more serious theological consequences.[3]

Realism of Duns Scotus. At the first blush of it, the realism of all previous schoolmen, at least since the twelfth century, may seem cautious, timid, reasonable, in comparison with the realism of the school whose teaching culminated in the system of Duns Scotus, said on insufficient evidence to have been originally a fellow of Merton, in any case a master of the anti-Thomist University of Oxford,[4] then a teacher of the anti-Thomist order of

[1] Gulielmus de Mara published his *Correctorium Fratris Thomae* in 1284 (Hauréau, iii. 99 *sq.*; Prantl, iii. 189; *Hist. Litt.* xxi. 299). Duns Scotus may thus have heard him. The actual master of Duns Scotus is said to have been William of Ware, the *Doctor fundatus* (cf., however, Rodulphius Tossinianensis, *Hist. Seraphicae Religionis*, Venice, 1586, f. 319 *b*), whose commentary on the Sentences is preserved in the Merton Library. [See F. M. Powicke, *The Medieval Books of Merton College*, p. 210. On William of Ware see A. G. Little, 'The Franciscan School at Oxford in the 13th century', in *Arch. Francisc. Hist.* xix (1926), 866-8, and the authorities there mentioned; Ueberweg-Geyer, ii. 480-90, 763; P. Muscat, O.F.M., 'Guilelmi de Ware Quaestio inedita de unitate Dei', in *Antonianum*, ii (1927), 335-50; H. Spettmann, O.F.M., 'Die philosophiegeschichtliche Stellung des Wilhelm von Ware', in *Philosophisches Jahrbuch*, xl (1927), 401-3, xli (1928), 42-9; A. Ledoux,

O.F.M., 'De gratia creata et increata iuxta Quaestionem ineditam Guillelmi de Ware', in *Antonianum* v (1930), 137-56. For proof of the connexion between Duns Scotus and William of Ware see E. Longpré, O.F.M., 'Le commentaire sur les Sentences de Guillaume de Nottingham, O.F.M.', in *Arch. Francisc. Hist.* xxii (1929), 232.]

[2] The indebtedness of all these writers to Bacon is carefully pointed out by Charles, *Roger Bacon*, p. 240 *sq.* He perhaps does not allow sufficiently for the possibility of the ideas being the common property of the Franciscan convent at Oxford, or of still wider circles.

[3] An angel being assumed to be 'form without matter', Thomas Aquinas was obliged to admit that there was no individual difference between angels: each angel was a different species.

[4] In 1300 a Franciscan named 'Johannes Douns' was refused licence to hear confessions by Bishop Dalderby (Linc. Reg. f.13; Wood, *City*, ii. 386): when, as

S. Francis at Paris and Cologne. To the modern mind the CHAP. XII,
§ 7.
system of Scotus is apt to appear a wild, luxuriant, rampant

Dr. Little remarks (*The Grey Friars in Oxford*, p. 220), he must, by the rules of the Order, have been at least thirty. The earliest—and indeed the only early—authority for the early life of Scotus is an entry in a Merton manuscript written in 1455: 'Explicit lectura doctoris subtilis . . . sc. doctoris Iohannis Duns nati in quadam villicula parochie de Emyldon vocata Dunstan, in comitatu Northumbrie pertinentis domui scolarium de Mertonhalle in Oxonia et quondam socii dicte domus' (also in some other Merton manuscripts). [See F. M. Powicke, *The Medieval Books of Merton College*, pp. 210–11.] It is very probable (as Bishop Creighton has suggested to me) that this represents only the conjecture of some scholar from Embleton (a Merton living), who was familiar with the Castle of Dunstanburgh and the hamlet of Dunstan in that parish, where is an old manor house with a 'peil' which local tradition makes his birthplace. There is no foundation for the tradition that he died at forty-four or even at thirty-three! It is certain that he went to Paris in 1304 and died at Cologne in 1308. In my estimate of Scotus I am much indebted to Erdmann, and still more to Pluzanski's penetrating *Essai sur la philosophie de Duns Scot* (Paris, 1887). Hauréau's account is singularly unappreciative. Particularly so is the attribution of a Spinozist tendency to a philosophy which insisted to extravagance on the arbitrariness of the Divine Will, which creates even the possibilities that are never actualized. [As a result of the researches of Fr. E. Longpré it is now known that Duns Scotus was born not later than 1265 at Maxton in Roxburghshire, that he was at school at Haddington

about 1278 and was sent to the Franciscan convent at Dumfries, where about four years later he entered the Order. Fr. E. Longpré has discovered from the register of Oliver Sutton, Bishop of Lincoln, that Duns Scotus was ordained priest at Northampton in 1291. Fr. A. Callebaut, O.F.M., has shown reason to believe that Duns Scotus was at Cambridge from about 1297 to 1300. Dr. A. G. Little in his 'Chronological Notes on the Life of Duns Scotus', *E.H.R.* xlvii (1932), 568–82, has pieced together the principal results of the researches of Longpré, Callebaut, Pelster, and Balič. For bibliographies of the works of Duns Scotus, and of the older commentaries and of literature dealing with his teaching, see C. R. S. Harris, *Duns Scotus*, Oxford, 1927, i. 313–53; E. Simonis, 'De vita et operibus B. Joannis Duns Scoti iuxta litteraturam ultimi decennii', in *Antonianum*, iii (1928), 451–84; Ueberweg-Geyer, ii. 504–17, 765–8. See also F. Pelster, S.J., 'Duns Scotus nach englischen Handschriften', in *Zeitschrift für Katholische Theologie*, li (1927), 65–80. The excellent critical survey of the literature by Fr. E. Longpré, O.F.M., in *Revue des questions historiques*, cxiv (1931), 400–10, should also be consulted. For the general study of the teaching of Duns Scotus reference may be made to E. Longpré, O.F.M., *La Philosophie de B. Duns Scot*, Paris, 1924; C. R. S. Harris, *Duns Scotus*, 2 vols., Oxford, 1927; P. Minges, *Joannis Duns Scoti doctrina philosophica et theologica quoad res praecipuas proposita et exposita*, 2 vols., Berlin, 1930; and D. E. Sharp, *Franciscan Philosophy at Oxford in the 13th Century*, pp. 279–368.]

outgrowth of hypostatized abstractions. Thus matter without form is conceived of as possibly, if not certainly, created
in time before any form.[1] A whole chain of 'acts' is interposed
between the *materia primarie prima* which *is* but does not
exist and the final union of form and matter in the concrete
thing or *compositum*. At first sight Scotus would appear to
assert the possibility of a really existing universal prior to the
particular: while the particular cannot be allowed to get its
very particularity without an individuating form called by
later Scotists its *haecceitas* or 'thisness'.[2] To the critic prepared
to find in the schoolmen nothing but a mass of absurdity it
will appear that every distinction that the imagination can
conceive becomes to Scotus a real, independent, separable
existence: to him the Scotist Universe will appear peopled
with these airy creations of the metaphysical imagination.
Closer study may perhaps suggest that there is in Scotus no
reactionary harking back to the crude realism of William of
Champeaux. Scotus knows nothing of real universals apart
from the particular in the ordinary sense of the word *real*.
The truth is that Scotus has divined the great secret of
modern idealism, the reality of mental relations and the part
which those relations play in the constitution of the world
which we know.[3] That in the works of Scotus and his
followers, as in all the schoolmen, there are absurdities and
exaggerations of subtlety, it would be vain to deny. The
same might be said of some of the greatest philosophers

---

[1] It is curious to see on this
point something like a recrudes-
cence of Scotism in Dr. Martineau's
Seat of Authority in Religion (London, 1890), p. 33, though he, like
some of the less orthodox schoolmen, makes this 'solidified extension' external.

[2] [The analysis which Rashdall
gives here of the teaching of Duns
Scotus is based on the assumption
that the treatise *De Rerum Principio* was written by him. Cf.
C. R. S. Harris, *Duns Scotus*, ii.
94–8. Dr. Harris has also accepted
the *De Rerum Principio* as a genu-

ine work of Scotus. Most modern
authorities, however, reject this
ascription. See D. E. Sharp, *Franciscan Philosophy at Oxford in the
13th Century*, pp. 284–6.]

[3] 'Intellectus facit universali-
tatem in rebus (a quotation from
Averroës); *ergo* illa est in re, non
intellectu' (*Opera*, Lyons, 1639,
i. 93). The proof is still more
idealistic: 'Forma non est extra
materiam, nec e conuerso; igitur
nec intelligible extra intellectum;
ergo nec modus intelligibilis extra
intellectum; igitur nec uniuer-
sale.'

whether in ancient or modern times; but in his most fine-
drawn distinctions there is always a meaning and sometimes
a flash of metaphysical penetration deeper than is to be found
in all the peripatetic common sense of Aquinas.

By the student of philosophy Scotus is not to be despised.
Nevertheless the impression which a superficial glance at his
twelve goodly folios is apt to give the modern reader is probably
the effect which a century of Scotism produced upon the world.
It is against Scotus and his still more spider-like successors
that the popular diatribes of sixteenth-century humanists and
reformers were mainly directed: it was upon Scotus that the
wrath of the New Learning fell most hotly, when for instance
Thomas Cromwell's visitors left the Quadrangle of New
College strewn with leaves of 'Dunce'.[1] And certainly it is
to the later phases of scholastic controversy ushered in by the
'Subtle Doctor' that the popular strictures on the scholastic
philosophy are most obviously applicable. The abuse of
distinction and of syllogism, the habit of spinning cobwebs
out of the philosopher's own inside, the multiplication of
barbarous technicalities and unintelligible jargon—these are
in popular estimation the characteristics of the scholastic
philosophy.[2] If these strictures will not be applied by the dis-
criminating critic without reservation to the works of Scotus
himself, there can be no doubt that they are applicable enough
to the writings of schoolmen without the genius of Duns in
what must after all be called the decline of scholasticism.[3]

---

[1] Layton thus describes their proceedings to Cromwell: 'We have sett Dunce in Bocardo and have utterly banisshede hym Oxforde for ever, with all his blind glosses, and is nowe made a comon servant to everye man, faste nailede up upon postes in all comon howses of easment, *id quod oculis meis vidi.* And the seconde tyme wee came to New Coleege affter we hade declarede your injunctions we fownde all the gret quadrant court full of the leiffes of Dunce, the wynde blowyng them into evere corner. And ther we fownde one Master Grenefelde, a gentilman of Bukynghamshire getheryng up part of the saide bowke leiffes (as he saide therwith to make hym sewelles or blawnsherres to kepe the dere within the woode, therby to have the better cry with his howndes.' Wood, *Annals,* ii. 62. [*Letters relating to the Suppression of the Monasteries,* ed. T. Wright (Camden Society), p. 71.]

[2] For a collection of scholastic absurdities see Binder, *Scholastica Theologica,* Tübingen, 1614, pp. 24–40.

[3] [On the activities of the

CHAP. XII, The system of Scotus may be compared to the flamboyant
§ 7. cathedral of the best period, supremely beautiful after its
kind, but exhibiting, in its wondrous intricacy of detail and rank
luxuriance of ornament, the gorgeousness of incipient decay.
Turning to the position of Scotus as a moralist and a theologian, our judgement of him must be a still more mixed one.
In the depth of its religious feeling his writing contrasts
favourably with the cold rationalistic orthodoxy of Thomas.
On the intellectual side, as well as on the religious, his doubts
mark an advance, though in his mode of meeting doubt there
is retrogression as well as progress. His intellect was acute
enough to see through much of the Thomist apologetic for
medieval dogma, but the dogma is none the less insisted on.
As a philosopher, he is, indeed, partially emancipated from
authority. But, if Aristotle and Augustine count for less with
Scotus than with S. Thomas, the Church and the Pope count
for more.[1] The Thomistic predestinarianism, the materialis-

Franciscan School in Oxford at the beginning of the fourteenth century, see E. Longpré, O.F.M.,'Jean Reading et le B. J. Duns Scot.
L'école franciscaine d'Oxford au début du XIVe siècle', in La France
francisc., vii (1924), pp. 99 sqq. See also A. G. Little, Grey Friars in Oxford (O.H.S.), passim, and Ueber-weg-Geyer, ii. 787. For Fr. Richard
of Conington, Provincial of the English Franciscans 1310, and a
supporter of the teaching of Henry of Ghent, see A. Pelzer, 'Godefroid de
Fontaines', in Revue néoscolastique, xx (1913), 368; and the biographical notice in A. G. Little and F. Pelster, Oxford Theology and Theologians, c. 1282-1302 (O.H.S.), pp. 260-1. On the attitude of Fr. Conington and another Oxford Friar Minor, Walter Chatton, towards
the subject of evangelical poverty during the controversy with John
XXII, see D. L. Douie, The Nature and the Effect of the Heresy of the
Fraticelli, pp. 149-50, 202-8. For Fr. William of Nottingham see E.

Longpré, O.F.M., 'Le Commen-taire sur les Sentences de Guillaume de Nottingham', in Arch. Francisc. Hist. xxii (1929), 232-3,
L. Meier, O.F.M., 'Wilhelm von Nottingham († 1336), ein Zeuge
für die Entwicklung der dis-tinctio formalis in der Universität
Oxford', in Philosophia perennis, Festgabe Joseph Geyser, Regensburg, 1930, and C. Balič, 'A propos de quelques ouvrages fausse-
ment attribués à Duns Scot', in Recherches de théologie ancienne
et médiévale, ii (1930), 160-88. For Robert Cowton, whose Commentaries on the Sentences were well esteemed in the fourteenth and
fifteenth centuries, see Ueberweg-Geyer, ii. 787, and H. Schwamm,
Robert Cowton, O.F.M., Über das göttliche Vorherwissen, Innsbrück,
1931.]
[1] [See E. Longpré, O.F.M., Le B. Jean Duns Scot. Pour le Saint-
Siège et contre le gallicanisme, Florence, 1930.]

tic doctrine of 'grace', the arbitrary 'scheme of redemption' are softened and spiritualized. On the other hand, the strenuously asserted free-will both of God and man approximates to arbitrary caprice.[1] With some of the harshness of Thomism there disappears also that noblest feature of the earlier scholasticism—its profound belief in the essential rationality of the great principles of morality and of religion both natural and revealed. By Scotus's time the great shock of the thirteenth-century scepticism had passed away: the Faith seemed to be in no peril: Scotus is for the most part content to let theology rest on the emotional prostration before authority popularly called Faith. By Duns Scotus the essential distinction between right and wrong was at least half-denied; morality was made to depend on the arbitrary will of God;[2] duty was reduced to a calculation of profit and loss; and while the fundamental basis of all religion was thus cut away, the theological energies of the 'Subtle Doctor' and of the Order of which he was the ornament were devoted to fastening upon the medieval Church, in the teeth of patristic authority and Dominican orthodoxy, the baseless fancy of the Immaculate Conception of Christ's Mother.

The intellectual monstrosities which emanated from the Scotist brain could not fail to provoke reaction. It is a striking tribute to the unquestioning submission of the Dominican intellect to the authority of S. Thomas that the reaction against Scotus came from the ranks of his own Order, not from those of its opponents. So long as he attacked Thomas, the Franciscan was free to choose his philosophical position. Scotus had complied with this essential condition

The Scotist theology.

---

[1] [On this subject cf. C. R. S. Harris, *Duns Scotus*, ii. 214–20. Dr. Harris (*op. cit.*, p. 219) remarks: 'It is a mistake made only too often to suppose that Duns reduces the will of God to a mere arbitrary caprice.']

[2] Scotus denies the *perseitas* of Good, and declares that murder would be right if commanded by God. (Opus Oxon. iii. Dist. 37, *Opera*, Lyons, 1639, vii. 857).

On the other hand he makes *beatitudo* consist in Love (Report. Paris. iv. Dist. 49, *Opp.* xi. 890 *sq.*). In fact his position is that man's love of God may be disinterested, his love of man not. [Rashdall's account of the theological position of Duns Scotus needs to be compared with that of subsequent writers on the subject. See D. E. Sharp, *Franciscan Philosophy in Oxford*, pp. 361–3.]

CHAP. XII, of Franciscan philosophy by a return to realism: William of
§ 7. Ockham complied with it by the revival of thorough-going
nominalism.[1] The way for Ockham was prepared at Paris by
the nominalizing Dominican Durand of S. Pourçain and the
secular Peter Auriol.[2] But it is fairly certain that Ockham
himself had studied and taught in Oxford before graduating
in Paris:[3] it is certain that he was an Englishman and that it
was in the English universities, in the English nation of Paris,
and in its daughters, the German universities—notably in the
Teutonic nations of Prague and the purely Teutonic university of Vienna—that Ockham's nominalism took the speediest
and firmest root, a fact the significance of which becomes
evident when it is remembered that Luther was educated
as a nominalist.[4] On its purely logical, its purely intellectual
side, Ockhamism represents the culmination of all scholastic
thought; and so far scholasticism supplied the weapons by
which it was itself destroyed.[5] Under Ockham's keen analysis

[1] [On the relation between the teaching of Duns Scotus and that of William of Ockham see C. R. S. Harris, Duns Scotus, i. 272, 300.]

[2] [Ockham, on his own admission, only read the works of Peter Aureoli hastily. See De Wulf, ii. 175–6.]

[3] 'The name of this great philo-sopher does not occur in the Old Catalogue, and his connexion with Merton College seems to rest al-most entirely on the authority of Sir Henry Savile, who cites an entry in a college manuscript which Kilner failed to find' (G. C. Brod-rick, Memorials of Merton College, p. 194). He is, however (as Sir H. C. Maxwell-Lyte points out, p. 118), mentioned in a eulogy of the uni-versity in Lambeth MS. 221, f. 308 b. Dr. Little, The Grey Friars in Oxford (O.H.S.), p. 224, also refers to Bartholomew of Pisa, Liber Conformitatum, f. 81 b, where he is styled 'Bacalarius formatus Oxonie', and to a Paris manuscript which shows that he entered the Order before leaving Oxford. [Ock-ham was known as an inceptor Oxo-

niensis, which meant that he had qualified to incept at Oxford, but had not proceeded to the degree of D.D. at Oxford. See Dr. A. G. Little's remarks on this subject, Oxford Theology and Theologians, c. 1282–1302 (O.H.S.), pp. 93–4. Ock-ham completed his Commentary in Oxford before 1324. See Car-dinal Ehrle, Der Sentenzenkom-mentar Peters von Candia, p. 82; J. Hofer, 'Biographische Studien über Wilhelm von Ockham', in Arch. Francisc. Hist. vi (1913), 209–33, 439–65, 654–69, and F. Federhofer, 'Ein Beitrag zur Bibliographie und Biographie des Wilhelm von Ock-ham', in Philosophische Jahrbuch, xxxviii (1925), 26–48. See also Ueberweg-Geyer, ii. 571–83, 781–2; and De Wulf, ii. 176–86.]

[4] He was especially a student of Ockham, d'Ailly, and Gabriel Biel. See Farrar, Hist. of Interpretation, p. 324.

[5] For this point of view see e.g. Lange, Hist. of Materialism (Eng. trans. by Thomas, London, 1877), i. 209 sq.

and vigorous criticism the realistic elements which still sur- vived in Thomas—his doctrine as to the *principium individuationis*, his 'ideas' in the divine mind, his 'visible and intelligible species'—were brushed aside as resolutely as the more chimerical entities of the Scotist system. From the point of view of the modern non-metaphysical man of science Ockham represents the perfection of common sense: 'Ockham's Philosophy is that of centuries later'.[1] On nearly every purely logical or psychological question Ockham gives an answer which, right or wrong, might still be maintained in almost the same terms by a modern philosopher. The distinction of matter and form, the fictitious intermediaries of sensation, the reality of universals outside the mind—all these disappear from his pages; nor, on the other hand, does he (in spite of a few passages which savour of the theory of *flatus vocis*) fall into the opposite extravagance of a nominalism which makes truth and falsehood merely a matter of words: in the language of modern philosophy he would be described as a conceptualist rather than as a nominalist. On his negative and critical side, he must remain for the modern as for the medieval world the 'Invincible Doctor'. Are we then to regard the great scholastic debate as closed and judgement given in favour of the so-called nominalism of Ockham? Such has been the conclusion of some modern historians of philosophy. To others it will appear that beyond the limits within which the mind of Ockham and the mind of the modern commonsense philosopher moves there is a region of truth into which the mere psychologist (and in Ockham's philosophical writings his psychology is perhaps the strongest point) cannot enter. Medieval realism dimly and blindly testified to the part which mind plays in the constitution of the objects of our knowledge —to the truth that in all our knowledge there is a rational element (if the expression may be allowed) which comes not from any supposed 'external object' but from the mind itself, and that these mental ideas, forms, relations—call them what you will—are not chimeras, illusions, imaginary entities, faint copies of unintelligible external 'things'; but, in the strictest

[1] Milman, *Latin Christianity* (1872), ix. 148.

CHAP. XII, sense of the word, realities—not indeed in abstraction from
§ 7.   that of which they are relations, but as real as any other
element in things. In the dim witness which it bore to this
metaphysical truth lay the strength of medieval realism; and
hence in part it was that medieval realism was not stamped
out by the 'Invincible Doctor'.

Ockham's   In the region of pure theology Ockham himself was
theology. enthusiastically, unimpeachably orthodox on all questions
except the authority of the papacy and its relation to the
civil power: he belonged, indeed, to that fanatical section of
the Franciscan order—the 'Fraticelli' as they were called—
who maintained in the teeth of Pope and councils the absolute
poverty of Christ and his Apostles and the obligation of such
absolute poverty on all his ministers.[1] In philosophy Ockham
was a sceptic: in theology he was as zealous a champion of
Franciscan superstition as the fantastic Scotus.[2] And this
union of philosophic scepticism with theological reaction was
effected by the expedient so tempting to the fanatics of all
ages, the division of the human mind into 'watertight com-
partments', the total divorce of faith from reason—in other
words by a blind prostration of the intellect, in matters of
religion and morality, before either external authority or
subjective religious emotion or some combination of the two.
We have observed the tendency to this divorce between
reason and religion even in Scotus; but it reaches a climax
in his pupil Ockham,[3] who positively revelled in demonstrat-
ing the uncertainty or irrationality of the dogmas which as
a theologian he was prepared to swallow with dutiful avidity.[4]

[1] [Ockham was one of the chief
supporters of Michael of Cesena,
but it is not true to say that he
belonged to the Fraticelli. See
D. L. Douie, *The Nature and the
Effect of the Heresy of the Fraticelli,*
p. 231.]

[2] [Ockham's chief disciple in
Oxford was Fr. Adam Wodham or
Godham, O.F.M. (†1358). See
A. G. Little, *The Grey Friars in
Oxford* (O.H.S.), p. 173; Ueber-
weg-Geyer, ii. 587, 588, 782–3.]

[3] Theologically Ockham was the
follower of Scotus, not his opponent—especially in his doctrine
of grace. It was the Scotist and
nominalist, not the Thomist, doctrines of 'Merit' against which the
Reformers revolted. See Ritschl,
*Critical History of the Christian
doctrine of Justification and Reconciliation* (Eng. trans. by Black,
Edinburgh, 1872), p. 73 *sq.*

[4] See especially his *Centilo-
quium Theologicum.*

It is in this respect that the scholasticism which originated CHAP. XII,
in the first half of the fourteenth century often falls so far   § 7.
below what may be called the moral level of the older scholasticism which it so largely supplanted.

Some appreciation of the teaching of Scotus and Ockham The
is necessary if we would realize the state of Oxford thought at Meta-
a period in which the debates of the schools had issues of *physicum.*
far-reaching ecclesiastical and political importance.[1] We are
familiar with the picture of medieval students ranging themselves under the rival banners of nominalism and realism and
fighting in the streets for these metaphysical abstractions as
vigorously as they would fight at other times for their nation,
their faculty, or their university. But it should be remembered
that it is only in the fourteenth century—after the development of Scotism and Ockhamism—that scholasticism assumed
the form of a philosophic feud mingling itself up with every
other national, political, and ecclesiastical question of the
day. And it is absolutely necessary to bear this fact in mind
if we would appreciate the position of Wyclif in Oxford
and in the medieval Church. The fate of Wyclif's Reform
movement was largely determined by its association with

---

[1] [On the study of philosophy at Oxford during the first half of the fourteenth century, Fr. C. Michalski has done valuable pioneer work; see his articles contributed to the *Bulletin de l'Académie Polonaise des Sciences et des Lettres; Classe d'histoire et de philosophie*: 'Les courants philosophiques à Oxford et à Paris pendant le XIVe siècle' (1921); 'Les sources du criticisme et du scepticisme dans la philosophie du XIVe siècle' (1924); 'Le criticisme et le scepticisme dans la philosophie du XIVe siècle' (1926); 'Les courants critiques et sceptiques dans la philosophie du XIVe siècle' (1927); and 'La physique nouvelle et les différents courants philosophiques au XIVe siècle' (1928). During the first part of the fourteenth century there were at work in Oxford masters of note among the secular clergy whose teaching did not exactly coincide with that of their Franciscan or of their Dominican contemporaries. Two of them, Simon of Faversham and Henry of Harclay, were chancellors of the university. See De Wulf, ii. 188; Ueberweg-Geyer, ii. 769. Mention may also be made here of the Carmelite School in Oxford, the activities of which are being explored by Fr. B. M. Xiberta, O.C. See his article, 'Robert Walsingham, Carmelità, mestre de teologia a Oxford, a primeries del segle XIVe', in *Criterion* (Barcelona), iv (1928), 147–74, 298–324. For article on him in *D.N.B.* see under John Walsingham. For Fr. John Baconthorpe, O.M.C., the friend of Archbishop Bradwardine, see below, p. 267, n. 3.]

CHAP. XII, what was, on the Continent, the weaker philosophical party.
§ 7.   In Paris, and still more in the German universities which
sprang out of the English nation at Paris, the nominalism of
Ockham was for a moment triumphant. But at Oxford the
development of realism does not close with Scotus: there was
a reaction against the extravagances of Scotism within the
realist ranks; and that reaction was led by Wyclif. Nothing
is more essential to an appreciation of Wyclif's position than
to realize that he was a famous scholastic thinker quite independently of his position as a theological and religious Reformer. It was Wyclif's prestige as a schoolman that gave
so much weight to the reform movement which he had
inaugurated. Since the days of Albert the Great, scholasticism, amid all differences between conflicting schools, had
been unimpeachably loyal to the medieval Church-system
and the theological premises on which it was based. The
importance of the Wyclifite movement consisted in this, that
now for the first time the established Church principles were
assailed, not by some obscure fanatic, not by some mere
revivalist, but by a great scholastic doctor in the 'second
school of the Church'.

Intel-   It was no accident that this movement took place in Oxford.
lectual
vitality of We have already insisted on the greater freedom of Oxford
four-
teenth- thought in the thirteenth century as compared with the theo-
century logical narrowness of Paris. At Oxford there was little of the
Oxford.
scepticism which at Paris was with so much difficulty driven
beneath the surface. There was no Inquisition: burning and
other punishments were all but unknown in England till the
reaction against Wyclifism in the reign of Henry IV. At
Oxford there was more intellectual freedom: on the other
hand there was that deeper and more earnest vein of religious
feeling which has been thought to be characteristic of the
Teutonic as compared with the Latin races. To appreciate
the number of the Oxford thinkers in the century after
S. Thomas's death, mention here may be made of the Franciscan Richard Middleton,[1] one of the early critics of

---

[1] [Fr. W. Lampen has thrown   tionality; see his articles, 'De Patria
doubt on Middleton's English na-   Richardi de Mediavilla, O.F.M.', in

Thomism, who paved the way for Scotism; the Scotist John CHAP. XII,
Dumbleton;[1] the Mertonian Walter Burleigh, a somewhat § 7.
original eclectic styled the 'Doctor planus et perspicuus';[2]
the Carmelite, John Baconthorp.[3] Not all the other nations
and universities of Europe between them could muster such
a list.[4] Of course, most of these men afterwards taught at
Paris or elsewhere on the Continent, but Oxford alone can
call them her sons.[5] In the generation which intervened
between Scotus and Wyclif Oxford was the scene of immense intellectual activity, and of an intellectual activity
which had more contact with the religious and political life

Arch. Francisc. Hist. xviii (1925),
398; 'War Richard von Mediavilla,
O.F.M.,Engländer', in*Franziscaner
Studien*, xv (1928), 170–2; and
'Richard de Mediavilla', in *France
francisc.* xiii (1930), 388–90. Dr.
F. Pelster has put forward the
suggestion that Richard of Middleton came of the family of
De Meneville or Meynill in
Northumberland. See his article
'Die Herkunft des Richard von
Mediavilla, O.F.M.', *Philosophische
Jahrbuch*, xxxix (1926), 172 *sq.*
Dr. D. E. Sharp (*Franciscan Philosophy at Oxford in the 13th Century*,
p. 211–76) has included Richard
de Mediavilla in her study. She is
disposed to hold to the tradition
that he studied at Oxford which
rests on the authority of the Scottish historian, John Major (1469–
1550). The evidence on either side
is not sufficiently complete to be
considered conclusive.]
[1] See the article by Dr. R. L.
Poole in *D.N.B.*; J. R. Magrath,
The Queen's College, i. 91–3; P.
Duhem, *Études sur Léonardo de
Vinci*, 1913, iii. 425–9, 460–9, and
passim.]
[2] [See the article by T. A. Archer
in *D.N.B.*, and C. Michalski,
'La physique nouvelle et les différents courants philosophiques au
xive siècle', *Bulletin de l'Académie
Polonaise des Sciences et des Lettres*,

Cracow, 1927, pp. 2–9, 27–32, 49–
51; Ueberweg-Geyer, ii. 619, 621–
2, 788.]
[3] [See Ueberweg-Geyer, ii. 617–
18, 787; B. M. Xiberta, O.C.,
'Joan Baconthorp i el dogma de la
Immaculada Concepció de Maria',
Estudi Franciscani (Barcelona), xl
(1928), 89; 'Addenda articulo De
Johanne Baconthorp O. Carm.',
Analecta Ordinis Carmelitarum, vi
(1929), 516–26; P. Chrysogone du
S. Sacr., 'Maître Jean Baconthorp',
in *Revue néoscolastique de philosophie*, xxv (1932), 341–65.]
[4] [It may well be doubted
whether Oxford merits in full
measure the claim which Rashdall
here makes for it. He was disposed
to under-estimate the importance
of Paris in the fourteenth century.]
[5] [The contribution made during the fourteenth century by
members of Merton College alone
to the study of logic and natural
philosophy is an imposing one. In
addition to Dumbleton and Burley
mention may be made of Roger
Swineshead, William Heytesbury,
Ralph Strode, Richard Billingham,
and John Chilmark. See P. Duhem, *Études sur Léonardo de Vinci*,
iii. 405–510; F. M. Powicke, *The
Medieval Books of Merton College*,
pp. 23–8; Ueberweg-Geyer, ii.
602–6, 784. For Bradwardine see
below, p. 268, n. 3.]

CHAP. XII, of the country at large than was the case with the Parisian
§ 7. scholasticism of the preceding century. Ockham himself was
no less great as a political thinker, as the champion of secular
authority against the usurpations of the pseudo-spiritual
papacy, than as the cleanser of the Augean stable of metaphysical absurdity. As a metaphysician Wyclif was his
opponent, though an opponent who knew how to profit by
his criticism;[1] but as a political and ecclesiastical thinker,
Wyclif's Ockham was distinctly one of his intellectual progenitors.[2]
prede-
cessors. Among the other influences that moulded Wyclif's mind
in the schools of Oxford and testify to the vigour and independence of Oxford thought at this period, two names may
be mentioned. The Mertonian realist[3] Thomas Bradwardine
(afterwards Archbishop of Canterbury), besides being distinguished as a mathematician, was the original and vigorous
exponent of that Augustinian predestinarianism which so

[1] It would be difficult to desire a more moderate or more reasonable realism than is expressed in the following: 'Et concordat ratio naturalis, cum Socrates et Plato magis conveniunt, quam Socrates et asinus; illud ergo, in quo conveniunt, est commune, ut primo conveniunt, est commune, ut primo conveniunt in specie, et sic gradatim in genere, quousque ad genus generalissimum sit adventum; sic omni individuo hominis (? *leg.* homini) esse hominem et per consequens communis essentia vel quidditas hominis est communis' (*Trialogus*, ed. G. Lechler, Oxford, 1869, p. 85). In the *De Ente Predicamentali* (ed. R. Beer, Wyclif Society, 1891, p. 41) he admits that 'ydee non sunt substancie formaliter, si non equivoce. . . . Ideo solum habent esse intelligibile aut possibile, necessarium et eternum'. Wyclif's 'ideas' have no existence apart from God; in fact he assents to Grosseteste's doctrine that 'Deus est forma rerum'.

[2] A papal Bull, in Walsingham, *Hist. Angl.*, ed. H. T. Riley (R.S.), i. 347, addressed to the chancellor and the university against Wyclifism complains of the revival of the doctrines of Ockham's disciples, Marsilius of Padua and John of Jandun.

[3] G. C. Brodrick, *Memorials of Merton* (O.H.S.), p. 188. [See the article on Bradwardine by Dean Stephens in *D.N.B.*; Ueberweg-Geyer, ii. 619, 622–4, 788; H. B. Workman, *John Wyclif*, i. 119–25; F. M. Powicke, *The Medieval Books of Merton College*, pp. 23–6; J. F. Laun, 'Thomas von Bradwardin, der Schüler Augustins und Lehrer Wiclifs', *Zeitschrift für Kirchengeschichte*, xlvii (1928), 333–56; and a French translation of the foregoing article without the notes but with addition of an appendix dealing with manuscript sources, 'Recherches sur Thomas de Bradwardin, précurseur de Wiclif', *Revue d'histoire et de philosophie religieuses*, ix (1929), 217–33. On Bradwardine's importance for mathematical and dialectical studies see P. Duhem, *Études sur Léonardo de Vinci*, 1913, iii. 294–9, 309.]

deeply coloured the Wyclifite and the Hussite movements. CHAP. XII,
Although Augustine contributed to the sum total of the §7.
scholastic theology not less largely than Aristotle, the general
effect of scholasticism was to throw into the shade the more
Pauline side of Augustine. However appalling some of the
Augustinian dogmas may sound to modern ears, it must be
admitted that a return to Augustine was a step towards a
return to spiritual Christianity. The return was begun by
Bradwardine, and carried on by Wyclif and Hus. Nearly
all medieval religious reformers were strong Augustinians:
even the Reformation of the sixteenth century was a return
to Augustine, or to an element in Augustine rather
than a return to the New Testament or to primitive
Christianity. But the most powerful influence of all those
which acted upon Wyclif's mind was that of Richard
Fitzralph, like Wyclif once a fellow of Balliol and
afterwards Archbishop of Armagh, the greatest scholastic
luminary of Wyclif's younger days, though better known to
us as the champion of the university and the secular clergy
against the encroachments, usurpations, and theological
corruptions of the friars. Recent researches have proved
that Wyclif's polemical works are more extensively and
directly indebted to the writings of Richard than had hitherto
been supposed.[1] Armachanus (as the Middle Age styled him)
was certainly a more vigorous and powerful writer than
Wyclif—perhaps the most intricate and obscure of all the
great scholastic host—though he is not to be compared to the
great Reformer either in moral intensity or in the range of his
speculation.

It is a striking illustration of the success which generally John
attends well-conducted persecution that Wyclif has been Wyclif as
almost ignored by the historians of philosophy. His great man.
school-

---

[1] See Dr. R. L. Poole's Preface
to his edition of Wyclif's *De
Dominio Divino* (Wyclif Society,
1890), to which is appended the *De
Pauperie Salvatoris* of Armachanus;
also his article on Fitzralph in
D.N.B. [On Richard Fitzralph
see C. Michalski, 'Le criticisme et

le scepticisme dans la philosophie
du xive siècle', in *Bulletin de
l'Académie Polonaise des Sciences
et des Lettres* (1926), pp. 9–14; H. B.
Workman, *John Wyclif*, i. 126–32;
the lecture *Richard Fitzralph, sometime Dean*, Lichfield, 1928, by his
successor Dr. H. E. Savage.]

CHAP. XII, works remained in manuscript up to the quincentenary of
§ 7.   his death. This is not the place in which to assign to Wyclif
his proper place in the history of the scholastic philosophy.[1]
But, although it is probable that he was not one of the greatest
or most original intellects of the Middle Age, the intellectual
movement of which Wyclif and Wyclifism were the outcome does represent the culmination of that speculative
fermentation of which fourteenth-century Oxford was the
centre.[2] The movement represents the last great effort of
expiring scholasticism: its fate may perhaps be considered to
have shown that scholasticism could not effect either the
intellectual or the religious emancipation at which Wyclif
aimed. The first of the Reformers was the last of the schoolmen—at least in England. The ecclesiastical repression which
followed the collapse of the Wyclifite heresy meant the ex-

Decay of tinction of all vigorous and earnest scholastic thought. Arch-
scholastic
thought bishop Arundel's triumph over the university in 1411 sounded
after 1411.

[1] [Dr. S. Harrison Thomson has examined Wyclif's philosophical position in an interesting article, 'The Philosophical Basis of Wyclif's Theology', in The Journal of Religion, xi (1931), 86–116. He has published for the first time an edition of the first two tractates of the Summa de Ente, Oxford, 1930. See also his articles, 'The Order of Writing of Wyclif's Philosophical Works', in Českon Minulosti, recueil d'études dédié à Václav Novotný, Prague, 1929, pp. 146–66; and 'A "Lost" Chapter of Wyclif's Summa de Ente', in Speculum, iv (1929), 339–46; and I. H. Stein's article, 'Another "Lost" Chapter of Wyclif's Summa de Ente', ibid. viii (1933), 254–5.]

[2] [On the subject of the life and teaching of Wyclif see the detailed study by Dr. H. B. Workman, John Wyclif, 2 vols., Oxford, 1927, and the authorities there given; and the valuable chapter on Wyclif, with bibliography, contributed by Mr. B. L. Manning to The Cambridge Medieval History, vii. 486–505,

900–7. Since the appearance of Dr. Workman's study some important additions have been made to Wyclifite literature. Besides the contributions noted above, Dr. S. H. Thomson has also written the following articles: 'Three Unprinted Opuscula of John Wyclif', Speculum, iii (1928), 248–53; 'Some Latin Works erroneously ascribed to Wyclif', ibid. iii (1928), 382–91; and 'John Wyclif's "Lost" De Fide Sacramentorum', in the Journal of Theological Studies, xxxiii (1932), 359–65. See also I. H. Stein, 'The Wyclif MS. in Florence', in Speculum, v (1930), 95–7; 'Two Notes on Wyclif', ibid. vi (1931), 465–8; 'The Latin Text of Wyclif's Complaint', ibid. vii (1932), 87–94; and 'An Unpublished Fragment of Wyclif's Confessio', ibid. viii (1933), 503–10; H. E. Winn, Select English Writings of John Wycliffe, Oxford, 1929; H. Kühn - Steinhausen, 'Wyclif-Handschriften in Deutschland', in Zentralblatt für Bibliothekswesen, xlvii (1930), 626–8.]

the death-knell of Oxford scholasticism.[1] The great realist and CHAP. XII,
nominalist debate lingered on for a century more; but all the §7.
life had been taken out of it: all real, fresh, intellectual activity
was beginning to divert itself into other channels. It was not
against the vigorous scholasticism of the thirteenth century,
nor even against the keen if over-subtle speculation of the
fourteenth, but against an effete traditionalism which per-
petuated and exaggerated the defects of the great thinkers
that the human mind rose in rebellion at the Renaissance and
the Reformation.

As a scholastic movement Wyclifism was almost crushed Perma-
in England before the Council of Constance proclaimed its Wyclif's
doom to the Catholic world. But none the less it can scarcely work.
be doubted (though certainly the evidence is scanty) that the
leaven of Wyclifism went on silently working beneath the
surface of Oxford life, while Bohemia was being torn asunder
by the religious revolt which the Oxford doctor's words had
done so much to excite.[2] It is a superficial view of history
after all which traces the English Reformation to the lusts
and the hatreds of a self-willed monarch. When the con-
flagration excited by Luther began to reach the English
universities, it found the flames already kindled by the Bible-
readings of Tyndale in Magdalen Hall and of the Cambridge
men both in their own university and in Cardinal College at
Oxford. It can hardly be doubted that those Bible-readings
of the English Reformers were ultimately the outcome of a
tradition of practical piety, of love for Scripture and of

[1] [Rashdall is disposed to make
too much of the effects of Archbishop Arundel's visitation on
Oxford. As Dr. H. E. Salter has
pointed out, the archbishop after
his visitation 'bore no ill will to
the University but made a liberal
present of books'. See *Snappe's
Formulary* (O.H.S.), pp. 113–15.]

[2] The full extent of Hus's dependence upon Wyclif has been for
the first time adequately demonstrated by J. Loserth in his *Wyclif
and Hus*. [See also H. B. Workman, *John Wyclif*, i. 8–9. On the

work of Peter Payne, sometime
Principal of S. Edmund Hall, in
championing the teaching of Wy-
clif in Bohemia, see F. M. Bartoš,
*Literární Činnost M. Jana Roky-
cany, M. Jana Příbrama, M. Petra
Payna* (Česká Akademie Věd
a Umění), Prague, 1928, and
Husitství a Cizina, Prague, 1931.
On Payne's Oxford career see
A. B. Emden, *An Oxford Hall in
Medieval Times*, pp. 133–54. Payne
died in Prague in 1455, having
spent over forty years in exile.]

CHAP. XII,
§ 7.
discontent with the prevailing ecclesiastical system, which lingered long after the days of Wyclif in the hearts of the English people and not least in obscure corners of the two university towns.[1]

Additional Note on the University of Oxford and the Great Schism

[At the close of the reign of Richard II the university was consulted on the subject of the Papal Schism, but its opinion was sought not by the King but by the University of Paris. In the autumn of 1395 delegates from the University of Paris came to England bringing with them a 'general epistle' and also a special letter addressed to the University of Oxford. See E. Perroy, *L'Angleterre et le Grand Schisme d'Occident*, pp. 365–70. The mission never visited Oxford, as Richard II was careful to retain its members at Westminster, fearing the national animosity which they would be likely to evoke in the university. The 'general epistle', however, was sent to Oxford together with the covering letter. Professor E. F. Jacob gives an analysis of this 'general epistle' in 'Some English Documents of the Conciliar Movements', contributed to the *Bulletin of John Rylands Library*, xv (1931), 362–4. The University of Paris urged the way of *cessio* as the only satisfactory solution to the Schism. In its reply the University of Oxford criticized this view and expressed preference for a General Council. Richard seems to have favoured the French proposal. According to Fr. Bliemetzrieder (*Archivum Franciscanum Historicum*, i. 577–600) the Minorite Provincial, Nicholas of Fakenham, wrote, at Richard's instigation in 1395, a treatise 'ad excitandum filios matris nostre Universitatis Oxonie', urging Oxford to take an interest in the efforts of Paris to end the Schism. In 1398, after the French king had withdrawn obedience from Benedict XIII, and approached Richard

[1] [On the subsequent history of Wyclifism in England see H. B. Workman, *John Wyclif*, ii. 323–404); J. Gairdner, *Lollardy and the Reformation in England*, i. 21–284.] The following inscription in a book in the Library of University College, Oxford (MS. 156), supplies interesting evidence on this head; 'Ego Johannes Russell, episcopus Lincolniensis, fatigatus hoc anno 1491 Oxon. cum multis hereticis, postquam peruenit in manus meas liber fratris Thome Waldensis, venerabilis doctoris, contra Wiclevistas, quorum in-sanissima dogmata multos nostre religionis Anglicane populares infecerunt, cogitavi aliqua excerpere ex eodem libro super sacramentalibus, in que Lollardi ipsi maxime invehentur, unde successores nostri et sui assistentes consiliarii in inquisitionibus heretice pravitatis aliqua paratiora inveniant ad confusionem errantium, quam aut nos ante habebamus aut ipsi successores habuissent istis non habitis.'

For some other evidence of the continued influence of Wyclifism see a note by Mr. F. D. Matthew in the *Academy*, No. 525, p. 378.

again with the suggestion that he should do likewise, Richard referred the question to the University of Oxford and in February
1399 received a reply in the same vein as before. At the same time
the university expressed its readiness to send over twelve of its
young doctors (*de nostris tironibus xii doctores electos*) to uphold its
thesis at Paris. See Prof. E. F. Jacob, *op. cit.* xv (1931), 366;
E. Perroy, *op. cit.*, pp. 386–7. No such mission from Oxford was
undertaken, for it was evident that there was no likelihood of
unanimity between the two universities being reached at that stage.
As M. Perroy says: 'Les Universités de Paris et d'Oxford ne par-
laient pas le même langage.' With the deposition of Richard in the
following July the attention of Oxford was diverted to more immediate considerations.

The part taken by individual Oxford men in the proceedings of
the successive General Councils is not the special concern of
academical history. The university was not called upon to send a
delegation to any of the Councils; but the Chancellors of Oxford and
Cambridge were members of the English delegation which attended
the Council of Constance. Oxford opinion, however, found expression in documentary form from time to time. On the eve of the
meeting of the Council of Pisa there appeared a treatise entitled
'Petitiones pro ecclesie militantis reformacione', by Richard Ullerston, Chancellor of the University, 1407–8. It was dedicated to
Robert Hallam, Bishop of Salisbury (it is printed by H. von der
Hardt, *Magnum Oecumenicum Constantiense Concilium*, i. 1126–70).
A memorandum of the university on the reform of the Church
(printed in Wilkins, *Concilia*, iii. 360–5) was issued shortly before
the departure of the first English delegation for the Council of
Constance. Like Ullerston's tract, to which it is related, and fairly
closely in places, this memorandum attacks appropriations, exemption, pluralities, dispensations, appeals, and abuses of privilege.

The influence of the opinion of university men, if not of the
Universities of Oxford and Cambridge, upon Conciliar proceedings
will not be under-estimated when it is borne in mind that it was
due to the proposal of the English and German delegations at the
Council of Constance that it was decided that voting should be
by 'nations' in accordance with academical custom in many universities. It was this decision that sealed the fate of John XXIII.[1]]

---

[1] [We are indebted to Professor E. F. Jacob for the information that
he has given for the preparation of this note.]

§ 8. THE UNIVERSITY OF CAMBRIDGE

Thomas HEARNE appended the *Historiola de Antiquitate et Origine Universitatis Cantabrigiensis* (by a Carmelite friar named CANTELUPE, who is said to have died in 1441) to his edition of Thomas SPROTT's *Chronica*, Oxford, 1719. It is almost entirely confined to the mythical *origines*. Dr. CAIUS, the college founder, who was the Cambridge champion in the Elizabethan dispute for precedence with Oxford, belongs to the same class of historians as Cantelupe. His *De Antiquitate Cantabrigiensis Academaei Libri Duo* appeared with a reprint of the Oxford *Assertio* of 1566 in 1568 (London); an enlarged edition, with a distinct *Historia Cantabrigiensis Academiae*, in 1574 (London), under the name of Caius Anglus. Archbishop PARKER added a few pages *De Scolarum Collegiorumque in Academia Cantebrigiensi Patronis atque Fundatoribus*, with a list of royal privileges, &c., to his *De Antiquitate Britannicae Ecclesiae*, 1572; he is quite as credulous as Cantelupe. Richard PARKER's Σκελετος *Cantabrigiensis*, written in 1622, was first published by Hearne in his edition of LELAND's *Collectanea*, vol. v (Oxford, 1715). It contains an account of the colleges and a 'Summa Privilegiorum'. A translation of this work (with CANTELUPE's *Historiola*) has been published as *The History and Antiquities of the University of Cambridge* (London, 1721). (LANGBAINE) *The Foundation of the Universitie of Cambridge* (London, 1651) is a very meagre account of the colleges. *The History of the University of Cambridge* by Thomas FULLER (with his *Church History of Britain*, 1655, ed. by Prickett and Wright, Cambridge, 1840) is the classical History of Cambridge, a much slighter work than Wood's *Annals of Oxford*, but in a style of still more charming quaintness. Edmund CARTER, *History of the University of Cambridge* (London, 1753), is chiefly confined to the colleges. *The History of the University and Colleges of Cambridge* by George DYER (London, 1814), though commendably free from antiquarian superstition, is a less important work than his *Privileges of the University of Cambridge* (London, 1824), a collection of documents with notes. *The History of the University and Colleges of the Univ. of C.*, 'printed for R. ACKERMANN', 1815, is a mere guide-book in folio; G. PEACOCK's *Observations on the Statutes* (London, 1841) is an interesting work of some research. C. H. COOPER, *Annals of Cambridge* (Cambridge, 1842–53), is the most detailed history that has appeared, but documents are unfortunately translated. [Vol. 5 of the *Annals of Cambridge*, edited by J. W. COOPER and published in 1908, contains additions and corrections to the four previous volumes.] The same writer's *Memorials of Cambridge* (Cambridge, . . . ; new ed. 1858–60) deal chiefly with the colleges. J. B. MULLINGER, *University of Cambridge from the earliest times to the Royal Injunctions of 1535* (Cambridge, 1873), is one of the most readable of university histories and is a real contribution to the history of medieval culture and learning, to which I am under great obligations. (This work is cited as 'Mullinger I.') He continues the narrative in *The University of Cambridge from the Royal Injunctions of 1535 to the accession of Charles the First* (Cambridge, 1884), and has also published a *History of the University of Cambridge* in CREIGHTON's *Epochs of Church History* (London, 1888), which is a popular abridgement continued to the present time. *The Architectural History of the University of Cambridge and of the Colleges of Cambridge and Eton*, by Robert WILLIS, ed. by John

Willis Clark (Cambridge, 1886), is a monumental work, the historical CHAP. XII, § 8. value of which is by no means limited to the architectural side. Mr. Clark has also published a more popular sketch, *Cambridge, brief historical and descriptive notes*, London, 1881.

The ancient statutes of the university, as well as the statutes of the colleges, are printed in *Documents relating to the University and Colleges of Cambridge* (London, 1852). But in the case of some colleges the statutes are only printed as revised under Edward VI; in these cases I have consulted the originals whenever extant. [James Heywood, *Early Cambridge University and College Statutes in the English Language*, London, 1855. This took the place of his *Collection of Statutes for the University and the Colleges of Cambridge, including various early documents*, London, 1840.] H. Gunning, *Ceremonies of the University of Cambridge* (Cambridge, 1828) is a useful record of ancient customs which are now too often matters of history. [Dr. H. P. Stokes (*Ceremonies of the University of Cambridge*, p. v) has pointed out that Gunning's volume is, in fact, a re-edition of Adam Wall, *University Ceremonies*, published in 1798, and that both writers are indebted to John Beverley, *An Account of the different Ceremonies observed in the Senate House, &c.*, published in 1788.]

Many miscellaneous documents and dissertations connected with the university are contained in the various proceedings of the *Cambridge Antiquarian Society*, especially a list of documents in the University Registry compiled by Dr. H. R. Luard, *Communications*, iii (1876), 387. Most of the charters and privileges of the university were collected in three manuscript volumes now in the University Registry. I have also consulted the enormous collection of manuscripts by Baker (part of which are in the University Library, the rest in the British Museum), and the Cole MSS. in the British Museum. The documents relating to the colleges are mostly calendared in the *Reports of the Hist. MSS. Commission*. [In 1894 the Cambridge Antiquarian Society undertook the publication of 'the Proctors' Accounts and Inventories, the Grace Books, and other documents relating to the early history of the University', as a memorial to Dr. H. R. Luard, registrary of the university from 1862 to 1891. *Grace Book A or Registra Procuratorum, 1454–1488*, edited by Sir S. M. Leathes, was published in 1897. This volume was followed in 1903 and 1905 respectively by parts i and ii of *Grace Book B, 1488–1511*, edited by Miss Mary Bateson. All three volumes contain valuable introductions. Other publications of the Society have made useful contributions to various subjects bearing upon the history of the university and its officers during the medieval period. Dr. H. P. Stokes has treated of *The Chaplains and the Chapel of the University of Cambridge, 1256–1568* (C.A.S., 1906), *The Esquire Bedels of the University of Cambridge* (C.A.S., 1911). and of *The Mediaeval Hostels of the University of Cambridge* (C.A.S., 1924). To the *Proceedings of the Cambridge Antiquarian Society* he has contributed a paper on 'Early University Property' (xiii, 1908–9, pp. 164–84), and Mr. J. W. Clark a paper on the University Chests 'with a transcript and translation of the deed of foundation and Statutes of the earliest of these, the Neel Chest, 1344' (xi, 1903–6, pp. 78–101).

The *Historical Register of the University of Cambridge to 1910*, edited by Dr. J. R. Tanner (Cambridge, 1917), contains chronological lists of university officers and admirable historical summaries under various headings. Dr. H. P. Stokes in *Ceremonies of the University of Cambridge*, has written a more popular record dealing with many of the subjects contained in the *Historical Register*.

In compiling *Alumni Cantabrigienses, A biographical List of all known Students, Graduates, and holders of office at the University of Cambridge, from the earliest times to 1751*, Cambridge, 1922–7, Dr. J. VENN and his son Mr. J. A. VENN have made all students of Cambridge history their permanent debtors.]

Myths and forgeries. A FEW words will suffice to clear away the cobwebs with which academic patriotism has surrounded the growth of the University of Cambridge. The exuberance of Cambridge imagination has, indeed, transcended that of our least scrupulous Oxford antiquaries. The foundation of Oxford by Alfred the Great being too circumstantially narrated to be shaken by fifteenth- or even sixteenth-century criticism, the champions of the eastern university were obliged to carry their inventive researches back into the mists of a still more venerable antiquity. The origin or 'restoration' of the university is variously ascribed to a Spanish Prince Cantaber, who flourished at a somewhat uncertain epoch, to King Arthur, whose charter bears date A.D. 531,[1] and (by more sober critics) to the Saxon King Sigebert in the seventh century; Bede and Alcuin (whose comparative chronology is not always clear to the historians) are named among its first teachers. A more detailed account of the university in a settlement of Crowland monks early in the twelfth century is derived from the continuation of the Ingulfine Chronicle attributed to Peter of Blois.[2] As to the authenticity of this narrative it will be sufficient to say that it makes an English monk teach the metaphysics of Aristotle about a century before there is any trace of their use in northern Europe.

The Oxford migration of 1209. The first appearance of the Cambridge schools upon the page of genuine history is in connexion with the great dispersion which followed upon the Oxford 'suspendium clericorum' of 1209. It is useless to speculate as to the character of the schools of Cambridge before this period. The same reasons which forbid us to make the University of Oxford a spontaneous development of the schools of S.

---

[1] Printed by Caius, *De Antiq. Cant.*, p. 50, and Twyne, *Antiq. Oxon.*, p. 45.

[2] *Continuatio ad Hist. Ingulphi*, ed. T. Gale, in *Rerum Anglicarum Script. Veter.*, Oxford, 1684, i. 114.

Frideswide forbid us likewise to seek the origin of the University of Cambridge (as has sometimes been done) in the Augustinian priory of Barnwell. In the case of Cambridge there is the additional difficulty that Barnwell is distant a good mile from the site of the later School Street, and that nothing whatever is heard of schools either at Barnwell or elsewhere in Cambridge before the historic migration of 1209.[1] It may be hoped that those who decline to accept the Parisian migration as the real source of the Oxford *studium generale* because it is not recorded in black and white that the English students recalled to England by Henry II repaired to Oxford, and because we do not hear of schools at Oxford before this date, will not have recourse to the gratuitous hypothesis of schools at Cambridge before 1209.[2] There may no doubt have been a priory school at Barnwell, and there were of course the grammar-schools which in the twelfth century were to be found in every town as large as Cambridge; but to seek in such schools a 'nucleus' of the later university would be as misleading as to talk of the cathedral school of Durham and the various charity schools of the same place as the 'nucleus' of the university founded there in 1833. It is to be regretted that so much dust should, even in recent years [as reckoned in 1895], have been thrown between the students' eyes and a very plain historical fact.[3]

Cambridge as a *studium generale* dates at earliest from

[1] 'Wahrscheinlich kam die Schule erst jetzt in Aufnahme' (Denifle, i. 368). In an interesting paper on *The Fenland* (*Archaeological Journal*, 1892, p. 272 *sq.*) Bishop Creighton recognizes the origin of the university in migration from Oxford and Paris. He rightly insists on 'ease of access' as the essential condition of its development, but still appears to me to attribute rather too much to the monasteries.

[2] [For a dissentient view see W, W. Rouse Ball, *Cambridge Papers*, pp. 181–7.]

[3] Even Mr. Mullinger speaks of the university as 'originating most probably in an effort on the part of the monks of Ely to render a position of some military importance also a place of education. The little school prospered; the Canons of S. Giles lent their aid; and when at length, as at Paris and Bologna, a nucleus had been formed', &c. (*Cambridge*, i. 334). But all known analogies are against the theory that monks founded schools or universities at a distance of twenty [actually, about fifteen] miles from their own monastery. The days of university extension were not yet.

CHAP. XII, 1209—at earliest because it is by no means clear that its
§ 8.
Dubious existence continuous existence really begins with that year. In the
existence ordinary course of things it is likely enough that the place
from 1214 to 1229. was wellnigh deserted by scholars after the return to Oxford
in 1214. At all events after 1209 we hear nothing definite[1]
of the Cambridge *studium* till 1229. In that year Henry III
offered an asylum to the dispersed scholars of Paris, promising to assign certain towns in England for their residence.[2]
One of the places to which they actually repaired was
undoubtedly Cambridge. It is only after the Paris migration
Royal re- of 1228 that any royal recognition or any distinct academic
cognition. organization becomes traceable in that town. Two years later
a royal writ gave the Chancellor of Cambridge—now for the
first time mentioned—power to signify to the Bishop of Ely
'rebellious clerks who would not be chastised by the Chancellor and Masters', whereupon the bishop was to invoke the
aid of the sheriff.[3] At the same time the sheriff was ordered
to expel from Cambridge all students 'not under the discipline
or tuition of some Master of Schools'.[4] In the same year the
'taxation' of halls is recognized in a writ which refers to the
'multitude of clerks from diverse parts as well on this side as

[1] Its existence may, however, be
inferred from the writ of Henry III
in 1218, directing the sheriff to
expel *clerici* who still remained
under excommunication for adherence to Louis and the Barons.
Document in Fuller (ed. Prickett
and Wright), p. 20, *note*.,
[2] Rot. Pat. 13 Hen. III, m. 6;
[*Patent Rolls, Henry III, 1225-32*,
p. 257]. See above, p. 83.
[3] *Royal Letters*, ed. W. W. Shirley (R.S.), i. 396. [*Close Rolls,
Henry III, 1227-31*, p. 586, dated
3 May 1231. A similar writ was
issued at the same time for Oxford,
but in the instructions for its issue
directions are given that 'ubi ponitur in primo brevi directo vice-
comiti Cantebrigie "ad mandatum
episcopi Elyensis, hic ponitur" ad
mandatum cancellarii et magistrorum Oxonie'. See also *Close Rolls*,

Henry III, 1247-51, p. 178; *1254-
6*, p. 94.] The chancellor received
the direct power of *Significavit* in
1242 (Cooper, i. 44); yet even
after this we find him signifying
through the bishop; Ely Reg.
Arundel, f. 9. [Dr. H. E. Salter
has drawn attention to evidence of
the existence of a chancellor at
Cambridge in 1226 to be found in
the transcript of a deed recording
a dispute between the prior and
canons of Anglesey and the prior
and monks of Longeville Giffard
over certain tithes in Bottisham,
Cambridgeshire. See *E.H.R.* xxxvi.
419-20.]
[4] *Royal Letters*, l. c. (Fuller, ed.
Prickett and Wright, p. 23); [*Close
Rolls, Henry III, 1227-31*, p. 586].
Fuller read 'scholarium', but this
would be a most unusual expression.

on the other side of the sea',[1] showing no doubt the effect of CHAP. XII, the royal invitation to the emigrant Parisians to settle in § 8. England. The first papal recognition of Cambridge occurs in 1233, when on the petition of the chancellor and scholars, Gregory IX authorized the Bishop of Ely to absolve scholars of Cambridge for *iniectio manuum*, and conferred a privilege by which scholars of Cambridge, willing to answer before the bishop or chancellor, were not to be summoned beyond the diocese.[2]

The history of the university privileges follows so very Constitu-much the same lines as the course of development at Oxford velopment. that it would be tedious to reproduce the various steps of the process in any detail.[3] Suffice it to say that the academic prerogatives and liberties were at Cambridge considerably slower in their growth and somewhat less magnificent in

[1] *Ibid.* (Fuller, p. 23); [*Close Rolls, Henry III, 1227–31*, p. 587].

[2] *Calendar of Papal Registers (Papal Letters)*, i. 135, 136. Cf. *ibid.*, pp. 126, 142.

[3] The parallelism of the two histories extends even to the buildings. The original hired schools were grouped about S. Mary's Church. The first University Schools at Cambridge were begun in 1470 (Fuller, ed. Prickett and Wright, p. 168 n.). [Work on the east side of the Schools Quadrangle was begun in 1470; but this was the last side to be erected. The north side is thought to have been completed by 1400; the west side was in existence in 1438; the south side was begun about 1458. See Willis and Clark, *The Architectural History of Univ. of Cambridge*, iii. 9–18; and H. P. Stokes, 'Early University Property' in *Communications and Proceedings of Camb. Antiq. Soc.* (1909), liii. 173–6.] S. Mary's was rebuilt in 1478 (*ibid.*, p. 170 n.). The great benefactor and builder of the Cambridge Library, Thomas Rotheram, Archbishop of York, was a con-temporary of Duke Humphrey. For the history of the Library see article by Henry Bradshaw in *Collected Papers* (Camb. 1889), No. xx. For the architectural history generally see Willis and Clark, vol. iii. [See also J. W. Clark, 'East Room of the University Library built by Archbishop Rotherham', in *Proceedings of the Cambridge Antiquarian Society*, x (1898–1903), 419–26; *Grace Book A*, ed. S. M. Leathes (C.A.S.), pp. xli–xlii; *Grace Book B*, ed. M. Bateson, pt. i, pp. xxxiii-xxxv, xxxviii.] It may be added that S. Benet's Church at one time had a certain connexion with the university. A dispute as to payment for ringing the bell of S. Benet's for extraordinary lectures (1273–4) is printed by Mr. Clark in *Camb. Ant. Soc.* 8o *Pub.* No. xvii, p. 56. Its bell was still rung, not only for this purpose but for Congregations, till after 1655. (R. Masters, *Hist. of C.C.C.*, p. 431.) It would also appear to have been used for English university sermons (*ibid.*, p. 433), like S. Peter's-in-the-East at Oxford.

CHAP. XII, their final development than was the case at Oxford.[1] Thus
§ 8.
it was not till 1268, after a migration to Northampton, provoked by the oppressions of the townsfolk, that the university
was granted the privileges in relation to the assize of bread
and beer, to the conservation of the peace, and to other matters
which Oxford had already enjoyed for twenty years.[2] It was
not till 1314 that her chancellor obtained the cognizance of
personal actions[3] of scholars against laymen—a privilege
which Oxford had enjoyed since the beginning of the preceding reign; and not till 1383 that the jurisdiction was
extended to all cases except felony or mayhem.[4]

Growth of ecclesiastical independence. Still more slow was the growth of the university's ecclesiastical independence. Up to the end of the thirteenth
century we find the bishop, through his official, deciding
internal disputes between the various faculties of the university, or hearing appeals from the chancellor's decisions.[5] We
even find traces of a claim to have the statutes of the univer-

[1] The earliest extant statute and
the first mention of the rectors
(i.e. proctors) is in 1275 (see above
pp. 57–9), [and below, p. 292, n. 4],
but the document implies earlier
statutes and a long-established constitution.

[2] Rot. Pat. 52 Hen. III, m. 25
(Dyer, *Priv.* i. 63). [*Cal. Patent
Rolls, Henry III, 1266–72*, pp.
195–6, dated 20 Feb. 1268.]

[3] Rot. Pat. 7 Ed. II, pt. 2 (Hare,
i. 65); [*Cal. Patent Rolls, Edward
II, 1313–17*, p. 102, dated
7 Apr. 1314].

[4] Rot. Chart. 7 Ric. II, No. 21
(Hare, i. 219); [*Cal. Charter Rolls,
1341–1417*, p. 29; *Rot. Parl.* v.
431. This latter privilege was
granted to the University of Cambridge in 1352, but it had to be
surrendered forthwith, as it was
found that it might result in financial loss to the Queen-mother to
whom the farm of the town had
been granted. See *Cal. Patent
Rolls, Edward III, 1350–4*, pp.
374, 392; *1361–4*, p. 510. On the

relations between the university
and the town during the fifteenth
century see *Grace Book A*, ed.
S. M. Leathes (C.A.S.), pp. xix–
xx; *Grace Book B*, ed. M. Bateson
(C.A.S.), pt. i, pp. xvi–xvii.]

[5] Hare MS. i, 44 *a*, 45 *b*; Bentham, *Hist. and Antiq. of Ely* (Norwich, 1812), p. 152. We find the
prior and canons of Barnwell successfully resisting the chancellor's
jurisdiction, and the official saying
to the university, 'Omnem iurisdictionem quam habetis, ex gratia
domini mei episcopi habetis, qui
vobis concessit iurisdictionem in
clericis. Archidiaconus autem
habet iurisdictionem in rectoribus,
vicariis, &c.; unum tantum sibi-
met reservavit scilicet viros re-
ligiosos.' *Liber Memorand. Eccl. de
Bernevelle*, Harleian MS. (Baker),
7036, p. 65. [J. W. Clark, *Liber
Memorandorum Ecclesie de Berne-
welle*, pp. 184–5.] Cf. *Hist. and Antiq. of Barnwell Abbey* in Nichols,
*Bibliotheca Topographica Britan-
nica*, v (London, 1790), 24, 25.

sity submitted to him for confirmation.[1] It was not till 1374 that the Cambridge chancellor even made a difficulty about taking the oath of canonical obedience, but after a long conflict and an appeal to the Court of Arches he was compelled to take it.[2] After this, however, the oath was sometimes dispensed with as a matter of favour; but the chancellors continued to seek confirmation from the bishop, and in some instances even to submit to the oaths of canonical obedience and respect for the episcopal rights, down to the year 1400.[3]

The earliest evidence which occurs of a claim to even a limited exemption from episcopal jurisdiction is in a royal order of 1392, which forbids the Bishop of Ely to withdraw into his own court causes pending before the chancellor.[4] In

Emancipation from bishop.

---

[1] Some difficulty was made by the official of Bishop Simon de Montacute (Reg. f. 2 b) in 1337 about the confirmation of the chancellor-elect. 'Non intendebat . . . aliqua statuta per universitatem Cantebrigiensem edita approbare, consensu ipsius Patris minime requisito, nec etiam ipsum electum aliqualiter confirmare, nisi secundum morem antiquum confirmandi huiusmodi electum in Cancellarium Universitatis predicte.' He compelled the chancellor to swear 'quod non innitetur alicui novo statuto in dicta universitate circa electionem dicti Cancellarii edito vel edendo quod quovis modo redundare posset in preiudicium ipsius Patris aut iurisdictionis sue vel ecclesie sue Eliensis', together with the oath of canonical obedience. It may be worth adding that the bishop used to issue during vacancies a commission to the doctors 'ad custodiendum iurisdictionem Universitatis Cantebrigiensis durante vacatione Cancellariatus', whereas at Oxford the university and its *Cancellarius natus* (the senior D.D.) used to exercise such jurisdiction with episcopal authority. See above, p. 124, n. 2, p. 125, n. 2.

[2] Ely Reg. Arundel, f. 75 a; Cooper, i. 112; Reg. of Consistory Court (Ely Registry, D. 2, ff. xix a–xx b). The chancellor is found 'pretendens . . . ipsum pro tempore suo ac predecessores . . . liberos fuisse et immunes ab omni obedientia Episcopis Eliensibus et . . . officiali eorundem et ministris prestanda'. It is to be noticed that the appeal was technically 'ad sedem apostolicam directe et pro tuicione Curie Cantuariensi'. This is usually explained as an appeal for the protection of the archbishop as *legatus natus, pendente lite* (see *Reg. Joh. Peckham*, ed. C. T. Martin (R.S.), ii. cvii), but, if we may generalize from this instance, it seems that practically the case was decided by the Arches Court in virtue of the archbishop's position as *legatus natus*.

[3] Ely Reg. Fordham, f. 181 b. In 1401 an appeal to the Arches from the chancellor in a civil suit was prohibited 'per breve Regis' (Lambeth Reg. Arundel, i, f. 554).

[4] The document is one of those which occur in Rysley's *Catalogue*, but are not now in the Registry. Luard, *Communications C.A.S.*, iii (1876), 389. [*Cal. Close Rolls, Richard II, 1389–92*, dated 13 Feb. 1392.]

CHAP. XII,
§ 8.

1401 Boniface IX dispensed with the episcopal confirmation of the chancellor-elect.[1] The early years of the fifteenth century were years of rapid progress at Cambridge; the university had now begun to be a formidable rival to Oxford. It was high time to assert their equality in medieval fashion, not merely prospectively but retrospectively. Accordingly a Bull was forged, purporting to emanate from Pope Honorius I, in the year 624. In this audacious document[2] the Pope is made to assert that he himself studied at Cambridge, and to confer upon the university the privilege of exemption from all episcopal and archiepiscopal authority. In the year 1430 the refusal of the chancellor-elect, John of Dunwich, to take the oath of obedience to the bishop, led to a suit in the Roman Court. On the strength of the Bull of 624 and other equally valuable documents the papal delegates,

The Barn-well process, 1432.

sitting in the chapter house of Barnwell in 1432, solemnly decided in favour of the university's entire ecclesiastical independence.[3]

When did Cambridge become a *studium generale*?

A more interesting matter than the claim of the university to ecclesiastical immunity is a question which has been raised by Denifle as to the date at which Cambridge became a *studium generale*. Nothing in Denifle's great work was more startling to English readers than to find Oxford and Cambridge treated as belonging to totally different classes or groups of universities. Oxford appears among the primeval

---

[1] Vatican Register An. 12. Lib. 2.6.77. I am indebted for this reference to Mr. Bliss's manuscript transcripts. [*Cal. Papal Registers (Letters)*, v. 370–1, dated 12 Jan. 1401.]

[2] It was admitted that the original was lost: copies survive in the Registry (Drawer, i. 19). It is printed by Twyne, *Antiq. Oxon.*, p. 60, also (p. 77) a Bull of Sergius I, produced on the same occasion. Both in Caius, *De Antiq. Cant.* (1574), pp. 58, 60, [in Cantelupe, *Historiola de antiq. et orig. Univ. Cantabr.*, appended to Sprott's *Chronica*, ed. T. Hearne, p. 253, and in G. Dyer, *Privileges*, i. 58–60.]

[3] The Bull of Martin V to the Prior of Barnwell delegating the affair is preserved in the Registry (i. 96), as also the ensuing 'Process' (Drawer, i. 18) and the confirmation by Eugenius IV in 1433 (i. 100)—all printed in the *Hist. and Antiq. of Barnwell Abbey*, App., p. 31. [See also *Cal. Papal Registers (Letters)*, *1427–47*, viii. 484–5. On the subject of fifteenth-century appointments to the chancellorship see *Grace Book A*, ed. S. M. Leathes (C.A.S.), p. xxxii.]

universities which were not founded but grew: Cambridge CHAP. XII,
§ 8.
is treated as having been for the first time erected into a
studium generale by the Bull of John XXII in 1318,[1] which Bull of
John
XXII,
1318.
is undoubtedly worded in the ordinary form of a foundation-
bull creating a new *studium generale* with the *ius ubique*
docendi and other privileges. Without discussing again the
correctness of Father Denifle's general theory as to the nature
of a *studium generale*, it may be pointed out that his treatment of Cambridge is upon his own principles somewhat
arbitrary. The term *studium generale* was perhaps less used
as well as less exactly defined in England than was the case
in Italy, while Cambridge was little known on the Continent.
It may be therefore difficult to cite passages in which Cambridge is explicitly styled a *studium generale* before the grant
of the Papal Bull. But it may still be contended that in the
thirteenth century the *studium* possessed all the characteristics which were included in the vague conception of a
studium generale then prevalent—a considerable number of
masters both in arts and in at least one of the superior faculties, students from distant regions, regular licences and inceptions, royal recognition and privilege. If we ask how far in
the early part of the fourteenth century the *ius ubique docendi*
would have been conceded to Cambridge on the strength of
ancient prescription, it is sufficient to say that at Oxford at
all events Cambridge degrees were in all probability fully
recognized;[2] and that therefore on the very strictest interpretation of Denifle's canons, Cambridge should at least be

---

[1] Printed by Fuller, p. 80, [and G. Dyer, *Privileges*, i. 60–1], *Cal. Papal Registers (Letters), 1305–42*, p. 172, dated 9 June 1318. See Denifle, i. 375. It is true, how-ever, that a chronicler speaks of the university as created *de novo* at this time: 'An. MCCCXX° de studio Grantebrigge facta est universitas sicut est Oxoñ. per Curiam Ro-manam', *Chron. Petri de Yckham* in the Library of C.C.C., Cam-bridge (No. 339).

[2] *Mun. Acad.*, ed. H. Anstey (R.S.), ii. 399. This statute is not dated; but, as Cambridge enjoys privileges over and above other universities, the concessions can-not be merely ascribed to the Papal Bull. An inference may possibly be drawn from the statutes of Peterhouse, which allow two or three scholars at a time to study at Oxford. They would hardly have done this unless they could be admitted *ad eundem* in that uni-versity. [*Stat. Antiq. Univ. Oxon.*, p. 46. Mr. Strickland Gibson dates this statute 'before 1350'.]

CHAP. XII, recognized as a *studium generale respectu regni* before the Bull
§ 8. of 1318.[1]

Insignifi-
cance of
medieval
Cam-
bridge.

Surprising as most Englishmen will probably think this particular application of the strict jurist theory as to the nature of a *studium generale*, Denifle's treatment of Cambridge will have a salutary effect if it awakens the English mind to the medieval insignificance of a university which at present divides so exactly the higher education of this country with her more ancient rival. Up to the end of the fourteenth century—that is to say virtually up to the downfall of scholasticism—Cambridge was a third-rate university; its position relatively to Oxford was the position of Erlangen or Greifswald as compared with Berlin, the position of S. Andrews as compared with Edinburgh, without that halo of superior antiquity which still enables little S. Andrews to bear herself proudly among the universities of Scotland. Not a single schoolman can be shown to have taught at Cambridge:[2] it is hard to produce the name, I will not say of a great man but of a prominent ecclesiastic, who studied at Cambridge before the middle of the fourteenth century. Its surviving statutes, late as they are, bear witness to the smallness of its numbers. It is contemplated that the whole number of its regents in

[1] A further argument may be drawn from the fact that Oxford applied for a Papal Bull conferring the 'ius ubique docendi' at the same time as Cambridge. (Above, i. 14; *Chartul. Univ. Paris.* ii, No. 756.) Oxford is admitted to have been already a *studium generale*. Too much must not be made of the fact that the Papal Chancery happened to draw up the Bull in the form which it was accustomed to use for the foundation of a new university. It is quite possible that the papal scribe had never heard of Cambridge in 1318.

[2] [This is too sweeping an assertion. Thomas of York was the sixth master of the Franciscan School in Cambridge, Roger Marston the twelfth, and Richard

Conington the thirty-first. See A. G. Little, 'The Friars and the Foundation of the Faculty of Theology in the University of Cambridge', in *Mélanges Mandonnet*, Paris, 1930, ii. 398, 400, and A. G. Little and F. Pelster, *Oxford Theology and Theologians, c. 1282–1302* (O.H.S.), pp. 74–5, 78–9, 81–2, 93–5, 260–1. Duns Scotus, O.F.M., is known to have been with the Franciscans in Cambridge in the closing years of the thirteenth century. See A. Callebaut, O.F.M., 'Le B[x] J. Duns Scot à Cambridge vers 1297à1300', in *Archivum Franciscanum Historicum*, xxi (1928), 608–11. See above, p. 257. Robert Holcot, O.P., and John Bromyard, O.P., leading opponents of Wyclifism, both taught at Cambridge.]

arts may not exceed twelve:[1] while it is necessary to make provision for the absence of even a single doctor in decrees or in medicine.[2] It was not till Oxford had become impregnated with the Wyclifite heresy that Cambridge came into fashion with cautious parents and attracted the patronage of royal champions of orthodoxy and their ecclesiastical advisers. The numbers grew rapidly during the latter half of the fifteenth century, and towards the close must have nearly equalled the much diminished population of Oxford.[3]

The organization of the University of Cambridge is so completely framed on the Oxford model that it will be enough to specify a few points in which the ancient Statutes of Cambridge exhibit original features of their own. In dealing with their contents, it is necessary to remember that we have no very ancient statutes belonging to the university. The University Archives were burned by the townsmen in the

---

[1] Non-regents may in this case vote in the election of chancellor. *Documents, Univ. and Colleges of Cambridge*, i. 309. So again *ibid.*, p. 361.

[2] 'Si doctor in decretis regens in villa non fuerit.' *Documents*, i. 365. So the proctors may present for medical degrees, 'si nullus regens vel non-regens in urbe fuerit'. *Ibid.*, p. 367. [On the subject of numbers see also *Grace Book A*, ed. S. M. Leathes (C.A.S.), p. xxix.]

[3] It appears from the MS. *Liber Gratiarium A* that in 1458 there were only six inceptors in arts. [Rashdall has overlooked other entries of inceptors in arts in the Proctors' Accounts for this year, which bring the total number up to fifteen. See *Grace Book A*, ed. S. M. Leathes (C.A.S.), pp. 17–18.] A great change seems to take place about 1459, when there were eighteen inceptors—almost equal to the Oxford average at about the same time. At the beginning of the sixteenth century, the Scotch historian, John Major, describes Cambridge as 'Oxonia paulo inferior tam in scholasticorum numero quam in literis' (*Hist. mai. Britanniae*, Paris, 1521, f. viii). He continues: 'In utraque vniuersitate quatuor aut quinque millia scholasticorum inuenies, omnes sunt adulti, enses et arcus ferunt, et pro magna parte nobiles. In collegiis autem grammatice non incumbunt. . . . In Europa opinione mea in musica sunt primi.' The evident exaggeration of the statement about the age of students, &c., detracts from his estimate of the numbers, which is clearly much too high for this period. [The last sentence in the passage here quoted by Rashdall does not refer to music in Cambridge, but to music in the parish churches of England. Sir Stanley Leathes, also basing his conclusion on the records contained in the Proctors' Accounts, considers that during the period 1455–6 to 1487–8 'the attendance at the University had increased, but not very greatly'. See *Grace Book A*, ed. S. M. Leathes (C.A.S.), p. xxix.]

CHAP. XII,
§ 8.

great 'Town and Gown' riots of 1381.[1] There are scarcely any statutes which can be with any confidence referred to a period before 1381: the great majority of them belong to the fifteenth century:[2] the earliest extant fragment of a statute-book dates from *circa* 1398,[3] the earliest proctor's book from 1417.[4] We are therefore prevented from tracing the growth of the academic constitution, which it would have been interesting to compare at each stage of its development with the successive changes at Oxford, and can only portray the constitution as it is presented to us, fully grown, at the beginning of the fifteenth century. And here the following points of contrast seem noteworthy:

Points of contrast: proctors and rectors.

(1) It has already been noticed that the proctors were at Cambridge habitually styled rectors. In the earliest statutes the title rector is often used alone: in others it is 'Rectores sive procuratores'.[5]

[1] *Rot. Parl.* iii. 108; Cooper, *Annals*, i. 120–1. It is worth while to cite Erasmus's character of the Cambridge townsmen: 'Vulgus Cantabrigiense barbarie inhospitales illos Britannos antecedit, qui cum summa rusticitate summam malitiam conjunxere' (Lib. VI, Ep. 27).

[2] The editor of the *Ancient Statutes* shows that the statute about the bedels must be 'ante 1276' (*Documents*, i. 354): does this owe its survival to a copy being in the possession of a bedel, and therefore less exposed to danger?

[3] Known as the 'Liber Procuratoris Antiquus', some leaves of which are bound up in the Junior Proctor's Book. See the preface to the statutes in *Documents*, i. 306. [See also G. Peacock, *Observations on the Statutes*, pp. 26–7.]

[4] Known as 'Markaunt's Book'; but the majority of the statutes are found only in the Senior Proctor's Book.

[5] [The use of the title proctor is far more common in the Cambridge

Statutes than Rashdall's statement implies. In the *Liber Procuratoris Antiquus* it is the usual designation, see *Documents, Univ. and Colleges of Cambridge*, i. 309, 310, 315, 323, 329, 332, 334, 338–49, 352–7, &c. In this collection of the statutes there are only two instances of the title rector being used alone, see *ibid.* i. 309, 311, and three of *procurator sive rector*, *ibid.* i. 310, 313, 338. John Markaunt's collection of statutes furnishes other instances of the use of the title rector, see *ibid.* i. 338, 340–2, 345. In the earliest known mention of a proctor by name, Hugh de Leveryngton, proctor 1314–15, is described as 'rector et procurator universitatis Cant. in arte dialectica actualiter regens', see W. G. Searle, *Grace Book Γ* (C.A.S.), p. xii; but in the Proctors' Registers and other records in which their names occur they are designated proctors, see, for example, S. M. Leathes, *Grace Book A* (C.A.S.), pp. 1–3, 5–12, &c. As the instances in which the title rector occurs in Markaunt's Book relate to early

(2) The taxors, whose primary function was the taxation of halls, were associated with the chancellor in the custody of the assizes of bread and beer[1] and of weights and measures, and in various ways were more important officers than at Oxford. It is no doubt owing to this circumstance that the office has at Cambridge survived till 1856.[2] Among other duties the taxors performed some of the functions of the Oxford Clerk of the Market.

(3) We have seen that the earlier code of legatine statutes at Paris issued in 1215 appears to recognize the right of the individual master to try causes in which his scholar was defendant. There is no trace of such a prerogative in the Oxford statute-book; but it is distinctly recognized at Cambridge[3] in the case of minor causes except when the scholar has 'expressly or tacitly renounced the jurisdiction of his master'.

(4) There is no trace of a 'Black' or 'Previous Congregation', a circumstance which explains the absence at a later date of proctorial veto.[4] How far there was any voting by faculties

statutes, it may be concluded that this title went out of general use in Cambridge during the course of the fourteenth century. For lists of the proctors during the medieval period see *Grace Book A*, pp. xxxv–xxxvi; *Grace Book Γ*, pp. x–xiv, xxxviii, and *The Historical Register of the Univ. of Cambridge to 1910*, ed. J. R. Tanner, pp. 35–6. On the office of proctor, see, in addition to the statutes, Sir Stanley Leathes's excellent introduction to *Grace Book A*, pp. vii–ix, xxxiv–xxxv; G. Peacock, *Statutes of Cambridge*, pp. 24–5.]

[1] *Documents, University and Colleges of Cambridge*, i. 349. Later (as it would seem) a statute was passed to restrict their powers. *Ibid.*, pp. 322–3. They ranked next to the proctors. *Ibid.*, p. 352. [See also on the subject of the taxors, *Grace Book A*, pp. xxxvi–xxxvii. An instance of a grant of exemption from 'taxation' for two hostels by the chancellor in 1246 shows the office of taxor to have been in

existence at Cambridge at any early date, see H. P. Stokes, *Outside the Trumpington Gates* (C.A.S.), pp. 16, 77.]

[2] [See H. P. Stokes, *Ceremonies of the University of Cambridge*, p. 76.]

[3] 'Magistri Regentes causas scholarium suorum ex parte rea existentium audiant et decidant universas, dummodo hoc postulaverint vel conventi hoc idem in iudicio allegaverint' (*Documents, University and Colleges of Cambridge*, i. 328). This and some other details of the statutes suggest that Cambridge sometimes borrowed its institutions direct from Paris, and not indirectly by way of Oxford. Cf. above, i. 292. [In his introduction to *Grace Book A* (p. xxxiii) Sir Stanley Leathes notes that no sign can be found in that record 'of this jurisdiction of masters over their pupils'.]

[4] [See *Grace Book A*, ed. S. M. Leathes (C.A.S.), p. xxxiii; *Grace Book Δ*, ed. J. Venn (C.A.S.), p. xxvi.]

CHAP. XII, is not clear; but it would appear that the doctors of the
§ 8.   superior faculties had some distinct voting power, since 'the
            consent of all the Doctors' is recited together with that of
            the regents and non-regents.[1]

The   (5) Another wholly peculiar Cambridge institution is
Master   the office of *Magister Glomeriae*—a superintendent of the
of Glo-
mery.   grammar-schools appointed by the Archdeacon of Ely, whose
            jurisdiction over these inferior schools dates no doubt from
            a time prior to the existence of the university.[2] A dispute
            arising between this official and the chancellor, Hugh
            Balsham, Bishop of Ely, in 1276 decided that the Master of
            Glomery should have jurisdiction in all disputes or causes
            of grammar-students (*Glomerelli*) among themselves or with
            townsmen, but that causes between the Glomerels and mem-
            bers of the university should go to the Chancellor's Court.[3]
            The Master of Glomery presented for degrees in grammar in
            the absence of a master of that faculty.[4]

[1] 'In plena congregacione regencium et non-regencium . . .
consencientibus omnibus doctoribus secularibus et religiosis'; MS.
Liber Gratiarum A ad ann. 1457.
[*Grace Book A* (C.A.S.), p. 8. See
also *Documents, University and Colleges of Cambridge*, i. 323–4; G. Peacock, *Observations on the Statutes of
Cambridge*, p. 24.]

[2] [Mr. A. F. Leach has shown
that the office of *Magister Glomerie*
was not peculiar to Cambridge, for
Merton College, Oxford, had its
Magister Glomerie in 1277, and
Salisbury its *Scole Glomerie* in 1308.
See A. F. Leach, *The Schools of
Medieval England*, pp. 171–2.]

[3] Document in Fuller, p. 47;
Peacock, App. A. [The *Ordinatio
de Iurisdictione Archidiaconi et Cancellarii Univ. Cantabr.* is printed in
full in the edition of the *Vetus Liber
Archidiaconi Eliensis*, by C. E.
Feltoe and E. H. Minns (C.A.S.),
pp. 20–3. For an analysis of this
ordinance see *ibid.*, Excursus B,
pp. 189–90.] Cf. Harleian MS.
7040 (Baker), 219. A building used

as a grammar-school was called
'Le Glomery Halle' (Willis and
Clark, i. 320). [On the subject of
'Le Glomery Halle' see H. P. Stokes,
*The Mediaeval Hostels of the Univ.
of Cambridge* (C.A.S.), pp. 43–8.]
The word 'Glomerellus' is used of
the grammar-boys in the school
founded by Abbot Samson at Bury
S. Edmund's. Brit. Mus. Add.
MSS. 14,848, f. 136 (privately
printed with the Statutes of the
Free Grammar-school at Bury,
and kindly communicated to me,
by my colleague, Lord Francis
Hervey). Cf. above, ii. 142, n. 2.
The *Magister Scolarum* at Bury had
a regular jurisdiction where one
of his scholars was a party, and
no one was allowed to teach within
the liberty of S. Edmund without
the permission of abbot and master.
[See also *Med. Archives Univ.
Oxford*, ed. H. E. Salter (O.H.S.),
ii. 279–80.]

[4] *Documents, Univ. and Colleges of Cambridge*, i. 374. The
archdeacon's commission to the
Master of Glomery (Caius Coll.

(6) The course in theology was shorter than at Oxford. A doctor's degree could be obtained in ten years, even by the candidates who had not been M.A.[1]

(7) In some of the earliest statutes of the university (one of them dated 1275) we find bachelors—perhaps bachelors of the superior faculties—present and apparently voting in convocation.[2] The anomaly is not unparalleled in very small universities. It disappeared at a later date.

(8) Our information as to the books required for degrees in various faculties in various universities at various times is so incomplete that it is hazardous to institute comparisons between them, but the Cambridge statutes do seem to give a prominence to mathematics in which it is tempting to find a prognostication of that devotion to the subject which has been the most characteristic feature of Cambridge studies for the last 200 years. The candidate for inception in arts was required to have been hearing mathematical

CHAP. XII,
§ 8.
Shorter
D.D.
course.
Bachelors
vote.

Studies.

S. No. 204, f. 216) beg ins: 'Cum ordinacio, disposicio et collacio scolarum grammaticalium et magisterii glomerie in universitate et magisterii glomerie in universitate Cant-(ebrigie) ad nos et Archdiaconum Elien(sem) quemcumque pro tempore existentem, dinoscitur notorie pertinere', &c. [The *Commissio Glomerie* to which Rashdall here refers is entered in a fifteenth-century hand in the Archdeacon's Book. See *Vetus Liber Archidiaconi Eliensis* (C.A.S.), p. 202, where it is printed in full.] Observe how this survival from the pre-university era shows the improbability that the university schools in any way grew out of the old schools of the town. Had there been any schools but grammar-schools in Cambridge before 1209, the archdeacon and *Magister Glomeriae* would doubtless have claimed jurisdiction over the masters and scholars who arrived from Oxford in that year. [The Rev. Dr. H. P. Stokes includes an interesting section on 'The Master of Glomery' in

The Mediaeval Hostels of the Univ. of Cambridge (C.A.S.), pp. 49–56.]

[1] *Documents, Univ. and Colleges of Cambridge*, i. 377. [See also *ibid.*, pp. 369–70, 378. It is not easy to discover how Rashdall arrived at the conclusion that the course in theology at Cambridge was the shorter. See *Stat. Antiq. Univ. Oxon.*, ed. S. Gibson, pp. cx–cxi. For *quaestiones* disputed in the faculty of theology at Cambridge see A. G. Little and F. Pelster, *Oxford Theology and Theologians, c. 1282–1302* (O.H.S.), *passim*.]

[2] So in the copy printed by Peacock, p. 23. The preamble disappears in the statute-book. *Documents, Univ. and Colleges of Cambridge*, i. 342; but cf. *ibid.*, p. 335, where we hear of 'maiores baccalaureos . . . specialiter in plena magistrorum congregacione ad hoc vocatos'. Cf. above, ii. 241. [There are two early instances of bachelors at Oxford being associated with masters in deliberation. See *Stat. Antiq. Univ. Oxon.*, ed. S. Gibson, p. xxii.]

CHAP. XII, lectures (in addition to Aristotle) during the whole three
§ 8.   years of his course between determination and licence.[1]
A later statute assigns the first year to arithmetic and music,
the second to geometry and perspective, the third to
astronomy;[2] but by this time six weeks' lecturing is counted
as a year.[3]

The Caput (9) In the year 1488, with a view to putting a stop to the
Senatus.   excessive and probably corrupt laxity with which graces or
dispensations were given by the regents, it was enacted that
no grace dispensing from the statutable requirements for
degrees should be submitted to the house without the previous consent of a board consisting of the chancellor or vice-
chancellor, and two doctors of superior faculties. Here we
have no doubt the first germ of the peculiar Cambridge
institution known as the head of the senate.[4]

Non-   (10) The non-regents, in certain cases at least, claim a share
regents. in the election of chancellor.[5]

[1] Documents, Univ. and Colleges
of Cambridge, i. 360. [As the
place given to arithmetic, geometry, and astronomy in the course
preparatory to inception that is prescribed in the Oxford statutes does
not appear to differ from that given
to these subjects at Cambridge, it
is not easy to discover the grounds
for Rashdall's suggestion as to the
prominence of mathematics in the
Cambridge curriculum. See Stat.
Antiq. Univ. Oxon., ed. S. Gibson,
pp. xciv, 33–4, 234–5.]

[2] Ibid., p. 382. The statute shows
that religious were here admitted
to arts lectures. [This later statute
does not seem to have come into
operation before 1501, in which
year a 'lector' in mathematics
appears for the first time in the
junior proctor's accounts as receiving the statutory fee of 2 marks.
See Grace Book B, 1488–1511, ed.
M. Bateson, pt. i, pp. xvii–xviii,
171. On the subject of mathematical studies at Cambridge during the medieval period see also
W. W. Rouse Ball, A History of

the Study of Mathematics at
Cambridge, Cambridge, 1889, pp.
9–11.]

[3] [For particulars concerning
degree courses and studies at
Cambridge during the fifteenth
century see Grace Book A, ed.
S. M. Leathes (C.A.S.), pp. xx–
xxxii.]

[4] 'Quod nulla gratia tempus aut
formam concernens de caetero pe-
tatur, nisi prius coram cancellario
praesidente aut vice-cancellario et
duobus doctoribus in congregacione
publice legatur ac per eosdem
petenda decernatur' (Documents,
Univ. and Colleges of Cambridge, i.
318). As to the later history of the
Caput Senatus see G. Peacock,
Observations on the Statutes, p. 21
sq. [See also Grace Book A, ed.
S.. M. Leathes (C.A.S.), pp.
xxxiii–xxxiv, 230; Grace Book Γ,
ed. W. G. Searle (C.A.S.), p. xxv.]

[5] There was an appeal on the
subject to the Arches Court in
1369. (Camb. Registry, i. 38.) Cf.
above, p. 285, n. 1. [So long as there
were as many as twelve regents, the

[There are other points of contrast to which attention may CHAP. XII,
be drawn. § 8.

(11) After approval had been given to a statute the congregation of regents and non-regents deputed certain of their body to reduce the statute into its final form. If eight days later the chancellor had failed to summon this committee, the proctors were required to do so; and they too were responsible for the insertion of the statute in the register.[1] But at Oxford, although there is evidence for the occasional appointment of a preliminary drafting committee, ordinarily the responsibility for the final drafting and registration of statutes was undertaken by the chancellor and proctors without the assistance of any committee.[2]

(12) In judicial matters the chancellor was not as free to act on his own authority as was the chancellor of Oxford: on occasions the regents were associated with him in the discharge of those functions. Besides having jurisdiction over minor cases in which scholars were concerned, the regents sat with the chancellor at the hearing of all cases in which 'the atrocity of the offence or the disturbance of public order requires the association and assent of the masters'.[3] If a regent were to commit an offence against the chancellor, it was provided by statute that the case should be heard by judges elected by other regents.[4]

(13) The vice-chancellor was elected by the regents, whereas at Oxford he was the nominee of the chancellor.[5]

(14) The division of graduates into 'gremiales' and 'nongremiales' does not appear to have been observed in Oxford. The term 'gremial' was applied, it seems, to 'permanent residents in the university and generally also associated members of it, living in some college, hall or hostel, as principals, fellows or scholars'.[6]

election was by the regents in arts; but if not, by the regents and the non-regents. See *Documents, Univ. and Colleges of Cambridge*, i. 309.]

[1] [*Ibid.* i. 309 (c. 3), 399 (c. 170).]
[2] [*Stat. Antiq. Univ. Oxon.*, ed. S. Gibson, pp. xix–xxi.]
[3] [*Documents, Univ. and Col-*

leges of Cambridge, i. 312 (c. 9), 325 (c. 29), 328 (c. 36).]
[4] [*Ibid.* i. 312–13 (c. 10).]
[5] [*Ibid.* i. 315 (c. 16), 338 (c. 52); *Stat. Antiq. Univ. Oxon.*, ed. S. Gibson, p. lxxiv.]
[6] [G. Peacock, *Observations on the Statutes*, p. 15, App. A, pp.

(15) The hostels where students resided were subject by statute to an annual visitation by the vice-chancellor, doctors, heads of colleges, and proctors. There is no evidence that the equivalent halls at Oxford were liable to any periodical visitation of this kind.][1]

(16) At Cambridge a man could be excused the statutory duties that attached to graduation by the forfeit of his *cautio*; but at Oxford a man was bound by oath to carry out these duties and could only be exempted by obtaining a grace from *Congregation*.[2]

I fear there may seem to be something almost disrespectful in the brevity with which I have disposed of so great a uni-
Lack of
materials. versity as Cambridge. But the fact is that it is almost impossible to find anything to say about medieval Cambridge which has not already been said of Oxford. It is surprising how rarely allusions to Cambridge and its affairs are found in the pages of historians—perhaps once for every ten or twenty times that the name of Oxford occurs in the chroniclers. If apology for my treatment of Cambridge be needed, it is supplied by the conduct of its own very learned historian, who has been driven for lack of material bearing upon medieval Cambridge to fill his pages with the history of Oxford. So scanty are the earlier records of Cambridge that we should be tempted even to exaggerate its medieval unimportance but for those standing memorials of its past which are supplied to us by her colleges, to the history of which we must now turn.[3] At Oxford the university had reached European fame before its earliest college was founded. At Cambridge there is reason to believe that the university was kept alive during its obscurer period and eventually nursed into fame and popularity very largely through the munificence of college founders.

---

xvii–xviii; *Documents, Univ. and Colleges of Cambridge*, i. 318. See also *Grace Book B*, ed. M. Bateson (C.A.S.), pt. i, p. xx.]

[1] [*Documents, Univ. and Colleges of Cambridge*, i. 316–17 (c. 18). The inclusion of heads of colleges suggests that this statute belongs to the close of the medieval period.]

[2] [See *Med. Arch. Univ. Oxford*, ed. H. E. Salter (O.H.S.), ii. 274–5.]

[3] [Dr, Little has brought to light three early statutes of the University: see his note on 'The Friars *v.* The University of Cambridge' in *E.H.R.*, l (1935), 686–96.]

§ 9. THE COLLEGES OF CAMBRIDGE

THE system by which halls were let to parties of students under a principal was exactly the same at Cambridge as at Oxford. At Cambridge, however, the more usual name was *hospicium* or hostel—not the only instance in which a Parisian usage has been preserved more faithfully at Cambridge than at Oxford.[1] It is still more clear than at Oxford that the principal was freely elected by the students;[2] and (whatever may have been the case at Oxford or Paris) their rights remained quite unimpaired down to the fifteenth century.[3] Eventually, when the majority of halls had passed into the possession of colleges, the colleges appointed an 'external Principal'—sometimes styled the 'Superior' or 'Con-Principal', while the students continued under the immediate government of an 'internal Principal', elected by themselves with the consent of the 'external Principal'.[4] The halls died out at Cambridge before the close of the sixteenth century.[5]

[1] The halls, at Cambridge known as *hospicia*, have died out. The bodies so called, 'Trinity Hall, Clare Hall', &c. are really colleges, just as Balliol used to be *Aula de Balliol*, &c. [On the subject of the hostels of Cambridge see H. P. Stokes, *The Mediaeval Hostels of the University of Cambridge* (C.A.S.), Cambridge, 1924. In this work Dr. Stokes has brought together a great deal of interesting information concerning all hostels whose names he has been able to discover.]

[2] See the thirteenth-century statute printed by Mullinger, i. 639. [As regards the evidence of the early Cambridge statute, it is to be noted 'that the two Universities in regulating the tenancy of all *Hospicia* and Schools were primarily concerned, not with any autonomous communities of scholars, but with those persons who were directly responsible for the engagement of such premises'. See A. B. Emden, *An Oxford Hall in Medieval Times*, pp. 22–3.]

[3] A statute—probably of this date—gives the chancellor power to visit hostels and remove an incompetent principal, but provides that 'alium principalem sociis eiusdem hospitii . . . eligendi libera facultas maneat' (*Documents, Univ. and Colleges of Cambridge*, i. 316).

The same statute forbids students 'alibi in villa quam in aula vel hospitio sub magistro vel principali moram facere'.

[4] See the testimony of Dr. Caius, *Hist. Cant. Acad.*, p. 49; Willis and Clark, i. xxi; ii. 417. [See also H. P. Stokes, *The Mediaeval Hostels of the University of Cambridge* (C.A.S.), pp. 34–7.]

[5] Seventeen lasted to Caius's time; for a list of twenty hostels, see his *Hist. Cant. Acad.*, p. 47; Willis and Clark, i. xxv.

CHAP. XII,
§ 9.
William of
Kilkenny's
bequest,
1256.

In the year 1256 William of Kilkenny, Bishop of Ely, died, leaving a benefaction singularly like the bequest of Alan Basset at Oxford a few years before. He gave 200 marks to the Prior of Barnwell on condition of his paying a stipend of 10 marks annually to two priests studying divinity in the Cambridge Schools, who were also of course to say mass for the bishop's soul.[1] At Cambridge, however, as at Oxford, the earliest patterns of actual collegiate life were supplied by the Mendicants.[2] The Franciscans came in 1224 or 1225 and established themselves in the Old Synagogue, whence fifty years later they moved to the site now occupied by Sidney Sussex College.[3] The Friars Preachers did not arrive till 1274.[4] In the course of the century Friars of the Sack, Friars

[1] James Bentham, *Hist. and Antiq. of Ely* (Norwich, 1812), p. 149; *Hist. and Antiq. of Barnwell Abbey*, in Nichols, *Bibliotheca Topographica Britannica*, pp. 53, 71, App. p. 23; Harleian MS. 7036 (Baker), pp. 29, 37. The case is contemplated 'quod universitas Cantabrigiensis processu temporis dissipetur' (*ibid.*, p. 38).

[2] ['I believe', writes Mr. W. W. Rouse Ball, 'that the presence in Cambridge of these great establishments, always housing a certain number of students, gave stability to the nascent University, and tended to prevent its dissipation in times of stress: this is a point in our early history which is sometimes overlooked.' See his *Cambridge Papers*, p. 185.]

[3] *Mon. Francisc.*, ed. J. S. Brewer, i. 10, 17; ed. R. Howlett, 9, 19. [Friar Thomas of Eccleston, to whose narrative Rashdall refers, does not mention any date for the arrival of the Franciscans in Cambridge. Dr. A. G. Little finds support for these dates in evidence drawn from another quarter. 'There is fairly good evidence', he writes, 'that Norwich, which was in the custody of Cambridge, was founded in 1226, and it is unlikely that the

foundation of the Cambridge house was later than this.' See his valuable article, 'The Friars in the University of Cambridge', in *Mélanges Mandonnet*, ii. 394–6.]

[4] [Dr. A. G. Little has pointed out evidence which proves that the Friars Preachers were in Cambridge thirty-four years before the date given for their arrival by Rashdall. 'The earliest mention yet found', writes Dr. Little, 'of the Friars Preachers of Cambridge is 1 August 1240, when a writ was issued to the Sheriff of Cambridge instructing him to send to the king at Westminster the heretic whom the Friars Preachers of Cambridge will deliver to him.' See Dr. Little's article, 'The Friars in the University of Cambridge', in *Mélanges Mandonnet*, ii. 393. The Close Rolls contain an earlier record than that to which Dr. Little draws attention. On 13 June, 1238, Henry III made a present of three oaks for the building of the chapel of the Friars Preachers in Cambridge. See *Close Rolls, 1237–42*, p. 61, and also *ibid.*, p. 185, for a reference to the site of their convent and burial-ground.] It appears that Cambridge, as well as Oxford, had its struggle with the friars, and at

of Blessed Mary, and Carmelites, Augustinians and Canons CHAP. XII, of Sempringham, established themselves in Cambridge.[1] The §9. Benedictine students from Croyland and the neighbouring monasteries appear to have lived in scattered halls till 1428, when they acquired a permanent college of their own,[2] afterwards known as Buckingham College,[3] the site of the present Magdalene.

PETERHOUSE (1284)

An account of the early foundation of the college is contained in Thomas BAKER, *Hist. of the College of S. John the Evangelist*, ed. Mayor, i. 13 *sq.* [A history of *Peterhouse*, by Dr. T. A. WALKER, was published in the Cambridge series of *College Histories* in 1906; a revised edition appeared in 1935. Valuable notices concerning the founder and the medieval members of the college are given by Dr. WALKER in *A Biographical Register of Peterhouse*, pt. i (1284–1574), Cambridge, 1927. M. R. JAMES, *Catalogue of MSS. of Peterhouse*, 1899, contains an article (pp. xvii–xxxii) on the library by J. W. CLARK.]

The first secular college at Cambridge was founded after the earliest Oxford colleges and in avowed imitation of the

about the same time. In the Parliament of 1305, the university complains that the preachers and minors deny the jurisdiction of chancellor and university, and have cited the chancellors and masters to the Roman Court. The answer is 'Non licet summonere aliquem ad curiam Romanam nisi per viam appellationis' (*Mem. de Parliamento*, ed. F. W. Maitland (R.S.), p. 34). As to the issue see Cooper, *Annals*, i. 70. [The controversy had begun in 1303: it was settled three years later on appeal to Benedict XI. See Dr. Little's note on 'The Friars v. The University of Cambridge' in *E.H.R.*, l (1935), 686–96.]

[1] The first three are mentioned in 1278–9 (*Rotuli Hundredorum*, ii. 360; Cooper, *Annals*, i. 59; the two last in 1291 (*Hist. of Barnwell*, p. 35). [See also J. P. Rushe, O.C., 'The Origin of St. Mary's Guild in connexion with Corpus Christi College, Cambridge', in *Proceedings of the Cambridge Antiquarian Society*, xvi (1911–12), 20–52, for the Carmelites; D. H. S. Cranage and

H. P. Stokes, 'The Augustinian Friary in Cambridge and the History of its Site', in *Proceedings of the Cambridge Antiquarian Society*, xxii (1919–20), 53–75, for the Austin Friars; and R. Graham, *S. Gilbert of Sempringham and the Gilbertines*, pp. 44, 135, 167, and 174, for the Gilbertines.]

[2] Wilkins, *Concilia*, iii. 424, 468; Dugdale, *Monasticon*, ed. Caley, ii. 123; Reyner, *Apostolatus Ben.*, App. p. 176; Cooper, *Annals*, i. 179. A Bull of Sixtus IV, cited by Willis and Clark, i. 1, mentions the surprising fact that the monks of Norwich were in the habit of residing with the seculars of Trinity and Gonville Halls, and sanctions the practice. [See M. R. James and C. Jenkins, *A Descriptive Catalogue of the MSS. in the Library of Lambeth Palace*, MS. 664, 48.]

[3] [The name of the college was given in honour of a benefactor, Henry Strafford, 2nd Duke of Buckingham, brother-in-law of Edward IV, beheaded by Richard III in 1483.]

CHAP. XII,
§ 9.
The Hospital of
S. John.

greatest of them. About the year 1280 Hugh Balsham, Bishop of Ely, introduced a body of secular scholars into the ancient Hospital of S. John.[1] The hospital was in the hands of a body of regular canons; and the attempt to unite seculars and regulars on the same foundation appears here, as upon a later and more celebrated occasion, when the experiment

Foundation of
college.

was repeated, to have conspicuously failed.[2] In consequence of the 'dissensions' which had arisen, the bishop in 1284 determined to separate the two bodies and divide the property between them. The Church of S. Peter without Trumpington Gate[3] was impropriated to the society afterwards known as S. Peter's College or Peterhouse,[4] though at first more usually styled 'The scholars of Ely'.

Certain hostels near the church became the habitation of the community; and the existing, though now much altered, hall was built with the founder's legacy soon after his death in 1286.[5] The house was at first but slenderly endowed with impropriations. In 1307 it obtained the adjoining property, hitherto occupied by the Friars of the Sack (*De Pœnitentia Iesu*), an Order doomed to extinction by the council of Lyons in 1274.[6] The bishop appears at first, like most Parisian college founders, to have reserved to himself and his succes-

[1] 'Nos igitur attendentes venerabilem patrem Hugonem Elyensem Episcopum proposito laudabili concepisse quod loco fratrum sc̄lariũ (i.e. *probably* scolarium) in hospitali suo Sancti Johannis Cantabrigie scolares studiosi subrogentur qui secundum regulam scolarium Oxonie qui de Merton cognominantur in Universitate Cantabrigiensi studentes' (Rot. Parl. 9 Ed. I, m. 28; *Documents, Univ. and Colleges of Cambridge*, ii. 1; [*Cal. Patent Rolls, Edward I, 1272–81*, pp. 420–1, dated 24 Dec. 1280]. Cf. Harleian MS. 7047 (Baker), f. 208 *sq.* Prickett and Wright (Fuller, p. 28, note) date the foundation in its earliest form from 1257, but do not state their authority.

[2] See above, p. 211.

[3] Rebuilt *c.* 1350, and styled S. Mary's-the-Less. It was used as the college chapel till 1632, though from 1388 there was also an oratory in college. Willis and Clark, i. 40, 50.

[4] Rot. Chart. 13 Ed. I, No. 103 [*Cal. Charter Rolls, 1257–1300*, p. 286, dated 28 May 1285]. *Documents, Univ. and Colleges of Cambridge*, ii. 1 *sq.*, and the Register of College Benefactions (*ibid.*, p. 45). [See also the article on the foundation of the college, T. A. Walker, *PeterhouseBiographicalRegister*,i.1.]

[5] Willis and Clark, i. 19. [See also T. A. Walker, *Peterhouse*, ed. 1935, pp. 6, 7; H. P. Stokes, *Outside Trumpington Gates* (C.A.S.), pp. 16–22.]

[6] *Ibid.* i. 5. [See C. H. Cooper, *Annals of Cambridge*, v (ed. J. W. Cooper, 1908), p. 250.]

sors the patronage of his college.[1] In 1338, however, Bishop Simon de Montacute resigned this right to the college—a striking illustration of the decisive influence upon the form and structure of our English college-system of the epoch-making foundation statutes of Walter de Merton at Oxford. He reserved to himself, however, the right of admitting the scholars-elect to these places.[2] From this prelate the college received its first extant code of statutes[3]—a code which was Statutes. superseded by an emended version confirmed by the same bishop in 1344.[4] Both codes incessantly appeal to the 'rule of Merton' and are entirely inspired by that model.[5] The college was to consist of a 'Master or Warden' and fourteen scholars, together with three poor grammar-boys who were to sing in the college church and serve the scholars in hall or chamber.[6] The scholars are to be at least B.A. on election, to proceed to M.A., and then to study theology; but two may

[1] [T. A. Walker, *Peterhouse Biographical Register*, i. 3.]

[2] Such is undoubtedly the provision of both codes of statutes (*Documents, Univ. and Colleges of Cambridge*, ii. 64, 65): as to the earlier practice the only authority appears to be Baker MSS. i. 33. The master was selected by the bishop from two candidates elected by the college.

[3] *Documents, Univ. and Colleges of Cambridge*, ii. 57 *sq.*

[4] *Ibid.* ii. 6 *sq.* [Dr. T. A. Walker, the historian of the college, describes the statutes of Bishop Simon de Montacute, dated 9 Apr. 1344, as 'the earliest extant expressly composed for the government of Peterhouse', see *Peterhouse Biog. Register*, i. 2; *Peterhouse*, p. 23. There appear to be no adequate grounds for Rashdall's conclusion that the code preserved in Brit. Mus. Harl. MS. 7032 and printed in *Documents, Univ. and Colleges of Cambridge*, ii. 6 *sq.*, is 'an emended version' of an earlier code framed by Bishop Simon de Montacute. The code

printed in *op. cit.*, ii. 57 *sq.*, which Rashdall identifies as that first issued by the bishop, is a later recension of the code of 1344: it contains several emendations and additions which must date from the first half of the sixteenth century, *e.g.* cc. 40 and 47. The code of 1344 contains references to *Statuta Antiqua Domus* (see *ibid.* ii. 39), by which must be meant the original directions of the founder, Bishop Hugh de Balsham.]

[5] [In the code of 1344 reference is only made to the 'rule of Merton' in ten of the sixty-one chapters of which these statutes are composed: in the later version of this code (*Documents, Univ. and Colleges of Cambridge*, ii. 57 *sq.*) all references to the 'rule of Merton' are omitted.]

[6] *Documents, Univ. and Colleges of Cambridge*, ii. 19, 20, 25. [These scholars in grammar became known later as *Bibliotistae* or *discipuli*. In Tudor times the college made provision for eight students to whom the designation 'poor scholars' was given. See T. A. Walker, *Peterhouse*, ed. 1935, p. 33.]

be allowed to proceed in the canon or civil law and one in medicine.[1] One or two scholars at a time may be licensed to study in Oxford—a good illustration of the relative positions of Oxford and Cambridge in the fourteenth century.[2] It is noteworthy that the distribution of fellowships among particular dioceses dates in the case of this as of many other English colleges from a comparatively recent period.[3] The full account which has already been given of the statutes of Merton will dispense from entering in greater detail into the constitution and regulations of Merton's Cambridge daughter.[4]

[1] *Documents, Univ. and Colleges of Cambridge*, ii. 10, 22, 23.

[2] *Ibid.* ii. 23. [It should be noted that according to the statutes this facility is allowed, 'cum boni scolares, quanto in pluribus universitatibus & diversis scientiis magis exercitati & excellentius informati fuerint, subtiles valeant effici, & ad proficiendum in iisdem merito promtiores.]

[3] From the episcopate of Bishop Richard Redman (1501–5): *Ibid.* ii. 66.

[4] [Although the statutes of Peterhouse approved by Bishop Simon de Montacute in 1344 contain certain provisions which are obviously based on Merton precedent, the points in which the two codes differ are sufficiently numerous and important as hardly to justify Rashdall's dismissal of the Peterhouse Statutes as too closely modelled on those of Merton to merit separate attention. The Peterhouse code is longer and fuller than that of Merton. It is not dependent upon the Merton code for its wording or its arrangement. It contains many chapters which deal with matters for which no adequate parallel can be found in the Merton code: viz. c. 5 concerning the oath due to the visitor, c. 7 concerning the assignment of rooms, c. 8 concerning the consultation of fellows by the master, c. 9 concerning the absence of the master, c. 17 concerning the purchase of victuals, c. 18 concerning the almoner and his duties,, cc. 19 and 20 concerning the porter and college servants, c. 29 concerning the precedence to be observed by fellows, cc. 35 and 36 concerning dress and discipline, cc. 37, 38, and 41 concerning recreations, c. 43 concerning the master and fellows joining religious orders, cc. 45, 46 concerning the fellows having employment or promotion outside the college, c. 52 concerning visitation by the Bishop of Ely, c. 53 concerning the books and muniments of the college, and c. 56 concerning the wills of the master and fellows. It is only in the following chapters that express reference is made to the Merton code: c. 2 concerning the compilation of the statutes, c. 16 concerning the bursars and their duties, c. 22 concerning objections to raising the number of the fellows, c. 28 concerning scholars in grammar, c. 30 concerning the emoluments of fellows, c. 39 concerning women entering college, c. 40 concerning the use of Latin, c. 49 concerning ejected fellows, c. 57 concerning the burial of fellows, and c. 58 concerning the holding of chapters or *scrutinia*. In several

KING'S HALL (*ante* 1316)

[Mr. W. D. CARÖE, *King's Hostel, Trinity College, Cambridge* (Quarto CHAP. XII,
Publications of Cambridge Antiquarian Society, 1909), describes the § 9.
medieval buildings of the hall as revealed by the discoveries made in 1905
when the outer coating of brick-work was removed. Mr. C. E. SAYLE contributed an account of King's Hall Library to the *Proceedings of the Cambridge Antiquarian Society*, xxiv (1921–2), 54–76.]

The earliest allusion to a body of scholars supported by
the royal liberality at Cambridge occurs in a writ of 1316,
ordering the Sheriff of Cambridge to pay the arrears of their
allowances, and to continue the same regularly henceforward.[1] They were then twelve in number and are described

of the chapters dealing with matters
common to the two codes there are
considerable differences: viz. Peterhouse, c. 3: Merton, c. 29, concerning the method of the election
of a master or a warden; Peterhouse, cc. 4, 21, 23; Merton, cc. 3,
13, 17, concerning the number,
nomination, admission, and qualifications of fellows; Peterhouse,
c. 10, Merton, c. 28, concerning
the accountability of the master or
the warden, and of college officers;
Peterhouse, cc. 15, 31, Merton, cc.
7, 10, concerning the number and
duties of the deans; Peterhouse,
cc. 24–7, Merton, c. 2, concerning
the studies and examination of
fellows; Peterhouse, c. 28, Merton,
c. 40, concerning scholars in grammar; Peterhouse, cc. 32, 33; Merton, c. 12, concerning guests and
lodgers; Peterhouse, c. 40; Merton,
c. 11, concerning the use of Latin,
French, and English; Peterhouse,
c. 42; Merton, c. 15, concerning
the composition of disputes, and
Peterhouse, c. 44; Merton, c. 4,
concerning allowances to infirm
scholars. Unlike that of Merton
the Peterhouse code contains no
specific provisions concerning
founder's kin, or a vice-warden
or chaplains, or *oeconomi*, or the
autumn progress of the warden.
Analyses of the Peterhouse Statutes
will be found in T. A. Walker,

Peterhouse, ed. 1935, pp. 23–7;
Biographical Register of Peterhouse,
i. 2–4.]

[1] *Documents, Univ. and Colleges
of Cambridge*, i. 66–7. In the
Parliament of 33 Edward I, the
King is petitioned 'quod ipse velit
esse fundator unius domus quam
eadem Universitas ordinavit pro
pauperibus scolaribus in eadem
universitate commorantibus sus-
tentandis', and praying for a licence
of Mortmain; in reply to which an
inquisition *ad quod damnum* is
directed. *Mem. de Parliamento* (Selden Society), p. 33. I cannot say
whether King's Hall was in any
way the outcome of this petition.
W. W. Rouse Ball (*Cambridge
Papers*, pp. 154–160) gives some
interesting details, gleaned from
the Exchequer Accounts, of a
journey taken in 1319 by the
warden and thirty-three members
of this house to York where they
had been commanded to spend
Christmas with the court. It may
be doubted, therefore, whether
Edward III is to be credited with
having increased the number of the
King's scholars when he placed
the foundation on a more permanent footing. King's Hall is
unique among academical societies,
as it was a royal foundation, 'supported by public funds, founded
in the first place for laymen and

CHAP. XII, as 'children of our Chapel'. They were then, it appears,
§ 9. recruited from the choir of the Royal Chapel. The King's
scholars had from the first lived together as a community,
though in hired hostels. Edward III increased their number
to thirty-two, placed the foundation upon a permanent
footing, built them a house of their own, and impropriated
the rectory of Northampton to the college.[1] Richard II gave
them a body of statutes.[2] A remarkable feature of these
statutes is the introduction of an age-limit: scholars are to
be at least fourteen on admission. The right of appointing the
warden, and the right of visitation were at first reserved to
the Crown; but the latter was transferred by Henry VI to the
Provosts of King's and Eton.[3] It is said that this is the college
which, under the name of Solar Hall, has been immortalized
by Chaucer in the Reeve's Tale. In the reign of Henry VIII
the foundation was swallowed up in the great college, whose
excessive size and predominance have been from that time
to the present such unfortunate features of Cambridge life.

MICHAELHOUSE (1324)

An account of the college is given by MULLINGER, *Univ. of Cambridge*, i.
234 *sq.*, who prints the statutes in an Appendix. [There is in *Michaelhouse*, privately printed in 1924, an interesting history of the college
written by Mr. A. E. STAMP at the request of the Council of Trinity
College on the six hundredth anniversary of its foundation. The text of
the Founder's Statutes has been included by Mr. Stamp as an appendix.]

especially for laymen connected
with the Court, and was for over
a hundred years under the King's
own eye to the extent that the
master was liable at any moment
to be called upon to give an account
of his charge, material and moral':
see A. E. Stamp, *Michaelhouse*,
p. 1.]
   [1] Rot. Pat. 11 Ed. III, p. 3,
m. 24, which founds (as if *de novo*)
a college of thirty-two scholars to
dwell together in the King's House
near the Hospital of S. John. At
the same time they are granted the
Church of S. Peter, Northampton.
Cf. Willis and Clark, ii. 682 *sq.*;
Documents, Univ. and Colleges of

Cambridge, i. 67 *sq.* [*Cal. Patent
Rolls, Edward III, 1334–8*, p. 541,
dated 7 Oct. 1337. The King subsequently found that this church had
already been granted in frankalmoin
to S. Katherine's Hospital by the
Tower of London, and so granted his
scholars in Cambridge the advowson of the church of Fakenham,
Norfolk, instead; see *Cal. Patent
Rolls, Edward III, 1338–40*, pp.
28, 29, dated 12 Mar. 1338.]
   [2] Printed in Rymer, *Foedera*, iii
(1740), pt. iii, p. 94.
   [3] Rot. Pat. 26 Hen. VI, p. 1,
m. 12; [*Cal. Patent Rolls, 1446–52*,
p. 121, dated 24 Jan. 1447].

Another Cambridge College which no longer retains a separate existence was known as Michaelhouse and was founded by Hervey de Stanton, Chancellor of the Exchequer and Prebendary of York and Wells, in 1324.[1] The statutes given by the founder are preserved and are earlier than the extant statutes of Peterhouse:[2] they are not detailed in their provisions and show no marked traces of the Mertonian influence, though the college-constitution is on the Mertonian model. As Balsham's scholars were intended to serve the Church of S. Peter, so the 'Scholars of S. Michael' were attached to the church of that name, a connexion which no doubt explains the provision—unusual in the early colleges —that all the students admitted were to be 'Priests or at least in holy orders', having the intention of being ordained to the priesthood within a year of their admission: all the fellows in priest's order are styled 'Scholar Chaplains'. All were to study theology.[3] [At its foundation the college consisted of a master and six fellows.[4] They were to have 'a common table and an uniform habit in so far as is possible'. The founder undertook to provide them with salaries until he should be able to furnish them with sufficient endowment: those in priest's orders were to receive 5 marks a year, those in deacon's or sub-deacon's orders 4 marks. Their meat and

[1] Rot. Pat. 17 Ed. II, p. 2, m. 12, and 1 Ed. III, p. 1, m. 24; [*Cal. Patent Rolls, Edward II, 1321–24*, p. 420, dated 1 June 1324; *Cal. Patent Rolls, Edward III, 1327–30*, p. 25, dated 3 Mar. 1327. See also *Cal. Patent Rolls, Edward II, 1324–27*, pp. 260, 324, 333; and A. E. Stamp, *Michaelhouse*, pp. 1–17.]

[2] Printed by Mullinger (*Univ. of Cambridge*, i. 640 sq.); [and by A. E. Stamp, *Michaelhouse*, pp. 41–7. A full analysis of them is given by Mr. Stamp (*op. cit.*, pp. 25–9). He considers them to be the original work of Stanton, not imitated from or based on those of any similar institution.] Most of the documents are copied in a book known as the Otryngham book, compiled by a master of that name (*c.* 1423–55), now in the possession of Trinity College. See Willis and Clark, ii. 669.

[3] Mr. Mullinger (*Univ. of Cambridge*, i. 234) states that fellows have to be on admission 'at least Bachelors incepting' in arts; this can hardly be got out of the words 'et qui in artibus incipere teneantur' (*ibid.*, p. 641), which mean merely that if not M.A. they must go on to that degree, and then apply themselves to theology.

[4] [In 1346 two more fellows, in 1429 'Turkes children', and in 1483 Sygo chaplains were added. See A. E. Stamp, *Michaelhouse*, pp. 24–33.]

drink were not to cost them more than 12*d.* a week each. Any surplus income was to be divided among them. They were to be allowed two servants who might receive 10*d.* a week each for their board: 40*s.* a year was to be allowed for the wages of these two servants, a barber and a washerwoman. If the master and fellows could obtain servants for less than this amount, they were free to divide the balance among themselves. The number of scholar chaplains could be augmented, if the resources of the college permitted. One of them was to be deputed by the master each week to superintend the catering; he was required to render account of his expenditure at the end of the week. A fellowship (*exhibicio*) was to be vacated, if a fellow became seriously ill,[1] or entered religion, or was absent for three months without permission of the master, or was lax in the pursuit of his studies or in the conduct of services, or became possessed of an income of 100*s.* a year.] The Chancellor of the University was made the ordinary visitor of the house with a power of appeal in difficult cases to the Bishop of Ely. [The Chancellor was to visit the college once a year, and more often if the master and fellows should so request him. The masses and other services to be said in S. Michael's church are specified by the founder in some detail; but Stanton expressly stated that the performance of these religious duties was not to interfere unduly 'with lectures and disputations in the schools'.] The individual existence of Michaelhouse was eventually extinguished in the great college which that munificent donor of other people's property, King Henry VIII, erected upon the ruins of more than one earlier foundation.[2]

UNIVERSITY OR CLARE HALL (1326)

[A history of *Clare College*, by Mr. J. R. WARDALE, in the series of *Cambridge College Histories*, was published in 1899. A handsomely produced history of the college in two volumes, entitled *Clare College, 1326–1926*, appeared in 1928, under the editorship of Mr. M. D. FORBES, in commemoration of the sexcentenary of the foundation of the college.]

[1] [This provision was soon modified and a sick fellow was allowed leave of absence and given 12*d.* a week for his keep. See *ibid.,* 27.]

[2] [See W. W. Rouse Ball, *Cambridge Papers*, pp. 12–13.]

This college derives its present name from Elizabeth de Burgh, Lady of Clare, and grand-daughter of Edward I. She and her two sisters had, between them, inherited all the family estates through the death of their brother, Gilbert de Clare, Earl of Gloucester and Hertford, who fell at Bannockburn.[1] But the work of the countess was merely an additional endowment of a small college known as 'University Hall', which the university itself had founded by royal licence in 1326.[2] This community certainly came into existence, but we hear no more of its history till in 1336 Richard de Badew, chancellor of the university, described as 'Founder, Patron, and Advocate of the house called the Hall of the University of Cambridge', grants all his rights in it to the Lady Elizabeth, in consideration of an advowson bestowed by her on the college.[3] The rights thus bestowed upon the countess were the 'advocacy' (or advowson) and 'patronage' of the college.[4] The object was evidently to make her the titular foundress, and from her no doubt most of the endowment was derived; but nevertheless there was no real breach of continuity, and the college must be considered to date from 1326. The statutes

[1] Cooper, *Memorials*, i. 25–30. [See also *Clare College, 1326–1926*, ed. M. D. Forbes, i. 3–29.]

[2] [*Cal. Patent Rolls, Edward II, 1324–27*, p. 244.]

[3] [The foundation of halls for the maintenance of scholars studying theology and logic in the university was contemplated by Roger de Northburgh, archdeacon of Richmond, the immediate predecessor of Richard de Badew in the chancellorship. Northburgh obtained royal licence in 1321 for the acquisition of the requisite advowsons for this endowment. See A. H. Lloyd, *The Early History of Christ's College*, pp. 28–9. Rashdall seems to under-estimate the assistance given by Lady Elizabeth de Clare towards the foundation of the college. In the first instance she came to the aid of Richard de Badew, chancellor of the university, by the grant of the advowson of Litlington, Cambridgeshire, when he found himself under the necessity of rebuilding University Hall after its destruction, it is said, by fire. After she had accepted the patronage of the Hall on its refoundation, she bestowed on it the advowsons of Great Gransden and Duxford in Cambridgeshire, and of Wrawby in Lincolnshire. See *Clare College, 1326–1926*, ed. M. D. Forbes, i. 31–2.]

[4] To speak with Mr. Mullinger (i. 251) of a 'greater liberality in the requirements respecting the professedly clerical element' in the statutes of this college is (as it appears to me) to put a somewhat anachronistic idea into the mind of a medieval founder. All the colleges were designed for ecclesiastics, whether they were required to take holy orders while still in the college or not.

CHAP. XII, were based on those of Michaelhouse.[1] By the statute issued
§ 9.   by the foundress in 1359 the 'perpetual Fellows and Scholars'
were to be, when the funds permitted, twenty in number, of
whom six must be priests. Two might study civil law, and
one medicine: the rest were to be artists or theologians. The
statutes were approved by the university, and the chancellor
continued visitor of the reconstituted college.[2] A new code
of statutes received the confirmation of Boniface IX in
1402.[3]

PEMBROKE (1347)

The *Documents* (ii. 189 *sq.*) print only the royal licence for the foundation
(Rot. Pat. 21 Ed. III, p. 3, m. 9 [*Cal. Patent Rolls, Edward III, 1345–8*,
p. 444]), and the statutes as revised in 1844. There are two manuscript
codes of statutes in the possession of the college: (1) the Statutes of 1347
(of which there is a duplicate in the University Registry); (2) an undated
code, in all probability of earlier date (see below, p. 306, n. 1). I am much
obliged to the kindness of the Rev. Dr. Searle, the present master, and of the
treasurer, Mr. Hadley, for giving me access to these documents. Mr. Mullinger (i. 236, 237) gives extracts from a manuscript account of the foundress
by Dr. Ainslie, late master of the college, which I have also seen. The
statutes as altered by Edward VI's visitors have been printed in a dateless
quarto (after 1733). [For an account of the foundress see H. JENKINSON's
article, 'Mary de Sancto Paulo, Foundress of Pembroke College, Cambridge', in *Archaeologia*, lxvi (1914–15), 410–46.]

The considerable number of colleges founded at Cambridge in rapid succession towards the middle of the fourteenth century testify to the marked progress of the university
at this time. The first of these was Pembroke or Valence
Marie, founded in 1347 by Marie de S. Pol, otherwise known

---

[1] *Documents, Univ. and Colleges of Cambridge*, ii. 117; *Harleian MS.* 7029 (Baker), p. 169.

[2] Vatican Register *De Exhibitis*, f. 46; [*Cal. of Papal Registers (Letters)*, v. 488–9. For an analysis of these statutes see J. R. Wardale, *Clare College*, pp. 5–11.]

[3] [Rashdall is incorrect in stating that Boniface IX confirmed a new code of statutes. It appears that on more than one occasion the chancellor of the university, in his capacity as visitor, had attempted by his ruling to make the statutes of the college sufficient authority

for certain changes in the administration of the college, and that the master had appealed to the Pope against this intervention. The Pope enjoins that the ancient statutes of the college shall be observed, 'notwithstanding revocations, injunctions, limitations made by the ordinary visitor or visitors', and expressly confirms certain provisions in the statutes which had formed the subject of the Master's petition. There is no mention of this episode in the histories of the college.]

as Mary de Valence, the widowed Countess of Pembroke,[1] CHAP. XII, and was designed for twenty-four major and six minor §9. scholars.[2] Only the former, of course, were full members of the foundation. All were to study arts and afterwards theology, except two canonists and one medical fellow. The college is remarkable as the only college in an English university in which a preference was accorded in the election of scholars to students of French birth [already at Cambridge or Oxford].[3] The provision is accounted for by the parentage of the countess, who was a daughter of Guy, Count of S. Pol. The earliest extant code of statutes was no doubt drawn up under the influence of the countess's Franciscan confessor. The college is placed under the authority of two annually elected, external 'rectors', who were to admit the fellows (elected, however, by the college) and to exercise certain very restricted visitatorial powers. One of the rectors was to be taken from the Friars Minor, of whom the foundress was a great patroness; the other was a secular.[4] This exact provision is found in the statutes of Balliol College, which, we have reason to believe, were based on Parisian models before the date of the characteristically English rule.

This provision disappears in another code of statutes, in the possession of the college, which is distinctly stated to have been issued in 1347. There is nothing decisive to show which code is the earliest, but the statutes would be more

---

[1] [The licence to found the college is dated 24 Dec. 1347, and the charter of foundation 9 June 1348; see *Cal. Patent Rolls, Edward III, 1345-8*, pp. 61-2, 444; *1348-50*, p. 349; and H. Jenkinson, 'Mary de Sancto Paulo, Foundress of Pembroke College, Cambridge', in *Archaeologia*, lxvi (1914-15), 422.]

[2] These places are also spoken of as 'exhibiciones minores'. If not elected 'major scholars', they were to leave the house when called upon to do so by the warden and scholars. [Mr. Mullinger (*Univ. of Cambridge*, i. 238) draws attention

to the inclusion of these 'minor scholars' as furnishing the earliest example of the admission of students in grammar to a college in Cambridge.]

[3] *Documents, Univ. and Colleges of Cambridge*, ii. 197. [On the French connexions of the foundress see the article by H. Jenkinson, 'Mary de Sancto Paulo, Foundress of Pembroke College, Cambridge', in *Archaeologia*, lxvi (1914-15), 409-12.]

[4] A minor peculiarity is the position of the dean, who is simply 'decanus capelle' (elsewhere 'cantor capelle aut decanus').

CHAP. XII, likely to be assimilated to the ordinary Cambridge type after
§ 9. a short experience of their working than so unusual a feature
as the supervision of the two *rectores* to have been introduced
at a later period. Moreover, on the latter supposition there
would be no evidence to show how the college escaped, as it
undoubtedly has escaped, from the tutelage in which it was
placed by the foundress.[1] There is indeed no evidence that
the undated code was ever in force.

GONVILLE (1349)

A paper entitled *Stabilitio Fundacionis per Rev. Patrem. Dnm̃. Willm̃.
Bateman. Norwici Episc.* exists among the Baker MSS. at Cambridge
(xxix. 271). In *Documents, &c.* ii. 213 *sq.*, are printed the royal licence to
Gonville (Rot. Pat. 22 Ed. III, p. 1, m. 33), Bishop Bateman's Statutes, and
some brief 'annals' by Francis Blomefield. There is a manuscript history

[1] Mr. Mullinger (*Univ. of Cambridge*, i. 237) says: 'The preamble in Heywood, *Early Statutes*, p. 179, and that in *Documents, Univ. and Colleges of Cambridge*, ii. 192, are calculated to give the impression that the Statutes of 1347 are still extant, but such is not the case. "Although no copy of them is extant," says Dr. Ainslie, "yet it is certain that they were enacted in the year 1347, since the revised copy of Statutes, by which they were superseded, though itself wanting in date, explicitly states that fact. The document containing the revised Statutes is in the form of an indenture," ' &c. I am at a loss to understand these remarks. I have seen both codes in the College Treasury—(1) the code of 1347, which is distinctly so dated, and (2) the undated indenture, which I take to be the earlier of the two. Dr. Ainslie rightly treats the indenture as the earlier, but seems to have in some way misunderstood the preamble of the 1347 statutes. Mr. Mullinger appears (1) to take the first of these documents for the Statutes of 1366, and (2) to assume that the indenture belongs to some period later than 1366. It is likely enough that the bishop or the university (both of them confirmed the dated code) objected to the rectors. There is a blank after 'hiis testibus', and the indenture may never have been executed. [Mr. Hilary Jenkinson, in his article, 'Mary de Sancto Paulo, Foundress of Pembroke College, Cambridge', in *Archaeologia*, lxvi (1914–15), 423–4, disagrees with Rashdall's conclusions and assigns both codes in the College Treasury to some date after 1347, confirming Dr. Ainslie's opinion. Dr. E. H. Minns and Mr. A. Attwater, successive librarians of the college, are both inclined to uphold Rashdall's view. Both codes refer to the foundress as 'illustris memorie', as if she were dead; but both contain provisions which speak of her as still alive. Mr. Attwater inclines to the conclusion that, while both codes were made after the foundress's death, the so-called 'indenture' represents a collection of statutes not all made at the same time, which was modified and rearranged in the code of 1347. A useful summary made by Dr. Ainslie, of the differences between the two codes, is quoted by Mr. Mullinger (i. 237, n. 2).]

(*Annales*) of the college by Dr. Caius in the College Library, for access to CHAP. XII, which and to some other manuscripts I am indebted to the Rev. E. S. Roberts, § 9. President of the College. [The *Annales* of Dr. Caius have been edited by Dr. John VENN, Fellow and devoted historian of the college, and were published by the Cambridge Antiquarian Society in 1904. Particulars of the careers of all known members of the college have been collected by Dr. VENN, in a *Biographical History of Gonville and Caius College, 1349–1897*, 3 vols., 1897–1901. The chief documents in the College Archives relating to the early history of the college are printed as an appendix to the third volume: these include Gonville's draft statutes and the statutes of Bishop Bateman. A history of *Gonville and Caius College*, by Dr. VENN, was added to the Cambridge series of *College Histories* in 1901. A note on fourteenth-century brick-work found in the chapel of the college was contributed by F. D. ATKINSON to the *Proceedings of the Cambridge Antiquarian Society*, ix (1894–8), 244–5. The medieval period is touched upon by Dr. VENN, in *Early Collegiate Life* (Cambridge, 1913), an attractive little book commemorating various incidents and occasions in the history of the college.]

In the year 1349 a college for twenty scholars in arts and theology was founded by Edmund Gonville, sometime [rector of Terrington in Norfolk and] vicar-general of the diocese of Ely.[1] It is characteristic of the difference between the great national University of Oxford and the more local reputation of Cambridge, that nearly all the colleges in the latter, down to the period of the reaction against Wyclifism, were founded by persons closely connected with the eastern counties. The original founder of Gonville Hall died a year after its first statutes were drawn up (1350), and the college was left very inadequately provided for.[2] The completion of the work was taken up by his executor, William Bateman, Bishop of Norwich, a distinguished Cambridge canonist from the Court of Avignon, by whom the statutes were remodelled with a

[1] *Documents, &c.* ii. 367. [The royal licence was given on 28 Jan. 1348; but the actual deed of foundation, which was executed at Gonville's rectory of Terrington, bears date 4 June 1349. See J. Venn, *Gonville and Caius College, Biog. Hist.* iii. 325–6; *Cal. Patent Rolls, Edward III, 1348–50*, p. 20. The letters patent of Edward III sanctioned the foundation of a college for twenty scholars; no particular number is specified either in the statutes drawn up by Gonville or in those of Bishop Bateman. Gonville's original foundation consisted of a master and four fellows, and, though at one time there appear to have been as many as nine and at another as few as two fellows, four was regarded as the normal number until 1478. See J. Venn, *op. cit.* iii. 213–14.]

[2] [These statutes do not appear ever to have been formally promulgated. See J. Venn, *Gonville and Caius College, Biog. Hist.* iii. 4, 341–5.]

CHAP. XII, view to the encouragement of his favourite studies.[1] The
§ 9. scholars, after completing their necessary regency in arts,
were henceforth free to betake themselves to theology or to
the canon and civil law: two might choose the faculty of
medicine.[2] At the same time the house was rechristened
as the 'College of the Annunciation'. Soon after this second
foundation (1351) the site of the college was moved from its
original position in Lurthburne Lane, now known as Free-
school Lane, to its present habitation, hitherto belonging to
the founders of Corpus, near the other foundation of Bishop
Bateman, of which we have next to speak.[3] The college,
originally consisting of a warden and four fellows, grew by
successive benefactions, and now bears the name of 'Gonville
and Caius College', after its refoundation in 1558 by Dr.
John Caius, the celebrated physician of Henry VIII, and the
earliest of Cambridge antiquaries.[4]

TRINITY HALL (1350)

The Deed of Foundation and Founder's Statutes are printed in *Documents,
University and Colleges of Cambridge,* ii. 415 *sq.* [H. E. MALDEN,
Trinity Hall, 1902. In *Warren's Book,* Cambridge, 1911, Dr. A. W. W.
DALE has edited the full collection of college records compiled with pious
care by the Rev. Samuel WARREN (1683–1744), sometime fellow and vice-
master of the hall. Interesting discoveries revealing medieval features in

[1] The deed of foundation, dated 1351, is in Ely Reg. Thomas de Insula, f. 45 *b*; [and is printed by J. Venn, *op. cit.* iii. 327. This *stabilitio* of the foundation bears date, 21 Dec. 1351.]

[2] *Documents, &c.* ii. 226. [According to the statutes drawn up by Gonville all the fellows were expected to pursue the study of theology after completing their course in arts, except that one or two of the fellows might, with the consent of the college, transfer to some other faculty, or any of them might for two years study canon law. See J. Venn, *op. cit.* iii. 213, 344. Bishop Bateman's elaborated code of statutes was issued in 1353. The bishop has been blamed for over-riding Gonville's wishes, but

see J. Venn, *op. cit.* iii. 6–7. Under Bateman's statutes a preference was given to the diocese of Norfolk in the election of the four fellows, see J. Venn, *op. cit.* iii. 210, 213. On the general question of the restriction of fellowships to certain counties see G. Peacock, *Observations upon the Statutes,* pp. 28–9, 110–11.]

[3] The original site was sold for the building of Corpus Christi College in 1353. Willis and Clark, i. 243. [For plans of the original and later sites of the college see J. Venn, *op. cit.* iii. 4, 26.]

[4] Rot. Pat. 4 and 5 Phil. and Mary, p. 7, m. 3 (41); *Documents, Univ. and Colleges of Cambridge,* ii. 215.

the buildings on the north side of the front court are recorded in *Trinity* CHAP. XII,
Hall, Restoration and Reconstruction, 1928–1929, by Mr. C. W. CRAWLEY.   § 9.
Professor E. C. CLARK contributed an article on the founder of the hall
to the *Proceedings of the Cambridge Antiquarian Society*, ix (1894–8),
297–336.]

Already, before taking up the unfinished work of Gonville
in 1350, Bishop Bateman had become the founder of a
college which he intended to be called 'The College of the
Scholars of the Holy Trinity of Norwich'. It is probable that
he had already established his scholars in a hostel hitherto
occupied by scholar-monks from Ely.[1] Here the bishop was
free to carry out his own ideas unfettered by the wishes of
another patron. The college was designed for the study of
the civil and canon law. The scholars were to be at least
B.A. on admission; and of twenty scholars, ten were to be
legists, and seven canonists (who were to take priest's orders
within a year of their election), though a doctor of canon law
might remain in the college with a view to graduating in
theology.[2] But the endowments of the college were never
sufficient to provide for this number.[3] The most noticeable
feature of Bishop Bateman's statutes is the liberality of his
allowances and the sumptuousness of his domestic arrangements.[4] While the annual allowance of a fellow of Merton
or Peterhouse was but fifty shillings, the budding lawyer of
Trinity Hall received (according to his degree) from six to
eight marks,[5] besides certain special distributions on festivals,

---

[1] Willis and Clark, i. 210, 237;
[see also H. E. Malden, *Trinity
Hall*, pp. 26–30].

[2] [H. E. Malden, *Trinity Hall*,
p. 26. The legists were not to
exceed thirteen nor the canonists
ten.]

[3] There are said to have been
only three fellows and three
scholars for more than a century
after the founder's death. Willis
and Clark, i. 217. The college
used the Church of S. John the
Baptist till 1445, when an 'Aisle'
was built for it in S. Edward's. *Ibid.*,
p. 220. [A licence for the erection
of a chapel or oratory was obtained

from the Bishop of Ely in 1352,
but it was not till some time
between 1445 and 1520 that a
chapel was built. See H. E. Malden, *Trinity Hall*, pp. 50, 51.] In
1481 a Bull of Sixtus IV permitted
Benedictine monks of Norwich to
live in either of Bishop Bateman's
colleges. Harleian MS. 7031
(Baker), 239. [See above, p. 295,
n. 2.]

[4] [For a careful analysis of the
statutes see H. E. Malden, *Trinity
Hall*, pp. 35–42.]

[5] [The master or *custos*, as he
is designated in the statutes of the
hall, was to receive 10 marks.]

CHAP. XII, so that a doctor-fellow might be in receipt of nearly three
§ 9. times the income of a scholar of Peterhouse. Clearly Bishop
Bateman, at all events, did not intend his fellows to be either
paupers or ascetics. A similar liberality, suitable to the
superior social position of a canonist, is evident in the establishment provided for by the founder, which consisted of a
dispensator or steward, a baker (who also acted as brewer),
a cook, an assistant to the baker, and an assistant to the cook.[1]
The visitation of the college was entrusted to the chancellor
of the university, who was required in certain cases to act
with the concurrence of the rectors or proctors of the university and two doctors. This regulation as to visitation, it
may be convenient to add, is substantially the same at Gonville, Corpus Christi, and Clare.[2]

CORPUS CHRISTI (1352)

The *Historiola Collegii Corporis Christi* by JOSSELIN (Latin Secretary to
Archbishop Parker) has been edited with some documents by Mr. CLARK
(*Camb. Ant. Soc.* 8°. *Publications*, No. xvii, 1880). This is the foundation of
the elaborate *History of Corpus Christi College* by Robert MASTERS (a former
master), Cambridge, 1753, and ed. Lamb, London, 1831. By the courtesy
of the Rev. Dr. Perowne, Master, I have been allowed the use of the
original Statutes of 1356. Large extracts are printed in MASTERS's
Appendix, p. 11. They are based on the statutes of Michaelhouse. Only
the royal licence and the statutes as revised in the time of Edward VI are
printed in *Documents, &c.* ii. 445 *sq.* [*A History of Corpus Christi College*,
by the Rev. Dr. H. P. STOKES, was published in 1898 in the Cambridge
series of *College Histories*. The history of the foundation of the colleges
and of its own connexion with the Guild of Corpus Christi and S. Mary
has been traced by Miss Mary BATESON in her introduction to *Cambridge
Gild Records* (C.A.S., 1903). An association with the Carmelite Order is
claimed for this Guild by J. P. RUSHE, O.C., in 'The Origin of St. Mary's
Guild in connexion with Corpus Christi College, Cambridge', contributed to the *Proceedings of the Cambridge Antiquarian Society*, xvi (1911–
12), 20–52. Dr. E. C. PEARCE, Bishop of Derby, sometime Master of
the college, contributed an article on the 'College Accounts of John
Botwright, Master of Corpus Christi, 1443–74', to the *Proceedings of
the Cambridge Antiquarian Society*, xxii (1917–20), 76–90. The oldest
catalogue of the library (*c.* 1376) is included by Dr. M. R. JAMES in
his *Catalogue of the MSS. of Corpus Christi College, Cambridge*, 1912,
i. ix–xi.]

[1] [The provision made by Bishop
Bateman for servants in his statutes
is not more liberal than that made
by the founder of the Queen's
College, Oxford, fourteen years

earlier.]
[2] *Documents, Univ. and College of
Cambridge*, ii. 123, 128, 230, 231,
448.

Although both of Bishop Bateman's foundations were com- pleted after the date of the Black Death, there is no ground for supposing that the great canonist was influenced either by any special religious zeal (except that zeal for ecclesiastical interests and that anxiety for his own soul which influenced all such foundations) or by any special desire to fill up the ranks of a clergy among whom (it is sometimes asserted) the ravages of the plague had been peculiarly appalling.[1] The latter was, however, the declared motive of the founders of the college now known as Corpus Christi, though long more usually styled Benet College. The same great calamity was, no doubt, one of the inspiring motives of the numerous foundations which had their origin at this period, both at Cambridge and at Oxford.[2] As its now prevailing name denotes, S. Benet's College was founded, in 1352, by one of the religious and charitable guilds of the Middle Ages—the Guild of 'Corpus Christi and the Blessed Mary' in the town of Cambridge. It was situated near the Church of S. Benet, which was impropriated to the college and served by its members.[3] The original master and fellows (only two in

[1] The impression *may* have arisen simply from the exacter statistics available in their case. See F. A. Gasquet, *The Great Pestilence*, London, 1893, p. 75. [Mr. H. E. Malden (*Trinity Hall*, pp. 13, 14) considers that the replenishing of the ranks of the clergy with well-trained men 'was a secondary or additional motive'. See also the article on Bishop Bateman in *D.N.B.*, and the paper on him contributed by Dr. J. W. Clark to the *Proceedings of the Cambridge Antiquarian Society*, xxxix (1896–7), 297–336.]

[2] See preamble to the statutes of Clare, New College, and even of King's. The formula survived its justification.

[3] The statutes [drawn up on 21 Mar. 1356] begin: 'Nos Henricus Dux Lancastrie Aldermannus et confratres Gilde Corporis Christi et Beate Marie Cantabrigie.' Mr.

Mullinger (i. 447) makes two distinct guilds, but the *Historiola* (p. 3) shows that they were amalgamated for the purpose of undertaking the building of a college. See the royal licence in B. Masters, *Hist. of C.C.C.* (1753), App., p. 4. The scheme had been begun by the Guild of Corpus Christi in the years 1342–7. [The two guilds that united for the erection of this college were the Guild of Corpus Christi and the Guild of S. Mary. On the enterprise of the joint guild Miss Bateson has well said that it 'was a remarkable event; not that this guild was the first or the last to take part in the endowment of education, for many founded or partly endowed grammar schools, but the foundation of a college was a more ambitious undertaking than is recorded of any similar society. It was further of peculiar interest as an effort made towards healing

CHAP. XII, number[1]) continued to perform all the duties of chaplains to
§ 9. the Guild; that is to say, they officiated at the obsequies of
its members. It was perhaps in consequence of this position
that we find the fellows bound by the wholly unusual obligation of saying the canonical hours daily.[2] The college was
gradually enlarged through successive benefactions by private
individuals. The alderman and six brethren of the Guild
conducted an annual visitation of the college in conjunction
with the chancellor of the university.[3]

GODSHOUSE (1441–2) [1439]

[A history of *Christ's College*, by Dr. John PEILE, Master of the college,
was published in the Cambridge series of *College Histories*, in 1900. Dr.
PEILE also compiled a *Biographical Register of Christ's College, 1505–
1905, and of the Earlier Foundation of God's House, 1448–1505* (Cambridge, 1910–13, 2 vols.) The statutes of God's House have been edited
by Mr. H. RACKHAM with an introduction, translation, and notes: *Early
Statutes of Christ's College, Cambridge* (Cambridge, 1927). Mr. A. H.
LLOYD has brought to light much new information about the first seventy
years of the history of the college in *The Early History of Christ's College,
Cambridge* (Cambridge, 1934).]

Godshouse, founded [in 1439][4] by William Byngham, rector
of S. John Zachary in London, forms the solitary instance in

an old feud between town and
university'. See *Cambridge Gild
Records* (C.A.S.), pp. xx–xxiii. In
furtherance of their scheme the
guildsmen obtained the patronage
of Henry, Duke of Lancaster, who
appears as alderman of the guild
in 1353. There is no contemporary
evidence for the statement that the
scheme had been begun in the
years 1342–7: see *Cambridge Gild
Records*, pp. xviii–xx.]
    [1] The number is to be increased
with the increase of revenue. The
basis of the foundation was supplied by a legacy for a chaplain
already bestowed upon the Guild
of S. Mary, B. Masters, *Hist. of
C.C.C.*, App., pp. 2, 3. [The provision for a guild chaplain, to which
Rashdall refers, was made in 1307
by Adam Elyot, alderman, not by
bequest, as Rashdall states, but

in his lifetime by deed of conveyance. See *Cambridge Gild Records*,
pp. xvii, 133.]
    [2] [They were to be graduates who
intended to devote themselves to
the study of theology or canon law.]
    [3] [On the early statutes of the
college and the connexion with the
Guild of Corpus Christi and S.
Mary see *Cambridge Gild Records*,
pp. xxv–xxvii. The guild appears
to have come to an end early in the
reign of Richard II; its disappearance was possibly not unconnected
with the outbreak in Cambridge at
the time of the Peasants' Revolt.]
    [4] [Byngham was already making
preparations for his foundation by
1436, but came into conflict with
the chancellor of the university
over his choice of site. See A. H.
Lloyd, *The Early History of Christ's
College*, pp. 11–34.]

the English universities of a college exclusively devoted to CHAP. XII,
§ 9. the study of grammar.[1] It was not, however, intended for mere grammar-school boys before entering upon the arts course, like the colleges for grammarians at Paris. It was designed as a nursery of grammar-school masters, and may fairly claim to be the first training or normal school on record. In the founder's petition to the King for leave to establish the house, it is recited that the petitioner had himself 'founde of late ouer the East partie of the wey ledyng from Hampton to Couentre and so forth, no ferther North þan Rypon, lxx scoles voide, or mo, þat weren occupied all at ones, within l yeres passed, bicause þat þer is so grete scarstee of maistres of gramer'.[2] Here we have presented to us one of the effects of the strange intellectual decadence of that fifteenth century of whom there are so many other indications. William Byngham's scheme seems to herald the age of reformed grammar-schools.[3] It may be noted as more than anticipation—as an actual indication—of the growth, not indeed of the New Learning, but of that humbler movement towards an improvement in grammatical teaching, which is traceable in many educational efforts of the later Middle Age, and which did in time prepare the way for the New Learning itself. At the same time, like many other reforming movements, it began long before the tendency against which it was a reaction

---

[1] [A wider scope was permitted under the royal licence of 1446 which approved of the foundation of a college consisting of a 'proctor and scholars to be instructed not only in the faculty of grammar but also in the knowledge of the other liberal arts'. See ibid., p. 75.]

[2] Documents, Univ. and Colleges of Cambridge, iii. 153 sq., where also the charters [i.e. those of 1442 and 1446] are printed. Cooper places the petition in 1439 (Annals, i. 188), and a royal licence was granted in the same year (Documents, &c. i. 42), when the establishment seems to be already in working order. [For the texts of Byng-

ham's petition and the royal licence dated 13 July 1439, see A. H. Lloyd, The Early History of Christ's College, pp. 356–9.]

[3] [Cf. H. Rackham, Early Statutes of Christ's College, Cambridge, pp. 26, 27, 141. The statutes of Godshouse required that every fellow unless he were elected a reader or lecturer of the college or became a parish priest should accept appointment as a master at any new grammar school where a competent salary was offered; otherwise he might continue to enjoy his fellowship until he had concluded the first year of his regency.]

had reached its culmination. The Old Learning did not
reach its lowest depth till long after the rise of the New. The
general tone of the universities continued to treat grammar
with contempt, and the general level of Latinity continued
to be low, in spite of such efforts towards better teaching of
grammar as are represented by the foundation of Winchester
and of Eton, of Godshouse at Cambridge and Magdalen
College School at Oxford.¹ [An important and novel feature
of Byngham's educational scheme finds place in the statutes
of Godshouse. Provision was made for the appointment of a
college lecturer who was required to lecture to the fellow
scholars and residents 'every day on which lectures are
usually read in hostels', and it is to be noted that the lectures
were to include not only sophistry, logic, and philosophy, but
also works appropriate to the study of the Latin language and
literature. It was directed, moreover, that these lectures
should continue to be given during the long vacation term,
by which arrangement it was made possible for country
schoolmasters to attend them.]² The history of Godshouse is,
however, shorter than that of the foundations with which it
has been associated, since in 1505 it was absorbed in the
Lady Margaret's foundation of Christ's College.³ While it

¹ Cf. above, p. 230.
² [See A. H. Lloyd, *The Early
History of Christ's College*, pp. 131–
7, 375–7; H. Rackham, *Early
Statutes of Christ's College*, pp.
22–5. Mr. Lloyd has discovered a
very interesting form of agreement
for the appointment of Ralph
Barton as college lecturer from
Sept. 1451.]
³ [Rashdall was under a misapprehension in supposing that
Godshouse was absorbed into a
new foundation. There was no
break in continuity between Godshouse and Christ's College. They
are, as Mr. Lloyd points out, 'one
and the same body', Godshouse and
Christ's College being equivalent
designations. See A. H. Lloyd,
*The Early History of Christ's
College*, pp. 129–30, 341–51. New

royal licences for his college of
Godshouse were obtained by Byngham in 1442, by which time he
seems to have been free from the
opposition at first offered him. In
1446 the site of his college being
required for inclusion in that
designed for the new royal foundation of King's College, move had
to be made to the present site, and
a new royal licence became necessary. These licences were superseded in 1448 by a royal charter
whereby Byngham's ambitions for
his college were consummated by
Henry VI making it a royal foundation. In 1505 the Lady Margaret
'as heir to all King Henry's godly
intentions' augmented, finished,
and stablished it. See. *ibid.*, pp.
50–6, 66–76, 86–104, 129–30, 280–
304.]

existed, it consisted of a proctor and twenty-four scholars, chap. xii, who were to be trained as grammar masters and then sent §9. out to teach country schools.[1] Though it constituted a separate college, it was placed under the government of the master and fellows of Clare Hall, to whom the power of framing the statutes was given by the royal charter.[2]

Its original site was part of what is now the ante-chapel of King's, from which it was transferred in 1446 to the ground now occupied by the college which has taken its place.[3]

KING'S COLLEGE (1441)

There is a notice of William Millington, the first provost, by George WILLIAMS, in *Camb. Ant. Soc. Communications*, vol. i, p. 288 (1859). A *Catalogus Alumnorum*, &c., appeared in 1730 (Eton); also 1740 and 1774. The statutes and charters have been edited by HEYWOOD and WRIGHT (*The Ancient Laws of the Fifteenth Century for King's College, Cambridge*, London, 1850). [A history of *King's College*, by the Provost, the Rev. A. AUSTEN LEIGH, was published in 1899 in the series of *Cambridge College Histories*. Mr. J. SALTMARSH has contributed an article on 'The Muniments of King's College' to *The Proceedings of the Cambridge*

[1] [See H. Rackham, *Early Statutes of Christ's College*, pp. 1–39.]

[2] [Mr. Lloyd refutes as 'a fiction of the nineteenth century' the view, which Rashdall reiterated, that 'the College of Godshouse was given to the College of Clare Hall in 1439, and that its subsequent foundation charters were of a college affiliated to Clare Hall', and shows that there is no evidence for assuming that the permission given Byngham under the royal licence of 1439 to place his college under the government of the Master and fellows of Clare was ever acted upon. The statutes of Godshouse are in part derived from those of Clare, but that is explained by the close friendship which is known to have existed between Byngham and the Master and other members of that society. The earliest extant version of the statutes of Godshouse is not dated, but as it is attested by Dr. William Stockdale, vice-chancellor of the

university, and William Cambrige, prior of Barnwell, it must have been sealed in 1495 or 1496. See *ibid.*, pp. 38–9; A. H. Lloyd, *The Early History of Christ's College*, pp. 238–43. The use of the designation 'proctor' for the head of Godshouse has been thought to indicate his subordination to the Master and fellows of Clare; but Mr. Lloyd compares the academical use of 'proctor' with that of 'president', which does not in all cases connote a representative quality. See A. H. Lloyd, *The Early History of Christ's College*, pp. 105–20. But it may be suggested that the unusual designation 'proctor' was chosen by Byngham in view of the possibility of his college becoming dependent on Clare Hall, as allowed for by the royal licence of 1439.]

[3] *Documents, Univ. and Colleges of Cambridge*, iii. 163. [See A. H. Lloyd, *op. cit.*, pp. 66–74, 97–8.]

Antiquarian Society (1933), xxxiii. 83–97, and 'A Hand-list of the Estates of King's College' to the *Bulletin of the Inst. of Hist. Research*, xii. 32–8. For the library reference should be made to M. R. JAMES, *Catalogue of the MSS. of King's College, Cambridge*, pp. 69–83.]

Object of foundation.
It has already been observed that the reaction against the ingrained Wyclifism of Oxford was at least one of the causes which attracted royal patronage to Cambridge. Oxford being regarded as hopelessly infected by traditions of heresy (however thoroughly its outward manifestations might have been suppressed), it was thought that in Cambridge a new school of the Church might be raised up to rival or supplant that 'second School of the Church' which had so grievously fallen from her first estate.[1] The most conspicuous manifestation of such a design is the foundation of King's College by Henry VI in 1441, originally known as the College of S. Nicholas.[2] The piety or ambition of an ecclesiastically minded king was fired by the desire to rival William of Wykeham's magnificent foundations at Oxford and Winchester:[3] the suppression of the alien priories decreed by Parliament in the preceding reign and carried out in his own provided a convenient means of carrying out the project.[4] The mere desire to found a college where the ground was less preoccupied may have had something to do with the selection of Cambridge rather than Oxford as the site of the King's College of our Lady and S. Nicholas, to which the College of Eton, newly erected hard by the royal castle of Windsor, was to occupy the same relation that S. Mary's College at Winchester bore to Winchester College in Oxford. The exact

[1] [Every scholar on his admission to a fellowship was required by the statutes of the college to take an oath that he would not maintain the 'damnable errors' of Wyclif or Pecock: see *Documents, Univ. and College of Cambridge*, ii. 623–4.]

[2] [See J. Saltmarsh, 'The Muniments of King's College', in *Proceedings of Cambridge Antiquarian Society* (1933), xxxiii. 86.]

[3] [The Rev. A. Austen Leigh (*King's College*, pp. 1–2) points to two persons as likely to have encouraged the King: John Langton, Master of Pembroke and Chancellor of the University, and William of Alnwick, Bishop of Lincoln, formerly tutor to the King.]

[4] The successive royal grants of the confiscated property (*Documents, Univ. and Colleges of Cambridge*, i. 43 *sq.*), among other feudal privileges, confer the right of having gallows on their manorial lands; Rot. Chart. 21–4 Hen. VI, No. 4; [*Cal. Charter Rolls, 1427–1516*, vi. 68–9, dated 3 Mar. 1446].

numbers of the two new foundations,[1] the intimate bond existing between them, and every detail in their organization, faithfully reproduce the splendidly original design of Wykeham. The statutes of King's College are almost a transcript of those of New College, reproducing even the now meaningless statement that the college was designed to repair the ravages of the Black Death of 1348.[2] As in other respects, so

---

[1] By the existing statutes: the original foundation was only for a rector and twelve scholars.

[2] [Although the statutes of King's College to a great extent reproduce the wording of those of New College, the reproduction is not as mechanical as Rashdall seems to suggest. The passage to which he refers does not expressly mention the Black Death of 1348, but is couched in sufficiently general terms as to be hardly less applicable in 1441 than it was in 1400. The passage in question refers to shortage of clergy 'ex pestilentiis, guerris et aliis mundi miseriis'. See *Documents, Univ. and Colleges of Cambridge,* ii. 482. In the statutes of King's College there will be found variations from those of New College which are not without interest. It is particularly noticeable that in almost all instances the salaries and allowances of college officers are fixed at a higher figure. For example, according to the statutes of King's College, the annual salary of the provost is fixed at £100, and his allowance of horses at £10; according to those of New College the salary of the warden is fixed at £40, and his allowance of horses at £6. Moreover, in the case of the provost, express mention is made of a personal staff to consist of an attendant of good birth (*generosus*), three valets, and two pages. The statutes of New College required that the joint number of civilians and canonists in the college should be twenty: the statutes of King's College, however, only stipulated for two civilians and four canonists. The three clerks assigned to the chapel under the New College statutes were doubled under those of King's College and one was to be able *iubilare in organis*. Two years was fixed by William of Wykeham as the period of probation for his scholars, but this was increased to three by Henry VI for his. William of Wykeham appointed five deans, Henry VI was content with three. The servants of the college are fully enumerated in the statutes of King's College, but not in those of New College. Among other variations it may be noted that in the statutes of King's College, unlike those of New College, fishing is included among the prohibited recreations, but chess is not; and the introduction into college is expressly forbidden of 'a monkey, bear, fox, stag, or hind, or any other unwonted or rarely seen wild beasts or birds'. On the other hand, the prohibition in the New College statutes with respect to 'the very vile and horrid sport of shaving beards which is a customary practice on the eve of the Inception of Masters' is omitted.

For an analysis of the statutes of King's College see A. Austen Leigh, *King's College,* pp. 7–16. See also J. Saltmarsh, 'The Muniments of King's College', in *Proceedings of Cambridge Antiquarian Society* (1933), xxxiii. 86].

CHAP. XII, in the history of its college architecture the foundation of
§ 9. King's introduced at Cambridge the new era inaugurated by
New College at Oxford: it is the first college in which architectural magnificence forms a prominent feature of the
founder's aim. In the magnificent scale of its chapel the
imitation has surpassed its model: King's College Chapel—
begun by Henry VI, continued by Henry VII, and completed by Henry VIII—fitly symbolizes the entrance of
Cambridge upon that period of her existence in which
she was for the first time fairly on a level with her elder
sister, and during a great part of which it was true that 'in
intellectual activity and readiness to admit improvement, the
superiority was . . . on the side of the less ancient and splendid
institution'.[1]

Special In one respect Henry endeavoured to do more for the
privileges. honour and glory of his new foundation than William of
Wykeham had been able to effect for New College. He
obtained a papal Bull exempting the college not only from
archiepiscopal and episcopal jurisdiction, but also from that
of the chancellor of the university.[2] And the university itself
in 1449 accepted this exemption on two conditions, (1) that
the members of the college should remain subject to the
chancellor and proctors in respect of the performance of
academical acts and exercises, though free from their judicial
and disciplinary authority, (2) that the whole agreement
should be void if the Bishops of Salisbury, Lincoln, and
Carlisle should pronounce it inconsistent with the 'statutes,
privileges, and laudable customs of the university'.[3] We are
not told what was the ruling of these prelates. But these
anomalous privileges seemed so outrageous even to those who
were to benefit by them that they induced the resignation of
the first provost, William Millington,[4] and led to a period

---

[1] Macaulay's *Essay on Bacon.*
[2] [A. Austen Leigh, *King's College*, pp. 13, 14. See *Cal. Papal Registers (Letters), 1431–47*, ix. 482–3, 511–12. The Bulls are dated 29 Nov. 1445. See also *Cal. Papal Registers (Letters) 1431–*

47, pp. 482–3.]
[3] Cooper, *Memorials*, i. 192; Hare MS. ii. 139.
[4] [Millington did not resign voluntarily. He was deprived in 1446. For the correspondence on this subject that passed between

of strife and confusion which was only ended in 1457 by an chap. xii, agreement between the college and the university, which § 9. reserved to the college only the jurisdiction over the founda- tioners, their tenants and servants, in civil or criminal cases arising out of acts committed within the college, including probate and administration.[1] The privilege of the college in

him and Bishop Bekyngton see *Correspondence of Bekynton*, ed. G. Williams (R.S.), ii. 157–74. See also *Grace Book A*, ed. S. M. Leathes, i. 5.]

[1] Rot. Pat. 35 Hen. VI, p. 2, m. 14 [*Cal. Patent Rolls, Henry VI, 1452–61*, p. 356]; Hare MS. ii. 141 *b*; Cooper, *Annals*, i. 207. In 1454 the university had refused to admit Kingsmen to degrees without their renouncing all privi- leges as well as swearing obedience to the chancellor 'simpliciter'. See Baker MS. at Camb. xxv. 447– 8. Mr. Mullinger (*Cambridge*, i. 311) appears to me mistaken in tracing the exemption of Kings- men from the necessity of suppli- cating for degrees to this some- what equivocal 'victory'. There is no more trace of this 'privilege' at King's than at New College till a much later period. See above, p. 221. [The Rev. A. Austen Leigh has reviewed the problem of the origin of the exemption of Kings- men from degree examinations in an appendix to his history of the college (see *King's College*, pp. 295– 8); but he is unable to solve it. 'It seems to be a case', he remarks in conclusion, 'in which all the evi- dence is on one side, and all the probability on the other. For, be- sides the improbability of the privi- lege being granted at any date later than Henry's reign, it is difficult to believe that the *same* abuse crept in, owing to *different* causes, at both Universities. Whereas, if William of Wykeham had already secured the privilege for his Foundation, the example set by Oxford might

not unnaturally be followed by Cambridge.' Dr. J. Venn, how- ever, on the evidence of the Grace Books, inclines to the view that at King's College 'the custom of claiming exemption began to pre- vail about 1510–25, but that ex- amination was not avoided till much later'. He founds this opinion on the following read- ing of the evidence. He first notes that in *Grace Book Δ*, which covers the years 1542 to 1589, the degrees of B.A. and M.A. are conferred upon Kingsmen 'sine gratia petita aut concessa', and turning to *Grace Book B*, which covers the years 1488 to 1544, he points out that 'we there find the same, or an equivalent expression, in general use for their degrees from 1528–9. Before that date the B.A. degrees of Kingsmen are seldom mentioned in the list of graces, which, of course, looks as if there was some- thing exceptional about them. The M.A. degrees, on the other hand, generally *are* recorded; and where recorded, it is significant that the expression used is exactly the same as for members of other colleges. There are many of them between 1510 and 1528, in which it is ex- pressly stated that the candidate had attended the ordinary lectures and performed the usual respon- sions. The B.A. degree, however, is not always omitted, and where it is recorded the customary expres- sion is used. Take the case of S. Simonds, B.A., 1508–9, a founda- tioner and fellow. It is plainly stated that he had kept the usual oppositions and responsions, &c.

CHAP. XII, matters testamentary was exercised up to the end of the
§ 9.   eighteenth century. The college was placed under the visitation of the Bishop of Lincoln.[1]

QUEENS' COLLEGE (1448)

The history of Queens' College by W. G. SEARLE (*Camb. Antiq. Soc.* 8⁰.
Publications, Nos. ix and xiii, 1867 and 1871) is the most careful and
complete history of a Cambridge college which has yet [i.e. before 1895]
been written. [His voluminous manuscript notes on the history of the
college are preserved in the library of the college.] I have been allowed,
by the kindness of the Rev. J. H. Gray, to see a copy of the original
statutes. The binding attributes them to Henry VIII and the year 1529,
but this is hardly borne out by their contents. They purport to emanate
from Elizabeth Woodville, and the educational provisions can hardly be
as late as 1529. They may have been very slightly altered in that year. [A
history of *The Queens' College,* by the Rev. J. H. GRAY was published in
the Cambridge series of *College Histories* in 1899. A revised edition was
issued in 1926. The Rev. J. F. WILLIAMS contributed an article on 'The
Muniments of Queens' College' to the *Proceedings of the Cambridge
Antiquarian Society* (1924–5), xxvii. 43–8.]

In 1446 Henry VI issued a charter founding a college of S.
Bernard for a president and four fellows.[2] It was refounded
on another site—that of the present Queens' College—in the
following year,[3] while in 1448 its charter was again cancelled
and a new one issued by Queen Margaret of Anjou, who had
petitioned her husband to be allowed to become foundress
and patroness of the college.[4] The college now bore the style
of the Queen's College of S. Margaret and S. Bernard, but
in 1475 was again refounded by another queen, Elizabeth
Woodville, once maid-of-honour to the fallen Margaret, and

His grace is in every way identical
with those relating to other colleges.' See *Grace Book Δ,* ed. J.
Venn, pp. xxi–xxiii.]

[1] Among its exceptional privileges were the power to create a
notary public, and licence to the
provost or a fellow named by him
to hear the confessions of all
comers: *Camb. Ant. Soc. Communications,* iii. 49.

[2] Rot. Chart. 25 and 26 Hen. VI,
n. 37; [*Cal. Charter Rolls,* vi. 74–5];
W. G. Searle, *The History of
Queens' College* (C.A.S.), pp. 3, 4.
[J. H. Gray, *The Queens' College,*

1926, p. 5.] [It is stated in the
charter of foundation that the
college was founded 'for the extir-
pation of heresies and errors and
the increase of the faith'. See *Cal.
Charter Rolls,* vi. 74.]

[3] W. G. Searle, *The History of
Queens' College* (C.A.S.), 1926, pp.
7–15; [J. H. Gray, *The Queens'
College,* 1926, pp. 5–7].

[4] *Ibid.,* pp. 15–17; [J. H. Gray,
The Queens' College, 1926, pp. 7–
10. See *Cal. Patent Rolls, 1446–
52,* pp. 143–4, dated 30 Mar.
1448.]

now consort of Edward IV, who aspired to the position of patroness and co-foundress of the society, henceforth known as the Queens' College.[1] It appears, however, very doubtful whether these royal personages gave the college much except patronage—a patronage which (as has been observed) it was at this time the deliberate policy of the court and its ecclesiastical advisers to extend to Cambridge rather than to the heresy-stained Oxford. The endowments of this college were gradually provided by a number of obscurer persons. The donor of the original site of S. Bernard's—Richard Andrew, burgess of Cambridge—has the best right to the title of founder, and the gradual enlargement of the very scanty foundation was primarily due to the energy of the first master, Andrew Doket.[2]

The earliest extant statutes appear to be those of the second foundress, Elizabeth Woodville, but slightly revised under the authority of Henry VIII in 1529.[3] By these statutes the college was to consist of a president and eighteen fellows (of whom fourteen were to be in priest's orders) with four poor scholars, two president's servants, and two cooks.[4] Fellows

[1] *Ibid.*, pp. 69–72; [J. H. Gray, *The Queens' College*, 1926, pp. 11–16]. [The title of the college can hardly be said to have undergone a change at this time, as it is still continued to be *Collegium Reginale sanctorum Margarete et Bernardi*, or more shortly *Collegium Reginale*, see W. G. Searle, *The History of Queens' College* (C.A.S.), pp. 62, 67–8, 70, 82, 85, 96, 98, &c.]

[2] [The historians of the college do not single out Richard Andrew in this way. 'The true founder of the College', writes the Rev. J. H. Gray, 'was Andrew Dokett,' and in the commemoration service of the college Dokett receives recognition as such. See J. H. Gray, *The Queens' College*, 1926, pp. 4–5.]

[3] See the Bibliography above.

[4] 'In hoc eodem collegio alantur quatuor scholares indigentes, duo seruitores Presidentis et duo coci.' The functions of the dean are limited to the chapel and its services. There were to be two censors, who were to preside over disputations and to lecture themselves, one on logic, the other on rhetoric. A lecture on 'Rhetoric or Cosmography' was to be given on festivals. One of them was also to give a daily lecture on the Bible or Sentences in the chapel. This last lecture appears to have been founded by some special benefaction. If no one was willing to give it for so small a stipend, he might preach English sermons instead. [Mr. Mullinger (*Univ. of Cambridge*, i. 316) and the Rev. J. H. Gray (*The Queens' College*, p. 31) state that on its refoundation the college was enlarged 'from a president and four fellows to a president and twelve fellows'. By subsequent benefactions the number of fellowships had been raised to seventeen before the death of the first presi-

were to be at least 'Questionists' in arts at the time of election.[1] All the fellows (after regency in arts) were to study theology, except two, who were to apply themselves to civil law and medicine respectively.[2] Not more than two fellows were to be elected from any one diocese (except the diocese of Lincoln, from which there might be three), or more than one from the same county. Provisions of this kind—found in many of the later medieval colleges—were made (as the Queens' Statutes say) to 'extirpate all partiality of countries' in elections. This is worth noticing as showing that the design of the founders was not to restrict, but to extend, the sphere of their liberality, though in practice these restrictions, once really necessary to avoid partiality, have operated in a precisely contrary direction. Certain visitatorial powers—that is to say the deposition of the president—were entrusted to the vice-chancellor and one other doctor or head of a college.

S. CATHARINE'S (1475)

The charters and original statutes (which are very short) are printed in *Documents*, iii. 75 *sq.*; also with an account of the foundation by the founder, and other documents, in *Documents relating to S. Catharine's College in the University of Cambridge*, by (Bishop) PHILPOTT, Cambridge, 1891. [*St. Catharine's College*, 1902, by the Right Rev. Dr. G. F. BROWNE, was added to the Cambridge Series of the *College Histories* in 1902. *MSS. in the Library of St. Catharine's College, Cambridge*, by M. R. JAMES (pp. 4–7), contains a catalogue of the books given by the founder, Dr. Robert Woodlark.]

S. Catharine's Hall was founded by Dr. Robert Woodlark, Provost of King's.[3] From whatever source the provost's income was derived, the fact that the head of one college should have been in a position to found another is an inter-

dent, Andrew Dokett, in 1484 (see J. H. Gray, *op. cit.*, p. 36). The eighteenth fellowship was founded in 1491 (see *ibid.*, p. 38).]

[1] The term 'Questionist' is still used for a fourth-year man.

[2] Notice the absence of canon law. This, together with provisions for Bible lectures in college and divers English sermons to be preached by the fellows, is a remarkable indication of a reforming spirit, if really belonging to the end of the fifteenth century. They may, of course, be due to Henry VIII.

[3] There is an account of his life by Archdeacon Hardwick in *Camb. Ant. Soc. Commun.* (1859), i. 329. [See also the article by Dr. Norman Moore in *D.N.B.*, and G. F. Browne, *St. Catharine's College*, pp. 1–6.]

esting indication of the growing importance of college-head-
ships, and (since Woodlark had begun life as a fellow of King's)
supplies another refutation of the mistaken idea that colleges
were designed exclusively to supply a meagre subsistence
to penniless students. The college originally consisted of a
master and three fellows.[1] All were eventually to study
theology, and were to be at least bachelors of arts in minor
orders at the time of election.[2] The college was actually
erected, and the fellows 'entered upon commons' in the year
1473, but the royal charter was not issued till 1475.[3] In the
founder's statute occurs the provision that no two persons
should be elected from the same county.[4]

JESUS (1497)

SHERMANNUS, *Historia Collegii Jesu Cantabrigiensis*, ed. Halliwell, London, 1840. [A history of *Jesus College*, by Mr. A. GRAY, Master of the college, was published in the Cambridge series of *College Histories* in 1902. A handsome volume containing *The Earliest Statutes of Jesus College, Cambridge*, appeared in 1935.]

A great deal of the property of English colleges is derived
in one way or another from monastic sources. Whatever may
be thought of the way by which, in other instances, monastic
property was diverted to educational purposes, it will be
difficult to construct an apology for the nuns of S. Rhade-
gund's, one of the earliest of Cambridge religious houses. We
are told that the nunnery had become corrupt and dissolute
'by occasion of its neighbourhood to the university'—a moral

[1] [Dr. Woodlark had intended his foundation to consist of a master and ten fellows, but his fortunes suffered through the downfall of Henry VI. See G. F. Browne, *St. Catharine's College*, pp. 16, 17. The statutes specify six fellows, with power to increase or decrease that number according to the income available. See *Documents, Univ. and Colleges of Cambridge*, iii. 81.]

[2] 'In ordine sacerdotii vel infra sacros ordines ad omnes minores constituti' (printed by Bishop Philpott 'ad omne minus!'). The charter speaks of three Fellows; Woodlark

himself speaks of it as 'fundata super uno magistro et *decem* sociis' (Philpott, p. 6). [Dr. Woodlark is particularly insistent in his statutes that his fellows should not study any other science or faculty than those of philosophy and theology. Bishop Browne has noted, in connexion with this injunction, that not one volume on the civil or canon law is included in the 137 volumes given to the college by its founder. See *St. Catharine's College*, p. 26.]

[3] [*Documents, Univ. and Colleges of Cambridge*, iii. 75–7.]

[4] [*Ibid.* ii. 82.]

degradation which had apparently carried with it the pecuniary ruin of the house, in which by this time but two sisters survived.[1] In 1497, John Alcock, Bishop of Ely, the patron of the convent in right of his see, procured the dissolution of the house by royal letters patent. If we may trust the extant statutes, the college was intended primarily for 'the study of Grammar, Rhetoric, Logic, Mathematics, and Philosophy'—an enumeration which (whether due to the original founder or to his sixteenth-century successor) reminds us that we have now arrived at the period of the New Learning, and that with Jesus our enumeration of Cambridge colleges must cease.[2]

[1] *Documents*, iii. 91. This impeachment of the nuns is supported by a contemporary Cantabrigian, John Major, *Hist. Mai. Brit.* (1521), f. viii. The timely suppression of the nunnery has saved the beautiful thirteenth-century church which still forms the college chapel.

[2] See note on p. 496.

CHAPTER XIII

THE NUMBERS IN THE MEDIEVAL UNIVERSITIES

[The matriculation lists, whose publication has been noted in the bibliographies of the various universities, make it possible to estimate the numbers in the German universities (including Basel and Louvain), and Paulsen's preliminary estimates, used by Rashdall, have been superseded by Franz EULENBERG's 'Die Frequenz der deutschen Universitäten von ihrer Gründung bis zum Gegenwart', in the *Abhandl. der Königlich. sächsischen Gesellschaft der Wissenschaften*; phil.-hist. Klasse, xxiv (1904), 1–323; cf. the same 'Die Frequenz der deutschen Universitäten in früherer Zeit', in *Conrads Jahrbuch für Nationalökonomie und Statistik*, 3rd ser., xiii (1897), 481–555.

The presence of foreign students in medieval universities, so frequently recognized as a normal or even necessary element in university life by the organization into nations, has received much attention since A. BUDINSKY published his essay, *Die Universität Paris und die Fremden an derselben im Mittelalter* (Berlin, 1876). It would not be possible here to survey the literature and, until more work has been done, any attempt to estimate results in a statistical form would be premature. Many of the books and articles have been noted in the bibliographical notes. The following may be noted as good examples: L. DAAE, *Matrikler over Nordiska Studerende ved fremmde Universiteter*, i (Prague, Erfurt, Rostock), Christiania, 1885; G. C. KNOD, *Deutsche Studenten in Bologna, 1289–1562*, Berlin, 1899, a biographical index to the 'Acta nationis Germanicae'; A. VARESS, *Matricula et acta Hungarorum in universitatibus Italiae Studentium*, i (Padua), Vienna and Leipzig, 1915.

We have been allowed to use an unpublished essay by Miss Hilda MOYNS in revising this chapter.]

IT has seemed advisable to bring together in a single chapter such information as we possess with respect to the numbers of the medieval universities at different times. Exact data on the subject only appear at a comparatively late period. The great northern universities kept no official records of students' names. At Bologna they are not preserved. Actual matriculation-books are only available for the latter half of our period and for some of the smaller universities. As to the population of the great parent universities at the most flourishing period of their history we possess only a few *obiter dicta* of medieval writers. It will be well first to collect the most famous of these statements and then to institute a critical inquiry as to their value.

The jurist Odofredus, writing in the middle of the thir-

CH. XIII. teenth century, tells us that at the end of the preceding century there had been 10,000 students at Bologna.[1]

Rabbanus Gauma, a Nestorian monk, puts the figures at Paris in 1287 at the favourite 30,000.[2]

Richard of Armagh, Wyclif, and Gascoigne. At Oxford we have the still more celebrated statement by Richard FitzRalph, Archbishop of Armagh, that there had once been 30,000 students there, though he admits that in his own time they had fallen to less than 6,000.[3] Some twenty years later Wyclif declares that there had once been 60,000 scholars, while now there were less than 3,000.[4] Gascoigne again tells us that he had ascertained from the 'rolls of the ancient Chancellors' that before the great plague there had been 30,000 students in Oxford.[5] No such 'rolls' now exist, and it is likely enough that what Gascoigne saw was simply a transcript of FitzRalph's plea on behalf of the university, or a conjectural estimate of a similar character, whether made by FitzRalph himself or some other chancellor.[6]

Emigration from Prague. In 1408 we have the alleged emigration of 2,000 German

[1] See above, vol. i, p. 180.

[2] *Chartul.* iii, p. xvii.

[3] *Defensorium Curatorum*, in E. Brown, *Fasciculus rerum expetendarum et fugiendarum* (1690), ii. 473.

[4] *De Ecclesia* (ed. Loserth, Wyclif Soc., 1886), p. 374.

[5] *Loci e Libro Veritatum*, ed. Thorold Rogers, p. 202.

[6] [Dr. G. G. Coulton has subjected FitzRalph's and Gascoigne's statements to careful criticism and confirms Rashdall's rejection of their figures as incredible. Dr. Coulton draws attention to a point with regard to Gascoigne's statement that was not noted by Rashdall, who relied on Professor Thorold Rogers's text, in which commas had been inserted that were not in the original. Gascoigne, who is remarking on the increase in the number of lawyers, writes: 'before the Great Pestilence in England there were . . . few lawyers in Oxford when there were 30,000 scholars at Oxford as I saw in the rolls of the ancient Chancellors of Oxford when I was Chancellor there.' Dr. Coulton points out that Gascoigne does not state that he computed the figure 30,000 from the rolls he had seen and suggests that the rolls to which Gascoigne refers must be those on which the records of degrees were kept. 'Gascoigne, naturally enough, could verify from these that fewer lawyers were created in 1300 than in 1450.' It may be presumed, as Rashdall indicates, that Gascoigne relied on FitzRalph's conjecture, or on what may have been a popular one, that once there had been 30,000 students in the university. See Dr. Coulton's article on 'Student Numbers at Medieval Oxford', in *History*, xix (1935), 324–7. See also Sir C. E. Mallet, *Hist. Univ. Oxford*, i. 138–9.]

students from Prague, a number which in some chroniclers
swells to 5,000.[1]

In estimating the value of these and similar statements two
or three *a priori* considerations should be borne in mind. In
the first place, the medieval mind was prone to exaggeration,
especially where figures are concerned. It delighted in good
round numbers, and was accustomed to make confident
statements entirely without adequate data. A familiar instance is the celebrated occasion when an English parliament
made a money-grant based upon the supposition that the
country contained more than four times the actual number
of parishes.[2] Then it will be observed that the most surprising statements as to Bologna and Oxford are not contemporary
estimates: they relate to what their authors were evidently disposed to look upon as an heroic age: the medieval was always
a *laudator temporis acti*. In the most astounding case of all—
that of Oxford—FitzRalph had a direct motive for exaggeration. He was anxious to prove that the university was being
depopulated in consequence of the kidnappings of the friars,
which made parents afraid to send their children to Oxford.
Hence the only part of the archbishop's testimony which
merits serious consideration is his statement that there were
6,000 students, or something less, in his own day,[3] and even
this is seriously discounted by Wyclif's estimate of 3,000.
The exceedingly narrow limits of the area inhabited by
scholars in medieval Oxford make even this reduced figure
somewhat difficult of acceptance. Odofredus again evidently
implies that he estimated the numbers of Bologna in his own
day at something considerably below the heroic 10,000. As to
Prague, there is reason to believe that the bulk of the expelled
Germans went to Leipzig, and Leipzig opened with a membership of less than 500. It is obvious therefore that these

---

[1] See above, vol. ii, p. 228.
[2] Stubbs, *Const. Hist.*, ed. 4
(1896), ii. 443.
[3] There is a still more extrava-
gant estimate in Rishanger for the
year 1294: 'Erat enim clericorum
numerus, quorum nomina scripta

fuerant in matriculis rectorum,
excedens .XV.M. multis fidedignis
(*sic*) hoc idem referentibus' (*Chronicon*, ed. Halliwell, Camden Soc.,
1840, p. 22). 'Rectores' must here
mean 'magistri regentes'.

CH. XIII. high figures must be very largely reduced.[1] It would be impossible of course *a priori* to say to what extent they should be reduced. But we shall be fairly safe in saying that they cannot be taken as even *prima facie* evidence for more than half the population to which they ostensibly testify.

Contemporary statements as to Oxford. With regard to Oxford it is possible to confirm this correction by more moderate contemporary statements. We have already noticed the 3,000 students who are alleged to have left Oxford in 1209.[2] In 1298 there took place one of the most memorable of the great encounters between Town and Gown in the streets of Oxford. The burgesses, in their subsequent petition against the university, allege that the attack upon them was made by '3,000 clerks or more',[3] or, according to another version, only 1,500 clerks. The occasion was a regular pitched battle between the opposing forces, at which few would be likely to be absent. At all events the burgesses would be likely to put the number as high as the known population of the university would render credible. Our conjectural halving of the archbishop's numbers as an outside limit is thus confirmed. The 3,000, if not the 1,500, would no doubt include many scholars' servants, who were always to the fore on these occasions. We have seen reason to conjecture that in 1315 the royal officials put the number of actual scholars at 1,500. We thus get 1,500 as the lowest, 3,000 as the highest estimate of the student-population of Oxford. There may well have been a slight increase between 1315 and the Black Death of 1348; but we shall be safe in assuming that the numbers could at no time have exceeded 3,000, and were probably always much below it.

Graduation at Paris. It will now be well to turn to Paris. It is not till the end of

[1] [F. Matthaesius, who has gone into this question, puts the numbers of seceders at 800 to 1,000; 'Der Auszug der deutschen Studenten aus Prag, 1409', in *Mitth. des Vereins für die Geschichte der Deutschen in Böhmen*, liii (1914), 58–111; also separately. See above, vol. ii, p. 228, n. 1.]

[2] See above, p. 33.

[3] 'Bien treis mil e plus clers de la Universite de Oxeneford' (Archives, Y. 12). [*Med. Archives Univ. Oxford*, ed. H. E. Salter (O.H.S.), i. 49, 57, 62, 64.] Another document in the same bundle has, however, 'bien mil e cink centz clers'—which illustrates the loose medieval way of dealing with numbers. [*Op. cit.* i. 60.]

the fourteenth or beginning of the fifteenth century that we CH. XIII. get actual records of the number of graduations at Paris or elsewhere. The register of the English nation, indeed, dates from 1333, but that by itself will hardly help us to an estimate of the total numbers. In the fifteenth century we have the registers of the other nations. If we confine ourselves to the nation of France,[1] we find that in the year 1450 there were conferred 156 bachelor's degrees and 111 licences. The numbers fluctuate to a surprising extent; in the year last mentioned they are exceptionally high. The year 1447 with 135 bachelors and 81 licences is a more normal one.

If we assume that four years was the average time of resi- Total dence before licence, 80 licences will represent 320 students numbers at Paris. who will eventually obtain the licence. From a comparison between the numbers of determinations and of matricula- tions at Leipzig, Paulsen estimates that between one-fourth and one-third only of those who matriculated ever took the bachelor's degree.[2] But at many of the German uni- versities a number of mere schoolboys and graduates of other universities resident in the town were placed upon the *matricula*.[3] At Paris, considering the number of students who came from other universities, it is not improbable that at least half the students who matriculated in arts must have even- tually become bachelors. 135 bachelor's degrees will represent about 270 matriculations in one year. Of these 270, 80 will proceed to the M.A. For the remaining 190 three years will be a high average residence. Thus we get 570 students who will not proceed to M.A. to be added to the 320 who will take that degree. That is to say, we get about 890 as the number of students in the French nation at one time. We may com- pute the proportion of French students to those of other nations from the fact that candidates were usually sent to be licensed in batches of eight, each of which contained three Frenchmen, two Normans, two Picards, and one Englishman

[1] Register in the Archives at the Sorbonne.

[2] *Historische Zeitschrift*, xlv. 293 sq. Only $\frac{1}{20}$ to $\frac{1}{16}$ proceeded to the licence.

[3] Grammar students are ex- cluded from the following compu- tation. If they are to be included we must add at least another 1,000, perhaps 2,000.

CH. XIII. or German.[1] If we assume that students from a distance would be rather more likely to complete their course than those from the country round Paris, it will perhaps be enough to double the number of French students to give us the whole number of students in arts at one time. That number will be some 1,700 students: 1,000 will be an outside number to add for the masters and the students of the superior faculties residing longer than the period allowed above for graduation in arts. This calculation will give us something over 2,500 students for the total membership of the university at this period.[2] A slightly higher estimate is suggested by a list of those who paid the *bursa*, a tax imposed by the university on all its members in 1464.[3] The names of about 2,300 students are actually recorded; but the manuscript is imperfect, and it is calculated that the whole list originally contained some 3,000 names. To these a small number ought possibly to be added for poor students who may have been excused payment, and for the non-graduate religious students, who were not technically members of the university, and would therefore not appear in these lists.

Paris in thirteenth century. There can then be little doubt that the academic population of Paris in the fifteenth century could not have ever exceeded some 3,500, if we include the students of the religious houses. The question now arises, 'Is there any reason to believe that at an earlier date the numbers were larger?' When we remember the numerous universities which sprang into being in the course of the fourteenth and fifteenth centuries, it is highly probable that at the end of the thirteenth and beginning of the fourteenth centuries the academic popula-

---

[1] Bulaeus, iv. 112; *Chartul.* ii, No. 1012. Sometimes the proportion could only be kept by sending up members of other nations as *Anglizati*, &c.

[2] This calculation was made before the facts mentioned in the next sentences became known to me.

[3] The document was published [from fragments found in the binding of a book] by Dr. Max Spir-gatis, *Personalverzeichniss der Pariser Universität von 1464*, Leipzig, 1888 (*Beihefte zum Centralblatt für Bibliothekswesen*, No. 1). [Thirty years later, in 1494, the German nation alone seems to have contained nearly 200 students; Ch. Jourdain, 'Un compte de la nation d'Allemagne de l'Université de Paris au xvᵉ siècle', in *Mémoires de la Société d'histoire de Paris*, i (1875).]

tion of Paris may have been considerably in excess of 3,500.[1] CH. XIII.
It is useless to conjecture the amount of this excess, but it will
be quite safe to assume that the students of Paris can never
at any time have exceeded 6,000 or 7,000. A number not
enormously short of this is suggested by the fact that in a
single year towards the end of the thirteenth century (about
1284) at least 400 licences were conferred in the faculty of
arts[2]—a number far exceeding anything that we meet within
the period of extant registers.[3]

For the fifteenth century at Oxford we get two sources Oxford in
of information: (1) lists of determinations and inceptions; century.
(2) lists of halls. The usual number of determinations in the
earlier part of the century was about 40, of inceptions about
20. Allowing that a third proceed to B.A., we shall get 120
matriculations in the year. The period of residence required
for determination seems, however, to have been practically

[1] As early as 1316 we find the
complaint 'nimium est illa scolarium multitudo contracta et
Parisiense studium incredibiliter
diminutum' (*Chartul.* ii, No. 729).
Of course, allowance must be made
for the medieval belief in a Golden
Age.
[2] At S. Geneviève alone. *Chartul.* i, No. 515, p. 616. But as the
faculty was at feud with the Chancellor of Notre Dame, it is not
likely there were many candidates
at the 'inferius examen'. From the
same document we learn that there
were about 120 regents. The statement that 4,000 clerks (not necessarily all students) were present
at the purgation of William of S.
Amour, deserves to be noticed.
Ibid., No. 256. High numbers are
also suggested by the statute of
1288, forbidding the examiners of
determinants to examine more than
forty-eight in one month. Bulaeus,
iii. 484; *Chartul.* ii, No. 544.
Another valuable source of information is supplied by the rolls
of supplicants for benefices presented from time to time to the

Holy See. In 1349, for instance,
the roll contains the names of 502
masters of arts, together with 32
masters of theology, 17 of decrees,
and 46 of medicine—597 masters
in all (*Chartul.* ii, Nos. 1162-5).
Unfortunately we do not know
what was the maximum standing
of these masters. Hence it is impossible to determine with any
certainty what number of resident
students they represent.
[3] 'D'après des calculs précis,
c'est à près de cinq mille qu'on
peut évaluer, vers 1350, le nombre
des maîtres et des écoliers—six
cents maîtres et quatre mille
écoliers—mais vraisemblablement,
dans la première moitié du XIIIe
siècle, il ne dépassait pas huit à neuf
cents' (Gréard, *Nos adieux à la
vieille Sorbonne*, p. 14). The first
part of this statement agrees fairly
with my own estimate (if the Grammarians are excluded); for the
thirteenth century I should suggest
a much higher figure. [See Additional Note at the end of this chapter.]

CH. XIII. a good deal longer than at Paris during the same period. Allowing six years for the sixth who incept, four for a sixth who only determine, and three for the rest, we shall get 520 students. If we add 300 for the students in religious houses, the masters, and the students of the superior faculties residing longer than the time required for graduation in arts, we shall get 820 for the total numbers. The number of halls existing in 1438 suggests a slightly higher figure. There were at this time seventy-one halls or students' houses in Oxford.[1] Considering that every house occupied by a single rich scholar and his family would appear in this list, ten will perhaps be a sufficiently high figure to take for their average population.[2] This would give us some 700 students, to which we may add perhaps 300 for the monastic and collegiate scholars.[3] We shall thus get 1,000 as the probable number of masters and scholars. In this very year 1438 the university presented a petition to Parliament in which they declare that of the 'many

[1] *Mun. Acad.* ii. 519 *sq.* [*Reg. Cancell. Oxon.*, *1434–1469*, ed. H. E. Salter (O.H.S.), i. 21–2, 39–41, 102–4, 123–5, 214–16, 247–50, 284–7, 337–9, 403–6; ii. 1–4, 48–51, 85–9, 291–2, 321–2. Dr. Salter estimates 'that the number of genuine halls was not more than 70 in 1435 and not more than 60 in 1470'; *ibid.* ii. 359.]

[2] The statutes of Ingolstadt restrict the number in each hall to eight or ten, with two poor students as servitors. Prantl, ii. 74. But at Rostock there might be thirty or, if there were two regents, forty. Westphalen, *Mon. ined. rer. Germ.* iv, c. 1027. The Oxford University Register for 1544 (f. 17 b) shows that Hart Hall paid an increased rent if its numbers amounted to thirty. But it is probable that Hart Hall was now larger than the average medieval hall. [Dr. H. E. Salter has arrived at a rather higher figure for the average complement of an Oxford hall. 'It is not impossible', he writes, 'that the halls of Artists contained on an average

20 members or more, while the halls of Legists had only 5 or 6.' He gives the total average as about 12. See his article, 'An Oxford Hall in 1424', in *Essays in History presented to R. L. Poole*, pp. 432–4, and his article on 'The Medieval University of Oxford', in *History*, xiv (1929), p. 59. An analysis of the list for 1438 and the similar lists contained in the Chancellor's Register does not confirm Rashdall's conjecture that these lists of halls included the houses occupied by rich scholars and their families. In making statistical use of these lists allowance, however, must be made for the inclusion of some halls that had become vacant, and of some that were annexes to larger halls. See *Reg. Cancell. Oxon.*, *1434–1469*, ed. H. E. Salter, ii. 358.]

[3] Allowing for a small number of 'Fellow-commoners' or 'Commoners'. There is no reason to believe that the system prevailed to any great extent at this date.

thousands of students who are reported to have existed in a CH. XIII. former age, hardly one thousand remained'.[1] We shall be allowing its maximum weight to such rhetoric if we take it as evidence of some considerable diminution in the numbers of Oxford.[2] The growing popularity of Cambridge would by itself make this probable. But when we have given its utmost weight to this consideration, these fifteenth-century data will be sufficient to make us feel that in giving 3,000 as a maximum for the fourteenth century, we were probably allowing a very handsome margin. The conclusions to which we have come in regard to the more famous Paris, which drew its students from an immensely wider area than Oxford, are another reason for reducing this figure.

It has already been intimated that with regard to the German German universities of the late fourteenth and fifteenth univer- sities. centuries, we have data for a tolerably accurate estimate of numbers. Paulsen arrives at the following results for certain selected periods at which the best information happens to be available. If anything, his estimates are probably too low. On the other hand it must be remembered that they must often include every sort of student down to the merest grammar-boy:

Prague   1,027 (1380–89).

Vienna   933 (second half of sixteenth century).

[1] 'Pauci aut nulli ad uniuersi- tatem accedendi habent volunta- tem; unde fit quod aule atque hospicia obserata vel verius diruta sunt, ianue atque hostia scholarum et studiorum clausa, et de tot milli- bus studencium que fama est istuc in priori etate fuisse non (MS. nam) iam unum supersit: at illi qui sane supersunt tedium quam maximum vite habent quod nullum fructum, nullum denique honorem post tan- tum studii sudorem consecuti fuerint' (from MS. Letter-book F, f. 46 a: printed in Peshall, p. 142). [Epistolae Academicae, ed. H. An- stey (O.H.S.), i. 156. The petition was presented to Archbishop Chichele and the Convocation of the Province of Canterbury, and not, as Rashdall states, to Par- liament.]

[2] [It may be learned from the rentals of the Hospital of S. John the Baptist, and from those of the Abbey of Oseney, that there was a steady decrease in the population of Oxford from the end of the thir- teenth century and a steady drop in the rent of houses, excepting some sign of a check in the decline in 1346, and during the period from 1366 to the end of the century. See Dr. Salter's detailed analysis of the evidence to be derived from the rentals of the Hospital of S. John the Baptist. Cartul. Hosp. S. John Bapt. (O.H.S.), iii. 28–31.]

CH. XIII.

Leipzig   662 (in 1472).
Heidelberg 285 (1386–1550).
Erfurt   506 (to c. 1450).
Cologne   852 (1450–79).
Rostock   350–466.
Greifswald 103 (1465–78).
Freiburg   143 (1460–1500).
Basel   280 (1460–80).
Basel   177 (1480–1500).[1]
Tübingen   233 (1477–1527).
Ingolstadt 220 (Foundation . . . –1493).[2]

[Some conclusions reached by Eulenberg may be set beside these figures. He considered that on the average a German student did not reside for more than a year and nine months. The majority took no degree. Some two-fifths became bachelors, and about one-twentieth studied in the higher faculties.[3] Taking the average period of residence and the numbers actually enrolled, and allowing a margin of error for omissions, he determined the average yearly attendance at ten German universities from the date of foundation until 1540 as follows:

Leipzig   504.
Erfurt   427.
Wittenberg 420.
Köln   388.
Ingolstadt 296.
Rostock   222.
Heidelberg 219.
Tübingen   161.
Freiburg   147.
Greifswald 84.

[1] [For the Basel matriculations see above, vol. ii, p. 275.]
[2] Paulsen, loc. cit., p. 296 sq.
[3] [At Freiburg between 1450 and 1465 the percentage of bachelors to the total enrolment varied from 25 to 39 per cent., of masters from 12 to 2 per cent. The total number of promotions to the degree of bachelor at Heidelberg between 1391 and 1454 was 2,001, or 22 per cent. of the matriculations. The total, 1454 to 1523, was 3,742, or 42 per cent. of the matriculations (Eulenberg, in Conrad's Jahrbuch (1897), p. 499).]

The estimate by averages conceals the local fluctuations in CH. XIII. numbers and the general effect of the disturbance caused by the Reformation, but its results are nearer the truth than those reached by Paulsen.]

The results of this investigation may be thus summarized: Results.

(1) It is improbable that the numbers of either Bologna or Paris can ever have exceeded some 6,000 or 7,000. At Paris at least it is pretty certain that this limit was approached during its period of highest repute—say, the beginning of the fourteenth century. (If all the grammar-boys of the city were added, we should possibly have to add some 2,000 more.) About the middle of the fifteenth century, however, the number at that university was probably nearer 3,000. In Italy the growth of new universities was so rapid and extensive and the decline in the reputation of Bologna so serious, that neither Bologna nor any one of its rivals can ever have approached the numbers of Paris after an early period of the thirteenth century.

(2) The maximum number at Oxford was something between 1,500 and 3,000.[1] By about 1438 the numbers had fallen to under 1,000.

(3) The numbers of Prague before the German migration in 1409 may have been 1,500 or more: Vienna and Leipzig may at one time have had 1,000. The numbers of the other German universities during the fifteenth century varied between 80 and 1,000, including grammarians.

(4) We may add that the population of other minor universities in France and elsewhere, wherever ascertainable, is always numbered by hundreds and not by thousands: at Toulouse alone there may have been as many as 2,000.[2]

---

[1] These calculations were completed before I noticed that Prof. Thorold Rogers describes the 30,000 as 'ten times more than the possible truth' (*Six Centuries of Work and Wages*, 1884, p. 167), while more recently he says, 'it is probable that the Colleges, Halls, and monastic institutions contained at least 1500 inmates' in 1380-1:

Oxford City Documents (O.H.S., 1891), p. 7. I am glad to find my estimate on the whole confirmed by a writer who knew medieval life so well. The civic population he estimates from the returns to the poll-tax as between 3,000 and 4,000 [1895].

[2] Above, vol. ii, p. 171. [The *rotuli* of some of these universities

CH. XIII. At the same time the relatively high and well-ascertained numbers of these and other less famous *studia*, at a time when universities were many, go to confirm the probability that when Paris was the sole or principal place of higher education for a large part of Europe its numbers cannot have fallen *very* far short of 6,000 or 7,000. This line of argument becomes particularly convincing when we compare Paris with Oxford. Oxford was recruited mainly, if not almost entirely, from the British Islands, and there was another, though considerably less populous, English university within a hundred miles of it. If we compare the population or the number of benefices and other posts to be filled by university men in England with the population or benefices in the enormously larger and more populous area from which Paris drew her students, it is probable that if there were ever anything like 3,000 students at Oxford, that figure must be, at the very least, doubled to represent the population of Paris at the height of its fame.

Many converging lines of evidence thus lead us to much the same result. We can say with absolute confidence that there can never have been 10,000 students at Paris: there may possibly have been 7,000 without the grammarians; there must have been something like 5,000, a limit which cannot well have been reached by any other university except perhaps Bologna in the course of the thirteenth century.

Additional Note on the Numbers at Paris

[The estimates of numbers at Paris are necessarily very unsatisfactory, for the evidence is generally contained in documents written in the heat of some crisis or occasioned by some special event. They are exceptional in themselves and are not logically comparable with each other. For example, in normal times an attendance of 200 at contain lists of all grades of students and masters, and, though these lists in all probability were by no means complete, they give a better idea than the Paris lists of graduates of the university population. In 1384 the rolls give 579 names for Angers, 444 (50 of whom were masters) for Montpellier, 1,287 (including 295 students of grammar) for Toulouse. In 1378 Cahors records 58, and in 1394 Perpignan records 207 artists: see Fournier, *Statuts*, i, No. 697 (Toulouse), ii, No. 1445 (Cahors), No. 1488 (Perpignan), iii, Nos. 1897–8 (Angers); the same, *Hist. de la science de droit*, &c., pp. 480–3 (Montpellier). For the figures in Spanish universities cf. above, vol. ii, p. 88, n. 6.]

congregation was exceptional, for normally only regent masters were summoned. But any master who had taken the necessary oath to observe the statutes, &c., *could* be summoned, and when we find enormous numbers taking part in university business, as in 1394 and 1406, we cannot assume that we are dealing with the normal population of masters, regents, and non-regents, in Paris. Nor, as Rashdall points out, can we assume that the numbers on the *rotuli*, e.g. the 790 masters of arts in 1403 (*Chartul.* iii, p. xvi), include graduates of the same standing, actually resident in the university. Hence we are inclined to reject Denifle's view (*ibid.*, p. xvii) that 10,000 *supposita* are not unthinkable, if by this he means the academic population. Rashdall's tentative 5,000 is a more likely maximum, even at the most crowded period.

The statement that 400 students received the licence in arts in 1289 (*Chartul.* i, No. 515, p. 616) comes in the long defence made to the Pope by the artists' proctor against the charges of the chancellor. The chancellor had accused the masters of arts of running about the *hospitia* to find young students and persuade them to take the licence at S. Geneviève. The reply was that this had been a very exceptional year. Not for twenty years had there been such a good list, and even of the alleged 400, not more than 120 had not taken the inferior examination. Obviously the figures were round numbers, and the circumstances unusual. In the same document it appears that at various times the chancellor had estimated the number of regent masters in the faculty at 300, 26, and 120! The faculty's spokesman accepts the last figure, 120 (*nam sunt tot vel circiter, ibid.*, p. 610; cf. p. 608). He also emphasized the intention of the faculty to insist on determination, and regarded 60 determiners in one year as a deplorably low number (p. 613). Here we seem to get near the facts for the time when the university was reaching the height of its influence. Four years later (1288) it was decreed that the examiners should not examine more than 48 bachelors in one month at S. Geneviève (*Chartul.* ii, No. 544). In 1338 the number was reduced to 16, of whom not more than 8 were to be heard at one time (*videlicet in qualibet auditione octo*; No. 1012). Since the number of *auditiones* in the year varied from 3 to 6 during the three months when examinations were held, the average may well have been lower; the *acta* of the English nation in the fourteenth century definitely contemplate fewer than 6 *auditiones* and the possibility of fewer than 8 candidates or even of none at all (see the references to the *Auctarium* collected by Boyce, *The English-German Nation*, p. 103 and notes).

This is the background against which we must set the most vivid statement which has come down to us about the numbers at Paris. It appears in the notes of a famous oration delivered by Jean Petit in a congregation held on 16 December 1406 (A. Coville, *Jean Petit*, pp. 73-80). After referring to an assembly in which 69 masters in

CH. XIII. theology had been present, he turned to the argument of Pierre d'Ailly that the question at issue (the recognition of Benedict XIII) was not a matter for the faculties of arts and medicine:

'Et quant ad ce, il a parlé que la Faculté de medecine n'a point à se entremettre en ceste matere, je m'en mervielle, et aussi de la Faculté des ars. Car premierement la Faculté des ars est teille qu'il y a bien mille maistres. C'est cy derriere me dist II mille.— Au mains en y a bien mille, de quoi il en y a bien deulx ou trois cens gradués en aultre science, comme bacheliers en theologie, en medecine, en droiz civilz et canons et en y a comme ces sont plus gradués, un theologien est de la Faculté des ars jusques à ce qu'il ait le bonnet sur la teste; le bonnet ne li amene point la science.[1] L'en parle a moy ci par derrier: il a grant paour que je ne l'oublie. Il me dist et dist vrai qu'il en y a moult crotés qui sont trés suffisans et bon clercs. En poureté croit la science et plus tost que en richesse. Il en y a des bacheliers cursoires à qui je m'en vois quant j'ay aucune cose à faire, qui y voient par aventure plus cler que beaucoup d'autres qui ont bien grant nom. Il y en a moult de bons clercs qui ne sont point maistres. Guignecourt,[2] qui estoit reputé le meilleur clerc du monde—il demourait au college de Charbonne—il ne fut oncques que bachelier cursoire.' (Coville, *op. cit.*, p. 80.)]

[1] [Cf. James of Dinant, *Summa de dictatoris officio*, ch. xix, in *Analecta Reginensia*, ed. A. Wilmart, Città del Vaticano, 1931, p. 148 note: 'Non credatur quod magistralis catreda istam solum modo conferat dignitatem . . . Nam et honor predictus debetur peritis quibuslibet in predictis scienciis, licet non ascenderint catredam magistralem.']

[2] [Jean de Guignicourt of the Sorbonne, master of arts 1361, bachelor in theology 1371, chancellor of Notre Dame 1386.]

CHAPTER XIV

STUDENT-LIFE IN THE MIDDLE AGES

[Throughout this chapter, and especially in the later sections, Rashdall spoke his mind freely and frankly. We have here his deliberate judgement on the medieval university and also on some fundamental issues in medieval history. These passages give the informed opinion of an English scholar in 1895 and we have left them without comment.

Although much has been written on medieval student-life since 1895, Rashdall's cool and racy description fortunately requires little revision. It would be possible to add a great many more details and to elaborate his arguments, but upon the whole his work stands. Extensive annotation would darken counsel. Moreover, those who wish to pursue the matter further would be better advised to read KAUFMANN, HASKINS, and ZACCAGNINI (to mention the more important scholars whom we have noted below) for themselves. BOYCE'S *English-German Nation* supplements Rashdall's discussion of the relief given to poor scholars in some important respects, and contains a good account of feasts at Paris. Marcel POËTE, *Une vie de cité: Paris*, deals to some extent with student life, mainly as illustrated by medieval poetry, e.g. i. 185–96 (Paris, 1924). G. REYNIER, *La Vie universitaire dans l'ancienne Espagne*, Paris and Toulouse, 1902, may be mentioned; also an article by J. ROBB, 'Student Life in St. Andrews before 1450', in the *Scottish Historical Review*, ix (1911–12), 347–60. R. S. RAIT, *Life in a Medieval University*, Cambridge, 1912, is a pleasant introduction. A delightful sketch by C. H. HASKINS, *The Rise of Universities*, New York, 1923, should be read. Perhaps the most helpful guide to the background of schools and to educational ideas, &c., is R. LIMMER'S *Bildungszustände und Bildungsideen des 13. Jahrhunderts*, Munich and Berlin, 1928, with its bibliography.

The German literature on the subject is much the most extensive. Since 1895 German learning has expressed itself in great encyclopaedic works, such as the 'Kulturgeschichte' of G. GRUPP and G. STEINHAUSEN and E. MICHAEL's *Geschichte des deutschen Volkes von dreizehnten Jahrhundert bis zum Ausgang des Mittelalters* (see vol. ii). These deal with university life, as, for a later period, does J. JANSSEN in his *Geschichte des deutschen Volkes* (vol. vii). F. SCHULZE and P. SZYMANK, *Das deutsche Studententum von der ältesten Zeit bis zum Gegenwart*, Leipzig, 1910, contains a chapter on the Middle Ages. For further references cf. Dahlmann-Waitz, ed. 9, Leipzig, 1931, pp. 206 *sqq.*

Rashdall rightly did not deal with the *goliardi* or wandering scholars who in recent years have attracted so much attention. The masters in the schools had no use for the vagrants. Commenting on Micah i. 13, 'Tumultus quadrigae stuporis habitanti Lachis: principium peccati est filiae Sion', Stephen Langton identifies Lachis with the roving spirit which demoralizes monks and scholars. They were gradually suppressed and deprived of the tonsure in the thirteenth century: see the chapter on the *ordo vagorum* in Helen WADDELL, *The Wandering Scholars*, London, 1927, with the bibliography and appendix; also PAETOW, *A Guide to the Study of Medieval History*, ed. 2, pp. 489, 490; HASKINS, *The Rise of*

CHAP. XIV. *Universities*, pp. 111–20; cf. G. Perna, *La vita goliardica nel medioevo e i privilegi di Federico II*, ed. 2, Naples, 1930. For Goliardic poetry see RABY, *History of Secular Latin Poetry in the Middle Ages*, Oxford, 1934, pp. 171–227. The French, German, and Italian literature is duly noted in these books.

Wandering, it is needless to add, was not confined to the irresponsible Goliards. Masters and scholars often passed from university to university, especially in Italy and later in Germany. The well-known medical scholar, Dino del Garbo (d. 1327), taught at Bologna, Padua, Florence, and Siena (R. DAVIDSOHN, *Geschichte von Florenz*, IV. iii. 172–3). Many instances could be given. The best-known wandering scholar, for he wrote an account of his wanderings, is Johannes Butzbach (1478–1526), but he was not typical of the student who moved from university to university, for his travels as a boy (1487–1500) did not bring him much in touch with university circles: see *Chronica eines fahrenden Schülers, oder Wanderbüchlein des Johannes Butzbach*, translated from the Latin manuscript by D. J. BECKER, Regensburg, 1869, reprinted Leipzig, 1923; also P. S. ALLEN, *Age of Erasmus*, Oxford, 1914, *passim*, and Malcolm LETTS in the *English Historical Review*, xxxii (1917), 22–33. Wandering from one university to another became more frequent in the humanistic age; cp. ALLEN, *op. cit.*, ch. iv. Erasmus himself was a wandering scholar: 'Non est in vicio commutare locum, sed perperam commutare vicium est. Nec est virtus diu mansisse in eodem loco, sed cum laude vixisse' (*Opus epistolarum*, ed. P. S. Allen, iii. 267).

In this connexion reference may be made to the students' guides which, though written in the sixteenth century, throw light upon medieval traditions. For example, in 1506, Thomas PENTZELT, of Leipzig, issued a little quarto of sixteen leaves, *Perutilis studendi modus* (Leipzig, 1506); and Horatius LUTIUS compiled for Italian students a more elaborate *Tractatus de privilegiis scholarium* (Padua, 1564) which deals with legal status, lectures, the rules for the copying of text-books by the authorized scribes, &c.]

I PROPOSE in this chapter to discuss a number of miscellaneous matters connected with the daily life of the medieval student which have not hitherto been dealt with. I shall confine myself for the most part to the universities of the northern type. In the life of the Italian law-student, living in his own way in his own hired house, there was no doubt much less that was distinctive and characteristic as compared with the life of the churchman or citizen of the surrounding world; and at all events the materials for the illustration of his life and habits are far less abundant than those which are available for the student-life of Paris, Oxford, and the German universities.[1]

[1] [Reference may be made to G. Zaccagnini, *La Vita dei Maestri e degli Scolari nello Studio di Bologna nei Secoli XIII e XIV*, Geneva, 1926.]

If we want to realize what manner of man or boy the medieval student actually was, we shall have completely to lay aside
most of the associations derived from modern universities,
colleges and schools of every description, whether in our
own country or on the Continent. When we are told that the
medieval student was younger than the modern undergraduate, we are apt to liken him to the modern schoolboy. When
we are told that he was regarded as a clerk, we are tempted to
compare him with the modern seminarist. When we are told
that some students begged, we are in danger of supposing
that the medieval student was usually a pauper sprung from
the lowest social grade. To remove these and similar misconceptions will be the object of this concluding chapter. If the
reproduction of the medieval student-life is a task which
strains to the uttermost all our powers of historical imagination, it is one which will richly repay the effort that it demands.
He who understands the life of a medieval university will
have taken no unimportant step towards understanding the
medieval Church and the medieval world. In speaking of
historical imagination, however, it may be desirable to add
that it is the reader's own imagination upon which the strain
will fall. The present writer has neither the power nor
the inclination to emulate the brilliant, if sometimes misleading, pictures which have been painted by several great
writers on medieval university life. His aim will be to bring
together facts and to allow the reader to paint his picture for
himself.[1]

Previous Education of the Medieval Student

The first question which it seems necessary to ask relates
to the equipment with which the average student entered
his university course. And that question is easily answered.
The lectures were given in Latin. Before the student could
profitably attend university lectures, he must have learned to
read, write, and understand such Latin as was used in the

[1] It will, however, occasionally
be necessary in the following chapter to make generalizations, the full
evidence for which cannot be exhibited in the notes.

CHAP. XIV. schools. Latin, it must be remembered, was not merely the language of the ordinary lecture-room, but theoretically at least of ordinary student-life. The freshmen must have been able to talk some Latin as well as to understand it. It is of course difficult to say to what extent the practice of the average student corresponded with the theory. There was no such thing as an entrance examination, except in the colleges; and the want of proper grounding in the Latin language constituted one of the most glaring defects of the medieval system. Still, in the first half of our period, when the universities were cosmopolitan, conversational Latin must have been almost a necessity of life to the university student. Even students from different provinces of the same country could hardly have understood each other without its aid;[1] and in the later period we find Latin-speaking in college and hall strictly enforced by statute. A statute of Paris makes the ability of a petitioner to state his case before the rector in Latin, without any 'interposition of French words', a test of his *bona-fide* studentship.[2] The certificate of 'scholarity' was to be refused if the applicant's Latinity proved unequal to the strain. So the founder of a chantry[3] which included provision for two scholars provides that one of them was to be sent to the university when he could 'read, sing, and construe well and compose twenty-four verses on one subject in one day'. These two illustrations will perhaps supply us with a sufficient idea of the attainments of the average student upon

[1] Englishmen then pronounced Latin in the continental way. See the testimony of Dr. Caius, in whose lifetime the melancholy change took place. *Hist. Cantab.*, p. 124.

[2] Bulaeus, iv. 218; *Chartul.* ii, No. 881. [An incident in the life of Pope John XXII illustrates this point. Jacques Duèse or D'Euse was a Cahorsin. In his youth he spent several years at the schools of Paris and Orleans; but he did not learn to speak the French of the Île-de-France. In 1323, as Pope, he was unable to make out a letter from King Charles IV of France and had it translated into Latin; N. Valois in *Hist. litt. de la France*, xxxiv (1915), 394.]

[3] This chantry or college, consisting of a chaplain and two scholars, was founded in the church of S. Bredgar (dioc. Canterbury). For admission to the college itself, the boys must 'competenter legere et cantare', and be not less than seven years of age. *Lit. Cantuar.*, ed. J. B. Sheppard, iii. 17. Elementary medieval education began with the Latin psalter.

entering the university proper as a student in arts. At the CHAP. XIV. same time it is probable that there was a residuum of men who understood even less of the lectures which they attended, or were supposed to attend, than an ignorant monk or 'hedge-priest' did of the psalter which he daily muttered. We have already seen that large numbers of students— probably a majority—never proceeded even to the lowest degree; there was no compulsion (except in the colleges) to enter for any examinations whatever, and numbers must have left the university knowing little more than when they entered it.

While we are upon the subject of medieval Latin, it may Medieval Latin. be well to remove some popular misconceptions. Among the students of a university and among the clergy generally (in so far as they spoke Latin at all) much villainous Latin was no doubt talked, just as much villainous French is or was encouraged by the rule of French-speaking in English 'Seminaries for Young Ladies'. But the Latin which was written by the theologian or historian, the Latin of the secretary's letter or the episcopal ordinance, was not so bad as is commonly supposed by those who have only heard it abused. The period of gross ignorance, of wrong inflexions and barbarous constructions, had passed away long before the beginning of the university era. Both the excellences and the defects of thirteenth-century or fourteenth-century Latin were due to the fact that Latin was still a living language, though its use was confined to the clerks and lawyers. J. S. Mill has rightly praised the schoolmen for their unrivalled capacity in the invention of technical terms. The Latin language, originally rigid, inflexible, poor in vocabulary and almost incapable of expressing a philosophical idea, became in the hands of medieval thinkers flexible, subtle, and elastic. And this enrichment of the language, which has had such immensely important effects upon the tongues of modern Europe, was carried on not only in the schools by the sophists and theologians, but (no doubt with less wholly satisfactory results) in the epistles of the ecclesiastic and even in the conversation of the ordinary schoolboy, until Latin as a living

CHAP. XIV. language was killed by the Ciceronian pedantry of the sixteenth or seventeenth century. The barbarism which shocks the modern scholar in the pages of the average medieval scribe consists in the introduction of new words, of vernacular idioms and combinations, and above all of new forms or derivatives of good Latin words demanded by the exigencies of new ideas, rather than in the violation of the ordinary rules of syntax or accidence.[1] There were of course different degrees of knowledge or ignorance even among the educated men of the Middle Ages. The average 'artist' heartily despised the mere grammarian or schoolmaster: the niceties of Latin syntax were beneath his notice: punctilious accuracy in such matters seemed unworthy of a philosophic mind. Consequently he wrote worse Latin than the monastic historian who perhaps loved his Virgil better than his Angelical Doctor. But still the average Oxford graduate could probably write Latin which was rarely adorned by the kind of blunders that the average modern passman will make in every third line. And the Latin of serious medieval books after the eleventh century is generally correct and its syntax

---

[1] [The most useful guide to the literature on this subject is L. J. Paetow, *A Guide to the Study of Medieval History*, revised edition, London, 1931, pp. 485–93. Instead of a list of books and articles we will cite two texts. In his comment on Psalm xxxvi S. Augustine says, 'Quid ad nos, quid grammatici velint? Melius in barbarismo nostro vos intellegitis quam in nostra disertudine vos deserti eritis'. J. Martin adds a significant criticism: 'aber gerade das pointierte Wortspiel disertudine—deserti zeight klar, wie wenig er sich von dem Pompe der heidnischen Beredsamkeit freizumachen verstand' (J. Martin, 'Volkslatein, Schriftlatein, Kirchenlatein', in the *Historisches Jahrbuch*, xli (1921), 213). The other passage comes from Walter Daniel's life of Ailred, who died in 1167, a level-headed Northumbrian: 'artes quos liberales uocant auctores iste magis palpando sensit quam bibendo gustauit, quantum attinet ad erudicionem illam que ore magistri discipuli pectus ingreditur. . . . Nec tamen ad modum rusticus in pronunciando sermonem innotuit, cui et diserto suppeciit splendissima et non parue glorie uenustam eloquiam habundauit. Habuit autem ad manum facile dicere quod uellet et ita proferre ut deceret' (F. M. Powicke, *Ailred of Rievaulx and his biographer Walter Daniel*, Manchester, 1922, pp. 90, 91; from Jesus College, Cambridge, MS. Q.B. 7, ff. 67 d, 68 a). Ailred, it should be added, had read a good deal. One of his writings was suggested by Cicero's *De amicitia*.]

free from most of the mistakes which are taken cognizance of CHAP. XIV.
at Responsions.[1]

In the universities (as has been seen) grammar formed one The
grammar
of the subjects of examination for degrees in arts; and students schools in
of that faculty were still (in the earlier part of their course) towns.
required to attend grammar lectures concurrently with the
course of logic and philosophy.[2] There were, however, in
every university town, as in other important places, grammar
schools proper, intended for the elementary instruction of
young boys and quite distinct from the schools of the faculty
of arts. In many cases, either by usurpation or special privilege, the university acquired jurisdiction over these schools.
This was the case in most German universities. In others
they remained under the ecclesiastical inspection to which
thay had been subject before the rise of the university corporations. Thus at Paris the chanter of Notre Dame retained
his control over the 'petty schools', including all elementary
or grammar schools in the city, whether boys' schools kept
by a master or girls' schools kept by a mistress.[3] There was,
of course, a special cathedral grammar school for the choir-
boys under his immediate supervision, but he also granted
licences to independent masters or mistresses (the former
might or might not be university graduates), and made rules
for the conduct of the schools, just as the chancellor had
done in early days for the schools of theology and arts.
At Cambridge the grammar schools were under the immediate control of an official who has caused great perplex-
ity to the antiquaries of that university—the 'magister

[1] There are, of course, a few exceptions. The inferior writers do
not distinguish between 'alter' and
'alius', between 'ejus' and 'suus',
and though 'ut' takes a subjunctive,
the niceties of that mood are not
appreciated, &c. The use of 'unus'
as an article, and of 'cum' in place
of an instrumental ablative, is
characteristic of the worst, and
especially of the latest, medieval
Latin.

[2] At least at Paris. There is some

reason for thinking that Oxford
Latin was worse than Parisian.

[3] Jourdain, Nos. 673, 738. A list
of 42 masters and 21 mistresses
licensed by the chanter is given by
Félibien, *Hist. de Paris*, iii. 449.
'Mixed' schools were not allowed
withoutspecial dispensations. *Ibid.*,
p. 447. Joli was Chanter of Paris,
and wrote his *Écoles épiscopales* to
defend the rights of the chantership.
Cf. *Chartul.* iii, Nos. 1237, 1713.

CHAP. XIV. glomeriae' who was appointed by and responsible to the archdeacon of Ely.[1]

Grammar schools at Oxford. At Oxford also it is probable that the archdeacon had originally, as part of his general ecclesiastical jurisdiction, a control over the grammar schools;[2] but here the chancellor of the university was too powerful for him to retain it. At the beginning of the fourteenth century we find the university legislating for the grammar schools, and appointing two masters from among its own graduates to superintend them. These 'superintendent masters' were remunerated by a tax levied upon the earnings of the inferior class of ordinary grammar masters.[3] Medieval dialectic brought even grammar into the region of debatable matter; and the masters of grammar were required to attend disputations in their faculty every Friday and periodically to observe a 'convenite', i.e. a kind of primitive Head Masters' conference held twice a term, to discuss matters of professional interest.[4] Their pupils were brought within the privilege of the university by being nominally enrolled in the *matricula* of a master of arts if their own master was not a graduate.[5] Otherwise they were not what

[1] See G. Peacock, *Observations on the Statutes*, App. A, and above, p. 288.

[2] I infer this from the fact that the first dated statute for the grammar schools (A.D. 1306) was passed 'In presencia venerabilium virorum domini archidiaconi Oxonie sacre theologie professoris videlicet magistri Gilberti de Segrave, et magistri Gilberti de Mideltona, tunc officialis domini episcopi Lincolniensis' (*Mun. Acad.* i. 85, 86). [*Stat. Antiq. Univ. Oxon.*, ed. S. Gibson, p. 22.]

[3] [*Stat. Antiq. Univ. Oxon.*, ed. S. Gibson, p. lxxxvi, n. 3.]

[4] *Mun. Acad.* i. 85–7; ii. 437–43. [*Stat. Antiq. Univ. Oxon.*, ed. S. Gibson, pp. 21–3. See also *ibid.*, p. lxxxv, n. 3.] An endowment was left for the payment of the superintendents in 1322. Document printed by A. G.

Little in *Eng. Hist. Review*, vi. 153. [Cf. *Med. Arch. Univ. Oxford*, ed. H. E. Salter (O.H.S.), i. 278–9.] This office was afterwards amalgamated with that of the 'magistri scolarum Augustiniensium', and the salary transferred to them. *Mun. Acad.* i. 363. [*Stat. Antiq. Univ. Oxon.*, ed. S. Gibson, p. 300, by statute dated 18 May 1492.] These were the masters who presided over the disputations of bachelors at the Austin convent. As misunderstandings have arisen on the subject, it should be mentioned that the Austin Friars never had anything to do with these disputations beyond lending their schools.

[5] *Mun. Acad.* ii. 445. [*Stat. Antiq. Univ. Oxon.*, ed. S. Gibson, pp. lxxxvi–lxxxvii, 173–4. Rashdall has misread the regulations concerning the enrolment of boys

we should describe as members of the university. The CHAP. XIV.
masters had no seat in Convocation: the boys were not keeping terms in any of the recognized faculties of the university.
The only difference between the position of their schools and
that of grammar schools elsewhere was that their masters
were licensed by the university authorities instead of by some
ecclesiastical dignitary. Sooner or later, however, it would Degrees in
appear that the process of admitting the masters was assimi- grammar.
lated to that attending admission to the regular degrees of the
university. In the fifteenth century we hear of regular examinations for the degree. In the sixteenth century there was a
bachelor's degree as well as a master's; and solemn inceptions
took place at which the master received as a symbol of his
office, not a book like masters of the other faculties, but
two to him far more important academical instruments—a
'palmer' and a birch, and thereupon entered upon the discharge of the most fundamental and characteristic part of his
official duties by flogging a boy 'openlye in the Scolys'.
Having paid a groat to the bedel for the birch and a similar
sum to the boy 'for hys labour', the inceptor became a fully
accredited master in grammar. When the mastership of
grammar had become a kind of inferior degree of the university, it was sometimes sought for by schoolmasters in other
places as an honorary distinction. These men were not necessarily required to reside in the university. Schoolmasters of
a certain standing were allowed to come up and take the
degree after performing some exercise prescribed to them by
the university. The exercise generally consisted in writing
100 verses in praise of the university. Had the ambition to
take these degrees in grammar been widely diffused, the
demand for whipping-boys might have pressed rather hardly

attending grammar schools in Oxford. It was the regent masters in
grammar who were required to
keep these lists of names; and any
teacher of grammar in Oxford who
was not a regent in the subject had
to enter the names of his pupils on
the roll of a qualified regent.] It is
interesting to note that some of

these boys were boarders in the
grammar masters' houses (commensales). For grammar degrees
at Vienna cf. above, vol. ii, p. 243.
[For the provision made for the
Merton College grammar-boys see
A. F. Leach, *The Schools of Medieval England*, pp. 171–4, 195–7.]

CHAP. XIV. upon the youth of Oxford; but very few of them are mentioned in the University Register.[1]

Grammar schools outside universities. There is no reason to believe that boys came to attend these inferior grammar schools in the university towns except from the immediate neighbourhood. The majority of scholars must have learned reading, writing, and the rudiments of grammar nearer home.[2] As to where and how this

[1] The documents do not enable us to trace the history of these grammar degrees with the fullness which one would like. The term 'incipere' is used of a grammar master in undated statutes (*Mun. Acad.* ii. 443) [*Stat. Antiq. Univ. Oxon.*, ed. S. Gibson, p. 21, l. 2], which had passed out of use before the middle of the fourteenth century, and which may well be extremely ancient. A rubric in *Registrum B*, written in 1477, describes these statutes as 'antique ordinaciones pro magistris in gramatica sed non sunt in moderno usu' [Mr. Strickland Gibson dates them: 'before 1350'.] The undated but much later statutes in *Mun. Acad.* ii. 436–42 [*Stat. Antiq. Univ. Oxon.*, ed. S. Gibson, pp. 169–73] regulate the examinations and speak of a licence by the chancellor. [Mr. Strickland Gibson dates these statutes: 'before 1380'.] The account of the inception ceremony is taken from Stokys' Book, the production of a sixteenth-century Bedel and Registrary of Cambridge. (Peacock, *Observations*, App. A.) An entry in the Oxford Register in 1509 shows that a similar custom was then in use at Oxford. A dispensation was granted in favour of a supplicant for the mastership of grammar, that 'traditio ferule cum virga sufficiat ad creandum unum magistrum grammatices, non obstante quocunque statuto in oppositum. Hec est concessa et conditionata. Una conditio est quod componat

50 versus, alia est quod disputet die veneris proxima' (Boase, *Register*, i. 64). For other instances of grammar degrees cf. *ibid.*, p. 298. In some cases a degree 'in arte rethorica' appears to have been given, and in these cases the graduate 'insignitus est laurea' (*ibid.*, p. 299). [See *Stat. Antiq. Univ. Oxon.*, ed. S. Gibson, p. lxxxviii.] The last degree in grammar is in 1568. *Ibid.*, p. 269. Dr. Clark (*Register*, ii, pt. 1. 8) says, 'I have found no trace of a "Master" of Grammar.' He appears to have overlooked the above-cited instance given by Mr. Boase (*Register*, i. 64). The formula 'admissus ad docendum' or 'ad instituendum pueros in grammatica', probably implies the master's degree. At Cambridge inception in grammar is mentioned in 1407. Reg. Ely (Fordham), f. 204 b. [On the grammar schools that existed in the fifteenth century see *Med. Archives Univ. Oxford*, ed. H. E. Salter (O.H.S.), ii. 278–80.]

[2] 'I am convinced that they (i.e. grammar schools) were attached to every monastery, and that the extraordinary number of foundation schools established just after the Reformation of 1547 was not a new zeal for a new learning, but a fresh and very inadequate supply of that which had been so suddenly and disastrously extinguished' (Thorold Rogers, *Six Centuries of Work and Wages*, London, 1884, i. 165). This is strongly confirmed by the statement of the Speaker in

knowledge was acquired, we have little detailed information. CHAP. XIV. An investigation into the grammar schools of the Middle Ages would be a subject for a separate treatise. Suffice it to say that the old ecclesiastical schools, in connexion with cathedrals or other important churches, were not destroyed by the growth of the universities, and other schools of the same kind were founded from time to time. Where the universities were within easy reach they were probably restricted for the most part to the study of grammar, and sometimes the rudiments of logic. In districts remote from universities there were ecclesiastical schools of a higher type, which certainly taught a full course of logic as well as grammar, and in some cases perhaps the whole range of a university arts course. In some countries the bulk of the inferior clergy must have received their education in such schools. At Vienna, Erfurt, and elsewhere, schools of this character became a nucleus for the later universities.[1]

1562, who told the Queen 'that at least an hundred (Schools) were wanting in England which before this time had been' (Strype, *Annals of the Reformation*, Oxford, 1824, i. 437). For the large number of pre-Reformation grammar schools see the list of thirty-six founded before 1509 given by Furnivall, *Education in Early England*, London, 1867, p. liii; and for further details as to their origin, Carlisle's *Endowed Grammar Schools in England and Wales*, London, 1818. Cf. also Edgar, *Early Scotch Education*, *passim*. As the mistake is often made, it may be added that the grammar schools connected with monasteries were secular schools, taught by secular masters, and quite distinct from the schools of the monks. [The existence of grammar schools in medieval England is one thing, the provision of schools by monasteries another. Thorold Rogers confused the two. See G. G. Coulton, 'Monastic Schools in the Middle Ages', *Medieval Studies*, No. 10, London, 1913;

and, for the schools, the works of A. F. Leach, *English Schools at the Reformation*, London, 1896, and *The Schools of Medieval England*, London, 1915.]

[1] [The bibliography of this subject is extensive. A good study and guide to the literature, old and new, is R. Limmer, *Bildungszustände und Bildungsideen des 13. Jahrhunderts*, Munich and Berlin, 1928, especially pp. 139–82. See above, vol. i, p. 90, for the earlier Middle Ages, and vol. ii, p. 1, 2, for Italy. R. Davidsohn's commentary on the well-known chapter in Villani's Chronicle (lib. xi, ch. 94) is an excellent introduction to the study of medieval education. He illustrates the nature of the three types of school in Florence in the early fourteenth century: those for the thousands of small boys and girls (reading and writing), those for 1,000–1,200 boys in arithmetic, and those in Latin and logic for about 550–600 boys. Lay masters, styled *ser* for courtesy, became frequent from 1275. (*Geschichte von Florenz*,

CHAP. XIV.   Where there was no cathedral, grammar schools were
Schools attached to some collegiate church or to ordinary parish
connected
with churches. Sometimes there was an endowment for such
churches.
schools: elsewhere they were supported by the municipality,
or, in places like Canterbury or Bury, by the monastery.
The great majority of the schoolmasters in the Middle Ages
were chantry priests. In other cases, no doubt, the boys were
taught by some poor priest in return for the scholars' fees
alone. Even in country parishes the canon law[1] required that
the parish clerk should be able to teach the boys to read as
well as to sing their psalter. How far such regulations were
actually carried out, it is of course impossible to determine
with precision. But it may be stated with some confidence
that at least in the later Middle Age the smallest towns and
even the larger villages possessed schools where a boy might
learn to read and acquire the first rudiments of ecclesiastical
Latin; while, except in very remote and thinly populated
regions, he would never have had to go very far from home
to find a regular grammar school.[2] That the means of educa-

IV. iii. 114, and the volume of notes,
pp. 26–7, where S. Debenedetti,
'Sur i più antiche doctores puerorum a Firenze', *Studi medievali*, ii.
327–51, is cited.]
    [1] 'Ut quisque presbyter, qui
plebem regit, clericum habeat, qui
secum cantet, et epistolam et lectionem legat, et qui possit scholas
tenere, et admonere suos parochi-
anos, ut filios suos ad fidem discen-
dam mittant ad ecclesiam, quos
ipse cum omni castitate erudiat'
(Decret. Greg. IX, lib. III, tit. i,
c. 3). [This decretal goes back to
the collections of Burchard of
Worms and Ivo of Chartres.] A
gloss adds, '*scolas*: docendo pueros
Psalterium et cantare' (Joli, p. 382).
The identity of the method pursued
in these elementary schools with
that in use in our day is illustrated
by the following: 'Et post breve
intervallum   resumebant   istud
idem, et cantabant: Pater, pater,
pater! eo modo, quo pueri, qui

instruuntur in scolis a magistris
gramaticalibus, solent facere, cum
per intervalla clamando repetunt
quod dictum est a magistro'
(Salimbene, *Chronica*, edit. O.
Holder-Egger in *Mon. Germ. Hist.*
xxxii. 1905, p. 264). It is noticeable
that even the grammarians on the
college foundations were required
to know some grammar on admission. Thus at the Collège de
Boissi: 'nullus vero Grammati-
corum recipiatur in dicta domo nisi
Donatum et Catonem (i.e. Dionysius Cato, see above, vol. i, p. 72)
dedicerit' (Bulaeus, iv. 354, 355).
Richard de Bury says that in his
book-hunting inquiries he did
not neglect 'rectores scholarum
ruralium pueryorumque rudium
paedagogos' (*Philobiblon*, ed. E. C.
Thomas, p. 79).
    [2] e.g. we hear of schools 'gram-
maticae et logicae' attached to a
parish church at Angers, the 'collation' of the mastership belonging

tion in reading, writing, and the elements of Latin were far CHAP. XIV.
more widely diffused in medieval times than has sometimes
been supposed is coming to be generally recognized by students of medieval life. The knowledge of reading and writing
and of the elements of Latin was by no means confined to the
clergy. The bailiff of every manor kept his accounts in Latin.
A grammar master often formed part of the establishment of
a great noble or prelate,[1] who had pages of gentle family
residing in his house for education. In other cases a boy of
a well-to-do family no doubt received his earliest education
from a chaplain or 'clerk' of his father, or from a private
tutor or neighbouring priest engaged for the purpose.

In the grammar school the rudiments of a classical educa- Method of
tion were imparted in much the same way as at the present teaching.
day. Donatus and Alexander of Villedieu were the grammars.
After some of the psalms had been learned (this was much
taught in the most elementary schools of all), Cato[2] served

to the Dean of S. Peter's. Ran-
geard, ii. 187. This may be taken
as a specimen of the higher class
of church school. The distinction
between the higher and lower class
of grammar school is well described
in a decree of the papal legate
Guido, who in 1267, on the petition
of the dean and chapter of Breslau, appoints 'ut infra muros ciuitatis Vratislauiensis iuxta ecclesiam
sancte Marie Magdalene scole fiant,
in quibus pueri paruuli doceantur
et discant alphabetum cum oracione
dominica et salutacionem beate
Marie virginis cum symbolo psal-
terio et septem psalmis, discant
eciam ibidem cantum, ut in ecclesiis
ad honorem dei legere valeant et
cantare (i.e. a song school). Audiant etiam in eisdem scolis Donatum, Cathonem et Theodulum (a
poet of the ninth century, author of
*Ecloga, qua comparantur miracula
V. T. cum veterum poetarum com-
mentis*) ac regulas pueriles. Qui
predicti pueri si maiores libros
audire voluerint ad scolas sancti

Johannis in castro Vratislauiensi se
transferant, uel quocunque voluerint.' The reason alleged for the
change is the inconvenience previously experienced through the
'parvuli' having to be sent to schools
(? supported by monasteries) outside the walls. The *scolasticus* of
the cathedral is to have the appointment of the rector of the new
school. *Breslauer Urkundenbuch*,
ed. Korn, Breslau, 1870, p. 35. As
to the smaller grammar schools of
Paris cf. Joli, p. 390.

[1] See Furnivall, *loc. cit.*, p. xi *sq.*

[2] See above, vol. i, p. 72. At
Perpignan 'Bacallarii legentes in
lectorio minori legant auctores con-
suetos, videlicet: Cathonem, Con-
tentum, et Thobiam (a twelfth-
century poem), et teneantur facere
duo proverbia de mane et duo de
vespere et reaudire lectiones lectas
et probare nomina vel verba in
proverbiis supradictis' (Fournier,
Statuts des Univ. franç. ii, No.
1485).

CHAP. XIV. for Delectus, after which the boy might be put into Ovid and possibly Virgil. In the absence of dictionaries the master no doubt literally 'read' the book to the pupils, i.e. construed it to them and afterwards required them to do the same. In England books were construed into French as well as English. Questions were asked in parsing and exercises set in prose and verse.[1] Disputations in grammar—perhaps something after the fashion in which candidates for King's Scholarships at Westminster used to challenge each other with hard questions—were also a favourite institution. After the boy had once entered the university all this ceased. No more classical books were construed, and we hear comparatively little of composition, though verse-making sometimes entered into university examinations. Lectures in grammar meant formal lectures on the grammatical treatises of Priscian and Donatus, or the more popular Alexander of Villedieu. But we have already endeavoured to show what and how a university scholar studied. Let us follow him to the university and see how he lived.

Life in the University

Age on entrance. In the first place, it is natural to ask the age at which a boy usually went up to Paris and probably most other universities. Twenty was the minimum age for the mastership, and the full course in arts lasted seven years. Fourteen might, therefore, be considered the normal minimum age for admission; but the Paris statute, which requires the 'determining bachelor' to be at least fourteen,[2] distinctly implies that some went up much earlier than this. Many would naturally have been older. On the whole it appears that the age of admission varied much more considerably than is now the case;

---

[1] 'Inter artes igitur quae dicuntur trivium,
    fundatrix Grammatica vendicat principium,
    sub hac chorus militat metrice scribentium'
(du Méril, Poésies pop. du moyen âge, pp. 151, 152); Mun. Acad. ii. 437, 438. [Stat. Antiq. Univ. Oxon.,

ed. S. Gibson, pp. 21, ll. 32–22, l. 7; p. 171, ll. 11–18.]
[2] Chartul. Univ. Paris. ii. 673. [This is queried by the editors (p. 674); see above, vol. i, p. 462, n. 4. Where the ages are given in later matriculation lists, few boys younger than fourteen are to be found.]

but as a rule the freshmen would be between thirteen and CHAP. XIV. sixteen.[1]

Quite young boys might, indeed, be canons or rectors of Beneficed parish churches; and in such cases entered as students in students. arts like other boys of the same age. But ecclesiastics of all ages frequently obtained leave of absence to study in the universities, and the older men naturally became students of canon law or theology. Between the years 1372 and 1408 there appear, on the matriculation-book of the faculty of law at Prague, the names of one bishop, one abbot, 9 archdeacons, 23 provosts, 4 deans, 209 canons, 187 rectors, 78 other secular clerks, and 25 regulars. So in the comparatively small university of Angers 138 beneficed persons (besides canons of the cathedral) obtained exemption from the tenth in 1413.[2] In the register of the German nation at Bologna more than half of the students are beneficed, most of them dignitaries or canons. Such men (whether graduates in arts or not) were of course, at least when living in their own houses and not in halls or other communities, only subject to much the same discipline as the university or the ecclesiastical authorities imposed upon doctors and masters; and many of them were among the most disorderly and troublesome of the academic population. In lecture the statute vainly prescribed that they should sit 'as quiet as girls'; and spiritual thunders had at times to be invoked to prevent them from 'shouting, playing, and interrupting'.[3] In what follows we are contemplating chiefly the career of the ordinary artist who usually entered the university at a more or less early age.

State of Discipline in University Halls and Colleges[4]

When we have grasped the fact that the medieval student Indepen- in arts was usually much younger than the modern under- boy-under- graduates.

[1] At the Collège de Laon, scholars before entering on the arts course are to be 'ad minus puberes' (Jourdain, *Index*, p. 107).

[2] Fournier, i, No. 457.

[3] *Mon. Univ. Prag.* I. i. 13; Tomek, p. 35. Odofredus (Sarti, I. i. 41) tells a story which illustrates

the mode of ironical applause or dissent in vogue at Bologna: 'scholares pulsabant libros contra eum.'

[4] [See especially the first three chapters in C. H. Haskins, *Studies in Mediaeval Culture*, Oxford, 1929: 'The Life of Medieval Students as

CHAP. XIV. graduate, we are very apt to fall into the mistake of seeing him merely the modern public-school boy, taught Aristotle instead of Cicero, and disputing sophisms instead of writing Latin verse. Such a view would, however, involve a complete misconception of his status. When we remember the youth of the medieval freshman, the unfettered liberty—not to say licence—which he originally enjoyed, is certainly one of the most astonishing facts about him. In some cases we do, indeed, hear of his being escorted from home by a 'fetcher', 'caryer', or 'brynger';[1] but the roads were dangerous, and protection of some kind was necessary even for men, while travelling in a carrier's cart was of course cheaper than riding. The proclamations against bearing arms often contain exceptions in favour of students travelling to or from the university. On arrival at Oxford or Paris our student had full liberty (unless his parents had made some provision for him, which would have been an impossibility for all but the rich) to choose the master to whose lectures he would go, and the hall or *hospicium* to which he would attach himself.

Touting masters.

While temporarily established at an inn before finding permanent quarters for himself, he would very probably be visited by some touting master or one of his students (who no doubt expected a commission on any business which he might introduce), anxious to secure the new-comer for his own hall or lecture-room.[2] In the matter of lectures, indeed,

illustrated by their letters', 'The University of Paris in the Sermons of the thirteenth century', 'Manuals for students'.]

[1] *Mun. Acad.* i. 346. [*Med. Arch. Univ. Oxford*, ed. H. E. Salter (O.H.S.), i. 245.] Cf. above, p. 103, n. 3, [and *Paston Letters*, ed. J. Gairdner, Edinburgh, 1910, iii. 77].

[2] The first Parisian statute against the practice was passed in 1290. Bulaeus, ii. 497; *Chartul.* ii, No. 570. So in 1452: 'Item circa predictos pedagogos et domorum principales magistros, statuimus et ordinamus, ne tanquam ambitioso

aut quaestui turpiter inhiantes per mansiones et loca concurrant, aut tabernas et hospitia circumeant per se vel per alios, ad rogandos sibi scolares.' At the same time migration was forbidden. Bulaeus, v. 572. [*Chartul.* iv, No. 2690.] So at Orleans: 'Nec doctor scholarem aliquem visitabit, antequam scolas suas vel doctoris alterius sit ingressus,' unless a relation or intimate friend. Fournier, i, No. 116. And at Basel: 'Nullos Magistros aut scolares . . . debere per se aut alium directe vel indirecte allicere practicare vel attrahere scolares advenientes vel qui de novo

a trial was respectfully solicited with all the accommodating obsequiousness of a modern tradesman. The pseudo-Boethius of the thirteenth century represents a scholar as advising freshmen not to commit themselves to a regent before they had attended his lectures for three days experimentally;[1] and the statutes of some universities provide that fees shall not become payable till after the expiration of that or some longer interval. With regard to residence, indeed, it was in the earlier period not necessary or even customary for the student, however young, to live under the nominal supervision of a master;[2] he might seek out his own lodgings in the town or join a party of students in hiring a hall.[3]

In the hall or *hospicium* one of the party was, indeed, called the principal and exercised a certain authority over the rest. But the principal was merely the student who had made himself responsible for the rent. His authority must have been derived from the voluntary consent of his fellow students. The owner could, indeed, transfer the hall to a new principal upon the retirement of the existing tenant; but, since there was nothing to compel a student to remain in the hall, the consent of the community was absolutely necessary to the

advenerint sue vie aut burse applicare, aut iisdem occurrere in ponte Reni aut quibusvis aliis locis' (Vischer, *Gesch. d. Un. Basel*, p. 153).

[1] Migne, *Patrol. lat.* lxiv. 1232. At Bologna the artist statutes provide 'quod quilibet scolaris possit experientiam facere de doctrina cuiuslibet doctoris et repetitoris spatio quindecim dierum', without fee (*Stat.*, p. 248). So Odofredus insists strongly upon the advisability of students exercising their private judgement upon the matter: 'Scolaris enim quemlibet debet audire et modum cuiuslibet inspicere, et qui si [*leg.* sibi] plus placebit ille debet per eum eligi, et opinione propria non alterius, non praetio . . . vel praecibus doctoris vel alterius' (*Proem. ined. ad Dig. vet.*, ap. Coppi, *Le Università Ital.*,

p. 257). [The bad master—self-advertising, pretentious, idle, quarrelsome, &c.—is described by the preachers; cf. Haskins, *op. cit.*, pp. 54-6.]

[2] The pseudo-Boethius advises the scholar to see as much as he can of his master 'mansionique eius, si possit, se inserat cohabitando, ut sic castigatus non solum se remordeat, verum etiam si locus adfuerit ad eum confluat inquirendo' (*Patrol. lat.* lxiv. 1230).

[3] For instance, the scholar who murdered a woman at Oxford in 1209 was attacked 'in hospitio suo, quod cum tribus sociis suis clericis locaverat'. Roger de Wendover (ed. Coxe, London, 1841), iii. 227. [Some letters give pleasant pictures of students who were fortunately lodged; Haskins, *op. cit.*, p. 18.]

CHAP. XIV. appointment. And in practice it appears that, upon the occurrence of a vacancy, a new principal was elected by the whole community just as the head is elected by the fellows of a college.[1] At Oxford, even after the effective nomination to the principalship had been secured by the chancellor in the reign of Elizabeth,[2] it was still considered necessary formally to convoke the members of the hall, graduate and undergraduate, and require them to elect the chancellor's nominee. The form has been gone through within living memory [in 1857]. There are, indeed, distinct traces that at one time the government of the hall was a democracy, the

[1] [It is not known upon what evidence Rashdall depended for this statement. It has already been pointed out that Rashdall's view of the democratic origin and character of the halls has met with criticism. See above, pp. 169-75, notes. 'It has been maintained', writes Dr. H. E. Salter, 'that in the Middle Ages the residents in a hall elected their own principal; this is quite incredible, but it would be reasonable that if a principal died or retired, the graduates of the hall should settle upon one of themselves to fill the post': see *Reg. Cancell. Oxon., 1434–1469*, ed. H. E. Salter (O.H.S.), i. xxix.]

[2] In the chancellorship of Leicester (Wood, ii. 232 *sq.*). The records of the election of the Principals of Hart Hall down to the appointment in 1710 of Richard Newton, the first Founder of Hertford College, state that the principal was 'elected'. The later form is that the election was 'confirmed'. See below, Appendix VII. So by the earliest statutes of Balliol (p. v) the scholars are to elect and obey the principal 'secundum statuta et consuetudines inter ipsos usitata et approbata'. We get another allusion to such statutes made by the *aulares* themselves in *Mun. Acad.* ii, 470 (headed 'ex privilegiis Universitatis in tempore Edwardi primi

concessis'), where the chancellor is authorized to over-rule any Aularian Statute and make new ones, 'et istud privilegium concessum fuit Cancellario quod olim Principales aularum et Scholares fecerunt statuta derogantia officio et potestati Cancellarii'. [The passage here cited by Rashdall is contained in a 'Nota pro statutis aularum in Oxonia' which was entered *c.* 1445 by Dr. Thomas Gascoigne in *Registrum A*, and is not supported by any other authority. See *Stat. Antiq. Univ. Oxon.*, ed. S. Gibson, pp. xix, n. 1, 224.] So at Vienna: 'Singulae conclusiones honeste et licite per Conventorem alicuius Bursae conclusae ex votis maioris partis Bursae sortiantur effectus executionis, nullo contradicente' (Kink, 1. i. 38). At Cracow we find the consent of students necessary to the purchase of plate, furniture, table-linen, &c. (*Regestrum Bursae Cracoviensis*, Buda, 1821). By the Oxford Aularian Statutes, each scholar was to have 'discos de propriis' (f. 6 a), [*Stat. Antiq. Univ. Oxon.*, ed. S. Gibson, p. 582, l. 23]. Eventually such things came by custom to be the property of the hall, and passed from one principal to another. On all these matters I know of no evidence as to Paris, but the system was probably much the same as at Oxford.

power of the principal being limited to the enforcement of statutes freely accepted by the community. It is likely enough that in practice the principals in the artists' halls were usually masters or at least bachelors; but it was not till the fifteenth century that the universities began to restrict the principalship to masters.[1] It was at about the same period that measures were taken both at Oxford and at Paris to suppress the class of martinets or chamberdekyns, and to compel all students to reside either in a college or in a hall or pedagogy presided over by a master or at least a graduate.[2] The statutes of the German universities throw still further light upon what was probably the state of things at Paris and Oxford before the universal requirements of residence. They for the most part enforce residence in Hall or college on all students in arts, with the exception of two classes—the sons of nobles or rich men who lived with a private tutor in houses of their own,[3] and the poorest students who could not afford the cost of residence in a pedagogy. With the great mass of students of moderate means residence in a hall was already the established rule long before it was actually enforced by university statute.

Gradual enforcement of residence.

[1] It is evident, however, that the statutes were long very imperfectly observed. In 1487 we hear, 'quod multi temeriter starent extra collegia et essent vagabundi errabundi et . . . starent cum quibusdam mulieribus in domibus earum et quedam mulieres tenerent pedagogia et collegia quedam' (*MS. Reg. Nat. Angl.*, No. 10, f. 35 b, Archives at the Sorbonne). [See above, p. 171.]

[2] [See *Stat. Antiq. Univ. Oxon.*, ed. S. Gibson, p. lxxxiii.]

[3] Cf. a decree of the University of Vienna: 'Anno 1401, 29 Maii in congregatione Universitatis declaratum fuit, quod ille teneret statum nobilium, qui tenet unum Magistrum in expensis et ad minus duos famulos' (Kink, *Gesch. d. Un. Wien*, I. i. 117). So at Cologne (A.D. 1457), students are required to reside in masters' *Bursae*, except poor students or 'nobilibus aut personis egregiis cum honesta familia ad studium missis; quos suorum regentium relinquimus arbitrio' (Bianco, *Gesch. d. Un. Kol.*, Anl., p. 76). At Leipzig, again, in 1441, we find a licence to reside 'extra bursas communes' (*Urkundenbuch*, ed. Stübel, p. 39. Cf. *Statutenbüch. d. Un. Leipsic*, p. 57, A.D. 1432). Cf. Kosegarten, *Greifswald*, ii. 308, and Westphalen, *Diplomatarium* (*Mon. Ined. Rer. Germ.* iv), c. 1016. Contrary to the experience of modern universities, this poorest class was undoubtedly disorderly. This is the account given of them at Oxford: 'Per dies dormiunt ac in noctibus circa tabernas et lupanaria spolia homicidiaque vigilant' (*Mun. Acad.* i. 320). [*Stat. Antiq. Univ. Oxon.*, ed. S. Gibson, p. 208.]

CHAP. XIV.   But even when the medieval undergraduate was fairly

State of imprisoned in his hall or pedagogy, it must not be supposed
discipline.
that he was forthwith subjected to the discipline of the
modern schoolboy. On this subject, indeed, there seems to
be an almost universal misconception. It is known that there
was a time when undergraduates in universities were birched;
and it is a somewhat natural assumption that the farther we
go back, the more Spartan will the discipline be found. Such
a supposition is, however, wholly opposed to all the evidence
within our reach. As to university discipline, as we should
understand it, there was in the thirteenth century really no
such thing.[1] For offences against the ordinary civil or ecclesiastical law, the undergraduate was of course subject to imprisonment or excommunication like other clerks. Offences
against the statutes of the university were punished in the
earliest period chiefly by excommunication, and later on
chiefly by fines; but the earlier university statutes hardly
attempted to interfere with the private life of students, except
with the view of preventing actual outrage or breach of the
peace, and perhaps of enforcing clericality of dress. It is

Corporal only in reference to the grammar school that we meet with
punish-
ment. any allusion to flogging; it is the grammar-master who was
presented with the birch as the symbol of his office. Among
the personifications of the Seven Arts which adorn the front
of Chartres Cathedral, grammar alone carries a rod.[2]   There

[1] [The general view, expounded
by preachers and moralists, was
that the master had disciplinary
authority over his pupil, though it
is not clear to what extent he
resorted to corporal discipline.
Error discipuli culpa est magistri,
both in learning and in conduct.
Cf. above, vol. i, p. 290, n. 1; and
below, p. 370.]

[2] In the poem of Theodulfus,
De VII Liberalibus Artibus (*Mon.
Germ. Hist. Poet. Lat. Med. Ævi*, i.
545), grammar is thus described:

'Huius laeva tenet flagrum, seu
    dextra machaeram,

Pigros hoc ut agat, radat, ut haec
    vitia.'

So Mapes, in *Apocalypsis Goliae
Episcopi* (ed. Wright, 1847), p. 3:

'Hic Priscianus est dans palmis
    verbera,
    est Aristoteles verberans aera.'

Kaufmann is the first writer who
has pointed out the absence of corporal punishment in the ordinary
discipline of medieval universities,
but he has omitted the needful
qualifications. The severity of the
discipline in the grammar schools
may be estimated from the terse

has always, indeed, been considered to be some peculiar and CHAP. XIV.
some mysterious connexion between the rod and classical
scholarship; a former age might have even attributed the
decay of classical scholarship in the medieval universities to
the absence of this stimulus. Certain it is that it was at about
the time when classical studies began to revive that the rod
reappeared in academical lecture-rooms. In all the university
records of the Middle Ages there is not a single hint or allusion to corporal punishment until the fifteenth century.
Then, indeed, the University of Paris, which was now for the
first time making a serious effort to put down the disgraceful
faction-fights which formed the favourite pastime of the
medieval student, did on rare occasions in solemn Congregation order that the rector and proctors should go to the colleges or pedagogies of the offenders—offenders, it should be
observed, who would now be liable to long periods of imprisonment or penal servitude—and there personally superintend the chastisement of the youthful rioters or bravoes.
It is not till 1469 that we find similar penalties denounced for
a mere university offence. In that year a new statute was
passed against the festive irregularities of the 'Feast of Fools',

statute of the college attached to
the Cathedral School of Reims:
'Singulis noctibus disciplinas acci-
piant' (Varin, *Archives Administra-
tives de la Ville de Reims*, i. 662 *sq.*).
It would appear, moreover, that if
the 'magnus magister' found at the
Saturday examination that the boys
under the 'parvi magistri' did not
know their lessons, 'verberat pueros
et magis magistrum eorum' (Robert
de Sorbon, *De Conscientia*, ed.
F. Chambon, Paris, 1902, p. 30;
cf. p. 8). In this discourse (according to the text of Bulaeus, iii. 227)
there occurs the startling statement
that 'si aliquis refutetur a Cancellario Parisiensi, verberatur'; a
'non' has dropped out (see Chambon's edition, p. 7, l. 20). The *De
Disciplina Scholarium* shows clearly
enough that no corporal punishment—indeed, no punishment at all

—was possible in the Arts Schools.
'Magister Franco in immansuetu-
dine prodeat in exemplum, qui ob
discipulorum suorum nobilitate sua
utentium irrefrenabilem arrogan-
tiam laqueo se suspendit; sapientius
autem egisset si mansuetudine usus
fuisset' (*Patrol. lat.* lxiv. 1235). It
is true that the master is required
to be 'rigidus . . . ut . . . proter-
vientes castiget'; but other instances of the use of 'castigare'
show that it is probably not to be
taken literally, and the remarks
which follow, on the treatment of
late scholars, make it plain that the
master had very little control over
his scholars. It is only the master
who leaves the university to teach
as a schoolmaster or tutor whose
pupil 'parentum assensu virgis
affligetur' (*ibid.*, c. 1237).

CHAP. XIV. and even then the correction is inflicted by university authority, not by individual masters or principals.[1] So at Louvain we find one or two cases of flogging ordered by the faculty of arts for homicide or other grave outrage.[2] These are the exceptions which prove the rule. They are new and extraordinary exercises of authority on the part of the university at large. It is almost as certain as such a matter can be made that the birch was quite unknown to the ordinary discipline of the university till towards the close of the fifteenth century or later. Even then such discipline continues to be the exception rather than the rule.

General laxity of discipline.   A few illustrations of the way in which even grave outrages were dealt with may illustrate the last statement. At Ingolstadt, a student having killed another in a drunken quarrel at a 'symposium', the university resolved on the 'confiscation of his scholastic effects and garments, and therewith contented did not proceed to the punishment of expulsion'.[3] It is satisfactory to add that a Prague master of arts,

[1] 'Quantum ad secundum articulum, deliberavit Facultas, quod transgressores sue conclusionis, scilicet portantes arma et assumentes habitus fatuorum, qui presentes sunt, corrigantur publice, in loco publico, puta in vico Straminis vel in Sancto Juliano, et in domibus eorum, coram Deputatis Facultatis; post correctionem vero susceptam, humillime si supplicaverint predicti transgressores, pro admissione ad gradus, tunc vult Facultas mite cum eis agere. . . . Facultas istos correctos scilicet admisit, si fuerint sufficientes, ad gradus vel baccalariatus vel magisterii' (Jourdain, No. 1369, anno 1469). Later on, in 1487, the rector, proctors, and 'pedagogues' are given a general power ' ad corrigendum, reformandum, et ad deponendum omnes abusus Universitatis absque ulteriori congregatione Facultatis' (Bulaeus, v. 784). It is obvious that they were not previously supposed to possess such

power. Goulet dates the general reform of university discipline from this period, and there can be no doubt that it constitutes an epoch in university history.

[2] Vernulaeus, Acad. Lovan., p. 58. Later we find corporal punishment denounced on any artist under twenty-five who sells his books without permission of his regent. Molanus, Hist. Lovaniensium, ed. Ram. ii. 930.

[3] 'Quidam studiosus Joannes Hohenburger Ambergensis, in symposio, cum ex altercatione verbali ad arma et pugnam deuentum esset, in ipsa dimicatione Christophorum Tobs itidem Studiosum interfecit. Facta est rerum ipsius Scholasticarum et vestium confiscatio, et ea contenta Vniuersitas ad exclusionis paenam non processit' (1479) (Rotmarus, Annales Ingolstadiensis Academiae, i. 19). To prevent exaggerated inferences from a solitary case, it may be well to contrast the Leipzig statute, 'quod quilibet

believed to have assisted in cutting the throat of a friar bishop, was actually expelled.[1] The statutes of the German universities are far more precise and detailed on matters of discipline than any that have come down to us from Paris: it was perhaps natural for new universities to embody in formal statutes regulations which had been merely sanctioned by custom and tradition in the older bodies from which they sprang. We see in these statutes—ranging from the last decades of the fourteenth to the end of the fifteenth century —a progressive attempt to introduce reasonable order into the undisciplined student-hordes of the earlier Middle Age. But the aims of medieval disciplinarians were—considering the youth of the pupils—of a very moderate order. It was as much as they could do (even in the fifteenth century) to compel the students to live in halls presided over by masters, to prevent students expelled from one hall being welcomed at another, to prevent the masters themselves condoning or sharing the worst excesses of their pupils, to compel fairly regular attendance at lectures and other university or college exercises, to require all students to return home by curfew at 8 or 9 p.m.,[2] to get the outer doors of the pedagogy locked till morning, and to insist on the presence of a regent throughout the night.[3] In some cases students are

Improved discipline of fifteenth century.

repertus in homicidio remittatur ad episcopum perpetuis carceribus mancipandus' (Zarncke, *Statutenbücher*, p. 60). It is, however, unlikely that such a sentence was ever carried out. At Greifswald a student who killed another in a quarrel is fined 200 florins (Kosegarten, ii. 188).

[1] *Mon. Univ. Prag.* I. i. 99, 100.

[2] At Erfurt it is enacted: 'Primo post campanam, que dicitur quinque solidorum, nullus scolaris absque necessitate vel racionabili causa vadat per plateas, et si causam rationabilem habuerit, vadat cum lumine aperto et per loca honesta' (Project for original Statutes in Weissenborn, *Acten*, ii. 7). So at Leipzig, college-doors are to be shut at 9 in winter, and 10 in

summer (Zarncke, *Statenbücher*, p. 182). 9 p.m. was the general rule in the colleges of Paris and Oxford; in the latter it is still retained, though ingress is allowed up to 12. Occasionally the hour of closing is earlier. At the Collège de Narbonne in 1379 the gate is to be shut 'post occasum solis', and 2d. charged to all who wanted to go in or out afterwards—the first instance I have met with of the still extant Oxford abuse known as a 'gatebill'. The Narbonne statute goes on to provide an increased penalty of 3 *solidi* 'si quis enormiter pulsaverit vel gravem strepitum duxerit', and of ½ mark (*plus* repairs) for breaking the gate (Félibien, v. 666).

[3] At Heidelberg in 1453: 'Item

CHAP. XIV. compelled to dine in their hall, and attend the subsequent disputation.[1] When the early habits of the community generally are remembered, it will be evident how much liberty or licence these regulations still allowed to boys of fifteen or sixteen living in the very centre of large and densely populated towns. They were in general perfectly free to roam about the streets up to the hour at which all respectable citizens were in the habit, if not actually compelled by the town statutes, of retiring to bed. They might spend their evenings in the tavern and drink as much as they pleased. Drunkenness is rarely treated as a university offence at all. In some statutes it is only on a third offence that a student is expelled for introducing suspected women into the pedagogy. The regular patrol of the proctors with pole-axe and armed attendants seems to be almost peculiar to the English universities.[2] In Louvain, and probably many German universities, the repression of 'night-walking' was entrusted to the 'promotor' of the university.[3] The penalties which are denounced and inflicted even for grave outrages and immoralities are seldom severe and never of a specially schoolboy character. In the most serious cases there was imprisonment[4] or excommunication; offences somewhat less serious, including many

quod in qualibet bursa vel eciam alia domo in qua scolares communiter dormiunt vel vivunt, in prandio et in cena sit ad minus vnus regencium eandem presens, maneatque in illa in hyeme a tempore cene, et estate a pulsu campane vini per integram noctem' (Hautz, Gesch. ii. 395). The same statutes provide for evening 'exercitia seu resumpciones'.

[1] e.g. at Rostock. Westphalen, Diplomatarium, c. 1029. These statutes seem to be given as the original statutes (circa 1419), but some things in them suggest a later date.

[2] In 1536 we find a citizen complaining that 'the proctor did thrust his pole-axe at him'. Document quoted by Boase, Oxford, p. 116.

[3] 'Promotor per dominum Rectorem iussus, noctu plateas obambulet, cum praetore vel sine praetore.... Quod si aliquem nocte illa apprehenderit, habeat ipse ab apprehenso octo stuferos et quilibet famulorum eius quatuor stuferos' (Statute in Molanus, Hist. Lovaniensium, ed. Ram. ii. 907).

[4] In some German universities there was a kind of genteel university prison for short periods. Thus at Leipzig a student may be required 'sedere in turri' for any period not exceeding six months. Zarncke, Statutenbücher, p. 55. Offenders were politely invited to go to prison (a custom still [1895] observed in some German universities), refusal involving expulsion. Ibid., p. 57.

which would now be treated as crimes (except, indeed, in chap. xiv. universities), are punished by postponement of the degree, expulsion from the college or pedagogy, temporary or permanent banishment from the university town; while ordinary breaches of discipline are expiated by fines.

Very curious is the minuteness with which in many university or college statutes a graduated scale of pecuniary penalties is adjusted to the various degrees of undergraduate enormity. Thus, in the statutes of the *Collegium minus* at Leipzig, drawn up in 1438, we find a fine of 10 new *groschen* provided for the offence of lifting a stone or other missile with a view of throwing it at a master, but not actually throwing it. For throwing and missing, the mulct is increased to 8 florins; while a still higher penalty is provided for the more successful marksman.[1] A later statute further distinguishes between 'hitting without wounding' and 'wounding without mutilation', for which the penalty rises to 18 florins, together with compensation to the injured master, while only for actual mutilation is the penalty of expulsion denounced.[2] The statutes of Vienna contemplate the possibility of flogging for the very poorest class of students.[3] With this exception it is not till the first year of the sixteenth century that we encounter a threat of flogging in the statutes of the University of Tübingen,[4] which seem to breathe a kind of Protestant

Tariff of fines for assaults.

[1] 'Item levans lapidem, cantrum aut consimile animo proiiciendi post corpus alicuius magistri, non tamen proiiciens, dabit collegio pro poena 10 novos grossos. Si vero proiecerit et corpus non tetigerit, dabit collegio 8 florenos pro poena. Si autem ipsum tetigerit citra vulneracionem, iuxta formam prioris statuti puniatur' (Zarncke, *Statutenbücher*, p. 227).

[2] *Ibid.*, p. 232.

[3] See above, vol. i, p. 527 n.

[4] The statute recites that whereas certain students had been imprisoned, and certain others to procure their liberation 'recusarunt bursalia exercicia et actus scholasticos solito more audire non sine quadam con-

spiracione' such attempts are prohibited 'sub prestiti iuramenti debito et pena exclusionis perpetue ab vniversitate aut correctionis publice virgarum duorum seniorum huic machinationi interessentium' (*Urkunden zur Gesch. d. Un. Tüb.*, p. 105). The provision is obviously an extraordinary expedient to meet an extraordinary emergency. In the thirteenth century students in the like case would have seceded and started a new university. In the very full records of Leipzig I find no allusion to 'virgae' till 1543, when we hear of 'castigationes' by the tutors or 'praeceptores', who were instituted in 1517. Zarncke, *Statutenbücher*, pp. 72, 90.

CHAP. XIV. austerity even before the dawn of the Reformation. The 'imposition' would also appear to be a sixteenth-century improvement in 'pedagogy'.[1]

Greater strictness in colleges.   It was, as has been already remarked, the growth of colleges that led to that great revolution in university discipline which reached its climax in the sixteenth century. The college introduced an entirely new relation between the teacher and the taught. The scholar who accepted a college endowment was no longer free to step across the road into a rival hall if dissatisfied with the treatment which he received from his own principal. Within the college walls he could be compelled to prepare his lessons, to 'repeat' them afterwards, or to take part in disputations or other exercises, as he could not be in the schools of the university regent, which he was free to leave at any moment. The college was under the supervision of a man of more years and more character than the average 'principal'; and neither he nor the subordinate college officers had anything to gain by condoning or winking at the irregularities of their charges. Even the boarder who was not on the foundation was probably placed there by his parents for the express purpose of subjecting him to a more real discipline than he was under at the hall; and it would be difficult to keep up one standard of discipline for the foundationers and another for the pensioners or commoners. Moreover, the mere character of the college building may have done something to facilitate discipline. A solid and substantial stone building, with a massive door well barred against the incursions of hostile mobs, offered smaller facilities for nocturnal escapades than the rickety tenement in the crowded

---

[1] The earliest instance I have met with is in the statutes of Corpus Christi College, Oxford (p. 99), in 1517, where the President may punish 'per iniunctionem ut per horam vel horas, cum minime vellet, aliquid scribat aut componat in Bibliotheca'. So in 1524 at Leipzig students are sentenced for lampooning each other ('mutuis libellis et iambis') 'ingredi carcerem et offerre domino rectori carmina greca', &c. (*Acta Rectorum*, ed. Zarncke, p. 7). The imposition is thus distinctly a product of humanism. It will hardly be believed by many persons now living in Oxford that impositions have been set and performed (*per se vel per alium*) by the dean of an Oxford college within the last few years [1895]. [Cf. W. W. Rouse Ball, *Cambridge Papers*, pp. 220–1.]

street which must often have served as the boarding-house CHAP. XIV.
of the ordinary student society. The hall-man must perforce
have been turned out into the street for any recreation that
he enjoyed. The college often included a garden, or at least
a quadrangle, which made it possible to restrain to some extent the unattached student's unbounded liberty to haunt
taverns and roam the town, alone or in noisy parties, at all
hours of the day or night.[1]

Yet even in the college the discipline was at first by no *College*
means that of the modern schoolboy. The college was a self- *discipline*
governing community, obliged to obey its own statutes and
its own officers, but still a community like a monastery or a *at first ec-*
clesiastical
secular chapter, every member of which (no matter of what *rather than*
standing) was under tolerably strict discipline himself, while *scholastic.*
he was expected to take more or less part in maintaining the
discipline of the house. At the annual chapter or scrutiny
every member was invited (after the monastic fashion) freely
to criticize the defects in his comrades' character and conduct;[2]

---

[1] The statutes of Harcourt provide that 'nullus . . . bibat in
taberna tabernarie sub poena sex
denariorum' (Bulaeus, iv. 156).
Does this mean 'tavern-wise' (i.e.,
perhaps, not as a 'bona-fide traveller') or 'of a female tavern-keeper'?
At the same college occurs a prohibition, 'ne aliqui de domo vadant
de nocte ad choream vel proces-
sionem Nationis' (*ibid.*, p. 159).

[2] An exceedingly amusing record
of the 'scrutinies' for 1338 and
1339 at Merton has been printed
by Thorold Rogers, *Hist. of Agriculture and Prices*, ii (Oxford, 1866),
p. 670 *sq.* [reprinted in Brodrick,
Memorials of Merton College, Oxford, 1883, pp. 340-7; retranscribed,
with facsimiles, in Allen and Garrod, *Merton Muniments*, Oxford,
1918, Nos. xiii–xv]. One fellow
complains that another called the
warden by his Christian name
'coram omnibus'. Another demands 'quod capellanus corrigatur
quoad calligas et eius vestes';

another is also exercised 'de caligis
Willelmi capellani'; another complains that the fellows 'uterentur
caligis inhonestis' [i.e. hose which
did not conform to clerical regulations, being tight and implying
doublet to match. Dr. Coulton
refers us to a parallel passage in
Visitations of Norwich Diocese, ed.
Jessopp, p. 201: *caligae* were not
boots]. Most of the complaints
relate to violent quarrels and assaults; one suggests embezzlement
of college funds. When there is no
scrutiny, students were constantly
called upon by the statutes to inform against one another. [At Merton a 'chapter' and a 'scrutiny' were
not, as Rashdall assumes, synonymous, nor were they held only once
a year. The statutes required that
'scrutinies' should be held three
times a year, and chapters periodically, at the request of the fellows.
At chapters inquiry was made into
the management of one or all of the
manors of the college, and decision

CHAP. XIV. and the college statutes frequently enjoin a system of mutual espionage.[1] Although the senior members of the house were admitted to a share in the government from which the juniors were excluded, there did not exist that sharp distinction between governing and non-governing members, or graduate and non-graduate members, which we find in the college of more modern times.[2] All alike were students, though some of them might be teachers also. In the earlier college statutes the discipline was much the same in its requirements for the theologian of thirty and for the artist of sixteen. The penalties are generally fines or forfeiture of commons, and, in cases of persistent obstinacy, expulsion.

Sconces. Occasionally we meet with the time-honoured custom of 'sconcing', still preserved in the college halls of Oxford for offences against an elaborate and arbitrary code of under-graduate etiquette. But in the Middle Ages even grave offences were expiated in this jovial fashion, as for instance at the Sorbonne, where a fellow who should assault or 'cruelly beat' a servant was to be mulcted in four gallons (*sextarius*) of the best wine, not for the benefit of the injured menial, but of his unharmed brother-fellows,[3] no less than for what, according to the modern ideas, would seem the minor offences of talking French or excessive hilarity at meals.[4]

taken how many more fellows the college could afford to elect. See *Reg. Annalium Coll. Merton.*, ed. H. E. Salter (O.H.S.), pp. xxxiii–xxxiv.]

[1] 'Iurabit etiam quod si aliquem de sociis nouerit ebriosum tabernas uel inhonesta spectacula communiter usitantem contenciosum luxuriosum uel notabiliter uiciosum custodi seu eius (MS. eius seu) locum tenenti quamcicius honeste si comode poterit indilate reuelabit' (Statutes of Pembroke College, Cambridge, in the College Treasury).

[2] Except, indeed, when the junior members were more or less the personal servants of the foundationers, as with the 'clerks'

of the Sorbonne or the 'poor boys' of Queen's. I am speaking of the relation between regular members of the foundation.

[3] *Chartul. Univ. Paris.* I, No. 448. [For the *sextarius* see G. G. Coulton, *Social Life in Britain*, Cambridge, 1918, p. 377 n.]

[4] At the Cistercian College: 'verbis latinis et non aliis, sub poena solutionis unius pintae vini qualibet vice assistentibus illico distribuendae, loquantur' (Félibien, *Hist. de Paris*, iii. 173 *b*). 'Sconces' are also imposed for other offences not serious enough to warrant 'disciplina regularis' (*ibid.*, p. 174). In the Collège de Cornouaille in 1380 scholars are required to behave themselves during meals and grace

The fifteenth-century Register of the Sorbonne—one of the very few documents of the kind which has come down to us—is full of amusing cases of 'sconcing' alike for serious and for trifling breaches of college discipline, imposed now upon grave theologians and now upon their humbler and younger servitors or 'clerks'. A doctor of divinity is sconced a quart of wine for picking a pear off a tree in the college garden, or again for forgetting to shut the chapel door, or for taking his meals in the kitchen.[1] Clerks are sconced a pint for 'very inordinately knocking at the door during dinner, 2s. for being very drunk and committing many insolences' when in that condition,[2] or a pint for 'confabulating' in the court late at night, and refusing to go to their chambers when ordered, or for asking for wine at the buttery in the name of a master and consuming it themselves.[3] The 'common clerk' or head cook is likewise sconced for 'badly preparing the meat for supper', or for not putting salt in the soup;[4] and it would appear that, while the fellows at least had the drinking of the sconces which they impose upon members of their own body, the clerks were at times 'sconced' for the exclusive benefit of the fellows. At all events, we find a clerk threatened with expulsion for saying that the fellows were in the habit, when unable to gratify their bibulous propensities at their own expense, of finding excuses for sconcing the clerks, and drinking at theirs.[5]

'cessante temporibus praedictis quocumque clamore, tumultu, risu, ludo et quacumque inordinatione; et contrarium faciens puniatur in aestimatione unius quartae vini mediocris . . . quod vinum inter socios compotabitur' (*ibid.*, p. 501). So it is forbidden to walk about the college 'cum calepodiis, id est cum patinis, sub poena unius pintae vini pro qualibet transgressione' (*ibid.*, p. 502). [*Patini* were fashionable pointed shoes, as worn by the laity.]

[1] *Bibl. Nat. Cod. Lat.*, No. 5494 A, ff. 2, 3, 6.

[2] *Ibid.*, ff. 2, 5.

[3] *Bibl. Nat. Cod. Lat.*, No. 5494 A, ff. 6, 40 ('nomine magistri sui ut fingebat et non sic erat'); though on another occasion immorality followed by perjury is punished by a sconce of a quart (*ibid.*, f. 8).

[4] *Ibid.*, ff. 12, 21. The same official (f. 23) is admonished and fined a 'bachelor' of wine ('unum baccalarium vini de meliori ad extra', i.e. not mere college wine) for being found 'penes Sanctum Andream de artibus (i.e. arcubus) cum una meretrice'. For having a 'meretrix' in his chamber on Lady-day a clerk is, however, expelled (*ibid.*, f. 29).

[5] 'Anno quo supra die x^{ma} octobris fuit potus clericus magistri nostri magistri Rolandi Guillelmus ad sex solidos parisienses propter

In some respects the discipline under which these boy-
The
medieval
under-
graduate
and the
modern. undergraduates were placed was less strict than that to which
men as old as the masters of arts of that day are subject in
modern England. At the College of Navarre, for instance, so
serious an offence as passing the night out of college was
expiated by a fine of two *solidi*, only half the amount of the
artist's weekly table allowance.[1] At the same college a student
might apparently have a guest to sleep with him for any
period under a week without the master's leave.[2] Where the
regulations savour of antique rigour, it is in general the rigour
of the monastery rather than the rigour of a strict school—as,
for instance, the requirement that all students below the
grade of bachelors shall ask leave to go out and only walk the
streets two and two, to avoid 'scandal'. The silence and bible-
reading in hall, the enforcement of punctuality at meals on
pain of bread and water, the appointment of spies to inform
against—not indeed (as in the cloister) all talking—but talking
in the vulgar tongue, are other features of collegiate discipline which show the influence of monastic ideas. Robert de
Sorbon, indeed, introduced into his college the rigid fasting
of the monastic houses, i.e. total abstention from food till
after vespers on all the fast-days of the winter season.[3] We
meet with the same ascetic rule in other colleges; elsewhere
the younger scholars are expressly let off with mere 'absti-
nence' from meat.[4] Occasionally, as for instance in the
very ecclesiastical colleges of Toulouse, the monastic penalty
of so many days' bread and water is prescribed for serious

verba scandalosa que de magistris
protulerat ut pote quod magistri
erant potatores et quando non
habebant unde potare gratis quod
ipsi inveniebant occasiones potandi
suos clericos. Fuit etiam dictum
quod si amodo in consimilia in-
cideret quod de collegio expel-
leretur quoniam *unica prava pecus
inficit omne pecus*` (*ibid.*, f. 2).

[1] Bulaeus, iv. 91.

[2] *Ibid.* It is possible that for a
less period the leave of the principal
of the artists was wanted.

[3] 'Diebus ieiunalibus a festo Omnium Sanctorum usque ad carnis-
privium non comedatur in domo
ista de bursa nisi in vesperiis et post
omnes lectiones diurnas' (*Chartul.*
i, No. 448). In 1315, in accordance
with the then general custom of the
religious houses, dinner was put
back to nones, but in 1362 the
house returned to its original usage.
Hemeraeus, MS. *Sorbonae Origines*,
ff. 33, 34.

[4] e.g. at a Toulouse college, all
under twenty. Fournier, i, No. 631.

offences;[1] but such provisions are not found at Paris or
Oxford.

At Paris there are no traces of corporal punishment in college statutes except for grammarians[2] before the sixteenth century. It first occurs in the exceptionally rigid code of statutes drawn up for the college of Montaigu by the great college reformer, Jean Standonck, and is then prescribed only in case of violence or rebellion.[3] As late as 1540 another French college confines this punishment to grammarians under fifteen years of age.[4] The register of the Sorbonne shows, however, that flogging was occasionally resorted to in dealing with serious offences on the part of the clerks, who, it must be remembered, were poor boys acting as the personal servitors of individual fellows. Even in their case it is confined to such offences as assaults on other clerks, 'even to effusion of blood though moderate', or kicking the 'common clerk', or repeatedly sleeping out. In one instance it is allowed in the case of the younger clerks as an alternative to heavy sconces for stealing 'apples, pears, cherries, and grapes, in sufficiently large quantities' from the college garden.[5] The general principle of college discipline at the Sorbonne was that each master was responsible for the behaviour of his clerk, for whose offences

[1] e.g. eight days for introducing a woman into college. *Ibid.*, No. 811.

[2] e.g. Félibien, iii. 511.

[3] 'Poenam subibit usque ad disciplinae susceptionem' (Félibien, v. 734). Stoppages of food and monastic prostrations are also features of Standonck's very peculiar system. It should be observed that students in the monastic colleges were, like other monks, subject to 'regular discipline'. In a college at Montpellier we hear of a student who said he was 18, but was believed to be over 21, forming a plot to wound or kill his master 'quia verberabat eum sicut alios studentes' (*Cartulaire de Montpellier*, i. 542; cf. pp. 547–8).

[4] In the College of Tours: 'Quas

quidem poenas pecuniarias non intelligimus habere locum in parvulis grammaticis minoribus quindecim annis; sed loco illarum poenarum pecuniariarum volumus quod puniantur per ipsum primarium virgis, moderate tamen et non saeviendo' (Félibien, iii. 421).

[5] MS. Reg. ff. 4, 7, 40. In one case a clerk is expelled because 'nec correctionem nec monitionem a magistris sustinere volebat' (f. 41). Where the offence was an assault on a comrade (who was of course a clerk), the offender was usually directed to go to the penitentiary for absolution. In one case of drawing a knife against another clerk (how far it was used does not appear) the college was satisfied with this penalty.

CHAP. XIV. he was himself liable to be sconced. When corporal punishment was thought advisable, the master was ordered to flog his own clerk or have him flogged by the boy's master in the schools.[1] The fellows were very much disposed to take the part of their humble companions, and sometimes have to be sconced themselves for not carrying out the flogging orders of the college. On one occasion the prior has to be likewise fined for not enforcing these sconces against a too indulgent fellow.[2] In all these cases it is to be observed that there is nothing to show the age of the boys: they may in all cases have been mere grammarians.

and in England. The prolongation of the whipping age to the verge of manhood is perhaps peculiar to the English universities. Even at Oxford, however, the sanctity of the human person seems to have been as jealously respected as in a modern French lycée during at least the first half of our period.[3] The earliest exceptions occur in the second half of the fourteenth century, and are essentially of the rule-proving order. The statutes of Queen's are the first statutes of a secular college which prescribe this mode of correction; and then it is only the 'poor boys' who are to be in certain cases offered the alternative allowed in the well-known inscription at Winchester,

'Aut disce aut discede; manet sors tertia caedi.'

These boys, it may be remembered, were some of them grammarians, who would be flogged as a matter of course like other schoolboys: some of them were or *may* have been artists, but all were foundationers of the poorest class, whose prospects would have been ruined by expulsion from the college; yet even in their case it is contemplated as possible that when they had reached 'marriageable years', they would kick against schoolboy discipline, and prefer the more serious but less

[1] 'Fuit etiam potus ad unum bachalarium de extra et iniunctum magistro suo quod ipse ipsum verberaret vel verberare faceret in scholis' (MS. Reg., f. 4).

[2] *Ibid,*, ff. 7, 8. In one case the master 'dixit magistro qui ver-

berabat in secundo ictu quod sufficiebat et per modum derisionis recessit'.

[3] [On the subject of corporal punishment see W. W. Rouse Ball, *Cambridge Papers*, pp. 199–214.]

humiliating alternative.[1] Even at Magdalen, founded in CHAP. XIV.
1458, corporal punishment is only contemplated in the
grammar school to which, it will be remembered, the
younger demies were sent. The statutes of Brasenose—
founded in 1509—are the first which exhibit the undergraduate completely stripped of all his medieval dignity, tamed,
and reduced to the schoolboy level, from which he did not
begin to emerge again till towards the close of the seventeenth
century. Here he is subjected to the birch at the discretion of
the college lecturer for unprepared lessons, playing, laughing
or talking in lecture, making 'odious comparisons', speaking
English, disobeying the lecturer, as well as for unpunctuality
or non-attendance at chapel, and other offences which fell
under the cognizance of the principal.[2] The statutes of Dr.
Caius for his college at Cambridge contain a precise definition
as to the age after which personal correction was exchanged
for a pecuniary fine. The founder, who was a great disciplinarian, fixed the age at eighteen.[3] Wolsey's statutes for
Cardinal College put it at twenty.[4] The sixteenth century was
the flogging age *par excellence* in the English universities.

[1] 'Sic vero de mea consanguini-
tate vel aliunde per socios admissi
ab huiusmodi elemosina non repel-
lantur, nisi ob defectum morum vel
profectus, . . . aut nisi, postquam
annos nubiles attigerint, castiga-
ciones concernentes delicta seu
erudiciones eorum sive in curialitate
sive in literatura a superioribus suis
quorum intererit imponendas sus-
cipere et servare contempserint'
(*Statutes*, p. 30), [J. R. Magrath,
The Queen's College, i. 46]. In the
same statutes 'castigatio' is denounced for not speaking in Latin
or French, 'quam si sustinere
noluerint poenam incurrant paulo
superius annotatam'. So, a little
earlier, at Durham College, the
monks thought 'castigatio' a suitable punishment for their poor
secular servitors. Wilkins, *Concilia*
(1737), ii. 614 *a*, 615 *b*.
[2] 'Secundum discretionem Lec-

toris puniatur, et hoc poena pecuniaria; alioquin virga corrigatur'
(*Statutes*, p. 15). 'Et volumus,
quod illa particula, scilicet "vel
virga corrigatur", conformiter in-
telligitur in omnibus aliis statutis
poenalibus poena pecuniaria' (*ibid.*,
p. 19).
[3] 'Adultos vocamus qui annum
exegerint decimum octavum.'
Caius seems to find a curious reason
for the definition in the fact that
'ante eam aetatem et antiquitus et
nostra memoria quoque braccas
inducere adolescentia non solebat'
(*Cambridge Documents*, ii. 271).
[4] 'Si graduatus non fuerit nec
vicesimum aetatis suae annum com-
pleverit, talis vel verberibus casti-
getur, vel praedictis poenis aut aliis
. . . ad arbitrium Decani et unius
censoris . . . puniatur' (*Statutes*,
p. 70).

CHAP. XIV.   In time the discipline of the colleges began to react upon

Reaction of colleges upon university discipline.

the discipline of the halls and of the universities generally. The very ample statutes of the German universities enable us to trace the gradual tightening of discipline which goes on till the sixteenth century is reached. The statutes become increasingly minute and restrictive in their interference with all manner of 'unacademical' pleasures, in the strictness with which they require attendance at university and college exercises, including the hall-dinner with its post-prandial disputations. A visit to the tavern, or even the kitchen of the college or hall,[1] becomes a university offence.[2] In France the younger students are confined to their halls, forbidden to pawn their clothes, and sent out to walk two and two under the supervision of a master, in the melancholy fashion still [1895] characteristic of the Parisian lycée.[3] In short, the beginning of the fourteenth century found the non-collegiate undergraduate a gentleman at large: the close of the fifteenth left him a mere schoolboy—though less completely so in Germany than at Paris and Oxford. The revolution is the

[1] A scholar in the *Manuale Scholarium* complains: 'Et quod plus me intus cruciat, quater in coquina arreptus sum: postulant a me denarios. *Bartoldus.* Quo iure hoc faciunt? *Camillus.* Rogas? Statutum fecerunt, ne quis intret coquinam, nisi famulus sit aut causam quandam habeat urgentem' (Zarncke, *Die deutschen Univ. in Mittelalt.*, Leipzig, 1857, p. 28. As to this dialogue see below, p. 378 *sq.*).

[2] We do, indeed, find such a prohibition as early as the statutes of Erfurt—or, rather, a project for the original code of statutes, which does not appear to have been ever formally enacted. The silence of many later codes—in spite of the general resemblance of the disciplinary clauses of different German university statutes—perhaps indicates that the provision could not be practically carried out. The statute provides: 'Item ad publicas taber-

nas non vadant in nocte seu in die nec ad alia loca inhonesta' (Weissenborn, *Acten*, ii. 7). At Leipzig a similar provision does not occur till 1458. Zarncke, *Statutenbücher*, p. 59.

[3] Cf. the following statutes of Angers in 1494: 'Caveant pedagogi, ne sui scholares sint vagabundi seu illicentiati domum exeant, et ne vestimenta sua aut libros in extraordinariis victualibus et superfluis aut ludis exponant, sed domum clausam teneant, maxime crepusculo adveniente' (Fournier, i, No. 497). So again: 'Quod scholares huiusmodi non mittantur ad campos sine magistro, qui eos ducat et reducat, regat et gubernet simul et in eodem loco, et omnes possit advertere, et bini incedant et redeant, maxime per villam' (*ibid.*). The discipline of the smaller French universities seems to have been particularly strict at this time: their arts faculties were, indeed, mere schools for boys.

more remarkable since the tendency seems to have been, if CHAP. XIV. anything, to come up to the University later than had been the case in earlier times.[1]

These remarks might be abundantly illustrated from the Aularian *Statuta Aularia* at Oxford. The mere enactment of a body of statutes for the halls by the authority of the university in place of the private statutes enacted by the scholars, marks an important step in the extension of college discipline to the unendowed societies. Such a body of statutes appears to have been enacted for the first time in the chancellorship of Gilbert Kymer (1431–4 and 1446–53) 'by the discrete and mature advice and consent of the venerable assembly of Masters and of the Principals of Halls'. Another body of statutes was passed in the chancellorship of John Russell, Bishop of Lincoln (1483–94),[2] and there can be little doubt that this is the code which is still extant. The regulations are of much the same kind as we find in college statutes, but (as is natural) less exacting. There are statutes against swear-

Marginal note: Aularian Statutes at Oxford.

---

[1] Leipzig forbids graduation 'nisi attigerit septimum decimum annum' (Zarncke, *Statutenbücher*, p. 331). [Rudolf Agricola apparently matriculated at Erfurt in 1456 at the age of twelve and proceeded to the B.A. two years later at the age of fourteen. He took his master's degree at Louvain in 1460, aged sixteen. See P. S. Allen, *Opus Epistolarum Erasmi*, i. 106 n.]

[2] *Mun. Acad.* i. 358. [*Stat. Antiq. Univ. Oxon.*, ed. S. Gibson, pp. 295–6.] This statute, dated 1489, provides for the periodical reading of the code in each hall. There can therefore be little doubt that the manuscript copy (Rawlinson Statutes, No. 34) was made at this date. Its existence has hitherto been quite unknown, the manuscript being uncatalogued. [It was printed as an Appendix in the original edition of this book, but has not been included in this edition as the text is printed in *Statuta Antiqua Univ. Oxon.*, ed. S. Gibson, pp. 574–88.]

Rashdall was mistaken in believing that the existence of these statutes was previously unknown. Both Twyne and Wood knew of them: see Wood's *Life and Times*, ed. A. Clark, iv. 105, 106, 130–1. See also A. B. Emden, *An Oxford Hall*, p. 197, n. 1. There is no evidence for the existence of the earlier body of Aularian Statutes which Rashdall presumed to have been enacted in the chancellorship of Gilbert Kymer. The statutes passed during Kymer's chancellorship, which principals were required by the statute of 1489 to read periodically to the members of their respective halls, may be identified with the statutes relating to breaches of the peace and other matters of academic discipline which were enacted during Kymer's chancellorship, but were applicable to the university as a whole, and were not specifically Aularian. See *ibid.*, pp. 197–200.]

CHAP. XIV. ing, games of chance, the art *bokelar*, 'unhonest garrulities', walking abroad without a companion, being out after eight in the winter or nine in summer, sharing a bed with a 'socius' without leave of the principal, entering another man's chamber without his consent, 'odious comparisons of country to country, nobility to ignobility, faculty to faculty', speaking English except at a 'gaude' or principal feast, and so on.[1] There are compulsory excursions into the country 'for the recreation, convenience, and honour of the community'; but on ordinary occasions students are merely required in the customary manner to walk with a companion if possible. They are free to be absent from meals and receive an allowance in respect of unconsumed commons; but attendance is enforced not only at the lectures, recitations, and disputations of the hall, but at the lectures and disputations of the university. All are required to hear mass[2] daily and to attend university sermons. After the evening potation[3] the community ended the day by singing the 'antiphon of the Blessed Virgin' or *Salve Regina* together. A definite penalty is imposed for every offence, ranging from $\frac{1}{4}d$. for not speaking Latin to 6s. 8d. for assault with effusion of blood. In most cases the fine is limited to a few pence. No other penalty than a fine is authorized except in the case of a boy placed under the charge of a 'tutor or creditor', who was to be excused payment of the fine if he had undergone

[1] 'Preterquam gaudiorum tempore et festorum principalium infra precinctum aule.' [*Stat. Antiq. Univ. Oxon.*, ed. S. Gibson, p. 579, ll. 20–1. For a full analysis of these statutes see A. B. Emden, *An Oxford Hall*, pp. 200–18.]

[2] 'Item quod quilibet infra aulam existens cotidie audiat missam et dicat matutinas et vesperas secundum exigenciam sui ordinis vel condicionis, sub pena oboli' [*Stat. Antiq. Univ. Oxon.*, ed. S. Gibson, p. 575, ll. 4–6]. Matins and vespers on ferial days can hardly be imposed upon persons not in holy orders. On Sundays and festivals all were to attend High Mass, matins, and vespers in the parish church. A chapel in the hall was exceptional. [The statute prescribes that a member of a hall shall hear mass and say matins and vespers 'according to the requirement of his order or condition'. The obligation, therefore, is not likely to have been so comprehensive as Rashdall supposed.]

[3] It is not quite clear whether this was observed only on Saturdays or every day. Sometimes we find this function specially associated with Saturday: elsewhere it seems to be a daily observance.

'corporal chastisement' in public at the hands of the principal CHAP. XIV.
on Saturday night.[1] As there is no indication that it was
necessary for even the younger scholars in halls to have such
a tutor, it may be inferred that it was a luxury of the rich.[2]

It should be observed that even these Oxford statutes, Traces left of ancient
which had for their object to assert the authority of the uni- autonomy in halls.
versity and of the principals, contain traces of the old aularian
self-government. Thus, though the principal when once
elected holds his office independently of the students, the
students every week elect an 'impositor' who is to enforce
the observance of the statutes. It would appear that he imposed the prescribed fines by his own authority and only
reported the offences to the principal at the weekly meeting
or chapter of the whole community after the singing of the
antiphon on Saturday night. The fines go to the 'community'. Moreover, offenders refusing to submit to them are
to be expelled 'by the authority of the principal and community'.[3]

One feature of the discipline of the later medievai college Latin-speaking and the 'lupus'.
is too curious to be passed over. We have already noticed
how invariable is the insistence in the statutes upon speaking
in Latin. How far such a regulation was really enforced in

[1] 'Quod vnusquisque scolaris
manens sub magistro, tutore, aut
creditore subeat in noctibus saba-
tinis publice correccionem cor-
poralem, aut alias multam pecuni-
ariam pro suis excessibus contra
prefata statuta . . . non obstante
quod magister suus, tutor, curator
aut creditor suus tunc dixerit se
illos excessus correxisse' [*Stat. Antiq. Univ. Oxon.*, ed. S. Gibson,
p. 587, ll. 9–15]. This is the first
occurrence of the word *tutor* that I
know of. [Earlier instances of the
use of the word *tutor* occur in *Registrum Cancell. Oxon., 1434–1469*,
ed. H. E. Salter, pp. i, xxx, 321;
ii. 215.] For the English 'creansyr'
in this sense see *Oxford Eng. Dict.*
It is perhaps implied that other
very young scholars were treated
in the same way.

[2] It was probably a tutor of this
kind who is alluded to in one of the
Paston Letters (ed. Fenn, London,
1787, i. 144 [and ed. J. Gairdner,
Edinburgh, 1910, i. 422]), where
the mother of Clement Paston sends
a message to his tutor (not in the
university) desiring 'that he wyll
trewly belassch hym tyl he wyll
amend; and so ded the last maystr
and the best that ever he had att
Caumbrege'.

[3] [*Stat. Antiq. Univ. Oxon.*, ed.
S. Gibson, pp. 585–6. It is possible
that the office of impositor was, as
Rashdall states, elective, but it
should be noted that the statute
upon which Rashdall relies for his
authority says no more than 'unus
alius sociorum deputetur aut duo
deputentur in impositorem'.]

CHAP. XIV. early colleges or halls it is difficult to conjecture. But, when the undergraduate had been fairly tamed, we find a widely spread system of spies called 'lupi', who were secretly appointed by the masters to inform against 'vulgarisantes', as the offenders were called who persisted in the use of their mother-tongue. We get constant allusions to this practice in the 'Manuale Scholarium' which emanated from Heidelberg towards the close of the fifteenth century,[1] and the appointment of 'wolves' is required by some of the German statutes.[2] There is no express evidence in any English college statutes of a corresponding practice, but it appears in the seventeenth-century statutes of Harrow School,[3] and was possibly not unknown in the universities at a time when there was very little difference between the discipline of a college and that of a grammar school.

Bachelors.   In the later medieval period, when the bachelorship of arts had acquired greater importance than it once possessed, the bachelor enjoyed a good deal more personal liberty than was accorded to the younger boys. At Navarre, for instance, he is allowed to walk abroad by himself, while the undergraduate was required to have an 'honest companion'.[4] Both classes of students were, however, it would seem, accompanied by the vice-master to university sermons and into the country, when leave was given for that purpose.[5]

The 'Bejaunus' and his Deposition or Initiation

Student initiations.   Amid all variations in the degree of his subjection to masters or university authorities, the medieval undergraduate was everywhere and at all times bound by a far more in-

---

[1] 'Bartoldus. Quid te sollicitat? Camillus. Obsecro, animadverte: duodecies fuerim in lupo! . . . B. Quis erat? C. Haut scio. . . . Dabo operam, perscrutabor ipsum; tandem postea iniuriam hanc ulciscar' (Zarncke, Die deutschen Univ. im Mittelalt., p. 28). So at Basel (Vischer, p. 152): 'Item rector burse diligenter provideat de signatore vulgarisancium quem lupum vocant, qui vulgarisantes fideliter

signet et se nulli manifestet sub debito bone fidei suo rectori debite' (c. A.D. 1466).

[2] Zarncke, Statutenbücher, p. 477 (A.D. 1499).

[3] The Commem. of the Tercentenary of Harrow School, Harrow, 1871, p. xxvii sq.

[4] Launoi, Reg. Nav. Gymn. Hist. (1678), i. 33.

[5] Ibid., p. 103 (A.D. 1404).

tolerant and inflexible code of student etiquette. We have CHAP. XIV. already noticed the hoary antiquity and the widespread prevalence of the custom of student-initiation. Three deeply rooted instincts of human nature combined to put this custom beyond the reach of magisterial suppression.[1] It gratified alike the bullying instinct, the social instinct, and the desire to find at once the excuse and the means for a carouse. First, the *bejaunus* or 'yellow-bill' (*bec-jaune*), as the academic fledgling was styled, must be hoaxed and bullied; then he must be welcomed as a comrade; finally his 'jocund advent' must be celebrated by a feast to be provided at his own expense. The development of these initiations

[1] A statute on this subject was passed by the University of Paris in 1342 (Bulaeus, iv. 266; *Chartul.* ii, No. 1057): 'Et quia plurimorum frequentius querelas accipimus, quod nonnulli per eorum potentiam bona simplicium scolarium occasione bejaunie sue rapiunt, nisi eis satisfiat de bejaunia, quam etiam, mala malis accumulantes, taxare nituntur pro libito voluntatis, et sic in hoc magnam partem sue pecunie coacti per raptores huiusmodi exponunt, de qua possent diutius in studio sustentari: hinc est quod nos attendentes predicta (nec non insultus, verbera, et alia pericula que solent exinde evenire, quodque etiam per talia plures a nostro distrahuntur studio, quod in nostri et prelibati studii redundat non modicam lesionem) . . . sic duximus ordinandum.' The statute goes on to forbid such exactions by any students 'exceptis sociis, cum quibus inhabitat, qui pro bejaunia domus poterunt recipere, dum tamen predicti bejauni hoc offerant spontanea voluntate'. 'Iurati' were to be deprived; 'non iurati' to be expelled 'a nostro consortio'; but how little control the university had at this time over the 'non iurati' is illustrated by the fact that it is obliged to order the proctors to proceed against the offenders before the Official. So at Ingolstadt: 'Venerabile nostrum collegium decrevit quod decanus potestatem habeat vexatores et tribulatores novellorum studentum, quos beanos vocant, arbitraria poena mulctare poenamque sic inflictam in suos convertere usus' (Prantl, *Gesch. d. Univ. in Ingolstadt*, ii. 103). A form of proclamation by a 'conventor' (the head of a hall) forbids his students 'cornua, ut ipsi vocant, deponere, aut contra scamna aut alio quocunque modo socios suos ducere, sub pena duorum solidorum irremissibiliter persolvendorum' (*loc. cit.*). The 'contra scamna ducere' probably implies the proceeding in vogue at Aix (see below, p. 384, n. 1). At Valence it is forbidden even to call a freshman 'bejaunus', or to put straws in his books, or to practise 'other vanities' (Fournier, iii, No. 1842). In 1465 'quedam secta abbatia bejaunorum vulgariter nuncupata' is suppressed at Montpellier (*ibid.* ii, No. 1166). At Paris in 1488 the statute of 1341 is only reenacted with the saving clause 'praeter spontaneam et moderatam Regis (Twelfth-night King) oblationem ac pecuniam noviter venientium qui vulgo bejauni nominantur' (Bulaeus, v. 783), which seems to imply that the 'bejaunia' is now compulsory.

CHAP. XIV.

Repression
gives way
to patron-
age.

is one of the most curious episodes in university history. At first we meet with severe and sweeping prohibitions against all exaction of 'bejaunia' from the unfortunate youth whose little purse, intended to meet perhaps his first year's expenses, was liable to be half emptied by what sometimes amounted to a raid upon the hard-earned proceeds of a parent's life-time.[1] Gradually we find restrictions upon the number of guests taking the place of total prohibition; and from the authoritative sanction there is a gradual process to the authoritative requirement of the 'depositio cornuum'. In the sixteenth century it has become in the German univer-sities an obligatory academical ceremonial like matriculation or determination.[2]

A medieval
'Verdant
Green'.

A curious account of a freshman's experiences has come down to us in an already mentioned 'Scholar's Manual' of the late fifteenth century—a kind of medieval 'Verdant Green'.[3] The story illustrates how the badgering or 'hazing'

---

[1] [Extant letters and forms of letters give numerous examples of the financial difficulties of students, and sometimes of their parents or guardians. See Haskins, pp. 7–16. A good case of the failure of sup-plies occurs in the *Rotuli litterarum clausarum*, ii. 89 b (12 Dec. 1225): King Henry III orders the mayor of London and others to provide 40 marks for the needs of six Portu-guese scholars in Paris; their relatives had sent money in a Portuguese ship for their main-tenance, but this had been lost when the ship was captured. The mayor is to provide the 40 marks from the proceeds of the mer-chandise in the captured vessel.]

[2] This stage would seem to have been reached at Greifswald by 1456: 'Item a beano pro ipsius beanii depositione non plus tertia parte floreni exigere aut exigi permittere debent bursarum rec-tores. Item depositio beanii fieri debet in collegiis aut regentiis, nisi deponens filius fuerit alicuius incole

huius ciuitatis, uel saltem licentiam habuerit decani et suorum asses-sorum specialem' (Kosegarten, ii. 304). So at Rostock earlier (*circa* 1419); Westphalen, *Diplomatarium*, iv, cc. 1014–16. A college statute at Paris as early as 1380 requires that 'pro iocundo . . . adventu solvat unusquisque secundum personae suae qualitatem et secundum quan-titatem facultatum suarum', &c. Félibien, iii. 504. [W. Fabricius, *Die akademische Deposition*, Frank-furt, 1895, takes a rather different view of the history of this institu-tion in the German university. He considers that the custom was al-ways practised in the *bursae*. Later the university took official sanction of it and imposed a fee. The 'un-lawful exactions' forbidden were those over and above the customary dues.]

[3] The book consists of a series of dialogues intended apparently in part as a *répertoire* of the latinity which a scholar would require for conversational purposes at the uni-

(as the American students call it) of the *bejaunus* has gradually CHAP. XIV.
assumed a stereotyped form. The raw youth from the
country is supposed to be a wild beast who has got to lay
aside his horns before he can be received into the refined
society of his new home. By this time the actual ceremony
of 'depositio' has become a solemn university function,
patronized though not actually conducted by the university
authorities. The student is first represented as conversing
with his new master, whom he asks to arrange for his
'depositio', and entreats to let the expenses be as moderate
as possible.[1] Then, after returning from matriculation before
the rector, he is visited in his room by two of the students.
They pretend to be investigating the source of an abominable
odour which has reached their nostrils. At last they discover
the cause; it is the new-comer, whom they take to be a wild
boar. A closer inspection reveals that it is a 'beanus', a
creature that they have heard of but never seen. Then follows
much chaff about the wild glare in his eye, the length of his
ears, the ferocious aspect of his tusks, and so on. Then with
mock sympathy it is suggested that the horns and other
excrescences may be removed by an operation—the so-called
'deposition'. The ceremony is apparently rehearsed in rough The
deposition
horse-play. The victim's face is smeared with soap or some- rehearsed.
thing of the kind by way of ointment; his ears are clipped; his
beard cut; the tusks removed with a saw; and so on. Finally,
they are afraid that the operation will be fatal: the patient
must be shriven without delay. One of them feigns himself
a priest, and puts his ear to his mouth. His confession is
repeated, word for word, by the confessor. The boy is made

---

versity. It was published as a dateless black-letter book, and is reprinted by Zarncke in *Die deutschen
Universitäten im Mittelalter* (Beitrag, I. Leipzig, 1857). [A collo-
quial English translation in R. F.
Seybolt, *The Manuale Scholarium*,
Cambridge, Mass., 1921.] I have
been quite unable to do justice to
the graphic and vivid presentation
of the scene.

[1] '*Disc*. Optime praeceptor, divi-
tiae parvae mihi sunt. Ne prorsus
sumptuosa collatio fiat, apprime
rogo, neque etiam volo, quod
nimium extenuetur ac honestas
offendatur in re, sed mediocritas
retineatur cum consuetudine. *Mag.*
Probe intelligo. Vocabo igitur tres
magistros et baccalaureos duos et
quosdam de sociis meis' (i.e. pupils
or boarders); *loc. cit.*, p. 4.

CHAP. XIV. to accuse himself of all sorts of enormities: as a penance for which he is enjoined to provide a sumptuous banquet for his new masters and comrades; and so he is led off to the 'depositio' proper.

The public deposition. The nature of the actual ceremony may be perhaps inferred from the anticipatory sketch of our two students. The victim appears to have been in some way dressed up in a cap adorned with horns and long ears to resemble a wild beast, and was then planed, sawn, or drubbed into shape with whatever varieties of insult or torture the wit, ingenuity, or brutality of different universities might suggest.[1] A little book published in the sixteenth century contains pictorial representations of the scene. There is a procession headed by a master in his academical dress and followed by students in a sort of masquerading costume. Then there is a representation of the planing down of the *bejaunus* extended upon a table, while a saw lies upon the ground, suggestive of the actual de-horning of the beast. Finally, his nose is held to the grindstone by one student while another turns the handle.[2] The work itself and later apologies[3] for the institution mention among the instruments of torture a comb and scissors for cutting the victim's hair, an *auriscalpium* for his ears, a knife for cutting his nails; while the ceremony further appears to include the adornment of the youth's chin with a beard by means of burned cork or other pigment, and the administration, internal or external, of salt and wine. In some universities the dose of salt was eventually reserved as a penalty for refusal to submit to a certain 'Musical Examination' with which the proceedings concluded—a feature of

[1] Cf. Ennen, *Gesch. d. Stadt Köln*, iii. 881.

[2] Dinkel, *De origine, causis, typo et ceremoniis illius ritus, qui vulgo in Scholis Depositio appellatur*, Erfurt, 1578 (a very rare work). It includes the 'Iudicium reverendi patris D. Doctoris Martini Lutheri, de Depositione', delivered on occasion of his taking part in one of these functions, and attempting to give a moral and symbolical turn to the

ceremony. The Reformer's words were often quoted, and may perhaps have helped to postpone the extinction of the barbarity for a century or two.

[3] e.g. Valentinus Hoffmann, *Laus depositionis beanorum*, Jena, 1657; Gellius, *De depositione academica*, Leipzig, 1689. The former contains a speech from a student who presided as *depositor* on one of these occasions.

the 'depositio' which will be recalled by readers of the
classical story of English public school life in the last century.

The particular ceremony of 'deposition', it should be Deposition
observed, is only heard of in the German universities; but peculiar to
Germany.
the system of extorting money and otherwise badgering or
initiating *bejauni* was all but universal.[1] In Germany the
'deposition' gradually paved the way for the so-called 'pen-
nalism', a system of brutal bullying and fagging of juniors
by seniors which exceeds in barbarity anything which the
annals of the English public schools in their worst days have
to record. The system reached its height in the seventeenth
century, and long defied all the efforts of professors and
governments to put it down.[2]

In southern France the initiation of *bejauni* assumed a Initiations
somewhat different form. Here the freshman was not a wild in France.
beast who had to be civilized, but a criminal who had to be
tried and admitted to the purgation of this peculiar form of
original sin. At Avignon the conduct of this 'purgation of
freshmen' was made the primary object of a religious confraternity, formed under high ecclesiastical sanction, with a Guild of
chapel of its own in the Dominican church. While, as the S. Sebastian at
preamble piously boasts, it was the object of the institution Avignon.
to put a stop to the 'nefarious and incredible enormities',
the drunkenness and immorality,[3] which usually charac-

---

[1] For the bibliography of the
subject see Pernwerth von Bärn-
stein, *Ubi sunt qui ante nos in mundo
fuere?* Würzburg, 1882, p. 103 *sq.*

[2] For a pathetic account of the
sufferings of a poor boy often reduced to the verge of starvation by
the depredations of the 'Bacchante'
or older student who lived upon his
beggings, see the *Autobiography of
Thomas Platter* (Eng. trans., London, 1839). I abstain from borrow-
ing further illustrations from this
source because (1) the date is somewhat too late; (2) the state of things
described seems to have been peculiar to Germany and Switzerland;
(3) none of the schools frequented

by these troops of wandering scholars were (so far as appears) universities.

[3] 'Adiicientes predictis ut morum
servetur honestas et viciorum ma-
cula profugetur ut prefati novicii
sive bejauni non audeant sumpto
convivio pro meretricibus consociis
aliquid impendere, per hoc illum
ritum dampnabilem annulantes',
&c. (Fournier, *Une corporation
d'étudiants en Droit en 1441*, reprinted from *Nouvelle revue historique de droit*, Paris, 1887, pp. 16,
17). The following details are
taken from the statutes and documents there printed.

CHAP. XIV. terized this celebration, the statutes still compel the *bejaunus*, except in cases of sworn poverty, to contribute six *grossi* to the funds of the guild. A noble or beneficed student paid double, and if on temperance principles he wished to limit the expense of the banquet usually given by a new-comer, he might redeem it by a further payment to the funds of the confraternity, to be spent 'to the honour of God and of S. Sebastian'. The 'purgation of his infection' was to be enforced by 'the capture of books'.[1] Once enrolled as a member of the guild, the freshman lost the 'base name' of *bejaunus*, and after a year's residence attained the 'honourable name' of student. By what ceremony over and above the compulsory subscription the purgation was carried out, does not distinctly appear; but, as we find that the guild appointed two officers called 'promotors' whose business it was to 'accuse' the freshmen, some sort of mock trial seems to be indicated. These fooleries contrast oddly with the provisions for masses and sermons with which the same statutes are largely occupied. To the medieval mind there was probably nothing incongruous in the juxtaposition, though it is curious to find apostolical sanction solemnly given to such a barefaced act of theft as the 'capture of books'. This particular instrument of extortion—strikingly suggestive of the workman's mode of enforcing class tyranny by the abstraction of tools—seems to have been the usual one in French universities.[2]

---

[1] 'Ad quorum solutionem per captionem librorum compellantur, sanctissime nostre confratrie utilitatibus et gloriosissimis operibus eiusdem fideliter applicandis' (*ibid.*, p. 15). It is not clear whether the banquet was defrayed out of these contributions or whether such entertainment was only expected in the case of the rich.

[2] At Orleans such extortions from *bejauni*, 'per captionem, ablationem vel subtractionem librorum, unius vel plurium, aut aliorum pignorum', is forbidden under pain of excommunication. Fournier, i,

No. 167. Two years later (*ibid.*, No. 174) the bishop again denounces any compulsion 'ut amplius expensis et iniuriis aggraventur ad solvendum huiusmodi beiannium suum seu suum novum adventum, ad tabernam ducentes et, ut ovis ad occisionem ducitur, accedere compellentes; . . . et ex hiis commessationes, ebrietates, turpiloquia, lascivie, pernoctationes tam in huiusmodi taberna, quam per villam de nocte incedendo, fractiones ostiorum, ut de aliis taceamus, oriuntur enormiter et insurgunt.' Cf. also No. 175.

From the same University of Avignon chance has brought down to us the 'Statutes of the venerable Abbatial Court of this famous College of S. Nicholas', i.e. the College of Annecy. This is the only documentary evidence that has come down to us as to the proceedings of those 'abbots' whom students are so often forbidden by university and college statutes to elect. The abbot holds a court twice a week. The object of the institution is not merely to conduct the 'purgation' of *bejaunia* (like the confraternity of S. Sebastian) when the freshman has served his time, but to enforce a series of minute regulations respecting his habitual behaviour. The freshmen are to serve the seniors at table, not to stand between them and the fire in the hall, to give place to them on all occasions, not to sit at the first table in hall, and not to call one another 'sir' (*domine*). Several statutes relate to the special duties of the junior man (*de officio ultimi*) in chapel and elsewhere. Some of the regulations bear on all members of the college, or 'monks' as they are styled, and are enforced by fines; but the offences of the *bejaunus* are expiated by a certain number of blows with a wooden spoon or ferule (*patella*). Moreover, every freshman received one such blow, apart from any special misconduct, every time the abbot held his court. After a certain term of good behaviour, the freshman was allowed to 'purge his freshmanship' by holding a 'repetition' upon an assigned *punctum* of the Institutes, and defending it against his brother-freshman (in imitation of the inception), after which followed the actual purgation, of which we can ascertain no more than that it was a ceremony involving the use of water.[1]

A statute of the neighbouring University of Aix enables us to fill up the hiatus in our knowledge of the 'purgation' at Avignon. It there appears that, after the freshman had been duly accused by the promotor, he was sentenced to receive a certain number of blows with a book or a frying-pan. On the highly philosophical principle that 'infinity may be avoided', it was, however, prescribed that each freshman

---

[1] Fournier, *Statuts des Univ. françaises*, ii, No. 1343.

CHAP. XIV. should not receive more than three blows from each of an unspecified number of students, but, if there were 'noble or honourable ladies' present, the rector might, upon their intercession, reduce the punishment to one from each operator.[1]

Similar customs at Paris,   No details happen to have come down to us of the customs in vogue at Paris, but they were no doubt very similar to those of the less famous French universities. The register of the Sorbonne contains a chance allusion to the election of an 'abbot' and to a 'washing' of freshmen on Innocents' Day, a ceremony which was preceded by a procession in which the unfortunate 'bejans' were carried through the streets upon asses.[2] Allusions to similar customs are found in other Parisian colleges.[3] As to the form which the bullying

[1] The details are difficult to make out. The rector is required to give notice that freshmen shall submit to purgation within a month 'cum pena purgationis fiende in studio, cum libro supra annum', but then goes on to prescribe that (apparently in all cases, even when there was no refusal to pay the bejaunia) 'quia nonnulli sunt alacres et iucundi, et in purgatione forte excederent, dando supra annum aut femora beianorum . . ., et ut infinitas sit vitanda, quod feratur sententia per dominum promotorem, quod quilibet det dicto beiano tres ictus aut minus, et non ultra, reservata misericordia domini rectoris ad preces nobilium mulierum sive honestarum, si ibidem reperiantur; et lata sententia, dominus promotor intimet sententiam domino rectori, et an demandabitur executioni, offerendo sibi sartaginem (a frying-pan), qua primo percutiet, si sibi videtur; et quod procedatur honeste' (Fournier, Statuts des Univ. Franç. iii, No. 1582). As to the meaning of 'quilibet', it is not clear whether this means every student present or the rector, promotor, and three students who were to be appointed to assist them

in the purgation. Dr. Chavernac (Hist. d'Aix, p. 108) mentions the interesting fact that the word bec-jaunes (corrupted into 'pigeons') was used in his youth among the students of Aix, and that he has heard peasants in the Basses-Alpes say 'vous payerez le béjaune'. The junior class in some of the Scottish universities was called the 'Bajan class' till very recently. [1895.]

[2] 'Anno quo supra (1476–7) condemnatus fuit in crastino Innocentium capellanus abbas Beannorum ad octo solidos parisienses exponendos in vino eo quod non expleuisset officium suum die Innocentum post prandium in mundatione Beannorum per aspersionem aque ut moris est quanquam sollemniter [mandatum] recepisset exercere suum officium ante prandium in ducendo beannos per vicum super asinum' (f. 73).

[3] Some idea of the universality of these customs may be gained from the fact that they had invaded the cloisters of the austere Cistercians. The statutes of the Cistercian College at Paris, drawn up in 1493, forbid 'omnes receptiones noviter venientium, quos voluntaria opinione Beianos nuncupare solent, cum suis

of freshmen assumed at the English universities we are CHAP. XIV. entirely in the dark, unless we may draw inferences from the and in England. 'tucking' and compulsory speech-making under pain of salt and water which lingered on, at Merton and elsewhere, to the end of the seventeenth century.[1]

Academical Dress and Clerical Status

A treatise on medieval universities must needs give some Undergraduate's account of the origin of those academical costumes which do dress clerical rather than academical. more perhaps to impress the imagination with a sense of the medieval origin of university institutions than is perhaps warranted by their real antiquity. It can hardly, indeed, be said that in the Middle Ages there was, for the undergraduate, anything which can properly be called academical dress at all. In the Italian universities the statutes contemplate that students will wear the long black garment known as a 'cappa', but aim rather at limiting the cost than at prescribing the form of his costume.[2] In the Parisian universities every

consequentiis, necnon baiulationes, fibrationes, reliquasque omnes insolentias et levitates circa quoscumque noviter venientes, tam in capitulo, in dormitorio, in parvis scholis, in jardinis quam ubiubi, et tam de die quam de nocte . . . fieri prohibemus . . . abbatis *Beianorum* nomen penitus delendo, ac deinceps nominari prohibendo'. The 'vasa, munimenta et instrumenta' used in these 'levitates' are to be surrendered (Félibien, *Hist. de Paris*, iii. 170). The interpretation of this statute must be left to the reader's imagination, aided by the evidence as to Avignon and Aix. 'Baiulationes' and 'fibrationes' would seem to denote some form of personal violence; but Ducange does not help us.

[1] At Merton the freshmen on certain evenings before Christmas had to 'speake some pretty apothegme, or make a jest or bull, or speake some eloquent nonsense' under pain of 'tucking' (i.e. cutting

open the chin with the thumb-nail), and on Shrove Tuesday had to make a speech which was rewarded by 'cawdle', or salted drink, or a mixture of the two (with more 'tucking' if necessary), according to its quality. These customs did not survive the Commonwealth. See the *Life and Times of Anthony Wood*, ed. A. Clark (O.H.S., 1891), i. 133-4, 138-9. At Exeter a similar custom was stopped by a rising of freshmen headed by the great Whig statesman, Anthony Ashley, afterwards first Earl of Shaftesbury. Christie, *Life of Shaftesbury*, London, 1871, i. 17, 18. At S. Andrews a custom lingers by which the senior has the right to demand a packet of raisins from any freshman he meets who has not previously paid this due. This is a clear relic of the *bejaunia*. [1895.]

[2] At Vienna in 1456 'desiderabant Consiliarii Regii, quatenus studentes aliquo signo notarentur, ut statuto more studentium in

C C

CHAP. XIV. student was supposed to be a clerk, and was required by custom or statute to wear the tonsure and the clerical habit.[1] We find statutes in abundance against various forms of 'indecent', 'unhonest', 'dissolute', or merely 'secular' apparel—such as 'trunkhose', puffed sleeves, pointed shoes, red or green hosen, and the like. At Heidelberg it was even thought necessary to forbid students from going out without boots 'unless clad in a garment reaching to the heels'.[2] But

Italia ab aliis differrent non studentibus' (*Conspectus Hist. Univ. Vienn.* i. 178). Was it just because the Italian student was not bound by master-made statutes that he did not object to academical dress?

[1] In the list of proctorial duties in *Mun. Acad. Oxon.* i. 110 [*Stat. Antiq. Univ. Oxon.*, ed. S. Gibson, p. 197, l. 27] we find a clause, 'Contra non habentes habitum et tonsuram decentes.' So at Prague (*Mon. Univ. Prag.*, p. 50) the B.A. was required to swear 'quod portabit habitum et tonsuram clericales'. In England we never find the clericality of a university student questioned. In some of the German universities it appears to have been possible to dispute his clerical immunities if he did not dress and shave clerically. Thus, at Leipzig, a scholar of law, who had thrown a stone at a master of arts while the latter was looking out of window, objected to the jurisdiction of the official of Merseburg on the ground that plaintiff 'non clericus sed laicus existat, quod ad oculum demonstro per eius barbe delacionem', which should be accepted till he proves 'se clericum ordinatum quod nondum credo'. It seems to be implied in what follows that a student on matriculation could claim to be a clerk or not, as he pleased (*Urkundenbuch*, ed. Stübel, p. 77). This was in 1445. A year later, significantly enough, there appears a decree 'quod nullus doctor, magister aut scolaris, in clericatu

existens, barbam nutrire praesumat' (Zarncke, *Statutenbücher d. Univ. Leip.*, p. 15). In 1496 (*ibid.*, p. 19) we find 'uxorati' exempted from some of the provisions as to dress, showing clearly that the original idea of academical dress was simply based on the fact that students were clerks. In Italy there is no trace of any scholars being treated as clerks except those regularly admitted by the bishop. Thus at Padua the bishop 'Vitalianum . . . scolarem . . . ordinavit in clericum' (Gloria, *Mon.*, *1318–1405*, ii. 28). So 'promovit ad primam tonsuram clericalem Petrum . . . scolarem' (*ibid.*, p. 33).

[2] 'Ita quod de cetero nullus incedat publice in via discaligatus, nisi inductus (i.e. indutus) fuerit veste talari, qua corpus suum de-center sit coopertum, sub pena vnius floreni' (Hautz, *Gesch. d. Univ. Heid.* ii. 398). At Cologne, the artist (unless a servitor) 'utatur honesta veste talari aut indecenter non accurtata, toga videlicet aut tabhardo plicas non ligatas habente, et capucio honesto cum corneta in plateis aut aliis locis extra bursam' (A.D. 1457) (Bianco, i, Anl., p. 74; cf. p. 51). So at Leipzig, in 1537, it is ordered 'quod nullus scholasticorum in collegio vel iuxta collegium scurriliter incedat, puta in diploide et tibialibus duntaxat, sine tunicella, in dedecus collegii et scandalum virginum et mulierum honestarum necnon ceterorum hominum intrantium et exeuntium

the shape and pattern of these garments would appear to chap. xiv. have varied a good deal according to the vanities of individual taste or changing fashion. No particular form of garment was prescribed by university authority: the undergraduate's dress was in no sense an official costume. The differentia of clerical dress was apparently supposed to lie in the outer garment being of a certain length and closed in front. But it was only in the latter part of our period that it was expected to reach to the heels, or at least well below the knee; and the restriction to black is not common[1] till even later. In the colleges only parti-coloured garments were regarded as secular: it was usual for graduate and undergraduate alike to wear a 'livery', i.e. clothes of the usual clerical shape but of uniform colour and material; just as the boys of Christ's Hospital wear a uniform dress of a particular colour, which is, however, in its general shape, merely the ordinary dress of the sixteenth-century schoolboy. The Christ's Hospitallers with their long coats and bands (which are of course merely a clerical collar) are a survival from a time when all students were supposed to be clerks. So at the College of Navarre the livery was to be of black;[2] at the College of Beauvais, 'blue or violet'.[3] The colour of the liveries in our English colleges is seldom prescribed by statute, though the Queen's men at Oxford were required to wear blood-red, but differences of colour and ornament as badges of different colleges still survive in the undergraduate gowns of Cambridge.[4]

A distinctively academical or official garment was at first confined to masters. This garment was not the modern gown or *toga*, but the *cappa* or cope, with a border and hood

The magisterial cappa.

---

collegium, sub poena quinque grossorum' (Zarncke, *Statutenbücher*, p. 240).

[1] It is found at Rostock, where the scholar 'incedere debet cum toga pro veste exteriori panni nigri ... undique clausa talari vel quasi', but coloured hoods are allowed (Westphalen, *Diplomatarium*, c. 1031). Cf. above, vol. i, p. 194 *sq.*

[2] 'Tabardas vel houssias de

bruneta nigra' (Bulaeus, iv. 92). As the statutes of Orleans allowed this garment to be worn in riding (Fournier, i, No. 26), it may be presumed that it was shorter than the *cappa*.

[3] Félibien, i. 669.

[4] [See H. P. Stokes, *Ceremonies of the University of Cambridge*, pp. 43–8.]

CHAP. XIV. of minever. The word *cappa* was indeed used to denote merely the ordinary full-dress outer garment worn by the secular clergy out of doors,[1] and it is difficult to say how far the early statutes on the subject do more than insist on masters appearing at all public functions in the full dress of the order to which they belonged. It is impossible to trace the stages by which the magisterial *cappa* acquired a more or less peculiar and distinctive aspect. Its use—at least its compulsory use—was confined to regents and sometimes to 'ordinary' lectures and other full-dress functions. A particular form of it—the sleeved *cappa*—came to be the distinctive dress of bachelors.[2] But though the strictness with which the use of the *cappa* is insisted on varies in different universities, colleges, and periods, it was, at Paris at least,

[1] See *Materials for Hist. of Th. Becket*, ed. Robertson, vi. 604; Labbe, *Concilia* (Venice, 1784), xxvi, f. 431. So in 1248 we hear (*Reg. d'Inn. IV*, ed. Berger, No. 4123) that 'Iudaei dioecesis Magalonensis et circumpositorum locorum, non sine ordinis clericalis iniuria capas rotundas et largas more clericorum et sacerdotium deferre praesumant, propter quod saepe contingit ut a peregrinis et advenis eis tanquam sacerdotibus honor et reverentia praestentur'. The external resemblance between a Jew and a doctor of divinity was still a joke in the days of the *Epistolae Obscurorum Virorum* (ed. Münch, Leipzig, 1827, p. 84). The *cappa* of the Oxford M.A. disappeared about the beginning of the sixteenth century, when we find the regents granting themselves wholesale dispensations from its use. The statutes of many universities allowed a 'tabard' to be worn at 'extraordinary lectures', or a 'cappa rugata' or 'cappa manicata'. The 'epitogium', or at least an 'epitogium longum', appears to have differed slightly from the 'cappa', but was generally allowed as an alternative to it. At other times,

however it is treated as synonymous with or equivalent to the 'tabarda'. Another form of the 'cappa' is styled 'pallium'. [See L. H. D. Buxton and S. Gibson, *Oxford University Ceremonies*, pp. 19–22.]

[2] Bulaeus, iv. 258: *Chartul.* ii, No. 1024, where it is also enforced on scholars at disputations. The statutes of Navarre provide that 'illi qui determinaverint, cappam habeant de perso vel alio uno et eodem colore honesto' (Launoi, i. 32). In the same house the theologians 'tabaldas seu houssias longas habeant cuiuscunque coloris voluerint, honesti tamen et unius coloris et eiusdem; et Baccalarii cappas rotundas eiusdem coloris' (*ibid.*, p. 35). From Bulaeus, iv. 280, it appears that the 'cappae' of determiners were 'manicatae' (with sleeves). At King's Hall, Cambridge, the undergraduate is required to wear 'robam talarem', the B.A. 'robam cum Tabardo gradui suo competentem' (Rymer, *Foedera*, III (1740), pt. iii, p. 94). [On the *cappa manicata* see L. H. D. Buxton and S. Gibson, *Oxford University Ceremonies*, p. 21, n. 1.]

quite open to an undergraduate to wear a *cappa* if he pleased.[1] At first this garment appears to have been black in the case of all faculties. But at some time between the middle of the thirteenth[2] and the middle of the fourteenth century a brighter hue was adopted by doctors of the superior faculties, usually some shade of red or purple. At Paris the rectors wore violet or purple, the masters scarlet, with tippets and hoods of fur.[3] The hood was not originally restricted to masters, Hoods. being part of the ordinary clerical dress of the period, and was not even exclusively clerical. It is only the material of the hood which was characteristic of degree or office. The use of minever hoods—still worn by the Oxford proctors— was generally confined to masters, except in the case of nobles and well-beneficed ecclesiastics. Bachelors of all faculties wore hoods of lamb's wool or rabbit's fur.[4] Silk hoods came

[1] Thus the ascetic reformer of the College of Montaigu, Jean Standonck, as late as 1501, orders that scholars of all degrees shall be provided 'de chlamyde seu pallio ante clauso, instar clamydum seu capparum quibus in vico straminis magistri artium utuntur . . . item de capitio seu camaldo', &c. The theologian's 'cappa' is to be black, the artist's 'de panno griseo ad nigrum magis tendente' (Félibien, v. 730). So at earlier colleges. Cf. *ibid*. iii. 376, 382; v. 641. A scholar (? of the thirteenth century) inveighs against rich men who turn their *cappae* instead of giving them to poor scholars (*Carmina Burana*, ed. Schmeller, p. 75). Cf. the statutes of Toulouse in 1304, where secular students, specially bachelors, are admonished, 'ut manticis longis vel cappis manicatis utuntur, prout in honorabili Parisiensi studio . . . observatur' (Devic and Vaissette, *Hist. Gen. de Languedoc*, vii. 545).
[2] Some say after the adoption of scarlet by cardinals during the pontificate of Innocent IV. Dubarle (i. 143) ascribes it to Benedict XII.

[3] At Paris (as at Oxford) the doctors of all superior faculties wore red; Bulaeus, i. 388. The rector wore purple with a cap, and apparently stockings of the same colour. *Ibid*. i. 227. Richer, describing the robes of his own day, says (*MS. Hist.*, f. 128 *b*) 'quattuor Procuratores Nationum purpurea induti, Doctores in Medicina et in Decretis capa purpurea ornati, Doctores quoque in Theologia cum capis et caputio pelliculis ornato'. 'Habits rouges' (*rubeae*) are often mentioned as characteristic of doctors of canon law. At Salamanca, in Rangeand's time, the latter appeared 'en habits rouges et verts', the doctors of theology in white, and the medical doctors in 'habit de couleur pâle' (*Hist. de l'Univ. d'Angers*, ii. 341). In England, however, scarlet was certainly worn by D.D.s. The M.D. of Caen (where Paris customs prevailed) was to appear 'in capa rotunda . . . de bruneta violetta et similiter in pileo illius coloris' (Fournier, iii, No. 1652).
[4] At Oxford, doctors of divinity also wore lamb's wool instead of

CHAP. XIV. in, perhaps towards the end of the fourteenth century, as a summer alternative for masters, whose winter fur hoods were something more than an honorary appendage in the unwarmed schools and churches of medieval times.[1] The 'Biretta' and 'pileum'. biretta,[2] a square cap with a tuft on the top (in lieu of the very modern tassel), was the distinctive badge of the mastership:[3] doctors of superior faculties wore birettas or other caps of red or violet.[4] In the faculties of law, medicine, and music,

minever. *Mun. Acad.* ii. 393. [*Stat. Antiq. Univ. Oxon.*, ed. S. Gibson, pp. 51–2.]

[1] *Mun. Acad.* i. 283, 301 [*Stat. Antiq. Univ. Oxon.*, ed. S. Gibson, pp. 233, ll. 21–8 ; pp. 239–40] ; *Chartul. Univ. Paris.* ii, App., p. 696. In 1444, Benedictine licentiates or bachelors of divinity or decrees wear 'caputia capparum scholasticarum cum buggio furrata . . . siue cum sindone nigro linita' (Reyner, *Apost. Benedictorum*, App., Pt. iii, p. 136). B.D.s still wear black silk hoods. At Oxford, undergraduates lost their hoods altogether in 1489, 'nisi liripipium consutum . . . et non contextum', presumably the little black stuff hood worn by 'Sophisters' in the schools till within living memory. [1895.] Cf. *Cambridge Documents*, i. 402. [See L. H. D. Buxton and S. Gibson, *Oxford University Ceremonies*, p. 25.]

[2] In general the term 'biretta' seems to be used where the cap was square, 'pileum' when round. Gascoigne, in his Theological Dictionary (ap. Bulaeum, ii. 257), tells us that at Oxford the round cap was worn by doctors in all the superior faculties : he declares that this ornament was bestowed by God himself on the doctors of the Mosaic Law. [On the use of the 'birettum' at Oxford see *Stat. Antiq. Univ. Oxon.*, ed. S. Gibson, pp. 229, 230; L. H. D. Buxton and S. Gibson, *Oxford University Ceremonies*, p. 27.] Later, the round velvet cap with coloured silk ribbon was worn

by doctors of law and medicine only, by whom it is occasionally still worn on state occasions at Oxford, and more frequently at Cambridge. [See L. H. D. Buxton and S. Gibson, *Oxford University Ceremonies*, pp. 27–8.] So at Caen : 'angulo carens in signum carentie sordium, quia ubi angulus, ibi sordes esse dicuntur' (Fournier, iii, No. 1718). A less gorgeous round cap is worn by the Oxford bedels. [See L. H. D. Buxton and S. Gibson, *Oxford University Ceremonies*, p. 46.]

[3] The undergraduate seems from an early period to have coveted this distinction. Cf. Prantl, *Ingolstadt*, ii. 113. Loggan's print of Oxford costumes (end of seventeenth century) shows the foundation-scholar wearing the square cap without the tuft, the B.A. wearing it with the tuft, other undergraduates and graduates in law and medicine wearing round caps. At a later period the tasselless cap was worn only by servitors and Bible-clerks. It is still worn by the choir-boys of Oxford colleges. At Paris students of theology in the Cistercian College were in 1493 allowed to wear a 'nigra bireta', though formerly worn only by bachelors. Félibien, iii. 175.

[4] Launoi, *Hist. Gymn. Nav.* i. 199, 200. At Perpignan white is the distinctive colour of theology, green of canon law, sanguine of medicine, and 'livid' of arts. Fournier, ii, No. 1517. Cf. *Chartul.* iii, No. 1708.

the place of the biretta was usually taken by a 'pileum'[1] more CHAP. XIV.
or less resembling the round caps still worn on state occasions
by Oxford and Cambridge doctors in those faculties, and at
Oxford also by the bedels. It is only in post-medieval times
that the biretta, first without, then with the sacred 'apex',
has been usurped first by bachelors, then by undergraduates,
and now (outside the universities) even by mere choristers
or schoolboys.

When the *cappa* was not required, master and scholar alike The
wore clerical garments of a less formal character, described ^{tabard.}
by a great variety of names, of which the commonest is
'tabard'. Cursory lectures, for instance, might be delivered
in this garment. Some statutes forbid the assumption of a
girdle round the waist by simple students; by others it is
prescribed and the removal of the girdle at graduation is Cincture.
treated as symbolic of emancipation from the *status pupillaris*.
In some universities it formed part of the distinctive costume
of graduates in law and medicine.

Oxford has not been conservative in the matter of costume: Conserva-
in that, as in more important matters, the Laudian age did dress at
its best to obliterate the very remembrance of the medieval Cam-
past. It is probable that no gown now worn in Oxford has

<hr>

[1] So Bulaeus, *Remarques sur la dign. du R.*, p. 24. The hood of the rector and proctors, but not the tippets, had disappeared in Du Boulay's day, though still worn by 'les adjoints des dits Procureurs' (*ibid.*, p. 25). It is curious that everywhere else throughout Europe, hoods have disappeared and tippets remained: in England the hoods remain while the tippets have disappeared, though Cambridge hoods retain traces of them, and the Cambridge proctors wear their hoods tippet-wise. A curious piece of rectorial and proctorial dress survives in a rudimentary form in the robes of Oxford proctors and pro-proctors, i.e. the purse now reduced to a triangular bunch of stuff at the back of the shoulder. It is presumably a survival from the very earliest period, when rector and proctors were primarily collectors and expenders of common funds (see above, vol. i, p. 313). This tippet is also worn attached to the gown of an M.A. who has held office as proctor. [Dr. L. H. D. Buxton and Mr. S. Gibson (*Oxford University Ceremonies*, pp. 26, 27) point out that this tippet is closely related to the tippets formerly worn by other members of the university, which makes it unlikely that it is really the survival of the purse.] At Paris the rector in Du Boulay's time and earlier the proctors wore 'une grande bourse violette à sa ceinture' (*Remarques*, &c., p. 25). A purse is also mentioned among the insignia of the D.C.L. at Oxford. *Correspondence of Bekynton*, ed. G. Williams (R. S.), 1872, i. 275.

CHAP. XIV. much resemblance to its medieval ancestor.[1] The Oxford
scarlet Convocation habit worn by doctors of superior
faculties over their ordinary gown is still called a *cappa*, but
it has not retained its ancient shape. If the antiquary wants
to see a true medieval *cappa* he must go to Cambridge upon
a degree-day. There he will find the presiding vice-chancellor and the professors who present for degrees in the
superior faculties arrayed in a garment which exactly resembles a fourteenth-century miniature of the chancellor
contained in the precious 'Chancellor's book' of Oxford. It
is a sleeveless scarlet cloak lined with minever, with a tippet
and hood of the same material fastened thereto.[2] The *toga*
was originally, it would appear, simply an unofficial robe or
cassock worn under the *cappa*—much the same as the tabard,
but probably longer. Gradually it assumed the form of a
distinctively academical dress, which, in the case of masters
of arts, has entirely superseded their ancient black *cappa*.[3]
The medieval *toga* was, however, originally by no means
distinguished by the sobriety of hue characteristic of modern
clerical tailordom. In Oxford the prejudice ran in favour

[1] [The history of the development of academical dress at Oxford
is the subject of an informative
chapter in *Oxford University Ceremonies*, pp. 19–32, but the authors,
Dr. L. H. D. Buxton and Mr.
Strickland Gibson, are careful to
point out that 'the history of academical costume is one of great
difficulty and one which at present
has no authoritative historian'.]

[2] That this was the original form
is clear from the question which,
according to John of Salisbury, was
often debated in the schools of his
day, viz. whether a man who buys
a 'tota cappa' had bought the hood
also (*Metalog*. i. 3). Cf. the following passages in the *Dictionarius* of
John of Garland (ed. Scheler,
*Lexog. lat. du XIIe et du XIIIe
siècle*, p. 25): 'Quidam declamatores
pelliciorum reparandorum discur-
runt per plateas civitatis et reparant

furaturas epitogiorum et palliorum,
eorum partem furando.' A statute
of Heidelberg requires the M.A. to
incept 'cappa nigra vario subducta
vel ad minus in habitu novo vario
vel serico subtracto' (Hautz, *Gesch.
d. Univ. Heid*. ii. 352). As to the
difference between the *cappa* and
the *pallium* (often prescribed as
synonyms or alternatives), cf. *Carmina Burana* (ed. Schmeller, p. 75):

'Contra frigus hiemis
Pallium cappare,
Veris ad introitum
Cappam palliare.'

[3] So at Prague, a statute of 1367,
forbidding masters to attend the
acts of the faculty 'absque tabardo
vel habitu sui gradus' (*Mon. Univ.
Prag*. I. i. 9), makes no mention of
the *cappa*, though still worn by doctors and bachelors of theology (*ibid.*,
p. 99).

of green, blue, or blood-colour.[1] In the universal change to
sombre black we may see a symbol of the way in which
sixteenth-century austerity eclipsed the warmth and colour
of medieval life.[2]

'The philosophy of clothes' in its application to the Meaning
medieval universities is a less superficial matter than might *of clericus.*
at first sight appear. It throws much light upon the relation
of the universities to the Church—a question often debated
with more zeal than knowledge by writers who imagine themselves to have some polemical interest in the issue. The
misconceptions which prevail on the subject are due to an
inadequate appreciation of the meaning attached to clericality in the Middle Ages. Even Savigny treats the term
'clericus', when used of a medieval student, as a synonym
for 'scholaris' without any distinctive meaning.[3] Bishop
Stubbs, on the other hand—if I may venture to criticize so
learned a medievalist—seems to have assumed that every
clericus was necessarily in minor orders.[4] The fact is that
clericality in the Middle Ages, though it did not necessarily

---

[1] See the numerous wills proved
in the Chancellor's Court at Oxford
(*Mun. Acad.* ii. 505–727 [*Reg.
Cancell. Oxon., 1434–1469*, ed.
H. E. Salter (O.H.S.), *passim*]),
which clearly show the distinction
between the *cappa* and the *toga*.
The first was an academical or at
least a clerical garment, the latter
was worn also by citizens.

[2] [Dr. L. H. D. Buxton and Mr.
Strickland Gibson describe black as
'not inappropriate since black has
always been associated with the
Faculty of Arts'; see *Oxford University Ceremonies*, p. 22.]

[3] Savigny, c. xxi, § 72. He adds
that the right of carrying arms
conferred by the statutes does not
suit the ecclesiastical state; but the
chancellor of Oxford, who was often
a priest, enjoyed a similar right,
which was a necessary protection
in the discharge of his duties. *Mun.
Acad.* i. 355. [*Stat. Antiq. Univ.*

Oxon., ed. S. Gibson, p. 293, ll. 28–
35. The statute to which reference
is here made is dated 1482.]

[4] In the *Report of Ecclesiastical
Courts Commission* (London, 1883,
Historical Appendix, p. 26), Bishop
Stubbs remarks: 'That the functions
of an ecclesiastical judge should be
exercised only by persons qualified
by the possession of Holy Orders,
seems to have been a principle so
universally admitted as to require
no general enactment.' In support
of his contention he quotes prohibitions of *laymen* exercising such
offices. It is probable that most
ecclesiastical judges had received
minor orders (which are not *holy*
orders) or at least the tonsure from
a bishop; but graduates in canon
law seem often to have acted as
ecclesiastical judges—at least in
Oxford—though only *clerici* in the
same sense as other scholars.

CHAP. XIV. imply even the lowest grade of minor orders, did imply a great deal. The adoption of the clerical tonsure and dress conferred, so long as the wearer continued celibate, the immunities and privileges of the clerical order—exemption from the secular courts, personal inviolability and the like—in as ample a measure as they could be enjoyed by the bishop or the priest.[1] The singers and servers of churches—predecessors of our modern 'parish clerks' and cathedral 'lay clerks'—the judges and practitioners of the ecclesiastical courts, at one time many of the secular judges[2] and lawyers, as well as a host of 'clerks' in the service of the Crown or the great nobles, belonged to this class. The relation between clerkship and the minor orders is an obscure subject. According to the canon law the conferment of the tonsure is quite a distinct act from the admission to the order of 'ostiarius'; but the ceremony has to be performed by the bishop or some specially privileged dignitary. It would be difficult to say what proportion of the medieval 'clerks' were actually in minor orders. As a rule it would appear from the episcopal registers that the tonsure was conferred at the same time as the lowest grade of minor orders—that of 'ostiarius'. But there is no evidence that the students of Oxford or Paris had as a rule received either the clerical tonsure or the order of 'ostiarius' from a bishop, and yet they are always regarded as clerks.[3] Had any formal ceremony been considered essential to clericality, it is one which would be certain to be sometimes neglected, and we should find attempts to enforce its observance; but there is no trace of any such attempts.[4] It would

---

[1] [This is a very loose statement of a highly technical matter which cannot be discussed here. See R. Génestal, La 'privilegium fori' en France du décret de Gratien à la fin du XIVe siècle, 2 vols., Paris, 1921-4.]

[2] An early commission of assize is always addressed to a certain number of clerici and a certain number of milites.

[3] [On the other hand, see the case of the schoolboy quoted from the Hereford episcopal registers, above, vol. i, p. 91 n.] I am informed that the tonsure is still sometimes conferred on seminarists of the Roman Church without any ceremony, but in that case it is not technically considered the tonsura clericalis.

[4] The only exception I have met with is at the Lombard College in Paris, where a statute provides 'quod predicte domus scholares sint et esse debeant clerici de Italia

appear therefore that nobody but the barber officiated at the CHAP. XIV. ceremony,[1] though no doubt the tonsure had to be formally made over again by the bishop before ordination. Large numbers both of graduate and undergraduate scholars were of course either in holy or in minor orders; but, if they took orders, it was in order to hold a benefice, not to qualify themselves for any university office or position. Only in the faculty of theology were holy orders—in some universities priest's orders—required for the doctorate. Orders were not required for even the highest university offices—such as the chancellorship at Oxford; or in the case of the earliest colleges, either for a headship or a fellowship. The gradual increase—at least in the English universities—of fellowships which required holy orders, was due mainly to two causes. In the first place the colleges were mostly designed for theologians, who had to take holy orders at that stage of their career at which it became necessary for them to preach; and secondly, it was a subsidiary object of most college-founders to get masses said for their souls, and a priest alone could say masses. In Germany and Spain the tendency to make university and college offices clerical, in the modern sense of the word, was promoted by the practice of endowing professorships with prebendal stalls.

Orders only required in theological faculties.

In the university of the northern type the teacher, like the

Celibacy of regents.

et de legitimo matrimonio nati, et quod illi qui ad presens clerici non existunt, promittent et facient se insigniri caractere clericali intra festum nativitatis beati Johannis-Baptistae proxime venturum' (Félibien, iii. 428). Here it is evident that a formal tonsuring by the bishop is meant. This was a regulation made by Italians for Italian scholars, and in Italy scholars were not treated as *clerici*, unless regularly admitted 'ad tonsuram clericalem' by the bishop. Even at Paris we find an oath administered to determiners, 'habebitis coronam irreprehensibilem, si gaudeatis beneficio corone' (*Chartul. Univ. Paris.* ii, App., p. 673). Still, the

enjoyment of clerical privileges in the university never seems to be dependent upon regular admission to the tonsure, and that a university scholar might be not *canonically* 'tonsewyrd', at least in England, is proved by *Paston Letters*, ed. J. Gairdner, 1872, ii. 239.

[1] A canon of the Second Council of Nicaea (embodied in Dec. Grat. P. I. Dist. lxix, c. 1) begins: 'Quoniam uidemus multos sine manus impositione a paruula etate tonsuram clerici accipientes, nondumque ab episcopo manus inpositione percepta super ambonem irregulariter in collecta legentes.' The irregularity would seem to have lingered in northern Europe.

CHAP. XIV. learner, though not necessarily ordained, was an ecclesiastic. But the only serious obligation which his ecclesiastical status imposed upon him was celibacy.[1] If a master married, he lost his regency.[2] It was not till the reform of Estouteville in 1452 that this regulation was modified at Paris even in the case of the least ecclesiastical of the faculties—that of medicine.[3] As to the marriage of the scholar, the case is not quite clear; it is possible that he would at one time have lost the privileges of 'scholarity', just as an ordinary *clericus* in strict law lost his benefit of clergy; but in fifteenth-century Oxford we find married scholars not unknown.[4] As he would be certainly incapacitated for taking a degree, it is clear that the married undergraduate would be at most an exceptional anomaly. The prohibition of marriage in college fellows—whether express or implied—was not due to any desire to make the colleges 'monastic', but was simply a part of the already established system of the universities in which they were situated.

Charivari.   In the less ecclesiastical universities of Southern Europe

[1] The tonsured clerk, though allowed to marry, lost the privileges of a *clericus*, and was exonerated from the duty of wearing the tonsure and *habitus clericalis*. Decretal. Greg. IX, lib. III, tit. iii, cc. 7, 8, 9. But there was much inconsistency both of theory and practice on this subject.

[2] He could, of course, retain it (just as he could become a priest or monk) by divorcing his wife. Jourdain, *Index*, No. 301; *Chartul. Univ. Paris.* ii, No. 565.

[3] Bulaeus, iv. 894–5. [*Chartul.* iv, No. 2690.] Before being admitted 'ad lecturam suorum cursuum', i.e. to M.B., the student was required to swear that he was not married. In 1395 it was decided that a licentiate who had married after taking his M.B. might be formally licensed though he might not continue his regency afterwards. Jourdain, *Index*, No. 928. Priests, it will be remembered, could not study medi-

cine without a dispensation. In the South German universities, married graduates and undergraduates are occasionally contemplated. Cf. Kosegarten, *Greifswald*, ii. 36. The often-cited case of the early German—not (as sometimes stated) Parisian—doctor, Manegald, whose wife and daughters were also teachers, is not to the point, since it appears that they were 'religione florentes' (Ricardus Pictaviensis, ap. Martène, *Ampl. Coll.* v, c. 1169), i.e. nuns. Of course, a married man could be a master when his wife had become a nun.

[4] In 1459 an indenture between town and gown at Oxford has a proviso 'that if eny clerk or Scoler, havyng a wyf and houshold within the precint of the Universite, or eny Scolers servant, selle eny opyn merchandise . . . as touching such merchandising, they be talliable with the burgesses of the said town', &c. *Mun. Acad.* i. 347.

there was, as we have seen, no objection to the marriage of CHAP. XIV.
either doctor or student, though the rectorship is often confined to the unmarried clerks in order that they might
canonically exercise jurisdiction over clerks. At the University of Aix a resident doctor or student who married was
required to pay 'charivari' to the university, the amount
varying with the degree or status of the man, and being
increased if the bride was a widow. Refusal to submit to
this statutable extortion was punished by the assemblage of
students at the summons of the rector 'with frying-pans,
bassoons, and horns' at the house of the newly married
couple.[1] Continued recusancy was followed by the piling up
of dirt in front of their door upon every feast-day. The statute
concludes by justifying these injunctions on the ground that
the money extorted was devoted to 'divine service'.[2] In
the colleges, even in Italy, celibacy was required because it
was the education of ecclesiastics that the pious founders
usually wished to promote.

Lectures

We must now endeavour to picture to ourselves the way in Hours of
lecture.
which the average student passed his time.[3] The records at
our disposal are seldom sufficient to enable us to say exactly
how many hours a day were usually or necessarily spent in
study. I shall not therefore attempt to reproduce in detail a day
in a medieval university.[4] It seems to have been usual to attend
as a maximum three lectures a day,[5] but it is hardly possible

---

[1] I am informed by a clergyman in a poor district of S.E. London that his parishioners are in the habit of going to other parishes to be married by stealth, to avoid similar demonstrations, which cannot now (it appears) be averted by the payment of 'charivari'. [1895.]

[2] Fournier, *Statuts des Univ. franç.* iii, No. 1582.

[3] [See Kaufmann, ii. 342-69, for a more systematic description of the lectures and other exercises in German universities.]

[4] [For a day at Louvain see Ap-

pendix in volume ii above, pp. 341, 342. The ideal day prescribed by R. Goulet for the scholars in colleges and pedagogies (*Compendium*, f. xviii) is suggestive: rise at 4, arts lecture at 5, mass at 6, breakfast, the regents in the schools 8-10 (9-11 in Lent), formal debates before the noon meal, repetitions, lectures 3-5, disputations 5-6, repetitions after evening meal, bed at 9.]

[5] At Heidelberg we find a statute 'ut scolares magis disciplinari valeant, ordinavit facultas (Artium),

CHAP. XIV. to say how long they lasted. Besides this there were 'exercitia' or disputations[1] of various kinds, and 'resumpciones',[2]

quod quilibet scolaris in posterum promovendus ad maius audiat tres lectiones in die cum diligencia' (Hautž, *Gesch. d. Univ. Heid.* ii. 347). At Leipzig (in 1410) a scholar is only allowed to hear 'duas lectiones in die de libris ad gradus'; no third lecture being counted 'nisi Priscianum breviorem et loyicam Hesbri' (Zarncke, *Statutenbücher*, p. 310). At Greifswald the student was to attend two or three lectures and two 'exercitia' a day (Kosegarten, ii. 308, 310).

[1] For the use of 'exercitium' and 'disputacio' as synonyms see Zarncke, *Statutenbücher d. Univ. Leipzig*, p. 394; Kosegarten, *Greifswald*, ii. 219, 301, 302, 310. In some universities it seems to have been usual to have disputations in the subject-matter of each book lectured on, as at Ingolstadt, where the lecturer on each book was to take the 'Exercitium eidem annexum' (Prantl, ii. 50). Perhaps in these cases the 'exercitium' was less sharply distinguished from the 'resumpcio'. [Cf. the evening exercise 'inter se' of the students of the Rosen Bursa at Vienna; K. Schrauf, 'Zur Geschichte der Studentenhaüser an der Wiener Universität', in *Mitth. der Geschichte für d. Erziehung und Schulgeschichte*, v (Berlin, 1895), 202.]

[2] In a statute of Leipzig in 1483 occurs the best explanation of the *resumpcio* which I have been able to find: 'Item placuit, quod omnes resumpciones publice, a quibuscunque fiant, debent fieri de licentia decani et seniorum et per modum examinis, ita quod scolares diligenter examinentur et audiantur, ut eorum ignoranciae succurratur. Si autem resumens voluerit aliquid pronuncciare, ut a scolaribus materia habeatur, faciat hoc uno die,

sequenti vero re-examinando, sub poena privacionis pastus eiusdem resumpcionis,' &c. (Zarncke, *loc. cit.*, pp. 394–5). Four masters were annually appointed to conduct such 'resumpciones' (*ibid.* 458–9). At Ingolstadt, a little later (1473), none are to resume to more than twelve scholars or eight B.A.s (Prantl, ii. 50). The 'resumption' was held twice a day for scholars, and once a day for bachelors (*ibid.*, p. 74). Elsewhere the *resumpcio* is explained as a 'summary examination' of the matter of a precious disputation. The *resumpcio* is no doubt much the same as the *repetitio* of Bologna, a term used at Cambridge at King's College, 'Quotidie fiat repeticio lectionis praecedentis ante lecturam novae lectionis' (Doc. ap. Rogers, *Hist. of Agriculture and Prices*, iii, Oxford, 1882, p. 741). In the old *Statuta Aularia* of Oxford [*Stat. Antiq. Univ. Oxon.*, ed. S. Gibson, p. 579, ll. 26–8] it is provided 'quod lecturam matutinam in aula et postmeridianam *recitacionem* eiusdem quilibet in facultate sua diligentur et attente obseruet'. This *resumptio* by the scholars themselves is no doubt the original form of the institution (see above, vol. i, p. 516), which at Oxford was not so early superseded by magisterial superintendence as elsewhere. [The *resumptio* in this source must be distinguished from the exercise in the theological inception at Paris and Bologna (above, vol. i, p. 486), and also from the 'resuming' of lectures which is frequently mentioned in the Oxford Statutes. Pelster unfortunately tries to relate these last two uses of the word (A. G. Little and F. Pelster, *Oxford Theology and Theologians* (O.H.S.), p. 52.)]

which seem to have been informal and catechetical classes CHAP. XIV. of small numbers, at which scholars were examined upon the subject of their lectures by the lecturer himself or some other master or bachelor. In the latter part of our period the scene of these less formal observances seems to have been the college or hall rather than the public schools; and there is a tendency to increase the number and the compulsoriness of these more private lessons.[1] No doubt the growth of these supplementary college lectures was connected partly as cause and partly as effect with the improvement in discipline which has already been noticed. The history of the medieval universities, regarded on their higher intellectual side, is in the main a history of decline and decay. In the universities of the fifteenth century the intellectual ferment of the days of Aquinas was no more: the intellectual life which always attends the discovery of new knowledge had passed away. But it is not clear that for the average student the fifteenth-century university was not a better place of education than the university of the thirteenth. The lectures may have been worth hearing in the public schools of thirteenth-century Paris; but—so far as the scantiness of the earlier records enables us to judge—the average student was compelled to do more work and given more assistance in the halls and colleges of the later Middle Age than he was in the days when the friars and the seculars were contending for the control of European education. It is no unfamiliar experience to find that what is the best education for the exceptional man is the worst possible education for the rank and file. In particular, as has already been incidentally noticed, that improvement in grammatical education and Latin writing which was quite independent of the Italian influence, but which to a large extent prepared the way for the reception of Renaissance ideas in Northern Europe, may be distinctly traced to the improved educational methods of

[1] See, e.g., Félibien, v. 669. [Contemporary opinion was not altogether of Rashdall's view. The Cardinal d'Estouteville (1452) wished to restore its old prestige to the Rue du Fouarre, and the *Advertissements sur la reformation de l'université de Paris*, a century later (1562), speaks of the wasteful and inefficient teaching in the colleges.]

CHAP. XIV. the Parisian and Oxonian colleges.[1] How well recognized this improvement and its cause were at the time may be inferred from the fact that in the course of the fifteenth century it was proposed to reform the University of Lisbon by establishing in it 'colleges on the model of those of Oxford and Paris'[2] with the express purpose of correcting the prevailing 'ignorance of Latin':

Divine Service

Mass not compulsory. In earlier times, as has been already said, it appears quite plain that the average student did not attend mass or any other religious service before going to lecture. It is recorded as a piece of extraordinary piety in canonized saints that they were in the habit of hearing mass at an early hour.[3] Among scholars, as in the community generally, church-going seems to have increased in the later Middle Age. At Vienna we hear that a bell rang for the whole hour between five and six to rouse those who wanted to hear mass before their day's work began.[4] But attendance was not compulsory. Even in colleges the earlier statutes enjoin attendance at church or chapel only on Sundays, holidays, and vigils.[5] At Oxford the statutes of New College are the first which require a daily attendance at mass; but towards the end of the fifteenth century we find that daily mass was enforced even on the students in the unendowed halls.[6] Such attendance was not,

[1] Thus at Leipzig, in 1499, the *resumpcio* included instruction in Latin verse-making and prose ('modum epistolandi'). Zarncke, *Statutenbücher*, pp. 458-9.

[2] 'Collegios a exemplo dos de Oxonia e Paris' (Braga, *Hist. d. Univ. de Coimbra*, i. 143).

[3] The University of Oxford, in asking for the canonization of Edmund of Abingdon, expressly says that he attended mass before lecture, 'supra morem tunc legentium' (*Collectanea* (O.H.S.), ii. 188). Cf. the case of S. Thomas of Cantilupe in *Acta Sanctorum*, October, i. 545.

[4] Kink (*Gesch. d. K. Univ. zu*

Wien, I. i. 37) cites the account of John Hindernbach, a student of Vienna (B.A. in 1437): 'Ante diem vero in ipso diluculo sub pulsu Primarum mos est, campanellam per horam ante diem compulsare, quo se studentes ad missarum solemnia praeparent.'

[5] At Nantes, as late as 1461, the *pædagogus* is only to take his scholars to mass 'ante ientaculum' on Sundays and Festivals. Fournier, iii, No. 1595.

[6] Goulet, *Compendium*, f. viii *b*; Oxford, *Stat. Aularia* [*Stat. Antiq. Univ. Oxon.*, ed. S. Gibson, p. 575, ll. 5, 6. See above, p. 374.].

however, necessarily before morning lecture. Lectures began CHAP. XIV. at about 6 a.m., though in some universities and colleges the hour of the first lecture or mass is as early as 5 a.m.[1] in the summer, and as late as 7 in winter.[2] In practice it is probable that the time varied with the season, though lectures often began in the dark without artificial light. Medieval lectures often lasted much more than the conventional hour of a softer age: in some cases the prescribed period for the first morning's lecture is no less than three hours.[3]

Meals

Mr. Anstey, the editor of *Munimenta Academica*, finding no record of any meal before dinner, confidently assumed that breakfast must have taken place not later than 7 a.m.[4] It is natural that an Oxford tutor should find it impossible to believe in the non-existence of that all-important meal of modern Oxford. But the empiricist might well point to

Breakfast a luxury.

By the statutes of S. Nicolas du Louvre at Paris the scholars are required 'interesse qualibet nocte matutinis' (Bulaeus, iv. 140), but such a provision is exceptional. The requirement of confession four times a year is rare: Félibien, iii. 510. Scholars are sometimes required to attend university *sermons*. A statute of the Collège des Cholets in 1415 requires mass to be said at 7 a.m.: 'itaque pro missis audiendis discurrendi occasio bursariis amputabitur' (Jourdain, p. 235).

[1] So at Leipzig *Statutenbücher*, p. 338), and Toulouse (Fournier, i, No. 691). A statute of a Paris college (undated) requires students to rise at 5, go to chapel, and attend lectures at 6 a.m. Félibien, v. 517. Cf. Péries, *La Fac. de Droit*, p. 109, where a law lecture begins at 5. A Paris statute of the fourteenth century complains that masters go to the schools at the hour of second mass, 'quo tempore suas lectiones secundum antiquam consuetudi-

nem merito pro maiori parte deberent finiuisse. Unde ipsis magistris eo quod lectiones suas in sacra pagina audire nequeant generatur praeiudicium scholaribus, eo quod aptiorem partem diei somno deducunt in damnum' (Bulæus, iv. 412).

[2] At Padua, lectures begin 'in crepusculo' (*Stat. Iur. Patav.*, f. 76 a). So at Cologne, 'disputatio ordinaria incipiatur in tribus quartalibus anni ante hyemem hora sexta, et in hyeme hora septima' (1392). Bianco, i, Anl., p. 62. Cf. Kosegarten, *Greifswald*, ii. 302. But as these passages refer to disputations, lectures may have begun earlier.

[3] e.g. at Perpignan (Fournier, iii, No. 1485, p. 667). This was in law: in arts a lecture would probably be much shorter to allow of a 'repetitio' immediately afterwards.

[4] *Mun. Acad.* i. lxxv. The passage which Anstey quoted to show that 'lectures began at 9 o'clock' refers to determinations.

CHAP. XIV. Mr. Anstey's incredulity as an apt illustration of his doctrine that inconceivability is no test of truth. It is abundantly evident that, so far as regular meals or college allowances are Dinner, concerned, no provision was usually made for any food before dinner at 10 a.m.[1] The earliest college statutes which contemplate anything of the kind treat it as an indulgence to weaker brethren: at one college it is only to boys under twenty that bread and wine may be 'temperately ministered' in addition to the two regular meals.[2] Even in the fifteenth and sixteenth centuries, when the 'jentaculum' or early breakfast had passed into a regular institution, it was still regarded as an 'extra' which the hardier and more economical student would dispense with, but we may conjecture that in practice the great majority of students did take some such

[1] In the thirteenth century, when we hear nothing of 'jentacula', dinner may have been earlier.

[2] A statute of the College of Verdala at Toulouse, in 1337, after a prohibition of any allowance of victuals away from the common table, continues: 'Per hoc autem prohibere non intendimus quo minus pueris minoribus viginti annis pro victu proprio indigentibus panis et vinum extra comestionem communem temperate valeant ministrari' (Fournier, i, No. 593). So in the statutes of the King's Hall at Cambridge in 1380 (Rymer, *Foedera*, 1740, III, pt. iii, p. 94): 'Quantum vero ad Gentacula, dictis scolaribus ministranda, ordinatione Custodis et Senescallorum volumus observari.' At Queen's, Oxford (*Statutes*, p. 19), 'gentacula preciosa' are forbidden, which may indicate that some breakfast was usually taken. An allowance of bread and wine is permitted in the sixteenth-century statutes of the College of Spain at Bologna. *Stat. Coll. Hisp.*, f. xvi. So Standonck (*c.* 1500) allows a crust of bread by way of 'jentaculum' to the boys, but not to the theologians. The old Oxford Aularian Statutes [*Stat. Antiq. Univ. Oxon.*, ed. S.

Gibson, p. 581, ll. 3, 4] forbid access to the 'promptuarium' or the kitchen 'causa prandendi, *iantandi*, cenandi, aut batellandi'. I may remark that 'battellare' originally meant to pay for something *extra* (like the Cambridge 'to size', or 'sizings'); 'battels' are always distinguished from 'commons', though the word is now applied to all college bills. (The Winchester colleger's weekly pocket-money is still called 'battlings'.) Even in the seventeenth century, breakfast consisted of a piece of bread and pewter of beer, consumed in the buttery or in the man's own room. It was thus the first meal that was taken in rooms. See C. Wordsworth, *Social Life at the English Universities in the Eighteenth Century*, Cambridge, 1874, p. 122 *sq.* Cf. also Erasmus, *Opp.* i, cc. 863, 865, 866 (references which I owe to Dr. P. S. Allen). [In striking contrast to the bad and sparse diet from which Calvin and Erasmus suffered in Paris was the generous provision made by the Elector Frederick of Saxony for the 'old college' at Wittenberg; see W. Friedensberg, *Urkundenbuch der Universität Wittenberg*, Magdeburg, 1926-7, i. 10-12.]

refreshment at an early hour. And in some colleges we meet CHAP. XIV. with traces of 'biberium' or 'bever', consisting of a drink of beer, possibly with a morsel of bread, some time between dinner and supper, and again at night before going to bed. The period from 6 to 10 was the most sacred time of the day for study and lectures. After dinner at 10 or (later) 11, followed perhaps by a post-prandial disputation, there was a short interval for exercise and relaxation, in so far as such indulgences were supposed to be necessary.[1] Lectures or disputations were resumed again perhaps at 12 or 1, and the ideal student was no doubt supposed to study till supper-time at 5.[2] On Fast-days in some colleges dinner was at 12 and supper disappeared. In many colleges and halls there was some kind of disputation (in Germany styled *exercitium bursale*) in the evening;[3] but on the whole it would appear that the evening, or part of it, was usually in the main considered the time for whatever amusement medieval student-life allowed. Amusement was, however, a thing which the medieval ideal of student-life hardly admitted at all; but the evening was certainly the time when the less industrious student took his amusement.[4] Even in the comparatively

and after dinner.

Supper: evening work or amusement.

---

[1] Islip's statutes for Canterbury College provide that 'cum post vesperas communiter scholares spatiari et aerem capere paulisper consueverant, volumus quod socii qui spatiari volunt, adinvicem se conferant et ambulent, bini et bini de doctrina vel de honestis solatiis conferendo, et sic simul redeant tempestivi' (Wilkins, *Concilia*, iii. 54). Walking alone was not merely unmonastic; it was considered undignified or 'bad form' for persons of the least consideration. We find masters warned against it in a commentary on the *De Disciplina Scholarium*.

[2] At Greifswald the regular hours for lecture (for jurists) appear to be 6 a.m., 9 a.m., 4 p.m., not including the 'vespertinum exercitium' after supper. (Kosegarten, i. 92.) At Ingolstadt the possible hours (in winter) were 8

and 11 a.m., 1, 2, 3, and 5 (*post cenam*) p.m. Prantl, *Gesch. d. Univ. Ingolstadt*, ii. 109 *sq.*

[3] At Ingolstadt (in 1473) this was followed by a 'publica conversatio', presided over by the 'conventor'— no doubt for practice in Latin, a note of the dawning Renaissance. Prantl, ii. 50.

[4] Cf. the *Carmina Burana* (ed. Schmeller), p. 73:

'Stratu contempto summo te mane levato,
Facque legendo moram quartam dumtaxat ad horam,
Quinta sume cibum, vinum bibe, sed moderatum,
Et pransus breviter dormi, vel lude parumper.

. . . . .

Si tempus superest, post cenam ludere prodest.'

CHAP. XIV. disciplined halls of the fifteenth century, the boys roamed
the streets freely till 8 or 9 o'clock; though by the end of
this period life in some of the stricter colleges had been
reduced to a round of lectures and exercises which left little
space for any recreation except what may have been supplied
by the 'honest jokes' with which the. tutor is sometimes
required to entertain the company after dinner and the half-
hour's light disputation which followed it.[1] Wandering in
the town or evening exercises over, at curfew the company
reassembled in the hall or parlour, and had a 'drinking' or
Collation (as it was called in monasteries) 'collation'[2] before going to
and even-
ing Anti- bed, a refection sometimes closely associated with the singing
phon. of the antiphon of the Virgin or *Salve Regina*—the usual
form of evening prayer in scholastic communities.

Standard of Living

Various   But before pursuing the subject of medieval amusements
standards
of comfort. it may be well to examine a little more in detail the ordinary
mode of life in the *hospicium* or college. Exaggerated accounts
are often given of the poverty of the medieval student—
especially of the class for which the colleges were intended.
The university students of that age were drawn from every
class of society, excluding probably as a rule the very lowest
though not excluding the very poorest. The scale of living
varied as widely as the social position of the scholars. There

---

[1] See the regulations for Louvain
in 1476, above, vol. ii, p. 342.

[2] Cf. statutes of New College,
p. 41: 'Post potationes in aula hora
ignitegii.' So in the old Aularian
Statutes [*Stat. Antiq. Univ. Oxon.*,
ed. S. Gibson, p. 585, l. 40]: 'Post
gloriose virginis antiphonam de-
cantatam et biberium completum.'
At New College the antiphon was
sung in the chapel after compline.
Cf. *Chartul. Univ. Paris.* ii, App.,
p. 689. At Jesus College, Cambridge, two *biberiae* were allowed
per diem, consisting of 'unam pin-
tam potus cum portiuncula panis'
(*Documents, Univ. and Colleges of*

Cambridge, iii. 114). The first of
these was no doubt the meal known
as 'nunsyns' or 'nuncheon' (whence
our 'luncheon') at nones (3 p.m. or
in practice earlier). Cf. Boase, *Reg.
of Exeter Coll.* (1894), p. xlvi. Dr.
A. Clark speaks of a 'biberium' at
Lincoln College at 9 a.m. Until
comparatively recently at Eton
boys on the foundation could procure a drink of beer at the College
buttery in the course of the afternoon; this was called 'bever'. [On
the subject of *biberia* see *Reg.
Annal. Coll. Merton.*, ed. H. E.
Salter (O.H.S.), p. xxxv.]

was the scion of the princely or noble house who lived in the CHAP. XIV.
style to which he was accustomed at home, in a hostel of his The rich.
own with a numerous 'familia', including poorer but well-
born youths who dressed like him and acted as his 'socii' or
humble companions, a chaplain,[1] and (if young) a private
tutor, besides the ordinary servants.[2] At the other end of the The poor
social ladder there was the poor scholar, reduced to beg for scholars.
his living or to become the servitor of a college or of a master
or well-to-do student.[3] At Vienna and elsewhere there were

---

[1] Thus, at Paris, the brothers
Thomas and Hugh de Cantilupe
'tenebant magnum hospitium et
habebant in familiam suam et ad
expensas et robas suas (*id est in
obsequiis et ad rem domesticam
curandam*) probos viros inter quos
erat magister Petrus de Buttevilt,
magister in Artibus, qui fuit post-
modum senescallus dicti domini
Walteri Wigorniensis episcopi'
(*Acta Sanctorum*, Oct., i. 544).
Afterwards, when Thomas lived
by himself, 'habebat secum continue in familia sua et de robis suis
unum capellanum, qui celebrabat
continue missam dicto domino
Thomae valde mane at antequam
iret ad scholas'. Moreover, his
valet 'dixit, quod in dictis studiis
continue dabat ad comedendum
quinque pauperibus ad minus in
domo sua, et aliquando tredecim;
et de fragmentis et micis mensae
suae vivebant saltem duo pauperes
scholares' (*ibid.*, p. 545). In smaller
French universities special privileges are conferred on 'nobiles ita
viventes', which is thus defined at
Dôle: 'Proprium habitet et teneat
domicilium, habeatque secum tenere socium honestum et sibi simili
panno vestitum, atque duos famulos honeste indutos, qui, aut saltem
unus eorum, cum prefato socio
ipsum per villam et ad studium vel
aliis locis et actibus scolasticis iugi-
ter associent, librosque suos, cum
opus fuerit, ad scolas sive studium

defferant, ac reportent,' &c. A
noble who only kept a master and
one servant took a lower place in
university functions (Fournier, iii,
No. 1616). At Montpellier the
student is esteemed 'noble' who
brings 'ad minus unum consocium,
duos scutiferos, unum coqum et
duos famulos' (*ibid.* ii, No. 1103).

[2] Even at Bologna we find in the
register of the German nation that
youths belonging to the higher
nobility came up attended by 'magister suus', or later 'pedagogus
suus' (see *Acta Nationis Germanicae*,
passim); e.g. Frederick Duke of
Austria thus came to the university
in 1332 (*ibid.* 92; cf. Malagola,
Monografie, p. 294). The young
gentleman was often already a
highly placed dignitary. Two provosts come up with 'magister
eorum' (*ibid.*, p. 99); and a Hun-
garian bishop is attended by a
doctor of decrees as his 'pedagogus',
a canon, a chaplain, and three
scholars as 'familiares' (*ibid.*, p.
215). In 1465, Wolfgang, Count
Palatine of the Rhine, matriculated
with a doctor of decrees as his
'pedagogus', a master and four
other scholars as 'familiares' (*ibid.*,
p. 210).

[3] For Prague cf. Tomek, p. 35.
At Leipzig, in 1443, 'servitores
magistrorum' are exempted from
fees; later, partial exemption is
granted to those 'qui in parte vel in
toto se suarum laboribus manuum

CHAP. XIV. halls (styled *Codrii* or *Domus Pauperum*) whose inmates were
Battelers regularly turned out to beg, the proceeds being placed in
and
beggars. a common chest.¹ In the Oxford halls there was a class of
students known as 'battelers' who were required to wait on
the others before sitting down to table.² Still poorer scholars

aut servitiis nutriunt et susten-
tant', and there is a still more
humble class of 'omnino pauperes'
(Zarncke, *Statutenbücher*, pp. 360,
397). The statutes of Toulouse
tell us that at Paris 'quelibet domus
scolarium . . . quamvis etiam de se
tenuis et exilis' supported 'unum
pauperem clericum' on its fragments (Devic and Vaissette, vii,
Notes, c. 546). Salimbene tells
a story of a nephew of Urban IV,
created a cardinal by him, who
'erat prius vilis scolaris in tantum,
ut etiam aliorum scolarium, cum
quibus studebat, carnes e macello
portaret' (edit. O. Holder-Egger,
in *Mon. Germ. Hist.* xxxii, 1905,
p. 170). So Piero della Vigna the
minister of Frederick II, 'cum esset
scholaris Bononiae mendicabat nec
habebat quod comederet' (Guido
Bonati, ap. Sarti (1888), I. i. 133).
Cf. Oxford *Reg. A a*, f. 87, where
'omnes scolares portatores librorum
magistrorum' supplicate to be allowed to count attendance at their
masters' lectures in lieu of those
prescribed by statute. At Greifswald every master could exempt
one 'famulus' from fees, in return
for which he is never to walk abroad
unattended. Kosegarten, ii. 304
(cf. pp. 265, 268).
  ¹ Kink, ii. 312. So at Leipzig
there was a common table for scholars too poor to live in the regular
halls, 'quibus non est tanta facultas,
ut hebdomadatim quinque grossos
pro expensis exponere possint'
(Zarncke, *Statutenbücher*, p. 72).
At Oxford we hear, in a list of
halls, of 'Spalding-Courte quae
fuerat una domus pauperum' (Merton Register, ap. Twyne MSS.

xxii. 320). Occasionally charitable
persons would receive a poor
scholar into their houses 'pro amore
Dei', or for the soul of a deceased
relative. Gloria, *Mon. d. Padova*,
1318–1405, ii. 329, 330.
  ² 'Quod batellarius quisquam in
refeccionibus comminariis de victualibus seruiat antequam se ad
reficiendum transeat, sub pena ij*d*.'
[*Stat. Antiq. Univ. Oxon.*, ed. S.
Gibson, p. 584, ll. 25–7.] The
learned Dr. Routh was once a
'batteler' of Queen's. At that time
he did not wait on others but
fetched his own victuals from the
kitchen and ate them in the hall.
(I am indebted for this piece of
tradition to Bishop Hobhouse.) It
is not quite clear whether he was
exactly the same as the 'semi-
comminarius'—probably he was
so: in any case the latter was no
doubt one who paid for and ate
smaller rations than the rest—
possibly only one meal instead of
two (a practice known elsewhere).
[For the semi-commoner see A. B.
Emden, *An Oxford Hall*, pp. 210–
11.] At Queens', Cambridge, the
two servitors of the president are to
receive their commons 'per modum
semi-commensalium' (*MS. Statutes*, f. 27). Originally, the 'batler'
was a poor scholar who acted as the
personal servant of the fellow who
appointed him. (Shadwell, in *The
Colleges of Oxford*, p. 112.) The
Paris *camerista* seems to have been
in the same position (see above, vol.
i, p. 487): so at a college at Caen,
the 'bursarius' who cannot pay
'portio sua' (by the aid of his
scholarship) 'poterit domo morari
sicut camerista' (Fournier, iii, No.

were granted licences to beg by the chancellor. It must, however, be remembered that the example of the friars had made
mendicity comparatively respectable. Many a man who
would have been ashamed to dig was not ashamed to beg;
and the begging scholar was invested with something like
the sacredness of the begging friar. To support a scholar at
the university or to help him on a smaller scale by giving him
something at the door, in return for a prayer or two, was a
recognized work of charity in the medieval world. Menial
service, again, implied less social inferiority in days when
gentle youths were habitually brought up as pages to bishops
or abbots. For these poor scholars the 'ladder' of a university
career was let down by the partial or entire remission of
university dues and lecture-fees;[1] though in some cases the

1713), though forbidden to live 'ut
martineti extra septa huiusmodi
Collegii'. The surviving Cambridge 'sizar' must once have fared
like the 'bateller'.

[1] At Paris the fees were fixed at
so many 'bursae', i.e. so many times
the weekly board. The pauper
scholar is entered as one 'cuius
bursa fuit nichil' (Registers, passim).
So at Prague in 1371 a scholar
'petens dimissiónem bursae propter
Deum' must swear 'quia in conscientia mea non habeo ultra libros
et vestes in praesenti de proventibus
quibuscunque res valentes tres
sexagenas aut duodecim florenos,
et quam cito habebo res tantum
valentes, libenter persolvam sine
dilatione'. (Mon. Un. Prag. i. i. 47.
As to Leipzig cf. Zarncke, Statutenbücher, p. 376.) At the Church-
schools attended before or as a
substitute for the university, poor
scholars were often received gratis,
e.g. at Worms: 'nulli tamen pauperi
advenae et mendicanti Scolarum
introitus praecludatur' (Schannat,
Hist. episc. Worm. ii. 161), and the
rich paid in proportion to their
means. At Ingolstadt the poor were
by statute admitted to lectures free
(Prantl, ii. 114), and the practice

was probably common even where
it could not be claimed as a right.
At S. Andrews an inceptor swears
to pay 'cum veniret ad pinguiorem
fortunam' (MS. Acta Fac. Art., f.
28 b). At universities of the Bologna type provision is made for the
admission of a very limited number
of poor graduates. As a rule no
doubt the poor scholars would leave
without the master's degree. [The
acts of the English nation at Paris,
which were not available to Rashdall, give much information about
the aid given to the poor scholars
in Paris. At Paris, as elsewhere,
this was so frequent that careful
regulation became necessary. Dispensation from payment of dues
was, at any rate after the middle
of the fourteenth century, 'granted
only through formal channels'. An
oath that the applicant was in
paupertate had to be taken by him
before the masters of the nation
assembled in Congregation (1369).
The names of those who had been
exempted from paying their burses
were, from 1405, entered in a
special book. All kinds of arrangements for future payment were
made, unless exemption was unconditional. The practice of

CHAP. XIV. scholar who graduated *in forma pauperis* was made to swear that he would pay the fees if he ever came 'to fatter fortune'.

The majority not paupers. But after all, as we see from the university records, it was only a very small proportion of the students in a university, and a still smaller proportion of university graduates, who belonged to the pauper or servitor class. The vast majority of scholars were of a social position intermediate between the highest and very lowest—sons of knights and yeomen, merchants, tradesmen or thrifty artisans, nephews of successful ecclesiastics, or promising lads who had attracted the notice of a neighbouring abbot or archdeacon. So habitual was this kind of patronage that a large proportion of university students must have been supported by persons other than their parents, whether related to them or not.[1] The colleges represent simply an extension of this widespread system.

Mode of living. Many university students no doubt lived in the direst poverty. There is a famous story of three students who were

sub-determination greatly assisted the poor scholar, for, as sub-determiner for another, he paid no burse or fee and his own weekly burse was kept low. 'The only claim to the position of sub-determiner was complete inability to pay the required burse.' See, for these and other details, Boyce, *The English-German Nation*, pp. 90–100, 164–7. For exception in German universities, Kaufmann, ii. 405–6.}

[1] How universal this system was may be judged from the Injunction of Henry VIII in 1535 (when the Dissolution of the Monasteries had no doubt diminished the supply of students), that every clergyman beneficed to the extent of £100 should maintain at least one scholar either in a grammar school or at a university. Wood, *Annals of Oxford*, ii. 66. [Urban V (1362–70), an assiduous benefactor of universities, is said to have maintained 1,400 students. In reply to remonstrances he observed that many of his protégés would not become ecclesiastics, but return to the world and live as fathers of families. Even as manual labourers, they would find their studies useful to them. In other words, while there were undoubtedly a great many scholars among the 'clergy, he was promoting a more general and hardly less useful interest in learning; this significant statement throws light on the academic *clerici*. See G. Mollat, *Les Papes d'Avignon*, ed. 2, Paris, 1912, pp. 107, 110. In the previous century the view was sometimes held that a scholar surrendered the right to support by his family; E. M. Meijers (in *Tijdschrift voor Rechtsgeschiedenis*, i. 112) quotes a suggestive story from the Orleans civilian, Jacques de Révigny: 'quidam erat scolaris. Pater suus nolebat sibi dare aliquid, nec libros nec aliud, et fratres sui ad hoc inducebant patrem, quia dicebant patri: ille clericus, frater noster, satis expendit et nihil lucratur.']

so poor that they had but one 'cappa' between them in which CHAP. XIV. they took turns to go to lecture.[1] Numbers must have lived on bread and porridge with a little wine and meat on Sundays and holidays. The annals of a modern university in Scotland or Germany, if not in England, would tell of not a few such stories. But it would be a mistake to infer that the majority of students lived in this way. No doubt it was not then considered necessary that an undergraduate should enjoy luxuries unknown to his father and sisters at home. The medieval student lived like the students of France or Germany, not like the average English undergraduate. When we remember the enormous supplies required in a university town, at a time when the cost of conveying provisions from a distance was greater than now, and the probable failings of manciples and clumsy male cooks, it is no wonder that 'Oxford fare' had a bad name.[2] But that does not imply that the ordinary undergraduate did not have regular meals, meat twice a day, and quite as much small beer as was good for him. From the graduation-lists of Paris in the fifteenth century it appears that the average 'bursa' or weekly expenses of a scholar varied between 2s. and 4s., the lower limit being the more common. The kind of living which even this represents was that of the middle classes rather than that of 'the poor'.[3]

[1] 'Nam, sicut narrare consueverat, ipse, et duo socii eius existentes in camera, non nisi unicam habebant cappam, et tunicam tantum; et quilibet eorum lectum infimum. Exeunte ergo uno cum cappa ad lectionem audiendam, reliqui in camera residebant; et sic alternatim exierunt; panisque et parum de vino cum potagio eis pro cibo sufficiebat. Non enim carnes aut pisces, nisi in die Dominica, vel die solenni, vel sociorum seu amicorum praesentia, eorum paupertas ipsos comedere permisit; et tamen saepe retulit, quod numquam in vita sua tam iucundam, tam delectabilem duxerat vitam' (Acta Sanctorum, April, i. 279). The story, here told of S. Richard of

Chichester, is repeated of many medieval personages, and Hatch (Hibbert Lectures, p. 36) traces it to Eunapius, Prohæresius (Heidelberg, 1596), p. 137.

[2] Mr. Mullinger (Cambridge, i. 371) quotes the words of the fallen Sir Thomas More: 'My counsel is, that we fall not to the lowest fare first; we will not therefore descend to Oxford fare, nor to the fare of New Inn, but we will begin with Lincoln's Inn diet.' Even in these luxurious days, the undergraduates' table in some college halls would represent a considerable comedown to an ex-Lord-Chancellor.

[3] It should also be remembered, before drawing exaggerated inferences from the existence of such

CHAP. XIV.   Nor did the standard of living in the colleges fall below
Standard the ordinary average. We have already seen something of
in colleges.
the domestic arrangements of the College of Spain at Bologna.
A pound of meat *per diem* may be the diet of hard-labour
prisoners but it is not the diet of paupers. And by the sixteenth century the allowance has been increased to a pound
and a half.[1] How little an endowed scholar's fare in the
Middle Ages represents a minimum scale is shown by the fact
that a servant's allowance of meat was only half a scholar's,
while a college servant's rations are luxury itself compared
with the dietary of many a medieval alms-house. The
increased allowance of the later statutes may be considered
to indicate a departure from the founder's intention; but the
reader may remember that from the first there was bread and
wine *ad libitum* at meals, and a 'collation' twice a day besides.
The household arrangements of the same college likewise
show anything but a niggard economy. At least as many
servants are provided for the thirty-four inmates of this
medieval college as would be required for that number of
students in our own day.[2] Among other enactments may be
noted the provision that the servants shall carry the canonists'
books to lecture for them. It is true that the whole scale of

charities as the loan-chests of Oxford (see above, pp. 35, 36), that a
medieval student was liable to be
reduced to great straits by temporary failure of supplies from
home. Communication was difficult, and the Jews (when and where
accessible) highly exorbitant. Malagola prints an interesting extract
from a letter of Copernicus when
studying at Bologna in 1499 to his
episcopal uncle, asking for fresh
supplies. He says that his brother
Andrew, who was in like straits,
'Romae servitiis se dare offerebat,
ut egestati mederetur' (*Monografie*,
p. 427). Yet Nicholas Copernicus
was already a canon of Frauenburg
(*ibid.*, p. 420), and the brothers paid
moderately high matriculation-fees.
Acta Nat. Germ., pp. 248, 252.

[1] MS. Stat. Coll. Hisp., f. xvi *a*
(Phillipps Library). Cf. above, vol.
i, p. 200.

[2] There was to be (1) a 'procurator seu yconomus' (not a scholar);
(2) a cook and an under-cook; (3)
two *canaparii* (butlers); (3) five
other servants. MS. Stat., ff. 8 *b*–
11 *a*. By the sixteenth century the
economic management of the college is transferred to *procuratores*
selected from the scholars, who
are all to learn arithmetic with a
view to serving in their turn—a
provision which (since they must
have resided three years in a university before admission) throws a
lurid light on the state of mathematical instruction among Italian
jurists. *Ibid.*, f. viii *b*.

living among the Italian students was rather more luxurious chap. xiv.
than that which prevailed among the mass of Parisian or
Oxonian scholars; and the Cardinal of Spain of course wished
his scholars to live as other students of moderate means were
wont to live at Bologna; but such statutes show that the
term 'poor scholar' was a more elastic one than would be
suggested by the moving pictures of academic poverty in
which the picturesque historian is wont to indulge. When we
turn to the colleges of Oxford and Paris, the facts are not
materially different. The allowance of wine at the College of
Harcourt was sufficient to make it expedient that college
meetings (*congregationes*) should not be held after common-
room (*post vinum*).[1] The different allowances for various
grades of students show that the diet of the seniors must have
been by no means austere.[2] It is contemplated that the college foundationer may be a man of sufficient social position
to entertain noble or distinguished guests.[3] It is not superfluous to provide that he shall not keep a private servant. In
some of the Parisian colleges he is allowed this luxury at his
own expense.[4] At New College, Oxford, a doctor of divinity
is even provided with a servant at the expense of the college.
It is quite true that the colleges were intended for 'poor
scholars'. But a 'poor scholar' in the sense of college founders Meaning
meant only a scholar unable to support himself at the univer- of 'poor
sity without assistance. Sometimes this is the interpretation colleges.
actually embodied in the statutes: in other cases there is a
fixed limit of income. When it is remembered that many of
the colleges were for theologians, that a theologian's training
lasted nearly half an ordinary life-time, and that his profession
even at the end of the period was not directly remunerative,
it is obvious that but for the assistance afforded by the colleges none but men of considerable means would have been
likely to enter upon such a career. It is, however, almost
assumed that the college fellow would, as a rule, have some

---

[1] Bulaeus, iii. 160.
[2] At Navarre a grammarian received 4 *solidi* a week, an artist 6,
and a theologian 8. *Ibid.* iii. 82.

[3] *Ibid.* iv. 156.
[4] e.g. at Narbonne (Félibien, v.
670) and du Plessis (*ibid.* iii. 414).

CHAP. XIV. small private means, since the college allowance was usually confined to bare food and clothing. At Paris it often ceased during the vacation.[1] In England founders were usually more liberal; but the mere fact that great prelates designed the colleges in part for their nearest relatives shows how far they were from intending their liberality to be confined to the lowest and poorest classes, or from expecting those who accepted it to live like labourers, although at that time there was less difference than now between the diet of the labourer and that of the classes immediately above him. The will of a fellow of Queen's in the fifteenth century shows that it was possible for a fellow to possess several horses, besides sheep and cattle, and to have lent his father as large a sum as £7.[2]

There was almost as much difference between the scale of living and social position of the fellow or full 'bursar' and the 'beneficiarius' who lived on the broken meats which fell from the college table or begged for alms at the college gates[3] as there was between the independent scholar and his student-servitor. Indeed, before the conclusion of the medieval Abuse of period we find it a matter of common complaint that the founda- colleges which were intended for poor, though not for pauper, tions. scholars were filled with men whose parents were quite well able to pay for the support of their sons at the university. John Standonck, at the beginning of the sixteenth century,

[1] e.g. at the College of Laon from June 24 to Oct. 1, except for the master and two scholars. Jourdain, *Index*, p. 108. The College of Dainville requires an entrance-fee of 40 *solidi*, with 'mappam sufficientem cum una thobalia' and 'de suo providere de linteaminibus et cooperturis' (Félibien, iii. 510). Elsewhere there is a contribution towards furniture. Fournier, iii, No. 1643.

[2] *Mun. Acad.* ii. 593. [*Reg. Cancell. Oxon., 1434–1469*, ed. H. E. Salter (O.H.S.), i. 199–201.]

[3] At the College of Narbonne, by the statutes of 1379, some poor scholars are to be selected by the

prior to receive 'fragmenta seu reliquie mensarum cum alio eorum proprio subsidio'. They were to be provided with a 'suitable place' in which to eat these remnants, and were in any case to have enough pottage to satisfy their hunger. In return they were to serve in the chapel with surplices, to ring the college bell, and 'do other things as commanded by the prior' (Félibien, v. 667). So at the Collège du Plessis in 1335 each scholar 'bursam habens quatuor solidorum' was to have a *beneficiarius* to live in the house, who was sustained apparently by his patron's leavings, and served in the chapel. *Ibid.* iii. 382.

attempted to correct this abuse by drawing up a body of CHAP. XIV.
statutes for the College of Montaigu whose austerity would College of
repel everything short of the direst poverty and the most excep-
intense devotion to study. Any one who will compare John tional.
Standonck's statutes with those of earlier foundations will see
how many degrees of poverty there were below that of the
'poor scholars' on an ordinary college-foundation.[1] The
statutes of this college are not, as has sometimes been supposed,[2] typical of university life in general, but the exception
which proves the rule.

It may be well perhaps to descend from these generalities The
to a few particulars. A fellow's weekly commons in the medieval
second half of the fourteenth century at an English college table.
varied (at ordinary times) from a shilling to eighteenpence.
Meat was then at about $\frac{1}{4}d$. per lb., butter and cheese at $\frac{1}{2}d$.
per lb., while 6 lb. of wheat could be bought for 1d.[3] Beer
good enough for a nobleman's determination feast could be
had at 12d. the quart;[4] but home-brewed small-beer must
have cost far less than this. Thus 1$\frac{1}{2}$ lb. of bread, 1 lb. of
meat, and $\frac{1}{4}$ lb. of butter and cheese per head could be provided for about 1d. a day or 7d. a week. This would form a
tolerably substantial basis for a student's diet, leaving at least
as much again for beer-money and 'etceteras'.

As to the English universities, it is customary to quote

[1] In these statutes he complains
of the 'potentum filii et divitum qui
caeteras pias pauperum fundationes
iniuste occupant' (Félibien, v. 735).

[2] e.g. Mullinger, *Cambridge*, i.
367, where some interesting remi-
niscences of Erasmus' days at this
college are cited.

[3] Rogers, *Hist. of Agriculture and
Prices in England*, Oxford, 1866, i.
57.

[4] *Ibid.* ii. 644. There is a more
expensive beer at 20d. the quart,
and an inferior at 10d. There is
also a payment to the 'pistor'.
These beverages were probably
strong ales like those which still
occasionally appear in wine-glasses
in college halls. [However strong

these beers may have been, their
prices as given by Rashdall are im-
possibly high. Rashdall does not
seem to have noticed that in the
same account there is record of
beer purchased at 1$\frac{1}{2}d$. a gallon. It
seems more likely that the beers in
question were purchased by the
quarter and not by the quart. Beer
was sold by the quarter in Oxford.
See *Med. Arch. Univ. Oxford*, ed.
H. E. Salter (O.H.S.), ii. 192. In
1579 the vice-chancellor 'setteth
the pryce of a quarter of the best
stronge ale at iiis iiijd'; see *Records
of the City of Oxford, 1509–1583*,
ed. W. H. Turner, p. 400. See also
L. F. Salzman, *English Industries
of the Middle Ages*, pp. 285–98.]

CHAP. XIV. the testimony of Thomas Lever, Master of S. John's College,
Lever's Cambridge, who draws a touching picture of the hardships
account of
S. John's, endured by the scholars of his college in a charity sermon
Cam-
bridge. preached on their behalf at Paul's Cross. He describes their
ten o'clock dinner as consisting exclusively of a 'penye pece
of byefe amongest iiii, hauying a few porage made of the
brothe of the same byefe wyth salte and otemell', and their
five o'clock supper as 'not much better'; while, for lack of
fire, they were forced 'to walk or runne up and down halfe an
houre, to get a heate on their feet' at bed-time.[1] But Mr.
Mullinger[2] has well pointed out that this was an exceptional
state of things—it represents the lowest ebb to which a college
could be reduced in a time of failing revenues; and after all,
two meals of soup, meat, and presumably bread or porridge,
is not so very bad. We have seen that, judged by the standard
of the age, the Oxford colleges at least had begun to earn,
long before the conclusion of our period, that character as
homes of substantial if not luxurious comfort which they have
never since lost. Any difference between them and the continental colleges (though there, too, we hear of the abuse of
colleges by well-to-do persons) must have been mainly due
to that life-tenure of fellowships which was peculiar to the
English universities.[3]

Hardships of Student-life

Hardships   In reading of the hardships of medieval student-life it
not pe-
culiar to must be remembered that many comforts and conveniences
students. which have become necessaries to the modern artisan were
then unknown luxuries except in the very wealthiest and
noblest homes. If the scholar's hardships were greater than

[1] *Lever's Sermons*, ed. Arber, p. 122.

[2] *Cambridge*, i. 371. [See also Sir H. F. Howard, *An Account of the Finances of St. John's College, Cambridge, 1511–1926*, pp. 26, 27.]

[3] This feature of the English colleges is censured by Polydore Vergil (*Hist. Anglic.*, Leiden, 1651, p. 140) who gives them a good character for morality in other respects but complains of the idle and elderly fellows 'qui omne vitae curriculum ibidem sese molliter curando transigunt, qui malis exemplis iuventuti plurimum interdum nocent'. The founders of Wadham College took the hint and limited the fellowships to twenty years.

those of his class elsewhere, they were largely those which CHAP. XIV.
were inseparable from his sedentary life. In the first rank of
such hardships must be placed his sufferings from cold. In
France and England we hear nothing of fires in the school, Want of
and there are very slight traces of them in college chambers. fire.
It is in fact certain that in the medieval lecture-room there
was no warmth but what was supplied by the straw or rushes
upon the floor: fires were certainly not a matter of course in
college rooms. A German winter must, one would think,
have been insupportable without fire even to the hardy
medieval, warm-wrapped in furs and dirt. In some of the
German colleges it was customary for the college to take its
meals in the kitchen during the winter season: in others we
hear of a common hall warmed by a stove or fire-place.[1]
But even in Germany we find that it is one of the duties of
the head of a college to make a periodical inspection of
college rooms lest perhaps their occupants should have
improvised for themselves grates or stoves.[2] Other statutes
denounce with much severity the practice of resorting for
warmth to the kitchen fire.[3] At the Sorbonne we do hear
of private supplies of wood for the fellows' rooms,[4] and at

[1] At Leipzig, in 1498, a contribution is to be levied 'ad emendum ligna ad calefatienda stuba magistrorum' (Zarncke, *Statutenbücher*, p. 233). So at Paris in 1540. Félibien, iii. 413.
[2] 'Ne . . . focos sive fornaces ibidem construant vel habeant' (Zarncke, *loc. cit.*, p. 234). [Cf. W. H. Woodward, *Vittorino da Feltre*, Cambridge, 1905, p. 35.]
[3] The following statute of the Collège de Foix at Toulouse (1457) I cannot find it in my heart to abridge: 'Sunt nonnulli qui ita gule et ingluviei sunt dediti quod ea que in coquina parantur videre cupiunt et eis exinde melius parari expetunt, neque contenti de his que apparata sunt refectionem sumere. Volumus, igitur, statuimus, et ordinamus ut nullus collegiatus sine licentia rectoris coquinam, paneteriam, sive

dispensam audeat intrare, sed si quid voluerit a rectore seu administratore petat. Si quis contrarium fecerit, puniatur pena arbitraria per rectorem indicenda. Non autem interdicimus quod si quis stomacho indispositus fuerit, possit intrare dictam coquinam et petere scutellam brolii, et coquus sibi ministrare teneatur, dum tamen talis non fingat se stomacho affligi, neque causa ad se calefaciendum in dictam coquinam intrare audeat' (Fournier, i, No. 840). The same statutes, however, provide for a fire 'in tinello' (the dining-hall) 'incipiendo in vigilia sancti Hieronymi usque ad festum Pasche'.
[4] In the MS. Register, f. 78, a dispute occurs 'super distributione camerarum et lignariorum': it is settled that two fellows shall share a 'lignarium'.

CHAP. XIV. Durham College, Oxford, the inventories of furniture contain allusions to andirons.[1] But the standard of comfort prevalent among monks of a lordly monastery like Durham was so much higher than that of the ordinary secular scholar that we cannot assume the existence of such luxuries as a private fire in Oxford colleges generally in the complete absence of other evidence. At Cambridge it seems that the parlour or (as it is now called) combination-room was largely intended as a place for the fellows to warm themselves in winter.[2] The cheerless picture presented by the fireless studies is completed by the wooden window-shutters, the clay or tiled floors either bare or strewn with straw, and the unplastered ceiling.[3] Glass windows were an exceptional luxury till towards the close of our period. At Padua the windows of the schools were made of linen.[4] In 1463 a glass window was for the first time introduced into the theological school at Prague.[5] In 1598 the rooms inhabited by some of the junior fellows at King's College, Cambridge, were still unprovided with this convenience.[6] Another melancholy detail is the

The 'parlour' at Cambridge.

Glass windows exceptional.

Expense of candle-light.

[1] Spelt 'awndyryns'. The inventories (a roll in the Chapter Library at Durham) were made in 1428. This fact was kindly communicated to me by my friend the Rev. Dr. H. E. D. Blakiston [now President of] Trinity College, Oxford. [These inventories have since been edited by Dr. Blakiston and are included in *Collectanea* (O.H.S.), iii. 41–55.]

[2] The early Cambridge colleges usually possessed such a room; at Oxford, oddly enough, the common-room seems to be a seventeenth-century invention. See the chapter on 'The Combination Room' in Willis and Clark, iii. 376 *sq.* At Durham College, Oxford, there was a 'loqutorium', but this was due to its monastic character. (Inventory of 1428.) [See 'Some Durham College Rolls', edited by H. E. D. Blakiston, in *Collectanea* (O.H.S.), iii. 45. Cf. Winkelmann, *Urkundenbuch*, i. 110

(1418) for Heidelberg.]

[3] Willis and Clark, iii. 320; Josselin, *Hist. of C.C.C. Camb.*, §§ 29–42.

[4] 'Bidelli scolas suas faciant cooper[i]ri et ipsarum fenestras lineis pannis vel aliter claudi' (*Archiv* vi. 451). At Paris there were windows 'de calce'.

[5] 'Item anno Domini 1463 ... comparatum est vitrum per facultatem artium ad fenestram unam in lectorio theologorum collegii Caroli, ne imbres et tempestates impediant magistros in legendo et disputando' (*Mon. Univ. Prag.* i. ii. 81).

[6] Willis and Clark, iii. 325. The inventory of furniture then taken mentions 'wyndowes glased', but in other cases only 'wooden leaves for the wyndowes'. The goods of a Sorbonnist in 1434 include 'unam parvam cortinam albam fimbriatam que inest fenestras camere dicti defuncti ad prohibendum ingressum venti pro pretio ii *sol.* viiid.' (Regis-

expense of artificial light in winter. When the average price CHAP. XIV.
of candles was nearly 2d. per lb., it is obvious that reading
by candle-light was beyond the means of the poorest
students.¹ No special allowance on this head was made by
the college. Hence, no doubt, the frequency of disputations
and repetitions as evening employments, at which a single
candle might suffice for the whole company.

The King's College inventory already mentioned and the College
various inventories of scholars' goods taken at Oxford² furniture.
enable us to form a tolerable idea of the ordinary furniture
of a student's room. The senior men usually had ordinary
bedsteads, in connexion with which various gorgeously
coloured coverlets,³ a 'celer and tester', or 'hanging linen'
and curtains are sometimes mentioned. The juniors often
slept in truckle-beds which could be put away under the
ordinary bedsteads. There is usually a table with a few chairs
or 'playne joyned stooles' or 'joyned formes'. 'A new cistern
or a troughe of lead', or 'a lead to wash with a cocke', or 'a Washing
picher and a bolle', are sometimes but not universally men- arrange-
tioned. (In some colleges there appears to have been a public ments.
lavatory in the hall.)⁴ A 'matteresse', a bolster, a 'pilowe',
and 'ii peyre of olde shetes' represent the bedding of a priest
who died at Vine Hall, Oxford, in 1455: he also possessed
'i candelstik of yrone' and 'i shere to snoffe candels'.⁵ In the

ter, f. 17). At Padua, by the statutes of 1556 (f. 126 b), the landlord
is to see 'quod fenestrae camerarum
et studiorum pannis lineis fulcian-
tur'.
¹ Rogers, Hist. of Prices, i. 414.
² Mun. Acad. ii. 525, 565, 582,
658, 663, &c. [Reg. Cancell. Oxon.,
1434–1469, ed. H. E. Salter
(O.H.S.), i. 110–11, 160–1, 162–4,
216–18, 237–40, 267–9, 315–16,
353–4, &c.] In the inventory discovered by Dr. Blakiston among
the rolls of Durham College belonging to the Dean and Chapter
of Durham—certainly the earliest
inventory of college-rooms in existence—are found a 'vertibulum', a
'lavacrum', and 'pelvis'. [See Col-

lectanea (O.H.S.), iii. 43–6.]
³ 'i coverlyt of reed and blewe
with estryche fetherys, pris iis. iiiid.
Item, i coverlyt of grene and yelow
poudred with roses, iis.' appear in
the inventory of a deceased chaplain in 1447. Mun. Acad. ii. 565.
[Reg. Cancell. Oxon., ed. H. E.
Salter (O.H.S.), i. 216–17.]
⁴ Boase, Reg. of Exeter Coll.
(1894), p. xli.
⁵ Mun. Acad. ii. 663. [Reg.
Cancell. Oxon., 1434–1469, ed.
H. E. Salter (O.H.S.), i. 353–4.] A
writer of the thirteenth century
thus describes the furniture which
the student expected to find in his
hostel, but, as the book is a word-
book, he probably exaggerates the

CHAP. XIV. case of humbler scholars blankets or counterpanes appear
without the sheets. The musical man had his 'lewt'. There
Books. was a chest or 'cofer' or 'canveisse' for clothes; if the occupant
were a serious student there would be a 'presse' or shelves
for books. In the inventories of more sporting characters,
knives and swords, bows and arrows, a hatchet or a silver
'misericordia' are more conspicuous than books. The aspira-
tions of Chaucer's clerk of Oxenford represent about the
maximum that an ordinary student would expect in this last
department—

'For him was lever han at his beddes hed
A twenty bokes, clothed in black or red,
Of Aristotle, and his philosophie,
Than robes riche, or fidel, or sautrie.'[1]

Beds. Separate beds are as a rule allowed by English college statutes, except occasionally in the case of the youngest boys.
At Magdalen College, Oxford, demies under 15 are to sleep
two in a bed.[2] The same arrangement is found in a monastic
college at Montpellier, and is allowed by special permission of
the principal in the Oxford halls.[3] In English college rooms the
usual arrangement was that each scholar had a 'study' of his
The
'study'. own adjoining the windows.[4] These studies were apparently
movable structures, being sometimes treated as part of the

completeness of the outfit: 'In
hospitio probi hominis debent
haec esse: mensa decens, mappa
candida, manutergium fimbria-
tum, tripodes alti, trestelli fortes,
torres, eremalia, focalia, stirpes
(some MSS. read 'stipes'), cippi,
vectes, sedilia, scamna, cathedra, spondae et fercula facta de
lignis levigatis, culcitrae, cervicalia
et pulvinaria, cribrum taratan-
tarum, haustrum, mulctra, casea-
rium, et muscipula' (Scheler, Lexi-
cographie Latine du XIIe et du
XIIIe siècle, Leipzig, 1867, p. 31).
Moreover, 'Haec sunt instrumenta
clericis necessaria: libri, pulpita,
crucibolum cum sepo, absconsa et
laterna, cornu cum incausto, penna,
plumbum et regula et speculum,

tabulae et ferula, cathedra, asser,
creta cum plana, pumex' (*ibid.*,
p. 31).
[1] Prologue, ll. 363–6.
[2] *Statutes of the Colleges of
Oxford*, ii (Magd. Coll.), p. 73.
[3] *Cart. de l'Un. de M.*, p. 542;
old *Stat. Aul.*, f. 2. [*Stat. Antiq.
Univ. Oxon.*, ed. S. Gibson, p. 576,
ll. 35–7.]
[4] Thus at New College: 'In in-
ferioribus . . . cameris . . . quatuor
fenestras et quatuor studiorum loca
habentibus, sint semper quatuor
scholares vel socii collocati' (*Statutes*, p. 88). We hear of such *studia*
in the friars' convents much earlier.
See references in A. G. Little,
Greyfriars in Oxford (O.H.S.), p.
55.

furniture. In their simplest form we may perhaps picture CHAP. XIV. them by the aid of the Eton boy's bureau or the Winchester scholar's 'toys'. By the time of the King's College inventory they have doors, and may therefore be supposed to have been something like the cubicles in the dormitories of some public-schools, though the structure was still apparently movable. In the Middle Ages, however, students slept in the part of the room left unoccupied by the separate 'studies' of its two, three, four, or occasionally more numerous occupants.[1]

Amusements

A very striking feature of medieval university life (at least in English eyes) is the almost total absence of authorized or respectable amusements. The statutes of the college founder or university disciplinarian on such matters are often more severe than they are in the repression of crime or vice. It is difficult to find in our records any allusion to recognized amusements except some vague mention of playing at ball out of doors, and within doors of singing or playing on the lute. But here again we are simply encountering one of the characteristics, not of the universities in particular, but of the age in general. The upper class of feudal society was an essentially military class: its amusements consisted in jousts and tournaments, hunting and hawking. Such recreations were not unnaturally considered too unclerkly and too distracting as well as too expensive for the university student, and were consequently forbidden in medieval statutes.[2] Contempt of the body was too deeply rooted a sentiment of the religious mind for a pious college founder to recognize

Absence of recognized amusements.

---

[1] On the whole of this subject see the most interesting chapter on 'The Chambers and Studies' in Willis and Clark, *Cambridge*, iii. 296–327.

[2] e.g. at Heidelberg: 'Item quod nullus capere presumat aviculas, aves seu feras quarumcunque specierum, seu capcioni illarum intersit, sub pena vnius floreni et confiscationis captarum' (statute of 1453, ap. Hautz, *Gesch. d. Un. Heidelberg*, ii. 393). 'Item quod nullus scolis dimicancium interesse, seu exercicio eorumdem se submittere presumat, nec aliquem ad docendum vel discendum huiusmodi vanitatem quoquo modo inducat, sub pena vnius floreni' (*ibid.*, p. 394). Cf. *Statutes of the Colleges of Oxford*, i (New College), p. 48.

CHAP. XIV. the necessity of bodily exercise and a free vent for animal spirits. Even 'playing with a ball or a bat'—the nearest approach to 'athletics' which we encounter—is at times forbidden among other 'insolent' games.[1] A sixteenth-century 'Indecent statute includes the machinery of tennis or fives among the instruments.' 'indecent instruments' the introduction of which would generate scandal against the college; though it charitably allows playing with a soft ball in the college court.[2] Though Gambling. gambling was not so strong a passion in the north as in the south of Europe, a good many statutes are directed against it even in northern universities. The sterner college founders forbade games of chance and playing for money altogether: the more indulgent contented themselves with limiting the stakes to eatables or drinkables and confining the games to Chess. festivals.[3] Chess is a pastime which might seem severe

[1] 'Ad pilam vel ad crossiam vel ad alios ludos insultuosos' (statute of Narbonne College, 1379, ap. Félibien, v. 670). [Rashdall is mistaken. The statute in fact forbids the playing of pitch and toss indoors.]

[2] 'Item, et quia multae querelae vicinorum ad aures nostras devenerunt de insolentiis, exclamationibus et ludis palmariis dictorum scolarium, qui ludunt scophis seu pilis durissimis ac ferulis reticulis et aliis indecentibus instrumentis, horisque et diebus indebitis, in scandalum collegii et detrimentum dictorum vicinorum; ideo ordinamus quod nulli,... de caetero ludant ad ludum palmarium, maxime in magna area dicti collegii, nisi pilis seu scophis mollibus et manu, ac cum silentio et absque clamoribus tumultuosis, neque ludant ante prandium', &c. (Statute of College of Tours, 1540, ap. Félibien, iii. 419, 420). It is surprising to find the martyr Ridley anticipating the manners of the nineteenth century by playing tennis or practising archery with a pupil. (The pupil was apparently, however, a junior fellow.) Strype, Memorials, III. i, Oxford, 1822, p.

386. I have come across no allusion to football before 1574, when it is forbidden at Cambridge, but in 1580 allowed only within the college precincts, non adulti offenders to be flogged. Cooper, Annals, ii. 321, 382. At Oxford in 1584 'any minister or deacon' convicted of this offence was to be banished and reported to his bishop, scholars over eighteen imprisoned and fined, those under eighteen to be flogged in S. Mary's. [See Stat. Antiq. Univ. Oxon., ed. S. Gibson, p. 432.] (Wood, Annals, ii. 220.) For football on Bullingdon Green in 1607 see Twyne MSS. xxi. 85. [See also the article on 'Sport and Pastime in Stuart Oxford', by P. Manning in Surveys and Tokens, ed. H. E. Salter (O.H.S.), pp. 104–5.]

[3] At Narbonne all playing for money is forbidden 'unless sometimes and rarely at honest and recreative games, for a pint or quart of wine or fruit, and without great noise and expenditure of time' (Félibien, v. 670). At Cornouaille (1380) playing at 'dice or tables' is allowed only 'for the recreation of some sick fellow . . . in the house

enough to propitiate the most morose disciplinarian, but it CHAP. XIV. seems to have enjoyed a curiously bad reputation with the medieval moralist, and is forbidden by many academical legislators. At Heidelberg, for instance, visits to the public chess-tables are forbidden 'especially on legible days'; at New College the stern Bishop of Winchester includes chess among the 'noxious, inordinate, and unhonest games' which are forbidden to his scholars.[1]

College statutes are not unnaturally full of prohibitions Musical directed against musical or other noises calculated to disturb ments. the studies of others.[2] Some few German statutes condescend so far to human infirmity as to permit at seasonable hours musical instruments, 'provided they are musical'. As to the keeping of dogs, hawks, ferrets, 'unclean beasts or birds',[3] Dogs, the practice was viewed by the college disciplinarian with a hawks, &c. traditional horror which (as regards dogs) still lingers in the breasts of the deans and porters of Oxford and Cambridge. As the grim sixteenth century is reached, the prohibitions against all 'profane games, immodest runnings, and horrid shoutings', become increasingly sweeping.[4]

or out of it on festivals, and for the sake of solace and for some moderate comestible or potable' (*ibid.* iii. 502). A court of justice might find the clause difficult to interpret: there is a further reservation in favour of Christmas and SS. Nicholas, Catherine, and Corentinus.

[1] *Statutes of the Colleges of Oxford*, i (New College), p. 48; Hautz, *Heidelberg*, ii. 394. [At Heidelberg to play chess on tables for a measure of wine was contemplated, 'dum modo fiat in solacium magistrorum et societatis gracia', Winkelmann, *Urkundenbuch*, i. 110 (1418).] At Louvain the legislator is more indulgent towards private games: 'Illos etiam a quibuscumque ludis taxillorum et chartarum (tutores) prohibeant, permittendo, tamen diebus et horis opportunis ludos virtuosos in domo vel locis privatis et non publicis . . .

sicut ad scaccos, ad pilam aut consimiles, absque tamen excessivo labore aut immoderata frequentia' (ordinance of Charles the Bold, Duke of Brabant, in 1476; Molanus, ii. 940). [Games of chess often ended in a fight.]

[2] 'Quod nullus ludat in domo cum cythara vel choro vel aliis instrumentis sonoris, per quod possent dicti scholares aliqualiter molestari' (Félibien, iii. 397).

[3] 'Nec etiam teneant bestias vel aves immundas vel alias nocivas' (*ibid.* iii. 386).

[4] Item placet, quod nullus scholasticorum intra vel prope collegium exerceat quoscunque ludos prophanos aut discursus immodestos seu boatus edat horrisonos, studiosorum interturbando negotia . . . sub poena septem grossorum' (statute of *Collegium minus* at Leipzig, ap. Zarncke, *Statutenbücher*, p. 240).

CHAP. XIV.   The institution of a sort of public university ball for the
Dancing. express purpose, it would seem, of introducing the students
to the 'most honourable and elegant daughters of magnates,
senators, and citizens', deserves to be mentioned as a rather
exceptional peculiarity of sixteenth-century Leipzig.[1] Much
more frequently we encounter stern denunciations of dancing
in any form whatever. But we may infer that the amusement
was a favourite one with the students from the fact that, even
in a college jealously guarded against female intrusion,
William of Wykeham found it necessary for the protection of
the sculpture in the chapel reredos to make a statute against
dancing or jumping in the chapel or adjoining hall.[2] His
language is suggestive of that untranslatable amusement now
known as 'ragging', which has no doubt formed a large part
of the relaxation of students—at least of English students—
in all ages. At the same college there is a comprehensive
prohibition of all 'struggling, chorus-singing, dancing, leaping,
singing, shouting, tumult and inordinate noise, pouring forth
of water, beer, and all other liquids and tumultuous games'
in the hall, on the ground that they were likely to disturb
the occupants of the chaplain's chamber below. A moderate
indulgence in some of the more harmless of these pastimes
in other places seems to be permitted.

Festivals   The ideal student of the Middle Ages probably amused
and eccle-
siastical himself little or not at all. The only relaxation which the
dissipa-
tion. university system provided for was the frequent interruption of the regular routine for the whole or part of a day
in honour of the greater holidays of the Church, or of the

---

[1] 'Ut in publico prudentissimi
senatus theatro doctores, nobiles,
magistri, studiosi iuuenes cum ho-
nestissimis et lepidissimis magna-
tum, senatorum et ciuium filiabus
choreas ductarent' (Zarncke, Acta
Rectorum, p. 34). On the other
hand, at Basel, in 1460, an agreement between the town and the
university provides 'quod studentes
per Rectores Bursarum et alios
inducantur ut non chorisent in
choreis civium publice nisi ad illas

specialiter fuerint invitati' (Vischer,
pp. 306, 307). So at Avignon dancing is forbidden 'salvis choreis
publicis que fierent in festis de
universitate (leg. universitatis) sup-
positorum' (A.D. 1441) (Fournier,
ii, No. 1334).
[2] Statutes of the Colleges of Oxford, i (New College), p. 100. In
Chaucer (Cant. Tales, l. 3329) a
scholar dances 'After the scole of
Oxenforde tho'.'

festivals of the patrons of a particular nation, or province, or CHAP. XIV.
faculty. For the faculty of arts the great days were the feasts
of S. Scholastica and S. Nicholas. Some statutes contain
severe prohibition of carnival-tide licence, but in Scotland
two or three days' holiday was expressly allowed for cock-
fighting at this season.[1] In all medieval universities—but
especially at Paris—the student enjoyed an abundance of
what may be called ecclesiastical dissipation. For the masters
at Paris there were national vespers and a national mass
once a week,[2] as well as on many festivals. These functions
were followed by a distribution of money or a dinner at the
expense of the nation. For master and scholars alike there
were frequent processions, university masses, and university
sermons, which at least afforded a welcome relief from morning lecture. The afternoons of holidays supplied the chief Half-
opportunity for country walks or recreation in the Pré-aux- holidays.
clercs.[3] In the German universities we find, however, a
growing tendency to abridge even this scant liberty by providing afternoon lectures on festivals. Mathematics are
sometimes introduced as a light study specially appropriate

[1] e.g. at S. Andrews: MS. *Acta Fac. Artium*, f. 1 *b*. The statute forbids the spending of a fortnight or three weeks 'in procuratione gallorum'.

[2] The vespers on Friday, the mass on Saturday. This usage was still kept up in the time of Goulet (viii *b*). At Oxford such entertain-ments appear to have been less frequent. But we find an annual item in the proctors' accounts, 'pro distribucione fienda inter regentes', amounting (at the end of the fif-teenth century) to £3 18*s*. 4*d*. Two great holidays were celebrated on the vigils of S. John the Baptist and of S. Peter, in connexion with which we find such items as the following: 'Item solutum in vigiliis sancti Io-annis Baptiste et sancti Petri in recreacione omnium graduatorum ex consuetudine laudabili ut placet iudicibus (i.e. the auditors, who

fixed the sum) . . . *vili. xiiis. iiiid*. Item pro cirpis consumptis in dictis vigilis et certis reparacionibus factis in locis ubi tenebantur dicte re-creaciones . . . *iiis*. Item, pro con-sumptione luminum in eisdem noctibus et in obitibus dominorum Ioannis et Thome Kempe, ducis Glocestrie et episcopi Lincolniensis . . . *xvis*.' from the accounts for 1494–5 in Archives, W. P—Y 28. [*Med. Arch. Univ. Oxford*, ed. H. E. Salter (O.H.S.), ii. 283, 351.]

[3] A statute at Ingolstadt re-strains what would appear to have been harmless country excursions: 'Retroactis temporibus nimium fre-quentare coeperint exitus cumula-tos ad loca nemorosa, quos exitus appellant fontonia'; henceforth they were only allowed 'semel in canicularibus . . . exire cum Decani licentia' (Prantl, ii. 113, 114).

CHAP. XIV. for such times, it being alleged that half-holidays were
Holiday usually spent in the tavern. In the evenings of festivals even
evenings. the sternest of college disciplinarians relaxed so far as to
allow story-telling or carol-singing, or the reading of 'poems,
chronicles of the realm, or wonders of the world' round the
fire in the college hall.[1] This was probably regarded as a
harmless substitute for the entertainments of strolling jesters
or actors or mountebanks largely patronized by the student
when free from collegiate restraints.[2] Only on Twelfth-night
were mummers allowed within the sacred precincts of the
college.[3]

Sundays.   By some universities we find even Sunday utilized for
lectures or disputations,[4] and there are traces of the same
institution in the early days of the Italian law-schools; but
this would appear to have been the exception rather than the
rule.[5] In general, the Sunday was free for worship and rest,
and seems to have been rarely abused by the outrages or
disturbances so common on other festivals.

Plays.   The comedies which began to be acted in the halls or
colleges towards the end of the fifteenth century form almost
the only amusement of an intellectual character which re-

[1] So at New College, where
lingering in hall is forbidden 'nisi
quando ob Dei reverentiam ac suae
matris vel alterius sancti cuiuscunque tempore hyemali ignis in
aula Sociis ministratur' (Statutes
of the Colleges of Oxford, i (New
College), p. 42). [See also Reg.
Annal. Coll. Merton., ed. H. E.
Salter (O.H.S.), p. xxi.]

[2] At the College of Cornouaille,
scholars are to abstain 'a quibuscumque ludis mimorum, iocula-
torum, histrionum, goliardorum, et
consimilium' (Félibien, iii. 502).

[3] Bulaeus, v. 782, 783, the number of 'mimi' being limited to one
'et ad summum duo'.

[4] At Leipzig: Zarncke, Statutenbücher, p. 339. So at Nantes (1461)
there are ethics lectures on Sundays
as well as other festivals: Fournier,
iii, No. 1595. We find 'questiones

dominicae' among the works of
Roffredus: Sarti (1888), I. i. 88.
The statutes of Salamanca forbid
'repetitiones' on Sundays: Denifle,
Archiv, v. 183. In modern Italian
universities, examinations are continued on Sundays. For an Oxford
Congregation on Sunday see Mon.
Francisc. (R.S.), i. 347. I have met
with a bulky treatise by a medieval
canonist in support of the thesis that
study on Sundays was permissible
except when pursued for gain.

[5] By a statute of the city of
Perugia in 1389 the Sapientes Studii
are to elect doctors to lecture on
Sundays or other festivals. Giornale
d. Erudiz. artistica, vi. 315, 316.
[Gerald of Wales says that at Paris
in his day (c. 1177) it was customary
to lecture on the canon law (causae
decretales) on Sundays; Giraldi
Cambrensis Opera (R.S.), i. 45.]

lieved the stern monotony of academic life. But these are not CHAP. XIV. heard of till the first breath of the Renaissance spirit had reached even Paris and Oxford: these comedies represent the first contact of the stream of academic culture with the now fuller and more vigorous current of popular literature, and exercised an important influence over the development of the modern drama both in France and England. It is needless to say that the innovation was looked upon with considerable suspicion, though not altogether prohibited, by the university disciplinarians.[1]

Alike in the universities and out of them the ascetism of Illicit the medieval ideal provoked and fostered the wildest indul- amusements. gence in actual life. If we want to realize what were the probable amusements of the un-ideal student we must turn to the things which laws and statutes prohibit rather than to those which they permit. For the bolder spirits there were sporting excursions into the country. Poaching in the king's Poaching. forests at Shotover or Woodstock was a favourite pastime of the Oxford scholar.[2] The University of S. Andrews with unwonted liberality actually allowed its students to go a-hawking, provided they went in their own clothes and not Hawking. in 'dissolute habiliments borrowed from lay cavaliers'.[3] On the roads round the university towns were even to be met parties of scholars—many of them expelled or banished for previous transgressions—who had turned highwaymen and Scholar now waylaid the more peaceful student approaching the highwaymen. university with his purse equipped for a nine months' residence.[4]

The proportion of idle men was perhaps not larger than Drinking, in most modern universities, but for the idle, as for the quarrelling. average student in his lighter moods, there were hardly any

---

[1] In 1488, at Paris, it was ordered that the principal should 'visit' comedies performed in his hall. Bulaeus, i. 785.

[2] Rot. Claus. 15 Hen. III, m. 10. [Close Rolls, Hen. III, 1227–31, p. 520, dated 22 June 1231.] Rot. Claus. 1 Hen. V, m. 29 dorso (Hare, Mem. 111) [Cal. Close Rolls, Hen. V,

1413–1419, i. 75, 76, dated 5 June 1413]; Macray, Reg. of Magd. Coll. i. 44.

[3] MS. Acta Facultatis Artium, f. 15 a.

[4] Rot. Pat. 15 Ed. III, Pt. iii, m. 8 (Hare, f. 68 a); [Cal. Pat. Rolls, Edw. III, 1340–1343, p. 363]; Rot. Parl. iv. 131 (9 Hen. V).

CHAP. XIV. amusements except drinking, gambling, and singing at taverns,[1] roaming the streets in large gangs under a 'captain' or otherwise, singing, shouting, dancing, throwing stones, breaking doors or heads, and fighting or quarrelling with townsfolk or students of a hostile 'nation'. Various forms of

Practical practical joking of the more violent order enjoyed a high joking. degree of popularity. Among the archives of the University of Leipzig is a 'libellus formularis' or collection of forms for rectorial proclamations against the various kinds of disorder which were wont to break out periodically in a medieval university like the recurrent epidemics of pea-shooting, catapulting, and the like at a modern school.[2] Among these is a form of proclamation against destroying trees and crops in the adjoining country, against 'wandering with arms after the town-hall bell', against throwing water out of the window upon passers-by, against wandering at night and beating the watch, against 'horrible shoutings and noisy and unwonted songs', against wearing disguises, masks, and 'rustic garments' at carnival-tide, against interfering with the hangman (*suspensor*) in the execution of his duty, against disturbing the inception banquets or 'Aristotle's feasts', against attending exhibitions of tilting, wrestling, boxing, and the like, against 'insolences' or practical jokes in general.

Contrast   The date of this document is as late as 1495. These were
between
earlier and the milder effervescences of medieval spirits at a period when
later the student had been already reduced to a semi-civilized
Middle
Age. condition. What his wilder outbursts of fun and frolic had been in the earlier days of unrestrained student-liberty, the reader will already have gathered from some of the Town and Gown narratives which have already been set before him. It may be well, however, to give a few further illustrations of the kind of violence of which the medieval scholar was alternatively the victim and the perpetrator. It is necessary that we should realize vividly what the treatment was

---

[1] A statute of Vienna (Kink, ii. 76) is directed against 'scholares brigosi, luxuriosi, ebriosi, disculi, noctiuagi cum instrumentis musicis uel alias ociosi, lenocinantes, fures, et precipue ciuium offensores, taxillorum lusores . . . et omnino ostiorum fractores'.

[2] *Statutenbücher*, pp. 102–19.

against which the medieval scholar—and indeed the medieval CHAP. XIV. clergyman of all grades—sought to be protected by his outrageous privileges, and on the other hand how much excuse there was for the bitterness and fury with which these privileges were opposed and resisted by the lay population. It is perhaps something more than an accident that the instances of lay oppression will be chiefly drawn from the history of Paris, and the illustrations of clerkly violence from the annals of Oxford and other towns wherein the clerkly element bore a larger proportion to the whole population.[1]

The wilder side of University life

The boundaries of the city of Paris had been extended by Feud Philip Augustus so as to include the suburb south of the Parisian river. The western. portion of this transpontine region and Moformed the students' quarter, in which were situated most of S. Ger the buildings used by the university and most of the colleges main. and hostels inhabited by the scholars. This *quartier latin*[2] (as it came to be called) extended from the Cathedral of Notre Dame on the island *cité* to the western wall near the site now occupied by the palace of the Institute. Medieval Paris, like medieval London, was surrounded by a belt of monasteries, whose abbots exercised a feudal jurisdiction over the districts surrounding their churches. Just outside the city wall, to the west of the students' quarter, stood the great abbey of S. Germain. Outside the abbey walls was an open meadow or waste ground which had from time immemorial been the promenade of the elder and the playground of the younger students. When the university had assumed the form of a definite corporation, that body or rather its faculty of arts claimed the Pré-aux-clercs as its freehold property. The property, or at least the free use of it, was

---

[1] [In what follows Rashdall gives instances of more or less organized turbulence. Another and more normal aspect of 'the wilder side of university life' at Paris is described in a vivacious chapter of P. Champion's *FrançoisVillon: sa vie et son* *temps* (Paris, 1915), i. 65–129.]

[2] Denifle has made it clear that the term was originally applied only to the island, but was gradually extended to the southern bank as the students deserted the former for the latter. See above, vol. i, p. 277 *sq.*

CHAP. XIV. recognized as belonging to the university by the statutes of the cardinal legate, Robert Curzon, in 1215. The monks, however, contended that the property had anciently been theirs and had been unlawfully alienated by one of the secular abbots in the ages of confusion; and the decision of the legate appears to have left at all events a boundary dispute between the abbey and the university unsettled. The unfortunate scholars were in consequence exposed to much annoyance, and at times to violent and organized attacks from the monks and their retainers. The first recorded outrage of this de-

A monastic scription occurred in 1278. At the morrow of the Translation
excursion. of S. Nicholas, the patron saint of scholars, the fields were crowded with the clerks, when the abbey bell was heard summoning the tenants and servants of the abbot and convent. By order of their black-robed masters an armed guard took possession of the three city gates which opened on to the Pré, so as to cut off the retreat of the scholars, while to the sound of horns and trumpets and with shouts of 'death to the clerks' the convent and its retainers, headed by their provost, sallied forth upon the unarmed and defenceless boys and masters, and fell upon them with bow and arrow, club, sword, or iron-tipped stave. Many were badly wounded, some mortally, but they were nevertheless dragged off to the 'horrible dungeons' of the abbey. Those who fled (a doctor of divinity and a doctor of medicine were among the number) were pursued far and wide over the country.

Punish-   It is significant of the lawlessness of the times that the
ment of
monks. ordinary course of justice seems to have been quite incapable of reaching ruffianism of this kind when committed by such offenders as the abbot and convent of S. Germain. The abbey claimed the 'justice' of the Pré; and was exempt from all episcopal or metropolitical jurisdiction. The university had no resource but to lay their complaint before the king and the papal legate, and to threaten a 'cessation' if redress were not granted within fifteen days. The abbot and the provost were deprived of their offices, but the penalties imposed were, as usual in such cases, mainly corporate. The monks were required to found and endow two chaplaincies,

one in the church of Sainte-Catherine, the other in the chapel CHAP. XIV. of Saint-Martin-des-Orges close to the walls of the abbey, with annual stipends of £20. At these chapels mass was to be said for the benefit of scholars 'before play-time'.[1] These chaplaincies were to be in the gift of the university, and formed the nucleus of the considerable patronage (chiefly in Paris) eventually acquired by the university.[2] The brutality of the monks was not, however, by any means effectually repressed by this humiliation. They were especially sensitive about the claim to fish in the city moat which divided the abbey grounds from the domain of the university. In 1318 it was necessary to procure a papal Bull empowering the bishops of Soissons and Noyon to investigate and punish an outrage upon some priests and other clerks who were enjoying this favourite amusement.[3]

In 1304 the provost of Paris hanged a scholar and gibbeted his body in flagrant contempt of the privileges of the university, and (as we are assured by a contemporary historian) unjustly to boot. A cessation of lectures compelled the king

Outrage by provost of Paris and its consequences.

---

[1] 'Ante ludum.'

[2] This account is taken from the *ex parte* statement of the university (Bulaeus, iii. 453 *sq.*; *Chartul.* i, No. 480); but the retribution which was meted out to so powerful a convent (Bulaeus, iii. 454; *Chartul.* i, Nos. 482, 484, 524; ii, No. 537, &c.) is sufficient to show that the monks cannot have had much to say for themselves. Very characteristic of the time, however, is the ample revenue assigned to the deposed abbot, who is rather praised for his readiness to resign than denounced for an offence which would now get him ten or twenty years' imprisonment or penal servitude in any civilized European country.

[3] Bulaeus, iv. 175; *Chartul.* ii, No. 762. There was, however, much subsequent litigation between the convent and the university. In 1345 the convent ceded to the university the patronage of two

churches in Paris—Saint-André-des-Arcs and SS. Cosmas and Damian—in consideration of the university giving up their claims on a piece of adjoining land. [Cf. *Chartul.* ii, No. 1109, and notes.] A significant clause provides that the abbey may build 'muros simplices . . . sine quernellio et fortaliis aliis a simplici muro, per quae scholares possent laedi'. Moreover, a door leading from the abbey grounds on to the Pré, through which, no doubt, the armed sallies had been made, was to remain for ever walled up (Bulaeus, iv. 287). Among the property bought in 1348 by the university as an endowment for one of the chaplaincies of S. Andrew's Church, we find: 'Item tam homines quam mulieres servilis conditionis ad voluntatem talliabiles et iusticiabiles altae, mediae, et bassae' (*ibid.* iv. 303).

CHAP. XIV. to punish the provost. The offender was required, besides suing for absolution at Avignon, to found two chaplaincies and present the advowson to the offended corporation. In addition to this substantial penalty, the wounded honour of the clerks was appeased by two characteristically medieval impositions. The provost was compelled to cut down the corpse, which had been hanging on the gibbet for some months, and kiss it; while all the clergy of Paris were solemnly convened by the official (the see being vacant) to march in procession with their respective flocks, each with cross and holy water, to the house of the offending magistrate, and there throw stones against it and utter a solemn exorcism or imprecation against the devil who was supposed to inhabit the building.[1]

'Affaire Savoisy.'   Another celebrated outrage on scholars occurred in 1404. The university was now at the height of its power, and the penalties which befell its oppressor were in consequence still more exemplary. A university procession was on its way to the church of Sainte Catherine, the patroness of scholars, to intercede for the peace of the church and realm and the health of the king. A party of pages and others in the service of the king's chamberlain, Charles of Savoisy, on their way towards the Seine to water their horses, met the procession, and, instead of waiting for it to pass, rode in among the scholars. A riot took place in which stones were thrown and some of the boys got trampled on by the horses of their assailants. Savoisy's retainers were not, however, satisfied with the results of the unpremeditated fray; but, retiring to their master's hotel, procured bows and arrows and other weapons, with which they made a deliberate and still more murderous onslaught upon the scholars, pursuing

---

[1] 'Recede, recede, maledicte sathana, recognosce nequitiam tuam dans honorem sancte matri ecclesie, quam quantum in te est dehonorasti ac etiam in suis libertatibus vulnerasti', &c. (*Chartul.* ii, No. 650). It is not quite clear whether the provost or his house is considered to be possessed, or whether the 'sathana' is meant to be a mere term of clerical abuse. A similar penalty was imposed for a similar offence upon a later provost in 1407, but apparently not carried out (Bulaeus, iv. 146; *Chronique du religieux de Saint-Denys*, iii. 726). In this case the scholar had admittedly committed highway robbery.

some of them into a neighbouring church where mass was CHAP. XIV. being celebrated. A crowd of indignant clerks, headed by the rector, proceeded at once to the king, and threatened to leave Paris in a body if justice were not done. The amplest satisfaction was promised; but a suspension of lectures and sermons for six weeks was necessary before it was obtained. Eventually, the master of the truculent household was sentenced to pay a fine of 1,000 *livres* to the victims, another 1,000 to the university, and to create a rent-charge of the annual value of 100 *livres* for the endowment of five chaplaincies which were to be in the gift of the university and to be held by masters. Finally, the chamberlain was dismissed from all his employments, banished from court, and his hotel ordered to be razed to the ground. The latter part of the sentence, we are told by the official record of the proceedings in Parlement, was executed by a great number of the triumphant scholars 'promptly and almost before it was pronounced'. Formal evidence having been given that Savoisy was a clerk, he was exempted from making 'amende honorable'[1] in person, but three of his servants (who were apparently the actual offenders) were ordered to go as penitents to three churches clad in their shirts only, and there carrying lighted tapers in their hands to be publicly flogged on behalf of their master.[2]

Another often-quoted illustration of academical morals in Proclamation by the thirteenth century is the proclamation of the official of official of Paris in 1269 in which he denounces a class of scholars, or 1269. pretended scholars, who 'by day and night atrociously wound and slay many, carry off women, ravish virgins, break into houses', and commit 'over and over again robberies and many other enormities hateful to God'.[3] Such were the kind of crimes in which the clerical tonsure enabled the Parisian scholar to indulge without the smallest fear of the summary

---

[1] 'Mulctam infamem, seu, ut vocant, honorabilem.'.
[2] Bulaeus, v. 95–109. The *Chronique du religieux de Saint-Denys* (iii. 186 *sq.*) makes the destruction a more formal proceeding, carried out by the king's carpenters marching in procession 'cum lituis et instrumentis musicis'.
[3] *Chartul.* i, No. 426 (wrongly dated in Bulaeus, iii. 95).

CHAP. XIV. execution which would have been the fate of an apprentice or a 'sturdy beggar' who essayed such pranks. As a means of preventing such outrages in future the official has nothing more deterrent to hold over the offender's head than the ineffectual threat of excommunication.

Coroner's inquests at Oxford.

If we turn to Oxford, perhaps the best evidence which comes to our hand is contained in the records of coroner's inquisitions. Over and over again occurs the dismal record, 'Such and such jurors on their oaths present that M or N, clerk, killed A or B, citizen or clerk (as the case might be—to do him justice it was nearly as often a brother-clerk as a citizen) with a sword or a pole-axe or a knife or an arrow; that he has fled and that there are no goods left' which can be distrained upon.[1] Rarely is the entry varied by the statement that the accused was obliged to take sanctuary, and after so many days abjured the realm. In those rare cases the culprit might be put to the inconvenience of continuing his studies abroad. In the majority of cases nothing worse happened to them than being compelled to go to Cambridge.

Town and Gown at Orleans.

Another illustration may be drawn from the annals of Orleans. In the year 1387, Jean Rion, a citizen of Orleans, employed two ruffians to waylay a bachelor of the civil law named Guillaume Entrant. Catching him on horseback outside the town, they threw him from his horse, and were only prevented from killing him by the arrival of timely succour. On another occasion they were more successful, wounded him 'atrociously and inhumanly in the head and other parts of the body', cut off a finger and left an arm hanging by 'a slender strip of skin' (*pellicula*). Finally they 'tyrannically' pulled out an eye, and left him for dead. Summoned before the Parlement of Paris, Rion pleaded that the scholar had seduced his wife, and continued the intrigue after having been forgiven and having solemnly pledged himself to abandon it. The fact was notorious and was not denied. The enormous damages claimed by the victim were

[1] See Twyne MSS. xxiii. 154, &c.; Thorold Rogers, *Oxford City Docs.* (O.H.S.), p. 150 *sq.* [All the surviving Oxford coroner's in-

quests not previously printed have been printed by Dr. H. E. Salter in *Records of Medieval Oxford*, Oxford, 1912.]

considerably reduced by the Court. Nevertheless, Rion was <small>CHAP. XIV.</small> condemned to pay 300 *livres tournois* by way of compensation, a fine of 100, and to make 'amende honorable' to the Court, the plaintiff, and the proctor for the university on bended knee and clad only in his shirt. The sentence led to a general outburst of rage and indignation against the scholars. Another scholar was beaten and mutilated 'so that he is expected to die rather than live'. At last there was a regular raid on the scholars 'to the ringing of bells and the sound of trumpets'. Houses were broken open, and scholars dragged out to the town prison. The citizens threatened that all the scholars should die. Nevertheless they do not appear to have done much in execution of their threats beyond beating a scholar's servant and pillaging a house. The scholars, however, fled the town *en masse*. The captain of the city guard rode through the suburbs with his men, shouting 'death to the scholars'. One noble youth was so frightened as to hide in a sewer 'for a long time'. The offenders—chiefly, it would seem, royal officials—were condemned to do penance and make 'amende honorable' to the university in the usual way, and to a fine, part of which was to be expended on a picture representing the offenders on their knees before the rector and other scholars.[1]

Yet another story from Toulouse. In the year 1332 five An Easter
scene at
Toulouse. brothers of the noble family de la Penne lived together in a *hospicium* at Toulouse as students of the civil and canon law. One of them was provost of a monastery, another archdeacon of Albi, another an archpriest, another canon of Toledo. A bastard son of their father, named Peter, lived with them as squire to the canon. On Easter Day, Peter, with another squire of the household named Aimery Béranger and other students, having dined at a tavern, were dancing with women, singing, shouting, and beating 'metallic vessels and iron culinary instruments' in the street before their masters' house. The provost and the archpriest were sympathetically watching the jovial scene from a window, until it was disturbed by the appearance of a capitoul and his officers, who

---

[1] Fournier, i, Nos. 212, 215.

CHAP. XIV. summoned some of the party to surrender the prohibited arms which they were wearing. 'Ben Senhor, non fassat' was the impudent reply. The capitoul attempted to arrest one of the offenders; whereupon the ecclesiastical party made a combined attack upon the official. Aimery Béranger struck him in the face with a poignard, cutting off his nose and part of his chin and lips, and knocking out or breaking no less than eleven teeth. The surgeons deposed that if he recovered (he eventually did recover) he would never be able to speak intelligibly. One of the watch was killed outright by Peter de la Penne. That night the murderer slept, just as if nothing had happened, in the house of his ecclesiastical masters. The whole household, masters and servants alike, were, however, surprised by the other capitouls and a crowd of 200 citizens and led off to prison, and the house is alleged to have been pillaged. The archbishop's official demanded their surrender. In the case of the superior ecclesiastics, this after a short delay was granted. But Aimery, who dressed like a layman in 'divided and striped clothes' and wore a long beard, they refused to treat as a clerk, though it was afterwards alleged that the tonsure was plainly discernible upon his head until it was shaved by order of the capitouls. Aimery was put to the torture, admitted his crime, and was sentenced to death. The sentence was carried out by hanging, after he had had his hand cut off on the scene of the crime, and been dragged by horses to the place of execution. The capitouls were then excommunicated by the official, and the ecclesiastical side of the quarrel was eventually transferred to the Roman Court. Before the Parlement of Paris the university complained of the violation of the royal privilege exempting scholar's servants from the ordinary tribunals. The capitouls were imprisoned, and after a long litigation sentenced to pay enormous damages to the ruffian's family and erect a chapel for the good of his soul. The city was condemned for a time to the forfeiture of all its privileges. The body was cut down from the gibbet on which it had been hanging for three years, and accorded a solemn funeral. Four capitouls bore the pall, and all fathers of families were required to walk in the procession. When they came to the schools, the citizens CHAP. XIV. solemnly begged pardon of the university, and the cortège was joined by 3,000 scholars. Finally, it cost the city 15,000 *livres tournois* or more to regain their civic privileges.[1]

It must be remembered that the violent scenes which crowd the records of a medieval university are only an extreme development of the violence which characterizes medieval life in general. It is, however, not so much the violence which distinguishes medieval society from modern as the status and position of the persons who abused, insulted, challenged, and fought each other like 'roughs' or small boys at school. At the present day party feeling sometimes runs high, but we do not hear of an ex-mayor of Cambridge wishing to fight the chancellor.[2] Scenes of disorder occur in modern universities, but the rectors and professors, heads and tutors take no part in them. Sometimes, too, violence of this kind was not merely the act of isolated individuals, however eminent, but the concerted resolution of grave assemblies. We have seen how at Oxford the bell of S. Mary's was wont to summon the gownsmen to do battle with the town when the bell of S. Martin's was set going by the mayor. At Paris we find the scholars of the Norman nation taking a vote in 'a congregation' as to the propriety of an attack upon another nation.[3] The attack was voted, with the result that 'one was killed and another mutilated'. Our knowledge of the fact comes to us from a 'dispensation from irregularity' granted to a clergyman, afterwards beneficed, who had voted for what is justly described as 'the war'.

Violence of medieval life in general.

Drinking Customs

The violence of medieval university life was almost equalled by its bibulosity.[4] Even the staunchest teetotaller

Bibulosity of medieval life.

[1] All the documents are printed by Fournier, i, Nos. 563-89.
[2] Cooper, *Annals*, i. 164; Hare MS. (Camb. Archives), ii. 57.
[3] 'In quadam congregatione scolarium nationis sue in qua fuit istud propositum, utrum placeret illis, qui erant ibi, quod forciores de natione se armarent et invaderent alios de alia natione' (*Chartul.* ii, No. 1072). [The narrative suggests that this was a meeting of students, not a formal congregation of masters.]
[4] Illustrations without number might be cited from the *Carmina*

CHAP. XIV. might well accord a certain toleration to drinking habits in a community which knew not tea, coffee, or tobacco, and in which life, unbrightened by wine or beer, must have been almost intolerably tedious. In this respect, it is true that it is but recently that our English universities have begun to throw off their medieval traditions: there are universities in which it reigns still. But there can be no better illustration of the nonsense commonly talked about the moralizing and elevating effects—I will not say of education—but of mere instruction than the annals of the medieval schools. The average medieval scholar was much better instructed, much more cultivated (in so far as purely intellectual training communicates culture) than the mass of the working class can ever be on leaving school. Yet his habits, his manners and moral tone generally were in many ways no better than those of the roughest and most uncivilized classes of modern society. From an evening tour through some of the worst dens and alleys of Seven Dials and Ratcliffe Highway, before the institution of the Metropolitan Police, there might have been gathered some faint conception of what life in a medieval university town must have been like, say at the end of the thirteenth century.

Drinking at Examinations, &c. To return to the subject of drinking customs—no important events of life could be got through without drinking. We have already spoken of the mode of celebrating 'jocund advents', determinations and inceptions; and many of the minor steps in the career of a university man were celebrated by feasts and drinking-parties given by the successful and elated candidate.[1] And it was not only after a university exercise

---

Burana; the well-known song beginning (p. 69) 'Meum est propositum in taberna mori' may serve as a type. Nothing can exceed the grossness of some of these songs; but the student-poetry of the Middle Age was not all bacchic or erotic or profane. A somewhat unfair impression in this respect is given by the collection translated by J. A. Symonds, *Wine, Women, and Song* (London, 1884).

[1] Thus by a statute of Ingolstadt there is to be no drinking at the chancellor's house after the examination, but it was provided 'ut licentiandus iam de recipienda licentia certificatus det de vino ytalico et speciebus doctoribus . . . et sociis venientibus ad congratulandum ei in loco ameno (? under the trees in front of the suburban wineshop) vel in domo sua' (Prantl ii. 66).

but during its progress that the need of refreshment was apt CHAP. XIV.
to be felt. Wine was provided for the distinguished visitors
to the schools at determinations. Many statutes allude—
some by way of prohibition, but not always—to the custom
of providing refreshment of the same kind for the examiners
by the examinees, whether before, during, or after an examination.[1] One of the main objects for which the nations
existed at Paris was the celebration of 'Feasts', which began
with a solemn mass and was concluded with a banquet in a
neighbouring tavern; from time to time it was long the
regular custom of the nations to consume their surplus
revenue by a carouse at the tavern.[2] The fee of the prelate
who celebrated on such occasions was paid by a present of
wine. The statutes of many German universities forbid the
rector to give 'propinationes' at the expense of the university
without its consent. A newly elected officer was required
to entertain his constituents with 'spiced wine'.

Oaths

Another characteristic feature of medieval life, vividly Frequency
illustrated by the history of the universities, is the inordinate of oaths.

[1] Bulaeus, iv. 391. Thus at
Heidelberg, 'examinandi . . . ipsis
temptatoribus nichil cibi aut potus
ad locum examinis sive temptationis
apportent'. But the examiners
could not do without refreshment:
'Scilicet ipse pro tempore decanus
de facultatis pecuniis potum dare
debet prefatis temptatoribus'
(Hautz, Gesch. d. Univ. Heid. ii.
353). So at Leipzig the candidate
is forbidden to treat (facere propi-
nam) the examiners before the
examination (Zarncke, Statutenbücher, p. 362). But here again
they were required to spend their
fees as examiners in 'prandia', 'bal-
neum intrando' (ibid., p. 363). So
at Ingolstadt, while bribes are forbidden, the examiners are to receive
a knife from each successful candidate in addition to the gloves pre-

sented to the rest of the faculty
(Prantl, ii. 115). In the medical
examinations at Vienna each candidate was required to spend a florin
'pro confectionibus' (Kink, ii. 163).

[2] [This custom was abolished or
rather suspended on various occasions during the fourteenth century
when other claims on the surplus
were pressing; cf. Auctarium, i. 363,
and Boyce, The English-German
Nation, p. 176 and note. But, as
Boyce shows in a previous and well-
documented chapter, the oppor-
tunities for revelry were frequent
(pp. 149–62). See also E. Chate-
lain, 'Notes sur quelques tavernes
fréquentées par l'Université de
Paris au XIVe et XVe siècles', in
Bulletin de la société de l'histoire de
Paris, xxv (1898), 85–109.]

CHAP. XIV. multiplication of oaths. The tremendous penalties involved by perjury supplied so convenient a sanction for all kinds of rules and regulations that their aid was invoked on the most trifling occasions. Modern common sense would naturally suggest that, when attendance at lectures was required, such attendance should be secured by calling over the names; in the Middle Ages the natural thing seemed to be to compel the supplicant for a degree to swear that he had attended the lectures. When a regulation was made, it was almost the invariable practice to require the persons affected to swear that they would observe it or that they had observed it. The candidate for an examination had to swear that he would not offer a bribe to the examiner; the examiner had to swear that he would not receive one. The candidate had, moreover, in some universities to swear not to wreak his vengeance by Prevalence knife or dagger upon a 'ploughing' examiner.[1] The authority of perjury. of every officer was enforced by an oath of obedience. The graduate was sworn in detail not to do almost all the things that previous university legislation had forbidden. College servants, like the retainers of great households, were sworn to obey their masters.[2] In earlier university legislation nearly every prohibition was made under penalty of excommunication or at least of incurring the guilt of perjury. It is instructive to observe in later statutes and ordinances a growing disposition to substitute written certificates for corporal oaths, and pecuniary penalties for spiritual terrors. It was found that practically a fine of half a crown was more deterrent than the most tremendous denunciations of posthumous vengeance, or of spiritual penalties in this life which depended for their enforcement upon the scrupulosity of the penitent and the severity of the penitentiary or the confessor.[3]

---

[1] So at Leipzig; Zarncke, *Statutenbücher*, p. 322.

[2] e.g. at the Collège du Plessis. Félibien, iii. 387.

[3] A late Paduan statute runs as follows: 'Primo ne tota universitas nostra pereat ac deinceps scholares periuri atque falsarii et infames habeantur, statuitur quod ubicun-que invenitur poena periurii in statutis, loco periurii ponatur poena quinque librorum et privationis uocis per annum' (*Stat. Artist. Achad. Patav.*, f. xxxii b). An Oxford statute of 1432 speaks of 'pena pecuniaria his diebus, ceteris plus timorosa' (*Mun. Acad.* i. 305 [*Stat. Antiq. Univ. Oxon.*, ed. S. Gibson,

We need not go back to medieval history to illustrate the
fact that an unwavering acquiescence in the reality of super- Irreverence
natural terrors may at times exercise but little deterrent effect stition.
upon the ordinary life of believers. It is only in the hour of
death that such terrors really appeal to the imagination of
the worst men; and in youth and health men do not think
they are going to die. Yet the close juxtaposition of superstition and the grossest irreverence is a rather startling
feature of medieval student-life. When we are shocked at
some of the secular things that medievals did in churches
which were supposed to be in the most material sense the
dwelling-place of Deity, the superstition may sometimes
perhaps be with us as much as with them. But it is strange
to find that it should have been necessary for William of
Wykeham to forbid dancing in his college chapel.[1] And it is
difficult to believe that, in the century which witnessed the
final triumph of the dogma of transubstantiation, it should
have been necessary to denounce excommunication against
students who played dice upon the very altars of Notre Dame Playing
de Paris by way of giving a finish to the dancing and singing altars.
processions in the public streets with which the feast of a
nation used to be celebrated.[2]

State of Morality

A still darker side of medieval university life must be Jacques de
glanced at if the reader is to be presented with a faithful testimony.
picture of things as they were. The *locus classicus*, as it may
be called, on the subject of student immorality in the Middle
Ages is a passage of Jacques de Vitry concerning the city of
Paris. Often as it has been quoted, it may be well to reproduce it once more in the original language:

'Tunc autem amplius in clero, quam in alio populo, dissoluta,
tanquam capra scabiosa et ouis morbida, pernitioso exemplo multos
hospites suos undique ad eam affluentes, corrumpebat, habitatores
suos deuorans, et secum in profundum demergens. Simplicem

p. 242, l. 9]), with reference to the   No. 470. It is characteristic of
futility of excommunication.   the time that the offence is aggra-
[1] See above, p. 422.   vated by being described as 'non
[2] Bulaeus, iii. 432; *Chartul.* i,   sine nota heretice pravitatis'.

CHAP. XIV. fornicationem nullum peccatum reputabant: meretrices publice ubique per vicos et plateas ciuitatis passim ad lupanaria sua clericos transeuntes quasi per violentiam pertrahebant. Quod si forte ingredi recusarent, confestim eos sodomitas post ipsos conclamantes dicebant. Illud enim foedum et abominabile vitium adeo ciuitatem, quasi lepra incurabilis et venenum insanabile, occupauerat, quod honorificum reputabant, si quis publice teneret unam vel plures concubinas. In una autem et eadem domo schole erant superius, prostibula inferius. In parte superiori magistri legebant, in inferiori meretrices officia turpitudinis exercebant. Ex una parte meretrices inter se, et cum lenonibus litigabant; ex alia parte disputantes et contentiose agentes clerici proclamabant.'

.   .   .   .

'Non solum autem ratione diuersarum sectarum, vel occasione disputationum sibi inuicem aduersantes contradicebant; sed pro diuersitate regionum mutuo dissidentes, inuidentes et detrahentes, multas contra se contumelias et opprobria impudenter proferebant, Anglicos potatores et caudatos[1] affirmantes: Francigenas superbos, molles et muliebriter compositos asserentes: Theutonicos furibundos, et in conuiuiis suis obscenos dicebant: Normannos autem inanes et gloriosos: Pictauos proditores et fortune amicos. Hos autem qui de Burgundia erant, brutos et stultos reputabant: Britones autem leues et vagos iudicantes, Arturi mortem frequenter eis obiiciebant. Lombardos auaros, malitiosos et imbelles: Romanos seditiosos, violentos et manus rodentes: Siculos tyrannos et crudeles: Brabantios viros sanguinum, incendiarios, rutarios et raptores: Flandrenses superfluos, prodigos et comessationibus deditos et more butyri molles et remissos, appellabant. Et propter huiusmodi cohuicia de verbis frequenter ad verbera procedebant.'[2]

Before drawing too sweeping inferences from this passage, some deductions must be made. Jacques de Vitry was a mystic, a monk, and a preacher of an impassioned, not to say fanatical type. He habitually paints the morals of his age in the darkest colours. It must, moreover, be observed that there were special circumstances which account for some of the most revolting features in the picture. In the early years of the thirteenth century the schools were confined by the

[1] [See George Neilson, 'Caudatus Anglicus': a medieval slander', Edinburgh 1896, reprinted from the Proceedings of the Glasgow Archaeological Society.]

[2] Hist. Occidentalis, Douai, 1596, pp. 277–9. Perhaps the fact that a master (collegiatus) should boldly

complain to the faculty against a bachelor for assaulting his 'focaria' (Mon. Univ. Prag. iii. 79) will illustrate the prevalent low standard in such matters as well as any more highly coloured denunciation. This was in 1499.

action of the capitular authorities to the densely crowded CHAP. XIV.
streets of the island round Notre Dame.[1] The habitation
of the sons of the prophets, as the masters themselves proclaimed, was too narrow for them. When the Quartier Latin
had enlarged its borders and the *vicus stramineus* had become
the centre of academic Paris, we may believe that quite such
open violations of external decency could hardly have been
the rule. But there is, unfortunately, only too much evidence
that de Vitry's picture of the scholastic life of his age, if
exaggerated, is not fundamentally untruthful.[2] In this respect, as in others, it is probable, however, that a considerable
improvement was effected by the stricter discipline of the
colleges and halls towards the close of our period.

Intellectual Enthusiasm

The character of any age, any country, any class, may no Intellec-
doubt be made to look very black indeed by the historian thusiasm.
who does nothing but summarize its vices. But where are
we to turn for materials to aid us in reproducing the brighter
side of university life in the Middle Ages? The nobler deeds
of active life may at times find their 'vates sacer': the life of
the virtuous student has no annals. If we want to appreciate
the nobler side of medieval scholastic life, we must contemplate the enormous intellectual enthusiasm which characterized its best period. The monastic ideal had consecrated
study so long only as it moved in a very narrow groove.
Secular knowledge was in the strictest sense the mere hand-
maid or rather the mere bondslave of theology; and theology
meant simply the interpretation of the text of Scripture and
the authoritative *dicta* of Fathers or Church. The intellectual
revolution of the twelfth and thirteenth centuries threw open
to the student the whole range of science in so far as it was
covered by the newly discovered treasures of Greek science,
medicine, and philosophy, and by the monuments of ancient
Roman jurisprudence. Theology remained Queen of the Medieval
ideal of
theology.

[1] But see above, vol. i, p. 277.   *Op. Ined.*, ed. J. S. Brewer (R.S.),
[2] A less suspected witness against   p. 412.
the morals of Paris is Roger Bacon,

CHAP. XIV. Sciences, but a grander and nobler conception of theology arose—a conception which the modern world, alas! has all but lost. Theology became not the mere Chinese mandarin's poring over sacred texts, but the architectonic science whose office it was to receive the results of all other sciences and combine them into an organic whole, in so far as they had bearings on the supreme questions of the nature of God and of the universe, and the relation of man to both. However much the actual methods and systems of the schoolmen fell below the grandeur of their ideal, the ideal was one which cast a halo of sanctity over the whole cycle of knowledge. The merely external accidental connexion of the universities with the ecclesiastical organization of the Western Church contributed to the same result. The interests of learning became associated, if not identified, with the interests of the Church: the pursuit of knowledge became an end in itself: a disinterested intellectual enthusiasm became an element of the churchman's ideal. So far from knowledge being valued only as a means to immediate edification and sacerdotal equipment, the educational blunder of the age lay rather in the opposite direction; the subjects of the churchman's education (if we except the narrowing and somewhat demoralizing study of law) had too little to do with his future work in life, either on its secular or its religious side. The great work of the universities was the consecration of learning; and it is not easy to exaggerate the importance of that work upon the moral, intellectual, and religious progress of Europe.

The average student. Some reserve is of course demanded in applying general reflections of this kind upon the character of an age, its institutions, and its ideals, to the ordinary life of its average representatives. The earnest students were probably—except perhaps in the age of Abelard or in the very first flush of the Aristotelian renaissance—a minority. Yet there must have been an immense mass of real intellectual enthusiasm for the development of a university to become possible. If we have any adequate appreciation of what a journey over half Europe, or even half England, meant to a poor man in a semi-civilized age, the movement which brought hundreds CHAP. XIV. or thousands of men and boys to the great centres of enlightenment will seem at least as noteworthy, as epoch-making a movement, as the stir in the active life of the period which produced the crusades. Undoubtedly this wild outburst of intellectual ardour which marked the age of Abelard cooled very rapidly as it crystallized into the institutional machinery of the university system. Yet the very absence of discipline, of compulsion, of domestic supervision in these universities of boy-students, the very ease with which (quite early in their history) degrees were obtained, the very laxity of discipline which has so often surprised us in the earlier portions of our narrative, testify to the existence of vast numbers of real students, or the machine could never have gone on as it did. The literary productivity of the universities is another piece of evidence tending to the same result. A university that is intellectually alive is not likely to be educationally inefficient. The almost superhuman diligence, the extraordinary concentration of reasoning power, the laborious subtlety of the great schoolmen must have had their fainter counterparts in vast numbers of keen and active and industrious brains. And it is to the moral discipline which all earnest intellectual work carries with it that we must look for the chief surviving evidence of a nobler life than that which is revealed to us by the brawls and the follies and the sensualities of university life—those light things which the stream of time has carried along on its surface and laid in almost bewildering abundance at the feet of the modern wanderer by its shores.

That newborn ardour in the pursuit of 'the pearl of science' which ushers in the university epoch has been already compared to the great outburst of crusading enthusiasm. The parallel is instructive in more ways than one. To suppose that every student of the twelfth or early thirteenth centuries, even if he were one of those who faced toil and privation in the effort to graduate at Paris or at Oxford, was moved by pure and disinterested enthusiasm for knowledge would be as absurd as to see a saint or a hero in every The universities and the crusades.

CHAP. XIV. impecunious baron or soldier of fortune who fought for the cross beneath the walls of Acre or of Damascus. The spirit of adventure, the desire to see the world, the ambition for distinction and promotion, even the baser thirst for booty, entered as largely into the motives of the average student as into those of the average crusader. Indeed, to the ambitious youth of the thirteenth century whose soul rebelled against the narrow limits of his native manor, his native farm, or his native shop, or against the still humbler lot to which numerous brothers might condemn a younger son, there were but two avenues of advancement open. For the man of sinew and of courage war offered chances: though to the humbly born the chances were small, at least in the first half of our period. To the boy conscious only of brains and energy the universities brought all the glittering prizes of the Church within the limits of practicable ambition; and, even apart from prizes, learning and academic position secured social status. As time went on, as the universities passed into the ordinary machinery of the ecclesiastical system and increased in number, the more romantic motives which had influenced the hearers of Aquinas and Grosseteste passed more and more into the background, and the universities became simply the ordinary door to clerical preferment.[1]

Aims and prospects of University students

Mixture of motives. The brilliant pictures which imaginative historians have sometimes drawn of swarms of enthusiastic students eagerly drinking in the wisdom that fell from the lips of famous masters have perhaps somewhat blinded us to the fact that the motives which drove men to the university exhibited much the same mixture and much the same variety as they do now. The pleasures of a university town bore their part in filling the halls. The picture which has been drawn of the life that went on in them may not commend itself to the

---

[1] By the statutes of some of the German chapters, study or graduation at a university was made a condition of enjoying the full rights of a canon, with or without exception in favour of 'de militari genere procreati'. For instances see Paulsen in the *Historische Zeitschrift*, xlv. 309 *sq.*

imagination of an age remarkable above all other ages for its CHAP. XIV.
ingenuity in the discovery of new amusements. But, at all
events, in a great university then as now men of the most
widely different tastes and interests found, in a perfection
rarely elsewhere obtainable, what is to most men the condition of all other pleasures—an abundance of varied, congenial,
but not exacting society. The principle 'nullius boni sine
socio iucunda possessio' was nowhere better understood than
in a medieval university. This motive was especially opera-
tive with those large numbers of older men who got leave of
absence from their benefices under pretext of study in the
universities. To such men the good company, the excite-
ments, the licence of a university town afforded a welcome
relief from the monotonous routine of the cathedral close or
the isolation of a country living.[1] To the great mass of the
younger students, however, the university was simply the
door to the Church; and the door to the Church at that time
meant the door to professional life. The key to a right idea of
the relation of the northern universities to the Church lies in
an appreciation of this fact. In southern Europe it was otherwise. Where the law of the country was more or less entirely
based upon the civil law (as was the case over most of Europe),
the universities were the ordinary places of education for the
great legal profession, which in the south was in the main
a lay profession. In Italy a degree in civil law was the passport to lay public employment of every description; while
the medical profession was at once more important and less
clerical than in England or northern France.

---

[1] Cf. a statute of Caen in 1439:
'Plerumque multi diversorum sta-
tuum sepe nituntur ad studia, non
causa proficiendi, transire sicut
nonnulli abbates, priores, curati,
viri ecclesiastici, seculares etiam et
plures uxorati, mercatores, mecha-
nici et alii inepti ad litteras, sed ea
solum intentione ut fraudent ecclesias divinis obsequiis, cessent ab
obedientia suorum superiorum, et
eximentur a iuridicione eorumdem, vexent indebite per citationes
pauperes, simplices, absolvantur a
tailliis et subventionibus regiis,
iuridictionem tam ecclesiasticorum
quam secularium dominorum effu-
giant et perturbent facientes diver-
sos transportus fraudulentos (i.e.
engaging in commercial transactions under cover of exemptions
from tolls, &c.) et similia commit-
tentes iuri dissona et statui eccle-
siastico penitus contraria' (Fournier, iii, No. 1652).

CHAP. XIV.   In the north of Europe the Church was simply a synonym

The Church and the profes- sions. for the professions. Nearly all the civil servants of the Crown, the diplomatists, the secretaries or advisers of great nobles, the physicians, the architects, at one time the secular lawyers,[1] all through the Middle Ages the then large tribe of ecclesiastical lawyers, were ecclesiastics. It is true, as has been already pointed out, that clerkship did not necessarily

Payment by bene- fices. involve even minor orders. But, as it was cheaper to a king or a bishop or a temporal magnate to reward his physician, his legal adviser, his secretary or his agent by a canonry or a rectory than by large salaries, the average student at Oxford or Paris—however little he might be looking forward to priestly duties as the real work of his life—generally contemplated holy orders as his eventual destination.[2] To the non-noble scholar ecclesiastical promotion could hardly come except through some of these secular professions. If he continued to reside and teach in the university, he might in time get a prebend or a living by means of the *rotulus beneficiandorum* and papal provision; or university distinction might directly recommend him for the highest preferment.

The uni- versities a road to prefer- ment. A chancellor of Oxford, for instance, was often made a bishop. Ecclesiastical reformers complained loudly of the way in which the universities were thronged by beneficed ecclesiastics hanging on in search of better preferment. But if they left the university, there was, as I have said, little chance for most men in the way of advancement except through secular work. A priest who had secured an important cathedral dignity might indeed, even in the retirement of his close, obtain a professional reputation, and so rise higher by favour of a chapter or a bishop. But a young man

[1] According to Pulling (*Order of the Coif*, p. 11), it was not till the middle of the thirteenth century that ecclesiastics were finally banished from the common-law bar and bench in England, but even after this it is probable that the bar was often recruited from clerks educated at the universities, and at times in minor orders which conferred no indelible 'character'.

[2] By canon law, though incumbents of benefices with cure were compelled to take priest's orders within a year after attaining the proper age, dispensations were very freely given to clerks in the service of kings or magnates, and to students in the universities. Many canonries could be permanently held by deacons or subdeacons.

who took a country living or a parochial chaplaincy and CHAP. XIV. devoted himself to the discharge of his spiritual duties would inevitably have remained 'not dead but buried' for the rest of his days. The idea of making a man a bishop or an archdeacon on account of his zeal, his energy, and success in the humble round of parochial duty is one which would hardly have occurred to sensible men in medieval times.[1] If a king had a mind for a saintly prelate, his choice would have fallen in the twelfth century on a monk, and in the thirteenth on a friar or a noble or an academic doctor who had a reputation for piety as well as for learning. Secular bishops were usually, especially in England, respectable men even in their youth, and still more often devout enough in their old age, but their sees were rarely won either by devoutness or by pastoral activity.[2] The professional work of the higher clergy consisted almost entirely in ecclesiastical administration, for which the study of canon law was considered the most important qualification.[3] The intermediate grade of clergy was for the most part content with a degree in arts. The lowest class—the curates or vicars of absentee rectors, the vicars of impropriated churches, the parochial chaplains and chantry priests, the great tribe of priest-vicars, secondaries, annuellers, and other very 'inferior' clergy who swarmed in amazing numbers round the precincts of the great cathedrals

No theology for the mass of clergy.

---

[1] Cf. the complaints of Clemengis as to the large number of idle absentees who crowded the universities (in Bulaeus, iv. 891): 'Et tamen cum hodie turbam Magistrorum cernamus, quorum pauci sunt, qui non curandas oues susceperint; cuncti pene in studiis aetatem conterunt.' If they retired to their benefices, they think they would get no further promotion: 'in locis autem studiorum multi ad opulentiorem sortem aditus patent. . . . Portantur Rotuli, quaeruntur ad Curiam legationes Principum.' And even when they did, this is his picture of their pastoral activity: 'Quis in universo regno, nisi forsi-

tan tu ille es' (he says to his correspondent), 'qui gregem suum pascere curet aut etiam nouerit, immo qui lana et lacte non assidue spoliet' (Clemengis, *Opera*, Leiden, 1613, ii. 339 *sq.*).

[2] [On the subject of appointments to the episcopate in England during the reign of Henry III see Miss Marion Gibbs's chapters on 'The Personnel of the Episcopate' in M. Gibbs and J. Lang, *Bishops and Reform, 1215-1272*, pp. 1-52.]

[3] Gerson, *De Examinatione Doctrinarum* (*Opera*, I, p. ii). Cf. Péries, *Fac. de Droit dans l'anc. Univ. de Paris*, p. 17.

CHAP. XIV. —of these it is probable that only a small proportion had a university degree: many could never have been at a university at all.[1] And, indeed, for most of such duties as these men had to perform academical learning was hardly required; it was enough if they knew the breviary by heart and could sing a .mass. Even for the parish priest with cure of souls 'pastoral' or 'spiritual' duties, over and above those of a purely mechanical nature, meant mainly two things—preaching and hearing confessions. A priest who had not had a theological education as a rule considered himself incapable of preaching: the silencing of the pulpits was one of the effects of the passion for the canon law on the one hand, and for the scholastic philosophy on the other, those effects being still further aggravated by the enormous expenditure of time required for a theological course by the university system. For the hearing of confessions the artist priest was equally untrained. Hence the really effective discharge of pastoral functions and the popular influence attaching to these functions was almost wholly abandoned to the Mendicants, among whom alone systematic theological training was enforced as a preliminary to the priesthood.[2] The consequences of this abandonment can hardly be adequately expressed in a few sentences. While the Mendicants were the best educated and the most active body of working clergy, while—at least in their earlier days—they absorbed

[1] Probably many had been for some short period at a university without taking a degree. This is proved by the large numbers of the universities compared with the comparatively small proportion of graduations. As to the rest, I know of little direct evidence. One must draw one's own inferences from, on the one hand, the large numbers of university students, and, on the other hand, the appalling ignorance —especially theological—of the clergy at the time of the Reformation.

[2] [Rashdall here expressed himself about the most difficult problem in the history of the medieval Church: to what extent were the parochial secular clergy in the Middle Ages a serious and competent set of men? The problem is apparently insoluble and in any case cannot be discussed here; but Rashdall undoubtedly exaggerated when he suggests that preaching and confession were practically abandoned to the Mendicants. For example, see the discussion, by no means favourable to the parish clergy, in G. R. Owst, *Preaching in Medieval England*, Cambridge, 1926, pp. 20–36, 71–7, 145–6, and *passim*.]

into their ranks nearly all the religious enthusiasm which
was to be found in the clerical order, they were also the
most conservative, the least progressive, the most ultramontane, and the most disposed to encourage every species
of lucrative charlatanry and popular superstition. It is
curious to reflect how largely the survival from the Middle
Ages of the traditions of secular university education for the
secular clergy, surviving to our own day, accounts alike for
the liberal culture, the social influence, and the somewhat
low standard of theological attainment by which, as a body,
the Anglican clergy in recent times have usually been characterized.

The comparison which has been instituted between the The Men-
dicants and
the Secu-
lars.
Mendicants and the secular clergy requires some qualification
as regards the last half of our period. The increasing corruption of the mendicant orders produced by the middle of
the fourteenth century a reaction in favour of their secular
rivals. Chaucer's ideal clergyman was a secular, whatever
foundation there may be for the tradition that John Wyclif
himself formed the model for his portrait. This turn of the
tide did not lead to any very widespread improvement in the
moral tone or the pastoral efficiency of the parochial clergy
as a body; but it probably did lead to not a few earnest men
remaining in their ranks who would infallibly have become
friars had they lived a century earlier. The Wyclifite and
Hussite movements differed from previous revivals above
all in being secular movements. Indeed, the Reformation
itself, though (as it chanced) inaugurated by a secular master
who had turned friar, was from one, and that not the least
important point of view, simply a restoration to its ancient
dignity of the parochial pastorate.

Religious Education

In view of current misconceptions as to the 'religious' No 're-
ligious
education'
for artists.
character of the medieval universities, it may not be amiss to
point out how little 'religious education' the medieval university supplied for the future priest. Except in so far as it
taught him to construe his breviary and qualified him to read

CHAP. XIV. a provincial constitution or an episcopal mandate in Latin, there was no relation between the studies of the artist and the work of the ecclesiastical order. That education might be a good—even an indispensable—foundation for the studies of the theologian; but in a large majority of cases that foundation must have remained with little or no superstructure. Even when college foundations had multiplied, but a small minority of the clergy could have obtained theological fellowships or bursaries within their walls. Outside the colleges, the wealthier and more ambitious students betook themselves to canon law rather than to theology; the poorer must usually have left the university with a degree in arts or with no degree at all, and consequently without even the rudiments of a theological education. Theological knowledge the artist had none, except what he might perchance have picked up at a university sermon. It is indeed a mistake to suppose that the medieval Church, at least in England, up to the reaction against Wyclifism, was actively opposed to Bible-reading even on the part of the laity; still less would it have had any disposition to interfere with it in clerks at the university. But a student in arts would have been as little likely to read the Bible as he would be to dip into Justinian or Hippocrates.[1]

Luther and the Bible. Much astonishment has sometimes been expressed at Luther's 'discovery' of the Bible at the convent library of Erfurt. The real explanation of his previous ignorance of its contents is that Luther entered the Order a master of arts who had never studied in a theological faculty. Even the highly educated secular priest, who was not a theologian, or at least a canonist,[2] was not supposed to know anything of the Bible but what was contained in his missal and his breviary.[3]

[1] A good illustration of this occurs in a Franciscan constitution of *circa* 1292: 'Nullus frater Bibliam vel Testamentum de elemosina habeat, nisi sit ad studium aptus vel ad predicandum ydoneus' (*Chartul. Univ. Paris.* ii, No. 580).

[2] As the Bible was one of the sources of canon law, we do occasionally hear of the canonist attending lectures upon it, though

the faculties do not appear to have required such attendance. But he wanted little more than a knowledge of texts to introduce into the pious preambles of legal documents.

[3] It is true that till he became friar, Luther had some difficulty in even getting access to a copy of the *whole* Bible, and that a doctor of divinity might be grossly ignorant even of the New Testament.

So much party capital has at times been made out of the supposed 'religious' character of the medieval universities that it is necessary to assert emphatically that the 'religious education' of a 'bygone Oxford', in so far as it ever had any existence, was an inheritance not from the Middle Ages but from the Reformation. In Catholic Europe it was the product of the counter-reformation. Until that time the Church provided as little professional education for the future priest as it did 'religious instruction' for the ordinary layman. Seminaries for the priest, catechisms, and careful preparation for first communion, whether at the universities or elsewhere, are the product of the counter-reformation, not of the Middle Age. The whole medieval university system, even the college system in the developed form which it had attained by the end of the fifteenth century, was about as unlike the modern seminary as anything that can well be imagined. If in one sense the seminary system is the great weakness of modern Romanism, in another it is its strength. It does at least secure careful religious and moral training and competent professional knowledge for the future priest; and this is just what the medieval university system hardly attempted to do.

Not only the universities but even the bishops seem, in so far as they required any real standard of learning from candidates for holy orders, to have insisted mainly on secular learning. The founder of a college at Avignon forbids his scholars to proceed to priest's orders till they had acquired a knowledge of physics and metaphysics and had had adequate practice in disputation and maintaining conclusions. The only piece of religious knowledge prescribed is the first (and mainly philosophical) part of S. Thomas' *Summa Theologiae*. The deacon must have studied the logic of Petrus Hispanus and the 'old logic' of Aristotle. The subdeacon was required merely to know the *Doctrinale* of Alexander of Villedieu, and the work of the Renaissance grammarian Perotus.[1] A bishop is said to have been degraded for being ignorant of Donatus: it may be doubted whether it could be shown that any one in medieval times was ever

Ordination examinations.

[1] Fournier, ii, No. 1399 (A.D. 1491–4).

CHAP. XIV. refused ordination—much less degraded when already ordained—for any degree of religious or theological ignorance which was not incompatible with ability to say mass.

Value of a Medieval Education

Educational value of a study distinct from intrinsic value.

What was the real value of the education which the medieval university imparted? That is quite a different question of course from the question of the intrinsic importance of the scholastic theology and philosophy, or again of medieval jurisprudence and medicine, in the history of thought; just as the intrinsic value of Greek literature and philosophy to the world is quite a distinct problem from the educational value of an ordinary classical education to the average boy. It is true that the problems are not unconnected, and it may sometimes be a melancholy necessity that to enable one man to study a subject with effect a dozen should be doomed to study it without profit. But for the present it is the educational value of the medieval university system that is in question.

Incompetence and neglect of teachers.

To the modern student, no doubt, the defects of a medieval education lie upon the surface. The external defects of the university organization have already been incidentally noticed. In the older university system of northern Europe there is the want of selection and consequent incompetency of the teachers, and the excessive youth of the students in arts. In the higher faculties, too, we have encountered a tendency on the part of the doctors to evade the obligation of teaching without surrendering its emoluments, while the real teaching devolved upon half-trained bachelors. It is, indeed, in the student-universities that the chairs would appear to have been most competently filled and their duties most efficiently discharged; in medieval times students were more anxious to learn than teachers were to teach. In the earlier period again there was an utter want of discipline among students who ought to have been treated as mere schoolboys. The want was partially corrected by the growth of the college system, but the improvement in this respect was balanced by the decay and degradation in the higher intellectual life of the universities. The Englishman, accustomed to divide all

No classification of students.

human intellects by the broad line which separates the CHAP. XIV.
'passman' from the 'honourman', will further notice a want
of classification in the system.[1] The *Organon* and the *de
Anima* must probably have been above the heads of a very
large proportion of the mere schoolboys who were set down
to them. It is perhaps to this cause (the want of funds was
another) that we must attribute the very small proportion of
students who ever attained even the B.A. degree, in spite of
the mildness of medieval examiners. There is considerable
reason to believe that in the Middle Ages a larger proportion
than at the present day of the nominal students derived
exceedingly little benefit from their university education.

'Oxoniam multi veniunt, redeunt quoque stulti.'

In the earlier part of our period this must have been peculiarly the case, when so little exertion on the part of the
student himself was required. A man was allowed year after
year to sit through lectures of which he might not understand
one word; later on this defect was partly remedied by the
multiplication of 'exercises' in college and hall.

For the fairly competent student the main defects of a Too dog-
medieval education may be summed up by saying that it too dis-
was at once too dogmatic and too disputatious. Of the putatious.
superstitious adherence to Aristotle or other prescribed
authority sufficient illustrations have already been given. It
is of course a direct outcome of the intellectual vice of the age
—a vice of which the human mind was by no means cured by
the Renaissance or the Reformation. It lasted longest where
it was most out of place. In the middle of the seventeenth
century a doctor of medicine was compelled by the English
College of Physicians to retract a proposition which he had
advanced in opposition to the authority of Aristotle under
threat of imprisonment. It may seem a contradiction to
allege that this education by authority was at the same time

[1] Foreign universities seem to
experience no such need—probably
because a large proportion of our
passmen have no business in a
university at all, and would not be
admitted to one in Germany; but
the German system does, no doubt,
compel men to write dissertations
who would be better employed in
reading for a pass or a fourth in
history.

CHAP. XIV. too controversial. Yet the readiness with which the student was encouraged to dispute the thesis of a prescribed opponent, and the readiness with which he would swear to teach only the system of a prescribed authority, were but opposite sides of the same fundamental defect—the same fatal indifference to facts, the facts of external nature, the facts of history, and the facts of life. Books were put in the place of things. This is a defect which was certainly not removed by the mere substitution of classics for philosophy. If in medieval times words were often allowed to usurp the place of things, they were not allowed to usurp the place of thought. For a moment no doubt the human mind was brought into real and living contact with a new world of thought and action, of imagination and art, of literature and history, by the 'New Learning'; but ere long classical education in turn became almost as arid and scholastic—as remote from fruitful contact with realities—as the education of the Middle Ages. The history of education is indeed a somewhat melancholy record of misdirected energy, stupid routine, and narrow one-sidedness. It seems to be only at rare moments in the history of the human mind that an enthusiasm for knowledge and a many-sided interest in the things of the intellect stir the dull waters of educational commonplace. What was a revelation to one generation becomes an unintelligent routine to the next. Considered as mere intellectual training, it may be doubted whether the superiority of a classical education, as it was understood at the beginning of this century, to that of the medieval schools was quite so great as is commonly supposed. If in the scholastic age the human mind did not advance, even Macaulay admits that it did at least mark time. The study of Aristotle and the schoolmen must have been a better training in subtlety and precision of thought than the exclusive study of a few poets and orators. However defective its methods of achieving that end, the scholastic education at least aimed at getting to the bottom of things,[1] although Renan (who gives it this praise)

Side notes: Indifference to fact. Scholasticism and classicism.

---

[1] 'Pour moi, qui crois que la meilleure manière de former des   jeunes gens de talent est de ne jamais leur parler de talent ni de

has also pointed out the supreme defect of scholasticism CHAP. XIV. when he says that its method was incapable of expressing 'nuances', while truth lies in the 'nuances'. But as a practical training in readiness and facility of expression the habit of disputation may have been quite as valuable an exercise as the practice of construing and composition, though the dialect acquired was different enough.

It is surprising how little the intellectual superiority of the eighteenth century over the fourteenth impressed itself upon the course of ordinary school and university education, especially in this country. That on the whole a good eighteenth-century education was healthier, more stimulating, and more rational than a good fourteenth-century education need not be denied; but our intellectual advance since the medieval period had less to do with the improvement in the substance or the method of education than the academic world complacently imagined. It was in the main what he picked up out of school and lecture-room that differentiated the educated man of the eighteenth century from the educated man of the fourteenth. *The fourteenth century and the eighteenth.*

But, because it is easy enough to pick holes in the education of the past, it must not for one moment be supposed that the education either of the scholastic or of the ultra-classical period was of little value. Up to a certain point—and this is one consolation to the educational historian—the value of education is independent either of the intrinsic value or of the practical usefulness of what is taught. The intelligent modern artisan educated at a primary school or the half-educated man of the world possesses at the present day a great deal more true and useful knowledge than a medieval doctor of divinity. But it can on no account be admitted *Value of education largely independent of subjects taught.*

style, mais de les instruire et d'exciter fortement leur esprit sur les questions philosophiques, religieuses, politiques, sociales, scientifiques, historiques; en un mot, de procéder par l'enseignement du fond des choses, et non par l'enseignement d'une creuse rhétorique, je me trouvais entièrement satisfait de cette nouvelle direction' (*Souvenirs d'enfance et de jeunesse*, Paris, 1883, pp. 253-4). Such is Renan's testimony to the semi-scholastic education of the seminary at Issy as compared with the classical education under Dupanloup which he had left.

CHAP. XIV. that this puts the uneducated man of modern times on a level with the educated man of the Middle Ages. And the educated man—the man who has spent many of his maturer years in subtle and laborious intellectual work—will generally show his superiority to the uneducated man even in the most severely practical affairs of life when once the former comes seriously to apply himself to them. It was emphatically so in the Middle Ages. Kings and princes found their statesmen and men of business in the universities—most often, no doubt, among those trained in the practical science of law, but not invariably so. Talleyrand is said to have asserted that theologians made the best diplomatists. It was not the wont of the practical men of the Middle Ages to disparage academic training. The rapid multiplication of universities during the fourteenth and fifteenth centuries was largely due to a direct demand for highly educated lawyers and administrators. In a sense the academic discipline of the Middle Ages was too practical. It trained pure intellect, encouraged habits of laborious subtlety, heroic industry, and intense application, while it left uncultivated the imagination, the taste, the sense of beauty—in a word, all the amenities and refinements of the civilized intellect. It taught men to think and to work rather than to enjoy. Most of what we understand by 'culture', much of what Aristotle understood by the 'noble use of leisure', was unappreciated by the medieval intellect. On the speculative side the universities were (as has been said) 'the school of the modern spirit':[1] they taught men to reason and to speculate, to doubt and to inquire, to find a pleasure in the things of the intellect both for their own sake and for the sake of their applications to life. They dispelled for ever the obscurantism of the Dark Ages. From a more practical point of view their greatest service to mankind was simply this, that they placed the administration of human affairs—in short, the government of the world—in the hands of educated men. The actual rulers—the kings or the

Marginal note: Medieval education a training for life.

[1] Kaufmann makes the remark of scholasticism: it may be extended to the whole work of the universities. [Cf. A. N. Whitehead, *Science and the Modern World* (Cambridge, 1927), ch. i, especially p. 15.]

aristocrats—might often be as uneducated or more unedu- CHAP. XIV.
cated than modern democracies, but they had to rule through
the instrumentality of a highly educated class.

In criticizing medieval culture and education, attention is Promi-
sometimes too much confined to the scholastic philosophy legal study.
and theology. The scholastic philosophy and theology do,
indeed, represent the highest intellectual development of the
period. But they do not represent the most widely diffused
or the most practically influential of medieval studies. Law
was the leading faculty in by far the greater number of
medieval universities: for a very large proportion of university students the study of arts, in so far as they pursued it at
all, took the place of a modern school rather than of a modern
university. From a broad political and social point of view The uni-
one of the most important results of the universities was the created the
creation, or at least the enormously increased power and lawyer-
importance, of the lawyer-class. Great as are the evils which
society still owes to lawyers, the lawyer-class has always been
a civilizing agency. Their power represents at least the
triumph of reason and education over caprice and brute
force. Lawyers have moderated or regulated despotism even
when they have proved its most willing tools: just as in
modern democratic communities their prominence must be
looked upon as an important conservative check upon democracy.[1]

Over the greater part of Europe the influence of the uni- Political
versities meant more than this. It brought with it the in- tance
creasing modification of legal and political institutions by the of Roman
Roman law, whether directly or through the canon law, studies in
whether by avowed adoption or by gradual and unconscious ties.
infiltration and imitation. This, too, was a civilizing agency,
though here again an increase of civilization had often to be
bought by a decline of rude, barbaric liberty. Our own
country is here the exception which proves the rule. Our
own universities are differentiated from those of the rest of
the world by the small extent to which they have been, or still

---

[1] Cf. the remarks of Lord Bryce,   iii. 376 *sq.* [Cf. new edition, 1910,
The American Commonwealth, 1888,   ii. 306–7, 665 *sqq.*]

CHAP. XIV. are, places of professional education. How far the different course which the development of our institutions has taken as compared with those of the Continent, and the large measure of Germanic liberty which they retained,[1] are due to the absence of civilian influence, is an inquiry which has perhaps been too much neglected by our constitutional England historians. It must not be supposed, indeed, that even in and the Roman England the influence of the universities upon our institutions law. has been small. To say nothing of the considerable infiltration of the Roman through the canon law into English law and still more into English equity, the common law escaped the modifications which nearly every legal system in Europe underwent at the hands of university-bred lawyers only by the creation of a rival legal science, and even of a virtual university of English law in London, which would hardly have been possible but for the example supplied by the Roman law and its academic professors.

Present influence of Medieval University Institutions

The uni- It is more directly relative to our subject to examine what versity a medieval have been the effects of the medieval universities upon our concep- modern educational system. The genius of the Middle Age tion. showed itself above all in the creation of institutions. The institutions of the Middle Age are greater—they may prove more imperishable—even than its cathedrals. The university is a distinctly medieval institution. By that is implied not merely that in the most altered and the most modern of the schools so called there are customs, offices, titles, for the explanation of which we must go back to the history of the thirteenth century with its guild movement, its cathedral schools, and especially its great struggle between the chancellor of Paris and the society of masters. The very idea of the institution is essentially medieval, and it is curious to observe how largely that idea still dominates our modern schemes of education. Persons to whom the term 'medieval' is synonymous with 'ideal', and those with whom it is a term of abuse, agree in the assumption that universities must

[1] [Cf. Kaufmann, i. 78–9.]

exist. And yet they did not exist in the most highly cultivated CHAP. XIV. societies of the ancient world. It is entirely misleading to apply the name to the schools of ancient Athens or Alexandria. If higher education is to exist, there must obviously be teachers to impart it, and it is likely that particular places will become famous for particular studies. But it is not necessary that the teachers should be united into a corporate body enjoying more or less privilege and autonomy. It is not necessary that the teachers of different subjects should teach in the same place and be united in a single institution —still less that an attempt should be made to make the teaching body representative of the whole cycle of human knowledge. It is not necessary that studies should be grouped into particular faculties, and students required to confine themselves more or less exclusively to one. It is not necessary that a definite line of study should be marked out by authority,[1] that a definite period of years should be assigned to a student's course, or that at the end of that period he should be subjected to examination and receive, with more or less formality and ceremony, a title of honour. All this we owe to the Middle Ages. Similar needs might no doubt in course of time have independently evolved somewhat similar institutions in a somewhat different form. But, in the form in which we have them, teaching corporations, courses of study, examinations, degrees, are a direct inheritance from the Middle Ages; and it would not be difficult to show that these inherited institutions carry with them not a few assumptions in educational theory and method which might have appeared questionable enough to an ancient thinker.[2] However much the modern mind may in certain directions be reverting to the ideas and spirit of the old world, education, like so much else in the modern world, will always exhibit a vast and

[1] This is, of course, less completely the case in some continental universities than among ourselves. Prescribed *books* are a *very* medieval institution.

[2] It is also true, no doubt, that parts of our educational tradition are an inheritance from the ancient world itself. The organization of education in the later Roman Empire involved a closer approximation to the university system than the education of the Platonic or the Ciceronian age.

CHAP. XIV. incalculable difference from the education of ancient Greece or ancient Rome just because the Middle Ages have intervened.

Its present influence. How much is lost and how much gained by the educational machinery which the Middle Ages have created for us would be a difficult inquiry. That something is lost is evident. Something of the life and spontaneity of old-world culture certainly seems to be gone for ever. Universities have often had the effect of prolonging and stereotyping ideas and modes of thought for a century or more after the rest of the world has given them up. It is surprising how slowly an intellectual revolution affects the course of ordinary education. But educational traditions are marvellously tenacious, quite apart from institutional machinery such as that of the universities; and education itself must always be, from the necessities of the case, a tradition. In all machinery there is some loss, and yet it is only by means of machinery that culture can be permanently kept alive and widely diffused. The machinery by which this process is carried on among ourselves is as distinctly a medieval creation as representative government or trial by jury. And it is a piece of institutional machinery which has outlived almost every other element in the education which it was originally intended to impart.

The reader who has had the patience to follow these pages thus far may, perhaps, be disposed to ask what message the study in which we have been engaged has for the modern educational reformer. And yet the attempts which have been made to impress university history into the service of the educational theory are not altogether encouraging. We have often had occasion to notice that features of the medieval university system which have constantly been appealed to as binding precedents were really less universal and less invariable than has been supposed. The University of London, after being empowered by royal charter to do all things that could be done by any university, was legally advised that it could not grant degrees to women without a fresh charter, because no university had ever granted such degrees: it had not heard of the women-doctors at Salerno.[1] We have been CHAP. XIV. told that the medieval university gave a religious education: we have seen that to the majority of students it gave none. We have been told that a university must embrace all faculties: we have seen that many very famous medieval universities did nothing of the kind. That it eventually came to be considered necessary, or at least usual, that they should do so, is due to the eventual predominance of the Parisian type of university organization, *minus* the very peculiar and exceptional absence of a faculty of civil law. We have been told that the collegiate system is peculiar to England: we have seen that colleges were found in nearly all universities, and that over a great part of Europe university teaching was more or less superseded by college teaching before the close of the medieval period. We have been told that the great business of a university was considered to be liberal as distinct from professional education: we have seen that many universities were almost exclusively occupied with professional education. We have been assured, on the other hand, that the course in arts was looked upon as a mere preparatory discipline for the higher faculties: we have seen that in the universities of northern Europe a majority of students never entered a higher faculty at all.

On all sides we find that a closer acquaintance with the facts results in a certain disillusionment. And it is chiefly perhaps in disillusionment of this kind that we must find the practical value of university history, as indeed of so much other historical study. The wide survey which we have taken of the universities of Europe will at least have taught us the flexibility and versatility of the medieval system in spite of much constitutional uniformity. It is only, indeed, in matters in technical constitutional law that medieval precedent can have any direct value to the modern university legislator. New needs must be met by new machinery. University

[1] I have been informed by an eminent judge, who was one of the counsel on whose advice the university acted, that a knowledge of this fact would have modified his opinion. [It is perhaps fortunate that the grant of degrees to women was not hastened by acquaintance with this legend. See above, vol. i, p. 85 n.]

CHAP. XIV. institutions must undergo perpetual modification in the future as they have undergone perpetual modification in the past. But it is well in this, as in wider fields of social, political, and religious organization, as far as possible to preserve historical continuity. We should avoid the wanton introduction of an historical solecism where an adhesion to ancient form and usage would be quite as easy, the wanton destruction of ancient institutions where a slight modification of them would serve as well, the wanton abandonment of ancient customs and traditions where they are neither harmful nor burdensome. Already, even in England, much has been lost that is past recall, but it may be hoped that a more extended knowledge and more intelligent appreciation of the old university system may prevent the further abandonment of a single piece of ceremonial, of nomenclature, or of procedure which will serve to connect the universities of the present with that medieval past out of which they have so directly and unmistakably grown.

Names are sometimes of more importance than is commonly supposed. Whether a particular institution should or should not be called a university may seem by itself to be a very small thing. But the name has got to be associated with education of the highest type: to degrade the name of a university is therefore to degrade our highest educational ideal. That universities should be multiplied is, within certain limits, natural and desirable; and it is by no means essential that all should conform exactly to the same pattern. It is natural and desirable again that efforts should be made to diffuse knowledge and intellectual interests among all classes by means of evening lectures. The English universities may well be proud of having taken the initiative in a movement of the most far-reaching social and political significance. But it would be a delusion, and a mischievous delusion, to suppose that evening lectures, however excellent and however much supplemented by self-education, can be the same thing as the student-leisure of many years, duly prepared for by a still longer period of regular school training. Examinations, too, and private preparation for them, are an excellent thing in their proper place; but it is a mistake to CHAP. XIV. suppose that an examining board can discharge any but the very lowest of a university's real functions. The two most essential functions which a true university has to perform, and which all universities have more or less discharged amid the widest possible variety of system and method and organization, hardly excepting even the periods of their lowest degradation, are to make possible the life of study, whether for a few years or during a whole career, and to bring together during that period, face to face in living intercourse, teacher and teacher, teacher and student, student and student. It would be a fatal error to imagine that either the multiplication of books or the increased facilities of communication can ever remove the need of institutions which permit of such personal intercourse. A university, therefore, must have a local habitation; if it embraces colleges in different places, you have virtually two or more universities and not one. Increased facilities of communication can never unite by the true university bond the inhabitants of distant towns: indeed it may be questioned whether the highest university ideal can be realized with the fullest perfection even in a single modern city of the largest type, especially where it does not possess a distinct university quarter.

It may in a sense be maintained that the bewildering accumulation of literature and the rapidity with which it is diffused have only emphasized the necessity for personal guidance and interpretation—for association in teaching, in study, and in research. Personal contact adds something even to the highest spiritual and intellectual influences—in all ages universities have been the great homes of 'movements' —and it adds a life and a power to the teaching of men whose books by themselves would be of comparatively small account. There is a kind of knowledge, too, which can only be secured by personal intercommunication, a kind of intellectual cultivation which is only made possible by constant interchange of ideas with other minds, a kind of enthusiasm which is impossible in isolation. To a certain extent of course these functions are performed by every sort of educational

CHAP. XIV. institution and every scientific or literary society. But it behoves us not to lose or lower the ideal of the university as the place *par excellence* for professed and properly trained students, not for amateurs or dilettantes or even for the most serious of leisure-hour students; for the highest intellectual cultivation, and not merely for elementary instruction or useful knowledge; for the advancement of science, and not merely for its conservation or diffusion; as the place moreover where different branches of knowledge are brought into contact and harmonious combination with one another, and where education and research advance side by side. If the study of university antiquities does something to keep alive this ideal and to add the charm of historic association to the institutions in which it has expressed itself, some practical purpose will have been served by what I have consistently endeavoured to make in the main a purely critical and historical inquiry. In education as in other matters some knowledge of the past is a condition of practical wisdom in the present, but the lessons of history seldom admit of formal deduction or didactic exposition.

APPENDIXES

[Certain of the appendixes which appeared in the original edition of this work are not reprinted here, as it has not been thought that their retention is necessary. Appendix XVIII—Schools in London —comprised an excerpt from Fitzstephen's *Description of London*, describing the grammar schools of the city. This passage has since been fully dealt with by Mr. A. F. Leach in *The Schools of Medieval England*, pp. 138–44. Appendix XX—Aristotle in Oxford—comprised an excerpt from Roger Bacon's *Compendium studii Theologiae*, the text of which is now available in Rashdall's own edition of it. Appendix XXIV—The See of Lincoln from 1173 to 1209—consisted of a list of the Bishops of Lincoln between these dates, showing the long vacancies which marked the intervals between each appointment. Appendix XXVII—The Cambridge Commencement—consisted of an extract from Gunning's *Ceremonies of the University of Cambridge*, to which reference has been made above, see p. 146. Appendix XXX—Statutes of the Oxford Halls, 1483–89—has not been reprinted as the *Statuta Aularia* which it comprised are now accessible in Mr. Strickland Gibson's edition of *Statuta Antiqua Univ. Oxon.*, pp. 574–88. Appendix XXXIII—The Present Constitution of the University of Oxford—has been superseded by the recent treatment of this subject in *The Government of Oxford*, Oxford, 1931.]

I

THE MIGRATION FROM PARIS

(See above, vol. iii, p. 29)

(1) Mr. A. F. Leach's criticism reprinted from a letter to the *Oxford Magazine*, vol. 30 (16 May 1912), pp. 331–3:

. . . . On what is this theory founded? On 'allusions' which previous inquirers had entirely overlooked, probably . . . because the allusions . . . are of a kind which would not be discovered by turning out the word Oxford in the indices of the various contemporary chronicles. These allusions are three in number. First, John of Salisbury records as a portent in 1167 the expulsion of alien scholars by France, 'the most civilized' or 'most polite'— which I suggest for a better rendering of *civilissima* than Dr. Rashdall's 'most civil . . . of nations'. This 'allusion', by the way, was 'discovered' by Dr. Rashdall by no more recondite labour than reading Denifle's *Chartulary of the University of Paris*, where John's letter, taken from the Rolls Series, appears among the

H h

APPENDIX I. earliest documents. Then come two edicts, or parts of one edict, called *constitutiones* in the original, of Henry II. Issued by way of bringing pressure to bear on Becket, then in voluntary exile in France, they were to the effect that (1) 'No clerk or monk or other religious shall be allowed to go abroad from or return to England without letters from the Justiciar for going abroad or from the King for returning', on pain of imprisonment. (2) 'All clerks having revenues in England shall be summoned in every country to come to England, as they love their revenues, and if they shall not come by the appointed time, their revenues shall be taken into the King's hands.'

Now, *prima facie*, there is no connexion between France expelling scholars and England recalling beneficed clerics. Moreover, while John of Salisbury's letter is placed by the editors in 1167, Henry's edicts are assigned to 1169. It is true, however, that Hoveden put them in 1164, and William of Canterbury, the recorder of Becket's miracles, in 1165. Therefore, says Dr. Rashdall, they really belong to 1167. This date no one else assigns to them and it has no argument in its favour, except one *ab convenienti* because it suits Dr. Rashdall. In his *History* Dr. Rashdall refers to the Constitutions only in the version of them given in the *Materials for the History of Thomas à Becket*, by William of Canterbury, and not to the ampler version given in the same series among Becket's letters. This latter version has a preface which gives an exact date; not indeed in so many words, but in the fact that it says they were brought into England from Henry by 'Wimer, a priest and a sheriff, and Walter of Grimsby, clerk and sheriff of Lincoln'. Now the Pipe Rolls of 1169–70 show Wimer, the chaplain, joint sheriff of Norfolk and Suffolk, and Walter of Grimsby, joint sheriff of Lincolnshire, and neither of them were sheriffs in any preceding year. Besides, there was no question of an interdict against England till May, 1169. It was to prevent its proclamation in England that the Constitutions were issued. Dr. Rashdall, however, further suggests that the two Constitutions are 'not quite consistent' with each other and 'are not placed consecutively, which seems to suggest that they may have been issued at different times'. Where is the inconsistency? The first Constitution is concerned to prevent any one importing papal interdicts or Becket's archiepiscopal excommunications and orders into England. The second attempts to denude Becket of the support of the clergy, English, French, or Italian, who, in spite of being in receipt of English revenues, used them against the English King in supporting his 'traitor and rebel'. It was a separate measure and therefore separately mentioned. It is certain, then, that the date of the edict is 1169 and not 1167 or any earlier year, and that John of Salisbury's expulsion of alien scholars by French authorities in the former year cannot be the same event as the recall by the English King of beneficed clerks in 1169. What John of Salisbury was referring to is still something of a mystery. But if the English scholars in Paris were supporters of Becket's, the last thing the French authorities, who supported Becket, would have done would have been to expel them. On the other hand, at the end of 1166 the German Emperor Frederick, who supported the anti-Pope, finally marched his forces into Italy to put down Alexander III; and this may well have given occasion to an expulsion by the University of Paris, the main support of Alexander, of its German students as schismatics and heretics.

It is impossible that if the English scholars were expelled we should not find a single word of it in John himself or any of the voluminous correspondence of and to the English exiles in France.

But, apart from dates, how can the recall of beneficed clerks to their benefices in England be the same event as the expulsion of scholars from France? No doubt in an appropriate context 'clerk' is used as equivalent to 'scholar', as in Chaucer's famous Clerk of Oxenford. But the clerks here mentioned are beneficed clerks, and those only. So Dr. Rashdall asserts that 'in the middle of the twelfth century scores, in fact, hundreds, of masters and scholars beneficed in England must have been studying in the schools of Paris'. The rarity of the description of *magister* appended to canons and other ecclesiastics before 1180 as compared with its frequency in the latter part of the following century of itself renders this assertion suspect. Dr. Rashdall seeks to bolster it by the register of the German nation at Bologna beginning in the thirteenth century, which, he says, shows that 'a large proportion of the students are archdeacons, provosts, canons, rectors, or the like'. This statement presumes a little too much on the readiness of your readers to accept his statements without verification. The register begins in 1289. In the first two years sixty-eight matriculated, none of them beneficed. In 1291, of thirty-one, three were canons of various churches. In 1292, two of the proctors were canons, and of fifty-seven matriculated one was a canon. In 1293, fifty-three students were admitted, of whom four were canons and one a provost. In 1294, fifty-nine were admitted, of whom one was a provost and one a 'custos ecclesie', i.e. probably the sacrist or treasurer of a cathedral or collegiate church. In one of the two years both the proctors were canons. So in six years, out of 268 admitted, eleven so far as we know, or a little over 4 per cent., were beneficed. I make no doubt that there were others who held livings. But there is no evidence as to their number. There is not the smallest justification for Dr. Rashdall's reckless assertion. We have not the smallest notion what the number of students at Paris was in the twelfth century, still less how many of them were English. In 1335 a list of all those assessable to Paris University gives some 800 persons, and as a page is missing at the beginning possibly there may have been another hundred. Of these names possibly thirty-two may be English, and about eighty are Scots, Scotland having then no university. In view of these figures it is impossible to believe that in 1167, when wealth was much less and university education a new thing, there were thousands of scholars and of these hundreds were English. What proportion of them would be beneficed? In 1335 only one beneficed scholar is mentioned, a certain archdeacon of Scotland, who was there with his brother. Among scholars of other nations appear three deans, two precentors, a *scholasticus*, i.e. schoolmaster or chancellor, and an archdeacon. Almost equally numerous are the lay magnates, the sons of Douglas with a master, the sons of the Count of Hamon, the sons of the Count of Heuntingen. It would be as reasonable to draw from them the inference that all or most of the Parisian scholars were of noble birth as to argue from the archdeacons, &c., that they were all or most beneficed. But we cannot argue from the numbers of Germans, who lived next door to Italy, at Bologna in the thirteenth, or the number of English and Scots at Paris in the fourteenth, to the number of English at Paris in the twelfth century. Dr. Rashdall might just as well cite the number of deaths of aviators in 1911 as showing that there were 'scores, nay hundreds' of aviators in 1900. The demand for university education was only in its infancy in the twelfth century, and was not a recognized excuse for non-residence of beneficed clergy till much later. It was not till 1219 that the canon law by a decretal of Honorius III provided that study at the university in theology was a valid excuse for non-residence as a canon of a cathedral. Before that, a special licence of non-residence in each case was required. The first mention in the canon law of attendance at a university as a legitimate excuse for non-residence appears to be a papal rescript in answer to a letter from the Archbishop of York in 1287. That such licence was in Becket's time a rarity would appear from Fitzstephen's Life of Becket himself. He records Becket's attendance at the school of the city, i.e. S. Paul's School, when he was a boy, and at the

University of Paris when he was a young man, without comment, APPENDIX
but when he mentions his going, after he had been beneficed by I·
Archbishop Theobald, to study law at Bologna and then at
Auxerre, he is careful to note that he went with the archbishop's
licence.

I maintain, therefore, that Dr. Rashdall's assertion as to the
numbers of English beneficed clergy at Paris in 1167 is as unproved
as it is improbable. The constant petitions of Paris and Oxford to
the popes in later days for the grant of papal provisions to benefices for even distinguished doctors and masters of the universities
go to show that at no time could the majority of university
residents have been beneficed. Dr. Rashdall, however, cites in
his *History* . . . as proving that beneficed clerks meant scholars, a
'passage in one of Becket's own letters, in which he complains
that the King wants all scholars to return to their country or be
deprived of their benefices'. I must confess to having overlooked
this reference. But culpable as my oversight may have been, what
are we to say of the carelessness of the writer who quotes as one of
Becket's own letters, a letter written to him by some unknown
correspondent, and that a letter which, as the Rolls editor points
out, is a tissue of misrepresentations by exaggeration of Henry's
edict? For while Henry merely directs the imprisonment and
trial of any one carrying into England papal interdicts or archiepiscopal mandates, this writer represents him as ordering the
instant and indecent mutilation of the offender. It is in the same
spirit that this anonymous letter-writer misrepresents the article
against absentee and non-resident parsons as an attack on learning in the person of scholars pursuing their education.

Very different is the view of the edict taken by Fitzstephen, at
once the sanest and the most detailed of Becket's biographers.
Fitzstephen, from the account of the schools of London which he
prefixes to his life of the archbishop, was evidently much interested
in schools and scholars, and if the King's edicts had aimed at them
or affected them to such an extent as Dr. Rashdall guesses, he
could scarcely have failed to mention it. Incidentally, he furnishes
the most convincing evidence that the real object of the edict was
not scholars at all, but the beneficed clerks of Becket's following.
For, after saying that the edict was issued to prevent the interdict being proclaimed in England in 1169, be it noted, he relates
that 'the King, earls and magnates of France interceded with
Henry for the greater clerks who remained with the archbishop
that *they at least* might have their revenues restored'. Henry
accordingly promised to see them, and Fitzstephen relates the

interviews at length and the result, which was that only one of them 'obtained restitution of his goods'.

Oddly enough there are certain constitutions of Henry given by Gervase of Canterbury, one of which does refer directly to scholars, and which Dr. Rashdall has omitted to mention. They seem strongly to suggest a university in England, and if in England, surely at Oxford. It is this: 'If any Welshman, clerk or layman, go to England without a passport from the King, let him be taken and put in ward: and all Welshmen at school in England shall be expelled.' Now we can hardly suppose that Welshmen went to English grammar schools, as they had plenty at home, e.g. at S. David's, where Giraldus Cambrensis was educated. The words must refer to university schools. They are an important addition to the evidence given in my book that a university, that is, a large collection of scholars studying in various faculties, viz. theology, canon law, and philosophy, was already in existence in Oxford in the first half of the twelfth century. To break this *catena* of evidence collected by Professor Holland, Dr. Rashdall resorted to several pages of wholly ineffective special pleading to remove the date of the famous Vacarius law lectures at Oxford from 1149 till after 1167, though vouched for by unimpeachable contemporary authorities. But let us assume that Dr. Rashdall's arguments are not a juggling with words or paltering with dates, and that the edict against beneficed clerks was aimed at English scholars at Paris, and so aimed in 1167 and 1169;[1] let us assume that the edict was obeyed, and these (mythical) hundreds of beneficed scholars flew back to England: Dr. Rashdall has still got to show that they went to Oxford and set up schools there, where were none before. But as to this, it is admitted that there is at least some evidence of schools at Oxford before 1150, that there is no allusion to Oxford after 1166 till 1180. The settlement of the returned scholars at Oxford rests on no more evidence than the single question asked by Dr. Rashdall, 'If the recalled scholars did not go to Oxford, where did they go to?' The answer is obvious: if the scholars recalled to their benefices obeyed the recall, they went where they were told to go, namely, to their benefices. Indeed, at the end of ten pages of argument, Dr. Rashdall in a note answers his own question with this remarkable admission: 'I do not assert that the connexion of the migration with Oxford is direct and immediate. For (1) the expelled scholars may have halted and temporarily studied in some other town or towns. (2) Or several *studia* may have been set up, while only

---

[1] Printed in error as '1149' in the *Oxford Magazine*.

one prospered, as happened with the migration from Oxford in
1209.' That is to say, the repatriated scholars may have gone to
half a dozen other places than Oxford, e.g. to Salisbury, to Reading, to Northampton, or to London (in all of which embryo
universities were formed), or to Lincoln or York. Not that there
is the smallest spark of evidence of their going to Oxford or coming
to England at all. He then adds a new, strange, and utterly
illogical guess of another origin of Oxford. 'The *studium* may have
been originally formed by students prevented from going to Paris.'
Really, if we are to take to guessing, we might as well guess that
it was originally formed by the students at the London schools
mentioned by Bishop Henry of Winchester, when between 1138
and 1140, as acting-Bishop of London, he prohibited any interference with the monopoly of the three privileged schools of
S. Paul's, S. Martin-le-Grand, and S. Mary-le-Bow, without a
licence from the schoolmaster of S. Paul's. That in Becket's
youth other schools had been allowed for any one specially
eminent in philosophy Fitzstephen expressly tells us, and that philosophy was effectively taught in these schools appears from his
description of the disputations held by the schools on saints' days.
But it is idle to set guess against guess. Dr. Rashdall really aban-
dons his own infant. . . .

(2) To this criticism Dr. Rashdall replied in the *Oxford Magazine*,
6 June 1912 (vol. 30, pp. 384–5):

. . . Mr. Leach has launched forth into a violent attack upon my
theory as to the process by which Oxford emerged into a *studium
generale*. I cannot re-state the whole of my argument—which
those who are interested in it can find in my *Universities of the
Middle Ages*, but I will briefly recapitulate the main points. There
are two steps in my argument—(1) an attempt to prove that the
migration of English scholars from Paris took place somewhere
about the years 1167–8, and (2) an attempt to show a probability
that this migration accounts for the rapid emergence of what was
already an important school at Oxford into the principal—and for
some forty years the only—*studium generale* in this country.

The evidence for the first step rests chiefly on three documents:
(1) A letter of John of Salisbury, dated by the editors 1167, saying
that 'France, the mildest and most civil of all nations, has expelled
her foreign scholars' ('aliegenas scholares abegerit'); (2) an edict
of Henry II that 'all clerks having revenues in England be summoned in every country to come to England . . . as they love their
revenues'; (3) a statement in a letter of the time saying that the

King 'vult etiam ut omnes scholares repatriare cogantur aut beneficiis suis priventur'.

In his statement of my case Mr. Leach omitted the last passage
altogether. He has now discovered that I made a mistake in
attributing this letter to Becket. It is a letter written by an anonymous correspondent of Becket contained in the collected Becket
correspondence. This was a serious slip on my part—the only
one which he has succeeded in pointing out; but it leaves my
argument quite unaffected. It is true that the writer misinter-
prets one of Henry's edicts, but that does not show that he is
wrong in his statement, which is a quite accurate reproduction of
the edicts whose text is before us as it was probably not before
the writer of that letter. The only point on which it adds to the
information contained in the edicts themselves is by showing con-
clusively that a contemporary recognized that an edict against
beneficed 'clerks' would necessarily affect some considerable
number of scholars, though of course it would not apply to
scholars only: that is why it is important for my argument, and
the reason perhaps why it was 'overlooked' by Mr. Leach.

Mr. Leach then tries to show that I am wrong in saying that
'in the middle of the twelfth century scores, in fact hundreds, of
masters and scholars beneficed in England must have been studying in Paris'. 'There is', he says, 'not the smallest notion what
the number of students at Paris was in the twelfth century, still
less how many of them were English.' One's impressions on such
a matter have to be arrived at by putting together a number of
small indications—the number of individual ecclesiastics who are
known to have studied there, the frequent allusions to the Parisian
schools by chroniclers and letter-writers, and so on. I cannot
expect Mr. Leach to attach any importance to my own estimate
based upon a study of pretty well all the available evidence, but
perhaps he will attach some weight to the authority of Bishop
Stubbs. 'I have already mentioned the two or three foreign schools
most frequented by English scholars. Paris was the centre of theological learning and general culture. Bologna was the school for
lawyers';[1] and he then mentions a number of the best-known Englishmen who were Parisian students, adding 'so probably were
Roger of Hoveden and most of those ecclesiastics of the time to
whom the name of *magister* is given in formal documents, of whom
it would be useless labour to give a catalogue'.[2]

As to the proportion of university students who were beneficed,

[1] W. Stubbs, *Lectures on Medieval and Modern History*, p. 138.
[2] *Ibid.*, p. 139.

I may appeal to Bishop Stubbs's statement (he is still speaking of English scholars), 'Bologna was the special university for the young archdeacons'. If English archdeacons (who specially required a knowledge of law) were numerous at distant Bologna, surely we should expect a still larger number of other beneficed clerks—cathedral dignitaries, canons, and rectors—at Paris. Mr. Leach seeks to discredit my view on this subject by appealing to the fact that 'it was not till 1219 that the Canon Law by a decretal of Honorius III provided that study at a university in theology was a valid excuse for non-residence as a canon of a cathedral'. The decretal made this a matter of right, but the custom was much earlier. Bishop Stubbs tells us that 'the statute of S. Paul's, drawn by Ralph de Diceto himself (who became dean in 1180), allowed not only non-residence but a pension of 40s. *per annum* from the *communa* or dividend; the student must go for not less than a year, he might go for two or three. This permission was freely used', &c.[1] This is a sufficient illustration that the practice was already common. Further than this I could only carry the argument by an accumulation of detailed testimony for which I could not ask you to give me space.

But now I must return to the authorities upon which the hypothesis of a migration is based. I ventured to suggest in a quite tentative way that possibly, since the edicts are assigned different dates by different chroniclers, the enigmatic statement of John of Salisbury may be a rhetorical way of referring to the migration consequent upon the edict. Mr. Leach gives reasons for believing that these edicts must all have been issued in 1169. I will not ask how far his argument is conclusive, but let us assume that it is so. That does not touch my main position. If 'France expelled its foreign scholars' in 1167, we must naturally suppose that these scholars would have included the English scholars; and thus there would have been a body of Englishmen obliged to leave the country, of whom we may assume that the majority returned home; and the edict of 1169 would have brought back any of the beneficed who had contrived to evade the expulsion or to return to Paris. By which body the expansion of the Oxford school into a *studium generale* was effected I cannot, of course, undertake to say. Or, if it be denied that there were any Englishmen at all among those expelled in 1167, then the exodus of 1169 would be sufficient for my purpose.

I now proceed to deal with the second step in the argument. He declares that 'the settlement of the returned scholars at Oxford rests on no more evidence than the single question asked

[1] *Ibid.*, p. 140.

by Dr. Rashdall, "If the recalled scholars did not go to Oxford, where did they go to?" The answer is obvious, if the scholars recalled to their benefices obeyed the recall, they went to their benefices', and then he goes on to insist that there is no evidence that they went to Oxford rather than to any of the other famous schools in England. My reasons may have been good or bad, but it is a mere travesty of an argument which occupies many pages in my book to say I have produced no evidence except what is contained in the question quoted. The main steps of the argument, though, of course, I cannot here reproduce the cumulative evidence for each, are as follows:

(1) There is no evidence to show the existence of a *studium generale* at Oxford before 1167–70, though there were certainly schools of a certain reputation here as at many other places. There is an accumulation of such evidence to show that there was a *studium generale* here very shortly after 1170. The suddenness of the transition suggests a cause operating somewhat suddenly. In the migration of a body of students from Paris (which I have given reason for inferring) we have such a cause.

(2) It is known that many other universities—in fact, most of the earliest universities—were started by such migrations from the very few original or archetypal universities. Up to 1167–70 there were many schools which were as famous as we have reason for supposing Oxford to have been. None of these developed into a *studium generale*; Oxford did so, and that with startling rapidity. Hence it is improbable that the Parisian immigrants went to any other school, or, if they did so, that they stayed there long. Knowing what we do know of the habits of medieval scholars suddenly compelled to migrate, we can feel sure that they would have re-established an imitation of the *studium* they had left somewhere or other in England. Such of them as were beneficed would accordingly have been unlikely permanently to remain in residence on those benefices when the statutes or customs of their cathedrals and the general law of the Church allowed them to be absent for purposes of study. As they did not (so far as we know) establish such a *studium generale* anywhere else, and yet a *studium generale* existed in Oxford soon after 1170, it is probable that they went there.

(3) There is nothing in the organization or institutions of Oxford which in the least suggests a gradual and independent development. All the institutions are modelled upon Paris, with such modification as was required by the fact that Oxford was not a cathedral city. Had the *studium* become 'general' by slow development, it is probable that the master's 'licence' would

have been granted by some local ecclesiastical authority, as was everywhere the case where a *studium* developed in this way. Instead of that, we find that the bishop was eventually obliged to appoint a chancellor, as it were *ad hoc*, a chancellor unattached to any church and existing solely to grant the licences and exercise jurisdiction over the scholars. This is just what would have been likely to happen if a great body of scholars from an organized *studium generale* settled down in a place where no system of graduation or other scholastic organization existed.

On this last topic I should like to quote the judgement of Bishop Stubbs: 'Our English universities, however far in historic distance we may throw back their origin, must have been framed on the model of the continental universities. I do not mean that they were not the successors of more ancient schools of study, many of which continued to exist for some time around the greater cathedrals; but that their university organization, their degrees and faculties, were borrowed from the established institutions on the continent.'[1] These words were written before the appearance of Denifle's book or mine. All subsequent investigation has confirmed their truth. The fact that the academical organization was copied from Paris does not by itself prove a migration from Paris. But the migration hypothesis entirely fits in with and explains the fact, and consequently the fact adds to the strength of the hypothesis.

I will add a brief reference to another document which Mr. Leach cites as strongly suggesting the existence of a university in England in the first half of the twelfth century, and 'if in England, then surely in Oxford'. Why so? There were plenty of cathedral schools in England and elsewhere at which many subjects were taught besides grammar. The Cathedral Statutes of Lincoln[2] require the chancellor 'scolas theologie regere'; so at York.[3] My space will not allow me to multiply evidence. Mr. Leach has himself called attention to the fact that in the London schools logic and occasionally philosophy were taught. There is no evidence that the schools of Oxford prior to 1167–8 differed in any way from those of Lincoln and York, Salisbury and London. The problem is why these schools never became 'general', while those of Oxford did so, and that with surprising rapidity. My theory accounts for the fact. Of course, I do not claim for it more than high probability. Mr. Leach fails to see that there is any problem to be solved.

[1] W. Stubbs, *Lectures on Medieval and Modern History*, pp. 141–2.
[2] *The Cathedral Statutes of Lincoln*, ed. H. Bradshaw and C. Wordsworth, i. 284.
[3] *Ibid.* ii. 96.

I will now allude to a point which strikingly illustrates Mr. Leach's controversial methods. I remarked that the indirect allusions to Oxford which I had discovered in the passages quoted above 'are of a kind which would not' (I wrote 'could not') 'be discovered by turning out the word Oxford in the indices of the various contemporary chroniclers'. Mr. Leach declares categorically: 'This allusion, by the way, was discovered by Dr. Rashdall by no more recondite labour than reading Denifle's *Chartulary of the University of Paris*, where John's letter, taken from the Rolls Series, appears among the earliest documents.' Now it so happens that I had quoted the passage in question (with the others referred to) and set forth my whole theory as to the origin of Oxford in a letter which appeared in the *Academy* in June, 1888. The first volume of the *Chartulary* appeared in 1889. As a matter of fact, that and the other passages which are not contained in the *Chartulary* were discovered by a laborious study of the seven volumes of the materials for the history of Thomas Becket, the writings of John of Salisbury, and much other contemporary literature. . . .

II (XIX)

LAW STUDIES AT OXFORD IN THE TWELFTH CENTURY

Twyne (MSS. xxii, f. 164) gives an extract from some lost portion of the work of Giraldus Cambrensis, no doubt the burned portion of the *Speculum Ecclesiae*:

'In altero MS° qui continet opera quaedam Sylvestri Gyraldi, viz. eius Distinctiones libris 4. Ubi in praefatione ad librum primum distinctionum suarum sic loquitur Gyraldus:

"Proinde etiam verbum illud quod apud Oxoniam nostris diebus a clerico quodam cui nomen Martinus, qui et Bononiae in legibus aliquandiu studuerat et literis tamen antea prouectus fuerat, pauperistis quorum ibi tunc copia fuit, dum pauperum S. liber ille sic dictus in pretio stetit, responsum erat, hic recitare praeter rem non putavimus. In quodam enim scholarium conuentu non modico ubi et causae coram iudicibus ventilabantur et controversiae cum aliis cunctis qui aderant aduocatis qui contra ipsum omnes esse consueuerant et ipse quoque contrarius uniuersis, lex una quae contra ipsum expressa videbatur, obiecta fuisset et conclamantibus cunctis et insultantibus 'per hanc legem Martine salies sicut et symiae saltandi dici solet perque legem istam velis nolis saltum facies,' curialiter ab ipso, mordaciter tamen et lepide APPENDIX
II. satis responsum est in hunc modum: 'Si saliendum est mihi, saliam quidem, sed saltum quem vos fecistis omnes et (?) cum animaduerterem scilicet usque ad Imperatoriam maiestatem si nempe debeatis et corpore medii, nec feci reuera nec faciam.'"'

The passage is paraphrased by Wood, *Hist. et Antiq. Univ. Oxon.* i. 56 (copied by Holland in *Collectanea* (O.H.S.), ii. 176). [The text as given by Twyne is clearly faulty in places.]

The allusion to the 'imperatoria maiestas' seems to betray the origin of the story. It is probably one of the numerous stories told about the disputes between Martinus and the other Bologna jurists (cf. above, vol. i, pp. 120, 259) at the Court of Frederick I, which Giraldus, consciously or unconsciously, transferred to Oxford in much the same way as university stories are transferred from Oxford to Cambridge, and from one great personage to another, at the present day.

III (XXI)

HONORIUS III AND OXFORD

Allusions to the Chancellor of Oxford appear in certain Bulls of Honorius III.

Twyne (MSS. xxiii, f. 67) gives the following account of a Bull which is not found in the published Registers of Honorius III:

'Bulla Honorii papae, dat. Laterani 3° Cal. Aprilis pontificatus sui a° 5°, in qua M^r. W. Scoto Archidiacono Wygorn., Cancellario Oxon., nec non Willelmo Rectori Ecclesiae de Cercell potestatem facit cognoscendi causas decimarum de diversis parochiis Osneyensibus debitarum, necnon testium qui decrepiti et senes iam erant in cautelam futuram examinandorum; deinde subiicitur illorum summonitio Rectori Ecclesiae de Bekele ut intersit receptioni huiusmodi testium si velit crastino Octabarum Apostolorum Petri et Pauli anno ab incarnatione domini 1221.'

Twyne continues:

'Haec omnia in uno eodemque scripto extant ubi simul cum illa summonitione recitatur bulla illa predicta papalis, et in fine illius chirographi sic habetur:

"Et in huius rei testimonium presenti scripto sigilla nostra apposuimus, haec autem a nobis duobus facta sunt quoniam tertius, scilicet Cancellarius, de quo in literis Apostolicis facta est mentio tunc temporis in rerum natura non fuit."'

This notice appears among 'Excerpta ex variis chyrographis et chartis tum Prioratus S. Frideswydae tum Monasterii Osney, in chartario Ecclesiae Aedis Christi Oxon.—sub aula eiusdem collegii.' As far as I can ascertain, the document must be lost. There is a marginal note: 'Vidi tamen aliud scriptum ad hanc ipsam formam, Walteri scilicet Archidiaconi Wygorn. et Cancellarii Oxon. sub sigillis suis de hac ipsa materia et absque sigillo Decani Oxon., a° domini 1221 die lunae proximo post festum sanctae Frideswydae super decimis de Kencote et Nortune.' Another Bull preserved in the University Archives is printed by Dr. H. E. Salter in *Medieval Archives of the University of Oxford* (O.H.S.), i. 10.

It begins:

'Honorius episcopus servus servorum Dei dilectis filiis . . . archidiacono Wigorniensi et . . . cancellario et decano Oxonie Lincolniensis diocesis salutem et apostolicam benedictionem': and ends 'Dat. Lateran. III Kal. Aprilis pontificatus nostri anno quinto' (30 March 1221; seal missing).

Other documents of the same kind and about the same date are also printed by Dr. Salter in the same volume, *ibid.* i. 11–17. [Dr. Salter has printed in the *Cartulary of Oseney Abbey*, iv. 185–7, a composition between the abbey and Richard Foliot concerning the tithes of Barton Odonis, which recites a Bull of Gregory IX, addressed to the Prior and the Dean of Abingdon and the Chancellor of Oxford, and dated 13 January 1228.]

A Bull about a similar tithe dispute, referring it to the Prior of S. Frideswide, the Dean of Oxford, and the Chancellor of Oxford, in 1231, with the decision of the delegates, is preserved among the manuscripts of the Dean and Chapter of Ely. The document runs: 'Omnibus sancte matris ecclesie fidelibus presens scriptum uisuris et audituris Prior sancte Fredeswide Decanus et Cancelarius Oxonie salutem eternam in Domino. Mandatum domini pape in hec uerba suscepimus. "Gregorius Episcopus seruus seruorum Dei Dilectis filiis priori sancte Fredeswide Decano et Cancelario Oxon. Lincolniensis dioc. salutem et apostolicam benedictionem. Querelam G. rectoris ecclesie de bluntesham recepimus continentem quod venerabilis frater noster Episcopus prior et conuentus Eliensis . . . Datum Reate 9 kal. julii pontificatus nostri anno quinto." Huius ergo auctoritate . . . In huius rei testimonium huic scripto signa nostra apposuimus. Anno incarnationis domini MCCXXXIII facta fuit hec compositio.' Other papal delegations to the Chancellor of Oxford in 1235 and 1236 occur in *Cal. Papal Registers (Papal Letters)*, i. 148, 151.

IV (XXII)

CONFLICT BETWEEN MASTERS AND SCHOLARS
AT OXFORD, ? 1338

(See above, vol. iii, p. 89)

'Quidam conflictus contigit Oxoniae die sabbati in festo S. Bene- APPENDIX
dicti Abbatis anno eodem (scilicet anno 1330) inter Magistros IV.
Oxoniae tam Regentes quam non Regentes ex una parte et communitatem scholarium eiusdem ex alia; eo quod quidam scholares
insolentes qui nolebant antiquis universitatis legibus circa pacis
conservationem et perturbatorum pacis punitionem ab antiquo
usitatis obedire liberius solito pacem perturbare volebant, unde
et multitudinem iuvenum sibi ad resistendum suis magistris
illicite adunabant. In ipso autem conflictu ex utraque parte quam-
plures vulnerati erant, et quidam interfecti; tamen victoria cessit
scholaribus 3° nonas Aprilis, videlicet die Veneris proxima ante
Dominicam in Ramis palmarum.'

These are copied by Twyne (MSS. xxii, f. 366), as 'excerptum
ex quodam veteri chronico quod olim pertinuit ad ecclesiam Lich-
feldensem', with the note 'Chronicon unde haec nota desumpta
est, pertingit ad annum domini 1347. Ibi etiam multa habentur de
ecclesia Lichfeldensi.' There is also a marginal note 'Mr. Allen',
but I have been unable to find the manuscript among Allen's MSS.
contained in the Digby bequest to the Bodleian, or to trace it
elsewhere. There must be some mistake about either the year
or the day: the dates given would be possible in 1338.

[It has been pointed out by Sir H. C. Maxwell-Lyte (*Hist. Univ.
of Oxford*, p. 132, n. 1) and Sir C. E. Mallet (*Hist. Univ. of Oxford*, i.
156, n. 1) that the dates given in this excerpt suit the years 1327
and 1349 equally well. Sir H. C. Maxwell-Lyte prefers 1327.
Sir C. E. Mallet seems to incline to 1349, 'apparently the year of
John Wylliott's stormy election as Chancellor'.[1] In his *Annals* (i.
442) Anthony Wood inserts a translation of this excerpt under the
year 1347; but Wood has failed to note that Twyne only mentions
1347 as the terminal year of the Lichfield chronicle from which
he extracted this passage, and does not suggest that year as an
alternative to 1330, the year given in the passage itself.[2] As 1349

---

[1] [See *Snappe's Formulary*, ed.
H. E. Salter (O.H.S.), pp. 305–6.]
[2] [The year 1347 is the terminal
year of the *Historia de Episcopis
Coventrensibus et Lichfeldensibus* of

Thomas Chesterfield, but this particular passage does not occur in the
text of the *Historia* edited by Henry
Wharton (*Anglia Sacra*, i. 421–
43).]

falls outside the period covered by the chronicle used by Twyne, it can hardly be admitted as a possible alternative. Of the other two alternatives to 1330 that have been suggested the year 1327 has most to commend it. The facts recorded in this excerpt agree well with the entry in the *Annales Paulini* (*Chronicles of the Reigns of Edward I and Edward II*, ed. W. Stubbs (R.S.), i. 332), which states under 1327 that a great division arose during Lent 'inter Cancellarium, magistros de Mertonhalle, et communitatem scolarium universitatis' over certain new statutes which were said to infringe ancient liberties. In the end 'the Chancellor and several masters of Mertonhalle' were deposed and a new Chancellor and proctor chosen. These events have an appropriate sequel in the statutes *De pacis perturbatoribus* which were promulgated by the university on October 16, in the same year (*Statuta Antiqua Univ. Oxon.*, ed. S. Gibson, pp. 128–31). It is known that one at least of the proctors who were in office in the early part of 1327 was a fellow of Merton—Thomas Bradwardine, subsequently Archbishop of Canterbury.[1] The year 1338, as a possible alternative, is unsupported by any corroborative evidence.]

V (XXIII)

AN OXFORD 'FORMA'

The following fragment, which has not been printed before, deserves preservation. It occurs in Twyne, MSS. xxii, f. 163 *sq.*, being copied by him from a manuscript which it would be difficult or impossible now to trace:

['In altero MS° quod sic incipit *utrum a sphaeris coelestibus continue mutabilibus, &c.*, vbi sic lego]:

Haec est forma incoeptoris in artibus Oxoniae, videlicet:

Liber Metaphysicorum per annum (connumerando dies festos).

Liber Ethicorum per 4 menses integros (con. dies fest.).

Geometria per unam septimanam integram (non con. d. f.).

Algorismus per 8 dies ⎫

Sphaera per 8 dies ⎬ non. con. d. f.

Compotus per 8 dies ⎭

Arithmetica Boetii per 3 septimanas integras (non con. &c.).

Priscianus magni voluminis vel liber Politicorum vel 19 libri de Animalibus connumerando libros de motu et progressu

[1] [See *Snappe's Formulary*, ed. H. E. Salter (O.H.S.), p. 326.]

animalium audiatur per 6 septimanas integras non. con. APPENDIX
V.
d. f.

Priscianus de constructionibus partium.

Liber coeli et mundi per terminum anni.

Liber Metheororum per terminum anni.

4us Liber Topicorum Boetii.

'Item oportet quod legat 2 libros logicales ad minus, unum de veteri Logica et alterum de nova vel ambos de nova et unum de libris naturalibus, videlicet libros 4 coeli et mundi vel 3^{es} libros de Animalibus, 4 libros Metheororum vel duos libros de generatione et corruptione vel librum de sensu et sensato cum libris de memoria et reminiscentia, de somno et vigilia vel librum de motu animalium cum duobus minutis libris naturalibus.

'Item oporteat (sic) quod bis respondeat et quater arguat in solennibus disputacionibus Magistrorum nec non disputando ad quodlibet, videlicet bis quaestioni et semel problemati. Item iurabit ante licentiationem quod provisum est sibi de scholis pro anno in quo debet regere.

'Item oportet quod unum librum Aristotelis, textum videlicet cum quaestionibus, in scholis publice rite legat.'

[Fr. C. Michalski, O.C.M., has pointed out that Twyne copied this *forma* from Corpus Christi College, Oxford, MS. 116, f. 30^v.

A similar *forma* is preserved on the last fly-leaf but one of Worcester Cathedral MS. F. 73. It is printed in the appendix to the *Catalogue of MSS. preserved in the Chapter Library of Worcester Cathedral*, ed. S. G. Hamilton, 1906, pp. 36, 176–7. It begins:

'Forma illorum qui incepturi sunt in artibus.

Ordinacio de forma audiendi libros.'

It omits the 'liber Metaphysicorum'[1] and the 'Quartus Liber Topicorum Boetii',[2] mentioned in Twyne's schedule. It gives five weeks, not one week, as the time to be taken in attending lectures on geometry. Instead of the last three paragraphs of the *forma* copied by Twyne, it concludes with the direction: 'Et omnes isti libri et omnes alii qui dicti sunt de forma legantur in scola rite secundum exigenciam inc(eptorum).' This *forma* corresponds exactly with that contained in the statutes of the university (*Statuta Antiqua Univ. Oxon.*, ed. S. Gibson, pp. 33–4).[3]]

Twyne (MSS. xxi, f. 761) copies another *forma* from the end

[1] [*Stat. Antiq. Univ. Oxon.*, ed. S. Gibson, p. 234.]

[2] [*Ibid.*, pp. 26, 200, 234.]

[3] [In the statutes the last sentence of the *forma* ends: 'secundum exigenciam materie.']

APPENDIX of a manuscript entitled 'Algorismus in prosa', in the Merton
v. College Library (which I have failed to identify):

'Nota quod hec est forma inceptorum in artibus:

In primis 4 libri Metheororum.

Item 4 de celo et mundo.

Item 4us Topicorum Boycii   a Marchal

Item Algarismus inicium (?)   a Payn

Item compotus cum spera.

Item Aritmetrica cum gemetria.

Item x libri Eticorum.

Item xii libri de Animalibus   a Play

Item xii libri Methaphysicae.' 2 4 5 6 7 8 9 10 11 12

[Memorandum quod J. T. (?) audiuit librum de sompno et
vigilia et librum de memoria et reminiscentia a M suo magistro
N. (?) K. (?) postquam gratia fuit. impetrata quod quilibet
istorum librorum staret pro quocunque libro sue forme volun-
tarie (?). Item librum de inspiracione et respiracione. Item librum
de sensu et sensato. Item librum de motu animalium.

Viue Deo gratus toto mundo tumulatus.

Crimine mundatus semper transire paratus.

Memorandum quod habui a Bokynham xii d(ies) in gemetria
et totalem literam 2 libri geometrie et a Wescot ix dies in
gemetria. Item a Bokynham literam totalem primi libri Arsmetrice
et xii dies Arsmetrice.

Item a Hobulam.

This *forma*, with the memoranda following after it, is written
in an early fourteenth century hand on the last leaf of Merton
MS. 261. It is printed by Professor F. M. Powicke as a footnote
in his introduction to *The Medieval Books of Merton College*, p. 34,
from a transcript made by Dr. P. S. Allen. Twyne's transcript
has here been emended and completed in accordance with that
made by Dr. Allen.]

VI (XXV)

LOST COLLEGES AT OXFORD

A. *Burnell's Inn or London College*

London College may perhaps be considered an exception to what
has been said above (vol. i, p. 533) as to the non-extinction of any
Oxford college founded in the medieval period. It is, however,
as will be seen, an exception which proves the rule. This college
has, indeed, perished so completely, that its existence has been

quite unrecognized by most of our university historians. The indefatigable Twyne, however (MSS. xxiv, f. 588), tells us that, when Edward I expelled the Jews from England, their synagogue in Oxford, with other adjoining buildings, was bought by William Burnell, Archdeacon of Wells and brother of the better-known Robert Burnell, bishop of that see, and was by him turned into a hall for students, known as Burnell's Inn. So far it might appear that this was a mere unendowed hall, and that the archdeacon's purchase was simply an investment of money; but the following passage from the *Chronicle of Mailros* would seem to indicate that the hall was meant as a habitation for the college maintained at Oxford during his lifetime by the purchaser's brother, Robert Burnell, Bishop of Bath and Wells. After speaking of the establishment of Balliol College, *sub anno* 1270, the chronicler proceeds:

'Et ibi [Oxoniae] alia domus Scholarium melior illa [Balliol], qui percipiunt ad communiam suam xii denarios per circulum septimanae de dono Episcopi Bathensis.' (*Chron. de Mailros*, ed. Fulman, ap. *Rer. Angl.*, Oxford, 1684, p. 241.)

Licence for an oratory was granted in 1291 (Lincoln Reg., Sutton, f. 25).

There is no evidence that the bishop endowed the college; and after his death in 1292 'Burnel's Yn' became an ordinary hall again, coming in 1307 into the possession of Balliol College (Wood, *City of Oxford*, i. 155).[1]

In the time of Henry IV, however, Richard Clifford, Bishop of London, acquired the inn,[2] and turned it into a college, henceforth known as London College, for a body of scholars whom he provided for during his lifetime, and to whom he left at his death in 1421 a sum of 1,000 marks. This sum was not, however, to be invested in land—then the only possible form of permanent investment. The executors were simply directed to pay £40 a year to the scholars as long as the money lasted. When this sum came to an end, the college must have been left without endowment;

[1] [Burnell's Inn and all his other houses in Oxford were left to Balliol by William Burnell, who died in the autumn of 1304. See *The Oxford Deeds of Balliol College*, ed. H. E. Salter (O.H.S.), p. 91. Dr. Salter places Burnell's Inn to the east of the synagogue, which was converted into an inn at one time known as The Pike, and at another as The Dolphin. See *ibid.*, p. 94, and Map 5 in Dr. Salter's *Medieval Map of Oxford*.]

[2] [In 1416 Bishop Clifford rented the inn from Balliol and made arrangements for purchasing it, if he should decide to do so. It is not known what happened to it after his death in 1421, but in 1450 it was in the occupation of Benedictine monks. See *The Oxford Deeds of Balliol College*, ed. H. E. Salter, p. 95.]

though, as the scholars were presumably in possession of the hall and paid no rent, the corporation must, it would seem, have survived, and vacant places been filled up by election. It remained as a college, with no endowment but its buildings. These are said to have been destroyed by Wolsey to make way for Christ Church.[1]

The following is an extract from Bishop Clifford's will:

'Item, lego mille marcas pauperibus scolaribus meis presentibus et futuris Oxonie in hospicio meo vocato Burnell commorantibus siue commoraturis et sociis dicti hospicii perseuerantibus et perseueraturis: ita quod de dictis mille marcis per executores meos Magistro et sociis antedictis pro eorum sustentacione quadraginta libre annuatim ministrentur, quousque summa dictarum mille marcarum sic ut predicitur sit soluta et plenarie consummata.' (Lambeth Reg., Chich. i, f. 347.)

The college was still extant in 1425, when we find a rental or payment 'de Johanne Hertipole modo tenente magistri et scholarium de quodam hospitio nuper vocato Burnell's Yn modo Lundon College pro tenemento nostro', &c. (Wood, *City of Oxford*, ii. 88). This passage is important as showing that the master and scholars had a corporate existence and held property. We hear of London College as late as 1616 (Archives, Reg. G. 6, f. 316 *b*), a statement which it is difficult to reconcile with Twyne's account of its fate. Wolsey may have bought the hall, but not destroyed it.

B. *S. Peter's House* (?)

A document is printed in Wood, *City of Oxford*, ii. 497, from the Register of Bishop Burghersh at Lincoln authorizing the collection of alms on behalf of the 'pauperes domum S. Petri Oxon. inhabitantes'. This may conceivably have been a 'domus pauperum' of the type mentioned above, p. 406, but there is nothing to prove that the house was for scholars.

[This was certainly not an academical foundation. See *Victoria County History of Oxford*, ii. 160.]

VII (XXVI)

RELICS OF THE ANCIENT AUTONOMY OF THE OXFORD HALLS

The following formal account of the admission of the last Principal of S. Mary Hall, the Rev. D. P. Chase, D.D., is a copy

---

[1] [London College was acquired by Cardinal Wolsey 'by good handling of the Master and company of Baley Colleage', see *ibid.*, pp. 97–8.]

(which I owe to his kindness) of the entry made at the time in the
Register of the hall.

This day at two o'clock p.m. the Rev. Drummond Percy Chase, Master of Arts, Fellow of Oriel College, was admitted Principal of this Hall in the presence of Edward Rowden, D.C.L., Registrar of the University and Notary Public.

The Aulares present were:

> Masters of Arts, two.
> Bachelors of Arts, three.
> Non-Graduates, seven.

Form of Admission

The Rev. D. P. Chase was, at two o'clock p.m., conducted by the Vice-Chancellor and Bedels to the Dining-Hall.

The Vice-Chancellor addressed the *Aulares*, stating that he was come in obedience to a letter, received on the day previous from the Chancellor of the University, to announce his Lordship's nomination of a Principal in the room of the Rev. Philip Bliss, D.C.L., lately deceased.

He next read the following passage from the *Statuta Aularia*, I. § 4. 1:

'*De Principalibus aularum eorumque substitutis*

Statutum est quod ad regimen aularum assumantur viri aetate matura et morum gravitate venerandi; saltem Magistri in Artibus, vel in Iure aut Medicina Baccalaurei; qui ad nominationem domini Cancellarii ab aularibus eligantur, et per Vice-Cancellarium ad praefecturam et regimen admittantur.'

He then read the letter of the Chancellor nominating to the vacant Principalship the Rev. Drummond Percy Chase, and submitted the nomination to the Aulares, by whom it was unanimously approved.

The Rev. D. P. Chase then took the Oaths of Allegiance and Supremacy, and the oath further prescribed by the *Statuta Aularia*, I. § 4. 2:

'Quod Principales . . . observari facient.'

The Vice-Chancellor then made the admission in the following words:

'Domine Principalis ego admitto te ad praefecturam et regimen Aulae Beatae Mariae Virginis', and, having briefly congratulated the Principal and the *Aulares* and made a cursory inspection of the Plate belonging to the Hall (a complete inventory of all the property being required, by the *Statuta Aularia*, I. § 6. 1, 'Statutum est ... iuxta verum valorem satisfacere', to be deposited with the Registrar of the University) he returned, accompanied by the Principal, to his own lodgings.

Dec. 5, 1857. D. P. CHASE, Principal.

The only other trace of self-government left in the still valid Laudian *Statuta Aularia* is the provision that any of the movables of the hall may be alienated, if of less value than 40*s.*, 'cum consensu majoris partis graduatorum' (§ 6. 2). If the value exceeds 40*s.*, the consent of the Vice-Chancellor is required. I may add that even this scant recognition of the society's autonomy seems scarcely consistent with the theory devised by modern lawyers, according to which the property of the halls is held in trust for them by the university. The fact is that the hall is a survival from a time when the modern notions about the incapacity of *collegia* to hold property without incorporation by the State had not been developed: our lawyers have accordingly not known what to make of the institution.

Dr. Chase's reply to my inquiries as to the ownership of the site and buildings of S. Mary Hall is perhaps worthy of preservation, as illustrating the position of a hall as a community occupying a house which is not its own.

'*The Buildings constituting the Quadrangle of St. Mary Hall* are in three holdings.

1. In the centre of the North side is a tenement, of two storeys, containing three sets of rooms, for which the annual Rent of Sixteen Pounds two Shillings is paid to Oriel College.

2. Adjoining this tenement on the East are Buildings,

   (*a*) of two storeys, containing three sets of rooms;
   (*b*) some "offices" behind the Quadrangle and not visible from it.

These are held from the Under-tenant of Magdalen College, originally at an annual Rent of £35; but since Michaelmas, 1862, £45.

3. The whole of the Eastern, Southern, and Western sides, and so much of the Northern as adjoins the Oriel tenement (1 above) are held of Oriel College at an annual Rent of £3. They include the Lodgings of the Principal.'

I have some recollection of having heard from the late Provost of Oriel [Dr. Hawkins] that a lease of this last-named portion (3) was in existence and that it contained power of re-entry by the college if the property should ever cease to be applied to academ- ical use.

Under the Statute for the Union of Oriel College and S. Mary Hall, 16 June 1881 (p. 321), Sections 1 and 2, this question will drop, 'on the first vacancy in the office of Principal of S. Mary Hall'.

All the halls are doomed to extinction except S. Edmund Hall, which in 1559 was placed under the government of Queen's College, by which the Principal has since then been appointed.

[On the death of Dr. Chase in 1902 St. Mary Hall was merged in Oriel. The separate identity and continuance of S. Edmund Hall were secured by University Statute approved by the King in Council in 1913.]

For the election of principals by students in the London Inns of Chancery, as late as 1854, see R. R. Pearce, *History of the Inns of Court*, p. 63.

VIII (XXVIII)

THE CHANCELLOR AND SCHOLARS OF SALISBURY, 1278

The following is the agreement between the Sub-dean and the Chancellor of Salisbury alluded to above, vol. iii, p. 88. It is taken from the *Liber Ruber* (f. 99) in the possession of the Bishop; to whose Deputy-Registrar, Mr. A. R. Malden, I am indebted for discovering the document, which I knew only from the imperfect copy given by Caius, *De Antiq. Cantab.*, p. 110.

'Die mercurii viii Idus Martii anno domini (*De iurisdictione Cancellarii Sarum.*) M°CC^mo septuagesimo VIII° presentibus in capitulo Saresberiensi dominis Waltero Decano, Domino Iohanne precentore, Simone Cancellario, Nicolao thesaurario, Stephano Berkensi et Henrico Wiltes'. archidiaconis, Willelmo Subdecano, Iohanne succentore, Willelmo penitentiario, Hugone de penne, Galfrido de Muleborn., Willelmo de Brimptoñ, Canonicis Saresberiensibus: Cum de iurisdictione inter scolares in Ciuitate Saresberiensi studiorum causa commorantes exercenda inter Cancellarium et subdecanum predictos, quorum uterque iurisdictionem ipsam ad suum officium pertinere dicebat, dissentio quedam exorta fuisset, tandem habito super hoc tractatu in capitulo die ipsa de utriusque [ipsorum] expresso consensu conuenerunt in hunc modum—videlicet quod dictus dominus Cancellarius, ad cuius officium pertinet scolas regere, inter omnes scolares, cuiuscumque facultatis existant, studiorum causa in ciuitate ipsa commorantes, qui tanquam scolares certi doctoris, cuius scolas frequentant, recom-

APPENDIX VIII. mendationem et testimonium habeant, de contencionibus ciuilibus et personalibus que pecuniarum interesse respiciunt, et scolasticis omnibus contractibus et eciam si laicus aliquem huiusmodi scolarium in consimilibus causis impetere voluerit, cognoscat et diffiniat et presbyteri ciuitatis decreta et precepta eiusdem cancellarii in hiis exequi teneantur. De aliis uero clericis et qui extra studium certi Doctoris scolas minime frequentantes ibidem moram fecerint [omnimodam], et de scolaribus ipsis, si forsan de lapsu carnis seu delicto alio ibidem commisso quod ad correccionem pertineat et salutem respiciat animarum, vocati fuerint, subdecanus ipse, qui est archidiaconus ciuitatis, iurisdictionem et correccionem habeat, exceptis tamen vicariis et clericis maioris ecclesie tam studentibus quam aliis, in quos Decanus cum capitulo et non alius ipso presente [Decano] et Subdecanus similiter cum capitulo Decano absente, secundum hactenus obtentam ecclesie consuetudinem, omnimodam iurisdiccionem et cohercionem exercebunt: ita quod Cancellarius ipse per se nullatenus intromittat de eisdem.'

This agreement is immediately followed by a deed of Giles (de Bridport), Bishop of Salisbury (1256–62), founding a college for a small community of scholars, to be called the *Scholares de Valle Scholarium* ('domum in usum et perpetuitatem scolarium qui vallis scolarium vocabuntur') with the consent of the dean and chapter and also of the brethren of the Hospital of S. Nicholas at Salisbury, the college being situated before the said hospital, between the cathedral and the King's highway. It was to provide for a warden and twenty 'honest and docible poor scholars' studying 'in divina pagina et liberalibus artibus'. The warden is given 'cohercionem plenariam ... tam in temporalibus quam spirtualibus' within the house and its precincts, with an appeal to the dean. The foundation of such a college, though it does not absolutely prove the existence of a *Studium Generale*, tends to corroborate it.

[This agreement has since been printed by the Rev. Canon C. Wordsworth in his edition of the *Cartulary of S. Nicholas' Hospital, Salisbury, with other records* (Wilts. Record Society), pp. 46–7, and is included by Mr. A. F. Leach in *Educational Charters and Documents*, pp. 168–9. Canon Wordsworth also prints the deed of Bishop Bridport founding the college (pp. 38–40). De Vaux college continued in existence until its dissolution by Henry VIII, at which time it consisted of a warden, four fellows, and two chaplains. Canon Wordsworth has compiled a list of its wardens. See *ibid.*, pp. lv–lviii, 36–49, and also the *Lectures on Bishop Bridport and De Vaux College* by the Rev. Canon J. M. J. Fletcher, reprinted from *The Wiltshire Gazette* of March 22 and 29, 1934.]

IX (XXXII)

THE PRESENT JURISDICTION OF THE CHANCELLOR'S COURT AT OXFORD[1]

By the ancient charters and statutes, as we have seen, this court APPENDIX
had the following jurisdiction: IX.

(1) Exclusive spiritual jurisdiction over resident members of the university and concurrent spiritual jurisdiction over citizens. This jurisdiction included probate of scholars' wills, which lasted till 1858.

(2) Civil jurisdiction in any case in which a member of the university [including a college] was plaintiff or defendant, exclusive of 'pleas which touch the crown', and of actions relating to a lay fee (i.e. practically all actions affecting real property). It appears to be doubtful whether it has jurisdiction in equity: in many cases it would clearly be without the machinery for enforcing equitable jurisdiction. (For contradictory decisions on this head see Grant, *Treatise on the Law of Corporations*, London, 1850, p. 523 *sq.*) The court would also at all times have been in practice incapable of exercising certain jurisdictions created by statute at a date subsequent to that of the university charters, e.g. by the various acts relating to insolvency and bankruptcy.

(3) Criminal jurisdiction in all cases in which a member of the university is prosecutor or defendant, except treason, felony, and 'mayhem'. It may be a matter of much antiquarian and some practical interest to inquire how far this jurisdiction has been affected by legislation in modern times.

1. If the judgement of Dr. Montague Bernard, then Assessor of the Chancellor's Court, in the case of Pusey and others *v.* Jowett (Oxford, 1863) is to be accepted, the spiritual jurisdiction has practically vanished. A suit being promoted against the Rev. B. Jowett, Regius Professor of Greek (afterwards Master of Balliol) for heresy, the Assessor ruled that by the Clergy Discipline Act of 1840 (3 & 4 Vict. c. 86), no proceedings could be taken against a clerk in holy orders except in the manner prescribed by that Act. The Act does not recognize the jurisdiction of the Chancellor, nor could the machinery which it provides be applied to the Chancellor's Court. Hence no proceedings can be taken against a clerk in holy orders in the Chancellor's Court for an

---

[1] [It is entitled 'The Court of the Chancellor commonly called the Vice-Chancellor's Court' in the Oxford University Act of 1862 (25 & 26 Vict. c. 26, § 12).]

ecclesiastical offence. The court no doubt retains the same power of excommunicating laymen for immorality, which is in theory retained by the courts of the bishops and archdeacons elsewhere, but the power is of course practically obsolete; though there is, it would appear, still nothing to prevent an archdeacon 'signifying' to the King in Chancery persons who refuse to perform a penance imposed by his court, and procuring their imprisonment by the writ *de excommunicato capiendo*.

2. In civil cases the jurisdiction remains absolutely intact, as was decided by the Court of Queen's Bench in the case of Ginnet *v.* Whittingham (1886), 16 Q.B. 761.[1] Under the Oxford University Act of 1854 (17 & 18 Vict. c. 81, § 45), the common law was substituted for the ancient civil law procedure of the court,[2] and under the Oxford University Act of 1862 and the Supreme Court of Judicature Act of 1884 the Vice-Chancellor may from time to time, subject to the concurrence of the authority for the time being empowered to make rules for the Supreme Court, make rules for the Chancellor's Court,[3] a power which was exercised in 1865, [1907, and 1918].

3. In criminal matters it is thought that the jurisdiction of the court has been seriously modified by the Summary Jurisdiction Act of 1879 (42 & 43 Vict. c. 49). It seems unnecessary to discuss the effects of the earlier Summary Jurisdiction Act of 1848. The Act of 1879 provided that summary jurisdiction should only be exercised in the manner prescribed by the Act; and it is contended that the practical effect of this measure is to abolish all the criminal jurisdiction of the Vice-Chancellor, except that which he exercises as an *ex officio* justice of the peace. This jurisdiction is of course much more limited than the old jurisdiction above described. Whereas under the old charters he might (without a jury) have tried a man for perjury, and sentenced him to two years' imprisonment or more, the maximum sentence which can be imposed by justices is six months' imprisonment. Moreover, in most cases, a justice of the peace must act with at least one other justice. Hence it has become the practice for the Vice-Chancellor to sit with some other justice of the peace for the County of Oxford, and (where the matter exceeds their jurisdiction) to commit for trial to the Assizes or Quarter Sessions. But the Act of 1879 required that justices should sit only in Petty Sessional

[1] [See J. Williams, *The Law of the Universities*, pp. 98, 99, 110, 135.]

[2] [See *ibid.*, p. 90.]

[3] [See *ibid.*, pp. 93, 94, and *Rules of the Chancellor's Court of the University of Oxford*, Oxford, 1933.]

Courts, i.e. in a place regularly appointed by the justices for the division. Consequently there was still an anomaly in the proceedings of the Vice-Chancellor who did not belong to any regular Petty Sessional Division, and held his court in a place not authorized under the provisions of the Act. Hence in 1886 an Act of Parliament was procured (49 & 50 Vict. c. 31) which provided that 'The chancellor, masters, and scholars of the University of Oxford may, from time to time, fix a place within the precincts of the University at which the chancellor of the said University, and his commissary for the time being (commonly called the vice-chancellor), and the deputy of the aforesaid commissary for the time being may sit and act as justices of the peace for the counties of Oxford and Berks., and when they, or any of them, sit in the place so appointed, and act as justices or justice of the peace for the county of Oxford or Berks., such place shall be deemed to be a petty sessional court-house within the meaning of the Summary Jurisdiction Act, 1879, and to be situate within the county of Oxford or the county of Berks., as the case requires, and any justice of the peace for the county of Oxford or the county of Berks., as the case requires, may sit and act with them or him as justice of the peace in such court-house.'

I venture to doubt whether this interpretation of the various Acts dealing with the matter can be sustained. The Act of 1879 relates exclusively to the jurisdiction of justices of the peace, and there is nothing whatever in it to curtail or modify any jurisdiction which the Vice-Chancellor exercises not as a justice. Moreover, this interpretation would make it exceedingly difficult to show whence the Vice-Chancellor derives his *exclusive* claim to try offences committed by or against members of the university. That jurisdiction was conferred upon the Vice-Chancellor as Vice-Chancellor, not as a justice of the peace. If recent legislation has destroyed his jurisdiction as Vice-Chancellor, has it not destroyed also his claim—at all events his exclusive claim—to try these offences? Such a jurisdiction he certainly cannot claim merely as one of the numerous justices of the peace for the counties of Oxford and Berks. Nor is there anything in the Act of 1886 to cure this defect in his position. That Act gives him special facilities for exercising his jurisdiction as a justice of the peace: it exempts him from the necessity of sitting with any number of other justices who choose to attend in the Petty Sessional Court of the district, though he must in certain cases sit with one justice of Oxford or Berks. But it does not confer upon him any jurisdiction which he did not already possess as a justice; and it does not exempt members of the university from the jurisdiction of the county or city justices. It cannot surely be contended that the charters are repealed in respect of the jurisdiction exercised by the Vice-Chancellor, while they are still in force in respect of the persons over whom that jurisdiction is exercised. If the jurisdiction of the Vice-Chancellor *qua* Vice-Chancellor is gone, members of the university can hardly be exempt from the jurisdiction to which other residents in Oxford are amenable; still less can the Vice-Chancellor claim the exclusive cognizance of cases in which a member of the university is the prosecutor.

There is a further anomaly in the position taken up by the university in this matter. Oxford is a county borough, with a separate Commission of the Peace. That being so, it is anomalous —though no doubt not illegal—for two justices of the counties of Oxford and Berks. to exercise jurisdiction in respect of offences committed within the City boundaries. If the Vice-Chancellor is by charter a city justice, the justice with whom he sits is not necessarily so.[1]

In this state of affairs it might be contended that *either* the Vice-Chancellor has lost all criminal jurisdiction beyond the right of holding a court for the trial of such offences committed in Oxford or Berks. as may be brought before him by the voluntary choice of the prosecutor, *or* that the old jurisdiction of the Vice-Chancellor's Court in all criminal cases but treason, felony, and mayhem remains intact.

The chief difficulty in the way of the latter view lies in two clauses of the Summary Jurisdiction Act of 1879 taken in connexion with two clauses of the Interpretation Act of 1889 (52 & 53 Vict. cap. 63. § 13). The clauses of the first-mentioned Act (42 & 43 Vict. cap. 49. § 20, c. 1, 2) run as follows:

'(1) A case arising under this Act, or under any other Act, whether past or future, shall not be heard, tried, determined, or adjudged by a court of summary jurisdiction, except when sitting in open court.

'(2) Open court means a petty sessional court-house.'

The clauses of the Interpretation Act, 1889 (52 & 53 Vict. cap. 63. § 13, cc. 11, 13) are:

'(11) The expression "court of summary jurisdiction" shall

---

[1] [The correctness of the interpretation which Rashdall has put forward in this paragraph is open to question. It may be suggested alternatively that the effects of the Acts of 1879 and 1886 have been to restrict the scope of the Vice-Chancellor's jurisdiction to that of a justice of the peace, but still to leave him within these limits the right to claim exclusive jurisdiction.]

mean any justice of the peace, or other magistrate, by whatever name called, to whom jurisdiction is given by, or who is authorized to act under, the Summary Jurisdiction Acts, whether in England, Wales, or Ireland, and whether acting under the Summary Jurisdiction Acts, or any of them, or under any other Act, or by virtue of his commission, or under the common law.'

'(13) The expression "petty sessional court-house" shall, as respects England or Wales, mean a court-house or other place at which justices are accustomed to assemble for holding special or petty sessions, or which is for the time being appointed as a substitute for such a court-house or place, and where the justices are accustomed to assemble for either special or petty sessions at more than one court-house or place in a petty sessional division, shall mean any such court-house or place.'

Now certainly the language of Clause 11 in the Act of 1889 is very comprehensive. It would be difficult to contend that the Vice-Chancellor is not a magistrate; and if he is a magistrate, it may be urged that he must conform to the provisions of the Summary Jurisdiction Act whether exercising his jurisdiction under the Summary Jurisdiction Acts, or any other jurisdiction which he possesses by law. But (1) in strictness the jurisdiction of the Vice-Chancellor, *qua* Vice-Chancellor, is not conferred by any Act of Parliament (though it is recognized in many Acts) or by the common law or by a commission, but by charter. And (2) if it be urged that the language of the clause is wide enough to cover the jurisdiction derived from the charter, it would seem that *pari ratione* it must cover all manner of courts and judges, even the judges of the High Court who are in the widest sense of the word 'magistrates' and specifically justices of the peace. Hence it would follow that even a judge of the High Court would be bound to exercise his jurisdiction in a Petty Sessional Court sitting with the other justices of the division. This being a *reductio ad absurdum*, it seems to me that it may still be contended that the Vice-Chancellor is not [solely] a magistrate within the meaning of the Act. The word must be understood to mean a magistrate with jurisdiction of the same character as that of a justice of the peace, e.g. the Lord Mayor or Aldermen of the City of London.

Up to 1894 the old process of Appeal to Congregation and Convocation described above (p. 136) remained in force. The last appeal which actually proceeded to a hearing was the case of Hampden v. MacMullen in 1843. An appeal was entered in 1894 but was abandoned before the hearing. An Order of Council of

23 August 1894 was procured (under the Supreme Court of Judicature Act of 1875, and Statute Law Revision and Civil Procedure
Act of 1883), by which an appeal is created from the Vice-
Chancellor's Court to a Divisional Court of the High Court (King's
Bench Division), and the old appeal is abolished. The Act of 1875
gives the King in council power to create an appeal from any 'inferior
Court of Record' similar to the appeal from county courts. It might
perhaps be doubtful whether this would apply to the criminal jurisdiction of the court, supposing any jurisdiction to remain other
than that which the Vice-Chancellor possesses as a justice of the
peace. Appeals from the Vice-Chancellor sitting in Petty Sessions must of course be made to Quarter Sessions on the facts,
and to the King's Bench on points of law, in the cases where
such appeals are allowed in the case of other Petty Sessional
Courts. If a case of a spiritual character were to occur, the old
appeal to Congregation and Convocation would apparently remain
in full force, since a spiritual court could hardly be covered by the
term 'inferior Court of Record'. The university has, however, itself
abolished the statute dealing with the appointment of Delegates
of Appeals. This would not, however, abolish the right to appeal
to Congregation or Convocation, supposing any such right to exist.

Besides the ordinary jurisdiction of the Vice-Chancellor, he
exercises a jurisdiction of a very peculiar character under the
Oxford and Cambridge Police Act (6 Geo. IV. c. 97). Jurisdiction over 'suspected women' is conferred by many old charters and
Acts of Parliament, but in practice all proceedings in such cases
are now taken under the Act of George IV.[1] The Proctors have
the power of arresting such women in the streets by means of the
Proctor's servants (who are sworn constables), and this power has
been exercised quite recently [i.e. recently, before 1895]; but of
late years it has been customary to bring up offenders who have
been observed by the Proctors loitering in the street or walking
with undergraduates by summons. As a rule this leads to the
disappearance of the woman. When the offender is brought before
the court, she is (for a first offence) usually discharged with a
caution. On a second offence she is imprisoned for a few weeks.
A jurisdiction which is thus very seldom really exercised produces
a much more extensive and beneficial effect than *a priori* objectors
to State interference might be disposed to expect upon the decency
of the streets and the morals of the town.[2]

[1] [See J. Williams, *The Law of*
the Universities, pp. 58–9.]
[2] [This power does not appear

to have been exercised since the
end of the nineteenth century.]

The jurisdiction of the Court of the High Steward of the Uni- versity, described above (p. 103), remains intact, but the privilege has never been claimed for a century or more, and the occasional cases of felony by members of the university are disposed of at Quarter Sessions or Assizes.

(I am indebted to Professor [subsequently Sir] T. E. Holland, sometime the learned Assessor of the Chancellor's Court,[1] for several pieces of information contained in the above paragraphs.)

[We are in our turn indebted to Dr. A. E. W. Hazel, Principal of Jesus College, the present learned Assessor of the Chancellor's Court, for help he has very kindly given in the revision of this Appendix.]

[1] [See Sir Erskine Holland's *A Valedictory Retrospect* (*1874–1910*), Oxford, 1910, pp. 19–20.]

[The earliest statutes of the college are those approved in 1514 or 1515 by James Stanley, Bishop of Ely. Apparently the only extant version of Stanley's statutes is the careful transcript made by Benjamin Newton, Fellow from 1746 to 1761. This transcript is reproduced in facsimile in *The Earliest Statutes of Jesus College, Cambridge*, where it is accompanied by a translation and notes. Rashdall followed Mullinger in mistakenly regarding the code printed in *Documents, Univ. and Colleges of Cambridge*, iii. 94–123, as that of Stanley's successor, Bishop West, whereas it seems to have owed its origin to the Commissioners of 1549. See *The Earliest Statutes of Jesus College*, pp. 46–9. Rashdall's remark, therefore, about the savour of the New Learning in the studies prescribed for the college loses its force. The foundation charter contemplated a college consisting of a master and six fellows: in Stanley's statutes the number of fellows is reduced to five. They were to be priests, of whom four were to be theologians, and one a legist. Provision was also made for four 'iuvenes' who were to be 'grammatici et dialectici', skilful in singing and apt for divine service; they were required to act severally as organist, sacrist, bible-clerk, and porter. There were also to be four 'pueri' to act as choristers. A school-master and an usher were to be appointed to have charge of them. See A. Gray, *Jesus College*, pp. 41–50, and *The Earliest Statutes of Jesus College*, passim. The impression given by Stanley's statutes is well summarized by their learned editor, who remarks 'that the Bishop hardly conceived of his college as participant in the educational business of a University. If he had any model of what a college should be it was taken from the many religious houses of Cambridge which in his day maintained a domestic independence of the University while their members had the advantage of its exercises and degrees. In the latter part of the fifteenth century, when the tares of Wycliffe and Pecock were taking root in the Universities, the Heads of the Church, as is shown in their Statutes of King's and Queens', had an anxious desire to protect the college student from such external tendencies as verged on heresy. Their ideal was an autonomous brotherhood, subject to episcopal control and emancipated, as King's was, from University restrictions.' See *op. cit.*, p. 48.]

INDEX

[Technical Latin terms are printed in italics.]

Aachen, i. 271.

Abano, Peter of, i. 265 n.

Abbasid Caliphate, i. 351.

Abbeville, College of, at Paris, i. 536.

Abbeville, Gerard of, i. 396, 490, 536.

Abbo of Fleury, i. 273–4, 275 n.

Abbot, election of, by students, iii. 377 n., 383, 384.

Abelard, Peter, i. 37, 43, 44, 49–66, 107, 128, 134 n., 135, 272, 276–8, 283, 287, 321, 349, 350, 364, 367, 492, 540, 565; ii. 152 n.

ABERDEEN, municipal schools of, i. 282 n.; University of, ii. 304, 307, 312 n., 318–20, 322 n., 324; bp. of, ii. 318.

Abert, J. F., ii. 257.

Abingdon, abbey of, iii. 7, 8 n., 11 n., 104 n., 185.

Abreu, J. M. de, ii. 108.

Abruzzi, nation of, at Bologna, i. 182 n.

Accursius, i. 163 n., 164 n., 180 n., 214, 256 n., 258; ii. 5 n.

— Cervottus, ii. 14 n.

— Franciscus, i. 209 n., 230 n., 256 n.; ii. 168 n.; iii. 163 n.

Ackermann, J. C. G., i. 75, 84 n.

— R., iii. 2, 274.

Acqui, bp. of, *see* Guido.

Act, the, at Oxford, iii. 146. *See* Inception.

Actors, *see* Mimi.

Adalbero, bp. of Verdun, i. 76 n.

Adalbert, abp. of Bremen, i. 86.

— abp. of Mainz, ii. 102 n., 119.

Adam, *see* Brome, Grand-Pont, Marsh, Petit - Pont, Victor (Saint).

Adamatus, physician of Salerno, i. 86.

Adamson, J. W., iii. 242 n., 246 n.

Ade, John, i. 550 n.

Adelard, *see* Bath.

Adoptionism, i. 56 n.

Adrian VI, Pope, ii. 268.

Advocati, i. 100.

Ægidius Romanus, *see* Giles of Rome.

— Fuscararius, i. 136 n.

Aeneas Sylvius, *see* Pius II.

Affò, ii. 334.

Age for degrees, i. 247, 303 n., 462, 472, 474; on entering university, i. 125 n.; ii. 89 n.

Agricola, Rudolf, ii. 55; iii. 373 n.

Aicardus, i. 283 n.

Aicelin, Giles, i. 537.

— Pierre, i. 537.

Aicelins, Collège des, at Paris, i. 537. *See* Montaigu.

Aides, i. 428 sq. *See* Généraux.

Aigrefeuille, C. d', ii. 116.

Ailly, Peter d', i. 401 n., 469 n., 550, 553 n., 563, 564 n., 566 n., 569 n., 572, 575–6, 578; iii. 246 n., 262 n., 338.

Ailred of Rievaulx, iii. 344 n.

Ainslie, Gilbert, iii. 304, 306 n.

Aix, University of, i. 469 n.; ii. 175 n., 186–9; iii. 377 n., 383, 384 n., 397.

Alais, schools of, ii. 332, 333.

Alardus, rector scholarum at Oxford, iii. 39.

Alban Hall, Saint, Oxford, iii. 174 n., 198 n.

Alban's, Saint, abbey of, iii. 26, 116. *See* John de la Celle, Nicholas.

Albany, nation of, at Glasgow, ii. 314.

Alberic of Reims, i. 67, 108, 493.

— — rector of University of Paris, i. 363 n.

Albericus Gentilis, *see* Gentilis.

Albert I, Duke of Austria, ii. 236.

— III, Duke of Austria, ii. 236 n., 239, 240.

— of Brandenburg, ii. 276.

— the Great, i. 263, 344, 354 n., 363–8, 382, 474, 490, 564 n.; ii. 255; iii. 245 n., 251, 266.

— *legis doctor*, i. 112 n.

— of Samaria, i. 21.

— of Saxony, i. 448, 449 n., 562 n., 564 n.; ii. 239, 240, 243 n., 305.

— Pastor at Gars, his College at Namur, ii. 239 n.

Albert, P. P., ii. 273.

Albi, schools of, i. 15 n.; ii. 173, 335; archdeacon of, iii. 433.

Albicini, C., i. 87.

Albigenses, i. 347; ii. 119, 161–2.

Albini, G., i. 240 n.